Law Enforcement

HANDGUN

Digest

(Revised Edition)

By Dean A. Grennell

DBI BOOKS, INC., NORTHFIELD, ILLINOIS

(FORMERLY DIGEST BOOKS, INC.)

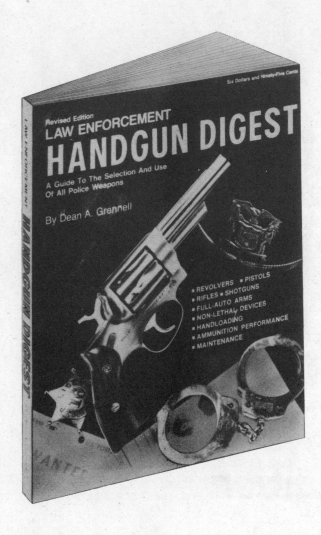

OUR COVER:

Ruger's Police Service-Six has found wide acceptance by law enforcers. Shown here in stainless steel with 4-inch barrel in 38 Special caliber, the popular revolver soon will be available in a 9mm blued version.

EDITORIAL DIRECTOR
JACK LEWIS

PRODUCTION EDITOR
BOB SPRINGER

CONSULTING EDITORS
MASSAD F. AYOOB
THOMAS G. FERGUSON
EVAN P. MARSHALL

ART DIRECTOR
JOHN VITALE

PRODUCTION COORDINATOR
WENDY WISEHART

ASSOCIATE PUBLISHER
SHELDON L. FACTOR

Produced by

Charger Productions

ISBN 0-695-80646-7   Library of Congress Catalog Card Number 73-186804

CONTENTS

NEW YORK STATE POLICE
STATE CAMPUS
ALBANY, N.Y. 12226

WILLIAM E. KIRWAN
SUPERINTENDENT

It is the sworn duty of every police officer to protect life and property. Such duty carries with it the obligation of the individual officer to insure the highest degree of proficiency in his use of firearms. It is the responsibility of the police department to require that their personnel are well trained in the handling of firearms as well as the laws governing their use.

In recent years, the courts have focused critical attention on the negligent use of firearms by police officers. Too often, municipalities have been required to pay large sums in damages where it was proven that the negligent use of firearms resulted in a direct lack of proper training.

Even more important than dollars and cents can be the extreme cost in loss of life resulting from a feeling of indifference which occasionally exists at all levels of the community, that the uniform and badge of a police officer offer him adequate protection. A police officer may carry a firearm for thirty years of service and never have to use it in the line of duty; however, in this era of accelerating crime rates, lack of respect for law and order and open violence, no officer or police administrator can afford a complacent attitude.

Skill in the use of firearms can be an insurance policy for the individual officer as well as a deterrent to claims against the department he represents. Certainly, firearms training is no remedy for the many problems of today's law enforcement officer but, if firearms proficiency bolsters the self-confidence of the individual officer or saves the life of one innocent person, it is worth the price.

W. E. Kirwan
Superintendent
New York State Police

The Author

DEAN A. GRENNELL was born near Humboldt, Kansas, in 1923, moving to Wisconsin some three years later, residing there until joining the Air Force in 1942. Graduating from Harlingen Aerial Gunnery School, in Texas, he went on to complete the course for aerial gunnery instructors at Buckingham Army Air Field, near Ft. Myers, Florida. Assigned to Tonopah Army Air Field, near the town of that name in Nevada — an operational training field for B-24 bomber crews — he served as a gunnery instructor until cessation of hostilities on V-J Day.

Returning to civilian status, Grennell worked for seventeen years as a sales engineer in heating and air conditioning and, for a portion of that time, served as a sergeant of auxiliary police with the Fond du Lac, Wisconsin, police department. Moving to Milwaukee in 1963, he worked for three years as a technical writer and, for a portion of that time, worked night and weekend shifts as a patrolman with the Germantown, Wisconsin, police department.

In the years since 1957, Grennell has served on the staffs of various firearms publications and has contributed to books such as GUN DIGEST and HANDLOADER'S DIGEST, specializing to some extent in technical discussions of reloading plus coverage of the manifold branches of the shooting sports. Since 1966, he has served as the managing editor of GUN WORLD Magazine and has written the book, ABC'S OF RELOADING, published in 1974 by DBI Books, Incorporated. He can be reached in care of Charger Productions, Incorporated, Box HH, Capistrano Beach, California 92624.

PART I: INTRODUCTION

THE REVOLVER -- AND WHAT TO DO ABOUT IT

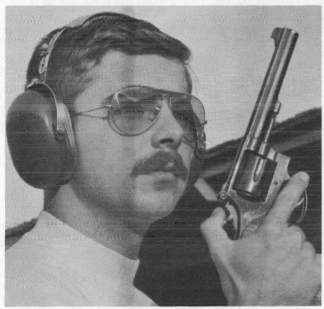

Target revolvers, such as this Smith & Wesson K-38, are preferred for range competition. Shooting glasses and ear-protection should be used as habit.

THE OFFICER'S HANDGUN is one of the most basic and important tools employed in law enforcement work. In the majority of instances, it rarely is drawn in line of duty and is fired in that connection even less frequently. However, its visible presence, in the officer's holster, is an effective deterrent to violence against the person of the officer or those under his protection. It offers proof to the general public, with which the officer must deal in normal routine, that he is prepared and equipped to back up his duly constituted authority with whatever degree of force that a given situation may require.

While the officer has access to armament of capacity and potential that is considerably in excess of the service handgun, the latter has the important characteristic that it is on his person and available instantly at all times when he is on duty and — in many instances — when he is off-duty in plain clothes, as well.

In the normal routines of law enforcement work, it is extremely rare for an officer to have any substantial amount of warning or time for preparation in those emergency situations which require the employment of firearms. The considerable percentage of police work is rather humdrum and routine, leading to a sense of complacency and no small amount of boredom. As a direct result, emergencies are apt to find an officer poorly prepared to cope with them.

All too often, an officer is not given the opportunity to correct a deficiency in attitude or preparedness. It is well to keep in mind that the next few minutes, the next stretch of highway, can — and sometimes do — present a drastic emergency situation in which familiarity with the service handgun, plus skill in its use under difficult and trying circumstances, can make the difference between survival, injury or death.

While recruitment and training procedures vary widely between departments, it is vital that the officer should be intimately familiar with the operation of his duty weapon and the procedures for making it shoot. In the example of revolvers, consider the matter of cylinder rotation. In the two makes of revolvers most widely used by law enforcement agencies, Colt and Smith & Wesson cylinder rotation is in opposite directions. Suppose an emergency situation has left an officer with but a single round of ammunition. In order for a single load to fire at the first pull of the trigger, the cylinder must be latched in place with the loaded chamber immediately next to the barrel: In "10 o'clock position" for the Colt, 2 o'clock for the Smith & Wesson. Yet the ignorance about this basic factor in revolver shooting has filled many a grave.

When the service handgun must be used in line of duty, split seconds usually are of vital importance. The weapon must be available instantly, without delay — not, for example, buried beneath the skirts of a uniform overcoat — and the officer's first shot should be effective. In many instances, the suspect will have fired the first shot and will be in the process of firing additional shots by the time the officer starts his draw. The importance of quick access plus accurate fire, under such circumstances, cannot be over-emphasized.

In view of the considerations just discussed, it is obvious that any officer who carries a handgun in the

Pencils point to next cartridge that will fire when
Colt (left) or Smith & Wesson (right) is cocked
or trigger pulled; importance is explained in text.

course of his duties should feel strongly motivated to
become as skilled in its use as possible. It is true that
many an officer has joined the force, performed his
duties for a number of years and retired without once
having had occasion to draw his weapon in line of duty.
However, for each officer so blessed, there have been
others who learned, in the final moments of their lives,
that they were not that lucky.

A pension is not much good unless you survive to
enjoy it. Your service handgun can make the difference,
either way. Few facts are more worthy of your careful
consideration than that.

Competence with handguns must be developed
through intensive and thoughtful practice and, once
attained, must be kept up through continuing practice.
Firing a handgun, for practice, is a pursuit that many
enjoy but, at the same time, many others view the
prospect with something less than anticipation. Regardless of the individual attitude, thoughtful and effective
practice is of vital importance and there are things which
can be done — and should be done — to reduce the
personal discomfort of practice firing.

Two areas of the human physique are vulnerable to
damage in routine firing: the eyes and the ears. While it
is not possible to employ protective equipment in
typical shooting situations in line of duty, there is no
excuse for neglecting this important consideration in
routine practice firing.

The eyes should be protected by suitable shooting
glasses and the officer should make it a matter of
absolute, inflexible habit to wear shooting glasses and
ear protectors at all times when firing, insofar as it is
possible and practical to do so. When bullets strike the
backstop of the target range, occasional particles of
bullet or backstop material may come flying back to the
firing position. Some revolvers may shave bits of bullet
and direct them to the sides. Thus, you need protection
over the eyes, not only from your own handgun but
from those being fired in adjoining positions.

Shooting glasses are available in an assortment of suitable colors: gray or dark green to ease eyestrain when
firing in bright sunlight, or yellow to aid in picking up
the apparent contrast on dull, dark days. Color response,
in the normal eye, gives the sharpest definition with
yellow light and the poorest with blue light. For this
reason, glasses having blue lenses should be avoided.

While a good pair of sunglasses is much better than no
glasses at all, it is best to obtain a pair of shooting
glasses, made specifically for that purpose, as these have
hardened lenses and are much more resistant to breakage
under the impact of the flying particles which may be
encountered.

In selecting a pair of glasses for shooting protection,
it is a good idea to look through both lenses at a distant
object, while holding the glasses at arm's length and
moving them about. When typical cheap sunglasses are
checked out in this manner, you will notice a rippling
distortion. To attempt to shoot while wearing such
glasses would impose a severe and unnecessary handicap,
besides causing eyestrain.

If desired and needed, it is possible to obtain shooting
glasses which have the wearer's optical prescription
ground into the lenses to afford the visual correction
required for optimum shooting capability. Alternatively,
clip-on shooting glasses of the appropriate color can be
used over the shooter's regular pair of spectacles, if
preferred.

We've discussed eye protection first, because eye
damage can be instantly and permanently disabling. Ear
damage, caused by loud sounds such as the reports of
firearms, requires a longer period of exposure, but is a
hazard only slightly less serious.

As with shooting glasses, any sort of ear protection is
better than no protection, but that time-honored
method, stuffing absorbent cotton into the ears, is quite
ineffectual and should not be relied upon if at all possible. Much the same can be said for the expedient of
sticking empty cartridges cases into the ears.

Ear-plugs represent the minimum in effective protection. Some, such as the Lee-Sonic, have valves which are
intended to permit the passage of normal sounds, closing
to block off noises of damaging intensity. Such devices
have the advantage that they permit a fair percentage of
the normal hearing ability and do not cut the shooter off
from commands of the range officer or similar important
sounds.

The so-called "ear-muff" type of ear protector is
more effective in controlling the noises of gun fire and
should be obtained and used at all times when firing, if
this is at all possible and practical.

Prolonged exposure, or even occasional exposure to
the sound of gunfire causes damage to the ear which is
permanent, irreversible and irreparable. Typically, such
damage first manifests itself in loss of sensitivity to the
higher sound frequencies. In time, this leads to the so-
called "nerve-loss" type of deafness in which the listener
can hear sounds, but has difficulty in distinguishing
words and conversation. Such forms of hearing loss are
difficult or impossible to treat successfully and do not,
as a rule, respond very encouragingly to the use of
artificial hearing aids.

In addition to protective devices for the eyes and
ears, the officer's shooting kit should contain such useful
accesories as cleaning equipment for the gun, a screwdriver for moving adjustable sights — if the gun is so
equipped — and a can of combination lubricant and rust
preventive.

Chapter 1

BASIC HANDGUN FIRING

The Techniques Discussed Here Can Improve Your Score On The Range Or In The Field, Where It Counts!

IT IS IMPOSSIBLE TO PLACE too much emphasis upon the importance of safety in the handling of firearms. A split-second of carelessness or inattention can result in an accident that is crippling or fatal to the victim, at the same time leaving the incautious person who caused the accident with a feeling of sick regret to the end of his days.

It is a prime responsibility of range supervisory personnel to instill proper safety habits in each new student and to enforce their observance in veteran officers.

Safe gun-handling habits can be summed up in a few short words: Handle any gun, all of the time, as if a bullet were about to blast out of the muzzle in the next instant.

Sometimes firearms are discharged unintentionally and accidentally. You can find positive proof of this in any indoor firing range, whether it's used by police or civilians: bullet-pocks on the walls, ceilings and, sometimes, through the partitions which separate the firing positions.

The inference is obvious: If you form an iron-clad habit of keeping gun muzzles pointed in a direction where a bullet will do no harm, should the gun discharge — as guns occasionally do — you will be spared nasty experiences such as lawsuits or the need for apologizing to the next-of-kin.

From the standpoint of safety habits, there is no such thing as an empty gun. If you treat all guns as though they are about to fire, it follows that you are not going to point an "empty" gun at someone and pull the trigger as a prank. The record books are full of instances such as

this, in which the victim of the joke fell down dead. And no one laughed.

The foregoing assumes that you are the one in control of the gun. The identical attitude toward firearms must be carried through in regard to guns in the hands of others. If someone is holding a gun and you see the muzzle moving toward you, move out of the way. Never voluntarily permit a gun barrel to line up with any portion of your anatomy. Let the offender know your feelings in this regard. Firearms safety takes precedence over Emily Post-type etiquette and courtesy, every time, all the time, always. Few people get a chance to die more than once.

DRY-FIRING PRACTICE

A useful amount of knowledge about sight alignment and trigger control can be acquired prior to firing with live ammunition and in conjunction with regular range practice. Proper gun-handling habits can be cultivated at the same time.

For example: Any revolver worth carrying is a masterpiece of precision engineering and manufacturing. The fine edge of built-in accuracy can be knocked out of it forever by improper handling and it doesn't take long. When the loaded rounds have been expended, the cylinder catch should be actuated with the firing hand and the cylinder should be eased outward without undue violence. After ejection of the spent cases and reloading

9

of the chambers, the cylinder should be eased back into place with the same care and deliberation: never by a sharp flick of the wrist, as it is done all too often in the movies or on television. Abrupt banging back and forth of the cylinder will spring the cylinder out of alignment, ruining the built-in accuracy of the gun and, if overdone, making it unsafe to fire.

As discussed in text, you can prolong the accurate life of a good revolver by many years if you take care to swing the cylinder out for ejection and latch it into position after reloading without the use of undue force.

Dry-firing can provide beneficial practice, as has been noted. The vital need for observance of suitable safety habits carries through into this activity, too. Never indulge in dry-firing without first verifying that the gun is empty: which means checking all chambers of a revolver or both the chamber and the magazine of an autoloading pistol.

You will not need a large amount of space for dry-firing practice. The appearance of a normal bullseye at typical range distance can be simulated by the use of a smaller mark at a closer distance. As a general guide, the aiming point should be a small black circle of an apparent diameter not much greater than the width of the front sight, as viewed in normal aiming position, with shooting arm extended fully.

SIGHT POSITIONING & ADJUSTMENT

As shown in the accompanying diagram, the sights are aligned with the shooter's eye in such a manner that the

tip of the front sight is level with both sides of the rear sight, with an equal amount of space visible between each side of the front sight and the corresponding sides of the rear sight notch.

When the sights are so aligned, the bullet's point of impact, at typical pistol distances, should be at or slightly above the tip of the front sight. With handguns having an adjustable rear sight, the shooter can adjust for any desired relationship between sight picture and point of impact for a particular load at a given distance. Handguns having fixed — that is, non-adjustable — sights must have their point of impact worked out by actual firing and this may change slightly from one make or type of ammunition to another.

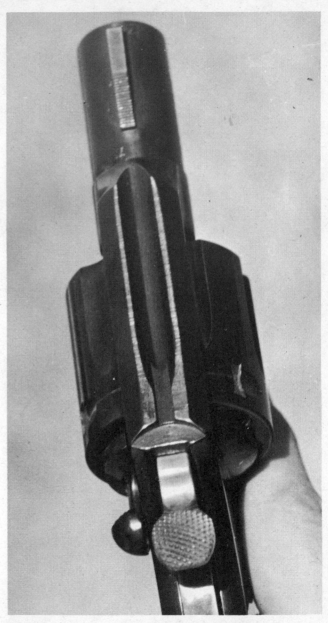

Fixed type of revolver sights employ a milled notch in rear of receiver, as in this Colt Lawman Mk III, as rear sight; though not adjustable readily, such sights are highly resistant to shifting under rough duty.

If a handgun is subjected to severe duty, as many police handguns are, the fixed sights are not as apt to be knocked out of adjustment as the target type. Fixed sights which are on the money are preferable in a gun

With handguns having fixed or non-adjustable sights, you may find that some loads do not strike at the desired place in the target. Changes in bullet weight or powder charge can have this effect. It may not be practical to file down, build up or bend the sights to correct them for the sight picture as shown in the center of this page.

As a rule, best results will be obtained by maintaining the same sight alignment and moving the aiming point. Instead of holding for the lower edge of the black circle, hold for a point the proper distance to the left, right, above or below. It is difficult to hold the front sight off-center in the rear notch by the same amount from shot to shot.

It is fairly common for a revolver with fixed sights to be "on the money" with full-power service loads, hitting low with light target ammo.

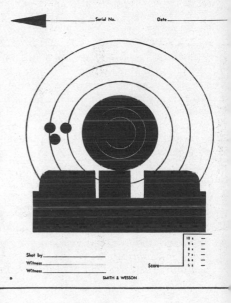

The illustration in the center of this page shows the proper sight picture for "6 o'clock hold." This is preferred by many target shooters, for it is more clearly visible than trying to see the black sights against the center of the bullseye, as with a center hold sight adjustment.

Adjustable sights will have to be set so as to put the group in the center of the bullseye with the selected holding technique. The rule is to move the rear sight in the direction you want the holes to move on the target. Thus, if hits are to the left, move the rear sight to the right; if hits are high, move the rear sight downward and so on.

Adjustment procedure for Smith & Wesson micrometer click sight is illustrated at the lower right.

SIGHT HIGH IN NOTCH — GROUP HIGH

SIGHT RIGHT IN NOTCH — GROUP RIGHT

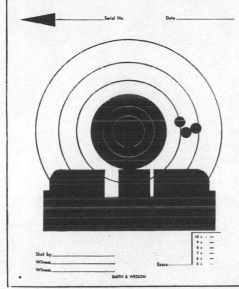

SIGHT LEVEL AND CENTERED IN NOTCH — GROUP CENTER

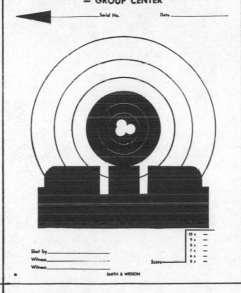

SIGHT LEFT IN NOTCH — GROUP LEFT

Before making any adjustments to the sights or to the sight picture, it is best to fire at least two or three groups of ten shots each. Find the center of each group, by estimate and base sight changes on its location.

These pictures show the hits close together. When firing, your groups may not be as small. Move the rear sight in the proper direction by a click or two and try again. Save the targets for comparison. This will help show the amount of movement per click of adjustment and this information can be noted for future use.

Usually, you'll have to change the sights or sight picture, if shifting to a longer or shorter distance. This will offset the effect of bullet drop.

SIGHT LOW IN NOTCH — GROUP LOW

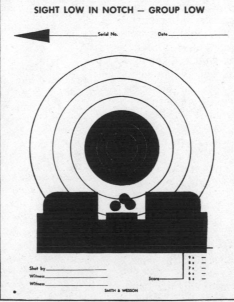

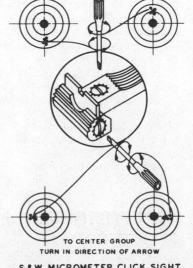

TO CENTER GROUP
TURN IN DIRECTION OF ARROW

S & W MICROMETER CLICK SIGHT

which must be carried and used, day after day under typical law-enforcement conditions.

Fixed sights which are off – that is, do not direct the bullet to the intended point of impact – are something else again. Any divergence from the point of aim will introduce an angular error, varying with the distance to the target. Often, it is possible to correct fixed sights, although the operation is better left to the departmental armorer.

Repositioning adjustable, or target type sights is a simple process, readily performed by the shooter on a trail-and-error basis, working toward the adjustment which places the center of the group precisely over the point of aim.

Bear in mind that it takes several shots to establish an average point of impact. Do not move the rear sight on the basis of a single shot. The usual procedure is to divide the target into quarters with a vertical and horizontal line and fire some given number, ten or twelve shots, into it. If about the same number of holes land in each of the four quarters, the sight adjustment can be regarded as satisfactory. If a substantial majority of the holes are below the horizontal line, the rear sight should be raised by a click or two. If there are more holes to the right than to the left of the vertical line, move the rear sight slightly to the left and shoot another test group.

The rule for adjustment of the rear sight is simple and easy to remember: MOVE THE REAR SIGHT THE WAY YOU WANT THE HOLES TO MOVE.

When working with a handgun having fixed sights, any correction of faulty alignment usually must be performed on the front sight by bending it right or left, or by filing down or building up. The rule, here, is to move the front sight in the opposite direction you want the holes to move. Thus, with a fixed-sight gun that shoots to the left consistently, you would warp the front sight slightly to the left, so as to move the point of impact slightly to the right.

SINGLE ACTION TRIGGER PRACTICE

It is conceded readily that formal, bullseye target firing has limited practical application to the type of firing that a law enforcement officer may be called upon to perform in a typical line-of-duty situation. Accurate firing under conditions of severe emergency will be covered elsewhere in this book. However, the officer may encounter occasional situations in which it is highly desirable to fire with care and deliberate aim, to obtain the ultimate accuracy of which his handgun and ammunition may be capable. That is the aspect of handgun marksmanship that we are discussing at present. Acquired practice and capability at this type of firing will not have any adverse effect upon your capabilities at combat shooting and a reasonable degree of skill at deliberate-fire accuracy could prove to be a useful asset under certain conditions.

In setting up your dry-fire practice facilities, refer back to the admonitions on firearms safety, as given earlier in this discussion. Dry-firing, by definition, is done without ammunition in the gun. This means that you check to make certain the gun is empty, before engaging in dry-fire practice. At the same time, you should make sure that no damage would occur that couldn't be lived with, even if the gun were to discharge a live round in the course of the dry-fire practice. Never forget that, so far as firearms are concerned, the first mistake is the one to avoid. The consequences of a mis-

take with firearms tend to be drastic, permanent and irreversible. Never let yourself forget that hard-but-true fact for so much as a moment.

Do not attach your dry-fire target to a wall where, were the gun to discharge, it could penetrate the partition and, possibly, kill or injure someone in the next room or apartment. So far as firearms are concerned, the only rule that will keep you out of trouble is to assume that anything that can go wrong, will go wrong.

Now, with that vital consideration taken care of, let's cock the hammer, line up the sights and commence squeezing the trigger. At once, you'll note a demoralizing fact: You can't keep the sights in a steady alignment with the target as you squeeze the trigger. Take heart: No one else can, either. With time and practice, you can reduce and minimize the wobble, but you'll never eliminate it altogether.

So this is what you do, or try to teach yourself to do: Build up the pressure on the trigger gradually. As you observe the sight picture wandering off of the intended point of impact, hold the pressure you've built up, but don't apply any more pressure until the sight picture starts wandering back toward the desired point of impact again. If you do this properly, the trigger will release and the hammer will drop on one of the times that the sights pass across the bullseye. Try to form the habit of making a mental photograph of the sight alignment at the instant of release, keeping track of it as a bullet hole in the target – high-right, low-left, right-on, etc.

Up to this point, assuming you haven't been doing any range practice with live ammunition, the muzzle of the gun will be rock-steady at the instant of hammer-drop. Your nerves will not have been subjected to the recoil, noise and general commotion which occurs when the hammer drops on a live round. As you go on to fire with live ammunition, on the range, and return to your dry-fire practice, you are apt to find that your nervous system has begun working against you. There is a strong tendency to squeeze the trigger, almost up to the point of release and then give it a yank and flip the muzzle off of the point of aim.

This is what is termed a "flinch," and it is the worst enemy with which a beginning handgun shooter must contend, so far as achieving the highest potential degree of accuracy is concerned. A flinch is perfectly normal, natural and quite involuntary. With practice, the effect can be wiped out or minimized and that's where the dry-fire practice comes into the picture. After firing with live ammunition, a few sessions of dry-firing can be of great help in bringing the tendency to flinch back under control.

If desired, a weight can be suspended from the muzzle of the handgun during dry-fire practice, serving to develop the muscles of the arm, wrist, shoulder and fingers and making the handgun seem lighter, easier to control during normal firing.

HOLDING THE HANDGUN

Correct grasp is an important factor in achieving accuracy. Assuming that you are firing right-handed, grasp the handgun by the barrel in your left hand, spread the thumb and fingers of your right hand and "bed" the butt of the handgun securely into the shooting hand, as shown in the accompanying illustrations. Note that the barrel should make a straight-line extension of the bones in the forearm and that it should be gripped as high on the stocks as is practical and comfortable. The reason for this is to direct as much as possible of the recoil force straight to the rear, where it can be absorbed by the mass of arm and shoulder.

The principle is easy to demonstrate: With the handgun empty, grasp it in your shooting hand from a point low on the grip and push rearward on the muzzle. You will note a strong tendency for the muzzle to pivot upward. Now, shift your grip to a higher point on the stocks and push the muzzle again, noting that the upward movement at the muzzle had been reduced to a useful extent.

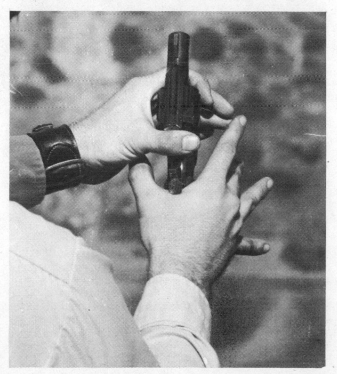

Binoculars or camera can be suspended from gun muzzle to add weight, develop muscles for steadiness, control. Below: Thumb ahead of cocked hammer, bed gun into shooting hand in line with bone of forearm, fingers wrapped about grip.

TRIGGER FINGER POSITION

Two positions of trigger finger: top, pushed through on first joint and, lower, with more sensitive tip of finger against trigger; latter way usually is preferred.

If you were feeling the texture of a surface — checking to see if smooth or rough — you'd use the tip of a finger, not that portion of the finger back at the first joint. This is because the nerves at the fingertip are closer to the surface and much more sensitive. This, in turn, means that the finger tip is the logical area to use in pulling the trigger for single action firing: that is, firing with the hammer cocked. As will be discussed, the technique must be modified for double action firing, but we are concerned with target type firing for ultimate accuracy in the present discussion.

Having grasped the handgun in the manner described here, it is likely that you will find that moving the fingertip to the trigger will, in turn, move the rearward portion of the trigger finger outward and slightly clear of the handgun frame. This serves two purposes, both of them beneficial: It affords maximum sensory control by placing the most sensitive area of the finger against the trigger and it gets the remainder of the trigger finger clear of the frame of the gun so that, when the trigger releases, there is much less likelihood that the finger will bump and deflect the handgun away from the intended aiming point.

So let's combine the factors of grasping the handgun, trigger finger placement and sight alignment to see how well the system works. Making certain that the handgun is empty and that it could not cause serious damage, even if it were loaded, cock the hammer, take aim at your dry-firing target and ease off the trigger a few times, observing the effect of the hammer's fall upon the sight alignment with the target.

Putting tip of trigger finger in contact with trigger has further benefit of moving the first two joints out of touch with frame, preventing deflection during release.

There is an old and useful technique used by marksmen who wish to improve their skill with the Government Model .45 auto pistol. This consists of balancing a dime upon the front sight and endeavoring to squeeze the trigger so carefully that the dime will not be dislodged when the hammer falls. It can be done, with practice (provided it's not one of the older, M1911 types with a sharp-edged front sight). Many handguns do not have front sights upon which a coin can be balanced. This need present no problem: You merely imagine that there's a coin balanced across the front sight and that you want to squeeze the trigger so steadily that it won't fall off. Naturally, you couldn't keep the dime in place when firing with live ammunition but if you can bring the handgun up to the instant of hammer-fall with the idea that you don't want to disturb that imaginary dime out there on the front sight, you will find that you have delivered the bullet to the point of aim with all of the inherent accuracy of which the arm and ammunition is capable. And that's what the entire business of handgun marksmanship is all about.

The essential trick is this: If your brain knows when the hammer is going to fall, you are almost certain to flinch and deflect the muzzle as release occurs. So the secret lies in easing back the trigger with such delibera-

tion and delicacy that, shot after shot, release occurs before the brain expects it, thus getting the bullet on its way to the target before the brain can transmit the flinch impulse to arm and hand.

When you have studied and absorbed the foregoing discussion, you will have learned — in theory — virtually all there is to know about achieving ultimate accuracy with the handgun. Putting that theory into practice is what requires patience and determination. Fighting and conquering the urge to flinch is an unending battle with your nervous system, a battle in which no clear-cut and permanent victory is apt to be won.

Learning the fundamentals is simple and easy. Putting them into practice with maximum efficiency is a process that can use up all the time you care to devote to the project. You can expect occasional sessions in which it will appear that, at last, you are on your way to complete mastery of the fine art of the handgun marksmanship. But, if you're human, don't be discouraged unduly if the next session at the range finds you making the same old mistakes and flinching bullet holes away from the ten-ring in a thoroughly demoralizing manner.

It's sad, but true: Handgun marksmanship is not like learning to ride a bicycle. It is not a matter of acquiring the basic knack and having it to enjoy forever. Accurate firing with the handgun requires regular practice, patience and determination. A reasonable level of competence can be obtained without too much effort, but progress beyond that point and maintaining that added degree of skill is what takes the regular practice and concentrated effort.

A highly beneficial dry-firing exercise is to balance a dime on front sight, attempting to drop hammer so delicately that it won't fall off — imagine the dime is out there in live-fire and try for same trigger-pull.

DOUBLE ACTION TRIGGER PRACTICE

Most revolvers, as well as certain auto pistols used in law enforcement work are of the design known as double action. That is, when the hammer is down, the trigger is well forward and a longer, harder pull of the trigger will cause the hammer to move back and drop without the need for cocking the hammer manually. This feature permits the handgun to be drawn and fired with the absolute minimum of delay.

It is possible to attain a surprising level of accuracy in double action firing of a revolver, by means of certain techniques to be described here. It requires a modification of the grip and hand position recommended for single action firing. The hand must be moved farther around the stocks, bringing the center bone of the index finger over the trigger. It may be noted that wide target triggers or trigger shoes offer a slight handicap for double action practice and firing.

If the trigger is pulled through double action with the fingertip in contact with the trigger, there will be a pronounced deflection of the muzzle as the hammer falls and this is ruinous to accuracy. The effect is caused by the abrupt release of pressure on the trigger after the hammer is released. The trigger finger then moves rearward to the limit of trigger travel and jars the gun in coming to a stop.

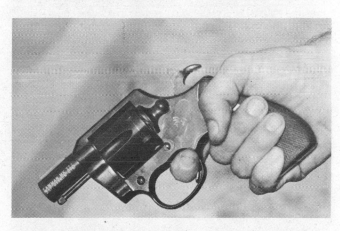

Above: In firing a revolver double action, grip is shifted to put more index finger over the trigger; this adds leverage and (below) brings fingertip in touch with frame before release to serve as steadying effect.

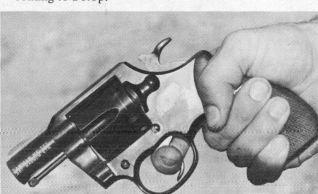

By repositioning the hand and trigger finger, as described, you should find it possible to touch the side of the frame with the tip of the trigger finger, just prior to release. This gives you a steadying effect and eliminates the uncontrolled backlash of the trigger finger after release.

Making certain the gun is not loaded, point it in a safe direction and try pulling the trigger through double action a few times. With most revolvers, you will feel and perhaps hear two faint clicks as the trigger comes back. Release will occur shortly after the second click, with just a little more trigger motion. It is at this point that the tip of your trigger finger should be touching the side of the frame, to the rear of the trigger. With a reasonable amount of double action dry-fire practice, you should find that you are able to pull the trigger

through the second click with a smooth motion, followed by a careful application of the final pressure before let-off. Given a smooth-working action, you will find that it is possible to dry-fire with little or no disturbance of the sight alignment. The basic principles will carry through and prove beneficial, even when firing rapidly in combat courses.

STANCE

Assuming that the shooter is right-handed, he positions himself with his body facing at an angle about forty-five degrees to the left of the target; vice versa for left-handed shooters. If you were to face squarely toward the target, you would find it uncomfortable and any unavoidable amount of rocking backward and forward would be converted into vertical dispersion of the bullet holes in the target. If you faced away from the target at right angles, the sway would result in horizontal dispersion. By splitting the difference with the forty-five-degree position, the effect is minimized in both directions.

Bullseye-view shows recommended stance: facing away at angle of 45 degrees to line of fire for solidity.

Facing squarely toward target puts tension on shoulder, causes an unsteady rocking back and forth of the feet.

Facing edge-on to the target may present the narrowest possible silhouette but it's not the ideal position. It increases left-to-right wavering of handgun muzzle, hurts scores.

Feet should be about 12-18 inches apart and angled as shown. Scuffle them about a bit to find a comfortable place for each and relax.

Place your feet about twelve to eighteen inches apart, toes slightly away from each other and shuffle them about as necessary to get them comfortably and securely planted. Your head should be erect, your body well balanced and relaxed, with weight distributed evenly between both feet. Your non-shooting hand can be shoved in a pocket, or the thumb tucked beneath the belt — dispose of it in any manner that feels relaxed and unstrained.

Your shooting arm, with the gun positioned in the hand for either single or double action firing, as described previously, is extended straight, without the elbow being locked. Likewise, both legs are straight, but without the knees being locked, so as to avoid muscular strain and nervous tension.

Extended arm should have elbow relaxed, not locked rigidly, assuring steadiness.

Check your stance and position by bringing the handgun up to eye level with your eyes closed, then look down the sights. If they are pointed to the right of the target, pivot slightly to the left, or vice versa, by moving both feet. Repeat as necessary, until the sights come naturally to the center of the target. Otherwise, you will be firing under a strain, caused by having to swing the muzzle toward the target for each shot. Unnecessary tensing of any of the muscles used in shooting can contribute to tremor and should be avoided.

Position of the shooting hand and trigger finger has been discussed here previously, in connection with

A useful test for suitability of position is to close eyes and aim gun toward the target. Check alignment by opening eyes and move feet, if necessary, so as to line up this way.

GRIP OF THE GUN

Typical grip for firing the .45 auto at targets features moderately firm, semi-relaxed hold, with thumb held high. Many combat shooters prefer to bring thumb down to touch middle finger, using the same hold for target work.

dry-fire practice. As to the matter of finger tension around the stocks of the handgun, experience at live-fire will indicate the degree of pressure which will give you the best results. Speaking in general, the handgun must be gripped with sufficient tightness so that it won't move around in the hand, even from the force of recoil. At the same time, you should not apply pressure so excessive as to set up muscular tremors. It is important to adopt and maintain a uniform amount of gripping pressure with your shooting hand, keeping it the same for each round fired. Any significant variation of holding pressure will contribute toward vertical dispersion of hits in the target.

When firing heavy loads in Smith & Wesson revolvers, recoil can peel the hide off the side of your thumb, if held close to the sharp knurling of the cylinder latch, as illustrated.

It is customary for right-handed shooters to extend their right thumb up along the cylinder latch of revolvers, keeping it in readiness to cock the hammer for the next shot. This may present problems in certain instances, such as firing powerful loads in Smith & Wesson revolvers, where the sharply checkered surfaces of the cylinder latch can abrade the skin of the thumb to an uncomfortable extent. You may wish to experiment with the possible advantages of bringing the thumb down and into contact with the tip of your middle finger — the upper of the three that are wrapped around the stocks. Some shooters find this beneficial, others obtain better results by laying the relaxed thumb alongside the frame, keeping it out of the way of the cylinder latch, if necessary.

The shooting arm, as has been noted, is extended with the muscles of the arm firm but not rigid. There should be no bending of the wrist or elbow at the instant of firing.

The trigger finger is placed so that pressure and motion is straight to the rear. The finger itself should be clear of the frame of the handgun, so as not to exert any horizontal deflection.

BREATHING CONTROL

The act of breathing in and out imparts some amount of motion to the body, thereby reducing the steadiness of your hold. During the interval of trigger pressure, prior to firing, it is best to leave off breathing temporarily. The most practical and comfortable method is to take a few deep breaths, let out about half of the last one and commence your sighting and trigger pressure at that time.

Normally, it will be possible to get the shot off within a few seconds, so that no discomfort results. However, if you become short of breath, do not fire hastily so as to be able to breathe again. Instead, ease off the built-up trigger pressure, take a few deep breaths, let half out and try again. If you hold your breath too long, shortage of oxygen is apt to cause unsteadiness and may have a blurring effect upon your vision, as well.

YOUR EYES AND THE SIGHTS

This is the ideal alignment of front and rear sights with bullseye for 6 o'clock hold when target shooting at a known range. The bullet strikes high to hit center of the bullseye.

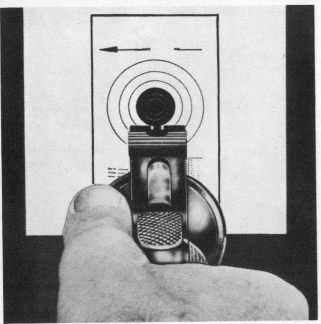

The correct alignment of the sights has been discussed and described here under comments on dry-fire practice. Repeating for the sake of convenience and emphasis, the top of the front sight is lined up, even with the top of the rear sight, centered in the rear sight notch, with an equal amount of space on each side of the front blade. The handgun must not be canted — that is, tipped away from the horizontal in either direction — and, insofar as possible, it must be held uniformly from one shot to the next.

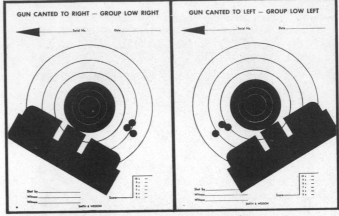

Gun must be held straight up and down for accuracy. Tilting or canting to one side or the other will throw hits to one side, as here.

The actual aiming point will depend upon the distance from the target to the shooter. The suggested sight picture with service arms having non-adjustable sights is to place the tip of the front sight over the center of the bullseye at fifteen yards and at six o'clock — that is, aligned with the lower edge of the black circle — from a distance of twenty-five yards. As has been discussed, actual performance of the given gun and load in the hands of the individual shooter may necessitate minor modification of the sight picture in order to bring the hits to the center of the bullseye.

Most shooters will find that they have a "master eye" and this is the one that should be used for sighting handguns. Identifying your master eye is done easily: Look at a point a few feet away and extend your empty hand so as to line up the tip of your index finger with the point. Now close one eye, leaving the other open. If the extended finger seems to remain motionless, your master eye is the one still open; if it seems to twitch to one side, you have closed your master eye.

There is no serious problem involved in holding the handgun in the right hand and aiming with the left eye, or vice versa, if your favored shooting hand is on the side opposite the master eye. This is not true of rifles or shotguns, of course, but the only personal adjustment necessary when firing a handgun is to turn the head slightly so as to put the master eye behind the sights.

If possible, try to train yourself to shoot with both eyes open. Your master eye will take over, automatically but you'll have the added benefit of vision from the other eye, as well. This is of further help in that it does away with some small amount of facial tension, permitting the shooter to be just that much more relaxed and comfortable. Certain shooters may find that they have considerable difficulty in aiming with both eyes open and, should this be the case, the master eye can be kept open for aiming, with the other closed.

The human eye is similar to a camera in that it focuses to provide the sharpest image to one given

FOCUSING YOUR EYES

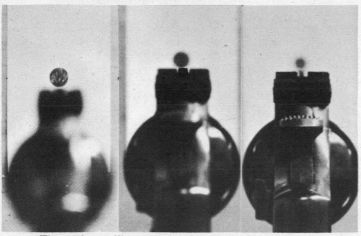

These photos illustrate the three points on which the shooter's eye can be focused in aiming. Left: when focused on the bull, both sights are blurred. Center: Focused on the front sight, both rear blade and bull are fairly well defined. Right: eye on rear sight makes front sight blade blurry, bullseye even worse.

distance, changing automatically to focus upon the object being given primary attention. This poses a minor problem in sighting, since you are dividing your attention between the target, front sight and rear sight, all being at different distances from the eye and thus impossible to focus upon simultaneously.

Therefore, you must select the most important of the three and focus your master eye for maximum sharpness at that distance. There is a natural tendency to focus upon the target, but this is the most distant and, with the eye focused on the target, there will be a badly blurred image of both front and rear sight, making it impossible to take accurate aim.

The best method is to focus your eye upon the front sight, allowing both rear sight and target to blur slightly. This is the approach that affords the greatest accuracy in aiming. It will require a certain amount of conscious effort to form the habit of focusing upon the front sight, although it will become instinctive with sufficient practice.

It may be noted that the blurring effect is most severe under conditions of dim light. As the light becomes stronger, the pupils of the eyes contract, thereby increasing the depth of sharp focus in the same way that a camera lens renders better detail when stopped down. As has been noted, the color of light has some effect upon apparent sharpness, too. Most people find that their vision is keenest when the light is predominantly yellow — as when wearing yellow shooting glasses — in comparison to normal, white light and light that is strongly tinted toward blue gives poor visual definition. Obviously, it would be inadvisable for most shooters to wear blue shooting glasses.

HOLDING & AIMING

It is important to understand that a handgun, held at arm's length in the customary offhand firing position, is going to move. No one can hold a handgun perfectly steady and motionless in this position. When you take up handgun marksmanship, you will observe a contin-

uous motion of the handgun during aim. Do not become discouraged, as this movement will be reduced to a considerable extent through training and practice. The strength of your muscles has some effect upon the amount of motion and this will improve through development of the muscles involved. However, the real problem lies in the ability of the brain to detect the direction in which the sights are moving away from the target and relay the necessary instructions through the nervous system to the muscles involved with arresting the wobble and moving the sights back toward the bullseye. Thus we see that the beginning shooter must work to develop this specialized ability of his mind and nervous system, as well as developing the muscles of shoulder, arm and wrist.

Even though the sights may seem to wobble over the target, if trigger is released in the proper manner, hits nearly always will stay inside the seven-ring, closer with practice.

Some amount of movement always will be present, varying between individuals and depending upon physical condition and prior experience. It may seem surprising and a little hard for the beginning shooter to believe but, no matter how much the handgun and sights may seem to wobble, if the trigger is pulled properly, without flinching, all hits on the target will remain inside of the seven ring, with most of these inside the eight ring. As capability improves, through the processes described here, this cone of fire can be tightened down to keep all hits inside the eight ring, the nine ring and, eventually, inside the bullseye.

The beginning shooter, if not familiar with these basic facts, is apt to feel discouraged by his inability to keep hits in or close to the bullseye. Unless the situation is explained to him fully, he is apt to feel that he is not natural-born marksman material and will not make the determined efforts to grasp, apply and practice the basic aspects of handgun shooting. There is not and never has been any such thing as a natural-born handgun marksman: Those who achieve superior skill are, simply, the ones who mastered every facet of the art through perseverance and practice.

LIVE-FIRE RANGE PRACTICE

While dry-fire practice is most helpful in becoming familiar with essential details, there is no substitute for burning powder and launching lead. Range firing can be sandwiched between alternate sessions of dry-fire practice for maximum benefit from both.

Usually, the officer will engage in his live-fire practice at a supervised range facility under auspices of his department. The rangemaster will outline the rules for safety and the mechanical details of the firing procedure before the shooters actually move up to the firing line. These will vary as to details from one department to another and, if there is any discrepancy between procedure at your range and the discussion in this book, you should follow the rules established for your departmental range. The firing procedures about to be discussed are typical, but not necessarily universal.

Make it a habit to keep muzzle of gun lined up with target and backstop. With hammer cocked over a live round, extend index finger outside the trigger guard, as in photo above. Bring the gun forward and up to eye level with a smooth motion, as in lower photo, putting the fingertip lightly on the trigger as the sights line on-target. Avoid the habit of dragging the gun back to a point next to your ear between firing each shot.

Try to form the habit of keeping the muzzle of your handgun directed in the general direction of the target and backstop at all times. You may observe that some shooters have a habit of bringing the muzzle back into the vicinity of their ear before coming down at the target. This is a dangerous practice, particularly if the handgun should be discharged unintentionally at that point — as can and does happen. Another bad habit is that of allowing the muzzle to point more or less straight downward between shots. This can cost you a toe or two, so don't let yourself fall into either habit.

Concentrate upon becoming familiar with the commands of your range officer, so that you will have a close estimate as to when firing will commence. Do not start your aim so early as to be tired when the signal to fire is given. On the other hand, do not start aiming so late that you must hurry unnecessarily to catch up with the clock.

The handgun can be held reasonably steady at arm's length for eight to ten seconds before a serious amount of movement will develop. In slow-fire, it is important that the shot be fired within this first eight to ten seconds. If not, even an experienced shooter and especially a new shooter may hold the handgun too long and, in trying to fight the movement, will fire a poorly aimed shot.

In slow-fire, it is helpful to lower the handgun — keeping the muzzle toward the target in the manner described previously — to relax the muscles and re-establish breathing control, then start over again if it did not prove possible to get the shot off properly within the first few seconds after the command to commence firing was given.

In timed-fire or rapid-fire, you will have to develop a system for controlling the distracting effect of having to fire within a fixed interval of time. The best answer to this is the ability to concentrate, being ready and reassured by the knowledge gained from previous experiences: the realization that a good performance can be made within the time limitations.

TRIGGER SQUEEZE

Most experienced and capable handgun marksmen would term this the most important single consideration in attaining handgun accuracy. As has been noted, your sight picture can be blurred, your hand can be trembling to a discouraging degree, your handgun and ammunition may have less than the ultimate, gilt-edged accuracy potential but, given the correct, jarless release of the trigger, the bullet will remain inside of a surprisingly tight cone of fire.

The opposite is true: You can have a superbly accurate handgun and ammunition which will put them all through one hole when clamped motionlessly in a machine rest. Your sight picture can be scalpel-sharp, with the barrel as steady as a human hand can hold. But, if you squeeze a few ounces and jerk the rest, it can throw the hit completely off the paper, perhaps into the ground, halfway to the target line!

You must understand and accept the fact that no one can make a handgun go off at a particular, anticipated instant without jerking the trigger and knocking the sights away from the aiming point. Many words have been used in describing the ideal hammer release: pull, squeeze, mash, milk, et cetera. One of the better descriptive terms is positive pressure. This can best be described as a steady, increasing pressure being applied against the trigger in a straight-rearward direction, thus allowing the hammer to release cleanly — and unexpectedly — to fall forward without disturbing the alignment of the sights.

Positive pressure can be built up slowly or rapidly, so as to accomplish the act of firing within a given time limit. But, if this method is not learned and used, whatever has been accomplished in sighting and steady holding is wasted.

Repeating for added emphasis, pressure must be applied to the trigger so that the handgun will fire without the shooter knowing or anticipating at which exact instant it will do so. If the shooter is aware that the handgun will fire at a particular moment, he is making it fire and, when this happens, pressure is built up all at once. As a result, the front sight is pushed, pulled or flipped out of alignment by the movement. In such a case, the bullet can go almost anywhere but it's most unlikely that it will endanger the bullseye.

The coordination needed to keep the sights aligned and release the hammer at the same time is great and cannot be accomplished without a large amount of effort, concentration and practice. Concentration, as the word is used here, can be defined as close mental attention or exclusive application of effort. This ability and willingness to concentrate, or the lack of it, is the chief factor which separates the good shooters from those less capable. There is no secret, "trick of the trade" involved in becoming an expert handgun marksman but, rather, it involves a thorough knowledge and understanding of good shooting techniques plus a determined concentration in applying them through practice, both with and without live ammunition in the handgun.

A competent handgun marksman is not born: He is made and, to a large extent, he is self-made. It is almost entirely a matter of personal choice for the individual to decide whether he is going to be a poor, mediocre, passable, adequate, excellent or brilliant shooter of handguns. Officers in the last two categories improve their expectations of surviving to collect pensions and, while still on active duty, are the kind you appreciate having around on details which could develop into bad situations.

It must be said that desire plays a vital role in the development of a handgun shooter. A man must have the desire to reach his utmost potential plus the determination and willingness to work at it before he can become a good shooter: Given these, he will become a good shooter.

FIRING THE BULLSEYE COURSE

Let's follow through the typical course and see how it develops, stage by stage:

First Stage: Slow-Fire. Ten shots in five minutes.

You know that you have much more time here, in comparison to the other two stages, but still you cannot afford to waste any. Having loaded five rounds into your cylinder or magazine, move a cartridge into firing position, with the hammer cocked. These steps are taken in response to commands of the range officer. At the command to commence firing, assume the proper position, with a good grip and breath under control as has been described here.

Extend the handgun to firing position, in a smooth motion, keeping the muzzle pointed toward the target. Take a final deep breath, let half of it out. At this point, your arm is as steady as it can get. If you can get off your shot in the next few seconds, it probably will be a good one.

You line the sights up — center or six o'clock hold, as required — with your master eye focused upon the front sight blade and commence to transfer pressure to the trigger in a steady increase. Bang! The hammer drops some little bit of time before you really expected it to. It was a good shot.

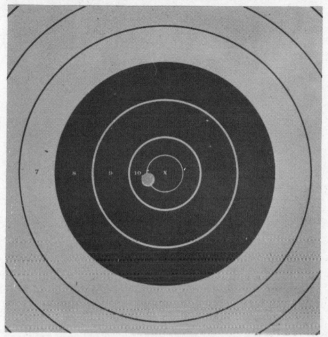

The object of the game: This bullet not only hit the ten-ring, but took a hungry bite out of the inner X-ring — featured on some targets as a means for deciding ties — and any bullet that cuts the line counts as the higher of the numbers.

Lower the handgun, its hammer still down on the fired cartridge, relax your arm muscles, breathe deeply and make your mental preparations for the next shot. Think about the things you are about to do and check them off on a mental list.

The handgun comes back up, extended toward the target, you cock the hammer and resume the same grip and hand position you used last time. You line up the sights and commence the squeeze. You continue to increase the pressure on the trigger. You squeeze harder, even harder, but the shot does not go off. You fight it and your vision commences to blur as the sights start to waver. But you won't lower the muzzle to relax for a fresh try: You're going to show this hunk of hardware who's in charge: Bang! It went off, at last and your trigger finger recalls it as a smooth release. You feel a sense of triumph that the gun didn't beat you.

So you focus your eyes on the target and you can see the hole, out in the white at six o'clock, well down into the seven ring. What happened? True, the shot was squeezed well but, in the meantime, you ran short on oxygen and you were so concerned with keeping the muzzle from sagging with your wearying arm that you didn't realize that the sights were no longer properly aligned.

It must be remembered that the shot will always go where the sights and barrel point at the instant the hammer drops. You promise yourself you won't make that mistake again. But you will. The next time you put pressure on the trigger and it won't go off, you recall what happened last time and try to squeeze faster. Bang! Off it goes and you made it go off. Knowing when the com-

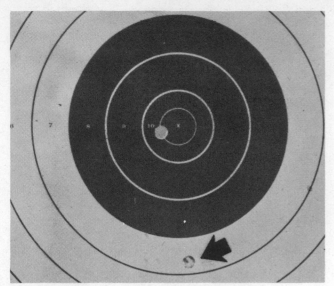

In target shooting, he who hesitates may not be lost, but it's apt to cost points! As noted in text, too much delay in getting off the shot will aggravate unsteadiness and sight wobble.

motion was due, you flinched up a storm. Count yourself as lucky if that hit is inside the count circles, or even on the paper.

So you continue on through the rest of your ten rounds of slow-fire; sometimes getting off a good one, sometimes not doing so well. It is hoped that you are learning all the while and profiting by the mistakes made.

So — as discussed — there is a natural urge to get the next shot off quickly, while you're still feeling steady. But if you anticipate the instant of trigger release, flinch puts it here.

Sorry about that! It can — and does — catch the best of shooters now and then. Only the most rigid concentration will prevent flinch.

SHOTS TOUCHING SCORING RING RECEIVE THE HIGHER VALUE. SHOTS OUTSIDE OF SCORING RING ARE SCORED AS MISSES.

Second Stage: Timed-Fire. Two five-shot strings at fifteen seconds each.

This is where readiness at the start becomes extremely important. Everything must be thought out and prepared for, prior to starting. In timed-fire, if you can pace yourself accurately, you will have at least three seconds for each shot. Here, the trick is to get off the first shot at or soon after the firing signal, leaving you the better part of fifteen seconds for the remaining four shots.

In timed-fire, as in rapid-fire, the thing to fight is panic. Pressure can be built up in the shooter and turned into panic by the realization that he must get off his rounds within the time limit. You know that, if everything doesn't go right at the start, you'll have to speed up or lose the rounds left unfired at the cease-fire signal.

Here is where the development of a steady cadence or rhythm in shooting can be of great help to you. Your pacing ability can be developed to a useful extent during your dry-fire practice. One suggested approach is to observe the second hand of a watch or clock while counting off seconds, either out loud or to yourself. In pacing yourself for timed-fire, with a round to be fired every three seconds, you might say something such as, "One thousand and one, one thousand and two, one thousand and (Bang!); one thousand and four, one thousand and five, one thousand and (Bang!)," and so on. With practice, it is possible to attain an excellent uniformity of timing by this or a similar technique.

Of course, it should be obvious that you must not squeeze the trigger so as to have the handgun discharge at a precise, anticipated moment or this is certain to cause flinching. The hammer must release unexpectedly, but within close limits to the paced intervals. When dry-firing or when practicing timed and rapid courses on the range, keep a check on your timing system by comparing it with a clock, firing timer or stopwatch.

At the start, you will find it helpful to concentrate primarily upon effective pacing of your shots: not rushing, but finishing within the time limit. Do not be too concerned with trying for a perfect shot in the center of the X-ring every time but, rather, devote your attention to pacing and proper release of the trigger — without flinching or jerking — and refine your aim to improve your scores later, after mastering the timing and triggering.

This does not mean that you should neglect the sight alignment: merely keep the sights lined up and pressure on the trigger constantly, so that the hammer falls within a set time limit, even if you are aiming into the eight or nine-ring at the time.

It is important here, in view of the time limit, to concentrate on keeping your master eye focused upon the front sight. Do not fall into the habit of looking down at the target to admire a good shot or cuss at a bad one. From the start, remember that once a bullet is fired, good or bad, it cannot be brought back and fired again so there is no point in worrying about it. The bullets to deserve your concern are those remaining in the gun, to be fired before the signal sounds.

Third Stage: Rapid-Fire. Two five-shot strings at eleven seconds each.

It has been observed that rapid-fire is just like timed-fire, only faster. This may be true up to a point but with a difference that, in rapid fire, you have but about two seconds per shot instead of a full three and the hazards of panic are that much greater in proportion, if not more so.

Naturally, rapid-fire requires more intense concentration, due to the closer time limit. Recovery of the handgun, from its recoil position to the aiming position must be accomplished more quickly. The grip must be secure enough to assure that the stocks will not shift in the hand from shot to shot. Sights must be brought back into alignment quickly and positive pressure applied with the same care as was exercised in slow-fire, but more quickly. It is much easier to neglect some vital portion of the firing cycle: You may find your eye focusing on the target instead of the front sight, for example.

Rhythm is absolutely essential and probably the lack of rhythm causes more bad shots in rapid-fire than any other factor. As was explained before, the first shot should be fired within one second after the firing signal has sounded. A common error occurs when the shooter tries to make the first round too perfect, losing vital seconds, becoming worried, trying to hasten his firing rate at the expense of pace and rhythm, sacrificing concentration and ending with a poor string.

A similar error, almost as common, is to get ahead of the normal pace and hesitate on the last shot, trying to make it perfect. In such cases, the last shot is almost sure to be a bad one because the shooter does not apply trigger pressure properly, becomes worried about the amount of remaining time and makes himself fire the handgun. In so doing, he is almost certain to disturb the sight alignment and either jerk or heel the shot.

In shooting rapid-fire, the shooter does not have time to correct minor errors in holding and sighting. Trigger pressure must be applied on the basis of sight alignment and sight picture. Every effort should be made to keep normal movements to a minimum, continue positive trigger pressure, maintain perfect sight alignment and pace your shots with a definite rhythm.

Nothing has been mentioned, up to this point, on breathing during timed and rapid fire. There will be some variation between what works best for one shooter and for another. Most shooters find that they cannot go the eleven seconds of the rapid string, much less the timed one, without replenishing their oxygen supply. Accordingly, it would be well for the individual shooter to experiment with incorporating breathing control into his dry-fire practice in connection with his personal system of pacing out the eleven or fifteen seconds. Strive to develop a system or habit of breathing during dry-fire, test it out under conditions of live-fire on the range and modify it as necessary during further dry-fire sessions until you have settled upon the pattern that works best for your own physique and temperament. Then work at making it a fixed habit, so that you don't have to think about it.

DOUBLE ACTION FIRING

Techniques for firing most revolvers and certain autoloaders by pulling the trigger through double action rather than cocking the hammer manually were discussed earlier in this chapter. It is a method that offers great practical advantages, once the basic principles have been mastered and it can be utilized to advantage in any situation involving shooting at short range or in which a shot must be got off for distracting or warning effect within the absolute minimum amount of time. In the hands of a practiced double action shooter, a substantially faster rate of accurate fire can be maintained than by cocking the hammer manually for each shot and pulling the trigger with the lighter, single action pressure.

Regardless of the thumb position you may have chosen for single action shooting, when you switch to double action, the tip of the thumb belongs down against the tip of the middle finger, exerting firm pressure and locking the stocks of the handgun in a solid ring of bone and muscle. Since you do not have to shift your grip or loosen your hold to cock the hammer for each shot, your hold is firmer, more uniform, for better control. In double action shooting, a moderately hard grip eliminates the problem of shifting and allows full time to be devoted to sight alignment and trigger control.

Unless the trigger finger is unusually long, the hand unusually large, or both, effective double action shooting requires a shift of the grip from customary single action positioning: moving the hand to put more of the index finger over the trigger. It must be remembered that typical double action pull will require at least two to three times as much physical effort as the normal single action pull.

You must keep in mind that, if you know the instant of firing, you will flinch; no one can help doing so. The principle of positive pressure on the trigger is as important in double action as in single action. Further, the added effort of pulling through double action will tend to deflect the sights to some extent and, in addition, the abrupt release of some nine pounds of rearward effort, as the hammer falls, will deflect the muzzle unless great care is taken.

Inherent accuracy in double action firing is dependent to some degree upon the individual handgun. Even guns of identical model and make can display markedly different characteristics when fired double action.

There are at least two schools of thought in regard to the best way to achieve double action accuracy — not at all an unusual situation in the field of handgun marksmanship theory — and, in the final resolution between the two, it is best that the individual shooter tries both to determine which has the greater advantage in his own instance.

The two-stage double-action pull has been described previously in connection with dry-fire practice: Get the index finger far enough through the trigger so as to put its tip in contact with the frame and control the backlash following release of the hammer. Squeeze through the two faint clicks felt in most revolvers during double action, brace the tip of the trigger finger against the frame and apply further pressure until the hammer falls. This technique need not involve a distinct pause. Further, the steadying effect of the fingertip against the frame should not be such as to deflect the sights from the bull's-eye at or after the moment of firing. Maximum effectiveness requires a handgun having a smooth double action pull, plus intensive practice; given those, a notable rate of fire combined with accuracy can be achieved.

On those occasions where the so-called classic offhand stance is not mandatory, the use of a two-hand hold will increase accuracy and control in double action firing to a remarkable extent. Often termed the Weston stance, the usual procedure consists of wrapping the weak hand over the shooting hand, pressing forward with the shooting hand and pulling rearward with the other hand. This creates a triangular shooting framework, with all of the steadying effect that a crossbrace provides for a wooden framework, such as a scaffolding.

Recent years have seen great gains in popularity for the two-hand hold in handgun training. Seemingly, those who prescribe and supervise handgun training programs have come to realize, albeit rather belatedly, the importance of striving for maximum effectiveness in favor of an impression of classic elegance.

It has been demonstrated beyond contradiction that the two-hand hold produces a sharp improvement in effective

Ray Chapman, of Sunland, California, demonstrates the two-handed hold that has come to be the accepted technique for combat competition firing. His gun is a customized .45 ACP auto with which he won the world's championship in a match held in Switzerland in the summer of 1975.

accuracy, particularly among those who do not have extensive experience and/or aptitude for handgun shooting.

At least as recently as WWII, the two-hand hold was a no-no in military handgun training and any attempt to brace a wavering pistol with the free hand would have been cause for roaring reprimands from the rangemaster. Within recent years, military trainers have recognized the virtues of the two-hand hold, with the result that it is being taught as the recommended method.

While hanging on with both hands offers decided advantages for firing revolvers, particularly in the double action mode, its benefits carry over into the firing of autoloading pistols, as well. The accompanying photo shows Ray Chapman's favored hold for firing the .45 ACP auto pistol. By way of credentials as to its effectiveness, it should be sufficient to note that Chapman, using the hold shown, turned in a score of 299 out of a possible 300 points to win the first International Handgun Combat Competition against a field of one hundred; Chapman's score was seven points over the next highest.

In the four years since the first edition of this book appeared, the emphasis in police firearms training has shifted to the two-hand firing technique, almost to the exclusion of all other methods. Modern training and qualification courses tend to include a considerable amount of firing from relatively short distances — seven yards or less — on the grounds that much of the shooting occurring under typical duty situation is at short range.

If your personal situation provides opportunity for casual, unsupervised handgun firing, there are a number of approaches that can improve familiarity and capability. Given a safe backstop, with no hazard of ricochets, it is surprisingly easy to develop the ability to hit fairly small targets without using the sights.

It helps if there is a little dust around the target, so you can spot where the bullets hit. Using a one-hand or two-hand hold, keep your eyes on the target and fire one round, noting the point of impact. Try to retain the "muscle memory" of where you were pointing for the first shot and make the needed correction, firing again. Make appropriate correction for the third shot and fire. With a moderate amount of practice, it is quite possible to develop the ability to walk in effective hits in firing just a few shots by use of this method. A similar approach can be quite helpful for developing the ability to hit close to the desired point on the first shot.

It should be underscored that safety considerations are of paramount importance. Avoid shooting alone in remote areas, lest even a minor injury make you incapable of getting out for treatment. There have been instances in which highly experienced shooters neglected this simple and obvious precaution, with more or less serious consequences. Since no one has invented a workable eraser for firearms, the basic philosophical outlook is, and should remain, "Never make the same mistake once!" Wry as that sounds, it makes good sense when working with firearms.

A MATTER OF CHOICE

Handguns For Law Enforcement Do Not Cover A Particularly Broad Spectrum, But There Are Variations For Specific Purposes!

Handguns used in law enforcement work fall into two categories: revolvers and autoloaders. With no more than rare exceptions, the revolvers are of the double action design wherein a longer, harder pull of the trigger will bring the hammer rearward and release it without the need for cocking the hammer manually. A few examples of auto-loading pistols are designed with the double action trigger feature, but most autos depend upon a thumb safety and/or an external hammer for safe carrying.

Each of the two basic types of duty weapon has its inherent advantages and disadvantages. Invention of the first practical revolvers dates from about 1836. Auto pistols appeared about sixty years later. Cartridge ammunition, as used today, was developed during and shortly after the Civil War, with the more efficient nitro or smokeless powder being introduced and developed in the closing years of the Nineteenth Century.

The revolver has been the accepted law enforcement handgun for upward of a century and has been refined and improved to offer a notable level of durability and reliability. Many departments require that only revolvers will be carried by reason of the fact that inexperienced personnel can be trained to handle the revolver with reasonable competence and safety more easily and economically than is the case with autoloading pistols. The resulting reduction of training and instruction time can save large departments

many thousands of dollars per year, particularly if there is a substantial amount of turnover in personnel.

With smaller departments, training and equipping is not such a heavy cost factor and many of these have been converting in whole or part to the auto pistols. While some departments permit their officers any reasonable option in choice of duty weapons, there is an obvious advantage in having all arms chambered for the same cartridge: a consideration which operates against the mixed use of revolvers and autos within the same department because, for the present, there are few if any cartridges which will interchange efficiently between the two types of handguns. True, the .45 ACP round can be fired in revolvers, but it requires the use of a special half-moon clip to facilitate rapid extraction and this would prevent rapid interchangeability between autos and revolvers in the thick of a firefight.

Thus, it comes to making a choice between the revolver or the autoloading pistol. Virtues of the revolver include the fact that it does not require some minimum amount of power from the cartridge to ready itself for the next shot. If the hammer drops and fails to fire the cartridge, a second pull of the trigger through the double action cycle will drop the hammer on a fresh cartridge. There are only two ways in which defective ammunition can stop a revolver: If the bullet should lodge in the barrel, due to a weak or defective

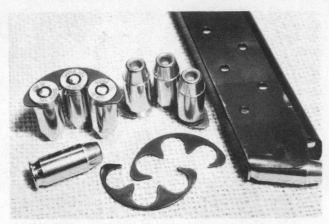

One of the few cartridges which can be used in both auto pistols and revolvers is the .45 ACP. However, the rimless case requires use of the half-moon clips for quick ejection, preventing quick interchange with magazine of auto, right.

powder charge and if the bullets move forward out of the case mouths, due to recoil until the tips project ahead of the front surface of the cylinder, preventing its rotation into line with the barrel. With factory-loaded ammunition of good quality, the likelihood that either of these conditions will occur is extremely remote and can be disregarded for all practical purposes.

With poorly crimped bullets, force of recoil can cause them to work forward in the case until tip projects from front of cylinder which catches on rear of barrel, stopping rotation of cylinder and effectively jamming the revolver.

Revolvers can handle many different types of ammunition, varying as to velocity, weight and design of the bullet, et al. Speaking in general terms, revolver cartridges tend to be capable of achieving higher levels of energy than do typical auto cartridges, although there is a broad area of overlapping between each.

It may be noted that some departments have taken the unusual step of deactivating the single action feature of their revolvers, so that the hammer cannot be cocked for firing by the lighter trigger pull. The reason given is that, on different occasions, an officer had been covering a suspect and — due to nervousness, being jostled or a similar cause — the gun discharged unintentionally. It was felt that the longer, more deliberate double action pull would minimize

As discussed, certain department have taken the step of modifying the service revolver so as to bypass manual cocking feature, making it necessary to fire with deliberate double action.

On the debit side of the ledger, revolvers are slow and clumsy to reload, particularly if it must be done one round at a time, under stress. This is offset by the availability of numerous rapid-loading devices which speed the operation to a useful extent. Few if any center-fire revolvers suitable for law enforcement work have capacity for more than six cartridges, while many of the small, concealable types hold but five rounds. With good revolvers of modern design, there is no benefit as to safety in carrying an empty chamber under the hammer, although some persist in this practice, reducing still further the number of available shots.

Revolvers are notoriously slow and clumsy to load, but several devices — such as these — are available to cut operation time to a small fraction.

The relatively open design of the typical revolver leaves it more than ordinarily vulnerable to dust, dirt, mud or similar foreign material and it is, likewise, rather vulnerable to damage from the rough usage to which a police weapon may be subjected. Hammer spurs can be broken or bent so as to prevent firing, ejector rods can be bent, as can the barrel; trigger guards can be bent in such a manner as to interfere with pulling the trigger while front sights or adjustable rear sights can be knocked askew or completely off. The revolver is, perhaps, slightly more susceptible to physical damage than are most autoloaders.

Minor drawback of revolvers is that tips of bullets — such as these hollow-points — can be seen or, if gun is empty, it's also visible.

Advantages of the auto pistol include, in general, slightly greater magazine capacity, considerably greater speed and convenience in replacing a loaded magazine — though, it must be pointed out, loading individual cartridges into a magazine is at least as slow and exacting a task as refilling a revolver cylinder, if not more so — a flatter, less bulky silhouette, slightly greater barrel length in terms of overall dimensions, slightly more massive and damage-resisting construction — this point varying between makes and types — plus the advantage that a covered suspect cannot tell, from the front of the auto pistol, whether it is loaded or empty; a minor disadvantage of large-caliber revolvers when viewed in good light. With many designs of auto pistols, it is possible to remove a depleted magazine, replacing it with a fresh

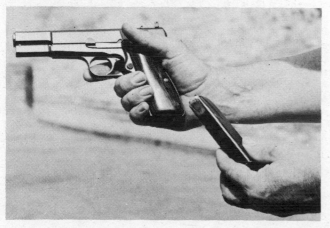

This Browning 9mm auto has been modified to take out magazine disconnector so that a round in the chamber can be fired, if needed, while magazine is removed, as in emergency covering of suspect.

one, meanwhile keeping the single round in the chamber ready for instant firing, should this be necessary. Some autos have a magazine disconnect device to nullify this feature although it may be possible to remove or deactivate the magazine disconnect feature, if desired.

Most liabilities chargeable against the auto pistol stem from defects in the ammunition or the magazine. You may hear caustic comments to the effect that "an automatic is apt to jam, just when you need it the most." Given a good auto, properly cleaned and maintained, stoppages are extremely rare unless the ammunition is defective or the feed lips at the top of the magazine have been bent or otherwise damaged.

A further consideration is the possibility that the duty weapon may be grabbed by a suspect with the object of using it against the officer or others. Operation of the average revolver is simple and straightforward, so that almost any unauthorized person can fire it with a minimum of delay. With auto pistols, depending upon the design, unfamiliarity on the part of a suspect could delay getting it into action, giving the officer an opportunity to regain control of his weapon.

The ideal handgun for everyday duty use is one that is rugged and reliable, to the greatest degree possible. The officer should resist the temptation to carry delicately tuned target arms on duty, even though they have proved capable of excellent accuracy in range practice. The same closely fitted tolerances which contribute to their inherent accuracy on the practice range can cause stoppages when subjected to the dirt and abuse of routine police work.

In fact, there are useful advantages in firing the everyday duty weapon during range practice and qualification, thereby maintaining the familiarity with its individual feel, balance, trigger pull and shooting qualities for the sake of building and retaining confidence in its ability to function properly under emergency conditions. In some instances, when departments place undue emphasis upon periodic qualification and competitive comparison of scores, this leads to the situation in which officers own and use a high-quality target arm and midrange wadcutter ammunition to punch out their bragging scores, then put the old duty clunker back in the holster, check to see that their belt loops or pouches are filled with standard service loads and hope that they can come fairly close to the mark, if a shooting situation should develop. Such situations tend to defeat the basic purpose of training and practice.

Minor roughness in the action, trigger pull or other operation of a handgun often will disappear with extensive use, as in dry-firing practice. If not, the conditions should be corrected by the departmental armorer or a professional gunsmith known to be reliable and competent. The temptation to indulge in do-it-yourself firearm modifications should be resisted, unless you have sound reason to consider yourself experienced and qualified for such projects.

There are many bright ideas which may occur and be put into practice without adequate investigation or inquiry; not always with satisfactory results. For an example, much common agreement exists as to the extreme reliability and dependability of good revolvers. But it is possible to make a high-quality revolver completely inoperable through improper lubrication. Facts are available in one instance in which the owner of a Smith & Wesson removed the side plate and applied liberal quantities of a mixture of castor oil and finely powdered molybdenum disulfide — a lubricating compound similar to graphite — to the moving parts of the revolver action; the object being to smooth up the trigger pull.

After a few firing sessions, in which the home-brewed lubricant seemed to be working all right, the revolver was

It is vitally important that lubricants used on handguns be of the non-gumming type, such as Brayco-LSA Gunlube or the five varieties above. From left: Testing Systems, Inc., TSI-300; Buchheimer's Gun Cleaner & Lubricant; LPS-1; WD-40 and Armite 1234 Formula. While others may prove acceptable, some popular oils can freeze and disable handguns.

stored away for a period of several months. When it was taken out for firing and loaded, a double action pull of the trigger resulted in a gentle click as the hammer fell between two cartridges. Further investigation showed that the little locking pawl, which comes up to engage one of the six crescent-shaped notches at the rear of the cylinder, locking a chamber in alignment with the barrel, had been frozen in retracted position by the lubricant, which had hardened to glue-like consistency with the passage of time. A thorough and careful cleaning restored the revolver to its normal condition of total reliability, but it was well that no one staked his life upon its ability to function during the time when it was incapacitated.

Specialized lubricants are available for firearms today which will deposit a rust-resisting and lubricating film on the surface of the metal without attracting and holding dust, dirt or similar harmful substances. TSI-300 and Brayco LSA Gunlube are two examples of non-gumming, non-attracting liquid lubricants which are well suited for use in firearms over the widest possible range of temperatures. Despite what may be proclaimed on labels, many common lubricants are not well suited for the purpose, due to gumming tendencies or similar qualities.

There are many people who consider themselves qualified to modify and improve the trigger pull on auto pistols, such as the Colt .45 Government Model and, in some small number of instances, such faith is justified. However, it should be emphasized that the sear and lock-work mechanisms of revolvers are not suited for this kind of treatment by reason of the fact that most of these parts are surface-hardened so that removal of a small amount of metal will expose unhardened areas to rapid wear. Further, the length and tension of the springs in revolvers should not be changed in any way from factory configuration, unless it is done by an authorized factory repair facility. Most factory warranties are worded to the effect that any unauthorized repair or modification will void the warranty.

If that is not a sufficiently thought-provoking factor, consider that injudicious tampering may result in a handgun that is out of order and therefore worthless — and such embarrassments have a way of cropping up just when you need the gun most desperately.

Chapter 2

STANDARD SERVICE REVOLVERS—

THE PRO & CON

The Traditional .38 Special May Not Be The World's Greatest, But Departments Rate It A Good Average!

CUTAWAY VIEW OF THE
38 MILITARY AND POLICE REVOLVER

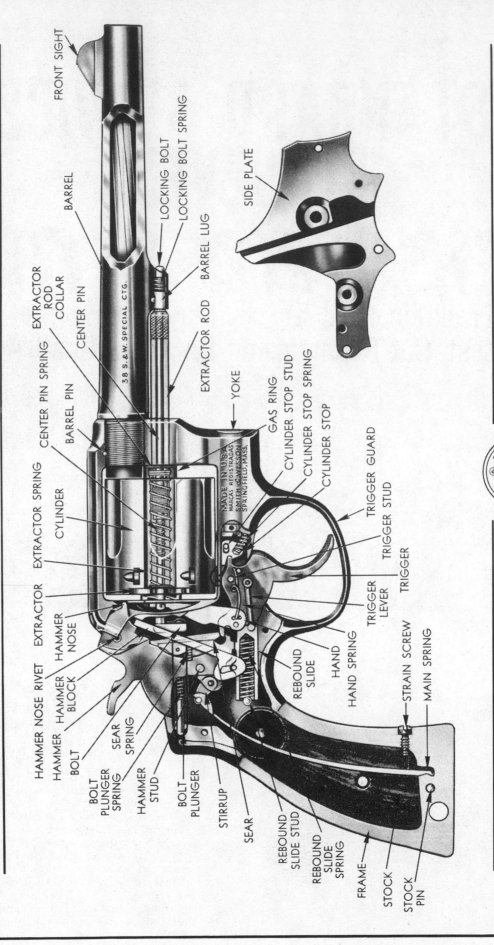

FRONT SIGHT

BARREL

LOCKING BOLT

LOCKING BOLT SPRING

BARREL LUG

EXTRACTOR ROD COLLAR

CENTER PIN

EXTRACTOR ROD

BARREL PIN

CENTER PIN SPRING

EXTRACTOR SPRING

CYLINDER

EXTRACTOR

YOKE

GAS RING

CYLINDER STOP STUD

CYLINDER STOP SPRING

CYLINDER STOP

TRIGGER GUARD

TRIGGER STUD

TRIGGER

TRIGGER LEVER

HAND SPRING

HAND

STRAIN SCREW

MAIN SPRING

REBOUND SLIDE

REBOUND SLIDE STUD

REBOUND SLIDE SPRING

SEAR

STIRRUP

BOLT PLUNGER

HAMMER STUD

SEAR SPRING

BOLT PLUNGER SPRING

BOLT

HAMMER BLOCK

HAMMER NOSE

HAMMER NOSE RIVET

FRAME

STOCK

STOCK PIN

SIDE PLATE

SMITH & WESSON SPRINGFIELD, MASS.

30

THE BASIC DESIGNS of the standard service revolver, as used in law enforcement work, have changed little since the time of their development in the early years of the present century. Such improvements as have been added are, for the greater part, in the nature of stronger, tougher metals, materials used in the stocks and in ballistic performance of the cartridges.

There is a fairly common consensus among many departments that no further improvement in the police revolver and its ammunition is necessary or desirable. In line with the trend toward greater urbanization and increasing population density, there has come a concern for the hazards posed by excessively powerful performance of police weaponry; this being particularly true in the consideration of effective range and penetration.

The primary mission of the service handgun is to immobilize a law-breaker, when required by the appropriate situation, ideally before he can inflict death or injury on others. By its nature and characteristics, the handgun is intended and suited for employment at short distances. It is most unusual for the police revolver to be fired at a target more distant than fifty yards and a high percentage of shooting is done at distances from twenty-five feet down to point-blank range.

Accordingly, it is regarded as a liability rather than an asset, if the police revolver and its ammunition pose severe danger to persons and property at distances greatly exceeding fifty yards. If used in buildings such as apartments, hotels or stores, bullets that penetrate walls, floors or ceilings carry a grave risk of inflicting injury or death upon innocent people: a contingency to be avoided at any cost. True, there is an application for more powerful handguns, as against vehicular crime on the highway or in more open, sparsely occupied areas and such armament will be discussed in a following chapter.

The most common type of police revolver has a four-inch barrel, fixed sights and is chambered for the .38 Special cartridge. Typical examples include the Smith & Wesson Model 10 or "Military & Police" and Colt's Official Police or Police Positive models. The blued-steel finish is used most widely, with nickel plating finding favor in those areas where rust and corrosion present severe problems.

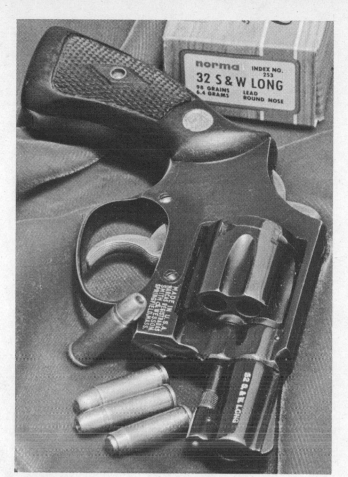

The .32 S&W Long is one of several cartridges below the .38 Special in power; now little used in police work for reasons discussed in the text.

Colt's "Diamondback," available in .38 Special or .22 long rifle, features protected ejector rod, adjustable sights, hand-filling grips and choice of polished nickel — as below — or blued steel.

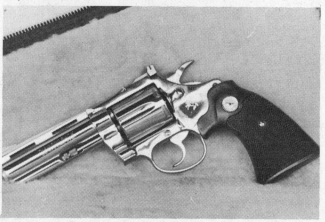

There seems to be general agreement, today, that the .38 Special cartridge represents the least powerful capability as ammunition for a service revolver, although, in bygone years, many smaller cartridges were used for the purpose. These included such numbers as the .32 Short Colt, .32 S&W, .32 Long Colt, .32 S&W Long, .32 Colt New Police, .32-20 WCF, .38 S&W, .38 Short and the .38 Long Colt.

Many of these old, small-caliber police weapons remain in use, being carried by bank guards, night watchmen and similar personnel for whom the gun is more a part of the uniform than something which is apt to be needed and used.

The .38 Special has been an odds-on favorite in police work for over half a century. In some instances, revolvers are fitted with barrels of five or six inches in length and some prefer the special heavy barrel model, due to its effect in reducing recoil.

Speaking in general, recruits can be trained to adequate familiarity with the .38 Special revolver within a moderate amount of time and its weight does not make it unduly burdensome to carry. For the officer who is seldom required to fire his weapon in line of duty, the .38 Special revolver can be a good, middle-of-the-road choice. In the hands of well trained personnel, firing suitable ammunition, this cartridge and revolver can be an adequate performer, free from the problems posed by excessive range and penetration.

For many years, the choice on double action revolvers for police work was fairly well limited to the various

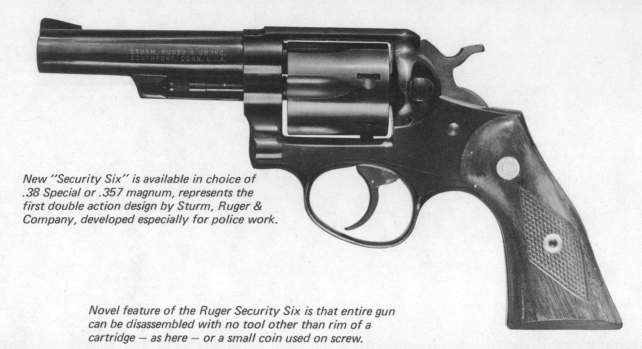

New "Security Six" is available in choice of .38 Special or .357 magnum, represents the first double action design by Sturm, Ruger & Company, developed especially for police work.

Novel feature of the Ruger Security Six is that entire gun can be disassembled with no tool other than rim of a cartridge — as here — or a small coin used on screw.

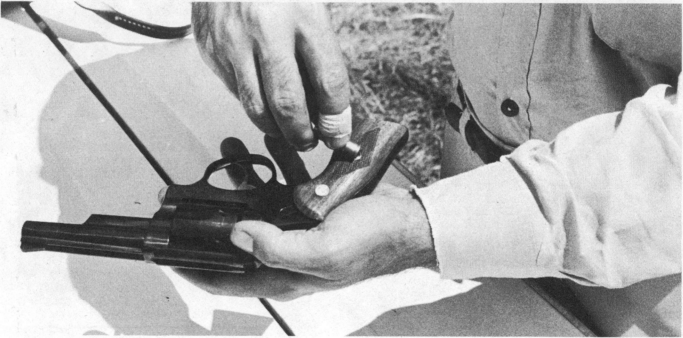

models by Colt and Smith & Wesson. Late in 1970, the firm of Sturm, Ruger & Company introduced their Security Six model, chambered for the .38 Special as well as the .357 magnum. In weight, proportions and performance capability, it compares favorably with the two older makes and the moderate cost of the Ruger Security Six offers a further advantage. Several importers have brought foreign-built double action handguns into the country, also, with an eye to garnering a segment of the police market.

In addition to the optional finishes of blued steel or nickel plating, there has been some trend toward having guns coated with teflon as an effective protection against rust and corrosion in situations posing severe threats to the steel of revolver mechanisms. The coating of teflon is about .0005-inch (half a thousandth) in thickness and does not affect operation of the gun materially. It is, however, uncommonly impervious to corrosion — not only from moisture but from practically any chemical — and is highly

resistant to normal handling and holster wear, as well. The usual color employed is black and the surface is moderately non-reflective. As a result, guns so finished do not have the showy, highly polished appearance of a nickeled or carefully blued finish, but are more practical in that they do not give off tell-tale reflections in dim light and do not pick up reflections to hamper the shooter's vision.

The teflon material was developed for the aerospace program and is used widely for covering the inner surfaces of cooking utensils. Cost of applying the coating — which includes disassembly and heat-bonding to the metal parts — averages between $25 and $35, depending upon the type and make of gun, with most handguns at or near the lower figure. One of the firms offering this service is Sportsman's Repair Center, Incorporated, 212 S. Patterson, Valdosta, Georgia 31601.

Once the officer has selected or been issued his duty weapon, there are several modifications which can be made or added to adapt it more usefully to this personal taste

Hard rubber grip adapter, as this one by Pachmayr, affords more holding comfort.

Custom stocks, discussed in detail later in this book, are favored by many. This is a Jordan Trooper, by Herrett; zebrawood.

Broad-spurred target-type hammer can be ordered as an option, makes cocking easier.

not touch the frame of the gun when held in the normal manner. This lack of support poses a handicap in holding the gun steadily in full control. The function of the grip adapter — usually made of hard rubber or moulded aluminum, with a thin copper bracket which goes under the wooden stocks and over the frame to hold it in place — is to fill in this gap and thus provide firm support for the gun against the top of the middle finger. Most makes of grip adapter are available in more than one size, as well as for the specific makes and models of revolvers.

Trigger shoe is held in place by two hex-head screws, gives effect of lightened trigger pull.

The broad, target-type trigger can be specified as a custom option on certain revolvers. However, many experienced shooters feel that it is none too helpful in double action firing and prefer the standard trigger because of this. A detachable accessory, known as a trigger shoe, is available for most makes and types of handguns and is held in place on the standard trigger by means of two small hex-socket screws. Such shoes are quick and easy to install, if desired for a specialized purpose such as target competition and can be removed as easily when no longer wanted or needed. In effect, the trigger shoe puts a larger area of trigger in contact with the finger tip and, in so doing, gives the impression that less pressure is required to drop the hammer. Although the exact weight of the trigger pull remains the same, it feels lighter when the trigger shoe is used.

A similar option is the broad-spur or target-type hammer, available as an option on several revolvers. This feature offers little if any advantage in double action firing, but is easier, quicker, more positive to cock the hammer in single action firing, as compared to the smaller, standard hammer spur.

and/or physical dimensions. Some handgun manufacturers offer deluxe grips or stocks as an optional, extra-cost feature, while several firms produce custom grips in a variety of patterns, sizes and materials. These are discussed in greater detail, elsewhere in this book.

Many officers prefer to retain the original factory stocks, as supplied with their duty weapon, installing a small device known as a grip adapter in the space between the grip and rear of the trigger guard. Although recent designs have tended to fill in this area, many guns continue in production in which the upper surface of the middle finger does

Chapter 3

M FOR MAGNUM!

Situations Can Arise In Which
The Medium-Powered
.38 Special Simply Isn't Enough
Gun And Cartridge.
Magnum Handguns And Loads
Are The Next Step Up!

As NOTED IN the previous chapter, many consider the .38 Special well suited for use at close quarters in predominantly urban — that is, densely populated — areas. However, many departments have experienced incidents in which it was apparent that the .38 Special, with standard police loads — i.e., the 158-grain, round-nosed lead bullet — was seriously deficient in stopping capability. Given the protection of a typical automobile, law-breakers are relatively safe from the effects of the .38 Special cartridge.

The .357 magnum cartridge was introduced about 1935 as a more powerful version of the .38 Special: the designation stemming from the actual diameter of bullets for the older caliber, .357-inch. Case diameter and rim dimensions remained the same as those of the .38 Special and the length of the case was increased by about .135-inch. This prevented the more powerful cartridge from being chambered and fired in guns built for the .38 Special, meanwhile permitting .38 Special cartridges to be fired in guns chambered for the .357 magnum.

Most revolvers in .357 magnum caliber have the rear of the chambers counter-sunk to accept the cartridge rims as a means of increasing action strength. The overall length of the cylinder differs little if at all, from that of most .38 Special revolvers, making it necessary for less bullet to be exposed at the front of the cartridge.

As a result, there is little if any gain in space available for the powder charge in the .357 magnum, as compared to the .38 Special. The difference between the two guns lies in the fact that the .357 employs alloys, heat-treatment and added thickness to increase the strength of the action, permitting the .357 magnum cartridge to be loaded to pressures roughly twice as high as those considered suitable for the .38 Special.

Typical velocities obtainable with the .357 magnum can be nearly twice as high as those of the .38 Special, resulting in substantially less bullet drop at extended distances and much higher energy. The number of foot-pounds of energy delivered or carried by a projectile varies directly as the square of the velocity: That is, if the velocity is doubled, the energy is multiplied by four.

A .357 magnum, left, with a .38 Special cartridge; outside dimensions are the same except for case length, .135-inch greater on the .357, to prevent it from being chambered in lighter .38 Specials.

Effect of gas leakage between cylinder and barrel can be seen clearly in this night photo of a .44 magnum revolver being fired. Flame from charge of powder provided sole light source for picture.

Smith & Wesson Model 27, in .357 magnum, can be had with barrel as short as 3.5 inches, as here. Right: Colt's Trooper Mk III — here in blued steel — is made only for the .357 magnum, comes with heavy barrel in choice of lengths and target sights.

It rarely is possible to duplicate factory-published velocities for handgun cartridges, as measured on a chronograph when fired from typical revolvers. The reason for this is that the gap between the front of the cylinder in a revolver and the rear of its barrel permits the leakage of a considerable quantity of high-pressure powder gases, with a resulting loss in driving force. Factory performance specifications usually are based upon measurements taken from unvented pressure barrels of about eight inches in length and, as a result, are correspondingly higher.

Barrel length plays a significant role in obtaining effective velocities, as well. A typical report on actual performance of a factory-loaded .357 magnum cartridge, with 158-grain jacketed soft-point bullet, notes the manufacturer's rating as 1550 feet per second, with actual measured velocity from a Smith & Wesson revolver with a six-inch barrel averaging 1298 fps; when measured in a 2½-inch S&W revolver barrel, velocity for the same load came to 1128 fps.

During the thirty-odd years of its career, the .357 magnum has gathered a considerable reputation for capability and, as sometimes is the case, a portion of that reputation verges into the legendary and is not fully supported by demonstrable facts. There seems to be a belief, widely held, that the .357 bullet will stop a fleeing automobile by smashing the engine block. Such claims are not entirely realistic. True, the bullet can crack relatively thin cross-sections of cast iron if it strikes at an angle close to ninety degrees without having to pass through other construction first. Tests, conducted on junked autos, indicate that critical quantities of velocity and energy are lost in getting through surrounding metalwork, such as fenders and hoods, so that the .357 magnum bullet cannot be depended upon to inflict disabling damage upon the engine of typical automobiles.

Many law enforcement agencies permit their personnel to carry the duty weapon of their choice, within practical limitations and on the condition that the officer can handle

Proportions of a magnum revolver with four-inch barrel are compared to those of standard Colt auto.

the given handgun efficiently. Frequently, this trend toward the use of more powerful guns and ammunition has been prompted by one or more incidents in which the traditional .38 Special has proved to be inadequate as to stopping power. Cases are on record in which the adversary in a shooting situation has been hit in nominally vital areas by as many as six rounds of .38 Special ammunition and has gone on to inflict fatal or serious damage upon others.

In such examples, the .357 magnum has been the popular choice as a more capable revolver cartridge. One obvious advantage is that, in departments where some of the personnel continue to use the .38 Special, the less powerful ammunition can be fired in the .357 magnum handguns, either in practice or if an emergency situation should call for extensive firing to the point of encountering shortages of available ammunition. At the same time, the stronger construction of the .357 frames, cylinders and

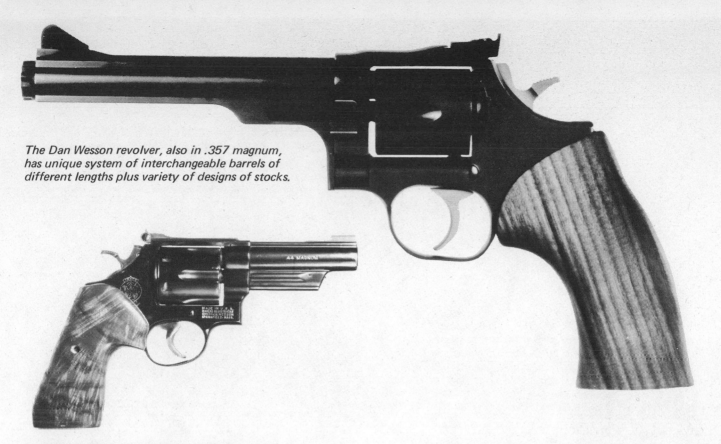

The Dan Wesson revolver, also in .357 magnum, has unique system of interchangeable barrels of different lengths plus variety of designs of stocks.

Smith & Wesson's Model 29, in .44 magnum, is the most powerful double action revolver currently available. This one has four-inch barrel, Herrett's Jordan Trooper stocks in walnut, adjustable sights.

barrels offers an ample margin of extra strength: a feature many consider advantageous.

While the major manufacturers of double action revolvers – Colt, Ruger and Smith & Wesson – offer the .357 magnum in barrels from 2½ to 8-3/8 inches, the six or 6½-inch is considered the most practical length for this caliber, rather than the four-inch length considered standard for the .38 Special. The added sight radius and increased velocity of the longer barrel are well worth the added increase in weight and bulk. Given the proper ammunition, in the hands of a skilled marksman, the .357 magnum is potentially capable of placing its bullet accurately at ranges as great as two hundred yards.

Another old cartridge – the .44 S&W Special – was and is factory-loaded to relatively low power levels, due to the fact that many revolvers chambered for this caliber are holdovers from the days when the cartridge was loaded with black powder. Modern guns, of strong construction, can handle considerably higher pressures and reloaders used to take advantage of this fact by making up handloaded ammunition for the .44 Special at substantially increased velocities and energies.

This resulted in the development of the .44 magnum cartridge, about 1956: again, a cartridge of the same diameter and rim dimensions as the .44 Special, but slightly longer to prevent its use in older, weaker guns. Bullet diameter for both calibers is about .429-inch for jacketed bullets or up to .431-inch for lead types. Bullet weights for the .44 range from about 180 to 240 grains, with the various manufacturers offering a broad choice of jacketed soft-point and hollow-point designs. This compares to a weight spread of about 110 to 200 grains for bullets offered in the .38 Special and .357 magnum loadings.

The .44 magnum has as much power as is apt to be required in a handgun cartridge but many shooters find the noise and recoil so excessive as to pose serious problems in training and duty use. It has been pointed out that a BB-shot which hits its intended target is more effective than a cannon shell that misses and the added capability of the .44 magnum is of little value unless it can be delivered dependably and accurately to the desired point of aim.

Consideration of these facts suggested the desirability of yet another caliber, midway in power and performance between the .357 and .44 magnums and this resulted in the development of the .41 magnum cartridge, early in 1964. Unlike the two older cartridges, the .41 magnum is not an elongated version of a previous caliber. Taking a bullet of .410-inch diameter, the .41 magnum case is appreciably larger in diameter than the all but obsolete .41 Long Colt round. Bullet weights for the .41 magnum range from about 170 to 245 grains in various jacketed and cast lead designs available.

Remington Arms Company, co-developers with Smith & Wesson of the .41 magnum cartridge and revolver, offers two distinct loadings. The less powerful of the two has a 210-grain lead bullet – advertised at 1050 fps muzzle velocity in an 8-3/8-inch barrel – and a 210-grain jacketed soft-point at 1500 fps. Actual velocity in a revolver with six-inch barrel, as measured in a chronograph, comes to about 972 fps for the lead bullet load and 1386 fps for the jacketed soft-point.

The theory behind this arrangement was that it would provide a comparatively mild load for practice or urban duty situations, with an alternate of a more powerful load without the need for reloading.

While the basic concept seems to offer desirable features,

Python, in .357 magnum, is Colt's top of the line model in double action revolvers. This one has been fitted with Hutson pistol scope to exploit long-range accuracy of .357 fully.

Ruger's Security Six double action also is chambered for .357 magnum. Weight and dimensions are no more than those of a typical .38 revolver.

the past twelve years have not seen widespread movement toward general adoption of the .41 magnum. Looking at the situation realistically, the large number of .38 Special revolvers still in service represents a sort of inertia effect. In those departments stipulating the use of a single caliber, changing over would mean the disposal of large numbers of a .38 Special or other given calibers and the acquisition of new guns plus new holsters, cartridge pouches, ammunition for training as well as for duty, plus the substantial number of man-hours represented by re-training of personnel. Viewed as a broad picture, the substitution of a caliber is not a step to be taken lightly.

There are a few other, non-magnum calibers, verging toward obsolescence, which possess sufficient power to qualify as suitable revolver duty rounds. These would include the .38-40, .44-40, .44 Special, .45 Auto Rim and .45 Long Colt. All are, in general, superior to the .38 Special in stopping power, but each suffers from the fact that there is a pronounced shortage of good, modern, double action revolvers chambered for them.

In this connection, it may be noted that the .357 magnum remains the preferred choice, by a wide margin, among those departments which choose to adopt a revolver more capable than the .38 Special and the popularity of the .357 round continues to grow at a moderate rate, some forty-one years after its initial introduction. Considering the historical aspects and the demonstrated slow rate of change in calibers, it seems probable that the .38 Special will remain a caliber with which to be reckoned for many years to come and the .357 magnum — capable of handling the same cartridge — will remain the strong second runner-up. In time, the roles may equalize and reverse, but it does not

seem likely that any wondrous new caliber is going to appear and capture the bulk of the police market within a short space of time.

The foregoing observation is made, not in a crusading or derogatory sense, but rather as a realistic assessment of a fairly obvious and stable state of affairs. Many factors weigh against each other and come into balance in the evaluation of a system of handgun and cartridge for law enforcement work, as has been outlined here. The special set of conditions which may apply to operations in one department and jurisdiction are less than valid when applied to those of another organization, whether nearby or far removed geographically. Circumstances alter cases. Conditions dictate policy.

The following pages contain accounts of testing sessions conducted in an effort to work up some firsthand information as to the effectiveness of various combinations of handguns and ammunition.

One test was conducted by a relatively small police department. Such exploratory tests remain fairly common in spite of a large and growing body of reports and opinions compiled by ambitious and expensive research programs. There is a perfectly natural desire to separate the facts of firearms effectiveness from the myth and folklore, of which a considerable portion seems to have gotten mixed into what often is accepted as fact.

In 1975, the Law Enforcement Assistance Administration published the preliminary findings of an extensive test program it had conducted with the assistance of the Law Enforcement Standards Laboratory, a subdivision of the U.S. Bureau of Standards.

At about the same time and for some while after, the

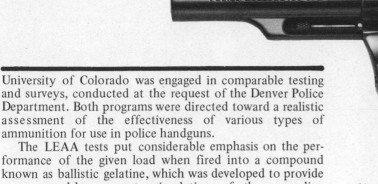

Newest entry from Charter Arms is their .38 Special Police Bulldog, with an empty weight of just 20½ ounces. With its four-inch barrel, overall length is 8½ inches and cylinder capacity is six rounds. A similar design, the .44 Special Bulldog, with three-inch barrel, weighing but nineteen ounces was introduced earlier to fill the need for a light, compact revolver holding five rounds of a heavy, large-diameter load.

University of Colorado was engaged in comparable testing and surveys, conducted at the request of the Denver Police Department. Both programs were directed toward a realistic assessment of the effectiveness of various types of ammunition for use in police handguns.

The LEAA tests put considerable emphasis on the performance of the given load when fired into a compound known as ballistic gelatine, which was developed to provide a reasonably accurate simulation of the wounding capabilities of the bullet in living flesh. Dimensions of the wound channel were recorded by high-speed cameras at the instant of impact. By means of sophisticated computer technology, wounds produced by the given load were evaluated against an inert mock-up of the human torso in terms of typical cones of dispersion obtained by having the loads fired by a representative cross-section of police officers.

Here, the thinking seems to have been that a load of high-stopping potential is of little value if the typical officer cannot cope with the noise and recoil, making him or her unable to employ it with the necessary degree of accuracy.

The LEAA findings were integrated to produce a series of numerical ratings called the Relative Incapacitation Index, or RII. No attempt was made to specify a minimum threshold, although it was suggested that any load with an RII of less than 10.0 might not be acceptable for general police use.

The University of Colorado program gave consideration to the social/political aspects, concentrating on three main points: severity of injury, stopping effectiveness and threat to bystanders.

Severity of injury was based upon the probability of a person's death within two weeks after being shot, assuming a hit in the torso that did not traverse a vital, such as the heart or a major artery. Further assumptions included the rendering of immediate and effective medical treatment.

Stopping effectiveness was judged upon the possibility that a 20 to 40-year-old man of average weight and height would be incapacitated and rendered incapable of returning fire or running away following a hit in the torso.

Threat to bystanders was evaluated on a basis of the remaining energy and tendency to ricochet characteristic of the bullet after passing through a man's torso at a distance of twenty-one feet.

Cartridges tested by the University of Colorado were the 9mm Luger, .38 Special, .357, .41 and .44 magnums and the .45 ACP. It was the consensus of the test crew that the recoil factor and noise level of the .41, .44 and .45 were of such severity as to make them poor choices for optimum employment by typical police personnel.

As in the LEAA tests, the University of Colorado crew utilized ballistic gelatine as their testing medium, taking note of the distance of penetration, maximum diameter of temporary cavity, the distance from the front surface where maximum temporary cavity diameter occurred, the degree of fragmentation or core/jacket separation of the bullet, the number of foot-pounds of energy lost in traversing 150mm of gelatine, original bullet diameter, weight and velocity, the maximum post-impact bullet diameter and its kinetic energy at muzzle and preimpact. Several shots were fired with each load and the results were averaged.

A series of loads placing well toward the top of the LEAA report incorporated the Glaser safety slug, available in loaded ammunition from Deadeye Associates and sold only to law enforcement agencies. This bullet employs a core of silicone-coated shot pellets in place of the usual solid lead, being enclosed by a copper alloy jacket and contained by a teflon nose cap. Upon impact, the bullet disintegrates into tiny fragments, producing a wound that is almost certain to be lethal with any solid hit in the torso, meanwhile minimizing possibilities of ricochet and hazard to bystanders.

The project of endeavoring to evaluate bullet and cartridge performance is by no means recent in origin. As early as 1904, a government commission, headed by Col. Louis A. La Garde, conducted a series of tests with the guns and ammunition available at that time. As ballistic gelatine had not been developed, they utilized ten cadavers which had been sent for dissection to a medical school, as well as sixteen living beef animals and two horses.

It is difficult, in reviewing the tabulated results of these and similar tests, to arrive at a firm judgment as to relative standings. Much depends upon the criteria on which the evaluation is made. If severity of the wound is held to be a minus factor, as in the University of Colorado tests, the Glaser safety slug would rank poorly, despite its high placement in the LEAA tabulations. The La Garde commission concluded that projectile diameter was a highly significant factor, with effectiveness varying in fairly uniform direct proportion, along with bullet nose shape. However, the University of Colorado test rejected all of the larger bullet diameters on grounds that typical personnel could not control them with the requisite degree of accuracy.

All of this tends to suggest that the interested student of such matters can find supporting data to uphold almost any preconceived beliefs. The difficulty lies in an accurate assessment of the optimum choice for a given application, still requiring a decision to be made at the local level of jurisdiction.

It Isn't What A Police Officer Carries, But What He Puts Into Its Chambers!

Smith & Wesson Model 19 Combat Magnum, with 2½-inch barrel offers excellent concealment capability with rounded butt, retains competent penetration with .357 magnum Super Vel ammo.

DESPITE A VAST amount of wordage that has been published on the subject, when a police department decides to consider something new in the line of weaponry, the usual procedure is to conduct some independent tests. Usually, they become interested in the capabilities and limitations of their present guns and ammunition after some startling incident in which the faithful old .38 Special has fallen woefully on its face — or muzzle, if you prefer.

When members of different departments get together, it's a safe bet that the bull session soon will take up the topic of weapon effectiveness. It is a subject of vital concern to any peace officer who takes a degree of interest in the performance of his job and in the preservation of his personal hide.

Since most departments are governed by some group or commission loosely termed the "city fathers," and since the governing group frequently shows more concern over the figures on the annual budget than over purely ballistic specifications, it becomes necessary for department members to muster convincing proof of the need for something better.

Changing over to new calibers or new guns can be a substantial item of expense and thus it is not a step to be taken lightly. For that reason, the frequent condemnations of their .38 Special in the firearms press have not as yet resulted in a country-wide shift to calibers and guns which — while more potent to some varying degree — would involve such an outlay of funds as to soak up the departmental budget for some few years to come.

However, the barrage of the anti-.38 propaganda has served at least one useful purpose: It has caused peace officers all over the country to re-evaluate the stopping power and overall effectiveness of the .38 Special revolver and cartridge with a searching and skeptical eye. In numerous instances, it has been the common consensus that it leaves something to be desired.

With that fact established, it becomes a matter of deciding what to do about the situation. Several approaches are available. Thanks to the developments of the Super Vel Cartridge Corporation in Shelbyville, Indiana, it now is possible to make a sharp improvement in the performance of existing .38 Special revolvers by the simple process of purchasing a few boxes of the Super Vel .38 Special ammunition and using that in place of the more conventional factory loads. The same firm offers ammunition for upgrading the .357 magnum to a comparable degree, as well as other calibers, such as the .380 auto, 9mm Luger, .44 magnum and .45 ACP.

If the .38 cartridge, in its standard loadings, is weak in barrels of four to six-inch lengths, it becomes plain downright helpless in the two-inch barrels of such revolvers as the Colt Cobra or the Smith & Wesson Chief's Special. And, in these shorter barrels, if the regular 158-grain bullet performs poorly, the 200-grain version is completely pathetic by comparison.

And still there are those who advocate the 200-grain

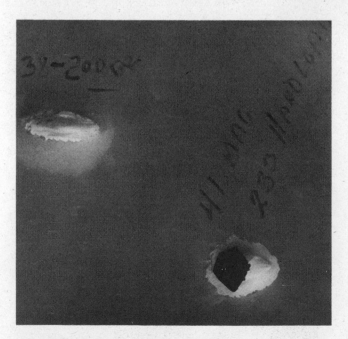

The .38 Special factory load with 200-grain slug merely left shallow dent when fired at 45-degree angle while .41 magnum penetrated deeply into car.

factory load as the ideal stopper, even in short barrels, pointing out that its low velocity keeps it from going completely through a target to waste a portion of its energy on the other side. In fact, I've heard some people advancing the rather startling theory that high velocity loads aren't as effective as slower ones, "because the bullet goes through so fast it doesn't have a chance to do any damage." While this observation may have a plausible sound, the idea is not supported by observed effects of high-velocity projectiles upon living tissue.

Previous tests had been made, by measuring actual bullet velocity through a chronograph. It was found that a typical 200-grain .38 Special factory load comes out of the two-inch barrel at about 572 fps, with an energy of around 145 foot-pounds rather than the claimed factory specs for a six-inch barrel: 730 fps and 236 foot-pounds.

In terms of bullet performance, 572 fps is not much velocity — you can beat that figure by 100 fps or so with certain of the more capable air rifles — and it must be

conceded that the 200-grain slug doesn't penetrate very much. In fact, you can't count on being able to drive one through the ordinary safety glass used in the side windows of a conventional automobile; a few may get through but, often as not, they'll flatten and fall to the ground, even at point-blank range.

Most back windows are designed to shatter into tiny fragments on impact, as this one did. Holes in trunk were from penetration tests of magnums.

Repeated tests with 2-inch barreled .38 Special showed inability to get through common auto body steel with anything short of Super Vel loads.

Point-blank hit with 200-grain .38 Special load in two-inch barrel still did not penetrate side window of test automobile.

Which brings up another key point: Often it happens that the police officer must use his weapon against felons inside an automobile. Few such anti-social types go to the bother and expense of equipping their cars with armor plate or bullet-proof glass. As it turns out, tests show pretty conclusively that almost any old jalopy is an armored car so far as the conventional .38 Special cartridge and revolver are concerned.

The test session under discussion was conducted by the Irwindale, California, police department, under supervision of Patrolman Harry Sibley. A small group of impounded autos, destined to be scrapped, had been hauled to an isolated area in the catch-basin of the Santa Fe Dam, where firing of live ammunition would pose no hazards to life or property.

Advance word on the project had been passed to several nearby departments and several of their officers were attending as spectators or co-experimenters; the latter having brought along some ammunition and guns which they proposed to try out on unperforated areas.

The old junker autos were fired upon with a broad assortment of loads, guns and lengths of barrel from front, sides and rear; from angles of ninety degrees to the target surface on down to more glancing hits.

Since there were no volunteers willing to sit inside and report on the experience of being shot at, Sibley had rigged a cut-out of ¾-inch plywood to serve as a sit-in. Usually, it's conceded that penetration of that much wood is about the equal of a dangerous and disabling wound. As the silhouette representing the driver and passenger of the getaway cars became noticeably moth-eaten, they were restored to duty by nailing patches over the wounds.

It should be explained that firing into or through the

coachwork of an automobile depends on chance to some degree. The lower part of the door conceals things such as armrests and window raising cranks and levers. If the bullet slams up against one of these obstacles, quite a bit of its steam will be wasted then and there.

However, the 200-grain .38 Special slug, launched at less than 600 fps from a two-inch barreled "off-duty gun," proved quite incapable of getting through the outer layer of stamped steel on the doors, even though the car in question was a popular member of the low-priced three. Viewing the shallow gouges left by the 200-grain bullets, one observer muttered wryly, "Halt or I'll scratch up your paint!"

Staying with the same two-inch barrel, but substituting .38 Special Super Vel ammunition with its 110-grain hollow-point bullet, made a world of difference. We've clocked this particular load at 1030 fps from the two-inch snubnosed barrel and it walks smartly through the outer paneling and makes respectable holes in the plywood dummies provided it does not encounter too much extra hardware within the door. The same load in the same gun goes through the glass, filling the air with an explosion of jagged splinters, and on through at least one three-quarter-inch thickness of plywood, expanding to about .45 caliber in diameter. There can be little serious doubt that this particular load offers a vast improvement in the capabilities of a short-barreled .38 Special revolver.

In fact, as we moved to a Smith & Wesson K-38, with its six-inch barrel and the 158-grain, full-jacketed .38 Special load from Norma-Precision — a combination that gives 850 fps and 250 foot-pounds through our chronograph — we found that its performance was closely comparable to that of the Super Vel in the two-inch barrel. Performance of this round is better than standard factory loads and its accuracy is outstanding, but the Super Vel load definitely is more formidable.

Regulation military "hardball" ammunition for the .45

ACP Colt auto, likewise, proved somewhat disappointing: a little better than the standard .38 Special, but not very much.

The 9mm Luger cartridge, fired by Sergeant George Visosky of the Covina, California, police department from his Smith & Wesson Model 39 auto, showed markedly better penetration than the .45 auto and its margin of superiority widened further when he switched to his pet reload using the 125-grain Speer soft-point bullet and 7.0 grains of Hercules Herco powder, which delivers about 1250 fps in the Model 39. For the first time, bullets began blasting through the trunk door, through the back of the rear seat and the back of the front seat to inflict painful damage to the plywood dummies.

The relation between velocity and capability rapidly became apparent. Of the three key factors — velocity, bullet weight and cross-sectional area — the speed of the projectile seems to be of primary importance. Admittedly, the energy in foot-pounds is not the sole consideration and energy retained by a bullet that has passed through the intended target is of no further use. But if the bullet doesn't have the energy at the muzzle, it can't deliver much damage at the point of impact.

A table of bullet energies and velocities, prepared by the makers of Speer bullets, illustrates this point quite graphically. Take, for example, the energy for a 100-grain bullet at different velocities:

600 fps	80 ft-lbs
850 fps	160 ft-lbs
1000 fps	240 ft-lbs
1200 fps	319 ft-lbs
1470 fps	479 ft-lbs

All of the above velocities are well within the capability

Reloads in the .41 magnum with six-inch barrel made the trio of holes indicated by arrow at left. Same three bullets made the exit holes at right, after going through car completely, right to left. The big "portholes" in the door at left were made by slug loads in a standard police riot gun.

of handguns, but note the sharp gain in striking force that accompanies each increase in velocity. If you want to hold the velocity down around 600 fps, meanwhile getting 479 foot-pounds, you've got to have a bullet that weighs about 600 grains; if you kept your barrel diameter at .38 dimensions, the projectiles would be something like three inches long. Or, if you kept bullet length the same, it would have to be nearly one inch in bore diameter.

Obviously, in the quest for more power in a handgun, it's easier, simpler, more practical to increase the velocity within reasonable limits.

But this brings up another factor to consider: the innocent bystander somewhere beyond the fleeing felon. Hardly anyone would question that it would be preferable to allow almost any sort of law-breaker to escape rather than run a serious risk of killing or injuring a guiltless tax-payer.

Here, again, the Super Vel design passes the test with blue-ribbon grades. The light 110-grain bullet, with its thin jacket of gilding metal and its exposed tip of soft lead, shows a strong tendency to upset and expand so as to transmit maximum energy at the point of impact, while its rather low cross-sectional density — particularly after expanding — causes a rapid loss of velocity to minimize the danger to someone a few blocks beyond the intended target. Essentially, the handgun is a short-range weapon with effectiveness limited to not much beyond fifty yards so far as combat accuracy is concerned. The Super Vel loads are intended to achieve maximum effect within this range, meanwhile reducing velocity more rapidly as they continue to plow through the air beyond that point. They are, of course, dangerous at distances a lot greater than fifty yards, but less so than heavier bullets of greater length for the same diameter, and the Super Vel tends to pancake, flatten and break up rather than take off on hazardous ricochets.

With the tests of .38 Special ammunition completed, attention was turned to some of the heavier magnum revolver calibers. While many consider the really heavy artillery to be impractical for standard police duty, there was considerable interest in finding out the exact effect which could be achieved with them.

Starting with a pair of short-barreled .357 magnum Smith & Wessons, a Model 27 with 3½-inch barrel and a 2½-inch barreled Model 19 Combat Magnum, we tried a few of the Super Vel .357 mag loads which our chronograph had clocked at 1300 and 1210 fps, respectively, through each barrel. Here, as with the 9mm Luger reloads by Covina's Visosky, we obtained fairly reliable penetration — except when the bullet encountered massive structural members — with impressive damage to the plywood dummies.

During a conversation with Lee Jurras, he mentioned that his .357 magnum Super Vel loads are checked during production and pressures are taken on their testing equipment to hold breech pressures below the 30,000 psi level. This is well within the capability of a well-made .357 revolver in good condition. Actually, the 110-grain jacketed bullets, available as a separate reloading component from Super Vel, can be driven to somewhat higher velocities than those of the loaded round which, as noted, averages 1300 fps from the 3-5/8-inch barrel. Experimentally, I've obtained as much as 1510 fps with the same bullet in the same barrel with no apparent ill effects in the test gun but I've no doubt that the pressures were running well beyond Jurras' 30,000 psi figures. The crucial point is that the Super Vel ammunition retains a margin of safety as to pressure when fired in the type of arms for which it is intended.

Switching over to the heavy stuff, we trotted out the Model 57 Smith & Wesson in .41 magnum with a six-inch

Jug of water explodes in spectacular burst when hit by experimental cup-point load in .357 magnum, driving water back toward shooter, who was standing at the left in this picture.

Sgt. George Visosky, of Covina, California, PD, checks out performance of his department's M39 S&W in 9mm Luger cal.

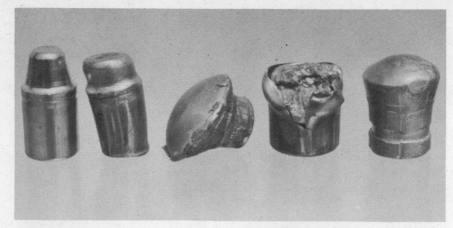

Left: Norma's 158-grain full jacket before and after firing; a 200-grain factory slug; .45 Norma HPt and a Lyman 410426, cast of type metal.

Hot reloads in the .41 magnum sliced through the heavy bumper as if it were tin, but none of the six rounds fired succeed in puncturing rear tire.

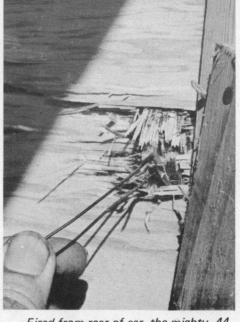

Fired from rear of car, the mighty .44 magnum blasted through trunk and seats, blowing this loop of wire gruesomely through ¾-inch plywood.

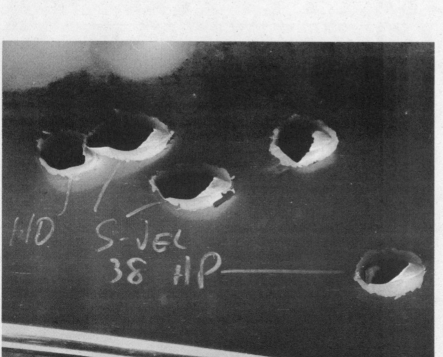

Super Vel's 110-grain bullet, in .38 Special, zipped on into the car with steam to spare, even when fired in two-inch revolver.

Alcan's AL-5 powder, behind the Speer hollow base wadcutter, seated with cavity to the front, develops 1340 fps velocity on a 10.0-grain charge, expand with great ferocity, meanwhile showing good penetration.

barrel and some hot reloads that deliver the Lyman No. 410426 cast round-nose — 233 grains, cast of type metal — at 1480 fps for about 1135 foot-pounds. Fired through the right front door at an angle of ninety degrees, the big slugs slammed through three thicknesses of plywood, blowing splinters all over the place and very nearly made it through the opposite door, leaving big welts and small holes in the paneling of the far side.

A Ruger Super Blackhawk, in .44 magnum caliber, firing Remington factory soft-points — Index No. 6844, "recommended for rifles" — performed even better. One three-shot burst into the test car equalled the performance of the .41, then went howling through the opposite door and made impressive dents in the front bumper of another car standing behind the first one. We switched to a .44 mag reload: the jacketed hollow-point 210-grain bullet by Super Vel, ahead of 29.0 grains of Hodgdon's H-110 pistol powder; this delivers right around 1680 fps out of the Super Blackhawk for a little over 1300 foot-pounds and it performs with enthusiasm. Fired from the rear, it blows a dime-sized hole in the tough, 1/8-inch steel of the bumper and keeps on going. The most impressive shot — in a grisly sort of way — from the .44 mag coursed through the trunk lid, through the backs of both seats, blowing a big loop of wire from the upholstery through the plywood "driver's" left kidney, through the dashboard and raised hob with the engine's air cleaner before coming to rest.

The traditional police riot gun gave a fine account of itself with double-ought buckshot and, particularly, with rifled slugs. The buckshot waltzed through the doors much better than did the .38 Special slugs from standard factory loads, with a few pellets getting part way through the opposite doors. But the rifled slugs left us thoroughly impressed, blowing great gaping holes through the doors and showering the interior with fragments of lead and door; again, no question as to capability. Lighter shot, however, doesn't even get through the first layer of paneling.

With little time remaining for that particular session, Sibley produced a number of jugs filled with water; the familiar plastic type used for laundry bleach. These were placed in an empty window and shot with various loads. Once again, the 200-grain .38 slug proved woefully lacking in knock-down power. After being shot, the jugs didn't even tip over but just sat there as water went glug-glug and slowly leaked through three-eighths-inch holes at front and back. Super Vel loads, in .38 and .357, slammed the jugs abruptly backward, ripped from top to bottom by hydrostatic shock, with a fine burst of spray dousing everything inside a ten-foot radius.

As one final sample of the reloader's art, we tried some of the maximum-effort .357 magnum cup-points. The bullets consist of a 148-grain Speer hollow-base wadcutter, with a .38 gascheck slipped over the step at the nose. They are seated backwards, crimped in the last grease groove, on top of 10.0 grains of Alcan's AL-5 shotgun powder; velocity is about 1300 fps in the 3-5/8-inch barrel but the expansion is impressive indeed. Expending most of its energy close to the surface, this load had the singular effect of blowing the water-filled jugs forward, rather than backward, with massive rents and rips in the front part of the jug. The water explodes in a thick cloud of droplets, leaving little doubt as to the shocking power of the .357 when properly loaded.

Oddly enough, this load and a similar one for the .44 magnum using point cast bullet both displayed good penetration through the car body, proving that expansion doesn't necessarily halt penetration if you have enough velocity behind it. But some amount of velocity — say, roughly 1000 fps or so — is necessary; were this not so, you could knock an adversary down by flicking marbles at him with your thumb...and it seems that the 200-grain factory slug from a snubnosed .38 isn't much more formidable than that.

As IF THERE were not enough problems involved with choosing the ideal handgun for carrying while on duty in uniform — a matter discussed elsewhere in this book — the correct choice becomes even more elusive in the area of a handgun for purposes of concealment when off-duty or working in plain clothes.

There are many factors which influence the final choice. Climate and temperature affect the amount and type of clothing worn and this, in turn, governs the amount of concealment available. The officer's proportions and physique play a significant role, as well. There are large, rawboned men who can pack a four-inch-barreled .44 magnum revolver under a suit coat with less betraying bulk than a smaller man might show if carrying a small automatic pistol.

There is no reliable way to predict the exact circumstances under which a concealed handgun may be needed and used. However, it is highly probable that the situation will be such that the gun must be drawn and fired with the greatest amount of speed and accuracy possible. The chances are that the adversary will have a loaded gun in hand and will be ready to shoot as quickly as his reaction time permits. Drawing "under the gun" is an adventure not to be undertaken lightly.

Assuming a typical situation in which the law-breaker has a gun in his hand, it becomes obvious that the concealed handgun must be brought into action quickly, accurately and — of equal importance — effectively. Unless the opponent is disabled almost instantly, he will fire one or more shots with his gun, endangering the officer and innocent people nearby. This consideration rules against concealable handguns whose stopping capability is below an arbitrary minimum level.

On the other hand, special circumstances can arise in which concealment is at a premium and the available space

in minimal. The considerations can be such that any gun — no matter how puny and diffident — is better than no gun at all. In an example such as this, one of the tiny .25 automatics may be indicated. Of such arms, the best that can be said is that they serve as a threat and a deterrent, rather than as a capable weapon in the customary sense of the term.

At the next level up from the .25 autos, we find the small pocket automatics for the .32 and .380 auto cartridges. The .32 auto, while remaining reasonably popular, cannot be rated as substantially superior to the .25 auto, although the .380 auto begins to approach the threshold of adequate capability: particularly with some of the more recently introduced ammunition such as the jacketed hollow-point loads by Super Vel.

A variety of small pistols, most of them foreign-made, are available for these two cartridges. Some feature the double action design, which permits the hammer to be carried down over a live round in the chamber, so that the gun can be drawn and put into action simply by pulling the trigger through a longer stroke.

The chief virtue of the autoloading pistols for concealment work lies in their somewhat slimmer profile, due to the absence of a cylinder. If the slight amount of added bulk is not objectionable, the indicated choice leans toward one of the several makes and types of short-barreled revolvers available.

Although some of these can be had in calibers lighter than the .38 Special — such as the .38 S&W Long — there is little advantage in the lighter calibers to offset the reduction in power as compared to the .38 Special. In fact, when fired from a two-inch barrel, even the latter cartridge is not particularly powerful, although the light weight of the gun itself does increase the apparent amount of recoil to a marked extent; particularly in those arms having aluminum alloy receivers to further reduce the net weight.

Chapter 4

THE UNDERCOVER HANDGUN

Out Of Sight, But Not Necessarily Out Of Mind, Routine Duty Poses A Challenge To These Guns!

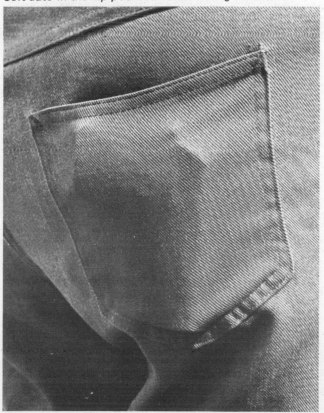

Even the smallest handgun can betray its presence by distinctive contours, as in the case of this .25 Colt auto in the hip pocket of close-fitting trousers.

Several designs are available in the short-barreled .38 Special revolvers. Some are of hammerless design, others have shrouds protecting the spur of the hammer; permitting the hammer to be cocked or lowered manually, if desired, meanwhile preventing the spur from catching on clothing so as to interfere with the draw. Various lightweight versions are made, such as the Smith & Wesson Airweight or the Colt Cobra. Finishes include the traditional blued steel, nickel plate and, as a further degree of resistance to corrosion, the Smith & Wesson Model .60, which has all of its metal parts made of appropriate stainless steel alloys.

For officers requiring more power in a concealable handgun that can be derived from the .38 Special cartridge, the next step upward is the .357 magnum. For many years, S&W has offered their Model 27 in a snub-nosed version with 3½-inch barrel. This brings the muzzle approximately flush with the front of the ejector rod housing. The frame and butt of the Model 27 retained the same dimensions as in conventional models, resulting in a moderately bulky weapon.

Within more recent times, S&W has added their Model 19, designated as the combat magnum, with barrel lengths available in 2½, 4 or 6 inches. A standard, square-butt version of the Model 19 is made, plus a round-butt model which trims a useful amount of bulk in this area for added concealability.

A comparable arm is the Colt Mk III Lawman model, with a heavy barrel in two-inch length and a butt which is a good compromise between shooting capabilities and concealability. Ruger's Security Six comes in 2½, 4 and 6-inch barrel length.

Only slightly larger than the 3½-inch Model 27 S&W are such designs as the same company's Models 57 and 58 in .41 magnum — available with four-inch barrel as well as six — and the Model 29 in .44 magnum, offered in 4, 6½ and 8-3/8 inches. Any of these offer close to the absolute maxi-

Aluminum alloy frame of Colt's Cobra cuts its weight to a feathery 15 ounces. Rounded grip corners offer a good compromise between solid hold and reduction of betraying bulges when worn.

In addition, the Colt Commander and Government Models are chambered for the .38 Colt Super as well as the .45 ACP; outside dimensions remain the same as for the 9mm Luger round and weight is about the same: slightly less in the instance of the .45 ACP, due to the larger amount of metal removed from the bore of the barrel.

The Spanish Star and Llama auto pistols are made in .38 Super and .45 ACP, basic designs being quite reminiscent of the Colt, with minor variations. All will be discussed in greater detail in a following chapter. However, they are mentioned here to stress the fact that, when the objective is the selection of a capable, concealable handgun, the auto pistol deserves thoughtful consideration and "equal time" with the short-barreled revolver, despite the fact that many officers rarely think beyond the snub-nosed .38 in reviewing this category.

A particular problem with certain of the snub-nosed revolvers, such as the S&W Model 10 Military & Police with two-inch barrel is that the design necessitates shortening of the ejector rod to the point at which a full available stroke of the rod is not enough to push the fired cases free of the

S&W's Airweight Bodyguard also employs alloy to keep its poundage down to 14½ ounces. Usually fired double action, design permits single action cocking, when desired, without hammer tang hang-up.

Snub-nosed version of S&W Model 15 Combat Masterpiece has two-inch barrel in place of the usual four. Featured are full-size grips, for those who prefer them, and fully adjustable rear sight.

mum amount of power and stopping capability within the dimensions of a handgun capable of being concealed from casual detection when wearing typical civilian garb, such as a business suit.

Neither Colt nor Ruger manufactures a double action revolver in calibers larger than the .357 magnum at the present time.

Several autoloading pistols are available in the medium to high-power categories and many of these are not appreciably more bulky than typical revolvers discussed here previously. Some are chambered for cartridges which do not give much edge to the .357 magnum, when fired in comparable barrel lengths.

The 9mm Parabellum — often termed the 9mm Luger — cartridge is the most popular round in the medium high-performance category of auto pistol cartridges. Typical guns chambered for it would include the Model 1935 Browning Hi-Power, the Smith & Wesson Model 39, the Colt Commander and Government Models, plus a host of European designs such as the Star, MAB, SIG-Neuhausen and Beretta. Many of these rival the snub-nosed revolvers in the area of practical concealability.

Colt's Diamondback also carries full-sized grips and adjustable target-type rear sight, vented rib. Same gun's available in other barrels, .22 version.

chambers. With the problem fully grasped and understood, often it is possible to accomplish complete and positive ejection by holding the muzzle uppermost and slapping the ejector rod down smartly. Otherwise, it will be necessary to pluck some or all of the empty cases from the chamber by hand. This poses a serious obstruction and delay in the reloading cycle and routine firing and reloading drill should be conducted in such a manner that the best procedure becomes conditioned instinct.

In this context, it is appropriate to bring up an important consideration. During normal firing practice on the range, revolver shooters become accustomed to pushing out the empty cases with some degree of care, returning them to a container or the shooter's pocket for reloading at a later date. The habits and conditioned reflexes so developed can constitute a serious handicap in an emergency shooting situation. Under stress, the mind tends to cling to habit patterns. When split seconds are of vital importance, instances have been recorded in which an officer lost more time than he could spare in punching out the empty cases carefully and wasting a moment in indecision over what to

S&W's Centennial is completely hammerless in design, can only be fired double action when the grip safety is depressed. Available as the Model 40 with steel frame or the M42 with aluminum alloy frame, respective weights are 19 and 13 oz.

Same gun shown in a pocket on page 47, Colt's .25 auto is about as small as it's practical to build a gun. Current model, here, has exposed hammer.

The S&W Model 60 is a recreation of firm's old Chiefs Special, with all metal parts of stainless steel alloys for maximum corrosion resistance.

Here's the Dan Wesson Model 14, with four-inch barrel and traditional grips. Chambered for the .357 magnum, these guns have unique feature of being able to change barrel to those of other lengths. Two-inch barrels can be had, with other stocks.

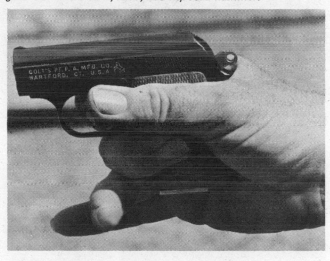

do with the empty brass.

Accordingly, while it may entail extra effort and time in routine practice sessions, it is sound strategy — on the range — to develop the habit of jabbing the empty cases out onto the ground each time the cylinder is emptied, reloading as smoothly and rapidly as possible and policing up the spent brass as a separate, later step. True, an occasional cartridge case may be stepped upon and ruined, but cases are infinitely more expendable than the lives and physical well-being of the officer.

While concealment handguns are equipped with sights — usually of the fixed, non-adjustable variety — the typical employment of such arms makes little if any use of the sights in the usual manner. Often, the concealed handgun is put into action from extremely short ranges, at which the instinctive point-and-pull technique is not only practical but mandatory under the circumstances.

While the discussion is elaborated in considerable detail in a later chapter, it is relevant to note at this point that the effective accuracy of the concealable handgun often can be improved to a most useful degree through the installation of stocks which have been engineered to function best in

Colt's Lawman Mk III features massive barrel, steel construction to help soak up the recoil of .357 magnum cartridge; this is two-inch type.

For those who prefer a longer barrel and a larger stock, Charter Arms makes this .38 Special model with three-inch tube and their Bulldog grip design.

S&W Model 36 Chiefs Special is in .38 Special, about the smallest gun that can be made for this cartridge. Five-shot cylinder helps cut bulk.

Colt's Diamondback is a scaled-down, .38 Special version of firm's popular Python model in .357 magnum, retaining many of big gun's features such as protected rod, vented rib.

Charter Arms' Undercover .38 Special here has standard size stocks of select wood, elaborate scrollwork engraving for those willing to pay extra for such features. Plain version shoots as well. Five-shot cylinder permits locating locking notches off-center for added chamber strength.

Smooth, slender, standard grips and nickel-plated finish distinguish this .38 Special from Charter Arms. Their Undercoverette is similar, made for the less powerful .32 S&W Long cartridge.

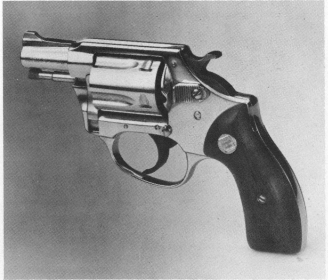

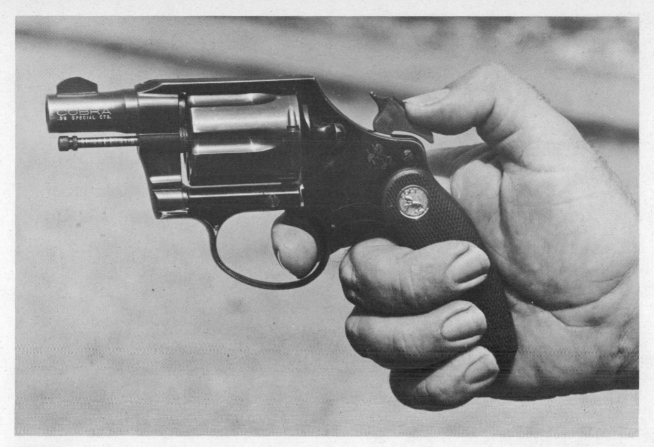

De-fanging the Cobra: Great care must be taken when lowering the hammer upon a live round in the chamber and muzzle pointed in safe direction.

Long a popular model in Colt line of concealable handguns, the Detective Special is chambered for .38 Special, has six-shot cylinder — as do all of Colt's revolvers — steel frame, squared stocks.

such types of shooting. As a rule, such stocks are slightly greater in bulk than the standard factory grips, but it may be felt that enhanced accuracy at instinctive shooting is a factor which more than offsets this minor sacrifice in concealability.

As has been noted, sacrificing barrel length toward concealability dictates a corresponding sacrifice in potential muzzle velocity which, in turns, gives away foot-pounds of energy at a steep rate — energy varying as the square of velocity, so that cutting the velocity in half cuts the energy down to one-quarter — and this consideration places vastly increased importance upon the accurate placement of the bullet. Given marginal power, a hit in certain small, strategic areas will do the required job whereas being off the intended mark by so much as a few inches will not have the same effect.

Which is to say that the responsibility of the concealed handgun is, if anything, more weighty than that of its larger counterpart which is carried in full view when on duty in uniform. This consideration mandates an even greater need for practicing with the concealed handgun to attain the highest possible combination of speed plus accuracy and total reliability.

The undercover handgun needs the greatest amount of power and capability which may be possible and practical under the given circumstances and these advantages must be exploited to the fullest degree possible, if there is to be any amount of assurance that the officer and his concealed handgun will be capable of coping effectively with a sudden emergency situation.

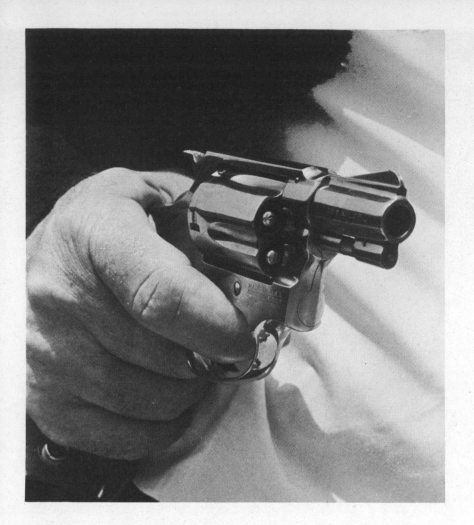

S&W's Stainless Model 60 Is Tested For Accuracy And Ballistic Qualities As A Clue To Snubnosed Performance!

THE MODEL 60 Smith & Wesson .38 Chiefs Special stainless revolver is an innovation from the standpoint of metallurgy, rather than design. The pattern is fairly well standardized, having been in the S&W catalogs for many years. Only the metal has been changed to protect against corrosion. Except for the stocks, which are nicely made of light-colored walnut in the familiar S&W contour, the entire revolver is made of various appropriate alloys of stainless steel. Even the little S&W medallions in the grips, as well as the escutcheons which hold them in place, are of stainless and all of the metal seems to be of highly ferrous alloys, since any given part is strongly attracted by a magnet. As you probably know, there are a great many different alloys categorically lumped under the name of "stainless steel," including a few paradoxical examples which are even capable of developing ordinary rust. The alloys chosen for the Model 60 allegedly will not rust from moisture, salt, humidity, sweat or any of the other agents which the gun may be expected to encounter in its normal — or, for that matter, abnormal — career.

The Model 60 may be considered an incorruptible modification of the older Model 36 .38 Chiefs Special, except for a few minor changes. For example, the flat, vertically serrated thumb piece used on the Model 36 and on the .38 Bodyguard Airweight has been replaced by the curved and checkered thumb piece found on the larger S&W designs; this makes it noticeably easier to unlatch the cylinder when swinging it out for loading.

Dean Grennell owns a conventional blued-steel Model 36 which he bought, second-hand, several years ago. Since it's almost identical to the Model 60, except for the metal, we planned to use it as a comparative standard.

Both of the guns — Models 36 and 60 — have barrels nominally two inches in length. We say "nominally," because the point is a little moot. One common way of measuring barrel length is from muzzle to bolt face; by this technique, the Model 60 measures 3.473 inches. Measuring from muzzle to the front surface of the cylinder, we get a dimension of 1.865 inches; from muzzle to the tip of the bullet in a typical factory load, the distance is 1.950 inches — which is about as close as we could come to the hypothetical spot two inches back from the muzzle. Measuring from a typical Remington or Western factory load, the base of the bullet travels approximately 2.5172 inches from its loaded position within the case until it exits from the muzzle.

We used a Schrader gauge to measure the single action (i.e., hammer cocked) trigger pull of the Model 60 and found it to be a clean, crisp fifty-six ounces. Grennell's Model 36, having been fired extensively for several years, has worked its single action pull down to a light forty-four ounces. The amount of double action pull was, in either case, well beyond the capacity of our measuring device. However, both guns display the velvet-smooth double action pull which S&W aficionados admire. By shifting the grip farther around, putting more finger through the trigger guard, you can rest the fingertip against the frame during the last fraction of an inch of trigger travel and, by means of this technique, let the hammer fall about as smoothly as if the hammer had been cocked. With a reasonable amount of practice, it is not too difficult to keep all shots "in the count" on a standard fifty-foot pistol target at that distance, when firing one of these double action.

The barrel of the Model 60 is rifled with a right hand

Remington's 158-grain Police Service load — Index No. 5138 — chronographed 685 fps in the two-inch barrel, for an energy rating of 163 ft-lbs at muzzle.

Except for the use of stainless steel instead of blued steel, the Model 60 is quite similar to M36 Chiefs Special.

twist, using the customary S&W rifling of five lands and five grooves. The lands and the grooves are of approximately equal width: roughly .115 of an inch. The S&W five-groove rifling is characterized by excellent accuracy but is slightly frustrating since that useful dimension, the groove diameter of the barrel, cannot be measured except with rather specialized and sophisticated gadgetry not ordinarily available. However, for all practical purposes, the groove diameter may be assumed to be .357 of an inch since cast bullets, sized to .358-inch, do not show any indications of fins or deformation at the base when fired with a light powder charge into cotton waste.

The snubnose revolver, in caliber .38 Special, is used extensively by law enforcement personnel whose duties require that they be inconspicuously armed with a handgun capable of speaking with some degree of authority. Since the two-inch barrel is used widely and because most of the ballistics data available on the .38 Special was obtained from longer barrels, we thought it would prove interesting to run some checks on the Model 60 with emphasis upon accuracy and power rather than on its non-corrosive qualities. We felt that its ability to emerge unscathed after being boiled in borscht was admirable and not to be lightly discounted. However, the prime function of a gun is to shoot.

One of the first things we did was to run some conventional factory loads through the chronograph out of the Model 60. Our ballistics tables usually rate the 158-grain lead bullet load in .38 Special at 855 fps from a six-inch barrel, with an energy of 256 foot-pounds at the muzzle. We wondered how much of that steam escapes when you bob four inches off the front of the barrel.

A round of Western Super-X, with a 158-grain Lubaloy-coated bullet (Index No. 38S1P), was clocked at 600 fps, right on the nose. For that weight and speed, the muzzle energy is 126 foot-pounds — which was rather disappointing, considering that even the lowly .32 auto cartridge is rated at 145 foot-pounds from a four-inch barrel. We

loaded in a round of Remington .38 Special Police Service (Index No. 5138) and triggered its 158-grain lead bullet through the chronograph: 685 fps was the reading, for a muzzle energy of 163 foot-pounds. That was better, but it was still far short of the rated 256 foot-pounds, claimed for the six-inch barrel.

The common approach to getting more power is to use a heavier bullet. We doubted if this would do the trick, but determined to try it anyway. We dug up five loose rounds of Western's 200-grain load. This is rated at around 730 fps from a six-inch barrel, giving 236 foot-pounds of muzzle energy. We flung one of these through the chronograph and got a reading of 572 fps. It seemed as though a person with well developed cheek muscles should be able to spit tobacco juice almost that fast!

Again we consulted the helpful tables in Sharpe's Complete Guide to Handloading and found that the good gentleman had not anticipated that anyone would mess around with velocities lower than 600 fps, because his tables started at that point. With a bit of interpolation and the aid of some scratch paper, we estimated the energy of 200 grains, loafing through space at 572 fps, to be in the neighborhood of 145 foot-pounds — again, in the same category as the .32 auto cartridge!

Grennell long since had established that his Model 36 shot precisely to point of aim, with its non-adjustable

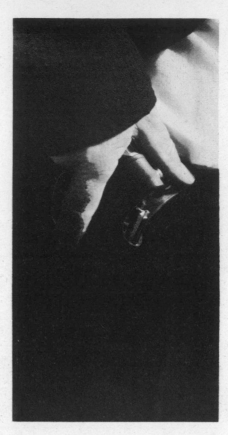
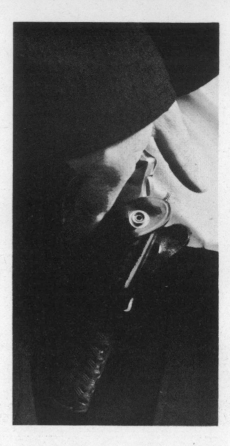

Stop-motion sequence of photos, above and at right, show the Model 60 being drawn from a thumb-break holster. Note that the index finger does not touch the trigger until the muzzle is safely clear of leather.

sights, at ranges within twenty-five yards, when fed a diet of Lyman No. 358250 cast bullets and 4.7 grains of DuPont P-5066 powder. Besides being able to take dead aim, the load grouped close together to a degree astonishing in so small a gun. We chronographed one of these loads — the round-nosed bullet weighs 154.5 grains, cast of hard alloy — and got an encouraging 748 fps out of the Model 60. That was good for nearly 193 foot-pounds and at last we had forged ahead of factory ballistics on the .32 auto and were now neck and neck with the .380 auto (factory rated at 955 fps for its 95-grain bullet with 192 foot-pounds from a 3.75-inch barrel).

Since the desired function of the snubnosed .38 Special is to inflict a wound which will disable a hostile opponent, rendering him incapable of further hostility within the shortest possible interval after being struck, we shifted our attention from the round-nosed bullet designs to more ferocious nasal configurations.

Several years ago, the late Charles Heckman — then president of C-H Die Company — introduced a bullet-making press called the Swag-O-Matic. Various nose punches were offered with this machine to turn out desired configurations up front where it counts. One of these is called the cup-point; it features a cavity approximately hemispheric in shape with a diameter only slightly less than that of the bullet. In the .38 (.358-inch diameter), this cavity is .275-inch diameter with a depth of .125-inch.

Originally, the Swag-O-Matic was designed for use with copper half-jackets together with cores of dead-soft lead. Swaged bullets, thus made, expanded well but tended to cause undesirable leading of the barrel. We recently had been doing some experimental work on swaged bullets, in connection with a testing program and had been getting promising results by starting with cast bullets — sized and lubricated in the usual manner — then putting them through the Swag-O-Matic press to re-form the nose. With this technique, the regular bullet lubricant remains in the grease grooves to provide discouragement to barrel leading, and mildly hardened alloys can be used without undue strain on the swaging press.

As a starting point, we chose the Lyman No. 35887 wadcutter design. This bullet, designed a few years ago by Charles Page, of Piqua, Ohio, is offered in two lengths, weighing 125 and 137 grains — the difference being a wider driving band at the base on the heavier version. We chose the 137-grain No. 35887, as made and sold by Green Bay Bullets, and put several of these through the Swag-O-Matic with the cup-point nose punch installed. The resulting bullets are .575-inch in length and the average weight is 138 grains; they are seated in the .38 special case to a depth of .550-inch.

Many people have suggested powders other than Hercules No. 2400 for high velocity handgun loads but No. 2400 still delivers good performance in most applications. We found that the two-inch .38 Special was no exception. Currently Hercules loading tables omit listings for No. 2400 in the .38 Special but the Lyman Reloading Handbook gives 13.5 grains as the maximum for a 148-grain bullet, while the Speer Manual for Reloading Ammunition (No. 6 edition) gives 12.0 grains as maximum for a 146-grain bullet. Since we were seating the cup-points rather deeply, we worked up to 11.5 grains of No. 2400 and stopped at that point. We suggest that 9.5 grains might be a good starting point if our readers wish to try this load and any heavier charges may be tried at the discretion of the individual reloader and/or shooter.

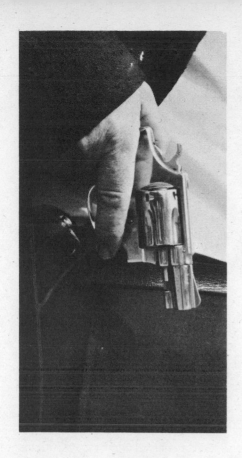  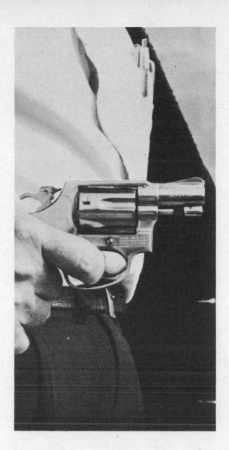

Maximum-effort load, with cup-point bullet, as described in the text, made these impressive exit holes in slab of hardwood. Standard, round-nosed bullets did not expand.

Exploded view of the Model 60 shows all component parts in relation to one another. All metal parts are of various appropriate stainless alloys, even to the grip medallions.

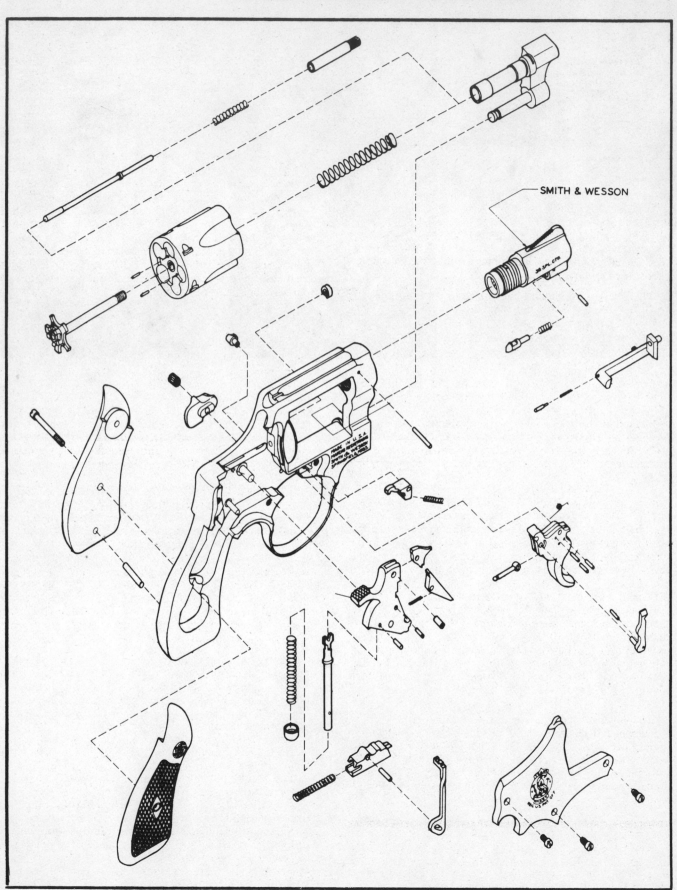

SMITH & WESSON

Reloaded cartridges in .38 Special Remington-Peters brass, CCI-550 magnum primers, using the modified wadcutter previously described, with a powder charge of 11.5 grains of Hercules No. 2400, gave a velocity of 910 fps from the two-inch Model 60 Smith & Wesson. This computes to a muzzle energy of 252 foot-pounds — which we considered to be acceptably close to the factory specifications for the .38 Special cartridge in six-inch barrels. Moreover, the expansion of the cup-point, at this or higher velocities, leaves little to be desired. When fired into a hardwood plank, one and one-half inches thick, from the two-inch barrel, exit holes averaged two by four inches in area. Round nosed factory loads, fired into adjacent portions of the same plank, merely pushed through, leaving exit holes slightly smaller than bullet diameter with a slight extrusion of fine splinters.

You may wonder if the cup-point displays reasonable short-range accuracy. So did we. Five rounds were fired through a Smith & Wesson K-38, fitted with a Bushnell Phantom optical sight, from an arm rest at thirty-five feet. The entire group went into one ragged hole which could be completely covered by a nickel, with room to spare. We felt that the accuracy of the cup-point could be considered adequate at combat ranges.

We observed no obvious indications of excessive pressure with the 138-grain cup-points and 11.5 grains of No. 2400. Empty cases extracted easily from the chambers and the appearance of the fired primer was comparable to primers from mid-range target loads.

We had recently received a test sample of the Super Vel Police ammunition in both .38 Special and .357 magnum. This is manufactured by the Super Vel Cartridge Corporation and delivery is restricted to duly constituted law enforcement agencies. Lee Jurras, the president of Super Vel and its companion enterprise, the Jurras Bullet Company, suggests that if civilians wish to obtain some of this ammunition, they may be able to order it through their local police department.

The samples of Super Vel ammunition are loaded in virgin — i.e., previously unfired — cases as supplied by Norma-Precision. The bullet is manufactured by Jurras, with a three-quarter length jacket and a hollow point in the exposed lead tip; weight is 110 grains, nominal: 110.2 grains by scale check on a pulled sample. Bullet diameter is .3564-inch — a good compromise for best results in either .357-inch S&W barrels or the undersized Colt barrels which may have groove diameters as small as .3535-inch. The jacket extends up past the tapering portion of the nose — diameter at front of jacket is .308-inch — so that no exposed lead touches the barrel. The hollow point cavity is tapered, being .140-inch at the top, .100-inch at the bottom, with a depth of .120-inch; lead tip is .150-inch long.

The powder charge in the .38 Special Super Vel weighs 8.2 grains and the propellant resembles Hercules Unique in appearance. The .357 magnum Super Vel seems to use the same powder in a charge that weighs 10.5 grains. Please note that while the powder resembles Unique, it probably is actually some type not available in canisters to the reloaders.

NOTE: *Do not interpret this discussion as a suggestion to load Hercules Unique in the weights given here since they might be considerably, in excess of recommended charges as given in various reloading manuals.*

We chronographed the Super Vel ammunition through various lengths of barrels readily available in the two calibers and obtained the following velocities:

| | .38 Special Super Vel | |
Barrel Length	Velocity, fps	Muzzle Energy, ft-lbs.
2.0"	1030	258
3.5"	1135	315
6.0"	1295	410
	.357 magnum Super Vel	
3.5"	1300	414

You will note that the actual delivered performance of this load in the snubnosed Model 60 — 258 foot-pounds — is slightly better than the (usually optimistic) factory rating for standard ammunition in guns with a barrel length of six inches. Further, from a six-inch barrel, the .38 Special closely approximates the power of the .357 magnum in the snubnose (3.5-inch) S&W version. Factory rating on the .357 magnum tends to be misleading since most such figures are taken from barrels 8.375 inches in length and such arms are generally impractical for law enforcement purposes because of their size.

We felt that we had found various means of putting adequate power into the snubnosed .38 Special and so we proceeded to check it out for accuracy. The Model 60 has the rather small, rounded butt commonly used on this type of S&W. Several firms offer stocks designed to provide a better grip. Unfortunately, such stocks add bulk to the gun, thus partially nullifying the purpose for which it was designed in the first place. Moreover, none of the snubnosed grips that we've ever tried have been any assistance in improving the shooting qualities of the snubnose. Indeed, we've never found a grip that shoots as well on these little guns as the stocks that the manufacturer provides as original equipment. However, this is a matter of personal preference.

At a distance of seventy-five feet, the 110-grain bullet of the .38 Special Super Vel loads printed below point of aim. This was not surprising since this is common when lighter-than-standard bullets are used in guns with non-adjustable sights. However, we understand the general thinking is that shooting low is something of a virtue since most inexperienced marksmen tend to shoot high. Firing the Model 60 with the Super Vel loads, we got a five-shot group from seventy-five feet which measured 4.310 inches, with four of the holes going into a 2.578-inch group. Center of the main group was approximately five and one-half inches below point of aim at that distance.

Factory ammunition with 158-grain lead bullets printed approximately to point of aim at seventy-five feet in the Model 60, with groups spreading from four to eight inches. Offhand, slow-fire groups rarely exceeded the size of the ten-count "kill area" of the standard seventy-five-foot police silhouette target.

We fired five rounds of the Super Vel .38 Special ammunition from the scoped S&W K-38 (six-inch barrel) from an arm rest at seventy-five feet and got a 1.712-inch group. This would have been more impressive if we had not just previously held four of the holes into an area nearly that small when firing the tiny Model 60 off-hand with fixed iron sights!

Summing up, it does not appear that the Model 60 has suffered in the slightest by being made of stainless steel insofar as accuracy is concerned. On the contrary, it generally shot tighter groups than Grennell's cherished Model 36 — which is made of blued but rustable steel.

Chapter 5

AUTO PISTOLS IN LAW ENFORCEMENT

The Self-Feeders Are Showing Steady Gains Against Revolvers And Here Are Notes On The Makes And Models Deemed Suitable!

THE EARLIEST PRACTICAL autoloading pistols began to appear in the final years of the Nineteenth Century. By that time, the basic revolver design had taken the form which remains little changed to the present.

Firearms design has remained relatively static in an era of competitive up-dating in most other fields. Perhaps this is because there are but a few areas in which a firearm can be improved.

You can make it shoot farther, faster, straighter, harder or through a greater thickness of barrier. You can increase the ammunition capacity, the reliability or the speed of replacing fired cartridges. You can make it more compact, lighter or lower in cost.

Most of these avenues toward improvement have been explored to the outer practical limits. Arms designers are faced by the problem that any extension of a key factor in one direction usually produces a corresponding effect in another. For one example, increasing the power — in terms of velocity or bullet weight — will increase the recoil and noise.

For that reason, the design of handguns reflects the end result of a chain of inter-related compromises: long barrels deliver more velocity but short barrels are less cumbersome; heavy bullets of large diameter offer better stopping power, but smaller, faster loads offer flatter trajectory and larger ammunition capacity within comparable gun size. Extremely precise fitting of parts contributes to accuracy, but may render the gun less dependable and certainly makes it more expensive to manufacture and purchase. These are but a few of the many considerations which must be weighed and reconciled with each other in designing any gun.

Let us briefly review the basic principles of the autoloading or semi-automatic handgun. In strict and precise usage, "automatic" implies a gun which continues to fire so long as the trigger is held back. In other words, a full-auto firearm. In a few rare instances, handguns have been manufactured that embodied a fire-selector which offered the option of full-automatic fire. Such guns were intended to be used in conjunction with a detachable shoulder stock which also was offered. In actual practice, a handgun firing

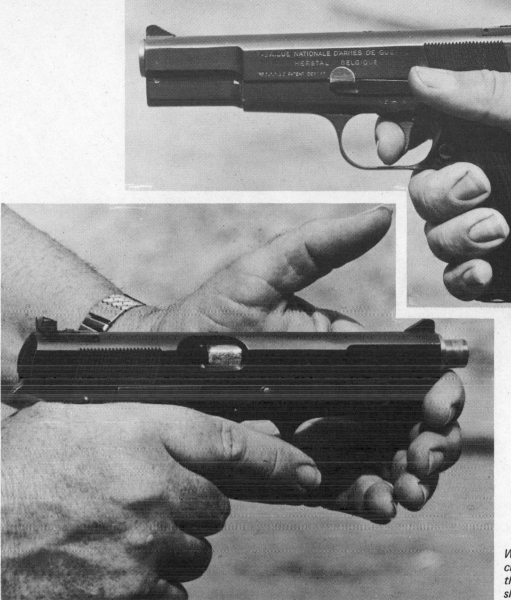

Thirteen in the staggered box magazine plus one in the chamber give the M35 9mm Browning a 14-round capacity. Lower portion of loop hammer spur has been removed on this one to stop nipping of shooter's hand when firing: This, with the added target sights make it a highly satisfactory auto.

With magazine in place, chamber can be checked by this method without locking slide open. With most autos, slide will halt before locking.

full-automatic is impossible to control. Which is the reason why handguns are designed to fire but a single shot with one pull of the trigger. Although they reload themselves automatically, it is necessary to release the trigger, allowing it to move forward and pull the trigger again to fire the next shot.

Autoloading and automatic arms are designed to function via several basic systems, but virtually all autoloading handguns harness the force of recoil to accomplish the operation of ejecting the fired case, re-cocking the hammer and chambering a fresh round. Depending upon the power of the cartridge being used, the system may be a straight-blowback or a recoil-operated, firing on a locked breech.

With cartridges, developing relatively low levels of force, such as the .32 or .380 auto calibers, the mass and inertia of the slide alone is sufficient to contain the forces generated at the peak of firing pressures. With larger cartridges, such as the 9mm Luger or the .45 ACP, the breech is tightly locked up for a brief interval after the cartridge has been

fired and the barrel and slide recoil as an integral unit for a short distance. As the pressure diminishes, the slide unlocks from the barrel and is free to recoil rearward to complete the remainder of the firing cycle.

In either case, as the slide separates from the barrel, a hook-like extractor drags the spent case out of the chamber, pulling it rearward until an ejector, stationary in the receiver, strikes the opposite rim of the case and flips it out through the ejection port of the slide. Simultaneously, as the slide moves rearward, it re-cocks the hammer, readying it for firing the next shot. At the same time, the slide is compressing a recoil spring which will force it back forward after completion of its rearward travel for the completion of the firing cycle.

Since all of this takes place in a small fraction of a second, it is impossible for the shooter to release the trigger during the process. Therefore, a device known as the disconnector is embodied in the design of the auto pistol. As the slide commences to move rearward, this disconnects the trigger from the sear, allowing the sear to resume its normal

Sandblasted nickel plated finish on this Colt Commander offers tops in protection, with bonus of attractive appearance.

position, so that it can engage the cocking notch of the hammer. It then becomes necessary to release the trigger, allowing it to move forward to re-engage with the sear so that the next shot can be fired by a subsequent pull of the trigger.

Were it not for the disconnector, the semi-automatic feature would not be possible. With the trigger remaining rearward in the instant following the firing of the round, the sear notch could not engage the hammer notch and the hammer would drop back down as the slide moved back forward under the impetus of the recoil spring. This might result in full-auto fire — impossible to control, due to the up-flip of the muzzle after each shot — or, more probably, it would result in a malfunction of the firing process, with the hammer dropping back down on the firing pin without setting off the next cartridge.

In well designed handgun systems, the force of the recoil is closely counterbalanced by the mass and inertia of the slide, together with the resistance to compression of the recoil spring. As a result, the slide retains but little force as it comes to a rest against the built-in stop at the rear of its travel along the receiver.

Once the slide stops its rearward travel, the force of the compressed recoil spring starts pushing it back into a fully closed or "battery" position. As the slide moves forward, a projection on its lower surface encounters the upper edge of the next loaded round, which has been forced to the top of the magazine and held in place by the magazine spring. The slide, traveling with considerable force, impels the next live round out of the magazine and shoves it forward until the nose of the bullet encounters the feed ramp — an inclined surface milled into the receiver and/or into the lower rear portion of the barrel. This deflects the cartridge upward, guiding it on into the chamber. At this point, the extractor hook will have engaged the rim or extractor groove of the chambered round, preparatory to extracting it after the next firing.

In a preceding section on revolvers, there has been a

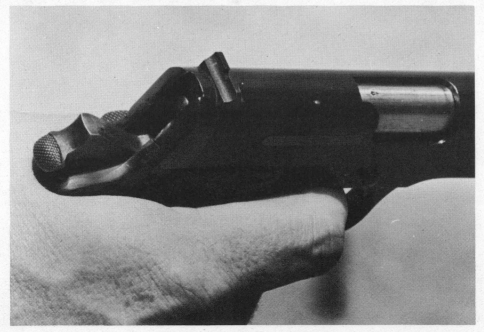

Broad hammer spur and large knurled safety of this 9mm Star afford positive operation.

discussion of the fact that virtually all revolvers depend entirely upon manual operation of the trigger or hammer by the shooter to prepare the gun for the firing of the next round. To plug up all loopholes, it is necessary to insert "virtually," because there once was a handgun called the Webley-Fosbery that sought to incorporate the best features of autoloaders and revolvers. It employed the force of recoil to cock the hammer and advance the cylinder to place the next chamber in line with the barrel. The Webley-Fosbery was not a great success and has been obsolete for many years, but is noted here for the sake of complete coverage.

Provided the revolver cartridge does not have a primer protruding excessively from the head, to hang up on the recoil plate, or does not have a bullet nose protruding from the face of the cylinder to prevent rotation behind the barrel, a pull of the trigger or cocking of the hammer followed by a pull of the trigger, will result in dropping the firing pin upon the primer of the next round. If the primer functions and if there is sufficient powder inside the cartridge, the bullet will be driven out of the muzzle of the revolver, leaving it in readiness for the firing of the next round, if unfired cartridges remain in the cylinder. In other words, all the revolver requires is a lack of mechanical interference, plus powder enough to clear the bullet from the barrel and it will continue to function in some minimal manner.

The autoloading pistol is slightly more demanding. In order to continue to function, the cartridge fired previously not only must have sufficient force to drive the bullet clear of the barrel but the recoil force so generated must be enough to slam the slide all the way to the rear. Further, if the primer was defective, the inert round will remain in the chamber, requiring the slide to be drawn fully to the rear manually in order to eject the dud load and chamber another for a fresh try.

If the cartridge in an auto generates insufficient force to work the action, any of several things may happen. Starting from the weakest example and working toward a normal load, there may not be enough force to extract the spent case and it will be rechambered or will remain in the chamber. With a bit more energy, the spent case will be extracted, but not ejected. Usually, in such cases, it will hang up on the side of the chamber, rather than going back in. This results in a stoppage or "jam." During either of the foregoing instances, the hammer may or may not be re-cocked for a second shot but, if it is, it will fall on an inert round, with no subsequent shot being fired. With just a bit more force being generated, the spent case will be ejected but the slide will not be driven back far enough for it to pick a fresh round out of the magazine upon moving back forward. In this example, the cocked hammer will drop on an empty chamber and no round will fire.

The foregoing discussion lists several instances in which an autoloading pistol will fail to fire if the previous load has not developed the full power required. Assuming that the previous round did generate sufficient force to drive the slide back to full-stop, it still is possible to encounter a malfunction in an auto pistol

The second series of malfunctions can occur, if there is any interference in feeding the next round out of the top of the magazine and on into the chamber. While not a common occurance, it can happen through a defect in the magazine or a deficiency in the ammunition. The angle and position of the next round is rather critical, to greater or lesser degree, depending upon the particular design of the handgun in question. A good magazine will hold it in the right place and position; a magazine with worn or distorted guide lips will not. The vast majority of all feeding problems in auto pistols can be rectified by replacing the worn

This two-handed hold affords maximum steadiness of aim. Gun is the Model BKS Star 9mm, with alloy frame which holds weight to a feathery one pound, eleven ounces, empty. Imports such as this one, from Spain, may be sole handgun source if laws are passed forbidding civilian handgun ownership.

Star Model BS, also in 9mm, has steel frame, boosting empty weight to two pounds, six ounces. Barrel is five inches: about five-eighths longer than that of the Model BKS Star. Both models have eight-shot magazines, plus one in chamber for nine.

As noted in text, the .38 Colt Super autoloader in one of the most capable of all gun/cartridge combinations, remaining unappreciated, due to wide availability of .45 ACP and 9mm Luger, for which companion guns of the Colt line are offered.

French-made MAB is offered with choice of eight or fifteen-round magazine, can carry ninth or sixteenth cartridge in its chamber.

or damaged magazine with one that is adjusted and contoured properly.

Even the best of magazines can produce stoppages if there are defects in the ammunition or in the remainder of the gun's mechanism. As has been noted, the feed ramp is designed to guide the nose of the bullet up and into the chamber at the rear of the barrel in a smooth, continuous movement. If the feed ramp is pitted, roughened or fouled with the powder and primer residue of rounds fired previously, it may offer enough added friction as a result so as to prevent smooth and reliable chambering. Alternatively, if the seated bullet differs too greatly from design limitations of the given handgun, this can produce a stoppage, even with a perfect magazine and an ideal condition of feed ramp.

If the bullet is seated so far out of the case as to give an excessive length over all, it can interfere with feeding up through the magazine. In handguns of marginal feeding capability, a bullet which has exposed areas of soft lead on its nose can set up enough added friction to prevent reliable chambering. A bullet which is unusually short, or is seated so deeply as to produce a too-short length over all, may be deflected upward too violently, so as to collide with the upper edge of the chamber, rather than being guided into seated position.

Beyond the basic principles discussed here — which apply to most if not all auto pistols — there are certain significant variations. Most of these are concerned with the method of getting the first shot off from the customary carrying mode.

Several pistols are of the "hammerless" design — which means that they actually have hammers which are enclosed by the rear of the slide and thus not accessible to be cocked or lowered manually. Other designs feature an exposed hammer, permitting the hammer to be lowered over a live round in the chamber, so that it only is necessary to cock with a flick of the thumb and commence firing.

In general, the exposed hammer is the more popular of the two and most of the more recently introduced designs have this feature. A second design feature which has been gaining in popularity and demand is that of double action for the first pull of the trigger. By this arrangement, a live round can be carried in the chamber with the hammer down and the gun can be fired with a single deliberate pull of the trigger, with no need to cock the hammer manually. Of course, the first pull requires somewhat more effort than subsequent shots, at which time the action of the pistol will have cocked the hammer, requiring only the shorter, lighter single action pull. A conversion device which allows this feature to be incorporated in several existing designs is discussed in detail, later in this book (section VII, Chapter 1).

One further notable feature is the staggered-column magazine design, which offers a substantial increase in magazine capacity. Such magazines are slightly wider than the single-column type, but provide room for nearly twice as many rounds. The French-made MAB pistol is offered with a choice of magazines which hold eight or fifteen rounds of 9mm Luger ammunition, while the Browning M1935 Hi-Power, which is manufactured in Belgium for Browning Arms Company, features a staggered-column magazine with a capacity of thirteen rounds. The staggered-column principle is impractical with cartridges

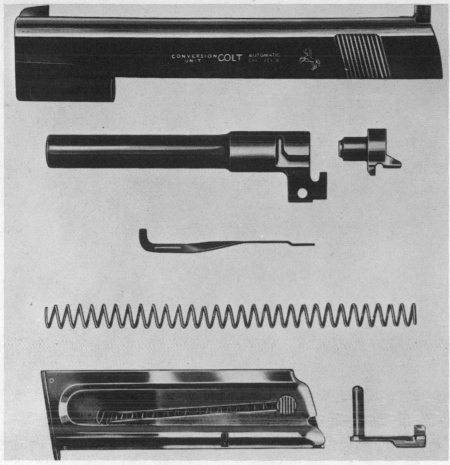

Snap-strap of the Safariland Model 55 holster can serve as added safety feature when carrying .45 Colt auto in its cocked and locked mode with a live round in the chamber.

Conversion unit for Government Model Colt auto pistols permits practice with economical .22 long rifle cartridge; not available for Commanders.

larger in diameter than the 9mm Luger, so far as pistols are concerned which carry the magazine inside the handle, although several submachine guns chambered for the .45 ACP use this system, the magazines being carried forward of the handle.

Performance and specifications of ammunition, both factory and handloads, will be discussed at greater detail in later sections of this book. However, brief notes follow on those calibers for which autoloading pistols currently are being manufactured.

The .22 long rifle is not usually considered suitable for use in law enforcement work, although the combination of velocity plus expansion capabilities of the high-speed hollow-point .22 LR are equal or superior to the .25 ACP and .32 ACP. Several imported pocket autos are available in this caliber, some of which are sufficiently small in dimensions to make them marginally practical for concealed or undercover applications.

The .25 ACP, or 6.35mm cartridge stands at the foot of the class, so far as velocity and stopping power are concerned. As with .22 LR and .32 ACP, about the best that can be said of it is that it is better than nothing, but not much. Its fully jacketed, round-nosed bullet has modest penetration and the low muzzle velocity achieved by the light powder charge, out of the typical short barrels of these guns, assures that the bullet will never expand after impact. Despite the unimpressive paper ballistics and meager stopping power, the .25 ACP, together with the .22 LR have a rather high mortality record, usually with death occurring several days after the shooting. For this reason, guns of this caliber should be treated with appropriate re-

spect when encountered in the hands of suspects.

The .30 Luger cartridge is not represented by any large number of guns suitable for law enforcement work and currently in production. The Mauser Parabellum, made to the basic design of the Pistole '08 or German Luger, is available in .30 Luger caliber and is in current production at the substantial price of $265, with a six-inch barrel. The same gun can be had at the same price in 9mm Luger with a four-inch barrel, although most would consider it priced out of the market for this particular application. Further, while the .30 Luger offers moderately high velocity from the six-inch barrel, no factory ammunition is available at present with expanding bullets and the small-diameter, full-jacketed, round-nose bullet offers much penetration but little in the way of stopping power. Several variations of the Luger have been manufactured in .30 Luger in past years and may continue to be encountered as used guns in assorted barrel lengths.

Much the same observations apply to the .30 Mauser or 7.63mm cartridge. Slightly longer than the .30 Luger, also with a bottle-necked case design, the .30 Mauser was designed for use in the Mauser Military pistol, late in the Nineteenth Century. Due to the fact that this gun carried its magazine ahead of the trigger guard, rather than in the handle, its dimensions were excessively bulky in terms of effective barrel length. A few "police models" were produced, with barrels of approximately four-inch length but these are rare collectors' items today and still are bulky for their performance and capability. The only other auto currently made for the .30 Mauser pistol cartridge is the Russian Tokarev: not a design likely to be adopted by police

Model 39 Smith & Wesson is one of the few auto pistols with double action design feature; only made in 9mm.

Until recently, Colt offered the 9mm Luger chambering only in its Commander series. Now available in the Government Model, as well, the five-inch barrel boosts velocities.

departments in this country!

The .32 ACP, or 7.65mm auto falls into the same category of inadequacy as the .25 discussed previously. Seriously deficient in stopping power, it serves as a deterrent when displayed, but a high-speed .22 LR hollow-point is slightly superior in stopping power. As with the .25 auto, no expanding-bullet factory loads are available for the .32 auto for the present. Even given a jacketed hollow-point bullet, it is doubtful if the small case and the short barrels typical in the .32 auto could generate sufficient velocity to assure reliable expansion in tissue. Most of the autos available in caliber .32 do not even offer the super-compact dimensions which are the sole virtue of some of the .25 autos. Were there an award for the world's most useless cartridge, the .32 auto would be a strong contender for that dubious title.

Moving up the ladder, we have the .380 auto, known in Europe as the 9mm Corto or 9mm Short. This can be regarded as the lower threshold of capability, so far as armament for law enforcement work is concerned and it achieves this conditional rating by virtue of high-performance ammunition recently introduced by manufacturers such as Super Vel Cartridge Corporation. The traditional factory load for this caliber, with a round-nosed, full-jacketed bullet of about 95 grains weight, is rated at

about 955 fps from a 3¾-inch barrel, giving muzzle energy of 190 foot-pounds.

As often happens, when off-the-counter factory ammo is fired through a chronograph to check the actual velocity, the results may fall a bit short of factory specs. Tested from a Browning .380 auto, with a barrel 4-7/16 inches in length, three lots of factory ammunition gave the following performance, based on five-shot averages:

Brand	Bullet Weight	Velocity	Energy
Browning	95 grains (FMJ)	925 fps	180 ft-lbs
Peters	98 grains (FMJ)	893 fps	168 ft-lbs
Super Vel	88 grains (JHP)	1104 fps	238 ft-lbs

The 9mm Luger cartridge climbs upward into those levels of energy and pressure too high for the straight-blowback action. With this round, it is necessary that the breech be locked for an interval after firing, until the bullet has left the muzzle and pressures have been reduced. Working at pressures which are relatively high in comparison to most handguns, the ballistics of the 9mm Luger reflect its efficiency to an extent surprising in view of its small size.

The past few years have seen great progress, insofar as factory loads and reloading components for the 9mm Luger

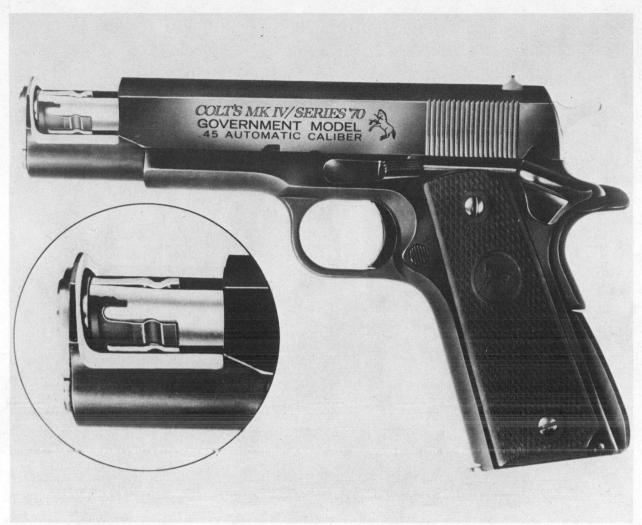

In 1970, Colt modified the design of their Government Model pistols by incorporating a split, collet-type barrel bushing that engages a tapered section at the muzzle with great precision, improving the accuracy of production guns to a considerable extent. Colt does not offer this in the shorter barreled Commander model, although Bar-Sto Precision can supply their stainless steel barrels with collet bushing for the commander in 9mmP, .38 Super and .45 ACP.

are concerned. Not long ago, it was impossible to obtain any load much more capable than the standard round which delivered a 125-grain, full-jacketed, round-nose bullet at about 1120 fps from a four-inch barrel, for energies of 345 foot-pounds at the muzzle. Although that represents a superiority of nearly 100 foot-pounds over the .38 Special revolver cartridge, the resulting load was long on penetration, but tended to carry much of the energy on beyond the intended target.

Today, several factory loads offer jacketed soft-point or hollow-point bullets of comparable weight, velocity and energy. These are quite capable of dependable expansion, so as to deliver virtually all of the energy to the target for maximum effect. Some of the factory loads, as listed in the section of this book discussing performance of ammunition, boast not only bullets designed to expand efficiently, but velocities and energies that are higher than the traditional 9mm load, by a substantial margin.

Considering that the compact dimensions of the 9mm Luger cartridge make it possible to design guns with a large magazine capacity, this is one of the most effective and suitable of all cartridges for an autoloading pistol in police work.

The cartridge known as the .38 Colt Super has led a marginal existence for several decades, without ever win-

ning any substantial portion of the popularity and acceptance that it probably deserves. Although available in a couple of Spanish-made autoloaders, the Star and the Llama, the primary firearms chambered for this caliber have been the Colt Government Model and Commander. Since both of these are offered in 9mm Luger and .45 ACP — both being cartridges widely used by the military forces of several nations — the .38 Super has been over-shadowed and overwhelmed, almost to the point of extinction: this, despite the fact that its ballistics will beat either of its contemporary calibers decisively.

The .38 Super is a victim of a vicious circle: Continuing in relatively limited use, it does not offer a large and attractive market to the ammunition manufacturer. As a direct result, no large amount of effort has been made to develop and market factory ammunition which will exploit the capabilities of this gun and its cartridge to the fullest extent. And this, in turn, hobbles the caliber against hopes of further growth and acceptance by the shooting public, including law enforcement personnel. All of which is somewhat depressing, because the .38 Super is capable of coming close to matching performance of the .357 magnum revolver cartridge. Whether the day will come when the .38 Super achieves its share of recognition before it is dropped from the ammunition manufacturer's list as an unprofitable and

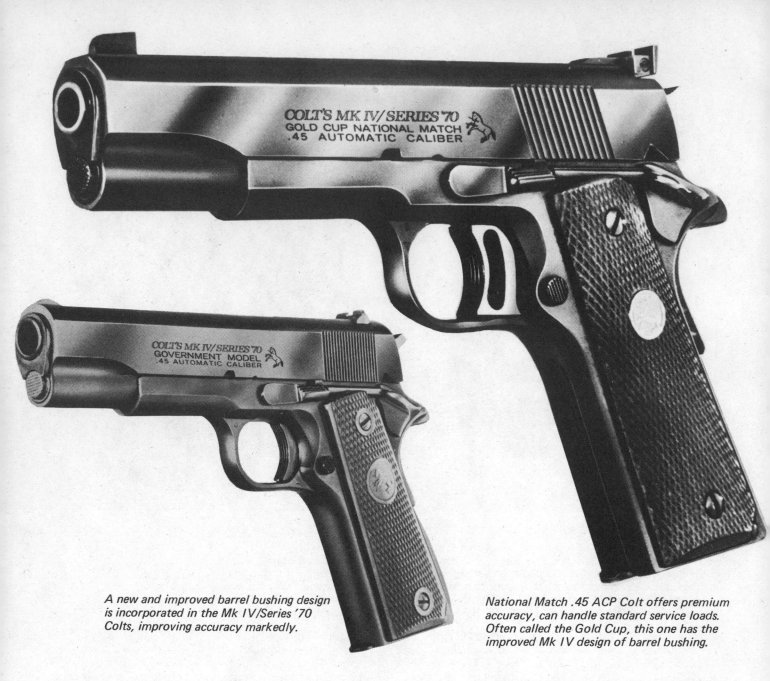

A new and improved barrel bushing design is incorporated in the Mk IV/Series '70 Colts, improving accuracy markedly.

National Match .45 ACP Colt offers premium accuracy, can handle standard service loads. Often called the Gold Cup, this one has the improved Mk IV design of barrel bushing.

obsolete number, only time can tell.

The .45 ACP – it stands for Automatic Colt Pistol – has seen enough guns and ammunition produced to its specs to assure a place in the sun for so long as handguns continue to be manufactured and employed. The relevant phrase, here, is: "Perhaps not the world's greatest, but one helluva good average." Again, as with the 9mm Luger, the popularity and wide acceptance of this gun and cartridge has encouraged the development of factory ammunition which upgrades its potential sharply over the levels long considered standard.

Although unable to operate at the pressures of the 9mm Luger, the .45 ACP offers the advantages of a large cross-sectional area, contributing to its effectiveness, even with non-expanding bullets. Add to this, the recent introduction of factory loads incorporating bullets which expand reliably at the velocities attained and you have a gun/cartridge combination which rates well up at the top of any ranking as to handgun capability.

The .44 AMP – standing for Auto Mag Pistol – reigns as undisputed heavyweight champ of the autoloading pistol

field and can give a good account of itself among revolver rounds, as well. However, as with the .44 magnum in revolvers, the gun and its cartridge are somewhat too lavish, both in physical bulk and performance – not to mention noise and recoil – to be considered seriously in law enforcement applications, except for highly specialized employment.

The .44 AMP was designed, primarily, for hunting large game with handguns and is well suited for this application. Much of the same observations apply to its companion cartridge, the .357 AMP, which is a necked-down version of the same cartridge, for use in an auxiliary barrel which can be interchanged with that of the .44 AMP, using the same receiver and magazine.

Comparative advantages and disadvantages of the revolver vs. the autoloader have been outlined and discussed in a preceding chapter. Much good and a bit of bad can be said of either and, in the final analysis, a selection must be based upon the factors and considerations of the specific situation.

With well maintained guns of suitable design and ammunition of high quality, reliability of the auto pistol will

Combat Commander has steel frame for added weight and durability, comes in choice of nickel or blue, calibers 9mm, .38 Colt Super or .45 ACP, as desired.

Original Colt Commander employs frame of aluminum alloy, thereby shaving about nine ounces of weight. Barrel of the Colt Commander is three-quarters-inch less than the five inches of Government Model.

compare favorably with that of revolvers. The more pertinent consideration is that of safety in routine duty use. In this area, revolvers are comparatively simple and straightforward. Regulations will vary between departments, in that growing number which have adopted auto pistols, as to the prescribed mode of carrying and use. Some specify carrying with a loaded magazine and empty chamber, requiring that the slide be drawn back and released to put the gun in readiness for firing. Obviously, this is considerably slower than drawing and firing a double action revolver. At the same time, it offers about the maximum degree of safety in the use of an auto.

With the M39 S&W pistol, as has been discussed, a live round can be carried in the chamber, with the hammer down and the gun can be drawn and fired as quickly as with a double action revolver, by simply pulling the trigger. In this particular pistol, if the hammer is cocked, moving the safety to its "on" position will cause the hammer to drop, interposing a sturdy bar of steel to keep it from striking the

firing pin. Certainly, this is a better system than the somewhat precarious process of lowering a cocked hammer over a live round by the use of a cautious thumb. However, it should be stressed that, with the safety of the M39 on, the gun cannot be fired until the safety lever is put down, even though there is a live round in the chamber and the trigger is pulled. Thus, vital time could be wasted in getting the gun into emergency action.

Some departments specify that autos such as the Colt Government Model be carried "cocked and locked," perhaps with the snap-strap of the holster beneath the hammer as an added safety precaution. This has proven a fast and effective mode. However, if the officer has done extensive practicing to develop speed at drawing and getting off the first shot — as with an empty gun — there is a distinct possibility that, in a sudden emergency, he may yank out the gun, mash down the safety lever and trigger off a shot from pure reflexive habit, even though he did not intend to fire at that time. This is a possibility which should be considered in personnel training.

Chapter 6

INSIDE YOUR HANDGUN

Although You're Urged Not To Explore The Inner Workings, Here Are Some Things To Know!

THE BETTER GRADES of modern handguns, as used in police work, are remarkably dependable. However, as with all mechanical devices, operation can become sub-standard, due to a number of factors.

Dust, dirt, residue from primers and powders, metal fouling and similar foreign matter can clog up the inside of a handgun, interfering with its functioning. If the gun is not kept clean and free of such accumulations, increased wear on the parts can result, as most such material is more or less abrasive.

Details on the cleaning, lubrication and maintenance of handguns are given in a following section of this book. Here, we're concerned with those minor irregularities which sometimes crop up in the best of handguns.

Beyond the point of field-stripping an autoloader for routine cleaning and lubricating, it should be stressed that the more the mechanism of the handgun is left alone, the longer and better it is apt to continue performing its intended functions.

Manufacturers of handguns have made intensive studies of the anticipated performance of their guns in any of the broad range of temperature and climate conditions in which such guns are carried and used. This research has been used to set up standards of adjustment and tolerances which are intended to assure reliable performance under any predictable circumstances.

For example, the setting for the hammer fall must exceed the minimum force required to set off cartridges in cold temperatures. Likewise, each part must function correctly under all conditions. Any tampering with the factory adjustments, particularly if done by personnel unfamiliar with the operation, can result in a gun that is unreliable or completely unworkable.

Any operating irregularities detected by the officer in routine firing of his handgun — as in range practice — should be brought to the attention of the department armorer for correction. If the staff does not include an armorer, it is common for a local gunsmith to handle such problems.

It should be noted that the people who style themselves as gunsmiths come in a wide assortment of capabilities. This is not said to belittle the many good gunsmiths. Indeed, most of the more capable members of the fraternity express at least as much concern over the situation as might any disappointed customer.

The other personnel of smaller departments should be able to suggest the name of a reliable gunsmith in the area, basing such recommendation upon experience with his work, delivery time and fees in the past.

After any work has been performed upon the mechanism of a handgun, it should be tested extensively — with practice ammunition and with at least one full magazine or cylinder of service loads — before returning the gun to duty status. Instances have occurred in which a defective handgun was sent in for repair and, upon being returned, was loaded and shoved into the holster without testing as

Circles indicate (top) the protruding portion of the disconnector of a Colt .45 auto and (lower) matching notch in lower surface of slide to depress this part as slide commences recoil.

Dinan recoil buffer, above, replaces Colt auto recoil spring guide, helps to cushion force of hot loads.

Condition of magazine lips plays vital role in feeding reliability; these two are good ones for Colt .45 auto.

Colt .45 auto has lower portion of its feed ramp machined into upper front of magazine well, going on to blend into beveled portion at lower rear of chamber. Both must be clean, smooth and well fitted to assure positive reliability of feeding.

described here. Later, when it became necessary to employ the handgun in the line of duty, it was discovered that the original malfunction had not been corrected, a new defect had turned up or, in a few unfortunate instances, both conditions were present. Obviously, such a state of affairs is most disturbing when it crops up in a duty shooting situation and it's best avoided.

Most revolvers have their internal mechanism enclosed by side plates which are fitted with great precision. These plates are held in place by screws. It is depressingly common to encounter a good revolver that has been disassembled by untrained hands. This is clearly apparent by the fact that the slots of the screw heads are burred badly. In addition it may be evident that the would-be gunsmith has used the screwdriver to pry off the side plate.

As has been noted, the disassembly of revolvers should not be undertaken by untrained personnel — and this includes most gun owners — but, if it is going to be done, it should be done properly. The screwdriver must fit the slot of the screw head precisely, both as to width and thickness. In many guns, this will require more than one screwdriver, merely to loosen and remove the securing screws.

The screws should be laid out in an orderly manner, on a flat surface, so that they will not be lost or put back into the wrong place. With all of the securing screws removed, the proper way to loosen and remove the side plate is by tapping down gently, all around the plate, using the butt end of the screwdriver: This assumes that its handle is made of plastic, wood or a similar, non-marring material. As the tapping is continued — not on the edges of the plate, but on the frame of the gun immediately around the plate — you will see the edges of the plate begin to work upward, due to the inertia of tapping down on the frame. Use patience and continue tapping for a bit longer, until the side plate can be lifted off easily with the fingers.

Although it has been discussed elsewhere in this book, it bears repeating here for emphasis: The engaging surfaces of hammer, trigger and sear on revolvers are surface-hardened. Any attempt to stone them down in an effort to lighten the trigger pull will remove the hardened surface, exposing the soft metal beneath. This will accelerate wear greatly, requiring replacement of the parts in a short time. Only those lubricants approved for use by your department should be used on the internal parts of a handgun.

COLT GOVERNMENT MODEL AUTOMATIC PISTOL
CALIBER .45

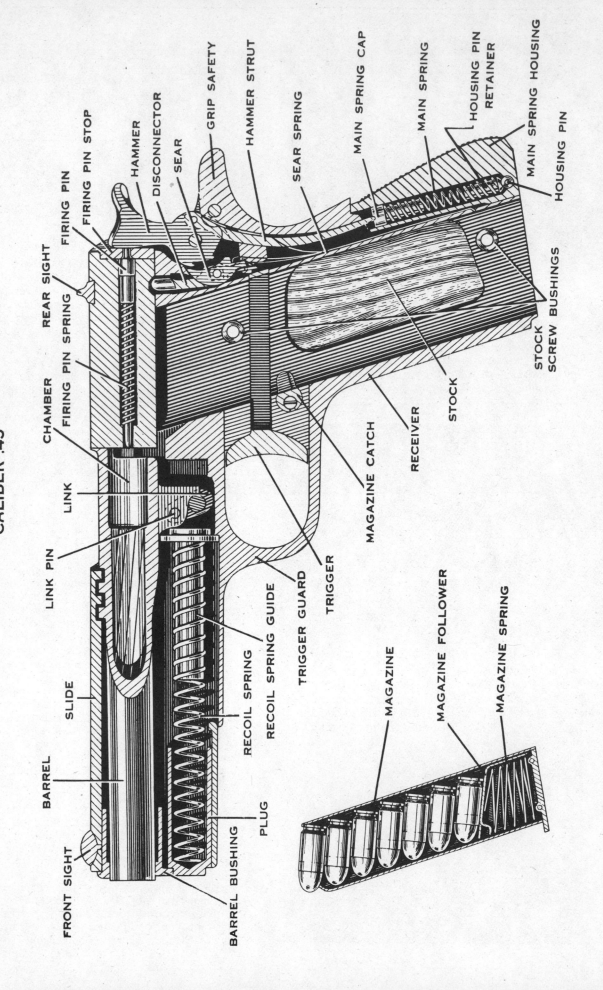

FIRING PIN STOP
FIRING PIN
HAMMER
DISCONNECTOR
SEAR
GRIP SAFETY
HAMMER STRUT
SEAR SPRING
MAIN SPRING CAP
MAIN SPRING
HOUSING PIN RETAINER
MAIN SPRING HOUSING
HOUSING PIN

REAR SIGHT
CHAMBER
FIRING PIN SPRING

LINK PIN
LINK

SLIDE

BARREL

FRONT SIGHT

BARREL BUSHING
PLUG
RECOIL SPRING
RECOIL SPRING GUIDE
TRIGGER GUARD
TRIGGER
MAGAZINE CATCH
RECEIVER
STOCK
STOCK SCREW BUSHINGS

MAGAZINE
MAGAZINE FOLLOWER
MAGAZINE SPRING

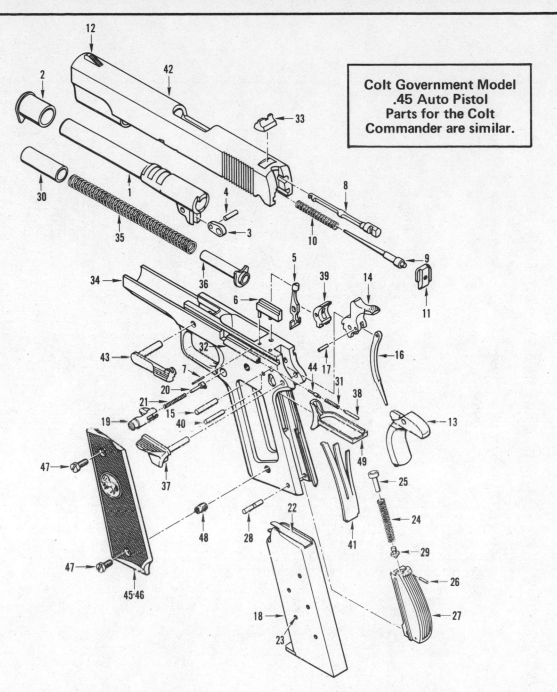

**Colt Government Model
.45 Auto Pistol
Parts for the Colt
Commander are similar.**

Drawing Number	Part Number
1 Barrel	50142
2 Barrel Bushing	50145
3 Barrel Link	50143
4 Barrel Link Pin	50144
5 Disconnector	50147
6 Ejector	50169
7 Ejector Pin	50170
8 Extractor	50184
9 Firing Pin	50185
10 Firing Pin Spring	50186
11 Firing Pin Stop	52434
12 Front Sight—1/10″	50189
12 Front Sight—.125	50193
13 Grip Safety	53821
14 Hammer	50150
15 Hammer Pin	50153
16 Hammer Strut	50151
17 Hammer Strut Pin	50152

Drawing Number	Part Number
18 Magazine Tube Detail Assembly	50201
19 Magazine Catch	50155
20 Magazine Catch Lock	50007
21 Magazine Catch Spring	50156
22 Magazine Follower	50199
23 Magazine Spring	50200
24 Main Spring	50158
25 Main Spring Cap	50159
26 Main Spring Cap Pin	50160
27 Main Spring Housing	50161
28 Main Spring Housing Pin	50163
29 Main Spring Housing Pin Retainer	50162
30 Recoil Spring Plug	50206
31 Plunger Spring	50165
32 Plunger Tube	50171
33 Rear Sight—1/10″	50190
33 Rear Sight—.125	50194
34 Receiver	

Drawing Number	Part Number
35 Recoil Spring	50204
36 Recoil Spring Guide	50205
37 Safety Lock	50174
38 Safety Lock Plunger	50166
39 Sear	50177
40 Sear Pin	50178
41 Sear Spring	50179
42 Slide	50191
43 Slide Stop	50195
44 Slide Stop Plunger	50167
45 Stock—Left Hand*	50207
46 Stock—Right Hand*	50208
47 Stock Screw—(4)	50209
48 Stock Screw Bushing—(4)	53665
49 Trigger Assembly	50180

Wood Stocks Available

*Stocks sold only in pairs, with Stock Screws

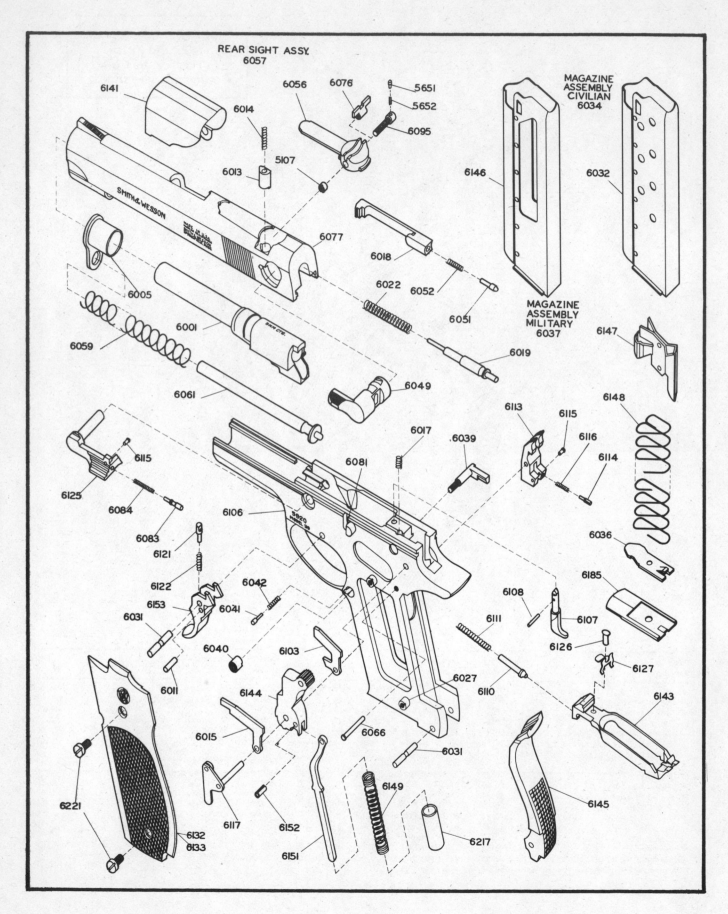

REAR SIGHT ASSY.
6057

MAGAZINE ASSEMBLY CIVILIAN 6034

MAGAZINE ASSEMBLY MILITARY 6037

SMITH & WESSON

SMITH & WESSON 9MM AUTOMATIC PISTOL
DOUBLE ACTION   MODEL No. 39

PARTS LIST

No.	Name	Price
5107	Rear Sight Windage Nut	$ .10
5651	Rear Sight Windage Screw Plunger	.15
5652	Rear Sight Windage Sc. Plg. Sprg	.10
6001	Barrel	14.30
6005	Barrel Bushing	1.65
6011	Trigger Plunger Pin	.10
6013	Ejector-depressor Plunger	.55
6014	Ejector-depressor Plunger Spring	.10
6015	Ejector Magazine Depressor	.55
6017	Ejector Spring	.10
6018	Extractor	2.20
6019	Firing Pin	.65
6022	Firing Pin Spring	.10
6027	Frame Stud	.30
6031	Insert Pin	.10
6031	Trigger Pin	.10
6032	Magazine Tube	1.65
6034	Magazine Assembly	4.25
6036	Magazine Butt Plate Catch	.30
6037	Magazine Assembly—Military	4.25
6039	Magazine Catch	.85
6040	Magazine Catch Nut	.40
6041	Magazine Catch Plunger	.15
6042	Magazine Catch Plunger Spring	.20
6049	Manual Safety	3.85
6051	Manual Safety Plunger	.15
6052	Manual Safety Plunger Spring	.10
6056	Rear Sight Leaf	4.15
6057	Rear Sight Assembly	6.60
6059	Recoil Spring	.65
6061	Recoil Spring Guide Assembly	1.65
6066	Sear Pin	.15
6076	Rear Sight Slide	1.10
6077	Slide	24.20
6081	Slide Stop Button	.45
6083	Slide Stop Plunger	.20

No.	Name	Price
6084	Slide Stop Plunger Spring	$ .20
6095	Rear Sight Windage Screw	.55
6103	Sear Release Lever	.30
6106	Frame (factory exchange only)	35.20
6107	Disconnector	1.10
6108	Disconnector Pin	.10
6110	Drawbar Plunger	.55
6111	Drawbar Plunger Spring	.10
6113	Sear	1.95
6114	Sear Plunger	.15
6115	Sear Plunger Pin	.10
6115	Slide Stop Plunger Pin	.10
6116	Sear Plunger Spring	.10
6117	Sideplate	.60
6121	Trigger Plunger	.30
6122	Trigger Plunger Spring	.15
6125	Slide Stop	3.30
6126	Trigger Play Spring Rivet	.10
6127	Trigger Play Spring	.35
6132	Stock, Right	2.20
6133	Stock, Left	2.20
6141	Dust Shield—Military	1.10
6143	Drawbar	6.60
6144	Hammer	3.05
6145	Insert	4.95
6146	Magazine Tube—Military	1.65
6147	Magazine Follower	.65
6148	Magazine Spring	.90
6149	Mainspring	.35
6151	Stirrup	.45
6152	Stirrup Pin	.10
6153	Trigger	2.20
6185	Magazine Butt Plate	.45
6217	Mainspring Plunger	.30
6221	Stock Screw	.10

SPECIFICATIONS

Caliber 9mm Luger and Parabellum
Magazine Capacity 8
Barrel Length 4 inches
Length Over All 7⁷⁄₁₆ inches
Weight 26½ oz. without magazine

Sights Fixed, ⅛-inch serrated ramp front; Patridge type rear adjustable for windage
Stocks Checked walnut with S&W monograms
Finish S&W Blue or Nickel
Ammunition 9mm Luger and Parabellum

NOTICE: Prices of parts are included for your information, but do not constitute an offer by the publishers of this book to sell such parts. If repairs are needed, order through your local gunsmith or supplier. If necessary, parts may be ordered directly from Smith & Wesson, Incorporated, Springfield, Massachusetts 01101. Prices are quoted, subject to change without notice and cannot be guaranteed.

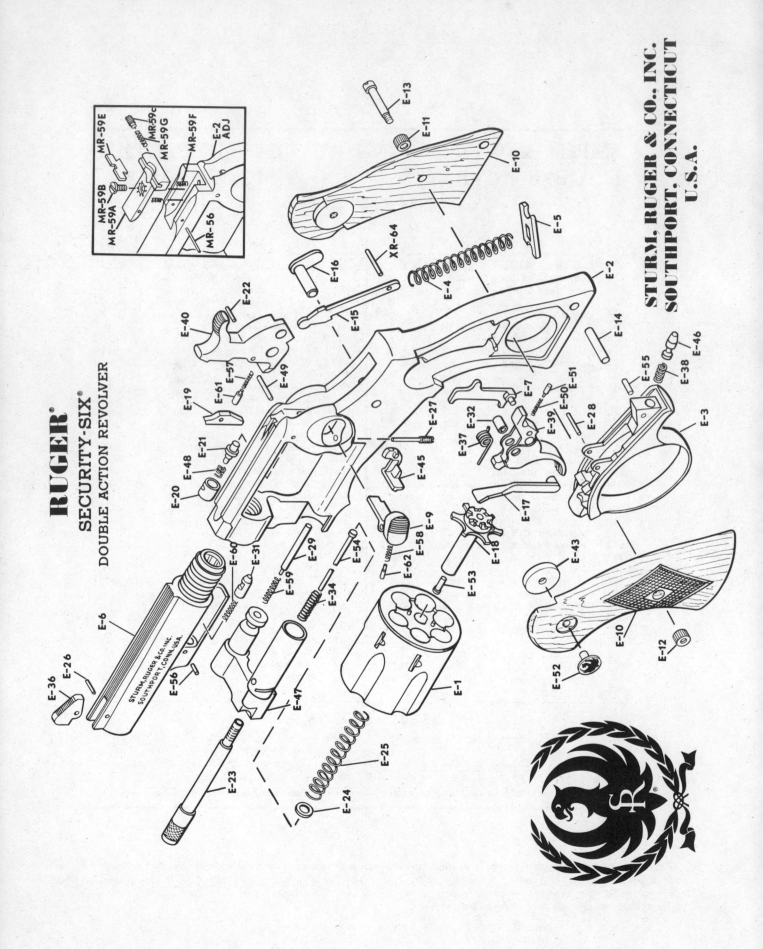

RUGER®

SECURITY-SIX®

DOUBLE ACTION REVOLVER

STURM, RUGER & CO., INC.
SOUTHPORT, CONNECTICUT
U.S.A.

74

RETAIL PARTS LIST

Part No.	Description	Price
*E-6	Barrel (Specify 2¾", 4" or 6")	$15.00
E-47	Crane/Crane Pivot Assembly	9.50
*E-1	Cylinder	11.00
E-53	Cylinder Center Lock Pin	.25
E-54	Cylinder Center Pin Rod	.50
E-34	Cylinder Center Pin Spring	.25
E-45	Cylinder Latch	3.00
E-29	Cylinder Latch Plunger	.50
E-59	Cylinder Latch Spring	.50
E-9	Cylinder Release Button	3.00
E-27	Cylinder Release Pivot	.50
E-58	Cylinder Release Spring	.25
E-62	Cylinder Release Spring Plunger	.50
XR-64	Disassembly Pin	.25
E-18	Ejector	7.50
E-23	Ejector Rod	3.50
E-24	Ejector Rod Washer	.25
E-25	Ejector Spring	.25
E-21	Firing Pin	1.00
E-48	Firing Pin Rebound Spring	.25
*E-2	Frame (Fixed Sight)	50.00
*E-2 adj.	Frame (Adj. Sight)	55.00
E-31	Front Latch	.50
E-56	Front Latch Cross Pin	.25
E-60	Front Latch Spring	.25
E-36	Front Sight Blade (Specify Bbl. Length)	.25
E-26	Front Sight Cross Pin	.25
E-43	Grip Panel Boss	.25 ea.
E-10L	Grip Panel (Left) Complete	4.00
E-12	Grip Panel (Left) Ferrule	.50
E-10R	Grip Panel (Right) Complete	4.00
E-11	Grip Panel (Right) Ferrule	.50
E-14	Grip Panel Dowel	.25
E-13	Grip Panel Screw	.25
E-40	Hammer	8.00
E-19	Hammer Dog	.50
E-22	Hammer Dog Pivot Pin	.25
E-57	Hammer Dog Spring	.25
E-61	Hammer Dog Spring Plunger	.25
E-16	Hammer Pivot Assem.	1.00
E-15	Hammer Strut	.50
E-4	Mainspring	.50
E-5	Mainspring Seat	.25
E-52	Medallion	.50 ea.
E-7	Pawl	1.25
E-51	Pawl Plunger }	.50
E-50	Pawl Spring }	
MR-35	Rear Sight Assy (Complete)	4.50
MR-59A	Rear Sight	3.00
MR-59E	Rear Sight Blade	.50
MR-59B	Rear Sight Elevation Screw	.25
MR-59F	Rear Sight Elevation Spring	.25
MR-56	Rear Sight Pivot Pin	.25
MR-59C	Rear Sight Windage Screw	.25
MR-59G	Rear Sight Windage Spring	.25
*E-20	Recoil Plate	1.50
E-49	Recoil Plate Cross Pin	.25
E-17	Transfer Bar	2.00
E-39	Trigger	3.00
E-32	Trigger Bushing	.50
E-28	Trigger Pivot Pin	.25
E-37	Trigger Spring	.25
**E-3	Trigger Guard (only)	6.00
E-46	Trigger Guard Plunger	.25
E-55	Trigger Guard Plunger Cross Pin	.25
E-38	Trigger Guard Plunger Spring	.25

*Parts must be installed at factory.
**Note: Sold in the white only unless fitted at factory.

NOTICE: Prices of parts are included for your information, but do not constitute an offer by the publishers of this book to sell such parts. If repairs are needed, order through your local gunsmith or supplier. If necessary, parts may be ordered directly from Sturm, Ruger & Company, Southport, Connecticut 06490. Prices are quoted, subject to change without notice and cannot be guaranteed.

FIELD-STRIPPING

RUGER "SECURITY SIX"

1. Unload revolver and close cylinder.
2. Remove grip screw and both grips.
3. Cock hammer. Insert disassembly pin about half its length into hole in mainspring strut, (See Fig. A). Pull trigger. Remove mainspring assembly. **(Caution: Do not remove disassembly pin until mainspring assembly is correctly reinstalled in revolver.)**
4. Pull trigger and remove hammer pivot and hammer while holding trigger back. (See Fig. B)
5. Use mainspring strut assembly to depress trigger guard lock plunger located inside frame at rear of trigger guard (see sectional view — Fig. C.) Simultaneously pull out and remove trigger guard assembly.
6. Open and remove cylinder. Remove cylinder latch. (See Fig. D) Disassembly is now complete.
7. Further disassembly should not be required and is not recommended.

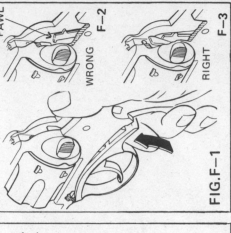

FIG.-A

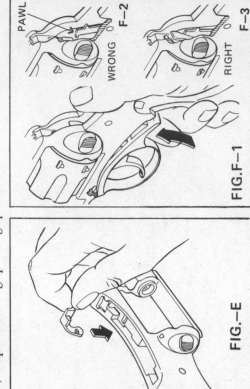

FIG.-B

FIG.-D

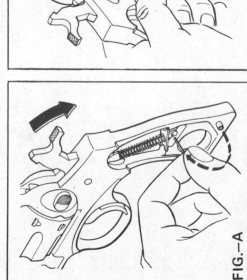

FIG.-C

REASSEMBLY

1. Replace cylinder latch (See Fig. E) Replace and close cylinder.
2. Hook front of trigger guard into recess provided in frame (See Fig. F-1) Align pawl in its recess in frame. (See Fig. F-2, 3) Check to be sure that *transfer bar* is in correct position in rear of firing pin. (Fig. F-3) Snap trigger guard shut. If solid resistance is felt or trigger guard will not shut, check position of pawl and transfer bar. (See Fig. F)
   (Note: At this point of proper reassembly, trigger will function to rotate and lock the cylinder. Pull the trigger once or twice to check functioning.)
3. Pull trigger and hold. Replace hammer and hammer pivot. (See Fig. G)
4. With hammer now forward, replace mainspring assembly. Key the two small notches in the mainspring support into place on the matching projections in the grip. Cock hammer. Remove disassembly pin. (See Fig. H)
5. Replace one grip. Replace disassembly pin in its storage compartment. (See Fig. A) Replace other grip and grip screw.

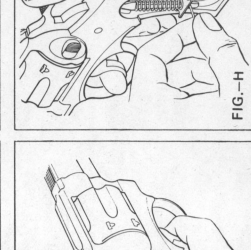

PAWL

WRONG F-2

RIGHT F-3

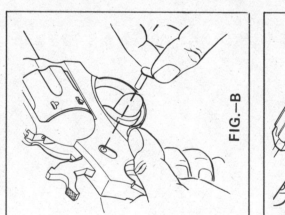

FIG.F-1

FIG.-E

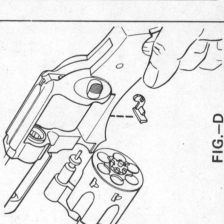

FIG.-H

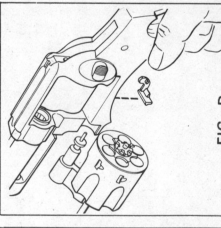

FIG.-G

*The French-built MAB, here disassembled, has
mechanical simplicity, large magazine capacity.*

Two conditions can be a source of difficult operation in revolvers. In the Smith & Wesson, the front of the ejector rod engages a lug beneath the barrel. It is not uncommon for the ejector rod to work loose, backing forward in its socket until the additional length interferes with latching the cylinder back into place. This condition can be corrected by the officer in the field on a temporary basis, by turning the ejector rod back into place with no tool other than his thumb and fingers. Usually, this is a left-hand

thread and must be tightened by turning opposite the usual direction.

A second source of revolver stoppages is the presence of unburned powder particles beneath the ejector star — that sprocket-shaped piece of metal which pushes the case rims from the chambers when the ejector rod is pushed. It does not take much dirt or unburned powder between the star and the cylinder to make it difficult or impossible to latch

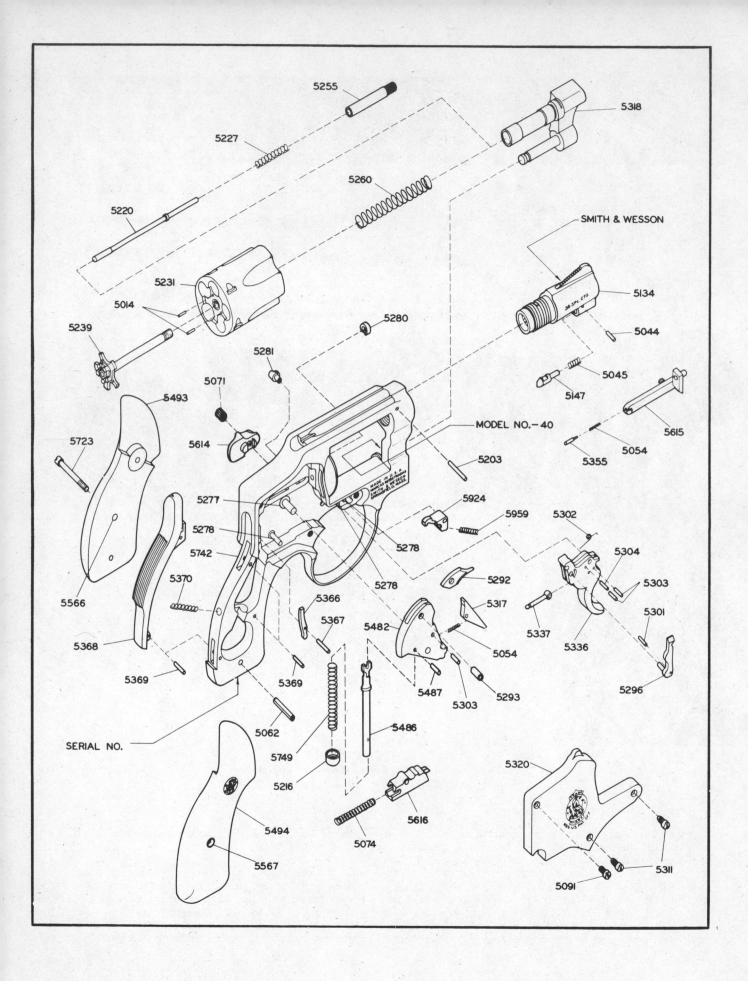

SMITH & WESSON

MODEL NO.-40

SERIAL NO.

NOTICE: The information on parts and prices, as it appears on the bottom of page 73, applies to this and the facing page as well.

SMITH & WESSON
.38 CENTENNIAL
MODEL No. 40

PARTS LIST

No.	Name	Price
5014	Extractor Pin	$ .10
5044	Locking Bolt Pin	.10
5045	Locking Bolt Spring	.20
5054	Bolt Plunger Spring	.30
5054	Sear Spring	.30
5062	Stock Pin	.10
5071	Thumbpiece Nut	.40
5074	Rebound Slide Spring	.60
5091	Plate Screw, Flat Head	.20
5134	Barrel, 2"	14.10
5147	Locking Bolt	.95
5203	Barrel Pin	.10
5216	Mainspring Rod Swivel	1.05
5220	Center Pin	1.20
5227	Center Pin Spring	.20
5231	Cylinder with Extractor and Pins	16.50
5239	Extractor	4.70
5255	Extractor Rod	1.20
5260	Extractor Spring	.40
5277	Hammer Stud	.70
5278	Cylinder Stop Stud	.60
5278	Rebound Slide Stud	.60
5278	Trigger Stud	.60
5280	Hammer Nose Bushing	.60
5281	Frame Lug	.60
5289	Hammer	4.10
5292	Hammer Nose	.90
5293	Hammer Nose Rivet	.20
5296	Hand with Stud	1.40
5301	Hand Pin	.10
5302	Hand Torsion Spring	.20

No.	Name	Price
5303	Hand Torsion Spring Pin	$ .10
5303	Sear Pin	.10
5303	Trigger Lever Pin	.10
5304	Hand Spring Pin	.10
5311	Plate Screw, Crowned	.20
5317	Sear	1.05
5318	Yoke	6.60
5320	Side Plate	7.65
5336	Trigger	4.45
5337	Trigger Lever	.60
5355	Bolt Plunger	.20
5366	Safety Latch	.60
5367	Safety Latch Pin	.10
5368	Safety Lever	2.95
5369	Safety Lever Pin	.10
5369	Safety Lever Disengaging Pin	.10
5370	Safety Lever Spring	.20
5486	Stirrup	1.90
5487	Stirrup Pin	.10
5493	Stock, Magna, Left	2.95
5494	Stock, Magna, Right	2.95
5566	Escutcheon	.40
5567	Escutcheon Nut	.40
5614	Thumbpiece	2.35
5615	Bolt	3.05
5616	Rebound Slide	2.95
5723	Stock Screw	.40
5742 *	Frame, with Studs, Bushing & Lug	35.30
5749	Mainspring	.70
5924	Cylinder Stop	1.75
5959	Cylinder Stop Spring	.20

* (factory exchange only)

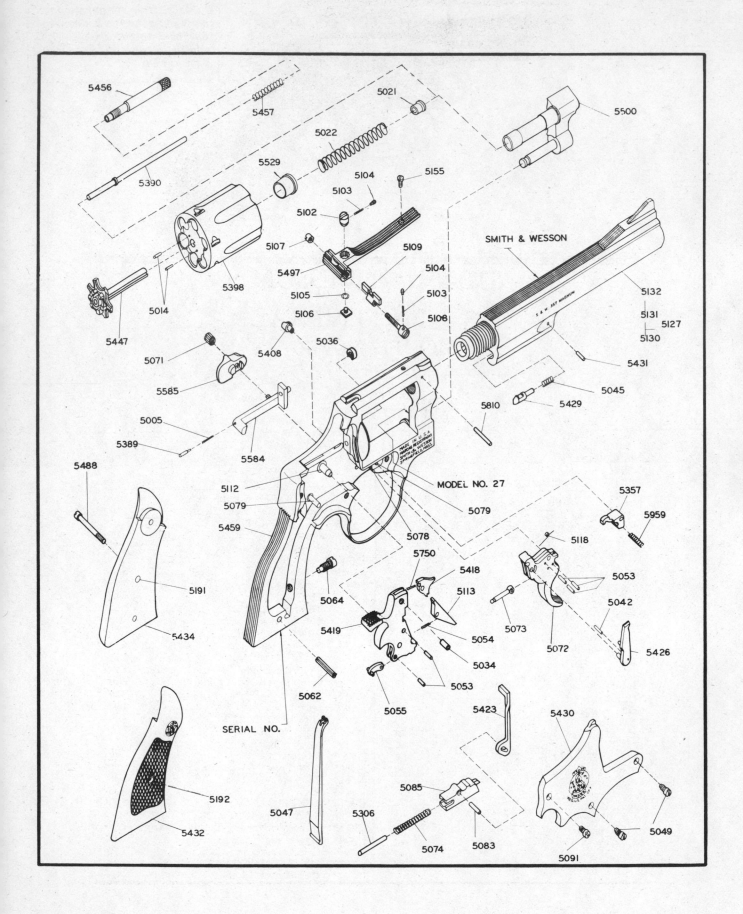

SMITH & WESSON

MODEL NO. 27

SERIAL NO.

NOTICE: The information on parts and prices, as it appears on the bottom of page 73, applies to this and the facing page as well.

SMITH & WESSON
.357 MAGNUM REVOLVER — MODEL No. 27
PARTS LIST

No.	Name	Price
5005	Bolt Plunger Spring	$ .30
5014	Extractor Pin	.10
5021	Extractor Rod Collar	.50
5022	Extractor Spring	.40
5031	Hammer Nose Rivet	.20
5036	Hammer Nose Bushing	.60
5042	Hand Pin	.10
5045	Locking Bolt Spring	.20
5047	Mainspring	1.40
5049	Plate Screw, crowned	.20
5053	Hand Spring Pin	.10
5053	Hand Torsion Spring Pin	.10
5053	Sear Pin	.10
5053	Stirrup Pin	.10
5053	Trigger Lever Pin	.10
5054	Sear Spring	.30
5055	Stirrup	.95
5062	Stock Pin	.10
5064	Strain Screw	.40
5071	Thumbpiece Nut	.40
5072	Trigger	4.45
5073	Trigger Lever	.60
5074	Rebound Slide Spring	.60
5078	Trigger Stud	.60
5079	Cylinder Stop Stud	.60
5079	Rebound Slide Stud	.60
5083	Rebound Slide Pin	.10
5085	Rebound Slide	2.95
5091	Plate Screw, flat head	.20
5102	Rear Sight Elevation Nut	.40
5103	Rear Sight Plunger Spring	.10
5104	Rear Sight Plunger	.10
5105	Rear Sight Spring Clip	.10
5106	Rear Sight Elevation Stud	.40
5107	Rear Sight Windage Nut	.10
5108	Rear Sight Windage Screw	.40
5109	Rear Sight Slide	1.20
5112	Hammer Stud	.70
5113	Sear	1.05
5118	Hand Torsion Spring	.20
5127	Barrel, 8⅜"	21.75

No.	Name	Price
5130	Barrel, 6"	$21.75
5131	Barrel, 5"	21.75
5132	Barrel, 3½"	21.75
5155	Rear Sight Leaf Screw	.20
5191	Escutcheon	.40
5192	Escutcheon Nut	.40
5276	Rear Sight Assembly	10.00
5306	Trigger Stop Rod	.20
5357	Cylinder Stop	1.75
5389	Bolt Plunger	.20
5390	Center Pin	1.20
5398	Cylinder, with extractor, pins and gas ring	23.55
5408	Frame Lug	.60
5418	Hammer Nose	.90
5419	Hammer	5.90
5421	Hammer, wide spur Target	7.65
5423	Hammer Block	.95
5426	Hand	1.40
5429	Locking Bolt	.95
5430	Side Plate	8.85
5431	Locking Bolt Pin	.10
5432	Stock, Magna, right	2.95
5434	Stock, Magna, left	2.95
5447	Extractor	5.30
5456	Extractor Rod	1.20
5457	Center Pin Spring	.20
5459	Frame, with studs, bushing and lug (factory exchange only)	41.20
5488	Stock Screw	.40
5497	Rear Sight Leaf	4.70
5500	Yoke	8.25
5529	Gas Ring	.60
5584	Bolt	3.05
5585	Thumbpiece	2.35
5750	Hammer Nose Spring	.20
5810	Barrel Pin	.10
5826	Stock, oversize Target, left	6.50
5828	Stock, oversize Target, right	6.50
5843	Trigger, wide Target type	7.65
5959	Cylinder Stop Spring	.20

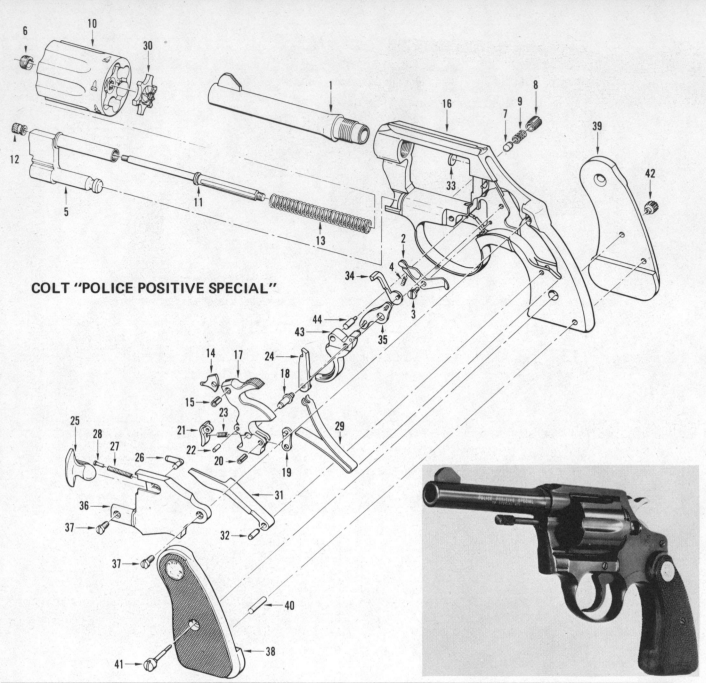

COLT "POLICE POSITIVE SPECIAL"

Drawing Number		Part Number
1	Barrel Assembly—4"— .32 New Police	56053
1	Barrel Assembly—4"—.38 Special	56063
1	Barrel Assembly—5"—.38 Special	56065
2	Bolt	56076
3	Bolt Screw	56173
4	Bolt Spring	50381
5	Crane	56159
6	Crane Bushing	56099
7	Crane Lock Detent	56078
8	Screw, Spring Retaining	56079
9	Crane Lock Spring	50516
10-12	Cylinder Assembly— .32 New Police	56145
10-12	Cylinder Assembly—.38 Special	56147
10	Cylinder—.32 New Police	56141
10	Cylinder—.38 Special	56143
11	Ejector Rod—.32 New Police	56129
11	Ejector Rod—.38 Special	56129
12	Ejector Rod Head	56165

Drawing Number		Part Number
13	Ejector Spring	50388
14	Firing Pin	56103
15	Roll Pin	95136
16	Frame	
17	Hammer Assembly	56082
18	Hammer Pin	50401
19	Hammer Stirrup Det. Assy.	56105
20	(Roll Pin) Stirrup Pin	56108
21	Hammer Strut	56107
22	Hammer Strut Pin	56108
23	Hammer Strut Spring	50400
24	Hand Det. Assy.	56086
25	Latch	56087
26	Latch Pin Det. Assy.	56088
27	Spring, Helical-Compression	A56367
28	Guide, Latch Spring	56089
29	Mainspring	56090
30	Ejector Ratchet .32 N.P.	56096

Drawing Number		Part Number
30	Ejector Ratchet .38 Spec.	56095
31	Rebound Lever	56091
32	Rebound Lever Pin	56092
33	Recoil Plate	56101
34	Safety Assy.	56171
35	Safety Lever	56094
36	Side Plate	56102
37	Side Plate Screw (2)	56176
38	Stock Assy. L.H. Sq. Butt	56115
38	Stock Assy. L.H. RND Butt	56124
39	Stock Assy. R.H. Sq. Butt	56210
39	Stock Assy. R.H. Rnd. Butt	56206
40	Stock Pin	95135
41	Stock Screw	C93116-3
42	Stock Screw Nut	56119
43	Trigger Assy.	B56372
43	Trigger	56371
44	Pin, Shoulder—Headless	B56357-1

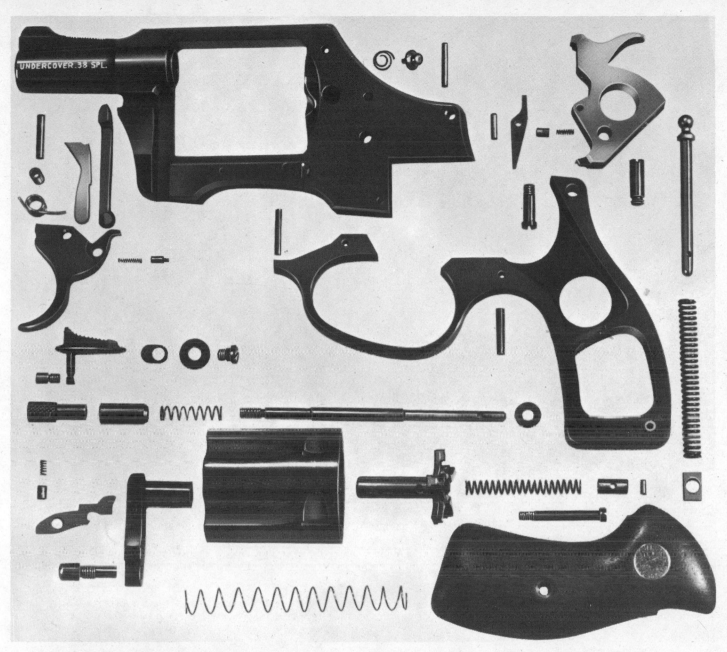

Component parts of the Charter Arms revolver underscore its simple and rugged design.

Loc-TITE sealant serves to prevent loosening of screws and other parts, as discussed.

Upper left: Screw holding thumb latch of S&W revolvers may come loose; check tightness and seal with Loc-TITE, if necessary. Lower left: The front screw holding rear sight on S&W revolvers should be checked for tightness periodically. Above: Incorrectly fitted screwdrivers, such as this too-small one, can mar or ruin screw head slots.

As discussed in text, after screws securing the sideplate have been removed, plate is loosened by gently tapping receiver around it, using the butt of a screwdriver or similar instrument.

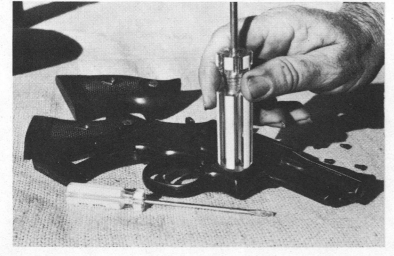

Revolver mechanism, such as this Model 27 S&W, can be cleaned and oiled with an approved lubricant, but, as discussed in text, contact points should be left alone.

Small build-up of unburned powder particles or other foreign matter beneath extractor star can make it protrude like this, interfering with closing cylinder.

Ejector rod of S&W revolvers has left-hand thread, may work loose and back out, preventing cylinder from closing. Hand-tightening restores to service.

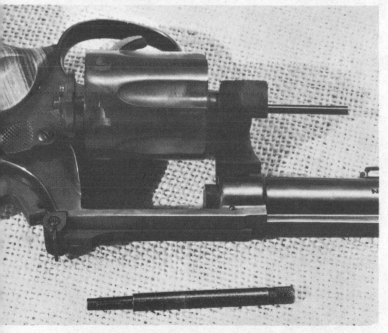

the cylinder back into place. This condition can be corrected easily by a thorough cleaning of both contacting surfaces.

A third disorder, fairly common to Smith & Wesson revolvers is for the screw holding the knurled thumb piece or cylinder latch to work loose. Often this can be detected by a looseness of the latch when opening the action. In extreme cases, the small screw may work off and be lost — perhaps together with the cylinder latch itself — before the condition is noticed.

There are a number of thread-sealing compounds available, such as Loc-TITE which can be most helpful in assuring that screws or similar threaded parts will not work loose amid the jar and disturbances to which a gun is subjected during firing. Loc-TITE is available in various grades, of which the one that is red in color is best suited to firearms applications. This compound often can be found in gun or motorcycle shops at about $1 for a small plastic tube. Due to its specialized penetrating properties, it is quite difficult to keep the opened container from leaking, no matter how tightly the cap may be turned into place. For this reason, it's best to store the unused Loc-TITE so that the tube is held against tipping, with its cap uppermost.

Although Loc-TITE and similar compounds are effective in preventing screws from working loose, it is possible — with a bit of effort and a properly fitted screwdriver — to loosen and remove screws which have been sealed in place. This may be necessary in the course of routine repairs or adjustments.

When using thread sealers, an extremely small amount is applied to the exposed portion of the thread, or to one of the areas before reinstalling the screw. The compound penetrates through the contact areas of the thread and hardens within a few hours. Obviously, it is important to take care that the sealing compounds do not leak down into the moving parts of the mechanism, where it could harden and make the gun inoperative.

Several cross-sectioned or exploded views are reproduced here to show the parts of popular handguns in relation to each other. These are included as a reference source only and the admonition is repeated one more time: Disassembly of handguns is a job for skilled technicians. Adventurous gun owners who disregard this advice are apt to end up with a gun that does not work, an expensive repair bill and an extended delay before the mistreated firearm returns to service.

Chapter 7

THE LONG BARRELS OF THE LAW

A Census Of Police Rifles Across The Country Would Reveal Astonishing Variety. Here Are Some Thoughts On Shrewd Selection, Rather Than Making Do With Hand-Me-Downs!

SHOOTING PLAYS an extremely small role in law enforcement work, although it's a vital consideration on those rare occasions when required. Recognizing this fact, the situations calling for accurate fire beyond typical handgun distance make up but a tiny fraction of the first fraction.

For all that, the police department cannot count itself adequately equipped and capable of coping with possible emergencies unless suitable rifles are available, along with personnel trained to use them effectively. The two ingredients are equally necessary, either being of little use without the other.

Anyone who has had occasion to poll a number of different departments will have encountered an improbable assortment of rifles stored in the gun lockers of the various stations. These may range from cheap, single-shot .22 rimfire plinkers through all manner of deer rifles — often quite dubious as to workability — on up to random samples of military weaponry. The usual justification for the presence of such potluck artillery is that it was acquired at little or no cost to the department. The .22 rimfire may have been confiscated from some kids using it carelessly in a vacant lot. The elderly, lever-action .30-30 may have been donated by the widow of a deer hunter, because a gun around the house made her nervous after his passing. Sometimes you'll see antique autoloaders, legacies from some nearby penal institution after the model had been phased out for use as guard rifles. Some of these are chambered for cartridges such as the .401 Winchester Self-Loader: long dropped from ammo-maker's lists and growing in value every year as a prized rarity among cartridge collectors. There is little to justify retaining such guns for police duty, since even a gun that cost nothing is worth less than that, if it cannot be made to fire effectively.

The relevant considerations boil down to this: On those rare occasions when police work requires a rifle, the chances are good that the emergency will need a rifle that is available with minimum delay, powerful, accurate and dependable. A sufficient supply of suitable ammunition should be on hand, along with personnel who can make it perform.

As with many other aspects of police weaponry, special aspects of the given situation will have the deciding vote as to the choice, deployment and employment of police rifles. In a jurisdiction having little historic record of rifles being needed, it's the usual custom to store them in the armory at

Conservatively priced, the Remington Model 788 offers good value and exceptional accuracy in the bolt action design. It's made in several calibers, of which the .308 Win is best suited to police use.

Also priced in about the same brackets as the Model 788, Winchester's Model 94 lever action carbine now is made only in caliber .30-30 Winchester chambering.

The St. Louis PD issues Browning autoloading rifles in caliber .30/06, with Redfield scope sights to selected personnel for anti-sniper work. Each man has one rifle, with which he works and trains to achieve complete familiarity, carrying it in a rigid, padded case in the patrol unit when on duty. Shifts are set up to keep at least one Marksman with a rifle on duty, ready for call at all times. Sgt. William Conreux, armorer for SLPD, is a member of the team, holds his issued rifle.

From left: The .30/06 Springfield, .308 Winchester, .223 Remington and .30 M-1 carbine cartridges are typical calibers discussed here.

Winchester Model 670 bolt action rifle is a lower priced version of their popular Model 70, available in several calibers for police use.

headquarters or sub-stations, breaking them out with supporting kits of ammunition and accessories in response to the rare emergency.

Given a higher level of social unrest, with a correspondingly greater likelihood that rifles will be needed — which tends to imply a city of greater population — one or more qualified rifle marksmen may be assigned to each shift, packing the rifles along in the cars while pulling tours of duty, taking them home or checking them back into the armory when off-duty, so that a capable gun/marksman team is never more than a few minutes away from readiness.

There is much to be said for assigning a specific rifle and shooter to each other on a permanent basis. A rifle used by many different shooters may have its sights adjusted back and forth between each contact that a single individual officer may have with it. As a result, it is unlikely that it will ever deliver its bullet to the same place from one practice session to the next. In police rifle work, it is of extreme importance that the first shot be placed with telling accuracy. Such shooting is apt to be done under conditions where it is impossible to "spot" the hit and make appropriate sight corrections or hold-off to compensate for the sight being out of adjustment. Further, the target is not apt to remain available for a second shot, if the first one misses.

With lives at stake, the shooter could fire and have no way of being able to tell if the bullet hit high, low, right or left of the aiming point: only that it had missed.

Alternately, if a competent rifle is issued to an officer and that man is trained to use it as effectively as possible, he will develop the confidence that is so important. As he takes his rifle to the range for periodic practice, takes it out of the case, loads and fires the first round, the appearance of a bullet hole within acceptably close distance to the point of aim will reinforce that confidence.

Then, should a serious emergency arise, requiring effective long-range rifle fire, confidence in his own capability and that of his rifle will be a steadying influence, prompting him to aim more carefully, squeeze the trigger more deliberately and put the bullet where he wants it.

Good rifle marksmen are not born with that capability, any more than are expert handgunners. But some men — as with the belt gun — will show more aptitude and, as a result, will learn faster. Interest and motivation, probably, play a bigger part than natural talent.

As is the case with most other branches of police weaponry, the final decision in the choice of a suitable caliber or cartridge will depend upon specific conditions and circumstances; also, to some extent, upon the experience and opinions of the personnel responsible for the final decision.

Among the suitable calibers, the .30/06 Springfield remains a popular number. Dating back to 1906, it was the primary military rifle cartridge of this country through two major wars. Vast numbers of surplus military rifles chambered for this caliber have been released to the civilian sporting market and the wide acceptance of the caliber keeps it high on the popularity polls among makers of commercial center-fire rifles, down to the present. A broad assortment of military and commercial loadings is offered in .30/06, all the way from light-weight, 110-grain bullets loaded to high velocity, through armor-piercing military designs to weights as great as 220 grains.

In coping with emergencies requiring rifle fire, based upon reasonable predictions, soft-point bullets in weights of 125 to 150 grains are the usual choice for maximum effectiveness in the .30/06 caliber. Some departments pack a small quantity of military armor-piercing loads in the kits for dealing with barricaded opposition, but great discretion is required in its use, due to high penetration and the risk of ricochets.

The standard NATO round, under its civilian designation as the .308 Winchester caliber, is used as widely as the .30/06 Springfield, if not more so. Although it develops slightly less velocity than the longer cartridge, the .308 Win is offered in a useful assortment of military and commercial rifles. Beside the bolt action — traditionally the most accurate and reliable design — the short length of the .308 permits it to be used in several autoloading and lever action designs. These have the advantage of a more rapid rate of fire, along with adaptability to right or left-handed firing.

This can be an important factor since even a shooter who is right-handed by natural choice may find it necessary to fire left-handed in order to take advantage of protection in the only firing position that may be available.

A third caliber, likewise gaining wider usage in police work, is the .223 Remington, also known as the 5.56mm in military circles. This is the cartridge used in the M-16 rifles which saw their first service in Vietnam. Rifles are available to police departments in this caliber, having fire-selector switches to permit full-auto fire or semi-auto — that is, a single shot with each separate pull of the trigger. Other arms offer capability only for semi-auto fire and these may be preferred on the basis of requiring less paper-work and red tape in purchasing, possessing and using. This is particularly true in instances where the rifle is purchased privately by the individual officer.

As is the usual case with military calibers, availability of surplus ammunition and empty cases has given impetus to the .223 Remington as a caliber for commercial sporting arms in bolt action designs and these have been adopted by some departments. The high velocity of the .223 — well over 3200 fps at the muzzle with a 55-grain bullet — coupled with its flat trajectory has proved the .223 to be a capable performer against hostile personnel in military applications. When using soft point bullets, the problems of

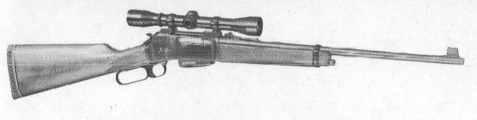

Browning Model BLR has four-shot magazine, comes in .308 or .243 Winchester calibers. Scope and its mount also are made by Browning.

Versions of the military carbine are made for commercial sale with five-shot magazines, as here, or fifteen and thirty round types.

Browning autoloader is available in several calibers, including the .30/06 with hinged five-shot magazine.

Colt's AR-15 police rifle is of semi-auto design, otherwise is similar to the military M-16.

Ruger Model 77 rifles are made in a long action, such as this one, for the .30/06 or a similar, but shorter action for the .308 Win cartridge, as well as several other calibers less suitable for the considerations of police use.

The Enforcer is a pistol-stocked version of the military carbine, offers magazine capacity up to 30 with compactness.

undesired penetration and ricochets is minimized since the high-velocity projectiles tend to disintegrate upon impact.

As has been noted, it would be difficult to name a caliber of cartridge that is not represented by a rifle in the racks of at least one department at present. However, the three listed here, probably, account for the considerable bulk of those in service.

Several — though not necessarily all — of the rifles suitable for police work are shown in the accompanying illustrations, with specifications in the captions. While it might be difficult to defend as an absolute evaluation, the general observation can be made that the primary target of the police rifle is more apt than not to be a hostile, armed man, probably concealed and protected to some degree by building construction — woodwork or masonry — or similar natural cover. As such, the target poses much greater hazard to the shooter than the largest, most ferocious big game species in the world, since even the biggest African elephant cannot pose a serious threat to the hunter who is several hundred yards away; but a cornered suspect, armed with a high-powered rifle can do so.

By ordinary hunting standards, Homo sapiens — to use the biological term for the human species — can be classified as a thin-skinned game animal in the weight category rarely exceeding two hundred pounds. In this light, any cartridge delivering energies much greater than the .30/06 is not justified by reasonable needs. A solid hit with the .30/06 will accomplish anything that needs doing. Use of a larger, more powerful cartridge may be justified on targets such as moose, polar bear or rhinocerous, but the power is wasted on H. sapiens.

In the same scale of values, cartridges delivering energies substantially less than the .223 Remington tend to be less than adequate. Note that the figure for muzzle velocities and energies are relatively meaningless. The normal function of the police rifle does not envision hitting the target at point-blank distances. Within the first fifty yards or so, it is more likely that the handgun would be em-

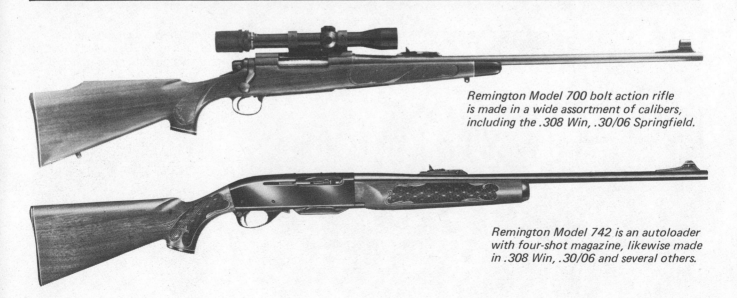

Remington Model 700 bolt action rifle is made in a wide assortment of calibers, including the .308 Win, .30/06 Springfield.

Remington Model 742 is an autoloader with four-shot magazine, likewise made in .308 Win, .30/06 and several others.

Armalite's Model AR-180 is a semi-auto design for the .223 Rem cartridge, can be fired with stock folded forward when compact dimensions are an advantage.

Browning's bolt action rifle has a Monte Carlo style of cheek pad for the right-handed shooter, but it can be fired from the left with equal comfort.

ployed. The significant data is that applying to ranges from one hundred yards on out to one thousand or more.

If some of the foregoing discussion seems cold-blooded and heartless to the sensitive reader, it is regretted and appropriate apologies are extended. However, it must be realized and accepted that there are occasions — quite rare, fortunately — similar to the one, several years ago in a southern city in which a deranged man barricaded himself atop a tall building with long-range armament and commenced picking off distant pedestrains in the coldest blood available. The ensuing turmoil served only to draw fresh spectators who, in turn, furnished additional targets for the homicidal maniac, many of them falling victims.

In such circumstances, it is impossible to protect bystanders from offering themselves as targets and the only way to staunch the toll of innocent lives is to put the predatory shooter out of action in the quickest, most positive manner possible. Comparable situations have turned up since that time and, in all likelihood, will turn up again. The

same person who finds the present discussion repugnant would, in the highest probability, be one of the first to denounce a police department which proved ineffective at controlling the murderous activities of similar felons.

In the final analysis, there are times when it is the duty of the police officer to terminate the unlawful activities of a manifest criminal in order to preserve innocent lives. If the criminal suffers fatal injuries in the process, it is regretted, but the situation is one of his own instigation and there is no obvious way of avoiding it.

One additional rifle and cartridge finding occasional use in police work is the caliber .30 carbine. Appreciated qualities include its compact dimensions and availability of large-capacity magazines. The standard military magazine holds fifteen rounds while a larger type — often known as the "banana clip" — holds thirty. In situations where large numbers of rounds need to be accessible quickly, it is a fairly common practice to overlap the lower ends of two thirty-round magazines and tape them together. Thus, when

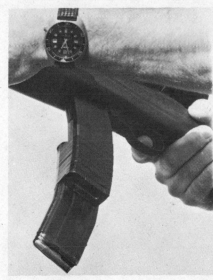

Thirty-round magazines are available for the Armalite AR-180 if conditions require more than standard 20-shot type.

As discussed, two of the 30-shot "banana clips" for the GI carbine can be butt-spliced for convenience.

one is emptied, the catch is released and the combination is given a half-turn to insert the fresh magazine. In this manner, sixty rounds can be fired within a short interval.

The military .30 carbine is made in at least two standard versions: the M-1 designed only for semi-auto fire and the M-2, which has a fire-selector permitting a choice of semi- or full-auto. There are firms which will convert the M-1 to the M-2 version for authorized users, such as police departments.

There is something to be said for the adjustable, aperture-type rear sight furnished on the .30 carbine, as-issued. Some sort of rough sight picture can be obtained quite quickly with it, thus being useful in short-range work where speed is essential. However, systems have been devised, permitting the installation of scope sights on the .30 carbine. One of the best of these is the S&K Instamount, made by the S&K Manufacturing Company (Box 247A, Pittsfield, Pennsylvania 16340). Installation consists of driving out the issue sight — tapping from right to left in the dovetail — after which the matching dovetail of the S&K base is inserted and secured by tightening a screw.

As many combat veterans can attest, the full-jacketed, round-nosed bullet for the .30 carbine is not one of the more outstanding man-stopper calibers. The bullet weighs about 110 grains and leaves the muzzle at about 2000 fps. Penetration is quite good for so small a cartridge but, as with other military bullets, it is not designed to expand upon impact.

Wide acceptance of the military and commercial version of the GI carbine among sportsmen has led to the introduction of soft-point bullets of the correct weight and diameter for this caliber. Since there is more than enough velocity available to assure positive expansion, use of expanding bullets increases the effectiveness of the .30 carbine round to a remarkable degree. Muzzle energy is about 975 foot-pounds and stopping power exceeds all but the largest handgun calibers.

If the .30 carbine is used with soft-point ammunition, it is important to make a thorough performance check with the ammunition and the magazines that are intended for duty use. The feed ramp of this rifle is designed to function

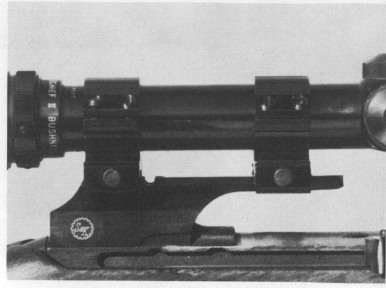

As discussed in the text, S&K's "Instamount" for the GI carbine offers convenient scope sight capabilities for this popular arm with minimum installation time.

with the full-jacketed military bullet and occasional feeding problems may be encountered with the soft-point bullets, due to the fact that the exposed lead tips offer more friction than the copper alloy of the jacket.

An important consideration, with police rifles, is the provision made for protecting them while being carried in patrol units or similar vehicles. The ideal method is to use one of the rigid cases lined with foam padding. Sights — particularly telescopic types — are quite apt to be knocked out of alignment by the rough handling to which an unprotected rifle is subjected, when carried in the trunk of a patrol unit. While the rigid, padded rifle cases are bulky and space is at a premium in most patrol units, such containers offer the only practical solution to the problem of having the rifle on hand and with the car. Further, they can

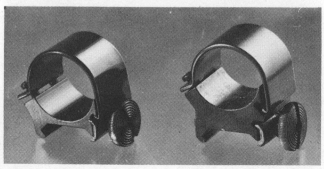

Pachmayr's "Lo-Swing" mount positions a scope for normal use but can be pivoted out of the way for use of open iron sights, when desired, swung back into position for use of scope without loss of scope zero.

Above, scope mounting bases by Weaver are designed to be attached easily to those rifles which are supplied drilled and tapped for scope mounting. Below: Regular Weaver scope ring is at left, with special high-rise ring at right for clearance in mounting large-lensed scopes.

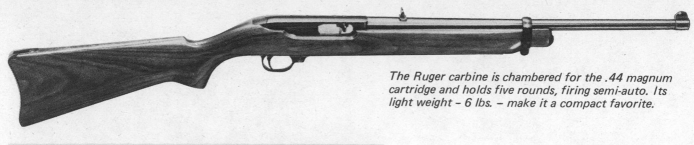

The Ruger carbine is chambered for the .44 magnum cartridge and holds five rounds, firing semi-auto. Its light weight – 6 lbs. – make it a compact favorite.

Rigid rifle cases offer useful degree of protection and convenience. This one will hold two rifles, plus miscellaneous supplies and foam plastic lining does not require custom-fitting of the rifles or other items.

be used to carry accessory items, such as cleaning gear, lubricants and assorted types of ammunition.

Even rifles which are stored in the departmental armory require some sort of protective case for transportation, since it is likely that the emergency requiring their use will necessitate breaking them out and hauling them to the scene with minimum delay. Under such circumstances, rifles with open, iron sights and, more particularly, scope-sighted rifles can be knocked out of alignment with their sights, reducing their usefulness by a large degree.

When it comes to a choice between open iron sights and optical or telescopic sights, there is much that can be said for — and some that can be said against — both types. Iron sights do not project as far above the barrel and, as a result, are less apt to be damaged or misaligned in rough handling.

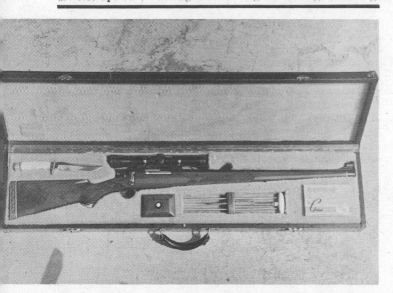

This rigid rifle case has been inletted to accomodate one particular rifle, with cleaning supplies, a box of ammunition and similar miscellaneous supplies.

Further, the iron sights are a bit quicker for obtaining a hasty sight picture when time is of vital importance. On the other hand, although highly skilled marksmen can attain remarkable accuracy with iron sights, the average shooter can do better, with much less training, when firing with optical sights.

The telescopic sight offers the obvious advantage of an enlarged view of the target, depending upon the amount of magnification of its optical system. Here, it should be noted, the powerful, high-magnification scopes are not practical for the probable circumstances under which police rifles are apt to be employed. Magnification is indicated by designations such as 2X, 4X or 6X, meaning that the image is made two, four or six times as large as when viewed by the unassisted eye. Telescopic sights are available in fixed-power and variable designs. A fixed-power sight will be listed as, for example, 4X, while the variable may be designated, for example, as a 2-7X or a 3-9X. The last terms mean that it can be adjusted across a range of magnifications from two to seven or from three to nine times the size of the naked-eye image. Usually, this is accomplished by rotating a ring around the eyepiece or objective lens of the scope.

For most practical purposes, the 4X scope is a good, all-around choice for typical police rifle applications. It offers an ideal compromise between the wide field of view of the low-power scope and the magnified image of the more powerful types. As is true in so many other instances, it is a matter of choosing the most favorable compromise. The low-powered scopes offer maximum brightness of image, the widest field of view and the largest amount of adjustment for aligning the sight with the bore of the rifle. At the other end, the high-magnification systems do not provide as much detail under difficult lighting conditions, their field of view is much more narrow, their exit pupil is more critical and parallax is more of a problem at varying distances.

Let's define a few of those terms: Exit pupil is the diameter of the image projected from the rear eyepiece of the scope to the shooter's eye. A small exit pupil, characteristic of high-powered systems, requires a steady, deliberate, precise positioning of the eye — or else you

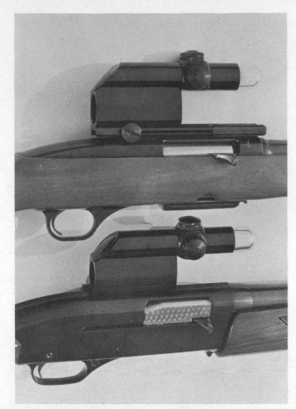

Novel Weaver "Qwik-Point" sights for rifles or shotguns are designed for work at short range. They do not magnify the image, but position a bright red spot, used in aiming.

Variable scope by Redfield can be set from 1X to 4X by a twist of the knurled ring ahead of the eyepiece. Redfield's extremely sturdy mounting base and rings secure it to this Remington Model 660 rifle.

Weaver K6 scope, here with Redfield mount on a Model 70 Winchester, is – at 6X – about the most powerful scope practical for use in police work.

Leupold's Vari-X II scope, variable from 3X to 9X, is mounted to this Mauser-type action by means of the Conetrol bases with unique, three-piece rings, also by Seguin, Texas-based Conetrol firm.

cannot see the image for aiming. The larger exit pupils as available in low-power systems, are less critical, quicker and easier to pick up.

Eye relief is the distance between the rear lens of the scope and the shooter's eye. This is quite short in the low-priced scope sights manufactured for use with .22 rimfire rifles and poses no problem with them, due to their modest recoil. The high-powered rifles require a longer eye relief, to assure that the force of the recoil will not drive the scope back to strike the shooter's forehead or eye.

Parallax is a shifting of the reticle (crosshair), as observed when the rifle is held motionless and the shooter's eye is moved about. Ideally, the crosshair should maintain its exact alignment with the aiming point as the eye is moved from viewing one edge of the image to the other. The shifting of the reticle with eye movement — parallax — is aggravated as the power of magnification becomes greater or the distance to the target becomes shorter. Most of the scopes of 8X or higher magnification provide a focusing

ring so that parallax can be neutralized for the given distance. This is fine for target shooting at known distances, but it is not practical when it becomes necessary to squeeze off a quick but effective shot at a small, concealed mark, an unknown distance from the shooter.

Most telescopic sights, in addition to providing adjustment for elevation and windage — movement between right and left — have a means for focusing the system to fit the shooter's eye. Usually, this is accomplished by loosening a lock ring just ahead of the eyepiece and turning the eyepiece in one direction or the other until the reticle and the target are seen with equal, maximum clarity. This is not as simple as it sounds, due to the natural tendency of the eye to adjust its own internal focus. The best means for checking the eyepiece setting is to focus the eye on a distant object, then move it to pick up the scope image, judging by the first glimpse, before the eye has a chance to re-focus.

Adjustments for elevation — up and down — and for

windage usually are made on two dials positioned midway up the scope. The dial on top of the tube is for elevation, the one on the right-hand side for windage. Usually, these are covered by protective caps, which must be turned off for access to the adjustment dials. The dials, themselves, may have knurled outer edges, permitting turning by the fingers, or — more frequently — have a curved slot in the center, for adjustment by means of a small coin or, if necessary, the rim of the cartridge.

While markings vary between models and manufacturers, the adjustment dials usually will have a small, curving arrow pointing to "R" for Right and "U" for Up or, perhaps, a two-headed arrow indicating the direction to turn the elevation dial for Up and Down; the windage dial for Right and Left.

The relationship between such markings and bringing the sight system to its proper adjustment is quite simple. If you want to have the bullet strike the target at a point higher than the previous shot, you move the elevation dial in the direction indicated by the arrow pointing to "Up." If you want the hole lower, move the dial in the opposite direction, or toward the letter D for Down.

In the same manner, if the hole in the paper appeared to the right of the aiming point, you want to move it to the left, so you turn the windage dial toward the letter L for Left or in the opposite direction shown for R/Right.

The instruction sheets accompanying scope sights often will show the value of one graduation or one click of adjustment in terms of minutes of angle. Often this unit is abbreviated as MOA. It is equal to slightly more than one inch of movement at a distance of one hundred yards, one-half at fifty, two inches at two hundred and so on. Thus, if your scope sight is graduated at the rate of one MOA per click of adjustment and your sighting shot struck four inches low at one hundred yards, you rotate the elevation dial four clicks in the direction indicated by the arrow toward the letter U for Up. If it's graduated at 1/2 MOA per click, you'd need to move it eight clicks. The informa-

Windage adjustment dial on the Leupold scope shows arrows indicating direction of rotation for moving point of impact to the left or right. Once Leupold scopes have been adjusted, outer ring can be rotated to align zero-mark with indicator line.

Ring on Bushnell ScopeChief offers quick choice of crosshair (CH) or Command Post (P), latter is for aiming under conditions of difficult lighting.

Bushnell's ScopeChief IV shotgun scope does not magnify, but features wide field, brightest image.

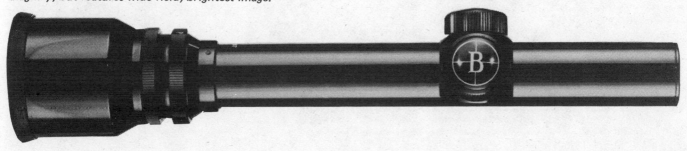

tion as to the amount of movement per click should be committed firmly to memory or, better, entered on a small sticker attached to the rifle where it won't be defaced or lost.

Scope reticles are made in a wide variety of configurations and several of these are shown in accompanying illustrations. The conventional thin crosshair type is fine, assuming good light conditions. The Duplex reticle, pioneered by Leupold, offers the dual advantage of heavy crosshairs at the outer edges, merging to fine wires at the center for precise or hasty aim, as required. The Command Post design, an exclusive Bushnell feature, permits the incorporation of a broad post which pops up magnetically, at the turn of a ring, when needed, meanwhile retracting at other times to allow use of a conventional crosshair. The Bushnell Nite-Site has a built-in lighting system, powered by a small battery, which can be turned on to outline the intersection of the crosshairs as a sighting aid under difficult lighting conditions.

Since bullets do not have wings, all bullets are drawn downward by the force of gravity as soon as they leave the gun barrel. If the bullet starts out climbing, gravity will commence slowing its upward motion until, at some point in the bullet's flight, it stops rising and begins moving back toward the earth.

The fall of a bullet — or any other unsupported object — is a uniform amount of downward acceleration, resisted only slightly by passage through the air. If a bullet is fired from a barrel that is absolutely level, it will drop about sixteen feet during the first second of its flight. At the same time, air resistance will be reducing the velocity.

These forces and factors combine, with the result that no bullet ever moves in an absolutely straight line — unless

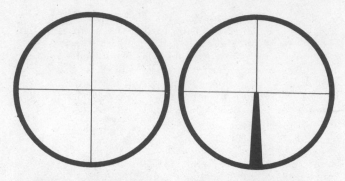

When it's too dark to see the crosshairs...
Switch instantly to Command Post!

Illustrated on previous page, Bushnell's "Command Post" reticle can be changed between standard crosshairs, at left, and the highly visible post version for use in dim light.

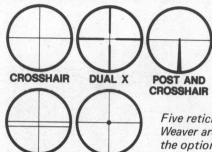

CROSSHAIR DUAL X POST AND CROSSHAIR

RANGE-FINDER DOT (at extra cost)

Five reticles offered by Weaver are typical of the optional choices available in scopes.

Equally effective against large, dangerous game or in police work, the unique "Partition Bullet" by Nosler assures expansion by foreportion, meanwhile assuring deep penetration by the base.

Four of the Browning scopes, one mounted on their auto has the novel "Widefield" eyepiece pioneered by Redfield, also available in that line.

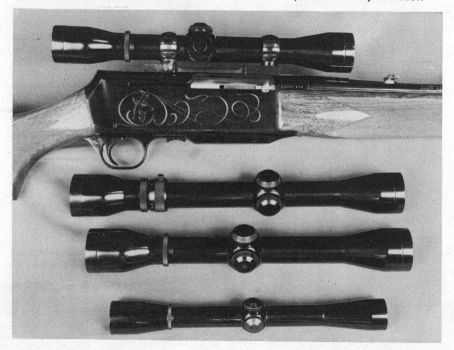

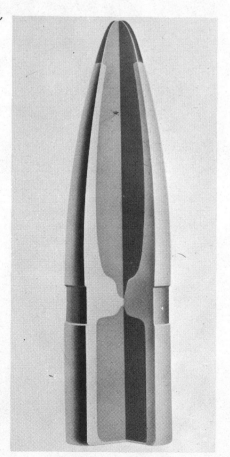

Duplex

CPC

Post & Duplex

Post & Crosshair

Crosshair

Dot ($10.00 add.)

Six reticle designs offered by Leupold include the popular "Duplex" which that firm introduced in 1962, with several other variations to suit tastes.

NOW WITH LIGHTED AIMING POINT!

Novel Bushnell ScopeChief V with Lite Site feature has the option of turning on a dot of illumination at center of the crosshairs to aid in aligning sights with dimly illuminated target. Scope is of 4X and requires some small amount of light on the target itself.

Bushnell's "DM" detachable mounting system uses bases compatible with those by Weaver, with special clamps that grip a rail moulded into scope body tube.

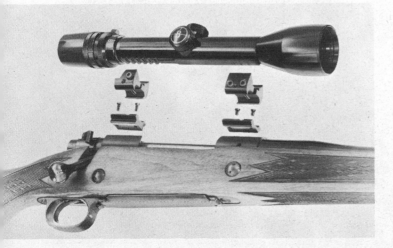

fired straight upward — but, rather, in a curved path which is termed its trajectory. In high-velocity rifles, this may be an extremely flattened curve, but it is a curve and it becomes progressively steeper as the distance from the muzzle increases.

The customary procedure is to sight the rifle so that the bullet is delivered exactly to the point of aim at some given distance — for instance, two hundred yards — and, with the sights so adjusted, the bullet will strike slightly higher than the point of aim at shorter distances or progressively lower as the distance increases beyond the range for which the sights are zeroed.

Most ammunition manufacturers can furnish charts which give the amount of bullet drop at appropriate distances. Most of the reloading handbooks provide similar information. By way of illustrating the effect of increasing distance on remaining energy and velocity of the bullet, as well as its drop, the following table — reproduced from the Hornady Handbook of Cartridge Reloading, page 320 — gives the data for the Hornady caliber .30 bullet of 150 grains weight, spire-point nose shape, for a muzzle velocity of 2700 fps.

| | Muzzle | DISTANCE (Yards) | | | | |
		100	200	300	400	500
Velocity (fps)	2700	2450	2210	1990	1780	1600
Energy (ft-lbs)	2429	2000	1626	1319	1055	852
Drop (inches)	0	2.52	11.51	28.86	58.46	100.57
Midrange Traj.	0	0.63	2.88	7.21	14.61	25.14
Bullet Path (in.)	-1.5	+1.73	0.00	-10.09	-33.94	-70.29

The Hornady Handbook contains many pages of similar data, carrying their bullets through the span of velocities practical for the given number. For example, the 150-grain bullet listed here is taken from 2200 to 3500 fps, in 100-fps stages.

In explanation of the last line — Bullet Path — the center of the scope sight is 1½ inches above the axis of the bore; hence the figure under the muzzle heading. With the sight adjusted to hit the point of aim at two hundred yards, the bullet will strike 1.73 inches high at one hundred yards, 10.09 inches low at three hundred and so on.

Although such tables are helpful in estimating the effect of bullet drop, it may be found that actual performance in a specific rifle varies to some extent from the figures given in the tables. For this reason, it is best to procure a sufficiently large supply of the given ammunition so that actual tests can be made, at measured distances, to determine the distance of bullet deviation above or below the point of aim.

When this has been worked out, the data can be entered on a chart fastened to the side of the rifle stock or in a similar, convenient location for future reference.

Remington 00-Buck
9 pellets - 12-ga
at 7 yards w/ A&W
Diverter

THE SHOTGUN IN POLICE WORK

Boasting Several Unique Qualities The Short Barreled Scattergun Fills A Special Niche — And Fills It Well!

Chapter 8

THE POLICE SHOTGUN is the major back-up weapon behind the officer's handgun and is a standard item of gear in most patrol units. Typically, such guns have a barrel bored to the improved cylinder choke, twenty inches in length. The slide action repeater seems to be the preferred design and many of these have been modified to increase the magazine capacity. Autoloading shotguns make up most of the remainder of such guns and, with rare exceptions, the chambers are for the standard length — 2¾-inch — 12-gauge.

Often termed a riot gun, the police shotgun is by no means restricted to such duty. In fact, it's apt to be brought into readiness on almost any occasion in which there seems to be a probability that firepower may be needed beyond the capabilities of the police handgun.

Regulations are by no means uniform through all departments, but the usual procedure is to carry the shotgun with the magazine full and the chamber empty. In this mode, it is a quick and simple matter to pump a shell into the chamber. If a live round is carried in the chamber — or left in the chamber after dealing with an emergency — there is a noteworthy risk of setting it off accidentally while in the car or when being removed. No small number of squad cars have suffered gaping holes in the roof or door as evidence of this particular hazard.

One of the great virtues of the shotgun for the varied demands of police duty is the broad versatility offered by the ability to modify its performance through choice of ammunition. Everything from non-lethal loadings of lightweight plastic pellets on through light loads with fine shot to heavy loads of buckshot and the various types of slugs can deliver anything from a tickle to instant demolition. In fact, as will be discussed later in this chapter, loads are available which give the shotgun performance capabilities comparing favorably with many rifles.

Further advantages of the shotgun include unmatched ability to score hits on elusive targets with the absolute minimum of time for aiming plus what well may be the most ferocious and impressive appearance — when viewed from the front — of any firearm capable of being picked up and carried by one man. There is something about that gaping, dime-sized hole in the muzzle of a 12-gauge that inspires some degree of caution and decorum in almost any beholder, no matter how provoked and berserk that person may have been before the exposure.

Quite apart from dealing with human adversaries, the police shotgun can be employed to excellent effect on diverse other targets, as well. Unruly animals, for example, can be handled with a shotgun or it can be used as a precautionary back-up by one officer while another attempts to secure the nuisance. If small-shot shells are available, their limited range can be invaluable in situations calling for gunfire in densely populated areas.

Properly supervised and effective training in the use of the police shotgun is as important as for the handgun and should be an integral part of periodic range firing for the personnel whose duty may include use of the shotgun. While appropriate adaptations of the practical pistol course — PPC — can be used to good effect in shotgun training, the conventional claybird aerial target, as used in skeet and trap shooting is excellent for familiarization. Practice with the clay targets can be carried out at trap or skeet ranges or one of the inexpensive spring traps, such as the Trius, can be installed at the regular departmental range. Another alternative is the use of a hand trap, available at modest cost. With a little practice, the claybirds can be thrown long distances with exceptional accuracy and control, using the handtrap. Speed, elevation and direction can be varied to infinite degree and the trainee can be presented with a variety of shooting situations limited solely

Left: Discussed on 107, A&W Shotgun Diverter modifies typical circular shotgun pattern, as left above, to a 4-to-1 flattened pattern, as at right.

Conventional skeet range offers excellent practice with the police shotgun, using number 9 shot loads in place of the usual buckshot. Range instructor at St. Louis PD is offering pointers to five-man squad.

by the imagination for the thrower.

There are certain problems connected with carrying the police shotgun in patrol units. The officer's handgun customarily is in its holster at his side and it is comparatively rare for unauthorized persons to attempt to gain possession of it. However, the police shotgun, if carried in the front seat or passenger compartment of the automobile, may be left unattended when the officer is handling a duty call. At such times, there is some risk that it may be stolen, perhaps even employed against the officer or fired by pressure on the trigger while resting in its mount or rack. The last factor mentioned is a prime reason for requiring that the shotgun be carried with an empty chamber when in the automobile.

Recognizing these problems, a number of racks, brackets and carriers are available for the purpose of assuring security of the police shotgun when not in use. The benefits of such devices deserve careful consideration as a means of preventing death, injury or costly lawsuits against the department and its supporting government.

The obvious measure of carrying the shotgun locked in the trunk is not a satisfactory solution, in most instances. Since, many times, it will be desirable to have the shotgun available as the officer dismounts, upon reaching the scene of the complaint, the delay caused by going around to the rear of the car to open the trunk can be a serious disadvantage. Further, firearms carried in the trunk tend to be subjected to hazards of damage from moisture to a greater extent than in the passenger compartment, which usually is heated during those times when moisture damage is most apt to occur through exposure to rain or condensation.

Cutaway barrel demonstrates a real shotgun hazard. Twenty-gauge shell, chambered accidentally, will drop down barrel, lodging ahead of chamber. If a 12-gauge shell is fired, the barrel will burst.

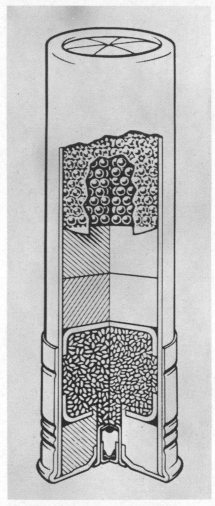

Typical shotshell is detailed in cutaway drawing. Super-X buckshot loads now include a filler of plastic powder among pellets to improve the pattern.

Gauge is determined by the number of lead balls of bore diameter making a pound. In 12-ga size, balls weigh 1/12 lb.

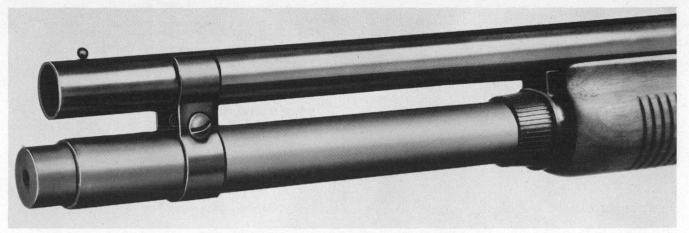

A useful accessory for police work is the magazine extension kit for the Remington Model 870R shotgun. Shell capacity is increased to 8 for 20'', 7 for 18''.

New from Remington is the folding stock kit, which can be installed in place of wooden stock on existing Model 870R police shotguns. Gun can be fired with stock folded, as above, or stock extends for normal use, as below.

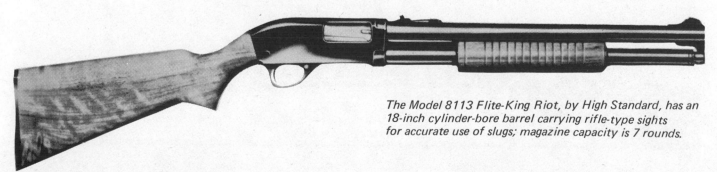

The Model 8113 Flite-King Riot, by High Standard, has an 18-inch cylinder-bore barrel carrying rifle-type sights for accurate use of slugs; magazine capacity is 7 rounds.

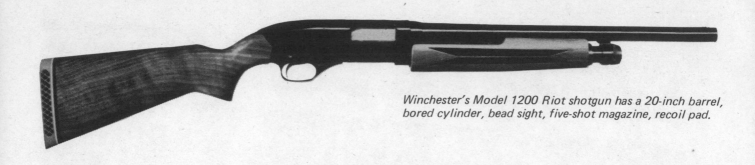

Winchester's Model 1200 Riot shotgun has a 20-inch barrel, bored cylinder, bead sight, five-shot magazine, recoil pad.

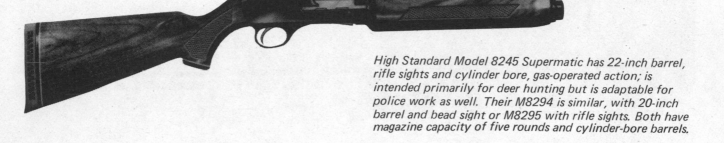

High Standard Model 8245 Supermatic has 22-inch barrel, rifle sights and cylinder bore, gas-operated action; is intended primarily for deer hunting but is adaptable for police work as well. Their M8294 is similar, with 20-inch barrel and bead sight or M8295 with rifle sights. Both have magazine capacity of five rounds and cylinder-bore barrels.

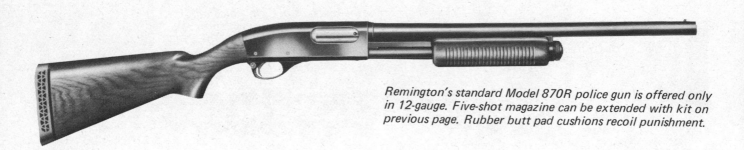

Remington's standard Model 870R police gun is offered only in 12-gauge. Five-shot magazine can be extended with kit on previous page. Rubber butt pad cushions recoil punishment.

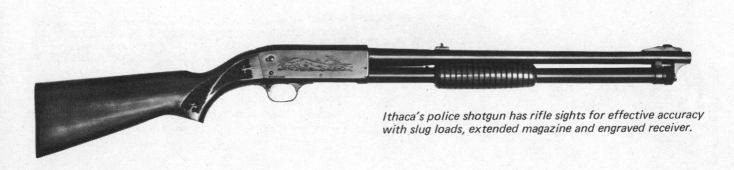

Ithaca's police shotgun has rifle sights for effective accuracy with slug loads, extended magazine and engraved receiver.

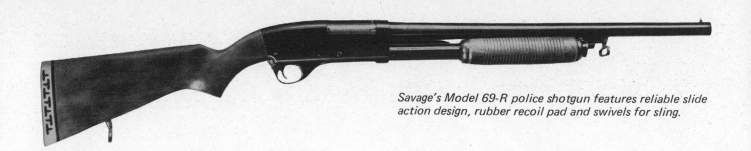

Savage's Model 69-R police shotgun features reliable slide action design, rubber recoil pad and swivels for sling.

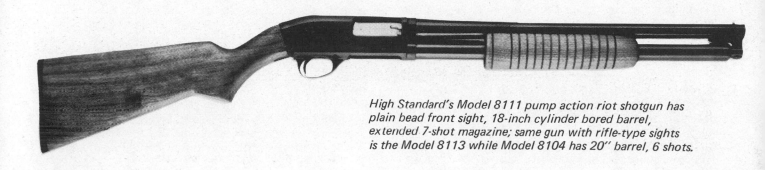

High Standard's Model 8111 pump action riot shotgun has plain bead front sight, 18-inch cylinder bored barrel, extended 7-shot magazine; same gun with rifle-type sights is the Model 8113 while Model 8104 has 20″ barrel, 6 shots.

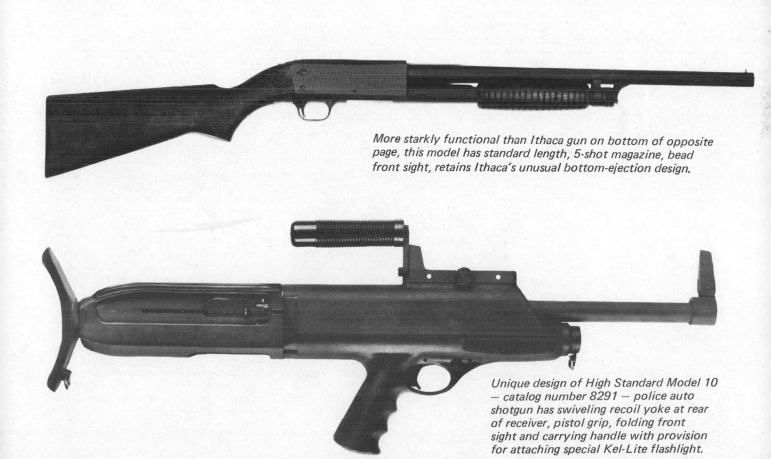

More starkly functional than Ithaca gun on bottom of opposite page, this model has standard length, 5-shot magazine, bead front sight, retains Ithaca's unusual bottom-ejection design.

Unique design of High Standard Model 10 — catalog number 8291 — police auto shotgun has swiveling recoil yoke at rear of receiver, pistol grip, folding front sight and carrying handle with provision for attaching special Kel-Lite flashlight.

And Now From The Horse's Mouth: A Police Officer's Philosophy On Shotguns!

PUBLIC CONTROVERSY IS seething in these United States over the use of high-powered police armament. It has focused lately on the American Civil Liberties Union's anti-dumdum-bullet campaign, but one part of the debate has been smoldering for years, and is doubtless due to erupt again.

The topic is the police shotgun; specifically, whether it should be standard equipment carried in every patrol car. On one side are the street cops themselves, backed up by most of the patrolmen's unions. They want the shotguns — indeed, they're pleading for them. They say it's suicide for one or two cops with .38 Specials to tangle with an armed robbery team packing sawed-off 12-gauge shotguns, .30 carbines and automatic weapons stolen from armories.

On the other side are a series of strange bedfellows who adamantly oppose the thought of a shotgun in every cruiser. ACLU, of course, is against it; so are many minority citizens' groups. But surprisingly, a number of police chiefs and commissioners, and even veteran firearms instructors, are also reluctant to make the riot gun standard equipment. They say that a mistake with a shotgun will be far more tragic than a misjudgment that turns loose only a .38 slug. They feel that in an urban firefight, a shotgun in the lawman's hands will mean nine to thirty times more projectiles flying about the scene; a scene occupied by perhaps dozens of innocent bystanders. They don't feel that their men are one hundred percent capable of controlling such a high volume of firepower.

The only solid arguments against the police shotgun in the cruiser come from the administrators. They don't think they can train all their men to handle the shotgun safely and accurately enough to keep all that buckshot from flying amok through a gunfight scene.

No dissertation on shotguns place in the scheme of police work would be complete without touching on the philosophy of the individual who is called upon to use such armament. We asked Massad Ayoob, a working police officer in New England, for his thoughts.

"It's a valid objection in many respects. To sportsmen, the shotgun is the easiest firearm to master, and the handgun, the hardest. But in police training, the situation reverses. Training focuses on the sidearm, yet one actually needs more practice time on the police shotgun to be completely safe and secure in its handling. It's a rare department that has a biannual or even yearly qualification with the shotgun to any degree. I've been out with enough under-trained cops in crisis moments to see them fumble dangerously with their unfamiliar shotguns. I can remember going into one or two situations where I was more afraid of the shotgun-armed cops behind me than of the unknown felons we were going in to face," Ayoob comments.

Still, this side of the argument doesn't weigh that heavily. Too many civilian appointees in police management think of the combat shotgun as a Wyatt Earp scattergun that throws a pattern wide enough to clean out a twenty-foot bar when fired from the bat-wing doors of the Long Branch Saloon. In actuality, police combat situations generally occur within seven paces and, at that distance, a charge of buckshot from the open or improved cylinder choke of a riot gun will just about fill the space between two shirt buttons on a human adversary. A day at the range will soon dispell notions of buckshot buzzing wildly in all directions.

"Moreover, it is my considered opinion that the presence of a shotgun in the cop's hands will reduce the volume of gunfire when lawmen confront criminals at the scene. We must always remember that in a gunfight in public, the great danger to the bystanders is the wanton gunfire of the desperate criminal, not the controlled firepower of the trained and disciplined police officer," Ayoob says.

Also to be considered is the psychological threat of the riot gun. Consider what happened in Boston last year. The police patrolman's union petitioned loudly for standard issue shotguns, because some fifty percent of the armed robberies in the city were being committed with sawed-offs. Civil liberties associations, black community groups and the Boston police commissioner all argued against the proposal, just as loudly. The debate was front page material and was played up on television news broadcasts.

The cops lost. Shotguns were issued, as a compromise measure, to district supervisors to carry in their command cars. Street cops complained bitterly that by the time the supervisor got there, they would be lying dead in the street, outgunned by an armed robbery team. But the real upshot of the controversy was that the criminals — who watched television and read the papers, too — saw how scared the cops were of sawed-offs and realized what a deadly edge they had. The number of sawed-off shotguns used in armed robberies shot up from fifty percent to between sixty-five and seventy-five percent.

This situation created two ugly dangers. First, gunmen who were confronted by cops now realized that they outgunned almost any lawman they faced, making them more likely to shoot instead of surrender. Secondly, the cops now were more likely to pull the trigger first and ask questions later if faced with an uncertain shoot/no shoot decison in a darkened robbery scene. It hasn't happened yet, but it's a potential tragedy that looms over any Boston cop who answers an armed robbery call.

As we have seen, the shotgun gives the officer a psychological edge over his criminal opponent that may forestall a shooting situation from the outset. If it comes to gunplay, the shotgun's massive stopping power can make the difference between an arresting officer and a candidate for an inspector's funeral. Still, the shotgun isn't the magic manstopper that you see on "Police Story": nothing stops one hundred percent of the time and there are documented cases of felons receiving several loads of buckshot in the torso and still being able to shoot and run for several minutes. A few gunmen have even absorbed 12-gauge rifled slugs in the chest and kept running.

Generally speaking, one shotgun blast is likely to neutralize a gunman instantly. One reason is the massive destruction that occurs when the pellet charge strikes en masse, as it will in most police gunfights because of the short range. Pathologists call the effect a rat hole wound. Secondly, a trained officer, firing the shotgun from the shoulder, is more likely to deliver a good center hit than he would with a handgun.

When a cop misses with a shotgun, it's generally because

In many cities, shotguns are issued only for special problems. Member of New York City Police Department emergency services unit breaks out Ithacas from their rack, which is carried in a big emergency truck.

he has fired from the hip. This is an archaic method of gun handling. In combat pistoling, most masters have gotten away from hip shooting, because they've found that they can bring the gun to point-shoulder in only a fraction of a second longer than it would take to fire from belt level and accuracy is increased greatly. Today's cop is trained to shoot from the hip only at point blank range — within arm's length — and only in those rare moments when he can't afford that fractional second; that is when he's looking down a gun barrel.

This doesn't hold true for the shotgun. The cop walking into a danger scene generally bears his smoothbore at port arms and, from there, it takes no longer to swing the butt up to the shoulder than it does to pivot the muzzle down to belly level for hip shooting.

In fact, shooting from eye level is even more important with the shotgun than with the sidearm. Fired from the hip, even when the elbow properly tucks the butt stock against the waist or floating ribs, the recoil still moves the shotgun in an unpredictable direction and makes it awkward to pull the slide for follow-up shots. Too, because the gun is held with one hand forward and one hand back, it is not instinc-

tive to index the target. Your eyes may be focused on your man's midriff, but your muzzle is probably pointing over his right shoulder.

Finally, the cop who learns to hit a silhouette from the hip with a riot gun, learns by practicing in a single position. In real life, he may have to twist to one side or the other to fire, and his feet will be placed wrong, throwing him off entirely. This is not a problem when the gun is fired from the shoulder.

A properly trained officer is unlikely to miss the target of his combat shotgun and jeopardize bystanders.

"The slide-action is the generally accepted riot gun. Personally, I could see a gas-operated autoloader like the Remington 1100 with a twenty-inch barrel, which I hear is being adopted by the Los Angeles Police Department's SWAT team. A man who doesn't have a lot of training won't have to fumble with the trombone action, which can cause problems: in his haste, he may not pull the slide all the way back, and in some models, he may forget to bump the slide forward to unlock it after firing. The gas auto's main advantage is the reduced recoil, which does allow for quicker follow-up shots.

"Still, the pump gun will remain standard for two reasons. First, it can be put in a stand-up dashboard rack like the Lecco holder with metal jaws clamped between slide and receiver, preventing unauthorized personnel from jacking a round into the normally empty chamber. Secondly, a swollen shell case that would jam an auto often can be pumped in and out of a slide-action's chamber by force. Firearms instructors will tell you that a pump is less likely to jam from neglect, but I think that's debatable," our expert contends.

A few departments are still using double-barrels with twenty-inch tubes. New York City Police Department issues this gun to detectives, on the theory that its simpler operation is better suited to men who have scatter-guns in their hands only occasionally. Their feeling is that the detectives will be using them mainly in raids, where they won't be likely to fire more than two rounds anyway. Stevens sells a lot of their short police-model doubles to private security guard firms, which don't have much time or money to train their personnel with more sophisticated shotguns.

A growing number of undercover narcs are carrying truly sawed-off doubles, cut back to the forend in front and to the pistol grip in the back, They feel that it's a counter-culture weapon that won't remind drug people of cops, yet it packs substantially more authority than the .25 automatic, which is so frequently issued to narcs that the street people are recognizing them as just as clear a police tip-off as a Detective Special. Still, this may not be the ideal weapon. The firearms instructor of an East Coast department told me recently, "Sure, our undercover people have sawed-offs, but they don't qualify with them. They just take confiscated guns out of the armory and put them under their van seats, without even checking to see if they work."

More practical super-short scatter-guns are growing in popularity amongst the boys in blue. These include the folding-stock option on the Remington 870 and the High Standard Model 10, a Supermatic auto of bullpup configuration that is seen most often in Dick Tracy comic strips.

"These stubby guns have one main purpose: they can be carried under an overcoat by a detective with one hand through a cut out pocket. But disadvantages are many. Recoil is more violent, and accuracy may suffer because of the awkard manner in which the instrument must be held. I tend to prefer the Model 10, because it can be fired from the shoulder with no alterations, though I admit that a 12-gauge magnum shell going off next to my cheek has never been a comforting sensation.

"In a standard riot gun, I like a twenty-inch tube for cruiser duty. There's a lot less flash and report than with an eighteen inch, and that's a vital consideration in a close-quarters gunfight in the dark. When the pump gun is cut down to between fourteen to sixteen, inches oddly enough, the blast isn't that much worse than with an eighteen incher, and portability is greatly enhanced, though at some negligible expense of velocity. I would approve of a super-short riot gun for a stakeout unit that works indoors where maneuverability is of the essence. I see no use for a twenty-two inch or longer barrel at all in police work: Bulk becomes noticeably greater, with no real reduction in blast or recoil. Best barrel length for the combat shotgun seems to be twenty inches

"There are three accessories I think should be mandatory on all police shotguns: the recoil pad, the extended magazine that gives the shooter six to eight-shell capacity instead of four, and rifle-type sights. The latter, coupled with slugs, gives the officer carbine capability within fifty, and in some circumstances, up to one hundred yards."

Ammo selection is vital. The buck, with nine .33 caliber pellets in the standard load and twelve in the short magnum, has long been the standard law enforcement loading, but more and more enlightened police gun experts are going to number 4 buck, which throws thirty-four .27 caliber projectiles. The feeling is that at maximum range — thirty-five to fifty yards — only about a third of the pattern is going to strike home. This means three .33s versus up to ten .27s. Since the buckshot pellet by itself delivers minimal shock, and does its work solely by destroying the tissue it contacts, No. 4 is more likely to puncture vital parts. Deer hunters who use buckshot are finding out the same thing. The 00 does, however, have greater penetration on auto bodies, which may make it a better choice for some rural and highway law enforcement agencies, though it's a good reason not to use double-ought in urban situations.

There are some good tear-gas loads for the 12-gauge, notably the AAI Ferret. It may not do the same job as a Flite-Rite out of a 37mm tear gas gun, but few cruisers carry the latter, and when an ugly barricade situation breaks so fast that the first patrolmen on the scene have to handle it, those 12-gauge Ferrets can be worth their weight in Law Enforcement Assistance Administration fund-granting forms. The only problem is that a lot of departments put Ferret shells in the cruiser trunks, but leave the gas masks at headquarters.

"Finally, there are the situations for which the gun is named: riots. I tend to be dubious about stun projectiles — bean bags, as they're known in the trade. When you're on the street in front of the television cameras, and you want to knock somebody down without hurting him, you don't do it by firing a shotgun in his direction. A lot of riot-training schools teach the officers to load No. 12 bird shot and fire it at the pavement several feet ahead of the advancing rioters, on the theory that the ricocheting pellets will sting the leader's legs and take the fight out of them. I can't see that. What I can see is a No. 12 pellet puncturing some teen-ager's eyeball, or a nervous rookie stuffing bird shot into his magazine and leaving a double-0 shell in the chamber, or a borderline crowd going berserk when the cry goes up, "The pigs are shotgunning the people!"

"I remember a crowd control situation where the officers fired rock salt out of their shotguns at the advancing crowd. Two kids were blinded for life as a result. Two young people were maimed when they hadn't done enough to warrant it, and two policemen were crucified for what they thought was a merciful exercise of nonlethal force — it shouldn't have happened," Ayoob recalls.

The shotgun is a combat weapon. Its function is to neutralize heavily armed, violent felons. The law enforcement arsenal has better crowd-control tools; bird shot and rock salt have no place in police work.

In a society where violent crime is on the increase, and where criminals steal M-16s from armories, the law enforcement officer is more and more likely to face homicidal felons armed with heavy weapons. A well-setup shotgun in an officer's trained hands will go far toward terminating that deadly criminal threat before it culminates in the death of an innocent citizen or a police officer.

It is essential that the officers be thoroughly trained with these potentially destructive tools in order to prevent the kind of tragedy that would totally alienate a public that already has little understanding of the lawman's job and the lethal weapons to which he must sometimes resort if he is to protect them from a danger they don't fully comprehend — a deadly danger that haunts him through his every working hour.

These are one man's thoughts.

The A&W Diverter Has The Capability Of Delivering Fan-Shaped Pellet Patterns, With Other Advantages, As Well!

Uncomfortable shooting stance was assumed to hold gun on its side to provide a vertical delivery of flattened pattern in paper as demonstration of its unique capability.

SHOTGUNS HAVE BEEN around for a long time and their unique to-whom-it-may-concern capability makes their use indispensable in certain applications. Until quite recently, no one has bothered to do anything revolutionary with the scattergun, since the introduction of the fixed-ammunition breechloader which supplanted the muzzle-loader some time toward the end of the previous century.

The typical pattern of a shotgun is approximately circular in cross-section and this seemed quite acceptable to most users, despite the fact that shotgun targets come in all shapes and sizes.

A definite need was recognized for a method of modifying the usual circular pattern insofar as specific military and police applications are concerned. The short-barreled shotgun still is in wide use by the military for guarding prisoners or guard duty in camps, where the population density makes the use of a high-powered rifle impractical. In addition, the police riot gun would be more effective, it was felt, if it could be made to control the height of its pattern in proportion to the horizontal spread. Often, it's desirable to discourage an unruly crowd without inflicting drastic or permanent injury upon the individual rioter. A flat, fan-shaped pattern would enable the officer to skim a charge along at ground level to deliver a highly distracting fire with minimum risk of lethal effect.

Certain other shortcomings of the standard 12-gauge riot gun were recognized and programmed for improvement, if such modifications could be incorporated practically. The recoil of the 12-gauge is jarring enough to pose a real problem when familiarizing untrained shooters with its use and the noise level is high, particularly in the instance of the shorter barrels. At the same time, most loads generate an objectionable amount of muzzle flash under dim lighting conditions. The flash is bad on at least two counts: It temporarily blinds and distracts the shooter and it betrays his location with the possible consequence of drawing return fire, if the adversary is armed.

Further specifications included the stipulation that

After a single shot through the A&W diverter from 20 yards, one empty beverage can of the original 16 remained standing in test illustrated in photos on opposite page, using size 8 shot.

Even the can that didn't fall was hit by a single pellet that went through both sides of the metal.

improvements in shotgun performance had to be made without reducing the muzzle velocity and, if at all possible, without eliminating the capability of firing slug loads with accuracy and safety.

The evaluation of performance and shortcomings was made by the Air Force's Directorate of Security Police for the benefit of the USAF and associated agencies. Several devices were tested in the search for a means of improving overall shotgun performance and eliminating the objectionable considerations. Early results were negative for any of several reasons: Some devices would fail by splitting or breaking in use, others gave an actual increase in recoil, or muzzle flash and none provided the desired control of the pattern on a uniform basis.

As the research investigation progressed, the firm of Kexplore, Incorporated, in Houston, Texas, was contacted with a request to assist in the project. Kexplore is an associate of A&W Engineering, Incorporated, specializing in kinetic research, the study of moving bodies.

Although one might assume that a shotgun pattern could be flattened to a horizontal plane by the simple process of flattening the barrel slightly at the muzzle, this does not prove to be true. Such a modification tends to produce an erratic dispersion of pellets, with objectionable gaps in the pattern at short ranges and, worse still, often creates a severe secondary peak of pressure near the muzzle where construction is not sufficiently sturdy to handle the added strain.

Research conducted by Kexplore resulted in the development of the device known as the A&W Shotgun Diverter. In its original form, the diverter produced patterns showing a consistent four-to-one dispersion, with excellent uniformity of pellet distribution at all practical ranges. The load used in testing and development was the standard No. 4 buckshot shell, with twenty-seven pellets and it was found that the same desirable dispersion and uniformity of pattern was maintained with other shot sizes, on down through No. 9 or smaller. At the same time, slug loads could be fired through the diverter with no appreciable loss of accuracy as compared to firing the same load through plain barrels without the diverter. If anything, accuracy seemed to be slightly better with slug loads through the diverter than when fired without it.

Complex pattern of diverting surfaces can be seen in this view of 4-to-1 model designed for police use. A 2-to-1 type also is made.

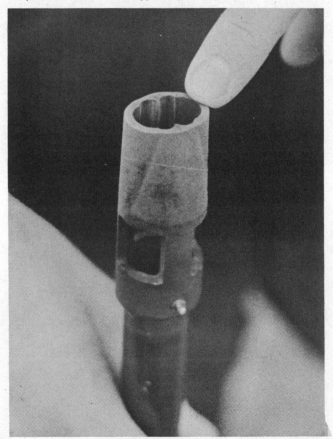

Sixteen empty cans were lined up for test of 4-to-1 unit at 20-yard distance.

High-speed photo, at the instant of firing, catches fifteen of the falling cans in mid-air.

Several subsidiary advantages were noted for the A&W diverter: Recoil was reduced by approximately twenty-two percent, according to laboratory measurements. There was a significant reduction of muzzle flash with the diverter, bringing it down to a level comparable to the firing of a heavy handgun.

Somewhat more astonishing was the fact that the diverter produced a useful gain in muzzle velocity over plain barrels of equal length with the same load. Using the No. 4 buck loads out of twenty-inch barrels, the standard barrels averaged a velocity of 1228 fps while addition of the A&W diverter boosted this figure to an average of 1301 fps.

Approximately 2500 rounds of the No. 4 buck loads were used in establishing these figures.

One further advantage turned up in the final evaluation: a slight but useful reduction in the level of the report, averaging about one decibel. Although this may not sound like a great deal, it should be remembered that the value of a decibel increases progressively at each higher level. When firing the diverter-equipped shotgun, there is a distinct subjective impression that the sound of the report is milder and less piercing to the ears than the same load from a plain barrel.

We were given an opportunity to try out the A&W diverter in two different modifications. Test arms were a slide-action riot gun with the four-to-one diverter silver-soldered to its muzzle and an autoloader with an experimental two-to-one diverter fitted to a threaded sleeve on its muzzle. The two-to-one version has been developed with an eye toward commercial application in the field of sporting firearms.

In basic form, both diverters are made of high tensile steel by the investment casting process, weighing slightly over four ounces. Each has three ports, approximately square and three-quarters of an inch long, just ahead of the end of the shotgun barrel. The ports are separated by solid extensions of the device, these being nearly 3/16-inch thick by 3/8-inch in width. The actual pattern control is accomplished by the contours of a mathematically determined area of the diverter ahead of the ports. This positions two tapering knife-edged ramps, one each at the top and bottom, with complex shaping of the tube as it leads to the front of the diverter. As you look at the muzzle of the device, the aperture might be compared to the spread wings of a butterfly — the resemblance being more apparent in the example of the four-to-one diverter.

Demonstrations consisted of working with the pattern board and a test on a conventional skeet range. The distinctive performance of the diverter was highly apparent on the pattern paper and one of us, at the expense of some slight physical strain, held the four-to-one equipped pump gun on its side to fire a vertical pattern followed by a conventional hold to superimpose a second shot to produce a neat, cross-shaped combination.

The reduction in recoil was quite apparent. As a test, some slug loads were fired into a safe backstop from the hip, using a one-hand-pistol-style hold without any

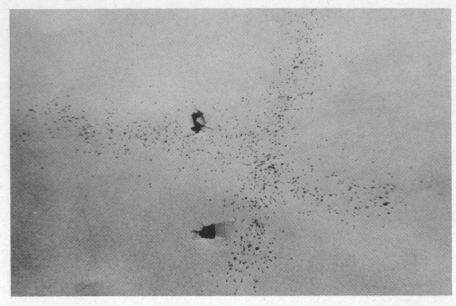

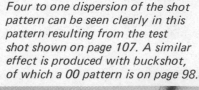

Two shots into the pattern paper with gun rotated 90 degrees gave this unusual, cross-shaped pattern. Large holes were made by wads of the number 8 loads.

Four to one dispersion of the shot pattern can be seen clearly in this pattern resulting from the test shot shown on page 107. A similar effect is produced with buckshot, of which a 00 pattern is on page 98.

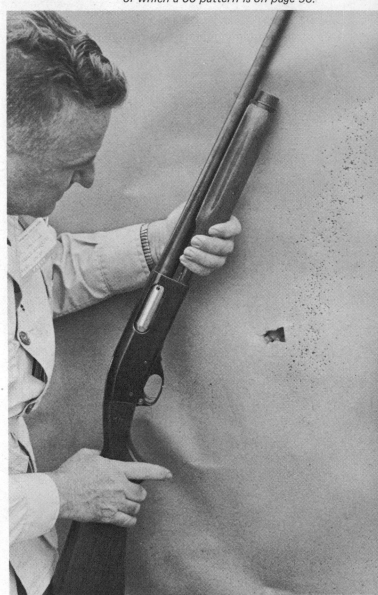

particular discomfort or difficulty of controlling the gun. When fired from the shoulder in the conventional manner, the recoil seemed quite mild. The general impression was that heavy 12-gauge loads felt similar to light field 16-gauge or heavy hunting loads from a 20-gauge.

As previously noted, the noise level did not seem as loud or as sharp as normally expected with heavy 12-gauge loads. We did not have an opportunity to check the reduction in muzzle flash in dim light although, in firing several rounds in the gathering twilight, no visible flash was observed at any time.

As a demonstration, sixteen empty beverage cans were lined up along the frame of the pattern board, extending for approximately six feet, horizontally. When fired upon from about twenty yards, fifteen of the cans were knocked off and examination of the remaining can showed that one pellet had gone through both thicknesses of tin without knocking it over; No. 8 shot was used in this test.

Firing offhand with the slug loads, there was no particular difficulty in holding the group within a six-inch spread at a distance of about forty yards. Mildness of recoil was a contributing factor here, since the deliberate aimed firing of a 12-gauge can be slightly nerve-wracking under ordinary circumstances due to the difficulty of controlling tendencies to flinch.

Moving on to the skeet range, which was not occupied by other shooters at the time, the demonstration became quite impressive. Using the fixed four-to-one diverter on the pump action gun, it was possible — in fact, surprisingly easy — to break both birds on doubles from station one and, with a trifle of practice, both could be broken with a single shell, if the shooter waited until they were meeting at the center of the range. It should be noted that skeet rules do not recognize getting two birds with one shot so it offers no great strategic advantage in that respect although it makes an interesting and challenging accomplishment as a pure tour de force.

Since the flattened pattern provided built-in lead in both directions, we went on to the number four skeet station where both birds cross in front of the shooter at angles of nearly ninety degrees. Again, the four-to-one diverter made its effectiveness known in no uncertain terms. So long as you were fairly careful about the elevation, it was all but impossible to miss powdering the birds from number four.

A&W Engineering designed novel pressure testing gun to measure levels at different points along the barrel in researching the diverter.

A threaded collar is silver-soldered to the barrel for installation. Four-to-1 diverter is at right, 2-to-1 in center. Both types carry round brass bead sights.

After the first few practice shots, shooters were calling for doubles from the fourth station and blasting them — with one shot per bird — so regularly as to be pleasantly monotonous.

The two-to-one diverter, being mounted on a threaded sleeve, can be rotated a quarter of a turn to provide a vertical dispersion rather than horizontal, if this seems desirable. We tried this with good effect on stations seven and eight where the birds move in or away at slight angles, and, again, found that the pattern control offers a distinct advantage. Indeed, several shooters discovered that it was astonishingly easy to break the low-house bird from the hip at station seven and a quantity of ammunition was expended to establish the ease of doing this particular unorthodox maneuver.

Personnel of the A&W firm, explained that, contrary to the obvious assumption, the diverter does not operate by deflecting the shot itself but, rather, by acting upon the inertia and pressures of the powder gases at the time they exit from the muzzle. This accounts for the excellent uniformity of performance since, were the pellets to be bounced off the inner surface of the diverter, they would be misshapen out of round, adversely affecting their flight characteristics.

If the A&W diverter did nothing beyond controlling the pattern to a flattened or rectangular pattern, it still would be a unique and valuable extension of the basic capability of shotguns. When you consider that it accomplishes pattern control with great efficiency and goes on to offer a gain in velocity, together with reduction in noise, recoil and muzzle flash, the advantages offered are remarkable, indeed.

The A&W diverter can be installed on existing single-barrel shotguns and it comes with its own gold bead front sight. Installation of the diverter may require some minor adjustment in sighting technique because of repositioning the front sight since the point of impact may not be in the same relation to the line of sight as before the diverter was installed. However, this presents no major problem and a short session with a few sheets of wrapping paper on the pattern board will establish the technique that delivers maximum effectiveness.

The short shotgun long has enjoyed high regard in law enforcement circles, because of its many advantages which include limited range — permitting its use in areas of relatively high population density — spreading field of fire to assure hits under the most difficult conditions and a formidable psychological impact upon persons who might, otherwise, be inclined toward belligerence. The latter virtue is not to be discounted lightly since, in many situations, the presence of the large-mouthed riot gun is so impressive that actual firing does not become necessary.

By extending the capability of the riot gun in all directions, the A&W diverter appears to make a good gun even better.

Patient, Dogged Research And Development Finally Paid Off With Proof That Projectiles Needn't Spin For Tack-Driving Accuracy!

ACCORDING TO Webster, "sabot" — pronounced sa-BOH or sab-OH, take your choice — is a kind of wooden shoe worn by the peasantry in various European countries, or a piece of soft metal formerly attached to a projectile to take the grooves of the rifling. Likewise, it's the root source for sabotage; presumably stemming from the practice of gumming the works by means of a wooden shoe, placed strategically.

A more specialized context, which many a dictionary overlooks, defines sabot as a sort of bushing, by means of which a projectile of relatively small diameter can be pushed down a barrel of larger diameter, thereby increasing the velocity substantially without a corresponding increase in pressure. Customarily, the sabot is sectioned into two or more pieces and these are designed to separate from the projectile as it leaves the muzzle for its flight to the target.

The basic principle of the sabot-accelerated projectile has been around for several decades and may have been applied to shotgun slugs before but, if so, we've not heard of it.

There can be little question that the field of shotgun slugs is one where improved performance would be welcome. Heretofore, the typical shotgun slug took the form of a lead cup, with rounded nose. Most of them had spiral ridges formed on the outer wall — hopefully, to impart a spinning motion as the slug traveled up the barrel or, if not then, from passage through the air after firing. There is quite a degree of doubt as to whether a "rifled slug" ever does, in fact, acquire any useful amount of rotary spin. It seems that the nose-foremost flight of the conventional shotgun slug is due, in large part, to the forward placement of its center of gravity; being guided by air pressure against the skirts, similar to the bird used in playing badminton.

This is borne out by the fact that slugs seem to shoot about equally well, with or without the rifling ridges on the outer surface. And some of the better slug loads perform with surprising accuracy.

The problem with most slug loads, heretofore, has been twofold: First, there is the difficulty of taking accurate aim with most shotguns and their rather rudimentary sighting facilities; second, the ballistic coefficient — that is, the ability to bore through the air — of the average shotgun slug is a bit better than that of a well-designed parachute, but one could wish it were a lot better than it is.

Recognizing the need for finding something better, two experimenters in Sebastopol, California — a bit north of San Francisco — expended an awesome amount of time and patience upon the project of developing a really efficient slug load for shotguns. William L. McAlvain and Dr. Ward Lewis Kelly collaborated in the development stages, with McAlvain concentrating upon the interior ballistics — powder charge, wad column, et al. — and Kelly concerning himself with the aerodynamics of the flight characteristics of the projectile after leaving the barrel.

It required a great deal of implacable determination to track down the proper shape, proportions and contour for the projectile. Kelly devoted over a year, twelve to fourteen hours a day, seven days a week, to design and trial of first one version, then another; making up test samples, loading them into shells, test-firing at the range and then "back to the old drawing board." Over 50,000 test rounds were fired.

Initial development was directed toward a load suited to meet the need of police departments; one which would offer the capabilities of a high-powered rifle, being fired from the short-barreled shotguns carried in most squad cars.

The product of all this exhaustive effort was christened the 12 Gauge/.500 Police Alloy Projectile and it's furnished, loaded into a 12-gauge shell, packed five rounds in a convenient carton. Several of the experimental prototypes had been equipped with fins for stabilization, but none of these designs proved effective. The jackpot configuration turned out to be about half an inch in diameter at front and rear, tapering to a wasp-waist of .317-inch diameter at a point just to the rear of its midsection. The final form was evolved through sheer trial and error techniques, with little if any help from Lady Luck.

Ballistic Research Industries, or BRI — the company organized to produce the 12 gauge/.500 projectile and ammunition — has an unsolicited report on trajectory test results, compiled on trials of the ammunition as conducted by Sergeant Roger W. Lenz of the Minnesota State Highway Patrol. Using the standard police riot gun issued to him, Sergeant Lenz fired at distances of fifty, one hundred and two hundred yards; at fifty, the point of impact averaged six inches above point of aim, twelve inches above at one hundred and back down to six inches above at two hundred yards. His report notes that he had no trouble in keeping hits within an eighteen-inch square from the kneeling position at two hundred yards. A three-shot group, fired from a rest at one hundred yards measured two and one-half inches, which Lenz considered outstanding, considering the inefficient bead sight on the issue riot gun used in the test.

Sectional density of the BRI slug is 134 percent greater than that of a typical shotgun slug of conventional design and this superiority is reflected in a proportional gain in effective range and retained energy at any given distance. Average velocity of the 12 gauge/.500 load, from a riot gun with its barrel of eighteen or twenty inches, is 1500 feet per second, which gives the 440-grain projectile a muzzle energy of 2200 foot-pounds. At three hundred yards, the BRI slug retains more energy than the bullet from a .30-30 rifle at the same distance.

At one hundred yards, the BRI slug will tear through a steel plate, one-eighth-inch in thickness, with plenty of wallop left for delivery to targets on the other side. By comparison, a conventional 12-gauge slug load will not penetrate the same material at fifty yards. Brick walls, concrete block and similar construction usually is penetrated by the first hit; if not, a second bullet to the same spot goes through. In effect, there is "no place to hide" from the 12 gauge/.500 load.

The projectile, in tests, proves able to blast through the near door and out through the opposite one on typical automobiles. Hits on the engine block result in massive damage to steel and cast iron construction, usually disabling the motor with a single round.

At the same time, the alloy of which the police slug is composed is designed so that, if it strikes a surface which it cannot penetrate, the projectile disintegrates into small fragments, minimizing any problems from ricochets.

Development has been carried forward to produce two additional versions of the Kelly-McAlvain sabot shotgun projectile for use by hunters. These are designated as the 12 Gauge/.500 Shock Point. The MK 9 is a complete round, packed five to the pocket carton and priced at $2.90 per carton, with a 440-grain projectile for use in cylinder or modified choke barrels; velocity is a bit below 1500 fps and pressure of the factory loading is reported to be approximately 9000 psi. The MK 5 is the identical projectile, complete with sabot and plastic base-plug, packed ten per carton at $2.95, for use in handloading shotshells. As with the MK 9 load, the MK 5 slugs are intended for firing from barrels bored cylinder, improved cylinder or modified choke.

For use in full choke barrels, the firm offers the MK 7 loaded round and the MK 6 bullet-sabot sets; prices and packaging are the same as with the MK 9 and MK 5 versions. Diameter of the projectile and sabots, likewise, is identical. However, the projectile is of a lighter, harder alloy, weighing 280 grains and delivering muzzle velocities of about 1700 fps. This results in muzzle energy of approximately 1800 foot-pounds and accuracy of the factory loaded round is exceptional, with comparatively modest recoil. It was necessary to go to the harder alloy to prevent the bullet from separating in the center when it encountered the constriction of the choke.

We obtained an assortment of the projectiles and loads for testing and, it must be conceded, factory claims as to accuracy were conservative in comparison to actual performance. The MK 9 loads went into one ragged hole from fifty yards, when tested from a pump-action High Standard Model 8113 police riot gun having an eighteen-inch barrel and rifle-type sights. The MK 8 police alloy load grouped between one inch to an inch and a half at the same distance.

At the same time, we tested one of the High Standard Model 10 riot guns. This is a rather futuristic-looking piece of equipment, measuring a hair more than 26½ inches in length overall. A curved and swiveling butt-plate is mounted to the rear of the action, having no stock in the customary sense of the term. We must confess that we experienced considerable qualms, prior to letting off the first MK 8 load in the Model 10. Recoil of the BRI loads had been sub-

A roll crimp is recommended for loading the BRI slug, rather than the usual star type. Lyman crimping head can be used in electric drill, although drill press is faster, easier. Slug is not made at moment, but probably will be.

stantial in the standard riot gun. Surprisingly, the kick was quite a bit less in the Model 10 than it had been in the more conventional design. Accuracy of the various loads was much the same, that is, highly satisfactory from the Model 10 unit, which is fitted with a mount for the Kel-Lite police flashlight.

A few groups were fired from a standard, sporting-type shotgun; a Model 25 Winchester which was fitted with a Cutts compensator. We removed the choke tube from the end of the Cutts for the tests and found that its brass bead front sight, lined up with the groove in the rear of the receiver, still was capable of close placement of the slugs, although not with quite the same degree of precision as from the rifle-sighted High Standard riot gun.

For some reason, the standard riot gun printed its group about ten inches to the left of the aiming point at fifty yards. With the initial sight setting, fresh from the box, point of impact had been about ten inches low, as well. It was no problem to move the sliding adjustment to raise the rear sight so as to obtain the correct elevation. There was no convenient provision for adjustment of windage. It would have been possible to drift the rear sight slightly to

Upper left: Here are several of the experimental slug designs which were tried in the process of arriving at the final design. Left: Brown sabots are slightly larger in diameter, produce bulges in most cases; white sabot avoids this problem when loading standard-thick cases.

Test shotgun grouped about 10" to left of aiming point, so a red paster was affixed 10" to right of bullseye, delivering this 5-shot, 50-yard group.

Three of the powders specified in BRI load data, as discussed in the text.

the right in its dovetail, but we did not do so, as the gun was on loan. So we took the easy alternate and pasted some Targ-Dot red aiming points about ten inches to the right of the bullseyes and had no further trouble in delivering groups neatly to the center of the target.

It would appear that the prospective user of these loads or projectiles should provide an ample supply for determining the grouping characteristics of the individual shotgun, plus enough extra rounds for the anticipated shooting.

It is recommended that the MK 5 and MK 6 bullet-sabot sets be handloaded into the virgin cases, that is, not previously fired. A further specification is that they be roll-crimped, rather than given a folded or "star" crimp.

A printed sheet of loading instructions is packed with each carton of bullet-sabot sets, giving detailed specifications for recommended procedures. Current sheets cover loads for Remington, Winchester and Federal plastic shells, plus both paper and plastic cases from Alcan.

When using the Remington type S-23470 plastic case, the sheet specifies use of the Remington 157 primer, which is a slight misnomer. Currently, Remington designates their small-diameter battery cup primer as the type 57-Star. Number 157 is used by CCI as the term for their so-called "Remington-size" primer.

The Alcan PGS — for plastic gas seal — over-powder wad is used with all of the various makes and types of cases for which loading directions are supplied. This wad has a small vent hole in its center to prevent shifting through air pressure built up during seating. An unlubricated nitro card of .200-inch thickness is placed over the PGS wad in all instances except for the Winchester type AA or high-brass cases; these require the use of a .250-inch filler wad.

A lightweight plastic plug is provided with each bullet to fill the hollow opening at the rear of the bullet. This is necessary to provide support so that the powder gas cannot come through the center vent and pierce the nitro card at that point. The plug fits rather loosely into some of the bullets and we found it necessary, in certain instances, to seat the bullet-sabot assembly with the head of the shell uppermost, to keep the plastic filler plug from dropping out of the opening. When this happened, it was impossible to steer it back into place and the shell mouth could not be crimped properly since the loose plug kept the bullet-sabot assembly from being seated fully.

The two halves of the sabot are moulded of polyethylene and the standard units are opaque white in color. A larger diameter is colored medium brown and is intended for use with shells having walls that are less than standard thickness. It virtually is impossible to produce an acceptable load by using the brown sabot in shells having standard wall thickness, because the over-size unit bulges the shell wall to the point of preventing chambering of the load.

With the white sabot halves, the reloading operation proceeds without difficulty. We found that the 12-gauge Lee Loader kit was ideally suited for most of the operations such as seating the primer, seating the wads and bullet-sabot unit. We used a Lyman 12-gauge roll crimping head on the case mouths and found that — while it could be done with an electric hand-drill — a drillpress made for vastly greater ease and precision. The load data sheet specifies 2-15/32 inches as the correct length of the loaded round after completion of the roll crimp.

The load for the Remington case, with Remington type 57-Star primers, is 28.0 grains of Hercules Herco powder topped by one Alcan PGS wad and one nitro card of .200-inch thickness. The two halves of the white sabot are held in place around the bullet and the assembly is inserted into the case neck and seated with a flat-faced punch having a diameter nearly equal to that of the bullet-sabot unit. Do not use the hollow seating punches supplied with most shotshell reloading presses for this operation. Seat the wad at eighty pounds, the bullet-sabot at twenty.

The load for the Winchester AA or high-brass shells does not specify the primer, though McAlvain suggests use of the primer from the maker of the shell, the Winchester number 209, in this instance. The powder charge is 31.0 grains of Hodgdon HS-6 powder, one PGS wad topped by one one-quarter-inch filler wad, such as an Alcan Feltan Bluestreak.

For the Federal plastic case, the recommendations are 27.0 grains of Hercules Herco powder; one PGS wad or one .200-inch nitro card on top of the powder, followed by a .200-inch nitro card on top of the over-powder wad, with wad seating pressure of twenty pounds. Primer is not specified on the sheet; McAlvain suggests the Federal number 209 primer.

For the Alcan LP7 plastic or L4 paper cases, the Alcan 220 primer is specified, with 34.0 grains of Alcan AL-7 powder, one PGS plus one .200-inch nitro card; no seating pressure specified.

In each of the foregoing instances, the bullet-sabot assembly, with plastic base filler plug in place, is seated atop the upper portion of the wad column — taking care not to dislodge the plastic base filler plug — and the bullet-sabot unit is seated snugly against the wad column, followed by a roll crimp to the specified 2-15/32 inches of loaded length overall.

There is an optional accessory, offered for use with the Lee Loader kit; a tapered, chrome-plated expander, having a knurled handle. We found this to be most helpful in expanding the ends of the cases slightly to provide easier starting of the wads and the bullet-sabot assembly.

Powder charges were dispensed from a RCBS Uniflow rotary powder measure, having the smaller (benchrest-size) of the two available chamber diameters. The charge weights were adjusted by means of a Lyman-Ohaus powder scale.

The sheet of loading data specifies that the handloads, when prepared according to directions, will generate pressures in the neighborhood of 11,000 psi and velocities of about 1400 fps. The quoted pressure is right at the uppermost limit of pressures considered permissible in shotguns, so care should be exercised in following directions to the letter, so far as components, charges and procedures are concerned.

Accuracy with the handloads was good, although not quite up to the remarkable performance of the factory-load ammunition. No significant variation was noted as to point of impact when firing handloading or factory ammunition.

No load data was available for use with the lighter, 280-grain MK 6 bullets. When loaded with data for the 440-grain bullets, recoil was quite light and the load did not generate enough push-back to operate the autoloading action of the Mark 10 police gun, which functioned perfectly with the 440-grain bullet loads.

The Model 8113 High Standard riot gun had an eighteen-inch barrel and a full-length tubular magazine, giving it a capacity of seven shots. Minor difficulty was noted with the standard, rifle-sighted riot gun and this seemed to stem from the lightweight firing pin or a slightly over-sized firing pin port or, possibly, a combination of the two conditions. At any rate, with the more energetic loads, there was a tendency for the primer cup to flow back into the firing pin and this would create some difficulty in operating the action to load the next round. The same effect was noted when standard fieldload shells were fired in the same gun, while the factory and the handloaded sabot loads did not cause this difficulty when fired in other repeating shotguns, such as the High Standard Model 10 police gun or the slide-action Winchester Model 25.

Evaluating the BRI bullet-sabot system, there was no slightest doubt that this offers a significant and valuable gain in both accuracy and performance when compared to conventional slug loads or buckshot shells. Effective range is boosted to double or better than of other ammunition for use in shotguns and overall performance capability equals or exceeds that of many a high-powered rifle.

Defense arms should be tested thoroughly with the given ammunition to establish the point of impact in relation to aiming point, as well as to verify reliability of function and operation. To stint upon the expenditure of ammunition for such purposes is false economy of the most foolhardy stripe. This observation should not be interpreted as a slur against the BRI bullet-sabot system, which we regard as excellent, nor against the High Standard police weapons, which performed well except for the primer-flow problem noted with the pump gun.

Rather, we are cautioning against the all-too-common outlook and approach wherein a gun and/or some ammunition is bought and put aside, untried and untested, until an emergency situation comes up. That, we submit, is much too late to conduct your field-testing.

The Shotgun Attached To A Motorcycle Offers Psychological As Well As Fire-power Potential!

WHEN THE ALARM is flashed, a motorcycle officer speeds through traffic ahead of the more cumbersome squad cars, leaps from his bike, digs his handgun out of its holster and all too often finds himself facing a man with a high-powered rifle or a shotgun loaded with deadly buckshot.

Such happenings, all too frequently, can do damaging things to the officer's morale and, if he pushes the issue, equally damaging things can happen to his health.

But in the seemingly quiet commercial community of Vernon, California, an independently incorporated city virtually within the shadow of the Los Angeles Civic Center, something is being done about this continuing possibility.

Like the outriders of the Old West, the cycle riders now arrive at the scene of a crime — still ahead of the larger police units — and dismount from their cycles with a business-like sawed-off shotgun in hand. The scatter gun, loaded with 00 buckshot, not only does a great deal to make the officer feel more adequate in the face of an emergency such as a bank robbery, but it can prove a deterrent to the suspected felon, who is quick to realize that he has no advantage in fire-power.

The infamous Watts riots of 1965 occurred not far from the Vernon city limits, some of the action spilling over the line of incorporation. While Chief of Police R. H. Bockhacker states rather positively that shotguns mounted on the motorcycles had been under consideration for some time prior to the riots, it was about six months later that their use as standard cycle equipment was approved and each of the bikes was suitably equipped for carrying such a

persuasive weapon.

Several types of shotguns have been used since the riders began carrying them. First was a Model 11 Remington automatic, but a special addition was necessary to the lock device on this to keep pranksters from pumping a round into the chamber and Bockhacker and his weapons sergeant, R. E. Shank, felt this was not particularly foolproof.

Next tried was the High Standard pump action riot gun and many of the officers favor this. Now under consideration, however, is Remington's Model 870 pump action, which is being thoroughly tested under field conditions. With its positive action, it is the feeling of some of the officers that this gun has definite advantages because of its simplicity for takedown and cleaning. That is one thing about carrying a riot gun on a motorcycle: It needs cleaning more frequently, since it is constantly exposed to grime of the city streets.

The device used to carry the short barrel guns on the cycles is called the Lecco-Lock Riot Gun Holder. Made by Lake Erie Chemical Company, it is familiar to most law enforcement officers, since it is the same electrically actuated lock used in many squad cars to retain the riot guns. Special brackets have been installed on the cycles and each unit of them is equipped with a hide-out button. The motor officer has only to push this concealed switch to release the lock and allow him to withdraw the shotgun from its holder. The button, of course, operates only if the key is in the ignition and is turned on. Yet it makes the gun instantly available, as the rider dismounts at the scene of trouble. It keeps it securely locked if in a crowd situation, where it might be better to leave it in its scanty scabbard.

The gun is carried muzzle down much in the manner of the rifle attached to a saddle in the Old West and the muzzle fits over a rubber or neoprene-fitted knob to hold it securely in place. Admittedly, the shotguns take a bit more jouncing about than in the security of a squad car. This is one reason for favoring the more positive slide action over an automatic model, where such treatment results in more things to go wrong with the more complicated and delicate mechanism.

Of the sixty-five men on the Vernon police department, only seven are assigned to motorcycle duty and these, according to Chief Bockhacker, all are senior men, most of them with more than a dozen years' service in law enforcement. The reason for this is obvious. Inasmuch as the motorcycle officers usually are the first on the scene of an incident, maturity is necessary, when one dismounts from his cycle with a shotgun loaded with 00 buckshot.

"Another reason for our selecting the slide action shotgun is the psychological effect," the chief states. "There is something quite positive in the action, when an officer jerks back that slide, then slams it forward to put a shell in the chamber. It makes one stop and think and, if that big muzzle is pointed in his direction, he's going to think even more before he does anything rash."

There are several banks in the city's five-plus square miles and, as it is heavily industrialized, this means payrolls. Since the cycle officers have begun carrying shotguns, there have been instances wherein the policemen have taken the shotguns from their cycles, but thus far a shot has not been fired in pursuit of a felon, although several have been captured. Again, the psychological factor and the suspect's knowledge of how many slugs that 12-gauge shell holds place the balance of power on the side of the officer.

There have been some problems with ammunition. With the guns carried on the cycles in the muzzle-down position, shotshells have a tendency to bounce a bit in the magazine, thus loosening the over-powder wads, it has been discovered. As a result of the loose powder, when the riot gun is fired with such a shell under the hammer, there is little velocity.

The only cure for this at present is to have the weapons training sergeant and these cycle officers make almost daily inspections of their ammunition and to replace the rounds frequently. To date, they have found that there is less problem with Peters ammo in the familiar blue plastic case and the Power Piston insert.

The suggestion has been made that the department utilize brass shell casings for this highly specialized type of loading and further investigations are being made in this direction, according to Sergeant Shank, although the logical source these days seems to be from European manufacturers.

The one thought that both the chief and the training sergeant have is that perhaps their men do not get enough individual and continuing training in riot gun handling and tactics. Each of the new officers goes through the standard sixteen-week course of the Los Angeles Sheriff's Academy, where they are checked out on the riot gun, but after that, shotgunning is pretty much on their own.

"We certainly do not have the kind of continuing training in this facet that we would like," Bockhacker says, "but we simply do not have the necessary facilities. They are given an occasional refresher course, although they requalify frequently with their handguns.

"However, in running down a roster of my men, I find that virtually all of them are bird hunters. That affords an opportunity each year to refamiliarize themselves with shotgunning under hunting field conditions if not necessari-

Lecco Lock is operated electrically and is similar to one used for holding shotguns in cars.

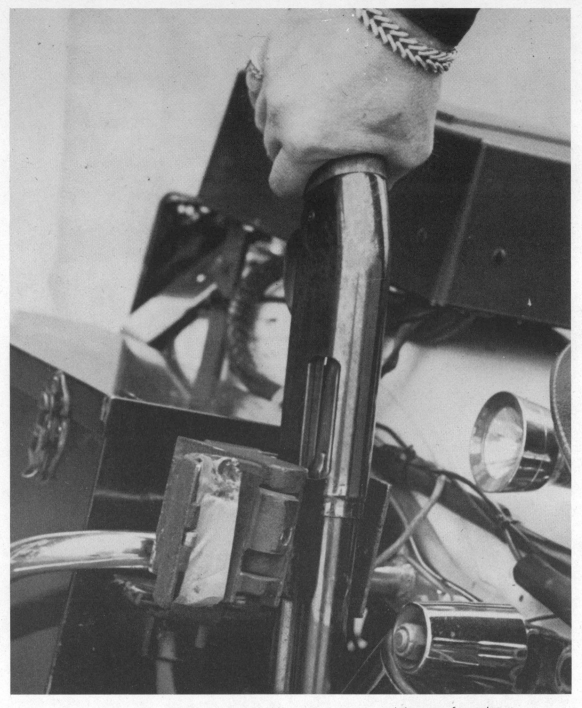

When lock is secured, padding prevents wear and damage of metal parts. Likewise, slide cannot be actuated to chamber a live round. Gun is carried with empty chamber to prevent firing when the motorcycle is unattended.

ly in actual law enforcement training."

In keeping with the idea of fire-power, the entire Vernon department in recent months have switched over from the .38 Special revolver to the .45 automatic as the standard sidearm.

"In the beginning," the chief admits, "the men didn't seem to care for the .45 auto, but we tried the .357 magnum and found that to be unsatisfactory."

The disappointment in the .357 came about after one officer had shot a felon with one. The bullet zipped through the man's body without visibly affecting him and it required another officer to knock him down with a blow from behind in order to put him out of action.

One of the chief reasons that the officers disliked the .45 auto when it first was adopted was the fact that they were carrying the guns without a round in the chamber.

"It was pretty logical to consider that an officer stopping a suspect for an ordinary traffic citation might have flashlight, pen and pad in hand. He would have to drop them all in order to actuate the gun and get ready to fire." Now, though, with proper training and especially designed

Business-like aspect of the police shotgun goes far to minimize chance that shooting is needed.

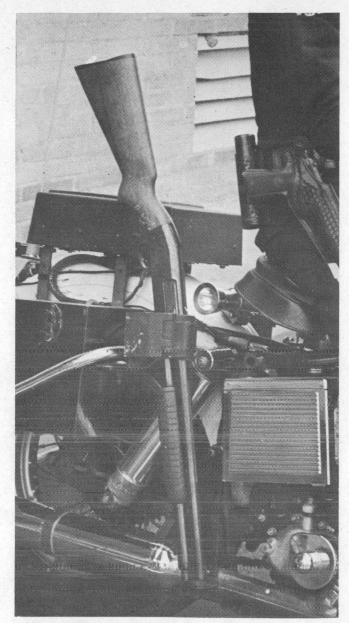

Above; Lecco Lock carries shotgun on right-hand side of cycle, quickly accessible when concealed switch is pressed to release the carrier.

Left: Muzzle of shotgun rides over a rubber plug to position it and cushion vibration while cycle is under way.

holsters, most officers are carrying the .45 automatics cocked-and-locked. Since adopting the .45, each man has received no less than twelve hours training with it.

Whenever one of the motorcycles equipped with its riot gun on full display is parked in public it creates a good deal of spectator interest, another interesting psychological factor, officers of the Vernon department feel. But it has gone beyond that. Numerous other law enforcement agencies across the nation have been keeping an eye on the operation with the idea of possibly equipping their own riders with the locked-in shotgun potential.

MACHINE GUNS AND SUBMACHINE GUNS

Chapter 9

These Capable, Ammo-Hungry Chatterboxes Can Be Useful In Certain Specialized Types Of Emergency, Given Proper Training!

Above: The Thompson remains the weapon coming first to mind when a submachine gun is mentioned. With its buttstock detached, length over all is but 23½ inches. Opposite: H&K's MP5A3 is modern in every detail, yet sells for about the same price as Thompson 50 years ago.

GETTING ACQUAINTED with those guns capable of continuous fire, so long as the trigger is held back, tends to be something of a disillusionment for the average shooter. There is a popular belief that all you need to do is point the muzzle in the general direction of the target, letting the garden-hose pattern take care of assuring a hit. It doesn't take long to learn that it's nowhere nearly that simple!

A full-auto arm chambered for ammunition nominally designed for use in handguns is termed a submachine gun; when chambered for rifle cartridges, it becomes a full-fledged machine gun, without the qualifying sub- prefix.

One fact becomes apparent quite early: Full-auto arms have a tremendous appetite for ammunition plus a nasty habit of running dry about the time the situation becomes truly interesting. An empty machine gun is precisely as effective as an unloaded flintlock musket; no more, no less.

Hand-held automatic weapons, intended to be fired from the hip or shoulder, present considerable difficulty in maintaining the desired point of aim during the firing cycle. This is caused by the fact that – in many designs – the axis of the bore does not line up with the point at which the gun is supported against the force of recoil. Usually, the support point is at the butt of the stock, or on a pistol grip: in either case, well below an imaginary line extending backward from the center of the barrel.

As an inevitable effect of this misalignment between rearward recoil and resistance to recoil, the muzzle tends to be deflected upwards each time a fresh round is fired. As several shots are being fired each second, it becomes extremely difficult to control the climbing tendency of the muzzle. The logical and most effective remedy for this problem is to fire in short bursts – three to five shots at a time – taking fresh aim each time before triggering off the next burst.

Certain modern full-auto designs recognize the muzzle-climb problem and make provisions to minimize and control it. The several arms designed for use with the .223 Remington or 5.56mm military cartridge – such as the

German Schmeisser, top, found its way from WWII Wehrmacht to a Southern California PD locker via a souvenir-conscious GI. The J&R M68 carbine, below, is semi-auto, fires the 9mm Luger round from 32-round magazine; its production is discontinued.

AR-16, AR-18, et al. — have stocks which are, essentially, an extension of the bore axis, with sights elevated well above the barrel for convenience of aiming. As a result, it is considerably more easy to maintain the desired aim during longer bursts.

The primary justification for full-auto weapons is for delivering as many shots as possible at a target which is within range for but a short time: an aircraft, for example, or an automobile attempting to run a road block at high speed. A secondary situation calling for the use of the machine guns is the presence of a large number of hostile personnel, an instance being a massed infantry attack in a military defense problem. In the latter example, it is crucial to note that all of the personnel within the target area must be uniformly hostile; no non-combatants, hostages or innocent bystanders, since the machine gun would endanger them impartially.

As noted in a previous chapter on police rifles, the full-auto weaponry on hand in various police departments represents a random assortment of makes, types and calibers. Donated or confiscated military souvenir weapons make up a substantial percentage.

The Thompson submachine gun remains one of the more common and popular designs. Most frequently, this is chambered for the .45 ACP cartridge, as used in the Government Model Colt .45 auto pistol. Several other calibers were produced in small numbers during development work on this gun in the early '20s. An early catalog lists other available calibers including a longer version of the

.45 ACP case which was designated as the Remington-Thompson caliber .45 military cartridge. This fired a 250-grain bullet at a muzzle velocity of 1450 fps. Other calibers were the .351 auto rifle, 9mm Mauser and 9mm Luger. The last named is perhaps the one most apt to be encountered, apart from the .45 ACP, but it remains a rarity.

Several design changes were made in the Thompson, following its introduction about 1921. Most of the original versions had cooling fins on the barrel and a second pistol grip ahead of the magazine. The charging handle was spherical, slotted through the center to prevent interference with sighting and was located on top of the receiver. A Cutts compensator was available as an option and most of the M1921 and M1928 guns have this accessory, which was mounted on the muzzle to reduce recoil and help control climb during full-auto fire.

Later models, such as the M1928A1 substituted a straight wooden forend for the forward pistol grip, retaining the finned barrel and the provision for the use of drum magazines. There had been a type C drum with a capacity of one hundred .45 ACP cartridges, but it tended to have problems in reliability of feeding. The type L, fifty-round drum is the one most commonly encountered, if at all. The drums were latched into place by means of crosswise slots in the receiver, with the alternate capability of accepting the staggered-column, box-type magazines of twenty-round capacity — designated type XX — which are inserted upward from beneath the receiver.

The Thompson M1 submachine gun was modified to put the charging handle on the right-hand side of the receiver. A rather rudimentary sheet-metal peep sight on the rear of the receiver replaced the elaborate adjustable rear sight of the M1928 and earlier models. The M1 retained the movable firing pin and hammer of the M1921 and M1928. The M1A1 version differed from the M1 solely in having a fixed firing pin, a small protrusion centered on the bolt face.

The M1A1 was extremely simple in operation. When cocked, the bolt was held to the rear, against the tension of the compressed driving spring, by the sear. When the trigger was pulled, the bolt drove forward, scooping a cartridge from the top of the magazine. As the cartridge came to rest in the chamber, the remaining inertia of the heavy bolt caused an indention of the cartridge primer via the protruding fixed pin, thus setting off the cartridge.

Earlier versions of the Thompson had employed the so-called "Blish hesitation principle," a somewhat dubious arrangement whereby a wedge of metal adhered under high pressure to keep the breech locked until pressure had diminished to safe levels. Sometimes called the delayed blowback system, this was replaced by the straight blowback design of the M1 and M1A1 in which only the inertia of the bolt assembly resisted the rearward thrust of the powder gases.

Upon firing, the bolt is driven back, compressing the driving spring, until it comes to a stop. If the sear remains down, as in full-auto setting with the trigger held back, the spring pushes the bolt forward again, repeating the cycle until the trigger is released or the ammunition is exhausted. When the fire-selector lever is rotated a half-turn rearward, to the "single" setting, a disconnector device is brought into play, so that the trigger must be released and pulled again for each shot.

The M1A1 was produced in large numbers during WWII, in which it saw extensive service. Toward the end of that conflict, the M3 submachine gun — often called the "grease gun" — was introduced. Being lighter, more compact and considerably less expensive to manufacture, it supplanted the Thompson to a considerable degree for military purposes.

An early version of the Thompson gun was manufactured, capable of semi-auto fire only; there was no provision for switching to full-auto. Despite the semi-auto feature, the Thompson carbine — as it was called — would not be legal for civilian use under present federal firearms regulations. Barrels of civilian sporting rifles must be of a length in excess of sixteen inches, as measured from muzzle to closed bolt face, with 26½ inches or more of length over all for the entire rifle. The Thompson carbine would meet the length over all requirement, but its effective barrel length remains about 10½ inches, well short of the minimum legal dimension. This is not to say that the Thompson carbine could not be possessed and used by authorized law enforcement personnel, but it is noted here as a relevant point in regard to private ownership.

At the present time, manufacturing rights of the Thompson are controlled by Numrich Arms Company, West Hurley, New York 12491. New units are available to qualified purchasers, as are spare parts and repair service.

Although many automatic weapons have been developed for military and police use since the end of WWII such as the M-14 and M-16 et al., little had been done in this country to develop a new and better submachine gun until Smith & Wesson went to work on the design of their Model 76 9mm submachine gun. The need for this type of gun in law enforcement and military work has become more evident in recent years with the increase of police shootings by criminals when, in many cases, the police were out-gunned by their assailants. The military has also found that, although the .22 caliber automatic M-16 gives the infantryman a lot of firepower, the small projectile is deflected easily when fighting in the dense jungle growth of Southeast Asia. The small bullet has extremely limited penetration power, as compared to heavier calibers.

The S&W 9mm submachine gun is a straight blowback, magazine-fed gun of rugged construction. The receiver is a length of seamless tubing. The sights are heli-arc welded to the receiver, as are the barrel-retaining bushing, magazine housing and two blocks which locate and retain the lockwork housing. A single large diameter screw bolt is used to both reinforce the grip, and to fasten folding stock, grip and lockwork housing to the gun.

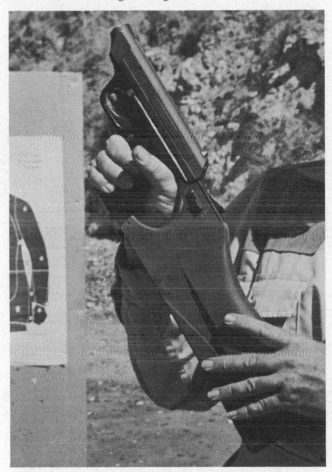

H&K's Model VP-70 becomes a machine pistol with the addition of this stock holster, functions solely as a semi-auto with stock removed. Fire selector is on the stock behind slide, can be worked from both sides.

A large-diameter recoil spring reciprocates that heat-treated alloy steel bolt in the receiver between the firing position and the rearward cocked position. Positive guidance is provided by the inside of the receiver, yet ample clearance is allowed to insure reliable operation even under extremely dirty conditions. This fact was brought home by a U.S. Navy test team in San Diego, California. The Navy men filled the magazine with sand while loading it, then successfully fired the gun without a jam. This is unheard of with most automatic weapons.

The S&W comes with a three-position selector switch, safe, semi-automatic and full-automatic. The switch is accessible from either side of the gun, making operation

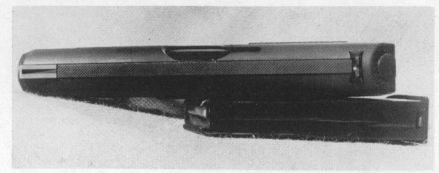

Front sight of VP-70 is of novel design with steel ramp to cast a shadow for a surprisingly effective sight picture.

Concealed hammer moves back and drops as trigger is pulled through long, heavy double action on the VP-70, being intended as a safety feature for carrying loaded chamber.

easy for left or right-handed shooters.

The gun has a thirty-six-round magazine of heavy metal construction. It is held securely within the magazine housing and can be used as a front hand grip or as a monopod.

The Model 76 is designed to take all 9mm Parabellum ammunition, both military and commercial. Recoil and muzzle climb are negligible, and the gun is quite accurate.

The firepower of the S&W is also superior to that of the Thompson and the M3 grease gun. Its cyclic rate of fire is 720 rounds per minute, which betters the others by thirty to fifty rounds per minute. With the stock folded, the gun is 20¼ inches long and, when the stock is extended, the gun measures 30½ inches in length. Barrel length is eight inches, weight when loaded is 8¾ pounds. This makes it nearly two pounds lighter than the loaded M3 and close to three pounds lighter than the Thompson.

The entire gun can be field-stripped in a matter of minutes without tools by using the tip on the butt end of the magazine. The eight-inch rifled barrel is changed quickly by unscrewing the barrel nut and heat guard. The field stripping breaks down into three major parts, the clip, barrel and heat guard, and receiver group.

The firm of Heckler & Koch GMBH, Oberndorf-Neckar,

John S. Wood, Jr., president of firm distributing H&K guns in USA, points out design features of the VP-70 to co-author of this book. A swivel button can be attached to belt for carrying gun in instant readiness to swing and fire.

When fired as a pistol, with stock removed, the VP-70's double action trigger requires a degree of concentration to hold sight picture. With loaded chamber, it holds nineteen rounds.

Relatively modest recoil of heavy gun plus light, high-velocity 9mm bullet can be seen is sequence photo taken at the instant of firing.

Firing three-round bursts from the hip, with stock attached, gave excellent seven-yard accuracy. Unique 3-shot burst control is a necessary feature, due to 2200 rpm cyclic rate.

Germany, produces several weapons applicable to police use. Distribution in this country is from Security Arms Training Affiliates, Suite 1004, 1815 North Fort Myer Drive, Arlington, Virginia 22209.

One of the more unusual guns in the H&K line is the VP-70 automatic pistol. It has a superficial resemblance to the French MAB pistol. The magazine of the VP-70 has a capacity of eighteen rounds of 9mm Parabellum ammunition. The novel feature is that the hammer is not cocked automatically after each shot. The spent case is ejected, a new round is chambered and the trigger must be released and pulled through a fairly heavy double action travel to fire the next round.

The theory behind the double action trigger system is that the gun can be carried with a live round in the chamber — giving nineteen shots before reloading — with a reasonable amount of safety, since it requires a long, deliberate pull of the trigger to set off the chambered round.

H&K manufactures a detachable stock-holster of their own design for use with the VP-70 pistol. The unique feature of this attachment is that an extension on the top foreportion of the stock enters the rear of the receiver of the pistol when the two are fastened together for firing. This extension modifies the operating system, permitting full-auto bursts of fire, only when the shoulder stock is in place. A selector switch on the stock offers a choice of semi-auto fire or full-auto in three-shot bursts. When the selector is moved to the figure 3, a pull of the trigger fires exactly three shots, after which the trigger must be released and pulled again to fire three more.

Since the cyclic rate of fire of the VP-70 in full-auto is about 2200 rounds per minute, a restricting fire control device is necessary, due to the difficulty of pulling and releasing the trigger quickly enough to keep the burst at a controllable length.

Another H&K design is their MP5, designated as a machine pistol, though the term is approximately interchangeable with submachine gun. It is available as the MP5A2 with a detachable stock of hard plastic, similar in shape to that of the M-16. Another version, the MP5A3, has a skeleton steel buttstock which telescopes into the receiver when not required.

The MP5 is chambered for the 9mm Parabellum — also termed the 9mm Luger — cartridge and the box-type magazine has a capacity of thirty rounds. The cyclic rate of fire for the MP5 on full-auto is about 650 rounds per minute. Weight of the MP5 is 5.6 pounds, not counting the magazine, which has an empty weight of 4.6 ounces.

The front sight is hooded to prevent damage and distortion, the rear sight is of novel design: A cylindrical sleeve carries four apertures, which can be locked in place by four detents to provide a rapid shift to four different sight settings for accurate fire at different distances. Sight radius is 13.77 inches, barrel length is 8.85 inches, length over all with stock extended is twenty-six inches, reduced to 19.29 inches when the stock of the MP5A3 is telescoped.

As with the fire-selector lever of the detachable stock holster for the VP-70, the control lever for the MP5 can be manipulated from the right or left side, making it usable regardless of which hand the shooter may favor. The fire-selector lever has four positions: a zero denotes the safe, a number 1 for semi-auto, a capital F for full-auto and a numeral 3 for controlled three-shot bursts at each pull of the trigger. Prices of the H&K guns are available from John S. Wood, Jr., president of Security Arms Training Affiliates, at the address given. As of shortly before publication date of this book, the departmental price of the VP-70 pistol system was quoted at about $160 in quantity; the MP5A2

H&K's MP5A3 features a telescoping steel stock to offer a choice of compact lines or firing convenience.

When MP5A3 stock is extended, as below, highly accurate, rifle-type fire is possible on semi-auto fire setting.

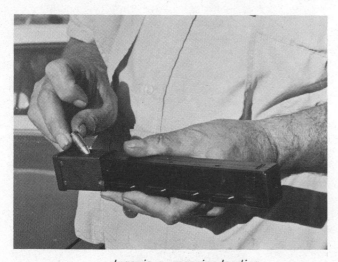

Ingenious magazine loading attachment for the MP5 speeds the operation: Just drop the round through the hole, press loader inward to seat cartridge in magazine.

Combination knife/bayonet for the Armalite AR-18 does not shift the point of bullet impact.

at about $185 and roughly $202 for the MP5A3 version. By way of comparison, the retail price on the M1921 Thompson submachine gun was approximately $200, back in the '20s when the purchasing power of the dollar was considerably more robust.

Armalite, Incorporated, 118 East 16th Street, Costa Mesa, California 92627, designed the AR-15 rifle, desig-

Top: Armalite AR-18 puts its stock in direct line with bore axis to prevent muzzle climb. Iron sights are raised for comfortable sighting.
Lower: Three-power scope is attached or removed readily without loss of scope zero, can be set quickly for ranges from 100 to 500 yards.

nated as the M-16 by the military, this gun having been produced by Colt since 1960 under license from Fairchild Aircraft Company, the former parent firm of Armalite.

Seven years after developing the AR-15, Armalite introduced a similar weapon of their own manufacture, the AR-18, incorporating several improvements over the original version. One of the more notable new features of the AR-18 is the addition of a folding stock, reducing the normal overall length of 38¼ inches to 28¾.

Two modifications of the basic AR-18 design have been produced. The AR-18S retains the auto/semi-auto capability of the originial, but has its barrel shortened to 10-1/8 inches, as compared to the 18¼-inch barrel of the standard AR-18.

The AR-180 is essentially the same as the AR-18, except that it is incapable of being switched to full-auto, offering semi-auto fire only. As the AR-180 is civilian-legal as a sporting arm, it is supplied with two twenty-round magazines which have been blocked to restrict capacity to five rounds each. This is required for hunting in certain jurisdictions. If desired, the blocking can be removed, restoring twenty-round capacity. Magazines of thirty-round capacity are available as optional equipment for use in any of the three models.

Other optional equipment for use with the AR-18 and its two companion models include a quick-detachable telescopic sight of 3X magnification. The scope can be removed in a matter of seconds, carried in the pocket — lens covers are provided — and re-installed as quickly, time after time, without loss of reticle adjustment or "zero." Once it has been sighted in on the given rifle, graduations permit rapid correction for bullet drop at all distances between one hundred and five hundred yards.

Grenades are available to qualified purchasers for launch-

Details of quick-detaching scope mount are simple: Spring-loaded plunger is pressed against rear sight, matching dovetail is snapped over the receiver base.

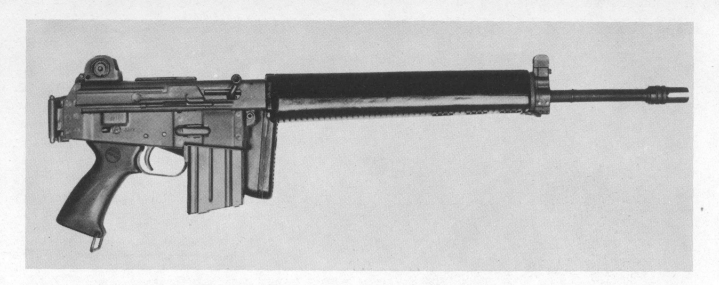

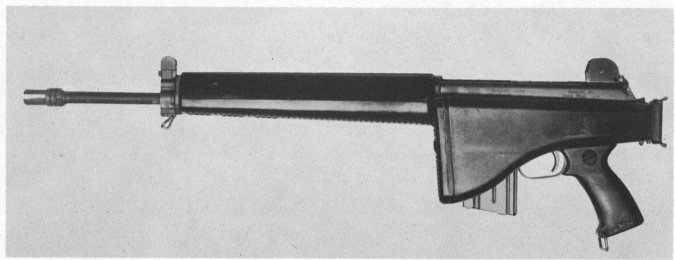

Top: Unusual feature of the AR-18 is its folding stock which pivots to the left and locks in place. Lower: View of the folded stock from left. Two-direction fire control lever cannot be operated from left with the stock folded, but is accessible from the right.

Below: The AR-18S is a short-barreled version of the AR-18, having a pistol grip on the forend and flared flash-hider in place of grenade-launcher/compensator of AR-18.

Three types of explosive grenades plus a practice variety can be launched from the AR-18, needing only the blank launching cartridge. Note position of sling and butt to avoid injury from sharp recoil.

Comparing the .308 and .223 cartridges, smaller magazine holds twice as many rounds, weighs less.

Details of design and construction of the AR-18 can be seen here. Bolt (center) is reversed from its normal position; note multiple locking lugs.

ing with the AR-18. No additional launching accessories are needed except for the specially loaded, bulletless grenade-launching cartridge. The hollow base of the grenade fits over the flash hider of the AR-18 and, in normal firing of ball ammunition, the flash hider neutralizes muzzle climb during full-auto fire.

The three types of grenades presently offered for launching with the AR-18 are a high-explosive/anti-tank type, 75mm in diameter, with a maximum range of 200 meters; a 62mm anti-tank type with a range of 260 meters and a 55mm anti-personnel type with a 300-meter range. While it is possible to launch grenades while hand-holding the AR-18, most shooters would consider the recoil excessive. The suggested procedure is to brace the extended butt of the stock against the ground, inverting the rifle — that is, with grip uppermost — to fire. Besides avoiding the recoil, this technique affords maximum concealment for the shooter and permits reaching the greatest possible distance. Inert practice grenades are available for personnel training.

The AR-18 and its two sub-models are chambered for the .223 Remington or 5.56mm cartridge. The cyclic rate of fire of the AR-18 and AR-18S, in full-auto, is about 750 rounds per minute. The fire selector lever has three positions on the AR-18 and AR-18S: Safe, Semi and Auto. The AR-180 is the same, except that the Auto is deleted. All three designs permit manipulation of the fire selector lever with either hand, from either side of the receiver.

The empty weight of the AR-18 is 6.7 pounds, plus one pound for the scope sight, if used. Sight radius is 20-7/8 inches. The front sight is a post type and is adjustable for elevation; rear sight is a peep or aperture type, adjustable for windage. If desired, a bayonet can be affixed to the muzzle of the barrel and, when installed, does not affect the point of bullet impact to any significant degree.

Muzzle velocity, with the military loading of the 55-grain, FMJ bullet, is rated at 3250 fps with the AR-18 or 2560 fps in the shorter barrel of the AR-18S. Even at the lower starting velocity, the 55-grain bullet will penetrate two thicknesses of a standard military steel helmet at a distance of four hundred yards.

A detailed discussion of all of the tactical considerations of full-auto employment would require more space than is available in the present volume. As a generalization, it may be noted that there is a trend, in the larger departments where the domestic climate so dictates, toward the formation of Special Weapons And Training teams, more conveniently abbreviated as SWAT. A typical example of such a squad may embody one trained marksman with a high-powered, long-range, scope-sighted rifle; four men trained with and carrying the AR-18 or AR-180 equipped with the 3X scope plus one man carrying a 12-gauge police shotgun.

SWAT — SHOCK WAVE AGAINST TERRORISTS

Chapter 10

Changing Social Patterns Have Dictated The Creation Of Squads Equipped To Cope With Extremists Of Every Type!

THE TERM SWAT has come to mean the magic answer in law enforcement just as FBI was equated with being the nemesis of all lawbreakers in the Thirties.

But it's not quite that simple. The letters stand for Special Weapons and Tactics; this force involves especially trained and equipped teams that can be drawn in for special duty in shooting situations that require more than the talents of the normal patrolman.

With interest in such techniques, many born of the terrorism tactics of small groups of revolutionaries and dissidents, a number of communities across the nation have instituted such forces. However, many of them are not properly trained and do not have the proper equipment.

An early consideration is to note that these units of the larger cities have a wider range of personnel from which to select, particularly military veterans with special training and, second, the SWAT members generally are already experienced police officers. Los Angeles picks its men from the Metro squad and these men must already have six years' experience, for example.

Subjects beyond the normal police training emphasize first aid, the psychological approach to crowd control and handling the mentally unbalanced individual.

Paramount are methods to protect any hostages involved. This requires the ultimate in discipline and teamwork. Everyone must know what is going on and no one man takes off on his own, unless cleared by the team commander.

Weapons training becomes sophisticated compared to normal police firearms work. Each man must be able to

SWAT gear is a blend of police and military. This Los Angeles officer carries a heavy-barreled Model 700 Remington, in .308 Win, topped by a 3-9X Bushnell variable telescopic sight.

determine and correct malfunctions in the dark in all arms used by the team; rifles (bolt or auto), shotguns and side-arms. Basic knowledge of common arms to be encountered can be important, particularly in attempting to disarm a suspect.

Rifle training with the anti-sniper rifle should start with the individual who will use it sighting it in at one hundred yards. At least one hundred rounds should be fired at one hundred yards, then at two hundred yards first using the one hundred-yard sight setting, then adjusting to two hundred. This training should be repeated periodically. This training is particularly critical for the anti-sniper as his skill may save the life of a hostage or a brother officer.

He should learn wind adjustment for two hundred-yard ranges and over. There will be little need for longer ranges, but the rifleman should have a three hundred-yard capability with the scope-mounted rifle. In rural areas for highway patrolmen, state police or sheriff departments, a five hundred-yard potential is highly desirable for circumstances where cover for closer approach may not be available.

After establishing ability at the bench at two hundred yards, shooting under natural conditions should be followed. Improvised means of concealment and protection should be used; that is, trees, buildings, walls, depressions, large rocks, etc. Don't depend on vehicle doors; a .223 will penetrate door and glass readily. It usually will not pass through both sides. A .308 or .30/06 and others will, regardless of all the television shows you have seen! In reality, one, lone vehicle is poor cover and it is hard to hide your

Trainee at left holds position, awaiting orders from team leader, so as to provide covering fire when the rest of the team moves up. Below, importance of concealment is stressed for the sake of surprise and safety in the course.

position. If at ground level, you can't lie on the ground without exposing one end or the other, but it is better than a two-inch sapling or a corral fence!

In long-range shooting — over two hundred yards — it is important to instruct on estimation of ranges; uphill and downhill, across a draw, the top of a building. A range finder is an asset — not for use during a shoot out — but for training. Estimation of ranges on uneven ground is a lot different than looking down an established, marked-off range. A study of the relative size and appearance of a man-sized target on the known distance range, using the rifle's scope, will help. Some scopes have range finder reticles, although practice remains paramount.

A major part of training is the importance of positive identification. The observer should provide assurance for the rifleman as to target identification. Usually the 3x9 variable scope can provide identification even in hours of near darkness, but the observer should verify the target, as he is under less tension, and use of high-power binoculars offers better light-gathering capabilities.

All team training should be in conjunction with those men who will be working together as a unit. Members should be cross-trained with all equipment, so they can replace a member in the event he is disabled. Too often one outstanding marksman is disabled and another takes over with only introductory-type training.

Training should be conducted under as realistic conditions as possible. A deserted farmhouse is ideal for an urban situation. Los Angeles Police Department personnel

Right, a vacant movie lot provides an excellent training ground for familiarization with SWAT specialized tactics. Below, trainees are taught techniques for entering safely.

use blank ammunition and have Universal Studios back lot and movie sets to work in during off-days when outsiders are excluded. This provides an opportunity for the trainees to try and locate where shots are coming from in residential, store or warehouse areas. This is particularly difficult in two and three-story buildings. A sniper standing back from an open window can fire from several feet back at personnel in the streets without revealing his position. Only binoculars or a high-power scope will locate him, if a muzzle flash is not spotted.

Dummies or wooden figures should be used to simulate a hostage and abductor. The abductor should be so rigged as to be movable approximately three inches by the tug of a cord. A rifleman should practice in this situation where the abductor may be moved only slightly, giving a small amount of clearance from the hostage, thus providing the rifleman a possible clear shot.

The objective is to develop the ability of the rifleman to hit the abductor without injury to the hostage only three inches away. The team should develop a procedure to create a diversion that might possibly cause the abductor to move slightly, providing an opportunity for the rifleman.

Incidentally, no consideration should be given to the use of an issue sidearm to attempt elimination of an abductor. This is a job only for a precision rifleman with stable nerves. The use of a revolver is hazardous and the safety factor for the hostage is a matter of mere inches, but such a situation is feasible for a good rifleman. Practice can provide an adequate margin of safety for a qualified rifleman.

Training should be conducted under hours of near darkness and the full potential of the telescopic sight should be determined. Other simulated situations should include the placing of hostage and abductor behind open windows and behind window glass at different street levels. This particular phase should be supplemented by all personnel surveying such areas with binoculars. The rifleman, using a scope sight, is not necessarily going to see the same details as the individual with binoculars. The telescopic sight becomes an important adjunct for the purpose of identification of another officer or innocent bystander.

For some reason, when trying to dislodge, frighten or hit a hidden sniper, the tendency is to shoot through the window from which he last fired. In the instance of the average dwelling or apartment building, even a .223 bullet probably will be able to penetrate six inches to two feet from the side window frame or below the window where a sniper will take cover. He won't move far, if he is trying to stop people from moving in on him, but trying to get an assured hit as the target is exposed for a fraction of a second is hard at best. Covering fire provides a great deterrent if it is going through the wall with a few splinters flying. Even cinder blocks will break up quickly from the .223 and other larger high-velocity calibers.

. Soft-nose bullets at high velocity will do no more nor no less damage than full-jacketed ones. Try this on half-inch steel plate — wearing good glasses at a distance of fifty feet. Automatic fire training should not start until this phase is completed to assured hits at two hundred yards on a six-inch bull.

Fire discipline is mandatory and the team leader should direct the need of auto fire. Too many departments purchase auto rifles; then decide they can't afford the ammunition for training, unless an emergency arises! The time to expend ammunition is during the training phase, or those issuing instructions are more to blame than the individual who hasn't had an opportunity to learn to control the bullet dispersion when using a rifle on automatic fire.

This portion is directed toward the two most common current weapons; the M-16 and AR-18 rifles. The AR-18

El Toro Marine Base's SWAT team Alpha moves out in MGM studios at Culver City, California. Speed and mobility are stressed. Below, Inspector Charles Steinmetz, of the Los Angeles FBI office, outlines a field problem for the students. Steinmetz was instructor for SWAT course.

Empty cases fly as a trainee familiarizes himself with full-auto operation of the Armalite AR-18 rifle. Throughout course, emphasis was upon realism, though the earmuffs are concession here.

has a bit better control factor against climb due to the position of slots in the flash hider. Both can be readily controlled with practice. The AR-18 utilizes a folding stock aiding concealability with an overall length of 28¾ inches.

The shooter must learn to shoot in short two and three-round bursts (there is no way he can get off one round on auto fire) and control the arm from going up and to the right for the right-hander. Firing is started at foot level to accommodate for possible climb. Auto firing should be restricted to relatively close ranges and usually for suppressing fire only. Most auto fire misses a man-sized target at fifty yards; the error is great if the shooter is in a hurry!

Training should include placing stress on the trainee. This is readily accomplished by use of a running course. Sophisticated equipment of several types is available to include a two-story building with six windows and six moving targets for setting up a variety of situations. This portable unit is produced by Caswell Equipment Company of Minneapolis, Minnesota. Another device is made by Advanced Training Systems Incorporated of St. Paul, Minnesota.

Night training is essential. Gas-operated weapons that are clip fed are a great deal different from the simple bolt-action systems but again the trainee must be trained to be able to clear malfunctions in the dark. These arms are not particularly complicated, but are unfamiliar to most officers without Vietnam experience.

A common fault in automatic fire is the natural tendency to put the arm on full-auto, then take deliberate aim with the sights! The first round is all that will be precisely aimed. If that type shooting is required, it should be done on semi-auto. The arm should be adjusted according to the

Lance Corporal Owen W. Reeves III moves up at double time as Corporal Barry W. Crawford, left, and Sergeant Daniel B. Robinson support him with covering fire. The trio are Marines, based in Yuma, Arizona, attending the two-week Swat course held at California's El Toro Marine Air Station under the instruction of specialists from FBI's Los Angeles office.

observed point of bullet impact. When the arm is fired from the hip, it is emphasized that the stock be tucked against the body under the right arm. Fancy positions should be avoided; such as holding the rifle inverted or swinging across the body, right or left.

The trainee must be taught not to let the rifle float from recoil, but to lean into the arm, pull the butt tight to the shoulder and use the forearm hand to hold the muzzle down on the target.

A second habit to be broken is the tendency for the target shooter to take a rifleman's stance where the body is erect and balanced. This is good for one shot! The balance of the burst will be far off target, as even the light recoil of the .223 will unbalance the shooter. He can recover only by releasing the trigger or running the magazine dry. About two twenty-round magazines will show the shooter what he must do. A bit of preliminary coaching can save much ammunition, however.

Firing from the hip should be taught in conjunction with running and stopping. No fancy side-canting positions for the arm should be permitted. Los Angeles has been using a quick-point system of poking the gun forward towards a target with out-stretched arms, eyes on the target, an instinctive type aiming procedure designed to speed up initial hits. Some have trouble adapting to this system that involves swinging the rifle forward. If they can't obtain a hit with it, they should try the hip position.

One-handed use should be developed using either hand in the event of a crippling hit. These arms are easily used with only one hand. The AR-18, with its folding stock, can be fired full-auto in the pistol position even from a moving vehicle or any other close quarter situation.

A telescopic sight on these arms provides a sniper capability out to four hundred yards. A fact often overlooked is that the trajectory of the military rounds of the 7.62 NATO (.308), the .30/06 and the .223 all meet at five

Above, five four-man SWAT teams, under command of Senior Team Leader Sam Platt — center, with shotgun — an El Toro MP, fan out in a wedge formation at the MGM studios. The wedge is an effective maneuver in riot control situations. Below, members of El Toro's SWAT team Alpha study a terrain map prior to embarking on a day-long exercise in land navigation.

Ever since the Austin, Texas, shooting incident on August, 1, 1966, metropolitan police departments have worked to provide effective countermeasures for similar situations. Here, two members of the Los Angeles PD SWAT team practice as a marksman/observer team from the top of a tall building commanding typical sniper sites. Official photograph, Los Angeles PD.

hundred yards! The .223 has the flattest trajectory up to that range, where it then loses velocity rapidly. The larger projectiles have two unassailable advantages; penetration and more wind resistance.

The 3X scope is adequate for virtually all ranges that will develop. Most will be one hundred yards or less. As to lethality, the .223 will penetrate both side of a government issued helmet at five hundred yards. The AR-18S, with its

10¼-inch barrel will penetrate one side of a helmet at 365-plus yards and also uses the 3X scope due to its inherent accuracy. Stock folded, it is only twenty inches overall.

Automatic fire requires a lot of space or a substantial backstop. Incidentally, the .223 will eat up any metal or wood backstop just about as fast as the .308 and .30/06. The Air Force — the first users of the M-16 — found it had

Careful planning and flawless execution of maneuvers is of paramount importance in successful, effective SWAT operations. Here, the team leader uses a blackboard to clarify strategy in much the manner of a football coach exhorting his men at halftime. Exercises often are carried out while wearing the bulky but effective flak-vest type of body armor seen here but, for reasons not entirely clear, the baseball cap is favored over steel helmets. Official photograph, Los Angeles Police Dept.

to use the regular .30/06 range backstop plans in spite of an anticipated saving on range construction.

Contacts across the country reveal less and less inclination toward the use of submachine guns of 9mm and .45 calibers. They offer only one advantage, which is in the price range. They are close-range weapons, using low-velocity, richochet-prone bullets; a hazard to innocent bystanders. Weight is close to that of the M-16/AR-18 weapons. They have no accuracy potential compared to the .223 high-velocity rifle cartridges. As the 5¾-pound AR-18S will stow in a briefcase, it can serve the other one purpose of the submachine gun, a "stake-out" concealable weapon.

Size of the team may vary from two to eight men, depending on local needs. Four or six-man teams are relatively common. A sheriff's department may not require the number needed in a metropolitan area.

A fairly standard organization would be the team leader with a bull horn and radio; a rifleman (anti-sniper) and observer (with shotgun) working together; two riflemen with AR-18, M-16 or semi-auto versions. Several teams carry both a shotgun and an auto or semi-auto .223 in the patrol unit, so they have immediate access to the weapon best suited to their needs. Bolt-action rifles should be the heavy barreled varmint models.

Submachine guns are considered handicaps due to lack of range and use limited to the inside of a building. Even there, one finds a hazard due to limited control, ricochets and lack of accuracy in an encounter with a barricaded individual. No officer psychologically wants to be out-gunned. The full-auto weapon has a decided advantage over the semi, if the suspect turns out to be armed with a stolen full-auto! For the same reason, if the word is out that the police are armed with full-autos, it has a decided deterrent effect on the criminal element. The automatic rifle, like the shotgun, is a strong deterrent to exposure or movement.

Standard equipment for a team should include two-way radios; a 40mm gas gun; binoculars; black jumpsuits; baseball caps; jump boots; gas masks; light, leather-palmed gloves, black rain gear; rappelling equipment; armored body vests; canteens; flashlights; shatterproof glasses; sidearms; cuffs; etc.

The subject of firearms can be discussed at book length but the sidearm draws the most controversy. The .38 Special places the officer in the position of accepting a calculated risk. There is no way that an officer, required to use his weapon, can be expected to hurt his opponent only a little. He should be able to protect his life and those of others at all possible minimum risk, not attempting to save the life of the individual trying to kill him!

In spite of the various opinions, the sidearm policy should be clear-cut. The .357 magnum should be the minimum revolver caliber and, if desired, the officer who can prove his ability with the .41 or .44 magnum should be permitted to carry the arm. How many times have you heard of an officer having to borrow ammunition from a buddy? If it's that big a fire fight, they need shotguns and rifles anyway.

Many departments are reverting to the .45 auto. The current 9mms have the advantage of greater capacity magazines and that is about all.

As to bolt-action anti-sniper rifles, the Winchester Model 70 and Remington Model 700 remain the favorites. The scope used is usually a 3X9 Redfield or Bushnell, although some fixed-power 4X are used and are probably adequate for virtually all ranges encountered. Other rifles, of course, will serve but the days of the .30-30 appear well past along with the old semi-auto .351 and .401 Winchester and the Remington slide actions.

The long favorite but ineffective .30 caliber carbine has probably contributed to more prolonged shoot outs than

Two high-powered rifles well suited for police work are the Winchester Models 70, above, here mounted with a 3-9X Burris variable scope in addition to standard iron sights and the Remington Model 700 BDL, below, which carries a 3-9X Leupold variable scope, plus factory iron sights. Text discusses appropriate calibers, sighting distances and training procedures.

any other arm. Any departments still using this arm are handicapped and there are a large number. Any criminal with a stolen sporting rifle of virtually any modern caliber from .222 up has the officer out-ranged with much greater lethality!

In the semi-autos, Ruger's Mini-14 .223 is a fine rifle that is less expensive but its walnut stock may lack durability to some extent for police abuse.

The shotgun remains a near essential in all police arsenals for close-in work. Most are pumps with eighteen or twenty-inch cylinder choke barrels. Autos, once considered too subject to malfunction, have the advantage of permitting prone fire without exposure to operate. There is no other real advantage, as a pump action can actually be fired faster than the autos, if there were such a need.

In recent years there has been a trend away from 00 buckshot due to limited hit potential beyond fifty-five yards with the nine or currently twelve pellets and the ricochet and dispersion problem in heavily populated dis-

tricts. Number 2 shot is deadly at the fifty-yard range, but velocity of the pellets drops off rapidly beyond this point. A hit on a man-size target is assured.

Calibers may range from .22-250 which is too often overlooked as a caliber of superior accuracy, extremely flat trajectory and has a penetration capability far beyond common knowledge, and full-jacketed bullets do not necessarily contribute anything. People overlook the fact that soft-nose sporting bullets will penetrate one-half-inch mild steel. Typical reaction to these high-velocity projectiles is the bullet's tendency (This includes .223 ammo) either to penetrate or disintegrate. There is no problem of ricochet. Ricochet is hard to attain with .223, .243, etc. and there has been a switch to obtain more penetration which is needed in this type of activity. The .30/06 remains a strong runner along with the .308 when the situation switches to penetration.

In recent months, some segments of the military have become interested in SWAT training, although it closely

Officers Beaver and Hillman, of the Los Angeles PD SWAT team, with some of the extensive equipment usually carried in the team's cruisers. Items include two shotguns, two M-16s, a Remington M700, an AR-180, tear gas gun and grenades, other gear.

Officer Hillman, of the LAPD SWAT team, prepares to fire 37mm tear gas projector by loading one of the canisters into breech.

parallels some of the training techniques taught ground troops in house-to-house fighting.

Among the first military units to undergo such training were three, eight-men teams of military policemen from the El Toro Marine Corps Air Station at Santa Ana, California, and a team of similar strength from the Marine Corps Air Station at Yuma, Arizona. With eight officers from California's Westminster Police Department, they underwent two weeks of rigorous training under instructors from the Los Angeles office of the Federal Bureau of Investigation. This constituted the first time the FBI ever has held such training in the field outside of the FBI Academy at Quantico, Virginia.

Although two weeks is a short time to learn every aspect

With action closed, now wearing full action gear, Hillman takes ready position, prior to firing a training round. Note that the sheath of the combat knife carried by the team even includes a pocket for a sharpening stone.

of SWAT, for the Marines participating it seemed like a rerun of infantry training with a lot of additional information and training that was never taught at Camps Lejeune or Pendleton.

According to Captain Robert A. Courtney, El Toro provost marshal, "The main mission of SWAT will be VIP protection, support if nuclear devices are moved through the El Toro area and prevention of aircraft hijackings. They will complement the standing Marine Police force with a highly specialized unit in critical situations, such as hostage incidents, snipers and armed suspects barricaded in built-up areas, requiring the use of special firearms, equipment and tactics."

During the two weeks of training, the select group of MPs and police officers covered everything from land navigation to criminal psychology and hostage negotiations. Additionally, each day started and ended with three to six-mile runs and plenty of calisthenics. Should an emergency arise, the SWAT teams may have to depend on the speed and endurance that go along with being in peak condition.

As training began, a friendly rivalry grew between the

Lance Corporal Stephen M. Davenport, an MP assigned to El Toro Marine Air Station, despenses a short-range load of Type CS chemical irritant fog, commonly termed tear gas, during the course of participation in chemical training phase of the SWAT course. A load such as this is used for close-in crowd dispersal. Under usual circumstances, the officer using the gas projector would be wearing a gask mask as protection, but training included exposure to the gas.

SWAT trainees as each tried to outdo the other during each phase of instruction, such as orienteering and land navigation. All agreed, though, that no one really wanted to go first during the chemical agent (gas) and chemical agent dispersing device phase. As one El Toro MP put it, tear gas has a tendency to humble a person.

Training began with FBI agent Jerry Crowe explaining "Why SWAT" and introducing the students to SWAT equipment, tactics and some of the history behind the formation of the concept.

Originally, the idea was developed by the Los Angeles Police Department and Marines at Camp Pendleton ten years ago to deal with armed militant groups and unusual or potentially dangerous situations requiring sophisticated tactics in built-up residential or business areas. Fireteam tactics in villages and towns where foes might booby-trap the area also were incorporated into SWAT.

The SWAT trainees learned the meaning of new phrases such as Extremist Activity and Urban Guerrilla Warfare and discussed examples which included a rundown of the much publicized SLA shootout in Los Angeles. The training also included police survival field problems and the use of new

types of firearms; new weapons were assigned to men which were far removed from the familiar .45s, M-14s and M-16s. Some men found themselves with a scope-mounted .30/06, a 12-gauge shotgun with grenade or canister launching device or an Armalite and all became reacquainted with bullet-proof flak-type vests and gas masks.

The El Toro SWAT trainees packed their gear and went to the MGM Studios in Culver City, California, to apply the techniques they learned by practicing on the Hollywood sets. There, the eight-man teams broke down into five-man teams and confronted situations set up by their FBI instructors.

During the day, they rappelled down the sides of buildings on the MGM sets, then climbed back up. They practiced riot control, hand-to-hand combat, searching procedures, camouflage and concealment and a variety of other skills needed to become a competent SWAT team.

Not all of the training was physically oriented. Many classroom hours were spent on subjects ranging from police ethics and decision making to criminal and militant psychology.

Under the FBI concept, each SWAT team is composed

SWAT trainees were required to gain first-hand experience in the effects of tear gas by passing through a cloud of it without the protection of gas masks. Here, Type CN gas has been released from a military-type grenade for training.

of five men, each man handling a specific weapon and job. The team leader maintains high mobility, supervises, provides covering fire and makes decisions. He normally carries an M-16 or rapid fire rifle. The second in the team is the marksman, who carries a scope-mounted rifle such as a .30/06 for long-range, difficult shots. The observer is the team's eyes and usually provides protection for the marksman. He also carries a rapid-fire weapon. The fourth man is the scout and does exactly what the name implies. Finally, the rear-guard provides protection for the team to the rear and flanks. Either of the last two SWAT team members may carry a grenade launcher, shotgun or M-16.

In the case of the eight-man El Toro and Yuma teams, the additional three men would be used as alternates or combine to form extra five-man teams, if needed.

Among the problems posed to the SWAT trainees was a fictitious case involving a combination kidnap, child-molesting and sniper incident.

At the same time police were investigating a child kidnapping and possible molesting, a call comes through about a sniper firing down at pedestrians and motorists. SWAT is dispatched to handle the sniper and after a struggle in which one officer is wounded, the sniper is captured and his car is found to have the bloody remnants of a girl's dress that matches the description of the missing child's clothing. Also it's discovered that the sniper has a previous record as a sex offender.

This is just one of the possible problems with which SWAT teams may have to cope. There seems to be no limit to the variety of emergency situations presented by lawbreakers and terrorists, no way of knowing what fresh challenge will materialize in the course of any given day's shift. For SWAT, coping is the name of the game. Both their training and equipment is designed so that it can be adapted to meet any unlikely situation.

Chief Ed Davis of the Los Angeles Police Department has made a statement that traditionally any crime wave has been eliminated when the citizens became motivated enough to move in and fill the breach. Police cannot do it all on their own.

If the citizens require or ask for more protection, the first basic factor is to hire people with needed qualifications and buy equipment that is required.

The police department of San Antonio, Texas, is one of the comparatively few major metropolitan agencies making fairly extensive use of the .41 magnum, some twelve years after its introduction in the Spring of 1964. This custom-stocked Model 58 S&W is carried by Patrolman Tom Ferguson, of the SAPD, who contributed his thoughts to this discussion.

A Controversial Point
On Which Few Are Neutral:
Is The .41 Magnum
The Ideal Police Handgun?

A .38 Special, with jacketed hollow-point bullet, is shown at left for size comparison with the .41 mag. Latter carries Lyman's No. 410610 cast bullet in gaschecked semi-wadcutter, weighing 215 grains.

THE PATROL CAR, one of the few moving vehicles on the darkened street at the late hour, glided forward silently. The solitary officer in the car drove slowly with what seemed idle nonchalance to his surroundings. He paid little attention to the two-way radio which had been speaking only infrequently until the dispatcher began reading off a series of stolen auto license plate numbers. The officer turned the volume up, as his relaxed attitude disappeared. The dispatcher had just read out the numerals on the plate of the car just ahead!

Quickly the officer asked for verification, got it, then hit his red light. The vehicle dutifully pulled to the right side of the road and stopped. With caution born of long experience, the officer approached the car with drawn revolver and ordered its two occupants out, hands held high.

As the driver emerged, the officer recognized a car thief, well-known in police circles, with his accomplice. Protruding from the offender's belt, hidden under a light jacket, was a fully loaded .38 Chiefs Special revolver. This particular thief was not known to go armed as a rule and, after relieving him of the gun, the patrolman asked why he carried it. Without hesitation the thief stated he was tired of the penitentiary and determined not to go back. Jerking his chin towards the officer's revolver, he said, "I intended to shoot it out, until I saw the size of that cannon."

The officer's revolver was a Smith & Wesson Model 58, caliber .41 magnum. This true story illustrates perfectly one reason thousands of policemen are switching from the .38 Special or .357 magnum to the big .41. A man may be so stupid he has to steal for a living, but he's smart enough to know when he's out-gunned. In this case, the impressive size of the handgun prevented a shoot-out with possible tragic results for all concerned.

The M58 Smith is big; a man-sized gun for man-sized chores. With the only barrel length available, four inches, it stretches 9¼ inches from tip to massive tail in its long dimension and nearly five inches from top strap to butt verti-

cally. Gun weight, emptied of its hog-nosed, butter-soft police loads is forty-one ounces, an appropriate figure.

The sights are fixed as a precaution against hard knocks in the field, making the gun look like an overgrown Military & Police M10, which it is. Size and barrel length give it a bulldoggy, pugnacious look few lawbreakers care to challenge. It is a nonflossy tool, built with the police market in mind.

Most of the .41's popularity with law-enforcement personnel stems from the effectiveness of the less powerful of its two factory-loaded rounds. To my knowledge, this is the only pistol or revolver cartridge ever developed specifically for the police officer. This round gives approximately 940 feet per second from the four-inch barrel of the M58.

Swaged from nearly pure lead, the 210-grain semi-wadcutter bullet yields up most of its 500-odd foot-pounds of energy on man-sized targets, seldom penetrating completely. With its two man-stopping edges, the bullet runs a true .410-inch in diameter, which translates into stopping power that the traditional and still mostly standard .38 Special cannot equal, no matter what the loading.

Performance-wise, the .41's closest ballistic brother is the obsolescent .38-40 WCF. Paper figures are close, with the old .38-40 throwing a flat-tipped 180-grain slug at around 950 fps from the 4¾-inch Peacemaker barrel. Bullet diameter ran closer than the caliber designation indicates; about .401, as opposed to the .41's true .410.

Years after the Model 73 and Model 92 Winchesters chambered for the .38-40 had given way to more powerful rifle cartridges, the Colt single-action and New Service revolvers chambered for the heavily tapered round still were earning reputations as good man-stoppers and hard shooters.

Though the .41 is close to the .38-40 in performance, its true ancestry goes back to experiments conducted in the late 1920s by Gordon Boser of Oregon. Boser utilized the now extinct .401 Winchester case for that firm's self-loading rifle. Cut off at the proper length for Colt single-action cylinders, Boser loaded it with heavy charges of 2400 pistol powder and cast 200-grain slugs of flat-tipped design. Special cylinders were built for .38-40 guns, and the original barrels retained.

This straight-walled design permitted higher pressures than the bottle-necked .38-40 hull, which owes its shape to the necessity of feeding through the actions of Winchester lever action rifles. Boser realized 1200 fps with this wildcat, a velocity not exceeded by most of today's cartridges.

None of this tells one much about the performance of the .41, unless you have some degree of familiarity with the .38-40. Does it kick? The answer has to be a carefully qualified no, unless you happen to be a complete novice to pistol shooting.

The same answer will suffice for the question, "Is it hard to shoot well?" Paper figures indicate a recoil factor in foot-pounds of energy as being 6.5 as opposed to the .38 Special's 3.3. This is not a substantial amount of kick compared to the .44 mag's upchuck of fourteen foot-pounds with full loads, and any police officer not related to a Munchkin should be able to handle it well.

Right, the S&W Model 57, here with six-inch barrel, is a refined version of the M58, supplied with target sights, broad trigger and wide-spur hammer. Shown with a Safariland Sight Track holster, the M57 is available with four-inch or 8-3/8-inch barrel, also. Below, Remington offers .41 mag ammo in two loadings, with lead SWC and high velocity JSP bullets, both weighing 210 grains. Recently Winchester-Western commenced making comparable .41 mag ammo.

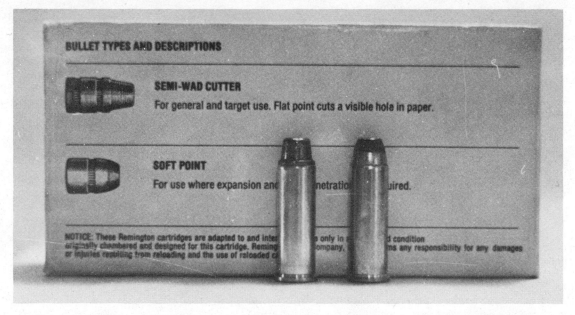

During this discussion of recoil, I would like to make one thing perfectly clear: We are speaking of the police load only, not the jacketed soft-point slug at magnum speeds. This round gets out at about 1250 from the M58's four-inch barrel, with appropriate energy and recoil figures. Meant for hunters of deer-sized game, it has no place in a police officer's revolver except under extraordinary circumstances; yet, paradoxically, it was the first to appear a decade ago when the .41 was exhibited to law-enforcement people. In my own opinion, this high-speed round with its excessive recoil is directly responsible for the .41's rather slow acceptance in police circles.

Only later did Remington cap off a lighter powder charge with the solid lead Keith bullet; and only now is the .41 making inroads into the realm of the .38 Special. This wise decision gave law-enforcement officers what they had asked for all along and, to my way of thinking, these loads should be headstamped and marketed as the .41 Police. As

a palliative to a brutality-conscious public, I believe the barrel markings on the gun itself should be changed. The right side of the barrel is now stamped ".41 magnum." For police issue, this should be changed to ".41 Police," a more descriptive term. Few, if any, policemen will care to utilize the jacketed soft-point magnum loads. They simply are not needed.

At the risk of repeating myself, I'll say again that officers used to shooting high-performance .38 Specials will find the .41 Police pleasant to shoot and easy to qualify with. The hot .38s now in common usage by many police departments are, in reality, "low-end" .357 magnums, with all the attendant nonvirtues of that cartridge. Not listed in order of importance, these include bright muzzle flash, heavy recoil, ear-splitting muzzle blast and a substantial risk of over-penetration. Add to this the factors introduced by inadequate barrel length. Most service .38s use four-inch barrels, fine for standard loadings of that cartridge. Most

users of four-inch .357s eventually discover that a large portion of the powder charge burns outside that short length adding nothing to energy or velocity figures, but much to muzzle flash and blast.

The still good .357 needs a six-inch barrel to be really effective and at least one large department, Detroit, has standardized this length. Even then, in order to gain more than merely increased penetration, it needs to expand its .357-inch diameter bullet. Now all handgunners know that expansion with pistol slugs is a sometime thing. If it does, fine and dandy, but the one well-directed slug a policeman may be able to let off could have a too thick jacket that wouldn't expand on a brick wall.

No such problems attend the .41 Police. The soft lead slug at 940 fps is not a magnum in any sense of the word, being merely a large caliber, heavy revolver load that achieves stopping power in candid manner. It doesn't need trick expanding bullets to be effective, thus avoiding neatly any charges of ghastliness from the public. Few unburned powder grains will be found in chambers or barrel after discharge; muzzle flash is reduced to a minimum. According to NRA-conducted tests, the .41 Police penetrates slightly less in any medium than the .38 Special, important in urban anthills.

Given all this good stuff, is the .41 Police really perfect? No, it isn't, but comes pretty close. For one thing, the soft lead bullet leaves healthy portions of itself inside the barrel, and after shooting a box or so it's time to scrub the lead out with a stiff wire brush and liberal doses of bore cleaner. To me, at least, this is always an onerous chore. If left unattended subsequent shots will keyhole before reaching the target.

Accuracy from a clean barrel is only ho-hum, being about on a par with full loads in the .357. Both calibers in good guns will shoot into three inches at twenty-five yards. It must be remembered that this round lacks the enormous amount of research and development to which the .38 Special is heir and no doubt the future will see changes in design, for the better we hope. A factory-loaded wadcutter of about 180 grains would be nice for practice and small-game hunting. The Police loads are not punishing, but they are full combat loads and full loads are expensive.

Handloaders, some of whom are police officers, will prefer the .41 in its fancy version, the M57 with adjustable sights. This fine gun is a dead ringer for the .44 mag M29 and is priced accordingly.

Despite any amount of loading bench alchemy, some fixed sight M58s mulishly refuse to deliver handloads to point of aim. Outside of long-term experimentation, the best solution is to develop a good load, then file or bend the front sight to fit. Although this satisfies most policemen and plinkers, it slices a good wedge out of gun versatility.

When loading combat loads, I try to keep velocities down around factory specs, slightly less than 1000 fps. I've had good results with Keith-type slugs weighing about 212 grains, cast hard to prevent leading. A dose of 8.0 grains of Herco throws these fairly close to point of aim, as does 7.0 grains of Unique or 7.5 of Red Dot.

My best bullet so far has been the excellent Speer 220-grain jacketed semi-wadcutter, riding 8.0 grains of Herco to about nine hundred feet per second. Apparently, longer barrel time at this velocity flips the heavy slug up to the correct elevation. Faster loads will shoot below point of aim.

The old magnum standby, Hercules 2400, doesn't burn well in the four-inch tube, unless magnum primers are used to light it off. This powder is meant for high velocities anyway, higher than practical for combat loads in the fixed-sights M58.

All of the listed loads using Unique, Herco or Red Dot are well below maximum and cases almost fall out of an upturned gun. All .41 loads should have a heavy roll crimp to prevent a slug working forward out of the case and tying up the cylinder. My small lot of Remington brass is on its tenth loading, and despite the need for a heavy crimp, I have lost only one case to date due to neck splits. My experience with the .41 shows it to be a remarkably good-natured round to load. Don't lose sight of the fact that, although we have a good deal of published loading data on the .41, it's still a great field for exploration, not fully mapped by any means.

Only time will tell if the .41 is destined to replace the .38 in police work. Expense is a factor to any budget-minded department, both for guns and cartridges. The one supreme, undeniable virtue of the .41 is the fact that it does what it's supposed to: stops an attacker instantly with one torso hit, with no increase in lethality over the .38 Special.

Users who know tell me it works fine, the true test of any tool. With this in mind, is it any wonder that many law-enforcement groups are asking, "What's so special about the .38 Special?"

A Hybrid
Between Our Own M-16
And Russia's AK-47
Resulted In The World's
Most Powerful
Semi-Auto Pistol.

THE BUSHMASTER

If receiver and magazine are pivoted in direction opposite to that shown here, the free hand can be used to grasp the magazine as an auxiliary handle.

The pistol grip of the Bushmaster swivels through 90 degrees of arc to put the magazine on either side of the shooter's forearm. Depending upon which way it's pivoted, the free hand can hold receiver or magazine as an aid in controlling recoil during fire.

THE ORIGINAL BUSHMASTER is a Central American pit viper, growing to about twelve feet in length, *Lachesis muta* to the herpetologists and called *surucucu* by some of the natives who co-occupy its turf. The snake is said to be a mean critter, more apt than not to aggressively pursue two-legged interlopers in its domain.

The latter-day namesake of the formidable reptile is nothing to dismiss lightly. In fact, the Bushmaster pistol might be a most welcome item of equipment to have along if there was likelihood of a nose-to-nose encounter with the serpent-type bushmaster.

Certainly, the Bushmaster pistol is not quite like anything else, before or since. Chambered for the cartridge called the 5.56mm or .223 Remington, it is fed from staggered-column magazines holding five, twenty or thirty rounds. Although there is a selective-fire version available — capable of semi-auto or full-automatic fire — the gun used in our tests is strictly semi-auto. The safety lever, tucked away at the lower left corner of the receiver, has two positions: safe and fire.

The pistol grip is placed well forward and the trigger actuates the sear by means of an extended linkage, somewhat in the manner of Remington's XP-100 pistol. The design principle is similar to that of the bull-pup rifles, whose action is located well to the rear, near the butt plate.

The Bushmaster pistol is manufactured by Gwinn Firearms (Box 1610, Rochester, New Hampshire 03867) and was designed by Mack Gwinn, Jr., the firm's president. It incorporates several parts that interchange with those of the M-16 or AR-15 rifles. These include the bolt, flash suppressor, magazines, pistol grip, trigger and numerous small pins and springs. The gas-operating system is closely similar to that used on the Russian AK-47 assault rifles, noted for its simplicity and trouble-free dependability.

Barrel length of the Bushmaster is 11-5/8 inches and empty weight is 5¼ pounds. The overall length, with standard flash suppressor, is 20-5/8 inches. The muzzle velocity, firing military 5.56mm ammunition, is about 2840-2860 feet per second. Gwinn Firearms can furnish ammunition, loaded with a faster-burning powder better suited to the shorter barrel of the Bushmaster, that, according to their spec-sheet, delivers 3040 fps.

If the Gwinn ammunition carries the 55-grain bullet — the literature does not specify the bullet weight — it would have a muzzle energy of 1128.6 foot-pounds.

On the basis of foot-pounds, that puts it about in the same general category as the .44 Auto Mag, shot for shot. In terms of the available foot-pounds without need to reload, presupposing the thirty-round magazine, it comes up with an impressive figure of 33,858 foot-pounds on tap, going far to justify the maker's claim that it is "the most powerful semiautomatic pistol in the world."

A unique and patented feature of the Bushmaster is its pistol grip that swivels forty-five degrees to the right or an equal distance to the left — putting the projecting magazine to one side or the other of the shooter's forearm — for convenience in firing either right or left-handed.

Chances are, you could stir up a lively discussion among a group of shooters as to which way to cant the action for firing with either hand. The manufacturer's literature shows right-handed shooters holding it with the pistol grip turned to the right, leaving the magazine extending to the left. Personally, I've developed a preference — being right-handed — for pivoting the grip to the left and letting the magazine project to the right. Trying it the other way, however, I find that the left hand can take a useful, steadying hold around the magazine, vaguely in the manner of the old Thompsons with the vertical grip in front.

The front sight of a heavy-gauge (0.125-inch) steel stamping that is secured to the pistol grip/barrel assembly by the flash suppressor. The standard rear sight is a small piece of 0.065-inch steel stock fastened to the rear of the receiver, with a tiny V-notch cut in the top and a punched detent to hold it in position. There is no provision for adjustment and the fact that one sight is attached to each of the two assemblies has the net effect of making the line of sight and the axis of the bore rather casual in their relationship to each other.

According to Mack Gwinn, it is possible to install a scope sight on the Bushmaster, although no details are available at present as to the method for doing so. I would say that the mounting of a suitable scope, such as Leupold's M8-2X with its extended eye-relief, in rigid alignment with the barrel, would be an improvement of major magnitude over the present arrangement of sights.

An optional accessory package offered for the Bush-

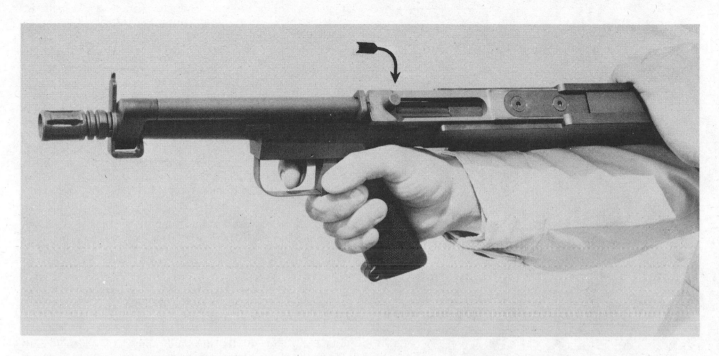

Details of gas actuating tube can be seen in photo above. It is adapted from the design of the Russian AK-47 assault rifle. Charging handle (arrow) cycles to the rear of the slot with each shot but hand is protected from action cover by a plate. Below, early production shows Bangor, Maine, but plant has been moved to Rochester, New Hampshire since starting.

BUSHMASTER PISTOL
GWINN FIREARMS
BANGOR MAINE

5.56 MM   001680

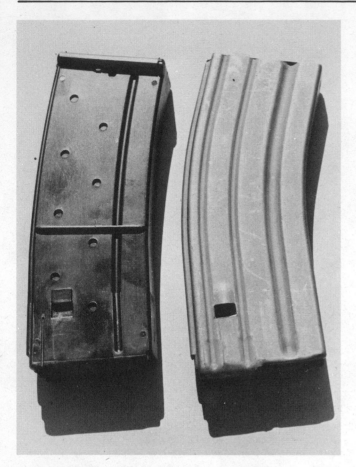

The Bushmaster pistol is designed to use the standard thirty-round magazine of the M-16 military rifle, or Gwinn can supply the plastic version, at left above, with the same capacity.

Both the standard flash suppressor and the extended one furnished in the optional accessory kit have front openings of about three-quarter-inch diameter. This confers the useful advantage of presenting the — if I may coin a term — coveree with an impressively large muzzle, slightly bigger than that of a 12-gauge shotgun, with a useful gain in psychological effect, contributing to the likelihood that shooting may not be necessary.

The effectiveness of the 5.56mm round is widely known and well documented, due to the extensive acceptance of the M-16 and AR-15 rifles in military and police employment. The moderate velocity loss of the shorter barrel would not impose a severe handicap to the cartridge's performance and the Bushmaster's compact dimensions suggest several effective applications for police work in the turbulent times of the later Seventies. It can be carried in patrol units and brought into action with considerably less difficulty than, for example, the traditional police shotgun. The utility of the Bushmaster for plainclothes stakeout situations is obvious.

In vehicular pursuit or barricade situations, the penetrating potential of the full-metal-jacketed, military 5.56mm round would be highly advantageous. I can't help thinking that the Laser-Lok sight, described in the February 1974 issue of GUN WORLD — still available at $1 per copy, postpaid, from the publisher — could be used as an extremely effective adjunct to the Bushmaster. As was noted in that discussion, the psychological effect of seeing that vivid, scarlet pencil of light impinge upon your personal real estate and knowing that it could represent a bullet hole at the touch of a trigger is immensely impressive.

One of the first things you notice, in firing the Bushmaster, is the virtual absence of recoil. None of the test crew felt in the least inclined to subject their shopworn eardrums to the unmuffled bark of the .223 cartridge from the short barrel and all wore David Clark earmuffs. Even so, enough sound came through to suggest that the sound effects would be more than slightly stupefying, if fired sans protection.

The full-auto version is said to offer the same absence of recoil as the gun we tested and has no tendency to climb during extended bursts. For those departments that are inclined to cope with the paperwork connected with full-auto ordnance, it should offer a number of intriguing and useful benefits. For but one example, it would be extremely effective in such situations as breaking through a door into a room where an armed suspect is known to be waiting or, for that matter, a number of armed and hostile suspects.

The semi-auto Bushmaster, in its present form, is civilian-legal. Quite frankly, it is difficult to visualize a valid recreational application for the gun, unless it could be fitted with an effective scope sight or, at least, a more accurate set of iron sights. With a more dependable system of sights, it would offer interesting possibilities as a survival gun for private pilots. In fact, as I understand, the design is somewhat derivative from military programs to develop survival guns for aircrews.

Trending back to law enforcement applications, it seems that the Bushmaster should offer excellent possibilities by way of a compact but effective armament for motorcycle officers, few of whom have been carrying anything much more potent than the regulation police handgun. By their very mobility, the cycle officers have a way of getting into thick and furious action, where a weapon such as the Bushmaster well could mean the difference between success or failure of the mission.

master consists of an adjustable, thirty-six-inch sling of heavy olive drab webbing and a rear swivel for the sling that carries a somewhat sturdier rear sight notch, as well as an extended flash suppressor and front sling swivel. We set the test gun up with the accessory package and found that the sights still are not compatible with the inherent accuracy potential of the cartridge.

Functioning of the sample gun, using various lots of military 5.56mm ammo on hand, was completely without flaw or difficulty. Accuracy, when firing from the hip, walking it in to targets such as tufts of grass and observing the dust puffs of previous shots, was excellent. It would appear that this is the firing technique envisioned as the one most apt to be used in typical police confrontations at short range. Not walking it in by dust puffs, of course, but firing at large targets from close up by instinctive pointing, rather than use of the sights.

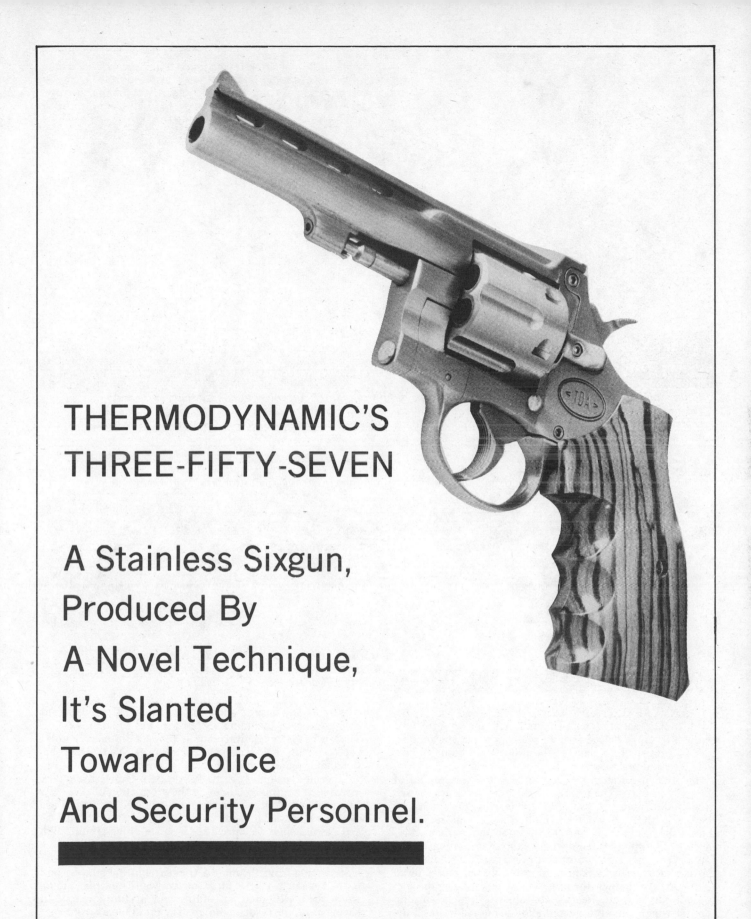

THERMODYNAMIC'S THREE-FIFTY-SEVEN

A Stainless Sixgun, Produced By A Novel Technique, It's Slanted Toward Police And Security Personnel.

Juncture point between the rifled inner sleeve and outer barrel shroud is indicated by arrow in above photo.

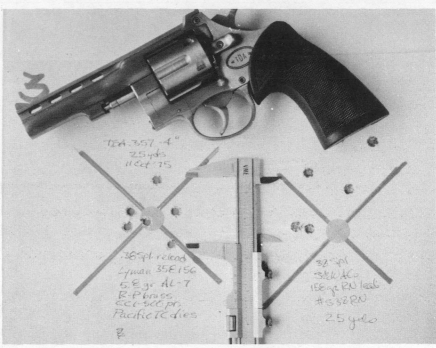

Test targets, fired from the TDA revolver at twenty-five yards varied from good to average. Six-shot group at left was obtained with the .38 Special reloads, described in the text. Group at right used factory loads.

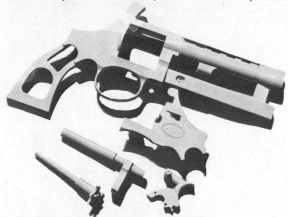

Left, five of the wax patterns, used in the investment casting process described here. Above, partially finished receiver for the 2½'' barreled model.

INVESTMENT CASTING — the technique of producing intricate parts in high-strength steel alloys — has developed to an advanced level of sophistication, and production of firearms by means of the process has come to be a well-accepted practice.

In brief, investment casting starts with a wax replica of the item or part to be formed. The wax patterns are formed in a mould, under pressure, complete with provisions for the sprues through which the molten metal will be poured during the casting step. After inspection and, perhaps, a bit of detail finishing by hand, the wax masters are sent to the foundry, where they are used in preparation of the mould. Casting medium is packed around the master and allowed to set up, after which the mould is heated, causing the wax to melt and run out. Heating continues to a high temperature, at which time the melted alloy is poured in to fill the space left open by the melted wax master and the mould, with its casting, is set aside to cool. When cooling has been completed, the mould material is broken away, leaving the casting ready for final finishing.

Almost any desired alloy can be used in the investment casting process, including several varieties of stainless steel. Thus, it becomes relatively simple to mass-produce complex parts at a much lower cost than that entailed in conventional machining techniques.

Thermodynamic Systems has made effective use of the investment casting technique in the production of their new International Police .357 magnum revolver, available in a choice of 2½ and four-inch barrel lengths. The entire frame and barrel is investment cast as a single, integral unit, with additional castings to form such parts as the side plate, trigger, hammer, crane and ejector star.

Emerging from the mould, the barrel of the receiver unit is solid steel. It carries an attractive ventilated rib, a ramp front sight .137-inch in width, and a sturdy rear sight having a .125-inch square notch. The ramp tapers from .475 at the rear to .375-inch at the muzzle. Ramp and sights, which are of the fixed or nonadjustable type, are left in a matte finish, colored a medium gray of the natural steel. Surprisingly, this offers excellent visibility under nearly any

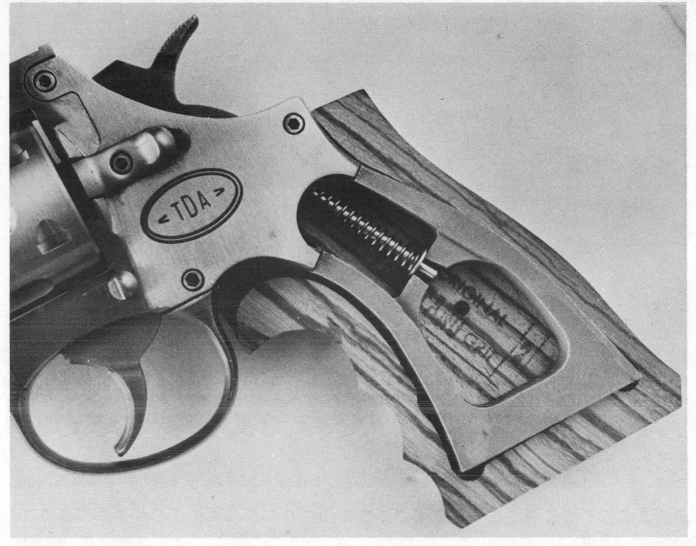

The handle of the TDA receiver is identical in dimensions to the medium or K-frame size of Smith & Wesson revolvers. Here, half of a set of Mustang grips, in lacquered zebrawood, is positioned for installation, showing modification of grip contours.

sighting conditions, showing up equally well against white targets or black bull's-eyes.

The barrel is drilled to accept a rifled tube, thus serving as the housing for the inner barrel. The tube, itself, is about .480-inch diameter, with a wall thickness of about .062-inch to the grooves. Groove diameter is approximately .3565-inch and there are six lands, about .055-inch in width, right-hand, at a pitch of about one turn to sixteen inches.

The barrel, nominally four-inch, has a net length of 4.085 inches from forcing cone to muzzle. The overall length of the cylinder — which is not recessed for the cartridge heads — is 1.57 inches in length by 1.55 in diameter. Thus, the combined length of chamber and barrel is 5.655 inches, not counting the gap between the front of the cylinder and the rear of the barrel, which is impressively scant in the sample gun. Sight radius is approximately six inches.

The trigger is a generous .4034-inch in width, with well-formed vertical serrations. The hammer spur is about .44-inch in width, with lateral serrations, likewise nicely executed. The International Police is supplied with well-made rubber grips, by Pachmayr, with moulded-in checkering, filling in the space at the top of the center finger of the shooting hand. Which is to say that the International Police

is furnished with target trigger, target hammer and target stocks at no extra cost.

The exact retail price is left somewhat to the option of the individual dealer and distribution is handled by EMF Company, Incorporated (Box 1248, Studio City, California 91604). Dealer inquiries are invited.

The International Police .357 tips the scales at just thirty-nine ounces, in the four-inch barreled model with the Pachmayr rubber grips, measuring 9½ inches in overall length. The frame is designed so as to accept the same stocks as those used on the K-frame S&W guns; a thoughtful touch.

The six-shot cylinder rotates in a clockwise direction, as viewed by the shooter; which is to say, the same rotation as modern Colt revolvers. The cylinder latch is pulled rearward to open and its contours as well as its operation are quite reminiscent of the Colt design. The cylinder, it should be noted, is machined from a block of stainless steel, not investment cast, being fluted in the usual manner. The sideplate is attached to the left side of the receiver, using hex-socket screws and that has the sound of an excellent idea. No more jiggered-up screw slots, for one thing!

The maker's emblem consists of a neat TDA, surrounded by two concentric ovals, on the sideplate. It's not entirely clear how this configurates with the firm's name, given as

Thermodynamic Systems on the right-hand side of the receiver, but it's not all that important, as problems go.

The hammer fall, in double-action, is quite short; not much over five-eighths-inch and about one inch in single-action mode. The coil mainspring shows a moderate but not serious inclination to stack in the DA pull, but it's entirely adequate for any normal need, unless you've been spoiled by the triggers of guns costing upward of twice as much. General appearance of the gun, as well as balance and handling qualities, are quite good.

However, handsome is as handsome shoots, so far as I'm concerned, so I rounded up an assortment of factory loads in .357 magnum and .38 Special for a trip to the range, tossing in a batch of .38 Special reloads from my privately operated munitions works. The last were comprised of Lyman's gas-checked semi-wadcutter, No. 358156, weighing about 150 grains, ahead of 5.8 grains of Alcan AL-7 powder. It is a load toward which my various .38 Specials seem to be somewhat prejudiced.

My long-term experience with fixed-sight handguns has not been encouraging. All too often, they tend to print well away from the aiming point and, in such cases, there is little you can do about it. When fixed sights are on the money, nothing could be finer, as there's no ready way for them to get knocked out of kilter, but I've never had much luck with the Kentucky windage approach.

Unpacking at the range, I set up targets on the twenty-five-yard line, put on my shooting glasses and Dave Clark earmuffs and performed a small ritual I consider mandatory before putting the first shot through a new gun: I peered up the bore to make certain the hole went clear through. Smile if you will but, on at least one occasion, this elementary precaution revealed the presence of a slug, lodged about an inch ahead of the chamber, in a new rifle I'd been sent for testing. It was the simplest way to find it out. It's a procedure I commend sincerely.

The bore was clear. They usually are. It's the exceptions that smart and sting. So I decided to initiate it with some of my .38 reloads. I seated myself at one of the rifle benches

Top, a close look at the wide, target-type trigger. Above, the test gun, with its four-inch barrel, employs the same length of ejector stroke as the 2½'' snubnosed version of the .357 TDE design.

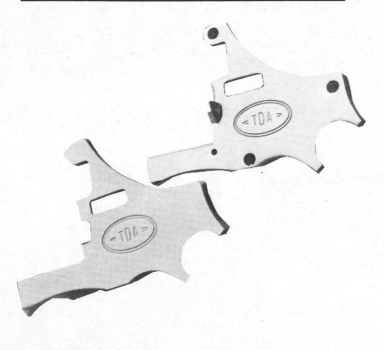

A wax pattern, at left, with a partially finished side plate. Right, the wax pattern for the trigger, with finished unit.

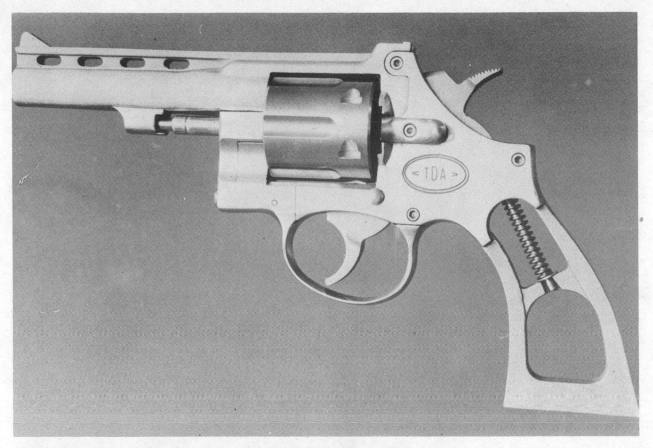

Like Ruger's Security Six, the TDA uses a coil-type mainspring, rather than the traditional leaf-type that is somewhat more subject to occasional breakage.

Side plate is held in place by hex-socket screws. Contour and operation of the cylinder latch is similar to Colt guns.

and bedded the heel of my shooting hand solidly into a nest of sandbags and commenced squeezing off half a dozen, single-action.

Viewing the resulting target, I felt impelled to mutter apologies to the gun's maker and designer. You couldn't ask for six hits centered more neatly around the point of aim. Forget about the Kentucky windage with this load, at least. Maximum spread for the six holes, center to center, was 2.030 inches up and down by 1.500 inches horizontally. As a maiden performance, I rated it highly satisfactory; in fact, downright impressive.

Since the gun is chambered for .357 mag, I went on to try a few factory loadings of that staunch cartridge through it. There was some amount of tendency for them to print a bit higher, though not off the paper, merely a matter of three to four inches.

I had installed a pair of Mustang custom stocks in lacquered zebrawood, made for the K-frame S&W, replacing the black rubber Pachmayr stocks. The primary reason was for the sake of photographing the gun in color. After a few six-shot bursts, the wooden stocks loosened enough to permit slight movement and caused some amount of interference with the hammer spur in cocking. When I reinstalled the Pachmayr stocks, these problems cleared up instantly.

JAC Associates, (Box 3355, Santa Monica, CA 90403), a subsidiary of TDA, specializes in a number of custom parts for the .45 auto. Upper gun has barrel and slide cut to 3¾'' and grip shortened. Lower gun carries firm's stainless steel barrel and adjustable stop trigger.

If I were planning to make permanent use of the Mustang stocks on this gun, I'd apply a little of Bob Brownell's Acra-Glas bedding compound to the inside, with appropriate release agent on the metal work, so as to take up the slack. Actually, the rubber Pachmayr stocks are superb for any usage except posing for color pictures.

As was noted, the matte gray finish of the front and rear sights proved surprisingly good from the standpoint of visibility. The single-action trigger pull is a bit over three pounds, but it is crisp and nondistracting on the let off, with none of the preliminary movement that my old K-38 has developed in recent years.

In a few rounds of combat competition-style shooting, double-action, from the seven-yard mark at the silhouettes, the International Police proved itself entirely adequate for normal needs. It points well from chest level with the two-handed hold and there was no hesitation in the pull. Despite the short stroke of the hammer on DA, there was no problem in failing to set off the primers of factory fodder or reloads.

The hammer, it should be noted, employs the system of a transfer bar which moves vertically into position as the hammer is cocked or the trigger pulled. It's quite similar to the arrangement employed with the Ruger Security Six and the redesigned Blackhawks. When the hammer is down, there isn't a way in the world for it to set off the round behind the barrel.

So the International Police .357 earned bouquets on any number of counts. It would be nice to say it didn't rate a single brickbat; nice, but not entirely realistic. In this im-

perfect world, hardly anything is completely without flaw. In this particular instance, in the ejection of the empty cases is the area that could get the most benefit from a little reworking. The ejection stroke is about 0.552-inch. The .357 mag case has about 1.232 inches of straight-walled body ahead of its rim. Deduct the .552-inch ejector stroke and you still have .680-inch of case left in the chambers. It seems just about impossible, with the gun horizontal, to smack the ejector rod so stoutly that you don't have to coax a few of the empties forth with your fingernails.

I suspect that the ejector stroke was kept to that length for the sake of the 2.5-inch barreled version. Short strokes are the usual rule with the snubnose revolvers and it would mean a lot of costly redesigning to lengthen the stroke for the four incher. It is not a hopeless fault by any means and you can clear all six chambers most of the time, if you point the muzzle straight up, so as to get gravity on your side, before slapping the end of the rod. It's much less a problem when firing .38 Specials in it.

It's a good bet that you'll be hearing more from Thermodynamics in the months ahead, as they've a number of intriguing projects under development. We hope to tell you about them as they're cleared for publication.

For the present, the International Police .357 represents an example of today's most popular pattern of revolver for the uniformed police officer, security guards and the like. If priced in the $130 brackets, it should be quite competitive with its contemporaries. To judge on the performance of the test sample, purchasers of the International Police .357 should find it well adapted to their needs.

Chapter 11

Remarkable Progress Has Been Made In This Field Within The Past Few Years!

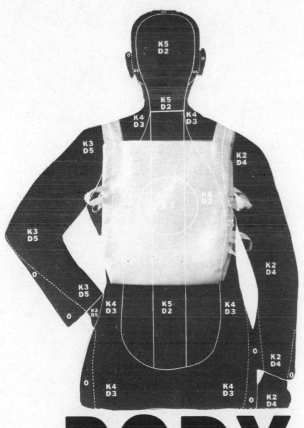

BODY ARMOR

IT SEEMS EXTREMELY ironic that, in a day when the American law-enforcement profession has made giant strides forward in every field from communications to public relations, the average street cop is forced to rely on what is essentially a medieval device to remain alive to accomplish his purpose.

Body armor is certainly nothing new but the demand for it has increased dramatically among police officers in recent years. The reason is a valid one. During 1964-73 a total of 858 policemen were killed in performing their duty. As might be expected, patrolmen accounted for the largest number in this brutal tally, sixty-eight percent. Of these, nearly twenty percent were killed with their own weapons while responding to what was thought to be a routine call. The killers? They ranged from irate housewives to stickup artists. Forty-two percent had been previously arrested for a crime of violence, fifty-nine percent had been convicted of a prior criminal charge, and an astonishing seventy-seven percent had a criminal arrest record. Facts such as these account for the current boom in sales of bullet-proof vests, and ought to make it plain to every police officer that he stands less chance of getting off duty alive than at any other period in our history. Today's policeman is painfully aware that the Old West never really died — it merely expanded its horizons, and is rumbling fitfully in every city from the Eastern seaboard to the Barbary Coast.

Until recently, personal body armor had been considered obsolete for centuries, in fact since the first early firearms appeared. Knights of the late Middle Ages who fought in chain mail or the later plate armor realized quickly that even the primitive muskets of that era could pierce their expensive metal armor with all the nonchalance of a modern .22 slug whistling through a bean can. Since that time, armorers never have been able to catch up with firearms technology, but due to the unreliable nature of early firearms certain vestigial items of personal armor lasted until the late Eighteenth and early Nineteenth centuries. Often seen in portraits dating from the American Revolution is the gorget, sometimes mistaken for a medallion, which it resembles. Draped around the throat, it was intended to foil a well-directed rapier thrust, but was mainly ornamental even in Revolutionary times. Better known is the high, hard leather collar issued to U.S. Marines early in the Nineteenth century. Intended to ward off or at least diminish the effects of a sword stroke, it was the origin of the term Leathernecks, who have admittedly established a good track record with or without such devices.

The revival of true body armor had to await the age of synthetic fabrics, only recently dawned. Today we have several good materials including ballistic nylon, but the better vests almost invariably are composed of several layers of material known by the trade name of Kevlar. Not so oddly, perhaps, Kevlar was introduced by the Dupont Company as a long-wearing material for automobile tires.

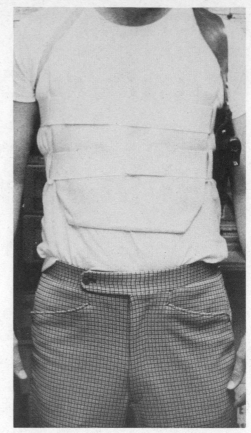

Left, Tom Ferguson models an early example of bulletproof vest from the Al Capone era; quite bulky, it weighs 35 lbs. Above, Second Chance vest weighs 2½ lbs., is unobtrusive, comfortable for routine wear, has better stopping ability.

Today, the tough fabric is produced by such firms as Burlington Industrial Fabrics and J.P. Stevens Company. It is probably safe to say that of the major firms now offering ballistic vests, the majority utilize Kevlar as a filler.

Tom Ferguson's experience with ballistic vests occurred in December 1974 during tests conducted by the San Antonio, Texas, Police Department on its underground range. Test results left him thoroughly impressed with the stopping potential of Kevlar. Shortly afterwards, in early 1975, the department bought and issued a large number of lightweight vests. Both the test and purchase were prompted by a shooting incident involving a patrolman in a neighboring city, during the previous October.

While on routine night patrol, the officer discovered an open door at the rear of a high school and went inside alone to investigate. This was common practice in his department, and his failure to call for a backup man doesn't necessarily reflect bad judgment. Midway through the darkened corridors, he was shot in the back at close range by an unknown assailant armed with a .380 automatic. Fortunately, he was wearing an early model Second Chance vest under his shirt which stopped the slug. He never saw his would-be killer, and had no chance to return the fire.

In describing the incident, he stated he at first thought he had been struck with a club, then noticed a stinging sensation. He was taken to a hospital for examination where doctors found a serious bruise under the left shoulder blade. The 95-grain round-nose projectile was recovered, having penetrated only two layers of the vest. Without it, the slug would have gone directly through his heart from the rear.

The SAPD tests began almost immediately afterwards and involved products from half a dozen firms. Since haste was paramount, they wasted no time pitting the vests against such puny performers as the .22s, various .32s or even the .380. "We wanted to know primarily if the vests would take a close range hit from a major caliber combat weapon, fully realizing that many officers are shot with their own revolvers," according to Ferguson.

SAPD regulations allow officers to carry revolvers of .38 Special caliber or larger, with barrel length not to exceed six inches. Plainclothes personnel are allowed to use a wide variety of weapons provided the .38 caliber floor is observed; therefore a comprehensive list of major calibers was readily available. Ammunition used in the tests was mostly commercial loads of virtually every type and description from FMJ to JHPs. To simulate the resistance offered by a human body and to prevent excessive give, each vest was draped over a large cardboard box filled with sand.

Firing began at fifteen feet after the following list of handguns had been assembled:

Handgun	Ammunition
1. Browning 9mm Hi-Power	FMJ, JSP, JHP
2. Colt .38 Super	FMJ only
3. S&W .38 Spl., M10, 4''	JSP, JHP, FMJ, (mil.), SWC, WC
4. S&W .357 mag, M19, 4''	JSP, JHP, SWC, W-W Lubaloy
5. S&W .357 mag, M28, 6''	JSP, JHP, SWC, W-W Lubaloy
6. S&W .41 Mag, M58, 4''	lead SWC, JSP
7. S&W .44 mag, M29, 4''	lead SWC, JSP

When the lengthy shooting session terminated, four of the six entries had been eliminated, having been penetrated by both the six-inch .357 magnum and the .38 Super.

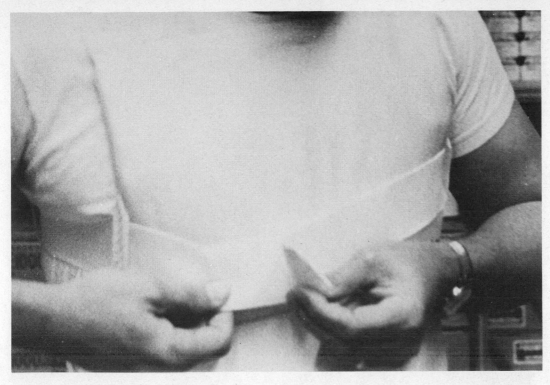

Straps that hold the Second Chance body armor in place are fastened with Velcro.

Few shooters appreciate the penetrating capability of the .38 Super, and may be surprised to learn that it was originally designed to blast through the primitive bullet-proof glass and body armor of the Prohibition Era. Before the advent of the .357 magnum, it was favored among FBI agents whose task was to confront various Al Capone types.

The vests eliminated were the Oshman, American Body Armor, Life Shield and Davis Aircraft Company. The .38 Super sailed completely through all four, while the six-inch .357 punctured the Oshman and the American Body Armor.

The remaining two vests were both lightweights, the 2½-pound Second Chance, and the Armour of America weighing the same. Both contain Kevlar as a filler material. The Second Chance vest is white in color, while the Armour of America vest is encased in a navy blue envelope of ballistic nylon.

"I was unable to drive any sort of handgun projectile through either vest. In attempting to do so, I laid each vest directly on the sand trap on the underground range and fired into each with the issue service revolver, the S&W .41 magnum. The ammo was Remington's 210-grain JSP which chronographs at 1250 feet per second from the four-inch barrel. The gun muzzle was approximately 2½ feet away. After firing I found each bullet balled up very nicely in a classic mushroom shape about halfway through each vest," Ferguson reports.

So much for handgun tests. Realizing that police officers face other deadly weapons, Ferguson utilized a favorite Buck hunting knife with a six-inch Bowie-type blade to prove another point.

"Each garment was placed on a sturdy wooden table with me leering over in a Jack-the-Ripper fashion; the ominous-looking blade clutched in my right hand. Arm muscles bulging, I gave each an overhand stroke which would have eviscerated a crocodile. Neither vest was punctured, and the outside cover was only slightly cut. Unsatisfied, I tried again using two hands, but the result was the same — no penetration.

"Being an astute, workaday-type officer, I seldom find myself going directly in harm's way, much preferring to manipulate a given situation in a manner which leaves a possible opponent in much greater danger from me than I am from him. Sneaking up from behind with a shotgun does not offend my moral code, and I have a fairly good repertoire of such gimmicks. However, if I were sent into a serious situation, either the Second Chance or the Armour of America vest would be eminently satisfactory to me. Both cover the vital area between collarbone and belt buckle, protecting such indispensable organs as heart, liver, pancreas, lungs and spleen."

After ballistic properties were resolved, several questions remained unanswered. Chief among these was the blunt trauma effect. Briefly, blunt trauma refers to the effect on flesh of a projectile that impacts with great force concentrated on a few square inches, but does not penetrate. The result can be a serious wound, or even death. Like body armor, this phenomenon is not new. In the era when the claymore was king of battles, many fighting men encased in chain mail died from sword blows that left no cut or slash on his body. Like a bullet, the sword's edge impacted on a small area, leaving a deep bruise which seldom healed. If such a concentrated contact occurred over a vital organ, death could come quickly. The force of impact is transmitted through armor, resulting in anatomic and physiologic derangement.

For the last two years, the U.S. Army has conducted tests of soft flexible body armor of the Kevlar type at Edgewood Arsenal's Biomedical Laboratory, Biophysics Division. Although the tests are incomplete, they have made several interesting findings. Over one hundred experiments have been made using anesthetized laboratory animals. Projectile velocity as well as bullet shape and type, and angle of impact, seems to be a major factor in producing serious blunt trauma. The scientists engaged in this project estimate a mortality rate of one to five percent might be expected if the wearer of a Kevlar vest were hit over a vital area with a really powerful handgun projectile, though the need for surgery would be reduced from eighty-two to one hundred percent. To the cop on the street — whose usual armor consists only of a thin blue shirt — these figures are quite acceptable. SAPD test personnel were divided in their opinions. Could an officer take a close range hit from a .41 or .44 magnum and remain in the fight, or would the

Today's body armor puts emphasis upon unobtrusiveness, as modeled here by Pat Reynoso. There is no obvious indication that she's wearing it. Refer to photo on facing page, at right.

trauma effect incapacitate him, leaving him helpless? Most held that a physically fit officer should be able to return the fire.

Neither the Second Chance vest nor the one from Armour of America offered protection from side shots. Each of the garments left approximately three inches of torso exposed between front and rear panels. Side panels are available from either manufacturer, but add much to bulk without contributing much to protection.

Present during the tests was a twenty-five-year veteran who expressed the opinion that this was immaterial to him.

"The average hood is such a lousy shot he would be doing good to get any sort of hit at all unless by accident," he contended. The rest tended to agree. Combined experience as police officers indicated that criminals are basically not firearms enthusiasts or good marksmen — they use firearms to intimidate unarmed victims.

Added to this is the fact that, nationwide, the hood population tends to prefer low-powered, badly sighted handguns, hardly conducive to good shooting. One claim, made by a current vest manufacturer in its advertising is that sixty percent of the handguns turned on policemen are of .38 caliber or less. If an officer can put just a few yards between himself and his assailant, the outcome will be in the officer's favor nearly every time. Side shots, and those directed at the officer's head will in most cases miss entirely, unless the range is very close.

For prospective buyers who prefer not to take a chance, the Protective Apparel Corporation of America, 333 Sylvan Avenue, Englewood Cliffs, New Jersey 07632, makes a wrap-around vest, giving side protection. For those unfortunate officers who may feel that their normal area of patrol takes them into a new World War every day, at least one company offers pants, jackets and vests. The Strong

Uniform Company, 14 W. Seventeenth St., New York, New York, is the only company to our knowledge that manufactures anything but vests. Their uniform pants and jackets are lined with Kevlar.

Wearability, both comfort and appearance, was the next item of discussion. Both the Second Chance and the Armour of America garments were light and easy to become accustomed to; in fact they give a feeling of invulnerability hard to put into words.

Appearance is another thing. Every uniformed officer present, including Ferguson, was wearing high-quality, superbly tailored shirts, tapered to fit the body. A good police officer is extremely self-conscious about his appearance. He wants to appear neat, unobtrusive and professionally attired. The officer you see every day on the street is probably wearing from $200 to $300 worth of uniform, as much as one would pay for a good suit. Needless to say, if a vest underneath all this excellent tailoring lends an air of untidiness, the vest will spend the majority of its career in the officer's locker, regardless of any bullet-stopping potential. If this is the case, the vest is useless. It is much better to have new uniforms tailored to fit over the vest, which can be accomplished with little effort. Most departments provide the officer with a uniform allowance. It should be used at the best uniform shop in town, buying clothing that won't betray the presence of the vest.

Plainclothes officers should have no problems of this sort. In fact, it is common for them to have their suits cut to fit unobtrusively over a shoulder holster, so why not a vest?

What about cleaning? Any officer wearing the same vest each day is certain to be concerned with body odor, and will want to know how to clean the vest. The following

Ms. Reynoso is wearing the Morgan Textured Body Armor, distributed by Safariland. Available to police only, the Morgan armor can be furnished for male or female officers, as discussed in accompanying text. The ballistic units are carried in a washable outer garment, don't need washing.

cleaning instructions come from Second Chance, and are applicable to all Kevlar and nylon vests:

Hand wash in lukewarm water with hand soap only. Let drip dry. Do not machine wash or dry. Do not use bleach. White nylon will yellow with age, but this will not affect your Second Chance's bullet-stopping power. We recently dry cleaned a super featherweight twenty times with no apparent loss of stopping power. This would indicate that occasional dry cleaning is not harmful.

According to Richard Davis of Second Chance, Box 578, Central Lake, Michigan 49622, water alone does not permanently degrade nylon or Kevlar. Once the vest dries out, it is back to full strength. Detergents or bleach, however, will weaken the ballistic effectiveness of both fabrics. It might be well for married officers to handle cleaning problems themselves, since it is their gizzard at stake. Many vests are sheathed in a detachable, washable envelope so there is no need to get the filler wet at all.

Due to the Equal Opportunity Law now in effect, many more women are being hired as patrol officers than formerly.Indianapolis, Indiana, started the trend in 1968 with paired female officers. In all fairness to the women, they have generally performed well as patrol cops, and are by no means immune to the hazards encountered by their male counterparts. Last year, in Washington, D.C., a uniformed female officer was killed by gunfire in an attempt to apprehend a pair of armed robbery suspects. Fortunately, many

manufacturers will custom-tailor a ballistic vest for female officers at slight additional expense.

Practically any center-fire rifle has the velocity necessary to pierce a soft, flexible Kevlar vest, unless steel inserts are used. This includes the .30 Carbine of which there are thousands in circulation. At least one maker offers a vest utilizing a rectangular steel panel covering the sternum to combat the effects of both high-velocity projectiles and blunt trauma — a worthy idea. This one is by American Body Armor & Equipment Company, 100 Ricefield Lane, Hauppauge, New York 11787. Fortunately for policemen, the rifle-armed antagonist is relatively rare. When practical, such situations are best handled by Special Weapons and Tactics teams (SWAT) with appropriate weapons and "hard" armor. The vests under discussion here are for everyday wear by street cops.

Tests are still in progress on soft, wearable armor, both by private manufacturers and at the Army's Edgewood Arsenal. In fact, some of the information contained in this article may be obsolete by the time it is read. Still, the combined opinion of all engaged in these tests is that lives are being saved by vests now on the market, and should be considered standard attire in every department in the nation.

During the tests by the SAPD, one oldtimer was admittedly impressed with the protection offered by the vests, yet was scornful. Somewhat bitterly, he remarked to Ferguson that, if he truly thought he needed such a device to protect himself from public he had served so long, he would resign.

The answer was: "Then you had better sign your pink slips and pull the pin, because that day is here."

At the time Tom Ferguson was participating in the evaluation testing of body armor for the San Antonio Police Department, at least one make was not included because it was not yet on the market. This is the Morgan textured body armor, presently distributed by Safariland, 1941 South Walker Avenue, Monrovia, California 91016. In the brief time since its introduction, Morgan body armor has been tested and accepted for duty wear by several major law enforcement agencies. Details and particulars can be obtained from the distributor by officially accredited agencies upon inquiry.

The Morgan body armor consists of armor packages and the garment. The armor packages are hermetically sealed and it is stressed that the seal should not be broken. They are designed to be worn with the printed side next to the body for maximum effectiveness and protection and should not be worn reversed. The armor packages can be cleaned with a cloth moistened in a mild soap solution; they should never be submerged in water.

The garment portion of the Morgan body armor is designed to carry the armor packages in the desired position and, for this purpose, it can be adjusted for optimum effect, being fastened with mating Velcro tabs. The garment is made of a blend of polyester and cotton. It is machine washable in mild soap and warm water and can be tumbled dry under moderate heat. No ironing is necessary. The manufacturer recommends that the garment be washed prior to the first wearing to eliminate color transfer. Standard color for the carrying garment is dark blue.

As an added convenience, the Morgan body armor can be ordered with a spare garment, permitting continuous use of the armor package while one of the garments is being cleaned or laundered.

Two patterns of the Morgan body armor are offered currently. One covers the front and back of the torso from collarbone to waistband. The second, termed the shirttail style, continues protection down to about the level of the hip joint on each side.

As shown in the accompanying photographs, the Morgan body armor can be supplied to the measurements of women officers, as well, and its presence beneath a properly fitted uniform is by no means obvious. This is a key consideration, whether the officer is male or female, because the typical officer has a natural concern for his or her appearance. Further, body armor that is clearly visible defeats its own purpose.

As Richard Davis, inventor of the Second Chance body armor, puts it, "If they see the armor, they aim for the head." In a recent conversation with Davis, I asked if he had been a police officer before turning to production of body armor. Davis replied that he'd never been a policeman, but had encountered more adventure than anyone really needs during his career as a night deliveryman for a pizza restaurant he used to own and operate in Detroit, Michigan.

It seems that Detroit's minor heist artists were much prone to call up the restaurant and order pizza, relieving the driver of his bankroll upon delivery and keeping the pizzas without paying for them, by way of adding insult to injury.

"One particular pair were so locked-in on their modus operandi," Davis recalled, "that they made the mistake of ordering two pizzas, both of a rather unusual combination of ingredients. The second time it happened, I went prepared and was able to aid in their temporary retirement from that field of activity."

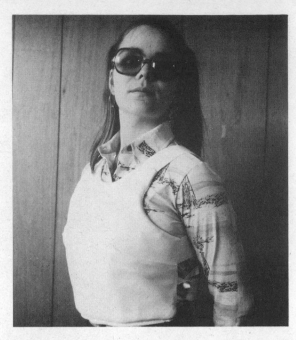

Above, Second Chance offers their body armor for policewomen, making it to the buyer's dimensions. It is designed to be worn beneath the uniform, worn outside here for clarity. Below, maker's label on oldtime vest shown earlier on page 162.

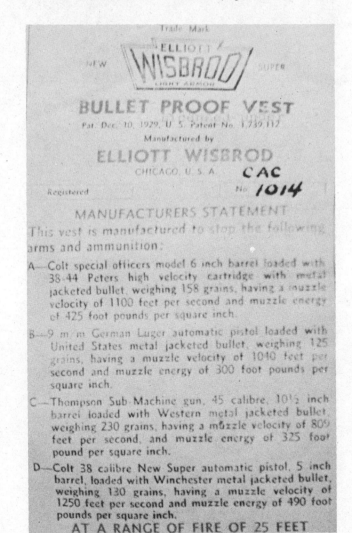

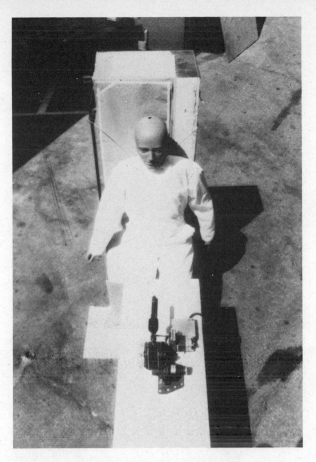

Above, the simulator setup at the labs of Sierra Engineering, as discussed in the accompanying text. Below, Second Chance panel Ferguson used in tests.

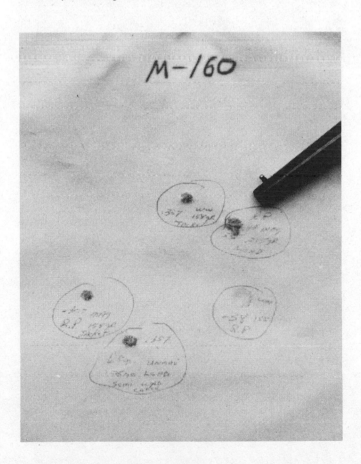

A gadget much beloved by science fiction writers is the robot, usually represented as looking and behaving much like a human being, but made of metal. Though it's not too well known, a highly specialized variety of robot has reached a notable level of development within the past ten years or so. More commonly, it's termed a human simulator and its particular value lies in its ability to react to trauma in a manner closely comparable to that of a human.

Human simulators have found wide and useful application in the training of medical personnel, for one example. The devices can be programmed to show specific vital signs — blood pressure, eye pupil dilation, pulse and respiration rate, et al. — which will be favorably affected by proper treatment administered within a prescribed time span. If the correct steps are not followed, the simulator may go into shock, regurgitate or even die.

Other types of human simulators have been used extensively in tests conducted by the Department of Transportation, intended to evaluate the trauma effect of automobile accidents upon the human body. Under controlled conditions, the simulators are subjected to the stresses of a collision and integral transducers measure and record the stresses involved. By this means, safety devices and different types of auto construction can be evaluated quite realistically without needless human suffering.

A firm called Sierra Engineering Company, 123 East Montecito Avenue, Sierra Madre, California 91024, has utilized a series of the human simulators, as developed for the DOT auto accident tests, in the evaluation of body armor. SEC has extensive experience in producing and testing prosthetic and protective devices and, in the course of a previous program, had occasion to set up a ballistic test range.

The simulator used in testing body armor has the same compression ratio in the thorax area as does the human body. It is comprised of all the components present in the human body, each being identical in dimensions, weight, center of gravity and location. The simulator is scaled to the ninety-fifth percentile dimensions — six feet two inches in height and weighing 210 pounds — which is to say that ninety-five out of every one hundred adult males will be no larger than the test unit.

Under impact, the simulator's thorax deflects in exact proportion — both in distance and time span — to that of the human body. Integral sensing units transmit the deflection forces to measuring and recording instruments. The usual procedure is to feed the readout to an oscilloscope or cathode ray tube (CRT). The CRT trace then is photographed for future reference, showing the exact amount of deflection as a graph line in relation to the time of duration.

The test simulator can be subjected to several typical forms of physical violence, such as blows with the human fist or clubs, kicks and similar stresses. The force thus involved is measured and recorded for comparison to the readings obtained when bullets are impacted against the thorax of the simulator. A bullet striking the protective body armor can transmit three hundred foot-pounds of kinetic energy or more and that sounds impressive. However, a lusty roundhouse clout from the human fist can transmit a greater force, over a somewhat longer duration, as can a well-swung length of a two-by-four or, for that matter, a croquet mallet.

Most ballistic impacts have a duration of no more than two or three milliseconds (1/1000th of a second), with the peak force spanning no more than one millisecond.

Dennis Salmans, manager of SEC's quality assurance department, recalls one maker of body armor who requested a test of his product on the laboratory's simulator under impact of the .44 magnum cartridge. The lab crew was assured that the armor under test would stop a .44

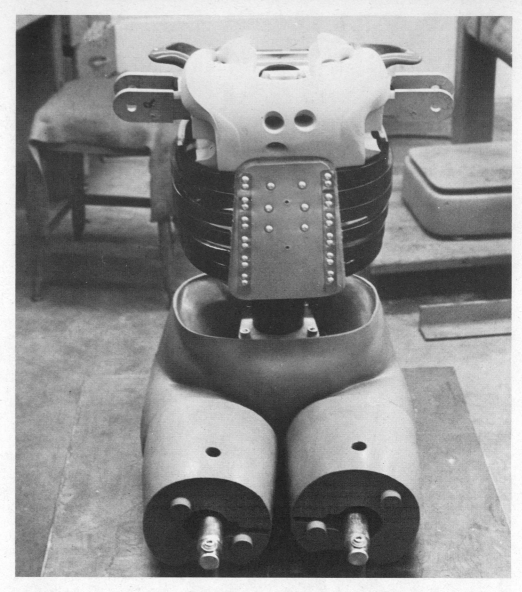

As discussed, the field of simulator robots has become quite highly sophisticated over the past decade. This is the torso mockup used for measuring blunt trauma effect of body armor.

magnum slug. Sadly, the slug whizzed through the armor and on through the thorax of the simulator, carrying away a section of rib. The client had to pay several hundred dollars for a repair of the rib cage, over and above the regular testing fees.

"Since then," Salmans notes, "if it seems at all doubtful, we run penetration tests against a block of clay before trying it on the simulator."

The simulators used in testing are reasonably lifelike in appearance, so much so that the ears are left off deliberately in their construction. This is done to keep anyone viewing photos of the tests from getting the impression that it is a real person.

SEC has made tests for a number of law enforcement departments and other governmental agencies. It is their policy to release specific test data only to the client who requests and pays for the testing, although they will comment in broadly general terms on the various aspects involved. SEC also conducts tests on allied subjects, using several sophisticated systems at their disposal. These include such things as comparative effectiveness of different calibers of cartridges or different loadings for the same cartridge, relative efficiency of other protective garments such as safety helmets, and so on.

The interest in and development of concealable body armor is of quite recent origin. At the time the first edition

of this book was published four years ago, the field was little explored. Body armor of that era was cumbersome, heavy, uncomfortable and designed to be worn over the regular clothing. Worse, it was by no means as effective as its users might have wished, being little refined from the flak-vests used in WWII and later conflicts.

It has been noted that wearing concealed body armor tends to confer a sense of invulnerability and the wearer is well advised not to let his or her judgment be unduly influenced by this. There is a substantial and growing number of police officers, still on duty, who owe their lives to the fact that they were wearing their armor when the need arose. Others, less fortunate, have staged an intrepid charge into hostile fire and have been killed by a bullet in the head. Still others have been killed shortly before they'd managed to save up enough money to order their body armor and at least one officer's experience was documented in the press when he was shot on the day his body armor was being cleaned. In that case, fortunately, the hit was not fatal.

In the final analysis, even the finest of today's body armor does not make one indestructible. The best it can do is to shade the odds in your favor. Considering the unattractive odds a police officer must face in routine duty, anything that improves the chances of collecting the pension merits serious consideration.

Speedloaders, from left to right, front row: HKS Six Second; Dade; Matich Qwik Load; (back row) Feathertouch; Second Six and Safariland. Text discusses good and bad points of each.

REVOLVER SPEEDLOADERS

Seconds Can Be Precious In A Firefight And Speedloaders Can Make The Vital Difference

SPEEDLOADERS HAVE BEEN around for a long time. Competitors in simulated combat matches were quick to adopt them, finding they provided the vital edge of speed needed for winning. But it's only in the past couple of years that they've begun to catch on among police. Massad F. Ayoob, a policeman and enthusiastic combat match competitor, is well qualified to give us his experiences and comments on today's array of speedloaders, with notes on the outstanding qualities of each.

His opinions are obvious. The single greatest shortcoming of the double-action revolver as a combat tool has been the slowness of reloading each of its five or six chambers. It was an argument that outweighed even cartridge capacity. Jeff Cooper has always maintained that, since reloading time is equal, a 1911 .45 auto was a better bet than a fourteen-shot Browning or S&W 9mm for the man who wanted shock power. For the man who wants double-action speed, accuracy and reliability, many feel, equalization of reloading speed would likewise make the revolver the weapon of choice over the automatic.

Dade loader pouch for N-frame .357 size will also hold a double stack of .45 ACPs in half-moon clips; the best ammo rig Ayoob has seen for the officers carrying .45 revolvers.

Ayoob recommends Bianchi Speed Strip for carrying spare ammunition when on duty in plainclothes.

How do speedloaders work? Some well, some not so good. Some are great for competition, while others are better for combat, and still others make a good compromise. Prices average $4.50 apiece, plus the cost of a pouch; an outfit of two loaders and a belt carrier sets you back around $20 no matter what the brand.

How do you decide on which you want? Speed is one factor. Another is security, that is, how likely the rounds are to spill out if the loader is dropped. There are two schools of thought on this: one is that the loader isn't going to be dropped; the other is that a secure loader allows one cop to throw a unit to an embattled officer in a tight position, who may be running out of ammo. We don't see the latter happening so much, but we like security for another reason: anybody reloading with bullets whistling past his head tends to get a bit fumble-fingered, and instead of groping for six scattered pieces of metal in the dark, one is better able to pick up the whole unit again. That's why we like the HKS for duty, and the Dade for combat competition and demonstrations.

The Dade loader is the increasing choice among combat masters for a simple and overriding reason: it's the fastest on the market. The margin is sometimes small, sometimes large, but always definite. The Feather Touch, which operates on a similar push-button/gravity drop system, comes close, but you have to feel around for its tiny button. On the other hand, the big head on the Dade comes instinctively under your finger the moment its payload

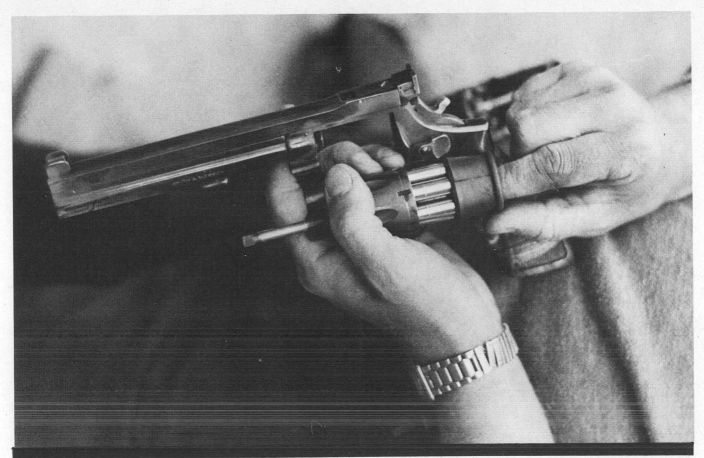

Inserting the Safariland speedloader in a K-38 modified for combat competition. Refer to photo on page 173 for further comments.

slides home into the cylinders.

A thin spring encircling the upper edge of the main body of the loader holds the cartridge rims in place; the six-petalled button pushes them past the spring and into the chambers. The three most common questions regarding this unit are, "Doesn't that little spring tend to snap?" "Won't the plastic break when it falls on the ground?" and "Won't the rounds fall out if you drop it?"

In heavy competition, where the shooter might be working the loaders a hundred times a week in practice and actual match shooting, they stand up remarkably well. I've never heard of the spring breaking or of any serious damage when the empty loader was dropped on the paved firing line after filling the sixgun. Scratches on the exterior surface are about all you need expect. But drop a loaded Dade and three to six rounds will probably bounce out.

"I did have one on which button assembly loosened up, allowing the push-out petals to get out of alignment, leaving the unit functional but awkward to manipulate," Ayoob reports.

"The Dade and the Feather Touch are about equally simple to line up with wadcutter ammo, second only to the Matich. The Dade comes with a variety of carriers. Their three-pouch, open-top rig is made for them by Tex Shoemaker leather; an excellent rig, though my sample didn't have quite the quality of workmanship I'd expect from the highly respected Shoemaker outfit. Dade is the only company to make a patent-leather-finish loader pouch, sometimes that's important to the growing number of officers who currently are buying or being issued shiny Clarino belt sets and must complement them with matching accessories. The duty pouches are half-plastic, half-leather, with or without top flap.

An outstandingly tough little unit, the Feather Touch loader manages to look bulkier than any other brand while being the most compact of all. One drops in the rounds and presses in the tiny top button to lock them in place; a second press drops them into the sixgun.

However, you don't feel a positive click when you press the button, and that can leave you with the nasty feeling that maybe nothing has happened. Secondly, our sample tended to drop only five of the six rounds every so often.

On the plus side, it can be just about as fast as the Dade and probably faster than any of the other brands. Also, you can bounce it off the floor without dropping any rounds so long as the loader doesn't land flush on its stubby button. The latter is unlikely, since the weight of the bullets would tend to make it land on the opposite end. Pouches are pretty much standard and as bulky as any around.

"For those who worry about losing rounds from a dropped speedloader, the HKS Six-Second Loader is the one to buy. I've thrown loaded HKS units to the concrete ten or fifteen times in rapid succession. Maybe once or twice, the metal detent knob would hit just so and turn barely enough to let a round slip out. On one occasion, I abused a K-frame HKS loader to the extent that four of the six chamber walls cracked, yet the loader functioned perfectly," Ayoob says.

"A knob-and-detent system is what gives HKS unit its sturdy feel and positive release. I find it a bit slower than the Dade, but a lot of other people don't notice any difference. And it can't be what you'd call slow. Gary Peach, 1974 United States Police Combat Pistol Champion, used HKSs to win the title and swears by them."

The feel of an HKS in action differs a bit from the others. For one thing, instead of a solid "stop" feeling when the cartridges are all the way in, there is a touch of springiness. This can lead a person unfamiliar with the loader to misjudge the point at which the cartridges are fully inserted and turn the knob too quick, resulting in one or two spilled rounds. This will not happen with full-length cartridges, though it does occur with wadcutters, if you're not accustomed to the feel of the product.

All in all, we rate the HKS as an excellent duty speedloader. It may prove itself to be the most popular for civilian shooters, as well. HKS honcho Bob Switzer has introduced a model to fit mid-frame six-shot .22 revolvers, either the K-22 or the Colt Diamondback. If it works as well as he says, it'll be a boon to plinkers and to combat shooters who practice with .22s on .38 frames to reduce ammo expense.

Our only doubt would stem from the fact that .22s with counterbored chambers tend to require a little pressure to get the rounds seated all the way into the chamber, especially when the gun is dirtied up from a little shooting. A gravity-drop loader like the HKS might leave the shooter with a couple of not-quite-seated rounds protruding from the cylinder of his K-22.

Possibly the greatest thing in the HKS line is the A-1 belt pouch, a trim over-under job that answers the main complaint about duty speedloaders: bulk. The A-1 loader is smaller than a Mace carrier. It's the best around, and the fastest of the duty rigs; the first one drops into your hand and you needn't dig it out.

One of the earliest successful speedloader designs, the Matich isn't seen that much today. The U.S. Service pistol team used them as recently as a couple of years ago, but have switched to the Dade.

The Matich is a flexible strip of neoprene with protruding ribs and a hook on one end. When the far end hooks to

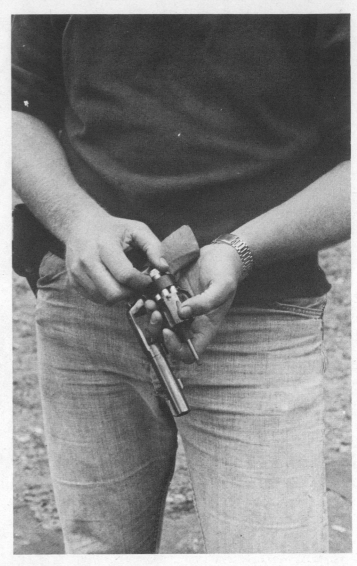

Knob release of the HKS Six Second unit gives a positive feel of release, even when used in the dark.

Most guns with target stocks need wood removed before speedloaders can be used without hanging up. These Dan Wesson PaceSetter grips have been modified. Many prefer standard grips and adapters.

the near, these ribs form a cylinder of the exact dimensions of whatever gun it's designed to fit. One end of the rubber strip extends beyond the hook. The shooter inserts the loaded unit into the revolver, making sure that the rounds go as far in as they can, and then grasps the tab and pulls straight sideways. The Matich unit then strips away from the cartridges, spinning the cylinder as the rounds drop in.

It has its good points and bad. It is totally impossible to dislodge rounds from a Matich loader when you drop it. Also, it is the only speedloader that holds the shells rigidly in line with the cylinder for which it's designed. Other loaders have a little play in them, for the obvious reason that the chamber of the loader must be the diameter of the cartridge rim which has to pass through it. This play re-

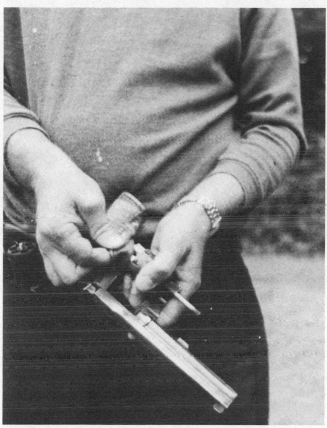

Peeling off the rubber Safariland speedloader must be performed with care, lest a jerky movement cause one or more cartridges to fall to the ground.

quires the shooter to jiggle the loader a bit to get all rounds lined up, especially with wadcutters. This is no problem with the Matich.

But if you pull that tab before the rounds are fully seated or if you pull it the least bit up and away, at least half of the cartridges are going to fly out of the cylinder. This is probably what killed the Matich for competitors, though it was quicker to line up than any of the others on the market and almost as fast as the Dades.

There is a more serious problem with the Matich, in my opinion, for policy duty in cold weather climates: the plastic will stiffen with only mild exposure to cold, making it extremely difficult to strip it away from the cartridges. Ayoob found this out at a winter combat match.

"The Matich is fast and secure, though. I used it for both competition and exhibition shooting and three-second reloads were easy. Its design was such that a smooth movement of hand-in/hand-away allowed for maximum reloading time," he recalls.

Not to be confused with the unit by HKS, the Second Six is exactly the opposite in terms of losing rounds when dropped. They come out easily, but it has other qualities that endear it to Southern California lawmen who are, right now, the only ones who've had a chance to work with it.

Inventor Bill Griffis takes pride in the fact that his is the only speedloader on the market sold to police only. To make sure that no one deviates from that policy, he has been reluctant to let a major distributor handle the line and, instead, sells them himself throughout the Southwest.

He admits that they'll readily lose their rounds if dropped, but like many who have gotten into speedloaders, he doesn't see that as a really significant factor. "I concede that they make lousy handballs," chuckles Griffis. "But I don't sell handballs. I sell speedloaders and my product does that job right well!"

"It's about the lightest unit around and it ties for the most compact. Its skeleton framework of fairly thin, hard plastic looks brittle and fragile, but I've had my set in action long enough to learn otherwise and a lot of that action was in the untrained fingers of fresh recruits. As far as them cracking when on the pavement, I can't really see that happening; they're so light they don't hit hard enough to break the high-impact plastic. (That's when they're emptied, of course. I do imagine that the weight of a loaded Second Six loader slamming to a hard surface a few times could do some damage,)" Ayoob says.

The Second Six gives the most positive delivery; that is, it's the only one that actually forces the cartridges firmly into the firing chambers. You draw the moving plastic ring back to the rear of the unit, where the little plastic teeth are located that hook on to the cartridge rim. You line up the rounds with the cylinder, push them halfway in, then, with fingertip pressure, slide the ring forward. This forces the rims over the plastic teeth and slams them into the cylinder.

The inventor stresses that this will allow a downed officer with a wounded arm to lay his revolver on the ground and recharge with a speedloader one-handedly. He's right; gravity-type loaders obviously wouldn't work sideways, and the Safariland unit, which we'll discuss shortly, might or might not. Ditto the Bianchi Speed Strip.

That extra push into the chambers eliminates the problem of the cartridges not being fully seated, which occurs often with handloaded ammo and dirty guns, and can result in a seized-up double-action trigger pull or worse.

The belt carrier is a trim little side-by-sider, probably the least bulky of the pouch-type speedloader cases.

In its various incarnations as the Hunt, Kel-lite and now Safariland Firepower unit, this little item has been around as long or longer than any other six-at-once number and is probably the most popular. There are several reasons why not all of them have to do with the efficiency of the product.

Its good points are that its totally neoprene composition makes it indestructible and it doesn't readily lose cartridges when dropped.

But since they're held only by the rims, the cartridges can splay outward, especially when carried for long periods in belt pouches. Like any speedloader, you generally can get round-nose ammo in, but wadcutters will require more jiggling than any other brand of six-at-oncer. Finally, you operate it by peeling the rubber clip off after cartridges have been inserted, and unless you do it slowly, you can bounce maybe four rounds right back out of the cylinder. A veteran competitor on the firing line can make this motion smoothly, but a cop in the heat of a gunfight makes jerky, fast movements, and can easily spill the cylinder he's just reloaded.

Note mashed noses of S&W hollow-points after gruelling test in paint mixer. HKS Six Second loaders took this beating with no damage, lost no rounds.

If this type is so inefficient, active combat competitors ask, why do you see so many on the firing line? Again, it has been around the longest, and the veteran masters use them out of familiarity and the newcomers buy what they see the old masters using. Many are, as we stated, getting away from this type and into the Dade and HKS loaders. (The heavy combat shooters also like the fact that they can bounce their discarded Safariland loaders all over a paved firing line without damaging them, but they're learning that the Dades and HKSs stand up nearly as well.)

The only unit presently on the market that can be called a speedloader yet doesn't drop in six at a time, the Bianchi is also the most popular revolver recharger around. There are several reasons why.

It's flat and compact, great for shirt pockets when working plainclothes or to back up the ammo supply on your duty belt. Don't carry them in trouser pockets, where they tend to hang up and spill rounds on being drawn. They fit the drop pouches that so many officers are required to wear on duty and which are about the only way of carrying spare ammo that is actually slower than a pocketful of loose cartridges. Some drop boxes are a tight fit, especially with .357 rounds and that may cause a hangup when you

whip out your speed strip; the rounds will clatter to your feet and you will be left holding an empty piece of steel-reinforced neoprene.

It's the loader most sportsmen have because it's the cheapest, and it's distributed along with the rest of the Bianchi line in sporting goods stores everywhere. It allows you to load rapidly one or two rounds at a time. It is slightly faster than the Matchmaker and Cirillo-type belt loops that combat competitors use when speedloaders are forbidden by local match rules.

Just for the hell of it, let's take a look at the old .45 ACP half-moon clips built for the Army 1917 revolvers, which were probably the first rapid-reload revolver system ever conceived. A lot of gun buffs still use these old pieces for self-defense and not a few cops — myself included — are known to pack either cut-down 1917s or chopped S&W 1955 Target revolvers.

"The half-moon clips are the second most compact speedloaders around, second only to the Bianchi strip. Coupled with the short length of the .45 ACP round, that makes for a lot of conveniently carried ammo. I found out early that the plastic-and-leather Dade pouch that carries two speedloaders for the "N" frame Smith will hold eight loaded

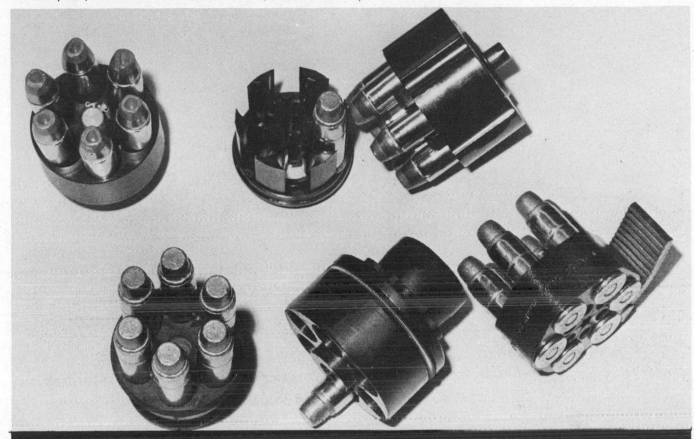

half-moons for my four-inch S&W 1955 Target — twenty-four rounds instead of twelve. Truth to tell, the Dade speedloader pouch in that size is the only practical way to carry half-moon clips on a duty belt. I specify the Dade, because it's cut away in front, allowing access to the half-moon clips at the bottom of the pouch," Ayoob says.

Reloading speed is generally figured in total time; counting the moments it takes to lower the sixgun, clear the empties, get the belt pouch open, reload, close the cylinder, and come up shooting. It is, as we say, the interval between the sixth and seventh shots.

From pocket or belt pouch, that interval takes most men nine to thirty seconds. From belt loops, a practiced man can do it in seven to ten. Safariland units, once you've got the feel of them, cut that to maybe five seconds. Bianchi strips go five to ten seconds.

"A Matich lets you reload in three or four seconds. So does an HKS Six Second or a Second Six or Feather Touch. The Dade gets you down to two seconds, with practice. These times are based on my own experience with each type, and I'm sure there might be fast-fingered fellas like Bill Jordan who can shave even the two seconds.

"A key factor, of course, is how long it takes you to get the loader clear. I predicate the above times on a loader that is either in a competition (open-topped) pouch, or hanging off my belt loops. A practiced man who has to dig his loader out of a flapped pouch is going to start en-croaching on the time it would take him to reload from a good set of belt loops."

But that's a practiced man. Only combat competitors reach that level of belt loader efficiency. For the rookie, we're talking about a six-second reload with a speedloader from a snapped pouch versus fifteen to twenty or more from the standard drop-box. And that's a lot.

Speedloaders have always been permitted in NRA combat matches, but until the past year or so, most locally run matches prohibited them on the grounds that they were not standard duty equipment and would give the well-equipped master an unfair edge over a newcomer carrying drop boxes. That sentiment is changing fast, for two reasons: speedloaders are selling like hot cakes to duty cops, and police instructors are finding that new shooters love them. It's the difference between learning to drive with an automatic transmission as opposed to a four-speed stick; there's a lot less to master.

In those regions where police combat shoots have a category open to civilians, the possibilities are obvious. For the man who carries a concealed handgun, they make sense, especially the Speed Strip. If you keep a revolver in the night table drawer it's a good idea to have a speedloader next to it to drop into your pocket when you pull on your pants and grab your gun to check out that noise in the kitchen. If you find an armed intruder down there and get into an extended firefight, it's worth ten times its weight in

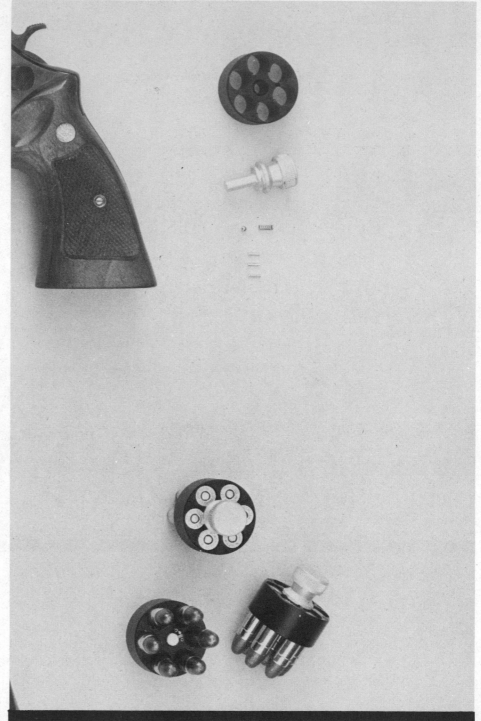

The HKS Six Second unit is comprised of seven parts, designed for reliable performance under severe duty conditions. Costing more than some of the others, it is available in sizes to fit all popular makes and types of revolvers in current law enforcement use.

burglar alarms. Civilians almost never practice the life-saving combat art of rapid reloading, and an HKS in your bathrobe pocket can make the difference between survival and the police finding your body on the kitchen floor with an empty .38 in your hand.

"The ultimate question, of course, is, 'How do speed-loaders compare with auto pistols' quick reloading?' Damn well is how they compare. In one exhibition, I got three gunloads out of a .357 in fifteen seconds, while the two experienced automatic shooters with me took seventeen and nineteen seconds, respectively, to put three gunloads through their 1911s. Figuring that they each had four more extra rounds to get off than I did, that made us equal in reloading time and, of course, gave them an edge in total firepower," Ayoob reports.

Until somebody invents a compact fifteen-shot wheelgun, the revolver will never equal the auto in total firepower. But the speedloader does make the sixgun's reloading time roughly equal to the self-loaders. When cops look at the bad points of the automatic — sloppy fifty-yard accuracy, high cost of practice ammo, greater maintenance and practice time requirements — it becomes increasingly apparent that a good double-action .38 or .357 backed up by speedloaders makes more sense as an issue weapon than a 9mm or .45 automatic.

We personally think that the new popularity of speed-loaders will strangle the trend toward automatics in police circles, at least until Colt introduces their double-action .45 self-loader. The speedloader simply negates one of the auto's major advantages over the revolver.

OF BADGES & BULLETS...

The Right Ammunition For A Given Purpose Involves More Than Making Sure That It Fits The Chamber. Here Are Points To Consider!

DEPARTMENTAL PROCEDURES and regulations vary widely between cities and there are few areas where this is so apparent in police work as in the ruling policy regarding ammunition to be carried by officers on duty. Some departments grant the individual almost unlimited free choice as to type and caliber of gun and the ammunition carried in it. Others issue some one particular make and model of handgun, perhaps even going to the extent of modifying the gun in some manner from standard factory production and go on to issue duty ammunition.

Supervisory personnel of the more strictly organized departments may make a regular practice of pulling surprise inspections of the loads in an officer's handgun at any given time and the man caught carrying non-regulation loads may receive anything from a reprimand through suspension or dismissal from duty.

Neither extreme would seem ideal from a practical standpoint. Total freedom of choice in guns and ammunition can and sometimes has resulted in some absurd and thoroughly impractical situations. As a salient example, we recall — not too many years ago — a deputy sheriff in the upper midwest whose sole duty weapon was an ancient .25 auto which he wrapped thoroughly in a large bandana handkerchief and stuffed the entire package in his right hip pocket.

At the other end of things, a few hundred miles from the bailiwick of the bandana-holstered deputy and at about the same point in time, the supervisory personnel of another department decreed that there was no sense in having to stock two different kinds of ammunition, one for practice and the other for off duty. Accordingly, all officers would carry midrange wadcutters in their revolvers while on duty. This, incidentally, was at a time when the quality of the practice ammo was so dubious that the rare practice sessions required ramrods and mallets for driving out bullets which had lodged in barrels, due to the absence of a powder charge in the occasional cartridge.

It is not the purpose nor the intent of this discussion to recommend uniform standardization of armament through all departments nor to advocate any specific handgun, caliber or cartridge. It seems likely that many would agree that the matter deserves to be evaluated on the basis of knowledge as to the performance characteristics of handguns and their ammunition. The final decision should integrate relevant and practical considerations which are numerous and varying to a confusing degree.

The ideal duty handgun and cartridge for a quiet little New England village obviously would be a poor choice on a tough waterfront beat of a major seaport, where patrolling in pairs is a matter of sheer self-preservation.

Recognizing this, we will discuss the basic facts of ballistics and cartridge performance in simple, non-technical terms — defining those terms which are critical to the considerations of the topic. This will be followed by comparative performance reports on a variety of typical factory loaded cartridges of different bullet weights and designs in the calibers considered appropriate for use in police handguns. It is hoped that the presentation will be helpful in developing a better understanding of the factors involved, toward the end of selecting combinations best suited for a given set or requirements.

Chapter 12

CARTRIDGE PERFORMANCE

To Be Effective, A Bullet Must Deliver Energy To The Target. Here Are The Mechanics Of That Process!

WE LIVE IN an endless ocean of air, which is fortunate since we need the stuff for survival. But, from a ballistic viewpoint, atmosphere is a mixed blessing. It is a rather glue-like medium through which to drive a bullet.

We hear the familiar phrase, "thin as air," but air at high speed is a powerful force and thin does not describe it well. If you've ever ridden a bicycle into the push of a strong headwind, your aching legs soon learned the meaning of "atmospheric resistance." View the aftermath of a tornado or hurricane; ride a fast motorcycle, an open cockpit airplane or a convertible with the top down: Yes, air is thick enough to make a lot of difference if you're moving fast or if it's moving fast or if you're both moving fast in the opposite directions.

Take the strongest wind, the fastest slipstream that the unprotected human can stand; multiply it three or four times and you get a general picture of the force through which a bullet must buck on the way to the target. It's not surprising that a bullet begins to lose speed as soon as it leaves the gun muzzle. The greater the speed, for any given bullet, the more rapid the rate of velocity loss from air resistance.

Obviously, a bullet that is long in proportion to its diameter will hold its speed better than one that has less length and/or greater girth. For the same reasons, a bullet with a pointed, streamlined nose will lose less speed over a given distance than another that is flat or blunt in front, assuming both start at the same velocity.

The long, thin bullet is said to have a high "sectional density." A shorter bullet of the same diameter has a lower sectional density. A bullet that is efficiently streamlined has a high "ballistic coefficient." Another bullet, of the same weight and diameter, but with a flat or blunt point has a lower ballistic coefficient.

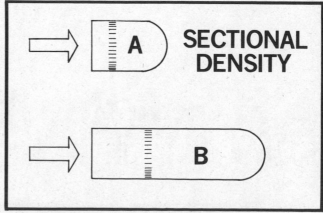

Although the same in nose shape, B is longer, heavier than A. As a result, if both start at the same speed, B will retain more velocity at any given point, due to its superior sectional density overcoming air resistance.

Sierra 125-grain JHC bullet, recovered from oil-base clay after high-velocity firing in a .357 mag revolver.

Sierra 110-grain JHC bullet, before and after firing, showing the extent of expansion — in oil-base clay — at moderate velocities typical of .38 Special revolvers.

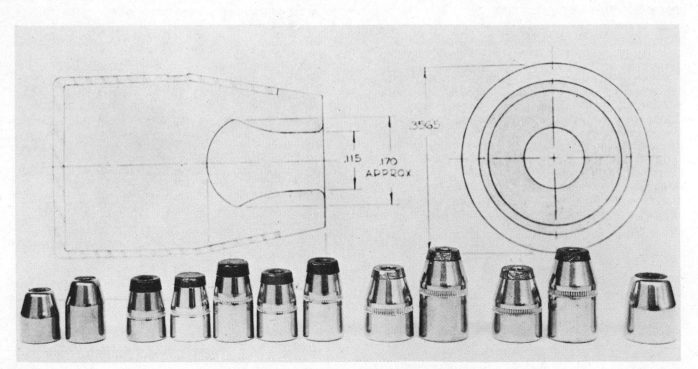

Jacketed hollow cavity — JHC — bullets are made by Sierra in five diameters: 9mm, .38/.357, .41, .44 and .45, with exclusive cavity profiled at top of photo.

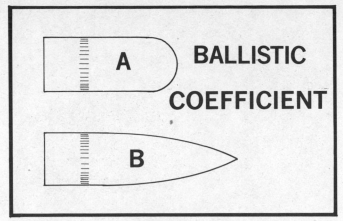

BALLISTIC COEFFICIENT

Although both bullets are of same weight and diameter, therefore having equal sectional density, bullet B is streamlined more effectively to minimize air resistance. Thus B will not lose velocity as rapidly as A, due to better (higher) ballistic coefficient.

Sierra's 150-grain in their heaviest JHC design in .3565-inch diameter, though a JSP — jacketed soft-point — design is made at 158 grain, lacking the unique nose cavity, with solid lead flat across tip.

Actually, the sectional density is a factor expressing the relation between a bullet's weight and its cross-sectional area, as viewed from the front and length is not the key factor. The ballistic coefficient combines the sectional density — weight and frontal cross-section — and incorporates a comparison of the given bullet's streamlining or lack of it.

The higher mathematics concerned with a bullet's flight through the air can require more study that the casual reader may wish to devote but a basic grasp of the meaning of sectional density and ballistic coefficient will be helpful in understanding the discussion that follows; hence the somewhat simplified explanations.

An object in motion possesses "kinetic energy." Its rate of motion is called velocity and, in discussing bullet performance, the customary measurement is in "feet per second," conveniently abbreviated to "fps." Bullet weight is measured in grains — there are 7000 grains in one pound, 437.5 grains in one ounce — and bullet energy is given in "foot-pounds." *

A foot-pound is the amount of energy that would be required in raising a one-pound object a distance of one foot. It is also approximately equal to the kinetic energy a one-pound object would acquire in the process of falling one foot.

*For readers who may wish to compute kinetic energy, the formula is fairly simple. Multiply the velocity in feet per second times itself, times the weight in pounds and divide by 64.32, which is the acceleration of gravity. When working with bullets, the weight of which is given in grains, it is necessary to square the velocity — fps times fps — and then divide by 7000 — the number of grains in one pound — and divide the answer by 64.32. This gives the amount of energy in foot-pounds for one grain. Multiply the answer by the weight of the bullet in grains to obtain the energy in foot-pounds.

Example: Determine the energy of a 158-grain bullet at 885 fps. 885 times 885 equals 783,255 divided by 7000 equals 111.889 divided by 64.32 equals (about) 1.74 times 158 (weight of the bullet in grains) equals about 274 ft-lbs.

Example: Determine the energy of a 3500-pound automobile, traveling at 60 mph (88 fps).

88 times 88 equals 7744 times 3500 (weight of car) equals 27,104,000 divided by 64.32 equals 421,393 ft-lbs.

Which may help to explain why automobiles, year after year, account for more casualties than bullets.

Here, the Sierra 110-grain JHC has been driven into oil-base clay at a velocity of 1600 fps, causing jacket to peel back, inside-out, creating perfect mushroom.

Apart from the number of foot-pounds carried by a projectile, a key factor is the manner of delivery to the target. One of the heavy medicine balls, used for exercise, can be thrown and caught without severe discomfort. However, in flight, the medicine ball is carrying some several foot-pounds of kinetic energy. It can be absorbed by the catcher without harm, due to the fact that the energy is distributed over an area of a good many square inches and it is absorbed over a relatively long time interval. The hands and arms act as springs to soak up energy and perhaps the catcher moves back a step or two in the process.

Try to catch a medicine ball — or a smaller one, for that matter — against the palm of your hand, with the back of the hand held solidly against a brick wall and it would be another matter, entirely! Here, the duration of the impact has been shortened greatly. Reduce the area of impact and it's much the same story. Position the point of a spike, three-sixteenths of an inch in diameter, against a piece of board, dropping a one-pound weight onto the head of the spike from 158 feet above and you have a rough duplication of the forces at work when a .22 long rifle bullet hits the same board.

Velocity plays an important part in transmitting kinetic energy. With the weight remaining the same, each time you double the velocity of a moving object, it acquires four times as much energy. Putting it in slightly more formal terms, energy varies in direct proportion to the velocity squared. As an example, a 100-grain bullet at 600 fps has about 80 ft-lbs of kinetic energy; double the speed to 1200 fps and the energy is about 320 ft-lbs; double it again, to 2400 fps and the energy quadruples to 1280 ft-lbs: about sixteen times as much as the figure for 600 fps.

Sierra's two JHC bullets for the .44 magnum or .44 Special, 240-grain at left, 180-grain at right, flank a cross-sectioned example of the 180, showing design.

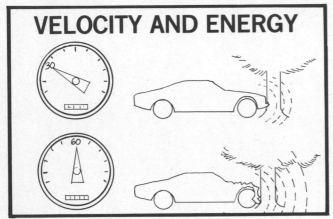

Any moving object has kinetic energy. If the speed is doubled, the object has four times as much kinetic energy. Thus it becomes capable of doing more damage.

In those bullets which have the capability of expanding upon impact, such as the soft-point or hollow-point, velocity is a key factor in expansion, as well. It is difficult to predict the probability of expansion on a hard-and-fast basis when bullets impact in living tissue since the target is by no means uniform in texture, consistency or resistance to penetration. If the bullet encounters a bone, it is quite apt to expand, even at relatively low velocities. Expansion in muscles or organs requires considerably more velocity before the odds become reasonably favorable. Other factors include such things as cross-sectional area and the shape of the bullet nose.

This poses a two-fold and slightly incompatible problem: It is desirable for the bullet to drill efficiently through the atmosphere on its way to the target without shedding any major portion of its starting energy in overcoming air resistance. At the same time, upon encountering the target, the opposite becomes true. As much of the velocity and kinetic energy as possible must be transmitted to the target. If the bullet penetrates completely and emerges with most of its original velocity, energy carried beyond the target can be regarded as waste and a decided disadvantage since it poses a hazard to property and personnel beyond the target.

As a rule, bullets whose profile and dimensions make them highly efficient for penetrating the atmosphere are likewise efficient for penetration of the target without significant transfer of energy. An example of such a bullet would be the typical military rifle bullet with its pointed tip and gently tapered nose, fully protected by a jacket of copper alloy. Such bullets rarely expand although, operating at much higher velocities than pistol bullets, any encounter with bone may cause them to tumble — go into end-over-end motion — and the impact may cause shattered fragments of bone to be converted into secondary projectiles which can cause as much damage as the original bullet, if not more.

Any substantial portion of the bullet tip which is flat or nearly so — that is, at right angles to the path of bullet flight — has a dual effect in transmitting kinetic energy to the target. First, it sets up a shock wave in the tissue, perpendicular in all directions to the bullet path, during penetration. Second, the impact of the flat area tends to initiate expansion, to an extent directly proportional to the effective area of the flat tip.

Thus, a bullet having a flat tip whose diameter is the same as that of the bullet — similar to a typical target wadcutter — rates high in efficiency of energy transmission after impact. Unfortunately, such bullets have the highest rate of velocity loss through the air for any given combination of bullet weight and diameter and it is difficult to maintain accuracy with them at velocities much in excess of the speed of sound through air — roughly, about 1150 fps.

Considerations such as these have guided the design of modern, expanding bullets for use in typical handgun cartridges. Such a bullet may have a flat tip whose diameter may be approximately half that of the bullet itself, followed by a rounded or tapered transition into full bullet diameter. The bullet core, of soft or slightly hardened lead may be enclosed by a jacket of copper alloy, extending over part of the nose, back along the sides and over the bullet base, serving as an effective means of preventing or minimizing bore-fouling problems at the higher velocities. A small amount of unprotected lead is left at the bullet nose and this may be a solid, flat surface or a rounded area — as exemplified by typical soft-point designs — or it may have a hole in the nose, extending back for a short distance into the lead core, as the hollow-point designs.

A recent innovation is the jacketed hollow cavity — JHC — design used in several of the Sierra handgun bullets. Here, the manufacturing process puts an orifice in the bullet nose which is considerably smaller in diameter than that of the cavity itself. As a result, once expansion commences, the cavity walls, supported by the mouth of the jacket, open outward to an expanded diameter which may be two or more times that of the original bullet diameter.

Simple arithmetic shows the effect of expansion upon transmission of kinetic energy. Suppose a caliber .38 bullet — .358-inch diameter — expands to three-quarters of an inch upon impact. This means that it has completed its passage through the air with a frontal or cross-sectional area of slightly more than one-tenth of a square inch. At or shortly after impact, the cross-sectional area becomes about .443 square inch: slightly more than double the diameter but well over four times the area. Such a bullet approaches maximum practical efficiency at carrying and transmitting energy to the target.

As has been noted earlier in this book, the traditional police service bullet, the 158-grain lead design with its rounded tip, is not apt to expand when encountering the target unless it impacts upon fairly substantial bones. The typical performance of such a bullet is complete penetration with relatively little loss of velocity. Energy transmitted to the target is easy to compute: Initial energy upon primary impact, minus remaining energy at the point of exit.

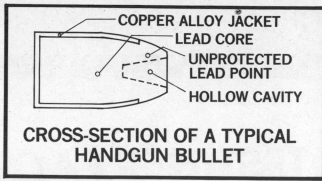

CROSS-SECTION OF A TYPICAL HANDGUN BULLET

Most of today's high-performance handgun bullets have a jacket — mostly copper with a small amount of zinc — covering the sides and base. The front is left with the lead core unprotected and an opening may be added.

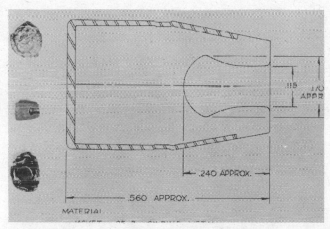

Engineer's drawing of the Sierra JHC design lists typical proportions of the cavity. Note the cannelure, for crimping the cartridge case neck into sides.

After firing a caliber .38 Sierra JHC 125-grain slug into oil-base clay, the resulting cavity was filled with plaster to produce this graphic channel casting.

As an example, take a 100-grain bullet which is traveling at 1150 fps upon entry and leaves at 850 fps: by no means unrealistic with a non-expanding bullet such as a round-nosed lead or fully jacketed design. Its initial energy is 293 ft-lbs and it still carries 160 ft-lbs after leaving the target so 133 ft-lbs was transmitted; only a trifle over forty-five percent of the energy carried to the target was effectively delivered and more than half goes on to endanger life and property beyond the target — even when the bullet has been aimed accurately.

By contrast, an expanding bullet — provided it scores a fair hit on the target — is much less apt to penetrate and, if it does not penetrate, the full cargo of kinetic energy will have been delivered, greatly enhancing the likelihood that the target will be disabled or immobilized. Since that can be assumed as the objective in firing at the target in the first place, the advantage of the expanding bullet becomes fairly obvious. If solicitude for the welfare of the target is a primary concern, then the indicated course is to fire so as to miss or — more logically — to refrain from firing in the first place.

Chapter 13

TESTING FACTORY AMMUNITION FOR POLICE HANDGUNS

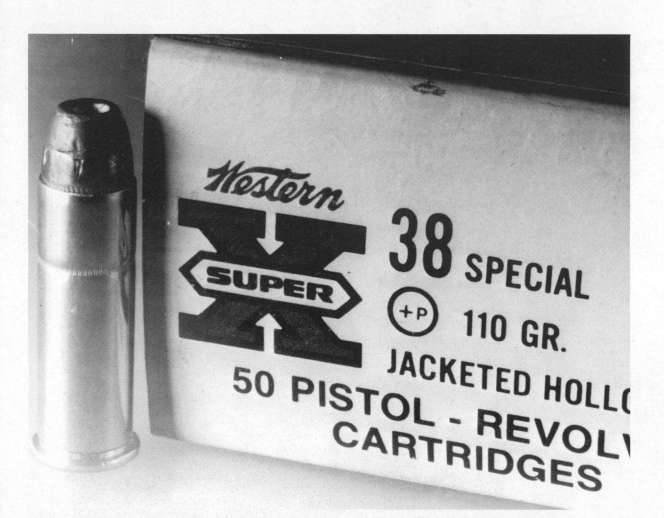

As discussed in Chapter 3, Western's Super-X loading of the .38 Special, their load number 38S6PH, with 110-grain JHP bullet, was tested by the University of Colorado for the Denver PD and its performance was rated as superior to nearly all the other loads tested. Introduced just prior to publication date, early test samples were available for inclusion here.

Comparing Paper Ballistics Of Cartridges To Actual Performance

CHOICE OF AMMUNITION is a critical decision and, at the same time, it is a highly complex one with a number of factors that must be considered. Not so long ago, the choice was much more limited, which made selection simpler, if not necessarily more satisfactory. At present, however, a bewildering variety of loads is available for most calibers of police handguns, often with little concrete information as to their comparative performance.

Sergeant Evan P. Marshall of the Detroit Police Department conducted the evaluation tests for the determination of the performance data listed in this section. In measuring velocities, he used a chronograph made by Chronograph Specialists (Box 5005, Santa Ana, California 92704). Careful comparison of velocities obtained with the CS instrument and those on other makes and types of chronographs showed uniform and accurate results. Since it is not at all unusual to encounter some amount of shot-to-shot variation in velocity for the same load out of a given gun, Marshall fired five rounds of each load to obtain the average figures given here.

Much of the credit for current interest in high-performance handgun ammunition goes to Lee Jurras, who began working with jacketed hollow-point (JHP) bullet designs in the basement of his Shelbyville, Indiana, home in the early Sixties. At first, Jurras produced and marketed only the bullets as a reloading component, and went on to organize the Super Vel Cartridge Corporation, which operated out of Shelbyville until it suspended operations in late 1974, large-ly due to difficulty in obtaining brass cartridge cases at that time. Since then, he has moved west, operating a custom pistolsmithing service as L.E. Jurras & Associates (Box 846, Roswell, New Mexico 88201).

During their decade or so of active operation in the production of high-performance handgun ammunition, Jurras and Super Vel proved beyond all doubt that handgun users and, in particular, law enforcement agencies were not completely satisfied with the capabilities of factory handgun ammunition available prior to that time. As a direct result, every major producer of handgun ammunition offers loadings today that are superior to the specifications of what might be termed pre-Jurras ammunition.

The common designation for such modern, extended-energy loads is +P, usually being incorporated on the headstamp of the cartridge case, as well as on the label of the carton in which the ammunition is packed. This serves as an indication that the load generates peak pressures in excess of those usually considered standard for a given cartridge by the Small Arms & Manufacturers Institute (SAAMI). The notice appearing on the bottom of Western Super-X ammunition, in a current +P loading, reads:

These center fire handgun cartridges are designed to deliver maximum accuracy and energy at normal shooting ranges. They are made of precision built components, assembled to rigid specifications. Non-corrosive priming will not cause rust or corrosion.

WARNING: Use only in arms in good condition de-

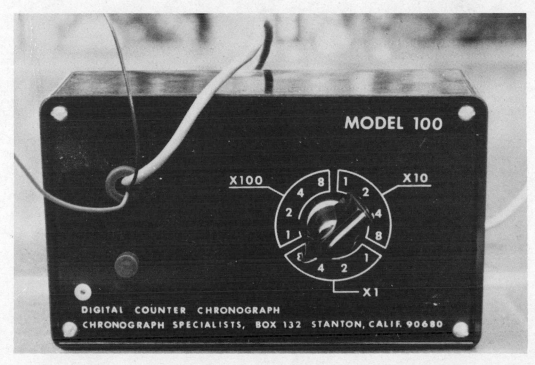

Sergeant Marshall used this Model 100 chronograph, by Chronograph Specialists, in measuring velocities of the factory ammunition covered in this test report.

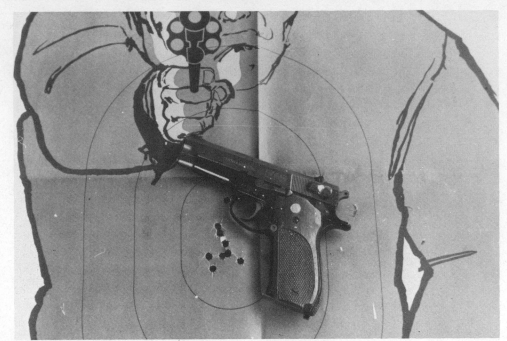

S&W's 90-grain JSP load for the 9mm showed good combat accuracy in M39 at distance of 25 yards.

Colt Lawman Mk III in .357 mag, has become a popular off-duty gun, being but slightly larger than a .38 snub.

signed and chambered by the manufacturer for this cartridge. If doubt exists, check with the gun manufacturer.

Cartridges with +P on the headstamp are loaded to higher pressures for greater velocity. Use only in arms recommended for this type of cartridge. Continuous use of +P cartridges in revolvers with aluminum frames or cylinders is not recommended.

Wear proper hearing protection. Repeated exposure to gun fire can damage hearing. Wear shooting glasses to protect eyes.

Most manufacturers of ammunition offer tables showing the velocity of their various loads. Often, these velocities are obtained by firing the ammunition in pressure barrels, usually without specifying the length of the test barrel. Considering the gap between the front of the cylinder and the rear of the barrel in revolvers, there is a natural desire to wonder if the specified velocity will be obtained when fired in a typical service revolver in which barrels rarely exceed four inches in length.

At the same time, it is important to know just how much velocity and performance will be sacrificed when the loads are fired from guns having extremely short barrels. In those calibers for which snubnose revolvers are available, tests have been made on two-inch or 2½-inch barrels, as well as on the more conventional lengths such as four-inch.

Of the several factors contributing to reliable performance, velocity tends to receive the most attention, since that is a highly relevant factor at the instant of impact with the target. It is, however, not the only factor to consider. The weight of the bullet and its capacity to expand for optimum delivery of energy likewise are of importance.

The bullet's net velocity at the instant of impact can be affected by several factors, including barrel length, amount of gap between cylinder and barrel, and the distance to the target. With the bullet's weight and velocity known, it is a simple matter to calculate the bullet's kinetic energy in foot-pounds. This is obtained by multiplying bullet velocity in feet per second (fps) times itself and dividing the product by 450,240, then multiplying the quotient times the number of grains of bullet weight.

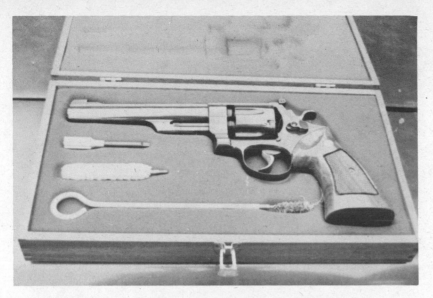

Above, not encountered commonly, the M25 S&W accepts .45 Auto Rim or ACP with half-moon clips, offering highly effective performance. Below, Marshall considers M58 S&W the best police revolver currently available for use.

Super Vel's 110-grain JHP load was the forerunner of today's high-performance factory ammunition. Its production was discontinued at the end of 1974, but most of the major ammo makers now carry loads of comparable ballistics.

As a typical example, let's find the kinetic energy for a 158-grain bullet at 1355 fps. First, we square the velocity: 1355 times 1355 equals 1,836,025. Dividing that by 450,240, we get 4.0778806 as the amount of energy for each grain of bullet weight. Multiplying that figure by 158 gives us 644.30513 foot-pounds. There is little point in carrying it beyond the decimal point and the operation is quick and simple with one of the small pocket calculators now in popular use.

As with velocity, bullet energy is by no means the sole or paramount consideration, although, like velocity, it is of considerable importance. Since energy varies in direct proportion to the velocity squared, doubling the velocity quadruples the energy and so on. Unless a projectile possesses substantial velocity, its kinetic energy will be low and, lacking energy, it can have no more than limited effect upon the target.

The chief criterion used in selecting the loads listed here was their ready availability to the typical police officer, as of early 1976. The test loads were purchased from open stock in retail outlets, which assured representative performance. There are or have been various loads for which remarkable properties have been claimed, which were not tested for the good and sufficient reason that they are not — presently, at least — readily available to the typical police officer, either as an individual or through departmental purchase channels.

All of the factory loads tested and listed in the accompanying tables proved completely reliable as to ignition and extraction. Occasional problems were encountered in reliable feeding of autoloading pistols. The Smith & Wesson Model 39-2, used in testing 9mm Luger loads, gave occasional stoppages with some of the factory loads. The same loads, it should be noted, functioned flawlessly through a Browning Hi-Power and a 9mm Star. The officer carrying an autoloading pistol should take pains to fire sufficient quantities of the load he proposes to carry on duty, so as to be as certain as possible of its functional reliability.

Here Are Tested
Performance Figures On Several Types Of Factory Ammunition, As Measured In Typical Guns Through A Chronograph!

VELOCITY TESTS — REVOLVERS

.38 Special

Test Guns:
2" Colt Detective Special
4" Smith & Wesson Model 10

Maker	Bullet Weight/Type	2" Velocity	2" Energy	4" Velocity	4" Energy
Remington		fps	ft-lbs	fps	ft-lbs
	95-gr JHP	1002	212	1072	242
	125-gr JHP	924	237	1089	327
	158-gr RNL	643	145	778	212
	158-gr RNL-HV	822	237	901	285
Winchester					
	110-gr JHP	967	228	1109	300
	158-gr SWC	853	255	978	336
	158-gr LHP	862	261	1023	367
Smith & Wesson					
	125-gr JHP	932	241	1084	326
	158-gr LHP	718	181	877	270
Speer					
	110-gr JHP	978	234	1109	300
	125-gr JHP	945	248	1154	370
	140-gr JHP	897	250	1086	367
	158-gr JSP	732	188	899	284
	158-gr SWC	759	202	829	241

.357 Magnum

Test Guns:
2½" Smith & Wesson Model 19
4" Colt Python

Maker	Bullet Weight/Type	2½" Velocity	2½" Energy	4" Velocity	4" Energy
Remington		fps	ft-lbs	fps	ft-lbs
	125-gr JHP	1267	446	1412	554
	158-gr SWC	1032	374	1152	466
	158-gr JHP	1126	445	1246	545
Winchester					
	110-gr JHP	1199	351	1387	470
	158-gr SWC	1143	458	1305	598
	158-gr JHP	1165	476	1265	561

Speer

	Bullet Weight/Type	Velocity	Energy	Velocity	Energy
	110-gr JHP	1187	344	1367	457
	125-gr JHP	1212	408	1394	540
	140-gr JHP	1141	405	1283	512
	158-gr JSP	1045	383	1156	469

Smith & Wesson

	110-gr JHP	1046	267	1152	324
	125-gr JHP	1011	284	1078	323
	158-gr JHP	1067	400	1202	507

.41 Magnum

Test Gun: 4" Smith & Wesson Model 58

Maker	Bullet Weight/Type	4" Velocity	4" Energy
Remington		fps	ft-lbs
	210-gr SWC	929	403
	210-gr JSP	1201	673

.44 Special

Test Gun: 3" Charter Arms Bulldog

Maker	Bullet Weight/Type	3" Velocity	3" Energy
Winchester		fps	ft-lbs
	246-gr RNL	693	262

.44 Magnum

Test Gun: 4" Smith & Wesson Model 29

Maker	Bullet Weight/Type	4" Velocity	4" Energy
Winchester			
	240-gr SWC	1195	764
Speer			
	200-gr JHP	1302	753
	240-gr JSP	1198	765
Remington			
	240-gr JHP	1223	797

VELOCITY TESTS — PISTOLS

9mm

Test Gun: 4" Smith & Wesson Model 39-2

Maker	Bullet Weight/Type	4" Velocity	4" Energy
Smith & Wesson		fps	ft-lbs
	90-gr JSP	1223	299
	115-gr JHP	1107	313
Speer			
	100-gr JHP	1286	367
	125-gr JSP	1104	338
Remington			
	115-gr JHP	1201	368
Norma			
	115-gr JHP	1112	316
Winchester			
	100-gr JHP	1299	375

.38 Super

Test Gun:	4½" Colt Commander		
Maker	**Bullet Weight/Type**	**4½" Velocity**	**4½" Energy**
Winchester		fps	ft-lbs
	130-gr FMJ	1156	386

.45 ACP

Test Gun:	4½" Colt Combat Commander		
Maker	**Bullet Weight/Type**	**4½" Velocity**	**4½" Energy**
Winchester		fps	ft-lbs
	230-gr FMJ	834	355
Remington			
	185-gr JHP	916	345
Speer			
	200-gr JHP	867	334

Left, Colt's .45 auto design has seen 65 years of use, but is far from being ready to retire. It's shown here in the lightweight Commander version with 4¼" barrel. Below, Charter Arms' .44 Special Bulldog is compact but offers outstanding stopping power for its size and weight.

Evaluation Of A Bullet's Expansion Is Tough Under Any But Combat Circumstances!

Marshall considers Winchester-Western's 158-grain LHP and 110-grain JHP loads to be two of the best currently available for the .38 Special, due to excellent expansion.

Long considered the traditional police load, the .38 Special in standard velocity, with 158-grain lead round-nose bullet is notorious for poor stopping power.

A BULLET'S VELOCITY is an important factor, but its performance upon striking the intended target is of even greater importance. Given two bullets of the same diameter, weight and velocity, the one demonstrating the greatest tendency to expand will be the most effective.

The obvious problem in evaluating this quality lies in the choice of the test medium. Many materials — such as ballistic gelatine and Duxseal — have been used, but they are not identical to the composition of the human body.

In conducting the tests to obtain the data listed here, Sgt. Evan Marshall of the Detroit, Michigan, Police Department used clean, dry sand, choosing this medium for a number of reasons. Since it is readily available, readers will be able to conduct their own tests of loads not yet released at the time of this book's publication, thereby affording a positive comparison to existing loads. Furthermore, sand is inexpensive; it can be used over and over and its consistency remains unchanged. The last consideration is a major problem in the use of clay or Duxseal, since minor varia-

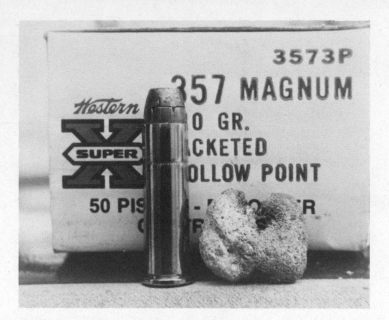

W-W's .357 magnum 110-grain JHP load offers excellent expansion for those who favor light-bullet loads in the .357 magnum, although Marshall's experience favors heavier slugs and tends to rate .357 mag as little above marginal.

R-P's .41 magnum JSP load offers impressive expansion but Marshall feels their lead SWC load is quite adequate for handling all but the most exceptional police combats.

Speer's 125-grain JHP load for the .38 Special offers good performance in this cartridge. The same bullet weight in a JSP version is the issue load of Michigan State Police.

tions in temperature of the medium have a considerable effect upon its reaction to impact.

While sand offers somewhat more resistance than flesh and, thus, produces a greater degree of expansion, it serves as a good indicator of expansion performance and provides a realistic comparison between one bullet design and others. If a bullet won't expand in sand, it is justified to assume its performance in tissue will be unsatisfactory, as well.

As a general rule, it is preferable that a bullet expand without excessive loss of weight, thereby assuring adequate potential for penetration. Sgt. Marshall recalls one episode in which an armed felon was struck six times with 110-grain hollow-point loads from a .357 magnum. All six bullets disintegrated on impact and did not have the desired effect of disabling the felon, who continued to return fire until struck by a load of 00 buckshot from a police shotgun. The recovered bullets had fragmented after no more than shallow penetration.

Marshall's experience indicates a direct correlation between a bullet's ability to expand reliably in sand without undue loss of weight and its demonstrated effectiveness in combat situations.

Speer 158-grain JSP is reliable in its expansion, despite relatively low velocity. Superior bullet construction is the key to its outstanding performance traits.

While not in wide favor, Marshall considers the .44 magnum as potentially a good police cartridge, provided requisite skill is maintained through practice. W-W's 240-grain SWC displays typcial performance of round.

W-W's 158-grain JHP load for the .357 mag offers reliable expansion from 4" barrel and is becoming the issue load of a growing number of departments.

As to the perennial controversy between proponents of the small-diameter, high-velocity, expanding bullet versus the heavier, large caliber bullets, Sgt. Marshall's experience leads him to prefer the larger diameters. For a period of fifteen months, Marshall was assigned to a unit responsible for investigating all shootings by and of police officers. During that entire time, Marshall did not encounter a single instance in which a small-bore weapon — .38, .357 or 9mm — stopped its intended target with one shot, regardless of the type of bullets used. In several incidents, the victim died later, but was not stopped by a single shot at the time of shooting.

The larger bullet diameters — .41, .44 and .45 — show a better stopping ability. The objection most frequently made against the larger calibers is that the typical officer has difficulty achieving accuracy with them, as compared to the smaller bores.

It should be borne in mind that the frontal area of a bullet varies in direct proportion to the square of the radius; that is, one-half of its diameter. Thus, what may seem a relatively small increase in diameter will result in a somewhat greater amount of area.

EXPANSION TESTS

.38 Special

Test Guns: 2" Colt Detective Special
4" Smith & Wesson Model 10

Maker	Bullet Weight/Type	2"	4"	Performance
		(inch)	(inch)	
Remington	95-gr JHP	.509	.604	good
	125-gr JHP	.525	.609	good
	158-gr RNL	.358	.358	poor
	158-gr RNL-HV	.358	.445	fair
Winchester	110-gr JHP	.535	.623	excellent
	158-gr SWC	.378	.526	good
	158-gr LHP	.539	.631	excellent
Smith & Wesson	125-gr JHP	.510	.612	good
	158-gr LHP	.516	.619	good
Speer	110-gr JHP	.481	.523	good
	125-gr JHP	.522	.609	excellent
	140-gr JHP	.501	.546	good
	158-gr JSP	.522	.578	excellent
	158-gr SWC	.399	.498	good

.357 Magnum

Test Guns: 2½" Smith & Wesson
Model 19 and 4" Colt Python

Maker	Bullet Weight/Type	2½"	4"	Performance
		(inch)	(inch)	
Remington	125-gr JHP	.692	.806	excellent
	158-gr SWC	.512	.603	fair
	158-gr JHP	.586	.661	good
Winchester	110-gr JHP	.679	.810	excellent
	158-gr SWC	.546	.612	good
	158-gr JHP	.648	.724	excellent
Speer	110-gr JHP	.659	.742	excellent
	125-gr JHP	.672	.755	excellent
	140-gr JHP	.644	.760	excellent
	158-gr JSP	.514	.581	good
Smith & Wesson	110-gr JHP	.529	.632	fair
	125-gr JHP	.519	.623	fair
	158-gr JHP	.546	.647	good

.41 Magnum

Test Gun: 4" Smith & Wesson Model 58

Maker	Bullet Weight/Type	4"	Performance
		(inch)	
Remington	210-gr SWC	.669	excellent
	210-gr JSP	.758	excellent

.44 Special

Test Gun: 3" Charter Arms Bulldog

Maker	Bullet Weight/Type	3"	Performance
		(inch)	
Winchester	240-gr RNL	none	poor

.44 Magnum

Test Gun: **4" Smith & Wesson Model 29**

Maker	Bullet Weight/Type	4" (inch)	Performance
Winchester	240-gr SWC	.752	excellent
Speer	200-gr JHP	.839	excellent
	240-gr JSP	.723	very good
Remington	240-gr JHP	.853	excellent

9mm

Test Gun: **4" Smith & Wesson Model 39-2**

Maker	Bullet Weight/Type	4" (inch)	Performance
Smith & Wesson	90-gr JSP	.609	good
	115-gr JHP	.541	good
Speer	100-gr JHP	.619	good
	125-gr JSP	.539	good
Remington	115-gr JHP	.499	fair
Norma	115-gr JHP	.601	good
Winchester	100-gr JHP	.662	excellent

.38 Super

Test Gun: **4½" Colt Commander**

Maker	Bullet Weight/Type	4½" (inch)	Performance
Winchester	130-gr FMJ	.417	fair

.45 ACP

Test Gun: **4½" Colt Combat Commander**

Maker	Bullet Weight/Type	4½" (inch)	Performance
Winchester	230-gr FMJ	none	poor
Remington	185-gr JHP	none	poor
Speer	200-gr JHP	.816	excellent

JHP — Jacketed Hollow-Point

JSP — Jacketed Soft-Point

RNL — Round-Nose Lead

RNL-HV — Round-Nose Lead, High Velocity

SWC — Semi-Wadcutter (lead)

FMJ — Full Metal Jacket

LHP — Lead Hollow-Point

NOTES ON RELOADING

Rockchucker press, by RCBS, is suitable for small departments or individual use. Here, it carries Pacific die for depriming and case mouth expansion. Note that prices in this section are approximate and are subject to change.

That Empty, Fired Cartridge Case Can Be Thrown Away — Wasting Money — Or It Can Continue Its Career, On And On!

Chapter 14

Reloading lets you do a lot more shooting for the ammunition allotment but economy isn't the sole motive. Rolling you own lets you tailor loads to get best accuracy for a given gun.

Mention RELOADS to the shooter who's never reloaded and you're apt to get any of several assorted negative reactions. Chances are, he knows someone who has had some sort of disillusioning experience with reloads — perhaps a damaged gun or a batch of loads that shot poorly, if at all. Many have the belief that the only reason for reloading is to cut corners in hopes of saving pennies.

Too, many shooters have the idea that there is something fearsomely complicated and formidable about the operations connected with reloading. As it turns out, this is not necessarily true. Actually, it's a fairly simple, straight forward mechanical process and, with a reasonable application of attention, common sense and following directions, reloading can be carried out with much satisfaction and few, if any problems.

Let's start by clearing up one minor point of confusion. We hear mentions of reloading and of handloading and the difference puzzles many people. You can buy empty brass cartridge cases which have never been loaded or fired before and, if you install primer, powder charge and bullet into such a virgin case, you will have assembled a "handload."

Fire a factory cartridge — in a center fire caliber such as the .38 Special, since the operation is impractical for rimfire cases such as the .22 long rifle — and take the empty cartridge case, putting it through the basic steps and, by the time it's ready to fire again, you will have assembled a "reload." Since you did it more or less by hand, using manually operated equipment, it would be correct to call it a handload if you wished. Actually, the two terms are pretty much interchangeable to any but the most fanatical hair-splitters.

If you went out and purchased a carton of fifty empty, brand-new cartridge cases, you became aware of one thing: The brass case is not cheap. In most calibers, the brass case is the most expensive single component of the loaded cartridge.

Therefore, throwing away your empty, center fire cartridge cases, once you've fired them, is not too different from throwing away a handful of shiny new dimes. Give or take the odd penny, depending on the caliber, that's about the going price for brand-new, virgin cartridge cases in the handgun calibers.

A further boggle, often put forward to explain reluctance to become involved with the reloading operation is that you need a lot of expensive equipment and materials in order to get started. Again: not necessarily true!

There long has been a demand for inexpensive kits of reloading equipment for the potential reloader who'd like to give it a try, though he's not sure if he can do it or if he'll find it sufficiently worthwhile to continue. Recognizing this substantial area of the market, several manufacturers have designed equipment which performs adequately

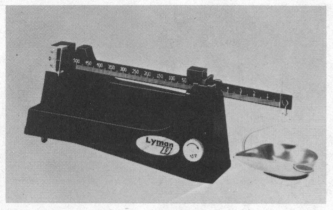

Reloaders' scales are highly sensitive instruments, needed for accurate check of powder charge and bullet weights.

and is priced quite modestly.

While the most common device used in reloading is the bench-mounted reloading press, there are several systems designed to operate without the need of the press. Examples would include the Lee Loader kits, the Lyman No. 310 tong tool and the Pacific Pakit.

The Lee Loader kit is one of the lowest in cost and, at the same time, is one of the most complete. Priced at $9.95 for the kit, offered in most calibers and gauges of handguns, rifles and shotguns, it includes a dipper-type powder measure and full, easy-to-follow instructions so that about all of the extra equipment needed is the assortment of components: primers, powder and bullets for handguns or rifles; primers, powder, wads and shot for shotgun reloading.

If you figure $1 for a pack of one hundred primers, $3-4 for a can of powder and $2-5 for a carton of one hundred bullets, that about covers the cost of your starter set of components. Total outlay: around $20 for enough equipment and supplies to reload your first one hundred rounds and half of the investment is non-expendable.

You may find that it doesn't cost that much, depending upon the competitive spirit prevailing in your source of supply, but we've tried to steer by the high side of the estimates in this discussion. The can of powder, in handgun calibers, will load a lot more than one hundred rounds so that your second hundred will cost even less. Yes, it's possible to spend more respectable sums of money upon equip-

ment for reloading and you may choose to do so after sampling the activity. But you should be able to get your feet wet for a $20 bill and stand a fair chance of getting some change back.

Let's trace the steps of the reloading operation now, selecting that evergreen favorite, the .38 Special as our demonstration caliber and discussing conventional reloading dies and presses in the process.

The neck of a properly loaded round of .38 Special grips the base of the bullet fairly tightly. The chamber of the revolver is slightly larger in diameter, by a few thousandths of an inch, than the outside diameter of the cartridge. This is intentional. It permits the neck of the case to expand away from the base of the bullet under the pressure of the powder gases, releasing the bullet for its passage up the barrel.

Since brass is no more than slightly elastic, the case tends to remain somewhat oversized in diameter after

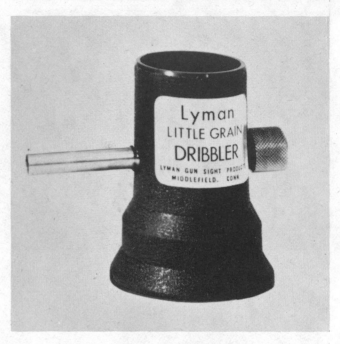

Powder dribblers are helpful in making up weighed charges, being used for adding the last few granules to balance the pan.

firing. Usually, you can insert the base of a new bullet easily into the neck of the fired case as it's a rather loose fit.

Accordingly, one of the first steps in reloading is to resize the cartridge case down to a suitable diameter so that it will grip the base of the next bullet properly. Since the thickness of the brass at the neck of the cartridge case will show some slight variation from one case to the next, the usual procedure is to size it back down a bit smaller than the intended final dimension. This is followed by expanding the neck by introducing an expanding plug of the desired diameter into it for a short distance. Only by so doing it is readily possible to have all of the cases emerge with the ideal inside diameter at the neck.

The resizing die consists of a round piece of heat-treated steel, threaded on the outside for inserting into the top of the loading press — the usual thread is seven-eighths-inch diameter, 14 threads to the inch — with a precision-reamed

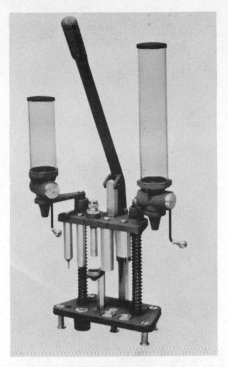

Two-cavity bullet mould
by Lachmiller is opened up to
show details of construction.

Lachmiller shotshell reloader
has attached powder, shot
measures on upper assembly.

hole up through the center. When the case is shoved up into the hole in the center of the die by operating the press, the brass is squeezed down to the intended, smaller diameter.

Sometimes, only the first half inch or so of the case is sized, this being termed neck-sizing. More customarily, resizing is carried as far down the case as possible: full-length resizing.

With standard steel reloading dies, it is extremely important to apply small amounts of a suitable lubricant to

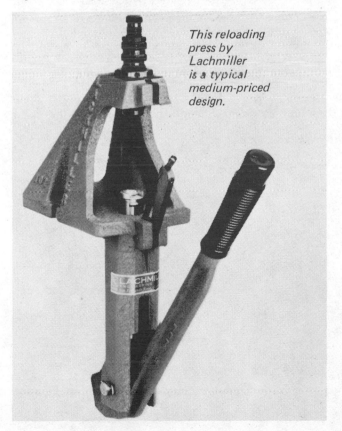

This reloading press by Lachmiller is a typical medium-priced design.

the outside of the case walls before resizing. If this step is neglected, dirt, grit and foreign material soon will imbed in the metal of the die, causing deep scratches to appear in the brass of the cases during sizing. This weakens the case and shortens the number of times it can be reloaded before being discarded.

In addition to the standard, heat-treated steel resizing die, there is a somewhat more elaborate type which has a small ring-shaped insert of tungsten carbide cemented into its lower end. Since tungsten carbide is one of the hardest substances known — second only to the diamond — this eliminates the problem of grit imbedding in the sizing ring and bypasses the need for lubricating the cases. This effects a double saving of time and labor: You don't have to apply lube to the cases before sizing and you don't have to remove it afterwards.

Tungsten carbide or t-c resizing dies are available for most of the straight-sided cases such as the .38 Special and the .357 magnum case can be reloaded with the same die used with the .38 Special. In the same manner, you can resize .44 Special brass with .44 magnum die or vice versa. Most .38 Special dies seem to work well with the .380 auto case, though you need a different sizing die for the .38 Super and the last can be used for the .38 S&W case. Price of the t-c resizing die will run from about $13 each to as much as $25, depending on the manufacturer. Price of a standard steel resizing die will be on the order of $6-8 each.

One manufacturer produces t-c resizing dies for tapered cases such as the 9mm Luger or the .30 M-1 carbine case. Since these require a much longer insert of carbide, the price is substantially higher.

Depending upon the manufacturer of the reloading dies, either the resizing die or the neck-expanding die will be equipped with a depriming pin which forces out the old primer. Here, it should be noted that there are two basic priming systems in use throughout the world, the Boxer and the Berdan. Most center fire cartridges made for sale in the USA are Boxer-primed and it is this type of case which standard reloading equipment is designed to handle.

The Berdan-primed case can be identified easily by the presence of two small flash-holes extending from the primer pocket into the powder space. These are seen easily when looking down into the case neck under good light. The Boxer-primed case has a single flash hole, somewhat larger in diameter, in the center of the case head when inspected from the mouth.

The Berdan priming system is used most widely by European ammunition manufacturers, including Great Britain. It is possible to reload Berdan-primed cases, but it entails considerably greater difficulty as well as supplies of the fresh Berdan primers. This is a minor problem in Europe, since reloading is by no means as popular and widely practiced there.

The decapping pin will be held to the end of a rod threaded into the sizer or expander die, usually by means of a collet arrangement. Check to be sure that this is well tightened before commencing to reload and make it a habit to check the solidity of the decapping pin periodically as you process the cases. It is not uncommon for the rod to work loose and be broken if its tip misses the flash hole.

When reloading straight-sided handgun cases, it is common for the expander plug to have a small flared area which bells the case neck slightly at the top of the expanding stroke. The expander stem can be turned up or down in the press head to adjust the amount of bell or flare given to the neck. You need a little flare, for ease of starting the bullet base into the neck later and to prevent shaving of metal from the side of the bullet. Avoid excessive belling of the case neck as this stretches the brass, making it brittle and it also causes difficulty in starting the case neck back up into the bullet-seating die at a later stage of the operation.

A good way to check the amount of neck-flare on the case after the expanding process is to grasp the head with the fingers of one hand and pull the neck between the thumb and fingers of the other hand. The amount of bell should be barely visible, though detectable to the touch when checked in this manner.

Usually primers are supplied in packs of one hundred and cartons of one thousand. It is a sound safety practice to keep them in the containers until used. Do not dump out a large number, loose in a container as this poses some hazard if one or more should be detonated accidentally. There is a lot of power in a modern small arms primer and they

Lachmiller powder measures use inserts to regulate weight of powder dispensed.

deserve to be treated with caution and respect. Do not subject them to intensive heat, nor to large amounts of jarring force. Small amounts of oil will deactivate the priming compound, so do not handle primers with oily fingers or allow case lubes or similar materials down into the interior of the case. Oils likewise will deactivate smokeless powder.

There are many methods and techniques for seating the primer and the one you're apt to use will depend somewhat

Set-up for weighing powder charges: Majority of charge is scooped from can with dipper, balance from trickler.

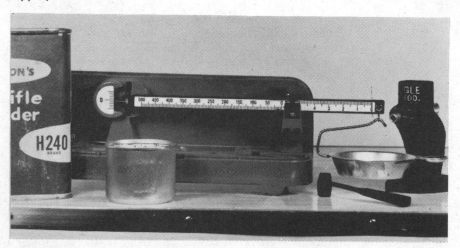

Winchester 630-P powder ignites more uniformly with magnum primers.

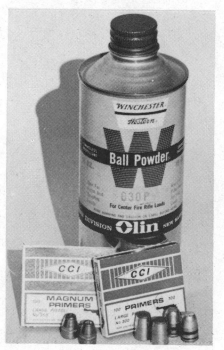

Priming press by Lachmiller easily converts to any caliber or size of primer.

An unmistakeable sign of excessively high pressure, primer pocket of case at left is expanded far beyond its normal diameter.

Several primer-seating defects can be caught by final inspection. Defective gun put off-center dent in center primer.

upon the make and type of loading press or other equipment you're using.

Primers are made in four basic types for handgun and rifle reloading: small pistol, small rifle, large pistol and large rifle. The small pistol and small rifle are of the same diameter — .175-inch — as are the large pistol and rifle types, which measure .210-inch in diameter. In general, the two rifle types measure slightly longer, front to back, so that they would protrude above the rear surface of the case head if seated fully in the primer pocket of a pistol case accepting the given diameter.

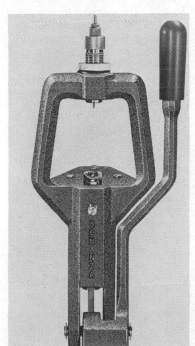

This loading press, by Bonanza will produce enough reloaded ammo to fill the needs of an individual shooter or of a small department.

Rifle primers are designed to withstand higher pressures and, as a result, have primer cups of thicker, tougher metal. Handguns deliver a comparatively light blow from their hammers and/or firing pins. Often the blow from a handgun firing pin is not strong enough to assure reliable ignition of a rifle-type primer. In addition, the pellet of explosive priming compound develops more force in the rifle-type primer and this would tend toward higher pressures if a rifle-type primer were substituted in reloading handgun cartridges. For these reasons, always use the proper type and diameter of primer when reloading.

Some manufacturers of primers offer two different versions — standard and magnum — of each of the four basic types and sizes of primers just listed. The magnum versions are designed to provide better, more uniform ignition with certain powders that tend to ignite with greater difficulty, by generating a spark or flash that is longer in duration. Such hard-to-light powders include the spherical or ball powders such as Hodgdon's H-110 or Winchester's 630-P. When using easily ignited powders such as Hercules' Bullseye and Unique or Hodgdon's TopMark, magnum primers offer no advantage and there is no sound reason to use them.

Moderation is the key in proper primer seating. If you do not seat them with enough force, the dome may protrude from the head of the cartridge and this will cause the cylinder of a revolver to hang up when that load rotates into firing position. If you use too much force, the primer will be seated deeply enough, but the primer cup will be distorted and the pellet of priming compound may be broken. In the latter example, misfires may result or, more rarely, it may cause a hang-fire: a noticeable delay between pulling the trigger and discharge of the bullet.

While there are devices such as primer micrometers on the market, designed to measure the distance the primer cup is below or above the surface of the case head, it is not necessary to use such tools in ordinary reloading. Just seat the primers with an easy, controlled amount of pressure so

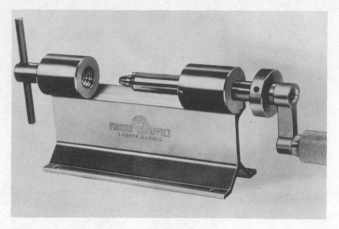

Forster-Appelt case trimmer restores stretched cases to their original length and can be used for other operations too.

Bonanza's fixed rotor powder measure is for pistol charges. Rotors are available for common run of Bullseye charges.

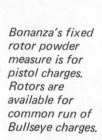

that you can feel the moment when the primer gets to the bottom of the pocket.

Inspection is an important step in reloading, particularly if the cases have been loaded a large number of times. Sooner or later, small, lengthwise cracks will appear in the case necks. This is caused by failure of the brass in being sized down and expanded back up, belled and crimped. The number of firings that can be expected will depend to some extent upon the make and type of case.

You can make a casual inspection of the fired cases at the time when first picked up in preparation for resizing and this is a good idea since any obvious defects can indicate rejection at that time. At the same time, continue to keep an eye on the condition of each case as you carry them through the various steps of the operation. Correct seating of the primer should be verified by additional inspection, following completion of that step. Sometimes you may detect primers that have been seated backwards — open-side-out — or sideways and such cases should be set aside for rejection or salvage at a later time.

Most reloaders prefer not to run the risk of expelling an incorrectly seated live primer on grounds that it could be

Some of the accessories available for use with the Forster-Appelt case trimmer: a primer pocket chamfering tool, universal hollow-pointer and bullet nose trimmer.

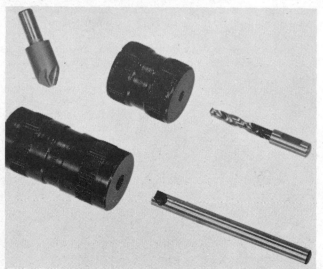

set off by the decapping pin. If you decide to salvage the case by removal of the primer, suitable precautions should be taken to guard against injury if it should detonate in the process.

There are two basic approaches to reloading: Starting with a single fired cartridge case and taking it through all of the steps of the operation to end up with a loaded round, ready to shoot. Alternatively, you can start with a given quantity of fired cases and put each of them through the particular operation before going on the next step.

The second technique is the one employed most customarily. With the typical reloading press that positions one loading die at a time, it would take up too much time to change dies for each cartridge case. The all-steps-at-once method can be followed with turret-top presses where it takes but little extra time to turn from one die to the next.

With all of the cases resized, deprimed, mouth-belled and re-primed, suitably inspected along the way, we are ready to add the powder charge. Initially, the given make and type of powder, as well as the weight of the charge, should be selected from one of the several reloading manuals, taking care not to exceed the recommended charge weights for that particular powder.

There are a great many different makes and types of powder available to the reloader, each intended for a fairly specialized range of application. Powders are by no means interchangeable with each other. For any particular caliber of cartridge and weight of bullet, there are specified charge weights for the more suitable makes and types of powder. These are listed in the reloading manuals and the specifications should be followed carefully, never exceeded.

Plain common sense can keep you out of trouble here. Buy your powder in the manufacturer's original can, from a trustworthy source and keep it in that container till it's used up. Avoid buying powder in bulk, no matter how attractive a bargain it may seem to be. Never use empty powder cans for storing powders of a different type than shown on the label. Never leave quantities of powder in a powder measure between reloading sessions.

The reasoning behind that last precaution is at least twofold: Many of the powders used in reloading pistol car-

Here the Forster-Appelt trimmer has been set up for cutting cavities in bullet noses with hollow-pointer.

Speer/DWM ammunition is packed in tough plastic boxes which can be used over and over to hold reload ammo.

Super Vel 190-grain JHP bullets are offered as a reloading component, permitting the duplication of factory load performance.

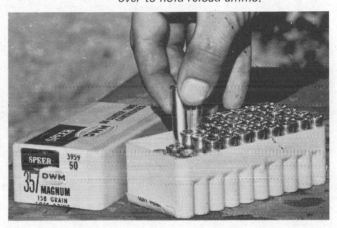

tridges are of the "double-base" type, that is, they contain a percentage of nitroglycerine in addition to the usual nitrocellulose. If a double-base powder is left in the powder measure for extended intervals, the nitroglycerine in the powder usually will attack the plastic of the reservoir tube, softening the plastic and making it opaque. Further, the next time you come to use the powder measure, it will be difficult to tell, for certain, the kind of powder remaining in the reservoir.

It is extremely difficult, nearly impossible, to identify a given make and type of powder by visual examination alone. Therefore, if you encounter a quantity of powder outside its original container and do not know for sure what kind it is, the only safe procedure is to discard it — flushing down a toilet is suggested as a safe disposal technique — because powder is much less expensive than the troubles that can turn up from mis-identification of it!

There are several devices for measuring powder and the most accurate and reliable is the powder scale. Most makers of reloading equipment offer one or more models of powder scale, with typical prices ranging from $10 to $25. Such instruments are extremely precise and sensitive, capable of detecting differences in weight of as little as one-tenth of one grain — 1/70,000th of a pound! — and typical reloader's scales offer weighing capacities from zero to 350 or 500 grains, permitting their use for checking bullet weight as well.

Another common item of reloading equipment is the adjustable rotary powder measure, also offered in the lines of most reloading equipment manufacturers. Since the weight of the powder charge may range from as little as 2.0 grains in handguns to as much as 75.0 grains or more in large rifle calibers, many rotary powder measures are made so as to offer sensitive accuracy in metering light charges at the expense of large-charge capacity.

Adjustability is afforded by means of a closely fitted plunger which can be moved back and forth in a cylindrical cavity by means of screw threads and locked in place by a lock ring. The cavity diameter governs the sensitivity of the measure for precise delivery of uniform, lightweight charges.

As an example, the RCBS Uniflow powder measure is offered with two different drum assemblies. One is intended for measuring relatively heavy charges of rifle powder and has a cavity that is larger in diameter. The second drum assembly, termed the firm's "benchrest" drum, has a cavity smaller in diameter but with limited maximum capacity. This and similar designs afford better sensitivity and uniformity in the lighter charge weights typical of handgun reloading.

Slightly less flexible but offering time-saving convenience is the fixed-rotor powder measure, as made by Bonanza, Pacific and Penguin-Lachmiller. These have a small-diameter, horizontal rotor which removes for substitution by loosening a locking screw. A series of interchangeable rotors offer a choice of charge weights in the range popular in handgun cartridge reloading. Usually, the rotor is stamped or etched on its end with a number corresponding to the number of grains of Hercules Bullseye powder that it

Browning is one of newest entries in the field of factory loads. Foam plastic liner can be used for reloads.

Though labeled for shotguns, Norma 2010 and 2020 can be used in handgun reloads if reliable load data is followed.

will throw.

Fixed-rotor measures tend to be lower in price than the adjustable variety and you can purchase only the rotors which deliver a charge called for by the manuals for a caliber and bullet-weight combination which you wish to reload. Additional rotors can be purchased separately as they become needed.

While most of the fixed-rotor measures are rated for but a single powder — usually it's Hercules Bullseye — if you have a powder scale, it is possible and practical to check the drop weight with other small-granule pistol powders, recording this data on a chart for future reference. Thus, for example, non-adjustable measures can be used with comparable powders such as Hodgdon's TopMark, Winchester 230-P, Alcan AL-5, Norma N-1010 and so on.

If the charged cases are "block-checked" before seating the bullet, it is likewise practical to use fixed-rotor measures in dispensing the slower-burning powders such as Hercules 2400 by depositing two or even three drops of powder into each case. Needless to say, it is necessary to verify the actual weight of the combined charges so dropped and be sure that it conforms to the charge weight specified in a reloading manual.

Reloading Can Be Performed Over A Broad Range Of Elaborateness And Cash Outlay. Here Are Some Examples Across The Board!

This Lyman hollow-base bullet mould has been opened up to show manner in which base punch fits into place. It's removed after bullet solidifies. Hollow-point types are closely similar to this in design.

The Pacific Mesur-Kit is an inexpensive and adjustable powder measuring system designed for use with the Pacific Pakit, but adaptable for other reloaders as well.

Here are examples of defective cases that should be caught and rejected before being reloaded.

If you are performing each operation separately on all of the cases being reloaded before going on to the next step, it is a simple and valuable procedure to place all of the cases, mouth-up, in a loading block, either before or after depositing the powder charge in each. Then, under good light, run your eyes up and down the lines of charged cases to make certain that each case has powder in it to the same level as the rest. This inspection step will prevent the accidental loading of a cartridge with a missing powder charge or a double powder charge. A missing charge is almost as bad as a double charge, since it will lodge the bullet in the barrel and, in rapid, double action fire, there is danger that a second round — containing the normal amount of powder — may be fired without noticing that the dud round did not deliver the customary report and recoil. Firing a normal round, with a bullet lodged in the barrel will almost certainly damage the barrel and may cause injury.

Many reloaders prefer the one-step-at-a-time method over the all-operations-at-once technique because there remains a faint possibility that the powder charge may not be added in the latter system. Only by visually inspecting each powder charge in each case before seating the bullets can you be absolutely certain that all charges are present and uniform.

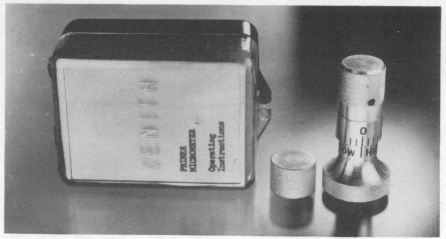

Zenith primer micrometer measures distance of primer above or below the surface of the case head with precision.

As discussed in text, case mouth at right has been flared or belled slightly to facilitate bullet seating.

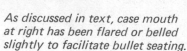

Taper crimping dies, as left and center, extend number of times a case can be reloaded. Die at right is a 45 ACP t-c type by RCBS.

If the case mouths have been given the correct amount of flare or belling, it should be easy to start the base of the bullet into the mouth of each case as the charged cases are positioned in the loading block. Then, with the seating die correctly positioned in the press and adjusted, it becomes a speedy process to pick up the charged cases from the loading block, with the bullets seated in the case mouths, and run them through the press one last time to seat the bullets.

This pre-supposes that it is feasible to seat the bullet and crimp the case neck, all at one stroke. This may not always be desirable. Some bullets have a crimping groove that is narrow or shallow or both. In such designs, if the neck is turned inward by the crimping ledge at the same time the bullet is being seated the last fraction of an inch, some metal will be gouged from the sides of the bullet and this contributes to inaccuracy, sometimes to bore fouling, as well.

The ideal seating technique — time and inclination permitting — is to seat the bullets as one operation and then to crimp the case necks as the final step. Some sets of reloading dies for handgun calibers have four dies: resizer, expander, bullet seater and neck crimper. Decapping, as has been noted, is performed simultaneously with either the resizing or the expanding operation.

Even with the conventional three-die set, in which the third die is intended to perform both the bullet seating and the neck crimping, it is an easy, simple matter to split the operation into two steps.

The body of the die is turned upward in the loading press until the case necks are not crimped at the top of the stroke. Then the seating stem is adjusted downward until the bullets are seated to the correct depth and all of the charged cases with bullets started by hand into the necks are run through the press to seat the bullets to the correct final depth. Following this, the seating stem is backed upward and the die body is turned downward until the desired amount of mouth crimp is applied to the case and the loads are fed through the press one final time.

Carbide Die Company, Box 226, Covina, California, makes a Lifetyme carbide die for the 9mm at a little over $40.

All of which carries the series of procedures to completion, starting with a fired case and concluding with one that is completely reloaded and ready to fire again. However, there is one final step that is neglected by many reloaders and that is the packaging and identification of the given load. Unless you have reached that uncomplicated point at which all of your reloads carry the identical bullet and powder charge for a given caliber, proper identification of reloads by listing the relevant load data is an urgent necessity.

It is a frustrating experience to lose track of the recipe

A typical three-die set, by C-H, has sizer, expander-decapper and seating die.

Powder and bullet scale by C-H has 450-grain capacity.

Powder funnel and trickler by C-H: base of latter can be filled with shot and capped for steadiness.

One way to record data used in making up a batch of reloads: Information is jotted on back of an old calling card, dropped in bag.

used in reloading a given batch of ammunition: particularly if it turns out to be uncommonly accurate. If you dislike the routine of bookkeeping, try jotting the pertinent data in a small, spiral-bound notebook, kept on the bench, entering the date of loading with the other data. The loads can be dumped into any sort of suitable container — a paper bag, one of the plastic bags which are supplied in rolls, to be torn off one at a time, or any container which will hold the loads until fired — then drop in a slip of paper with the date of loading on it and it becomes an easy matter to check back to that date in the notebook for a full rundown

on the recipe involved. If you load more than one batch of ammo on a given day, merely differentiate by a letter of the alphabet after the date: 6-10-73-A, 6-10-73-B and so on.

Up to this point, we have assumed that the bullet were purchased, all ready for seating in the necks of the charged cases. Now, let us look into the steps connected with the home production of bullets.

The most popular, widely used system for producing bullets is by casting them in moulds, using a molten alloy of which lead is the chief ingredient. Bullet moulds are produced by several manufacturers, including Hensley & Gibbs, Lyman Gun Sight Corporation, SAECO, Lee Custom Engineering, Penguin/Lachmiller and Ohaus Scale Corporation. Addresses of these firms are given in the directory section of this book and any of them will furnish an illustrated price list of their moulds, showing the bullet designs they offer, free on request.

Besides the mould, you will need equipment for melting the lead alloy, a dipper or ladle for pouring it into the top of the mould and a mallet for striking the sprue cutter and tapping the solidified bullet free of the mould. As will be discussed shortly, you will need equipment for sizing and lubricating the cast bullet, as well.

Bullet alloy consists, usually, of lead, tin and antimony. Other metals may be present as impurities and do not pose severe problems in trace amounts. Pure lead does not make a satisfactory cast bullet since it is prone to cause bore fouling or barrel leading. Tin must be added to the lead to harden it and minimize bore fouling. Proportions of about sixteen parts lead to one part tin are customary for handgun bullets. Anything in excess of one part tin to ten parts lead produces no further advantage and is apt to cause bore fouling.

Additional hardening of the alloy can be accomplished by the addition of antimony. However, the latter metal alone is not sufficient to assure bullets of good quality. Antimony melts and re-solidifies at a much higher temperature than does lead. As a result, a lead-antimony mixture,

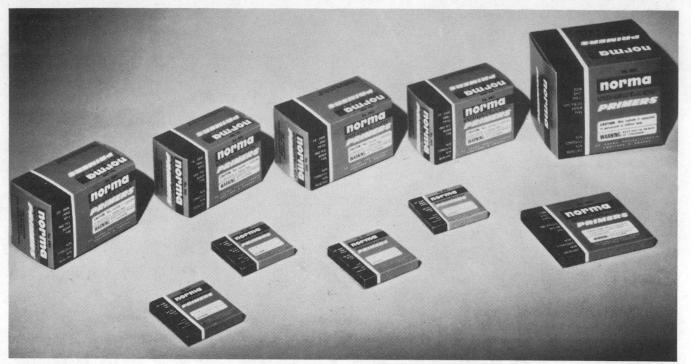

Five types of Norma primers: large and small rifle, large and small pistol with Winchester-size (larger) shotshell type.

Typical half-jacketed hollow-points, these are for .41 magnum by Speer with exposed, soft lead front half.

Aluminum blocks are a feature of the Lee mould. Lines are for air venting.

upon hardening, will be found to consist of crystals of antimony surrounded by almost pure lead. A bullet of such an alloy will present almost as much tendency to bore fouling as a pure lead one. It is necessary to add a small amount of tin, which remains mixed with the lead as they both solidify, serving effectively to minimize bore leading.

Sources of suitable metal for making into alloy are important to the bullet casting reloader since there never seems to be enough raw material on hand. Garages and tire stores often have quantities of wheel weights that have been removed. Sometimes such weights can be purchased for a cost on the order of five to ten cents a pound. This is not clear profit since the weights have the little steel clips attached and the whole works must be melted down. Once

melted, the steel clips can be skimmed off the top of the molten metal.

At this point, a small amount of tin must be added to the mixture, since wheel weights tend to run about 95 lead/5 antimony in percentage. Tin is comparatively expensive and one of the more reliable sources is bar solder, which can be purchased from hardware stores or similar suppliers. Get the large bars rather than wire solder, since it tends to cost less and is more convenient. Avoid, in particular, the wire solder which has a core containing acid or rosin; this will cause popping and spattering if dropped into melted metal in large quantities.

Take suitable precautions when working with melted metals. Do not have supplies of powder or primers nearby where a splash or spill of alloy could set it off. Wear safety

Standard steel resizing die, such as this one by Eagle, requires the cases to be lubricated before being sized for reasons explained in text. Press is the RCBS Rockchucker with lube pad, lube by same firm.

Lyman's Mould-Master electric furnace has thermostat control. Top of GI mess kit makes a good pig mould or cast iron type such as the Ohaus can be used. Plastic mallet is for hitting sprue cutter.

glasses or a face shield to protect your eyes. Don't work while barefoot or wearing bedroom slippers, sandals or such type of footgear as a spill of liquid lead on unprotected hide is an experience not quickly forgotten!

After the metal has melted and the alloying ingredients have been added, it is necessary to flux the mixture. A small amount of beeswax — about the size of a pea — is dropped on top of the metal and stirred in with a metal stirring stick. An old spoon works well and can be used for skimming off the impurities which will rise to the surface when the flux takes effect. Be careful not to stir so vigorously that the metal spills and splashes. Since the heat of the metal may be above the flash-point of the beeswax, it is possible that you may have flame for a foot or two above the metal for a brief interval. Be sure to keep flammable materials out of this area.

Whether the beeswax flares up or not, you will have quantities of smoke after fluxing and provision should be made for ventilation. Further, prolonged exposure to molten lead without adequate ventilation can pose a severe health hazard — the same being true of exposure to lead dust in an unventilated indoor range.

With the metal alloyed, fluxed and skimmed clean, we're ready to commence casting operations. Holding the mould in one hand, with the handles pressed firmly together, use the ladle to skim a spot of bright metal on the surface of

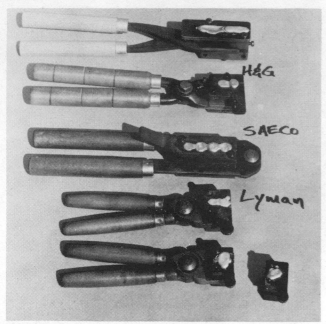

Typical bullet moulds, from top: Hensley & Gibbs 4-cavity; SAECO 2-cavity; Lyman four, two and single cavity, separate block.

An assortment of Lyman moulds, opened and closed to illustrate construction details.

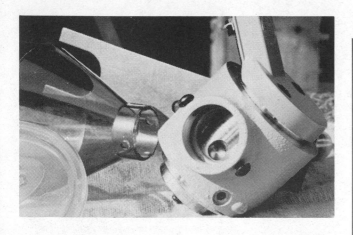

Ohaus Model 7200 Du-O-Measure has unique design in which the drum can be unlocked by loosening a set screw, rotated half a turn to use small-diameter handgun chamber — at top — or large chamber for rifle charges.

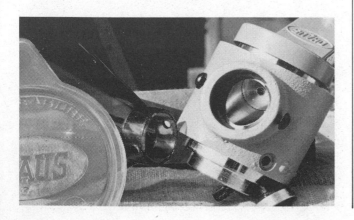

the alloy and dip a moderate amount up to pour into the sprue hole on top of the mould. If you are using a mould that turns out more than one bullet at a time, run the ladle down the groove separating the respective sprue holes, pausing at each to pour enough metal to fill that cavity and leave a moderate amount of excess metal for the sprue.

Be deliberate and unhurried in your motions but, at the same time, fill each mould cavity as quickly as possible. Once dipped from the melting pot, the metal will be cooling rapidly and the hotter it is when it reaches the mould cavity, the better the finished bullet will be.

You can expect to be disappointed by the appearance of your first several case bullets. Usually, it takes several fillings before the metal of the mould block heats up to operating temperature. At the same time, though you may have used solvent to remove most of the preservative oil from the cavity — applied to prevent rust — it takes a while for the heat to remove the last faint traces of oil from the cavity and, so long as any small amount remains, the heat will act upon oil residue to produce gas, resulting in creases and imperfections of the finished bullet.

In striking the sprue cutter, a non-metallic, non-marring instrument should be used, so as to prevent damage to the mould. A hardwood stick, a mallet or the plastic handle of a large screwdriver are among the things that work well for this.

Usually, the bullets will remain lodged in one side or the other of the mould block, requiring taps on the side of the mould tongs with the mallet to loosen them. Allow the bullets to drop onto a relatively soft surface, such as cardboard, so as to prevent them from being battered and damaged when they are hot and somewhat softer than they'll be after cooling.

The cut off sprues, as well as all imperfect bullets should be dropped back into the melting pot. However, avoid dropping the rejected bullets directly from the mould blocks into the molten metal. Droplets of liquid metal are

The Texan three-place reloading press for pistol or rifle cartridges permits installing three dies at once, simply moving the case from station to station in reloading process.

Super Vel's bullet for the .45 ACP should be seated to depth as shown for sure functioning.

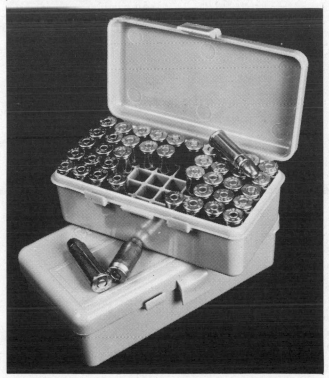

Case-Gard ammunition boxes by MTM have self-hinged snap-lock tops, come in sizes to fit most calibers of handgun, or rifle ammo.

apt to spatter up and get between the two halves of the blocks, preventing them from closing together tightly. This would result in a bullet with fins at the juncture line between block halves.

In melting the metal, an old frying pan on top of a gas or electric stove will serve reasonably well. If a large pan of melted metal is handled, it is a good precaution to grasp the rim opposite the handle tightly with a pair of pliers, rather than trying to maneuver the pan by the handle alone. The considerable weight of the metal can slosh to one side and cause upsets and spills.

SAECO and Lyman produce electric melting pots intended for casting bullets and these are excellent investments for the man who plans to cast in extensive quantities. SAECO has one model which rests on the bench top, with the metal being dipped from the upper surface of the metal. At somewhat higher prices, both firms offer more elaborate models which position the pot on a pair of metal legs, with a valve controlled by a handle on the side which delivers metal through a spout in the bottom of the pot. Most such units feature thermostatic temperature control, so that a knob can be turned to cut off electricity to the heating coils when the metal reaches the desired temperatures.

The temperature of the metal must be such that well-filled bullets are produced after a reasonable warm-up period but, at the same time, the metal should not be so hot that the finished bullets have a "frosty" appearance. These are your guidelines in controlling the temperature for best results.

An unusual feature of the Lee moulds is that the blocks are made of aluminum rather than the iron or steel used by most other mould makers. The Lee moulds are available only in single-cavity designs at present and the aluminum offers two advantages: solidified lead has less tendency to cling to it than to iron or steel and aluminum has excellent heat-conducting properties, making it possible to heat up the blocks quickly and uniformly.

The Lyman No. 45 lube sizer, above, has been replaced by the No. 450, an improved but similar version. Gas checks and several lubes can be used.

As discussed, C-H Swag-O-Matic is designed solely for swaging bullets, can be used to modify shape of cast and lubed bullets.

This basic design is termed a C-type press, offered by most manufacturers. This is by Texan.

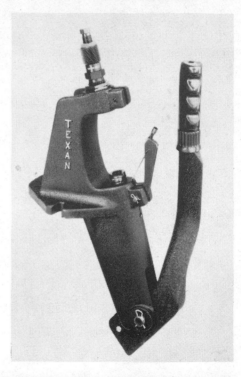

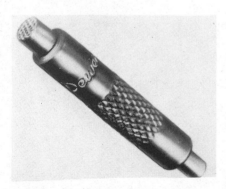

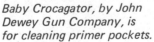

Baby Crocagator, by John Dewey Gun Company, is for cleaning primer pockets.

Lyman blocks are offered in single, double and four-cavity block designs. They have several hollow-point or hollow-base designs, which are produced by clamping a removable punch into the bottom of the block before pouring the metal, removing it from the completed bullet. Not surprisingly, this restricts the hollow-point or hollow-base designs to use only in single-cavity moulds. In general, double-cavity blocks are but slightly faster in production rate than single-cavity types and do not provide a doubled output, as might be assumed.

Ohaus moulds are produced in single and double-cavity for the present and may be offered in a four-cavity version at some future time.

Hensley & Gibbs bullet moulds are sold only on a direct-to-the-customer basis — that is, not through dealers or distributors. Prices are as follows, plus postage to the applicable zone for the weight indicated from Hensley & Gibbs, Box 10, Murphy, Oregon 97533. Four-cavity mould (3 lbs.) $29.50; six-cavity mould (5 lbs.) $47.50; ten-cavity mould (7 lbs.) $75 — when the ten-cavity mould is cut for bullets of .44 or .45 caliber, the number of cavities is reduced to eight. A pouring ladle, suitable for use with these moulds, is priced at $2.25. Note that prices are subject to change without notice and cannot be guaranteed.

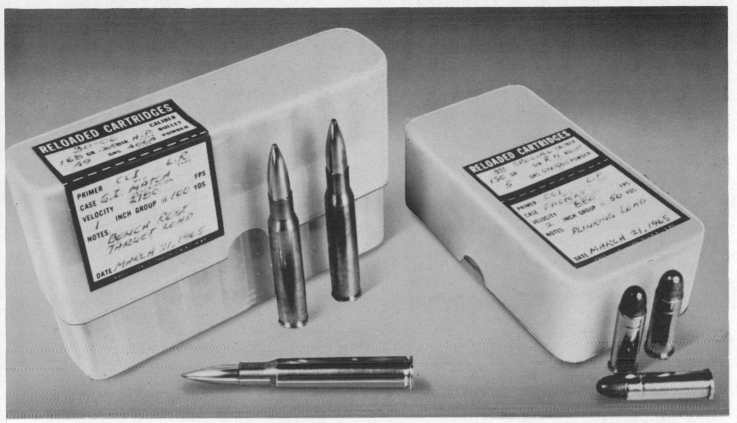

Ammo reload data labels, by JASCO, provide handy means of recording info.

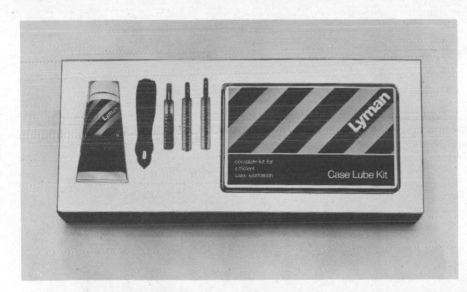

Lyman's case lube kit includes pad, lube, neck brushes and handle.

Hensley & Gibbs design charts are shown in two accompanying full-page charts. They request the following information:

Number of cavities: four, six or ten (eight for .44 or .45).

Bullet number, as shown in the chart.

Plain, bevel or gas check base.

Anticipated sizing diameter and make of sizer you use.

Weight desired, if more than one is shown.

The alloy you plan to use.

Firearm for which bullets are primarily intended.

The following notes apply to the chart illustrations:

1. Also available with bevel base.
2. Also available with gas check base.
3. Bevel base standard.
4. Gas check base standard.
5. This is H&G's standard .357 magnum bullet.
6. Either base, plain or bevel is suitable. Usually sized .357".

Darkened lines in the drawings indicate crimping grooves. Drawings are not drawn to exact scale, but are approximately actual size. Bullet weights are only approximate, due to variation in composition of alloys. Top figure in each box is H&G's bullet number. Lined base denotes gas check design. Shaded numbers are standard designs.

Mr. James Gibbs, of H&G, offers the following instructions and recommendations for the use of his firm's bullet moulds:

1. All oil should be cleaned from the mould before it is heated. Use gasoline or other solvent. Wipe all solvent from the blocks and cavities. Any residue left on the mould will form carbon. This carbon will cause gas for a long time and prevent the casting of full, sharp bullets.

2. Place mould alongside pot to warm while the alloy is melting. Use care not to overheat the mould. Do not dip mould into molten metal to heat it quickly.

3. Always close the mould gently. If the heated mould is roughly slammed closed the dowel will be injured and spoil the alignment. While holding the grips firmly rap the mould lightly once on one side. This seats the dowels home and prevents alloy from running between partly open blocks. To operate the sprue cutter and to rap the mould closed use nothing other than a light wooden implement.

4. The dowel pins, in a new mould, are quite tight and if mould is overheated they may bind and not allow the mould to quite close. If the pins seem to stick, and the mould opens with a snap, close the mould gently, give it a light rap on one side and hold up to the light and observe whether much light shows through between the blocks. In the larger moulds a bit may show without harm as one can see through a very small space when looking against the light. If the mould is standing open it is only necessary to drive the dowels back into the block very slightly as they are made to be adjusted in this manner. They are so adjusted, by us, after heating and testing the mould and this treatment is usually not needed unless the mould is grossly overheated. As wear occurs the dowels should be driven out a bit to adjust for the wear.

5. Allow time for metal to set and harden and then strike sprue cutter with the wooden mallet. Here you can tell whether the mould and/or the alloy is at correct casting temperature. If the sprue hardens almost instantly it is too cold. If it takes more than three to five seconds to harden then the mould or the alloy is too hot.

6. After casting for awhile, especially when working fast, the mould blocks may become too hot and, although the metal on sprue cutter appears to have set, upon cutting it off the bullet will be found to be still soft and semi-molten metal dragged across the top of the mould. Now, with the bullets still in the cavities (to prevent water getting in) the mould may be quickly plunged into hot water for only an instant. Properly done this will keep the mould at correct casting temperature even when working at top speed. Long, heavy bullets require more time to set than do short light ones.

7. The ratio of mould temperature to temperature of the molten alloy is important. The alloy should be considerably hotter than the mould. If the mould is working too hot there is less shrinkage in the bullet and it may not fall freely from the cavity. If the mould is cooler and the metal hotter, more shrinkage occurs and the bullet will drop out easier.

8. Our four, six, eight (.44 and .45 cal.) and ten cavity (.38 cal. and smaller) are all equipped with the fast pouring, trough-type sprue cutter plate. For pouring these moulds use only an open pouring dipper. We can supply these in proper size, made of stainless steel and designed for the purpose. The tube-snout pouring dipper will not pour a stream heavy enough for good results with this type of pouring plate. Pour a good, heavy stream of alloy from a slight height and move the dipper rapidly from one hole to the next. Vary the height of pouring and the speed of progress from one hole to the next one until good results are obtained. With practice, this is the most rapid method

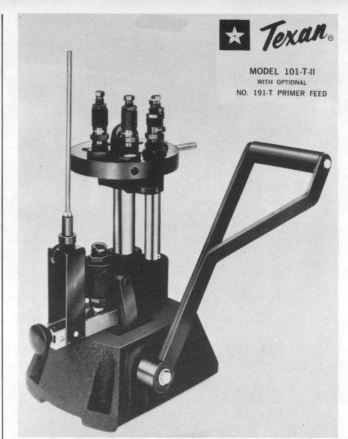

An example of a typical turret-top press is Texan's Model 101-T-11 with optional No. 191-T primer feed in which knob is actuated to drop each primer into place on priming post. Turret has seven stations and is rotated manually to move dies into place above cartridge case being loaded.

Cast and half-jacket bullets tend to be more favorably priced than the JHP and JSP types, thus favored for practice.

of producing good bullets.

9. It is probably easiest to make good bullets if only new tin and new lead are used for the alloy. However, if scrap lead pipe, plumber's lead or sheet lead is used, usually no trouble will be had. Tin in the form of scrap pipe is good. The local junk dealer is usually the source for these. Linotype metal may be used in place of tin for hardening the alloy. Linotype metal used just as it is makes an excellent rifle bullet alloy. Lead cable covering may be used if the

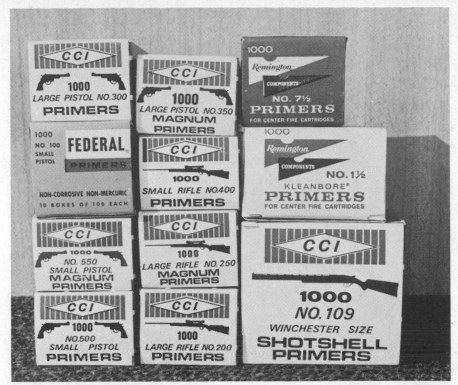

Micro-Mist is an excellent preservative for use on bullet moulds and its Micro Solv offers easy, quick removal for next use.

Primers come in a bewildering array of makes, sizes and types, of which this is but a small sampling. The key point is to use right one as discussed.

Lee Target Model loading kit is for rifle calibers at about $25, offers high precision. A similar kit, at $9.95, extends inexpensive entry into the reloading field for handguns, rifles, shotguns.

Lachmiller 400 press is a sturdy, inexpensive design, suitable for reloading modest amounts of ammo.

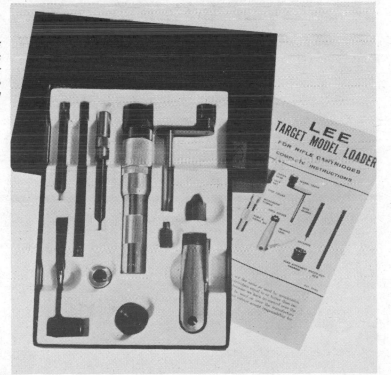

soldered ends are cut off and discarded. A very small amount of this solder (not to be confused with tinner's solder) will spoil a whole pot of alloy. Old storage battery lead may be used to harden the alloy if it does not make the alloy too hard or too large a bullet because of its high antimony content. When lead alloys are repeatedly reheated or when bullets are recovered and used a number of times the alloy becomes short and brittle. This may be mixed with good lead to restore proper hardness.

10. If used frequently and the climate will allow the mould may not need oiling to protect it from rust. Usually if stored in a wooden container (and not wrapped in cloth or paper) a mould may be left unoiled. This is left to the judgment of the user. Do not use wax, tallow, or anything that cannot be readily cleaned from the mould before heating. Never oil the mould when it is hot.

11. Do not tighten the sprue cutter plate screws so there is any bind. The plate must be left free to swing of its own

Expansion of the hollow-base wadcutter, seated backwards, is demonstrated graphically. Cartridge is the .38/45, a necked-down .45 ACP case.

Texan adjustable powder measure can be installed in station of turret-top press to dispense powder in turn.

weight. Tightening the screws will cause endless trouble by holding the blocks apart and will sooner or later cause either the screws or the plate to break.

12. Do not dump bullets from the mould directly into the pot of molten metal as the splash will cause flakes of metal to cling on the faces of the mould and hold the blocks apart. Lead flakes should be removed, using a sharp knife or razor blade. The flakes should be picked off rather than scraped off so the lead is not rubbed into the mould block.

13. After considerable use, and especially if direction No. 3 is not followed burrs may form around the dowel holes. This will hold the blocks apart. The burrs may be removed by careful use of a No. 3 cut file.

14. Great care must be used when working on the mould faces so that edges of the cavities are not dulled.

15. If the screw pins, that hold the blocks to the handles, become worn they may allow the handle to bear against the bottom of the block slot and cause the mould to stand open on one end. To correct this, remove the handles and observe the worn spot where they bear on the block. File the handle at this point until pressure is restored to center of the block on the screw pin.

16. If mould is allowed to rust, the cavities may be cleaned by revolving a bullet, coated with fine grinding compound, in each cavity.

17. Abuse, in the form of the wire brush probably ruins more moulds than any other form of misuse. Never, under any circumstances, use a wire brush on any part of a mould.

18. Every mould is tested by pre-heating and actual use of the mould. The mould then receives final adjustment. The bullets are measured, weighed and are sized. All this is done to determine with certainty, that the mould works properly and that the bullets are suitable for intended purpose.

19. Federal law forbids supplying sample bullets.

Lachmiller — a division of Penguin Industries, Incorporated (Box 97, Parkesburg, Pennsylvania 19365) — makes two-cavity and three-cavity blocks with a pair of handles that will fit either block. Accordingly, their complete double-cavity mould is priced at $17.50, the three-cavity being $19.50; blocks alone are $13 for the double, $15 for the triple and handles only are $4.50.

Current handguns designs from Lachmiller include one for the 9mm, five for the .38 Special or .357 magnum, one for the .41 magnum, two for the .44 Special or magnum, two for the .45 ACP and one for the .45 Long Colt. They also have three round-ball moulds, diameters of .357, .451 and .454-inch, plus moulds designed for casting rifle bullets.

Lachmiller offers several other useful items of equipment, including their unusual Lube-A-Matic sizer-lubricator which can use their own sizing dies or those made by Lyman. A ratchet arrangement maintains tension on the grease pressure piston automatically as the handle is moved up and down to size and lubricate the cast bullets. Other equipment includes shotshell reloading presses, handgun and rifle reloading presses and dies, adjustable powder measures, fixed powder measures — the last accepting three different drums and having the capability of measuring rifle as well as pistol powders, a shotshell reconditioner, a separate priming tool, case length gauges and numerous other items, all fully illustrated and priced in the catalog that's free on request.

SAECO prices their mould blocks and their handles separately or together as an assembly — with the difference that the cost of a complete mould with handles is $1 less than that of the blocks plus separate handles — and they offer blocks with one, two, three or four cavities. All blocks are useable on the same handles. Cost of the complete mould, by number of cavities, is $18.50 for a single, $24.50 for a double, $29.50 for three and $33.50 for four. The handles are $6.50 and the cost of the set of blocks alone can be determined by subtracting $7.50 from the price of the complete mould having the same number of cavities. SAECO also makes moulds for rifle bullets and these are available only in single and double-cavity patterns.

The same firm makes three electrically heated melting pots: the Model 31 is a utility design with its temperature being manually controlled by disconnecting the cord periodically; price is $24.50. The Model 32 has a thermostatic heat control, to hold the molten metal at the pre-selected temperature automatically. Like the 31, the 32 is an open-topped pot, designed for dipping the metal from the pot with a ladle. Price of the Model 32 is $36.50. Both pots will hold twenty pounds of lead.

Lower in capacity — eleven pounds of lead — but offering much more in convenience and production capability is SAECO's Model 24 electric melting pot at $44.50. It has the thermostatic temperature control, graduated from 450 to 850 degrees F., plus a valve-controlled bottom delivery spout which is beveled to fit the sprue plate of most bullet moulds. As with the other two models, the M24 draws

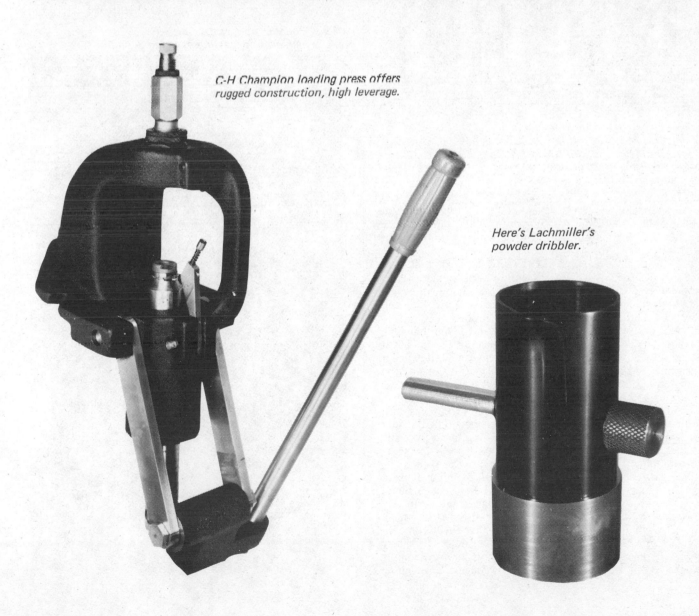

C-H Champion loading press offers rugged construction, high leverage.

Here's Lachmiller's powder dribbler.

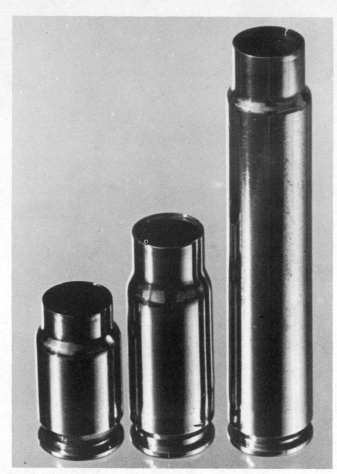

Essentially similar, except for their powder capacity, .38/45 (left), .357 Auto Mag Pistol and .35 Brown-Whelen rifle cartridge have same diameter of case head and bullet, as can be seen.

Company, Box 881, Chandler, Arizona 85224. The present version — Model 2400 Mk2 — is fifty-two inches high, thirty inches long and sixteen inches wide. Current consumption is 20 amps of 220-volt, single-phase.

Magma is working on the design of a matching automated lube-sizer to go with their Bullet Master but late word at press-time was that it's not yet ready for production.

Most of the reloading presses and similar equipment discussed up to this point have been of the type suited to the needs of the individual shooter who wishes to reload for his own needs. We turn our attention to some reloading machines which, in consideration of their cost and capacity, are better suited to the requirements of police departments.

One of the oldest, best known of these is the Star progressive reloading tool. It's manufactured and sold by the Star Machine Works of San Diego, Incorporated, 418 Tenth Avenue, San Diego, California 92101. First patented and produced in the early '30s, the Star has changed but little over the past four decades. They still make a one-caliber model, handling only the .38 Special, at $240 — this and any of the others listed can be had with a tungsten carbide resizing die at $12.50 extra — and a Universal Model at

Magma Bullet Master, as discussed in text, is high-capacity casting machine.

1000 watts and the pot is elevated on a pair of steel legs, so that moulds can be slid underneath for filling. Any of these electric pots can be obtained for use with 220-volt current at an added cost of $4 per pot.

An unusual device is SAECO's lead hardness tester, at $28.50, designed to perform accurate measurement of the comparative hardness of samples of lead alloy, including cast bullets. This affords an unusual degree of precision and control over this aspect of bullet production.

SAECO's lubri-sizer, at $36 — plus $4 for the matching C-clamp, if desired — is most convenient to use in that it has a spring-loaded grease piston which can be put under pressure by a few turns of the handle. This permits the sizing and lubrication of a sizeable number of bullets before taking up a few more turns on the pressure handle. Forty-four diameters are offered in the sizing dies to fit this unit, from .2240 to .4580-inch, with top punches to fit the nose of nearly any cast bullet design, including those from the moulds of other manufacturers. The dies — including bottom punch — are $6.50, the top punches $2.50 each.

Larger police departments, with a corresponding demand for cast bullets, may wish to investigate the Magma Bullet Master, an automatic casting machine with a rated capacity in excess of two thousand per hour of cast bullets for small arms. Designed and manufactured to utilize SAECO mould blocks, it can be used with blocks of other makes if slightly modified. Priced at $1495, FOB Queen Creek, Arizona — weight is 222 pounds — it's made by Magma Engineering

$275 in the steel resizing die. The universal version can be converted over to reload the .45 ACP and, probably, other calibers as well, depending upon popularity and availability. A set of dies for conversion to another caliber is $49 or a complete head, tooled up for one caliber is $90.50 — both with steel resizing die, carbide available as above.

The Star can be described as a semi-automated progressive. It is capable of producing one loaded round with each stroke of the operating handle, once all the six stations are filled and in operation. The primers and the powder are fed automatically. The empty case must be inserted manually and the bullet must be started into the case manually at the bullet seating station.

As with all progressive reloaders, heads-up and attentive operation is mandatory if results are to be satisfactory. The instruction sheet that comes with the Star tool minces no words about this.

Production capacity of the Star reloading machine is on the order of four hundred rounds per hour when worked by a single, reasonably skilled operator. Add a helper to start the bullets into the charged case and the production rate is nearly doubled. Note that safety systems can be bypassed,

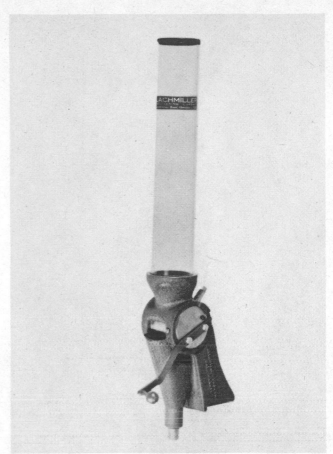

Lachmiller adjustable powder measure has large capacity hopper, mount base.

Star loader feeds primer and powder with each pull of the handle, carrier for cases must be turned by hand.

but should not be, due to the danger of double-charging a case and damaging a gun and possibly the shooter or a bystander. This can happen and it has happened.

With most sizer-lubricators, you position the bullet, as cast, beneath the top punch, operating the handle which forces the bullet down into the sizing cavity at which point grease is forced into the bullet grooves through grease ports in the die. It then is necessary to raise the handle, bringing the sized and lubricated bullet up and out of the sizing die.

Through an ingenious design, the Star lubricator and sizer pushes the processed bullet on down and out the bottom when the next bullet is forced in from the top. Thus an entire step — removal of the finished bullet — is saved and the time needed for the operation is reduced to about one-third of that required when using other machines.

The Star lube-sizer is made by the same firm that produces the Star progressive loaders just described. Price of the Star lube-sizer is $52.50, extra sets of dies and bullet punches are $10 and a convenient die extractor is offered at $3.50.

All of the Star machines are shipped with complete operating instructions and an illustrated parts list. It is important that all personnel operating the equipment become thoroughly familiar with the instructions and follow them implicitly. This will assure long, satisfactory service of the equipment and trouble-free performance of the ammunition produced on it.

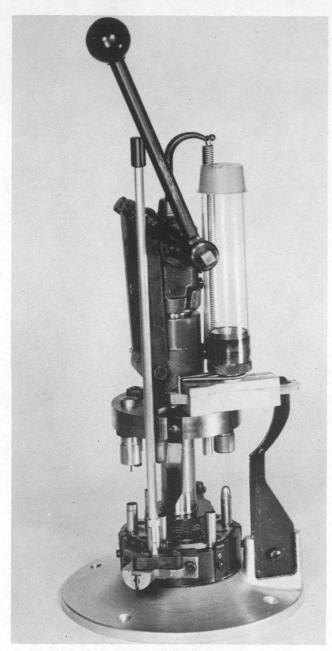

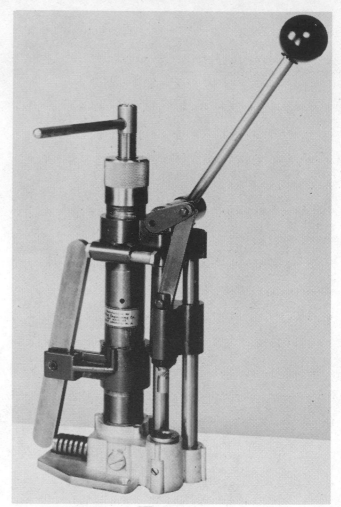

Phelps sizer-lubricator handles cast bullets rapidly, as discussed in text.

Phelps progressive loader requires moving shell carrier and seating the bullets by hand, feeds primers and powder charge with each handle pull.

A second progressive reloading press for handgun cartridges is the Phelps, made by Phelps Reloaders, Incorporated, Box 4004, East Orange, New Jersey 07017. In design, principle and general mode of operation, it is closely similar to the Star. It's available in a standard model, handling the .38 Special only, at $252.50 — all prices are FOB East Orange — a deluxe model for .38 Special or .45 ACP at $287.50, extra tool head for caliber conversion of the deluxe machine at $97.50. Extra tool heads for the deluxe machine are available in many other popular handgun calibers and all tooling is supplied with tungsten carbide resizing dies at the cost quoted.

As with the Star, the Phelps requires advancing of the six-station shell carrier by hand after each stroke of the operating handle. Primers are dispensed by an auto primer feed, with a capacity of one hundred primers and an arrangement which halts operation of the loader when the primer feed tube is empty. Powder is dispensed automatically with each stroke of the handle from an integral

measure having a transparent reservoir of hardened glass. Bullets must be started into the flared neck of the charged case by hand and, as with the Star, this can be handled by a second operator to increase production capacity.

Phelps reports that their customers are able to produce as many as 1100 rounds of reloads per hour — presumably in two-man operation.

Phelps also produces a sizer-lubricator and, as with their progressive reloader, the general appearance and functioning is closely similar to that of the Star previously described here. Price of the Phelps lube-sizer is $55, complete, FOB East Orange. Extra die is $7, extra bullet punch, $2 and they'd like to have a sample of your bullet to assure correct fit.

Both the Star and the Phelps are designed for manual feed of the empty case into the shell carrier. Some twenty-five years ago, Hulme Firearm Service, Box 83, Millbrae, California 94030, commenced producing an automatic case feeder for use with the Star or Phelps machines. Current

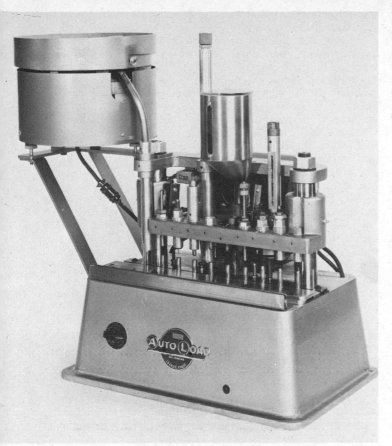

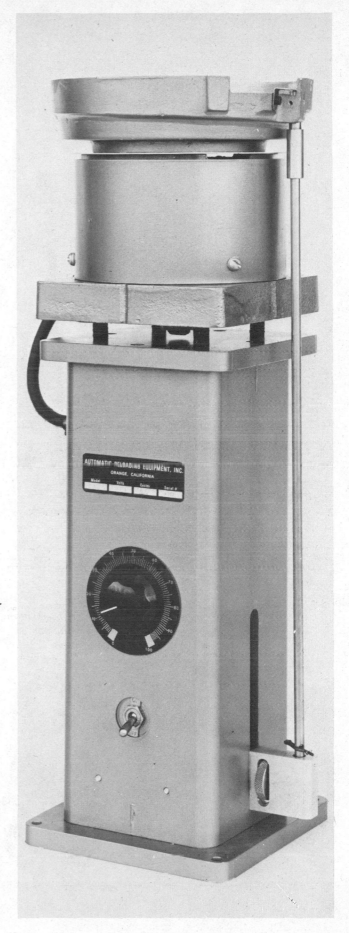

Rosan Enterprises, of Newport Beach, California, makes this fully automated reloading machine, since renamed the Ammo-Load, for full-auto reloading to production rates as high as 5000 rounds per hour, with option of being able to convert it to handle various calibers of cartridges. The cost is substantial and subject to change, so current quotes should be requested. For departments with high-volume needs, the saving in labor tends to offset equipment cost.

Accessory for Ammo-Load is this auto primer tube filling device by same firm.

prices for the Hulme case feeder run a trifle under $50 and the device is available in most of the common handgun calibers.

As the departmental appetite for reloaded cartridges goes on up, requiring higher rates of reload production, the price tag for the appropriate equipment tends to escalate rather sharply. Not that it's out of proportion because you don't have to save a vast amount of man-hours before the cost of the equipment begins to earn its own keep and pay its own invoice.

Rosan Enterprises, 2901 West Coast Highway, Newport Beach, California 92663, makes and sells a fully automated, electrically driven cartridge reloading machine with a production capacity of about 5000 rounds per hour. It's now called the Ammo-Load (formerly the Auto-Load) and the cost is well into the four-digit brackets. It is suggested that a current price or lease quotation be requested from the maker at the address given here previously. There are several arrangements available whereby the machine can be

Ponsness-Warren Model 800B is a high output reloader for shotshells. The only manual operations are to put in empty case on the down-stroke, a wad on the upstroke. Load data can be varied.

leased for varying time intervals, with option of converting a portion of the lease payments to apply on purchase of the equipment. Leasing can run as low as $130 per month on up, depending upon details of the agreement, length of lease and similar factors.

Conversion of the Ammo-Load machine to handle a different caliber requires about one hour of set-up time, involving change of four dies, feeds and shell rails. Accuracy of the powder charge is within two-tenths of one grain and dies are available for any center fire, rimmed or automatic handgun ammunition using American — Boxer-type — primers. Weight is 228 pounds and standard motor is ½ hp, 110-volt, single-phase, 60-cycle. Other electrical specs can be matched at extra cost.

All surfaces subject to extreme wear are either tungsten carbide or heat treated. Some of the early units have now reloaded in excess of thirty million rounds. Adjustments such as primer seating, bullet depth and so on require but a few seconds. Periodic cleaning and maintenance takes only a few minutes. Normal operation is by means of a foot switch, leaving the operator with both hands free to service the feed tubes. Powder supply is visible through a sight glass and each charge is visible before being dropped into the shell. Due to the necessity in many organizations for stretching the useful reloading life of the brass as long as possible, a tapered crimp is suggested. A final sizing die is included as the last operation to iron out any minor imperfection in crimping due to imperfect cases.

Several items of auxiliary equipment are made by the same firm to make full use of the Ammo-Load's production capacity. There's an automatic washer-tumbler for cleaning the cartridge cases before loading or the finished reloads afterward. It has a capacity of four thousand cases per

Texan's progressive shotshell reloader indexes the carrier automatically for high output.

From left: a Hornady .38 half-jacket, a Lyman 311240 cast bullet, the pair as ready to swage and the finished .38 slug.

operation and can be used with liquid or dry cleaners. Then there is a vibrating case inspection table which removes foreign objects from fired cases before loading, being equally well adapted to inspection of loaded rounds and counting and/or packaging into bulk containers or cartons at the rate of 250 rounds per minute.

There's an automatic primer tube filler which replaces the tedious hand operation, filling tubes at the rate of better than 5000 primers per hour. Last but not least, there's an automatic case separator which sorts and segregates mixed brass at the rate of well over 6000 assorted-caliber cases per hour.

Many commercial producers of bullets offer their bullets in feed tubes suited for use with automatic reloading machinery as an optional packaging. The usual system is that the empty tubes can be turned in for credit on the next shipment. This saves the chore of loading the bullets into tubes for use with the machines.

The second basic technique for bullet production, apart from casting, is by swaging: cold-forming under high pressure. At least two firms continue to produce and sell equipment for swaging partially jacketed handgun bullets: C-H Tool & Die Corporation, Box L, Owen, Wisconsin 54460, makes the Swag-O-Matic press which can turn out bullets from .308 to .454 inches in diameter, each with an assortment of nose shapes, by changing the lower dies and the nose punches. Half-jackets for making handgun bullets continue to be available from Speer, Hornady and Herter's.

The last-named firm — Herter's, Incorporated, Route 1, Waseca, Minnesota 56093 — presently offers various bullet swaging presses as well as die sets designed for swaging bullets in regular reloading presses of their own and other makes.

Most swaging presses are designed to use cores cut from

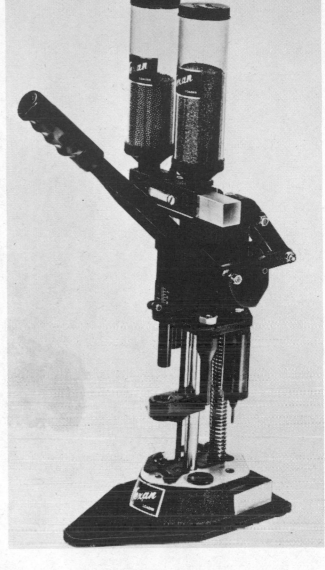

This Texan shotshell reloader is lower in price and capacity, requires more hand operations.

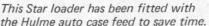

Plastic ammo boxes, such as these by MTM, are available to fit most calibers, empty cases can be put back for reloading.

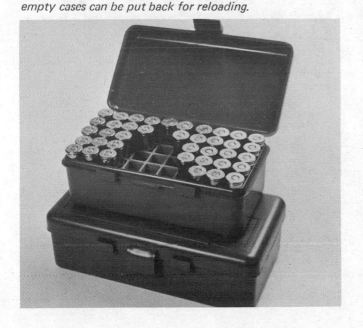

This Star loader has been fitted with the Hulme auto case feed to save time.

Ponsness-Warren Model 375 is lower in cost and output than same firm's 800B but can be set up for fast change between either of two gauges of shell.

Texan Model LT is lowest-priced shotshell loader in firm's line.

Texan
MODEL
LT

Not content with seating the primer sideways, an inattentive shooter tried to fire it, luckily without success!

Three popular jacketed .38 bullets: Super Vel 125, Speer 140, Sierra 150.

soft lead wire. The cutter is adjusted so that the combined weight of the core and the jacket add up to at or just over the desired weight of the finished bullet. When the die is adjusted so as to extrude a small amount of excess core material, excellent uniformity of bullet weight is obtained.

Since lead wire tends to be both expensive and difficult to find, many reloaders have used cast bullets as their core, usually with reasonably satisfactory results. Bullets are cast in the next caliber smaller — using caliber .30 bullets for making swaged .38 size, for example — and a fairly soft alloy is used to minimize strain on the bullet-swaging press.

As has been detailed elsewhere in this book, it is possible to cast a bullet of the finished diameter — give or take a few thousandths — run it through a lubricator-sizer in the usual manner and follow this by running it into a C-H Swag-O-Matic bullet press. In so doing, moderately hard alloys can be employed and the lubricant remains in the original grooves after it has been swaged. A hollow-point or cup-point nose punch can be used in the Swag-O-Matic to produce finished bullets which expand quite dependably and the time required for the entire series of operations is

but little more than for making conventional cast hollow-point bullets. Usually, it's possible to insert a gas check into the swaging die before starting the base of the lube-sized bullet and the gas check will be pressure-fitted accurately, even though the original design did not have provisions for a gas check. By so doing, the bullet can be driven to some-what higher velocities than one with an unprotected base.

It is entirely possible that some police personnel and/or their departments may wish to reload shotshells for practice sessions with the police shotgun. Probably, this will entail light loads with small sizes of shot for use on the skeet-range or with claybirds thrown from a handtrap or one of the inexpensive little spring traps made by Trius.

Depending upon the quantity of reloaded shotshells required, there are several excellent reloading presses avail-able. Manufacturers of reloading equipment, such as MEC, Lyman, Pacific, Texan, Lee, Lachmiller, Herter's or Ponsness-Warren include shotshell reloading equipment in their lines and will be pleased to provide detailed informa-tion upon request.

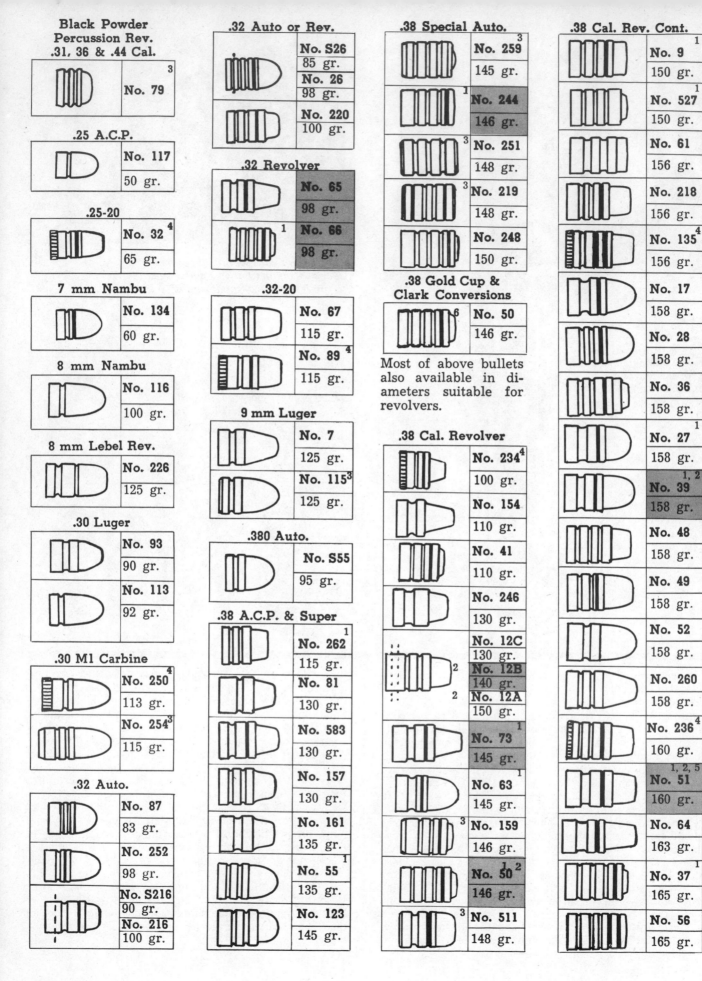

Black Powder Percussion Rev. .31, 36 & .44 Cal.

No. 79 [3]	

.25 A.C.P.

No. 117
50 gr.

.25-20

No. 32 [4]
65 gr.

7 mm Nambu

No. 134
60 gr.

8 mm Nambu

No. 116
100 gr.

8 mm Lebel Rev.

No. 226
125 gr.

.30 Luger

No. 93
90 gr.
No. 113
92 gr.

.30 M1 Carbine

No. 250 [4]
113 gr.
No. 254 [3]
115 gr.

.32 Auto.

No. 87
83 gr.
No. 252
98 gr.
No. S216
90 gr.
No. 216
100 gr.

.32 Auto or Rev.

No. S26
85 gr.
No. 26
98 gr.
No. 220
100 gr.

.32 Revolver

No. 65
98 gr.
No. 66 [1]
98 gr.

.32-20

No. 67
115 gr.
No. 89 [4]
115 gr.

9 mm Luger

No. 7
125 gr.
No. 115 [3]
125 gr.

.380 Auto.

No. S55
95 gr.

.38 A.C.P. & Super

No. 262 [1]
115 gr.
No. 81
130 gr.
No. 583
130 gr.
No. 157
130 gr.
No. 161
135 gr.
No. 55 [1]
135 gr.
No. 123
145 gr.

.38 Special Auto.

No. 259 [3]
145 gr.
No. 244 [1]
146 gr.
No. 251 [3]
148 gr.
No. 219 [3]
148 gr.
No. 248
150 gr.

.38 Gold Cup & Clark Conversions

No. 50 [6]
146 gr.

Most of above bullets also available in diameters suitable for revolvers.

.38 Cal. Revolver

No. 234 [4]
100 gr.
No. 154
110 gr.
No. 41
110 gr.
No. 246
130 gr.
No. 12C
130 gr.
No. 12B
140 gr.
No. 12A
150 gr.
No. 73 [1]
145 gr.
No. 63 [1]
145 gr.
No. 159 [3]
146 gr.
No. 50 [1,2]
146 gr.
No. 511 [3]
148 gr.

.38 Cal. Rev. Cont.

No. 9 [1]
150 gr.
No. 527 [1]
150 gr.
No. 61
156 gr.
No. 218
156 gr.
No. 135 [4]
156 gr.
No. 17
158 gr.
No. 28
158 gr.
No. 36
158 gr.
No. 27 [1]
158 gr.
No. 39 [1,2]
158 gr.
No. 48
158 gr.
No. 49
158 gr.
No. 52
158 gr.
No. 260
158 gr.
No. 236 [4]
160 gr.
No. 51 [1,2,5]
160 gr.
No. 64
163 gr.
No. 37 [1]
165 gr.
No. 56
165 gr.

.38 Cal. Rev. Cont.

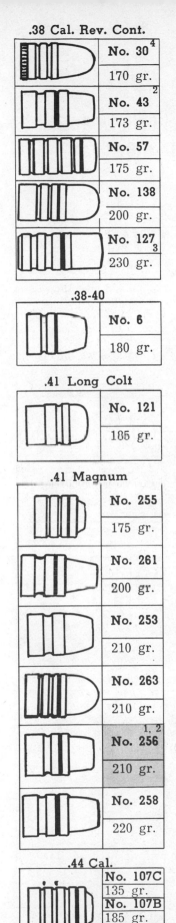

No. 30 [4]	170 gr.
No. 43 [2]	173 gr.
No. 57	175 gr.
No. 138	200 gr.
No. 127 [3]	230 gr.

.38-40

No. 6	180 gr.

.41 Long Colt

No. 121	185 gr.

.41 Magnum

No. 255	175 gr.
No. 261	200 gr.
No. 253	210 gr.
No. 263	210 gr.
No. 256 [1,2]	210 gr.
No. 258	220 gr.

.44 Cal.

No. 107C	135 gr.
No. 107B	185 gr.
No. 107A	245 gr.

.44 Cal. Cont.

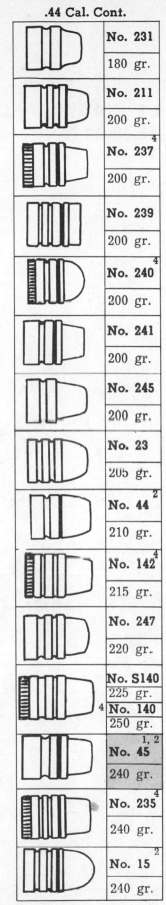

No. 231	180 gr.
No. 211	200 gr.
No. 237 [4]	200 gr.
No. 239	200 gr.
No. 240 [4]	200 gr.
No. 241	200 gr.
No. 245	200 gr.
No. 23	205 gr.
No. 44 [2]	210 gr.
No. 142 [4]	215 gr.
No. 247	220 gr.
No. S140	225 gr.
No. 140 [4]	250 gr.
No. 45 [1,2]	240 gr.
No. 235 [4]	240 gr.
No. 15 [2]	240 gr.

.44 Cal. Cont.

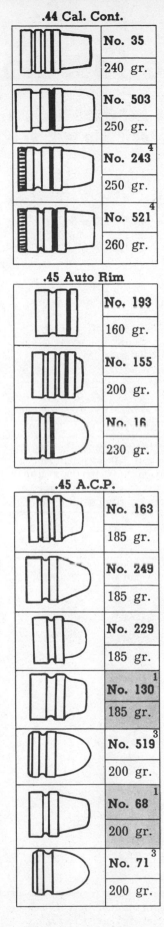

No. 35	240 gr.
No. 503	250 gr.
No. 243 [4]	250 gr.
No. 521 [4]	260 gr.

.45 Auto Rim

No. 193	160 gr.
No. 155	200 gr.
No. 16	230 gr.

.45 A.C.P.

No. 163	185 gr.
No. 249	185 gr.
No. 229	185 gr.
No. 130 [1]	185 gr.
No. 519 [3]	200 gr.
No. 68 [1]	200 gr.
No. 71 [3]	200 gr.

.45 A.C.P. Cont.

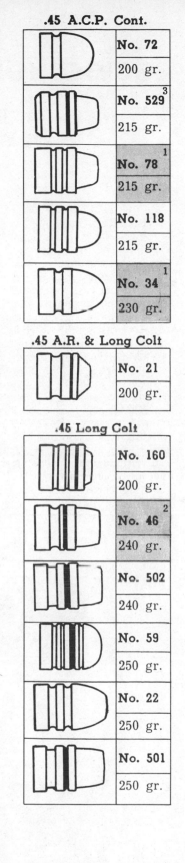

No. 72	200 gr.
No. 529 [3]	215 gr.
No. 78 [1]	215 gr.
No. 118	215 gr.
No. 34 [1]	230 gr.

.45 A.R. & Long Colt

No. 21	200 gr.

.45 Long Colt

No. 160	200 gr.
No. 46 [2]	240 gr.
No. 502	240 gr.
No. 59	250 gr.
No. 22	250 gr.
No. 501	250 gr.

Hensley & Gibbs bullet mould designs. Refer to data on pages 212-3.

Tested Reload Data

Favorite Handload Recipes, Developed By A Working Police Officer And Evaluated In Typical Duty Weapons For The Given Caliber.

The reloads listed here were developed and tested by Sergeant Evan P. Marshall of the Detroit, Michigan, Police Department. In instances where applicable, Marshall chronographed the given load through short barrels as well as the customary four-inch length.

Each load in the accompanying table has been assigned a number for convenient identification. In those examples tested in more than one barrel length, a letter has been added to the number, such as 5A and 5B. The purpose is to simplify reference between the captions of accompanying photos and the corresponding data listing.

Muzzle energy, in foot-pounds, has been calculated by the following process: The muzzle velocity in feet per second (fps) is squared — that is, multiplied times itself — and the product is divided by 450,240 to obtain the amount of energy per grain of weight for that velocity. The resulting figure is multiplied times the bullet's weight in grains to obtain the final figure for the muzzle energy of that particular load. The factor 450,240 is employed as a convenient time saver. It is the product of 64.32 times 7000; respectively, the constant for gravity and the number of grains in one pound. The accepted equation for kinetic energy is velocity squared, divided by 64.32 (sometimes rounded off as 64), divided by 7000 (to convert between pounds and grains) to obtain the muzzle energy in foot-pounds.

Text describes method for calculating the number of foot-pounds of kinetic energy for any moving body, including bullets, provided information on weight (in grains) and velocity (in feet per second) are available for the equation.

With the present ready availability of small pocket calculators, computing kinetic energy of any moving body becomes a quick and simple operation. A foot-pound is defined as the quantity of energy necessary to raise a weight of one pound a distance of one foot against the normal gravity of the planet on which we live. Alternatively, one foot-pound is the energy acquired by a one-pound falling body after dropping one foot. Energy of, for example, 414 foot-pounds is equal to that of a one-pound weight that has fallen 414 feet or to that of a 414-pound weight that has fallen one foot and so on.

Here are six examples of reference works containing added information on reloading. Book at upper left gives details on reloading procedures, while handbooks/manuals from Sierra, Hodgdon's, Hornady, Speer and Lyman prescribe exact weight of powder by bullet weight and cartridge.

Reloading should be performed by those having adequate familiarity with the process and suitable equipment for proper operations. Several excellent and reliable manuals or handbooks on reloading are available and it is recommended that one or more such books be consulted as a guide to selection and use of load data. Extensive firing of high-performance ammunition will accelerate the wear of any firearm and shorten its useful, accurate service life in the process. Accordingly, high-performance loads should be employed judiciously, with sensible restraint and only in modern arms known to be in first-class condition.

Since we have no control over methods and equipment employed in reloading, neither the author nor the publishers of this book can assume or do assume any responsibility, either expressed or implied, for consequences arising from or alleged to have arisen from the use of the accompanying load data.

Reload Data Test Report

Load No.	Cartridge Caliber	Case Make	Primer Type	Powder Weight (Grains)/Type	Bullet Make/Weight and Type	Muzzle Velocity (fps)	Muzzle Energy (ft-lbs)	Expansion Diameter (inch)	Comments
1	9mm Luger	W-W	CCI-500	9.0 gr Blue Dot	115-gr Sierra JHC	1306	432	.713	4″ S&W Model 39-2
2	9mm Luger	W-W	CCI-500	8.2 gr Blue Dot	125-gr Speer JSP	1161	375	.662	4″ S&W Model 39-2
3	.38 Colt Super	R-P	CCI-500	9.6 gr SR4756	115-gr Sierra JHC	1436	526	.802	4¼″ Colt Commander
4	.38 Colt Super	R-P	CCI-500	10.1 gr Blue Dot	125-gr Speer JSP	1284	459	.688	4¼″ Colt Commander
5A	.38 Special	R-P	CCI-500	13.7 gr 630	110-gr Hornady JHP	1040	264	.604	2″ Colt Detective Special
5B	——	——	——	——	——	1203	352	.657	4″ S&W Model 10
6A	.38 Special	R-P	CCI-500	10.2 gr 630	146-gr Speer JHP	867	242	.521	2″
6B	——	——	——	——	——	956	295	.567	4″
7	.38 Special	R-P	CCI-500	6.8 gr SR4756	148-gr Speer HBWC	922	278	.682	2″ bullet seated backwards
8A	.38 Special	R-P	CCI-500	10.4 gr 630	158-gr Hornady JHP	802	226	.502	2″
8B	——	——	——	——	——	906	286	.564	4″
9A	.38 Special	R-P	CCI-500	9.9 gr 630	160-gr Speer JSP	795	223	.489	2″
9B	——	——	——	——	——	892	263	.512	4″
10A	.357 magnum	Speer	CCI-500	10.0 gr Unique	110-gr Hornady JHP	1302	414	.675	2½″ S&W Model 19
10B	——	——	——	——	——	1465	524	.823	4″ Colt Python
11A	.357 magnum	Speer	CCI-500	14.5 gr 630	125-gr Hornady JHP	1122	349	.652	2½″
11B	——	——	——	——	——	1302	470	.845	4″
12A	.357 magnum	Speer	CCI-500	18.0 gr 296	146-gr Speer JHP	1225	486	.655	2½″
12B	——	——	——	——	——	1357	596	.708	4″
13A	.357 magnum	Speer	CCI-500	17.0 gr 296	158-gr Hornady JHP	1102	425	.645	2½″
13B	——	——	——	——	——	1234	534	.742	4″
14A	.357 magnum	Speer	CCI-500	16.5 gr 296	160-gr Speer JSP	1125	448	.612	2½″
14B	——	——	——	——	——	1267	566	.709	4″
15	.41 magnum	R-P	CCI-350	20.0 gr 2400	170-gr Sierra JHC	1325	661	.778	4″ S&W Model 57
16	.41 magnum	R-P	R-P 2½	14.7 gr AL-8	200-gr Speer JHP	1102	538	.703	4″ S&W Model 57
17	.41 magnum	R-P	R-P 2½	11.0 gr AL-7	220-gr Speer JSP	905	398	.637	4″ S&W Model 57
18	.44 Special	W-W	R-P 2½	7.5 gr Unique	200-gr Hornady JHP	806	288	.655	3″ Charter Arms
19	.44 magnum	W-W	R-P 2½	12.0 gr Unique	200-gr Hornady JHP	1167	604	.816	4″ S&W Model 29
20	.45 ACP	W-W	R-P 2½	7.8 gr Unique	185-gr Hornady JHP	882	320	.691	4¼″ Colt Commander
21	.45 ACP	W-W	R-P 2½	8.5 gr AL-5	225-gr Speer JHP	894	398	.691	4¼″ Colt Commander

NOTE: Makers or distributors of the listed powders are: Alcan (Smith & Wesson Ammunition Company): AL-5, AL-7 and AL-8; E.I. du Pont de Nemours: SR4756; Hercules, Incorporated: Blue Dot, Unique and 2400; Winchester-Western: 630 and 296.

Load No. 1 put 9.0 grains of Hercules Blue Dot behind the 115-grain Sierra JHC bullet in the 9mm Luger for 1306 fps velocity. Jacketed hollow cavity bullet expanded to .713".

The No. 2 load for the 9mm used Speer's 125-grain JSP and 8.4 grains of Blue Dot for velocity of 1161 fps.

Speer's 148-grain hollow-base wadcutter, seated backwards, on top of 6.8 grains of du Pont SR4756 powder, makes an extremely efficient .38 Special snubnose load; No. 7 load.

In the .38 Super, No. 3, Sierra 115-grain JHC, ahead of 9.6 grains of SR4756, went 1436 fps, expanded to .802".

In the .357 magnum, Nos. 10A and 10B, the Hornady 110-grain JHP reached high velocities in both barrel lengths and displayed excellent expansion when fired into the sand.

Moving up in weight for the .357 magnum, No. 11 A&B has Hornady's 125-grain JHP ahead of 14.5 grains of W-W 630 powder, continuing to show good velocity and expansion.

Load No. 12 A&B carries Speer's 146-grain JHP ahead of 18.0 grains of Winchester-Western 630 powder, with good expansion and muzzle energies of 486 and 596 foot-pounds.

Sierra 170-grain JHC bullet, Load No. 15, displayed fine accuracy in Sgt. Marshall's four-inch S&W M58 .41 magnum.

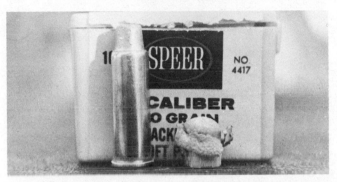

Load No. 17 for the .41 mag used Speer 220-grain JSP and 11.0 grains of Alcan AL-7 powder for 905 fps velocity.

Fired from the 3" Charter Arms .44 Special Bulldog, Load No. 18 put the 200-grain Hornady JHP out at 806 fps.

A light-bullet load for the .45 ACP, No. 20 carries the Hornady 185-grain JHP and 7.8 grains of Hercules Unique.

Speer's 225-grain JHP, Load No. 21, hits 882 fps on 8.5 grains of Alcan AL-5 and expands to .691" diameter.

Compare the FMJ bullet with the recovered 125-grain Speer bullet, Load No. 4, for .38 Colt Super, both being fired into the sand test medium employed by Sgt. Marshall for series.

Another .38 Super — No. 4 again — continued to produce the excellent expansion that increases cartridge effectiveness.

Load No. 6 A&B, for the ever-popular .38 Special, put Speer 146-grain JHP ahead of 10.2 grains of W-W 630 for energy of 242 foot-pounds from the two-inch barreled test gun.

Chapter 15

Law
Enforcement
Requirements
Differ
From The
Traditional
Military
Needs
For This
Round!

POLICE LOADS FOR THE .45 ACP

THE CARTRIDGE generally known as the caliber .45 ACP — for Automatic Colt Pistol — has been around since 1905, having been designed by John Moses Browning for the Colt Model 1905 auto pistol. That arm was produced in an effort to upgrade the performance of the .38 military auto, but the first version of the M1905 proved unacceptable for a number of reasons, among them, a shortage of safety features. The improved version, known as the Model 1911, was adopted by the U. S. government and a few refinements — such as the arched mainspring housing, an extended grip safety tang to cure the nasty back-biting tendencies and a shorter trigger — resulted in the present M1911A1 shortly after the end of the First World War.

The cartridge developed in 1905 was loaded with a 200-grain bullet which had a velocity of approximately 900 fps at the muzzle. The U. S. Ordnance Board requested a heavier jacketed bullet and the familiar version carrying the 230-grain slug was designed at Frankford Arsenal. For some years thereafter, ammunition companies produced the 200-grain load in addition to the 230-grainer, but the lighter of the two was discontinued sometime prior to 1930.

So the 230-grain, fully-jacketed load settled down into a long and successful production run. Like most bullets termed "full-jacketed," the gliding metal jacket encloses the nose and sides, with the central portion of the base having the lead core unprotected. Velocities with this bullet average 800 fps from the autoloader and somewhat less from revolvers chambered for the same cartridge, such as the M1917 Colt or Smith & Wesson.

To cite a couple of examples, a typical round of military ammunition, headstamped WCC/64, gave 618 fps from an M1917 S&W with another from the same box producing 775 fps from an auto: about 193 and 303 foot-pounds, respectively. Velocities of around 850 fps are claimed for most factory loads today, equivalent to 370 foot-pounds at the muzzle, 335 at fifty yards and 305 at one hundred yards. Mid-range trajectories for this load average about 1.6 inches at fifty yards and 6.5 inches at one hundred yards.

Although primarily a short-range cartridge, i.e., fifty yards or closer, you can lob them uncomfortably close to a man-sized target out to about three hundred yards provided certain conditions prevail: the target is a bit dusty so that you can see where the ranging shots strike. The amount of holdoff, or Kentucky windage, at three hundred yards is on the order of twelve to fifteen feet, usually requiring a yard or so to the right or left. However, a fairly skilled marksman usually can put a few holes in a silhouette target at that distance after firing three or four magazines-full at it.

Although the cartridge has enjoyed a few minor improvements over the past fifty-odd years — such as non-corrosive primers in the early 1950s — the basic bullet design has varied but little. The reasons for this static state of affairs would include such considerations as the fact that the rounded, jacketed nose assures the utmost

No longer in production, these DD half-jacketed softpoint bullets once were made by International Bullet & Ammunition Corporation in three weights: 180, 200 and 225-grains. Loaded and fired bullets are of the 180-gr weight.

reliability of feeding and functioning through the auto-loading action, the broad and shallow rifling grooves of the barrel, designed to handle the jacketed bullet, do not perform well with lead alloy bullets unless of a hardness of one part tin to fifteen parts lead or better.

One further reason for the dearth of change in bullet design is simply that the old copper-clad punkin ball does a pretty fair job of man-stopping, given a solid hit in any fairly strategic area of an adversary. Although one sometimes hears lurid claims that it is so horrendously formidable that a graze of the tip of pinky-finger will send a man spinning like a top to lie unconscious for hours, there is little factual basis for such claims. It's a good, capable cartridge for use on unprotected man-sized target out to fifty yards. It's a fact that the .45 ACP leaves something to be desired when it comes to getting inside an automobile without opening the door first.

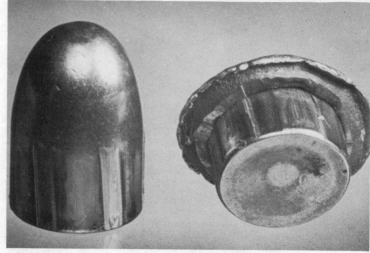

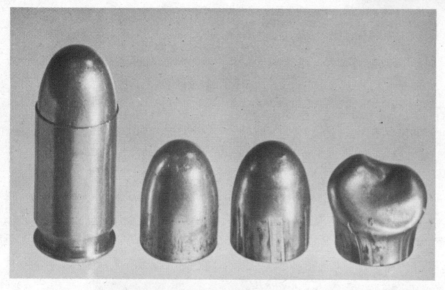

Both of these bullets were fired into water-soaked phone books. The 230-gr military full-jacket, left, displays no expansion, while 180-gr softpoint shows classic mushroom shape.

Standard jacketed military round but rarely expands unless encountering hard objects, as did slug at right.

Expansion of the 230-grain Norma hollow point, although superior to full-jacket load, failed to expand the jacket at the 810-fps velocity level.

234

Another factor that cast a blight upon development of really effective combat loads for the .45 ACP was that, until recent times, few used the .45 for combat except for the military and they were restricted to the jacketed load by provisions of the Geneva Convention. Although widely used by civilians as a target round, most manufacturers felt — perhaps correctly — that the potential demand for a maximum-performance load was too scanty to warrant the expense of its development. There was the metal-piercing load, available to law enforcement agencies, with a slightly more pointed 230-grain bullet at 945 fps, but its expanding properties were, if anything, inferior to the standard load.

One of most astute and readable commentaries on gunshot wounds is to be found, guest-authored by Colonel Frank T. Chamberlin, Medical Corps, U. S. Army, Retired, in the second volume of P. O. Ackley's Handbook for Shooters and Reloaders. Colonel Chamberlin notes that he had tried, a hundred times or more, to rupture or knock the jacket off of a military .45 bullet: boring holes in the tips, making saw cuts across the nose and similar approaches. Despite firing them into every imaginable sort of media, he was unable to shoot the jacket loose from the core.

We corroborated Colonel Chamberlin's findings by pulling the jacketed semi-wadcutter bullet from a 185-grain Remington Targetmaster cartridge, hollow-pointing the tip and reloading it ahead of 9.3 grains of Hercules Unique: a rather stiff load and not necessarily recommended, producing approximately 1240 fps and 632 foot-pounds. Although about half again as fast as the military load, when fired into a stack of pulp-wet telephone directories, the cavity in the nose collapsed inward, forming a sort of chisel-shaped point and leaving a wound channel less impressive than that of the unmodified bullet at the same velocity.

Introduction, a few years ago, of popular-priced equipment for swaging half-jacketed bullets — such as the C-H Swag-O-Matic press — opened a new area of exploration in maximum-performance .45 ACP reload-ing. Of the several nose shapes available by simply changing the nose punch, the spire and round nose types offered little promise in the way of expansion. The semi-wadcutter functioned quiet well, provided weight was kept below about 225 grains and preferably a bit less. The hollow-point version of the semi-wadcutter offers the best compromise between feedability and expansion. The cup-point, while possessing the maximum amount of sheer ferocity, is unsuitable for use in the .45 ACP because of its shape. The cup-points can, however, be used to excellent advantage in the M1917 revolvers.

In conducting a series of tests, we used a No. 255 Hensley & Gibbs mould — that's their light wadcutter for the .41 magnums — to turn out cores of pure, soft lead and, together with Speer .45 half jackets, processed them into hollow-point semi-wadcutters with the Swag-O-Matic. The resulting bullets weighed 196 grains and had about one-sixteenth of an inch of full-diameter exposed lead showing above the top of the half jacket. It's necessary to seat these with the shoulder flush with the case mouth; approximately 1.110-inches LOA. Using a charge powder, velocities averaged 1000 fps for 415 foot-pounds of energy. Expansion was good and feeding, generally, no great problem.

Reliability of feeding is the crucial problem when you commence working up combat loads with bullets having exposed lead at the tip. Lead, in its natural state, is not particularly slippery and it tends to bind instead of sliding up the feed ramp and into the chamber. Various remedies have proved helpful. A product called Dri-Slide, being a suspension of molybdenum disulfide in a petroleum solvent vehicle, can be applied to a common flannel cleaning patch and the noses of the bullets dabbed or twirled on the moist cloth after loading. Set the cartridges primer-down until the Dri-Slide dries and it seems to reduce feeding problems substantially.

Lacking Dri-Slide, a twirl of the bullet tip on an un-inked stamp-pad lightly saturated with the case sizing

Swaged, half-jacketed hollow point showed good shocking power, but usually lost most of its exposed lead.

lubricant seems to help. You should take care not to be too lavish with the lube, however, since an excess amount of oil within the chamber could subject the breech mechanism to increased strain due to the un-checked back-thrust of the case at the moment of firing. Polishing the surfaces of the feed ramp is, likewise, help-ful and the ramp itself can be coated with Dri-Slide if desired. Worn or spreading lips on the top of the maga-zine often are a source of feed stoppages.

Don't stick your neck out with any combat load, until you have made and tested a sizeable quantity to them through the gun — and magazines — in which you intend to use them. The most potent cartridge, if it doesn't get into the chamber and fire for some reason, is dangerously useless.

Still casting about for a means of producing the ideal core for swaging into the HPSWC half-jackets, we tried the Lyman No. 358156 design: a semi-wadcutter intend-ed for the .357 mag and .38 Special. The volume of metal in this bullet proved perfect for the jackets and swaging dies being used, producing a well formed bullet with just a thin sliver of exposed lead above the top of the jacket. When made with cores of pure lead, the resulting .452-inch diameter bullet weighed 173.5 grains and, with a couple of stiff and not necessarily recom-mended test loads, 9.0 grains of Hercules Unique gave 1300 fps and 650 foot-pounds. Increasing to 9.5 grains of Unique gave 1340 fps and 690 foot-pounds — nearly twice the energy of the standard factory load.

One final experiment with the swaged bullets con-sisted of using linotype metal instead of pure lead, casting with the Lyman No. 358156 mould to form the cores . . . a process having much to recommend it over cutting lead wire into short sections. With the harder core, the volume was the same, but the weight was reduced to 165 grains and, with a fingers-crossed increase to a not necessarily recommended charge of 10.0 grains of Hercules Unique, we obtained a velocity of 1400 fps, right on the nose, with 720 foot-pounds of muzzle energy.

We feel that this represents the upper practical limit of output for this cartridge in the Colt autoloader and strongly counsel that it be approached with caution, if at all. Even if the gun seems to handle this load with no trouble — as did our GI test arm, made by Remington-Rand — frequent use of such loads should be avoided and periodic inspections should be made to check for signs of battering or incipient cracks in those areas of the barrel, slide and receiver which bear the brunt of stopping the slide in its rearward motion. Installation of a recoil buffer, by a competent gunsmith, has merits for this application.

Recently Norma-Precision added the .45 ACP to its line of loaded ammunition in the form of a 230-grain jacketed hollow-point bullet; index number 264. Speed checks indicate typical velocities at the muzzle of 810 fps in the auto and 780 fps in an M1917 Smith & Wesson revolver; 333 and 308 foot-pounds respectively. The jacket material used in this bullet is the usual triclad soft steel favored by Norma and most European ammu-nition makers. At those velocities, the steel jacket does not upset too reliably. We tested several by firing them into saturated telephone directories and found that they rarely achieve a greater diameter at the nose than the usual .452-inch base dimension. This is not to say that they are ineffectual. On the contrary, there is no doubt that their shocking power exceeds that of the conven-tional full-jacket bullet. The flattened tip sends shock waves in all directions through the penetrated medium at right angles to the path of the bullet, while a round nose tends — at .45 velocities — to insinuate itself through the

target with a minimum of commotion.

The best, most effective, commercial bullet that we tested from a standpoint of expansion, was the DD variety formerly made by International Bullet & Ammu-nition Corporation of North Lindenhurst, New York. This firm was the corporate successor to Shooting Associates, Incorporated, and produce the DD bullets for auto pistols and its companion, the Nuro Shok bullet for revolvers and certain rifles. DD bullets for the .45 ACP were offered in three weights: 180, 200 and 225 grains. The exposed soft lead tip had a broad and shallow cavity which might be described as a dimple-nose, rather than a hollow-point. Whatever you choose to call it, there can be little doubt that it was effective.

We chose to do our experimenting with the 180-grain version, admiring the way that the top of its half-jacket tapered in slightly, so that little if any of the soft lead came in contact with the rifling of the barrel. Further, being the lightest, it has the highest potential velocity and, when you're after expansion and stopping capa-bility, there is nothing quite as useful as being able to boost the feet per second well beyond the thousand mark.

As with all of the other velocity tests listed here, we used FA/60 Match brass and Alcan Large Pistol primers. Initial resizing/decapping was performed in a Lyman T-C tungsten carbide die, followed by a pass over the ex-panding plug of a die furnished with the No. 310 Lyman tong tool, adapted for use in conventional reloading presses by one of the Lyman bushings made for the purpose. Bullets were seated, without crimping, in a C-H seating die for the .45 auto rim — chosen because it offers the option of crimping, if desired, or not crimping by screwing the die body slightly higher in the press.

The exact amount of crimp for the .45 ACP round is

Imressive muzzle flash from heavy charge of Unique powder provided sole illumination for taking this photo.

a question upon which there is everything except agreement. We prefer to perform a very slight crimp, just sufficient to assure that the loaded round will chamber without hang-up or resistance caused by a flared neck dragging its way up the walls of the chamber. For this purpose, it's hard to beat the taper crimp dies, such as those available from Gil Hebard Guns or RCBS, Incorporated, and that constituted our final production step. In adjusting the taper crimp die, it seems to work well to field strip the pistol and hold the barrel, chamber-up, dropping the loaded rounds into place. If they don't drop all the way by their own weight, chances are, there will be problems in the feeding, so the crimp die is turned down in the press until the cartridges chamber easily, without any extravagant degree of crimp being visible.

We started our tests with Hercules Unique and obtained results so gratifying that we never got around to trying anything else. Apparently, it's the logical choice for top velocity with light bullets in the .45 auto. There is a rather copious amount of muzzle flash when firing it in a dark dim area, but the velocity, coupled with good accuracy, compensates for that.

Starting at 8.0 grains of Unique behind the 180-grain IBAC DD bullet — a load suggested by IBAC president Walter Maryanov — we obtained 1050 fps for 440 foot-pounds; 8.5 grains of Unique gave 1180 fps and 556 foot-pounds; 9.0 grains gave 1250 fps with 622 foot-pounds. Tested by firing into soaked phone books, the expansion of the 180-grain IBAC bullets was, indeed, excellent. With 8.0 grains of Unique, penetration was six inches, nose expanded to .600-inch and weight of recovered bullet was 178.9 grains. With 9.3 grains of Unique — not necessarily recommended — penetration was seven inches, nose expanded to .675-inch and recovered weight was 178.2 grains.

Both test loads plowed impressive "wound channels" through the wet paper, leaving a pulped and macerated trail that averaged about 1½ inches in diameter near the entrance.

As noted, the unmodified military ammunition for the .45 auto has, in countless instances, proved effective out of all proportion to its paper statistics. Police departments that have changed over to carrying the .45 auto as a service weapon, report stopping capability vastly superior to that of the traditional .38 Special, even with standard commercial loadings.

The department in El Monte, California, for example, converted to the .45 auto. Just prior to that time, they had had three fire fights in close succession, all with the .38 Special and all with unsatisfactory results. The sight of the big auto's on the hips of the uniformed officers serves as a deterrent to violence — and, on that one occasion, a holdup in progress, the .45 restored peace with awesome finality. Detective Clarence Johnson of the El Monte department, in charge of the production of target ammunition for the force, reports satisfactory proficiency on the part of individual officers, contradicting the usual argument that the .45 auto is too hard to learn to shoot.

With the prospect of being able to produce combat loads that nearly double the energy of the factory load, expanding to .675 caliber without appreciable loss of bullet metal, the big self-feeder comes solidly into its own as a stopper with few if any peers. With eight rounds instead of the revolver's six and the added edge of a lightning-fast refill, the .45 has a lot going for it.

The .41 Magnum Is Meant To Fill A Hole In Police Armament; Special Loads Can Help!

These three guns were used in test firing. From Top: S&W Model 57 with 6-inch barrel; S&W Model 58 with 4-inch; Ruger Blackhawk with 4-5/8-inch.

THE .41 MAGNUM came along during the winter of '63-'64 in response to considerable clamor from a number of those who felt — not without reason — that there was a need for a caliber suitable for adoption by police departments to replace the traditional .38 Special. The supporters of the .41 were off-set by an equally vociferous group who maintained that there was something pretty underhanded about ringing in yet another caliber when we already had the .44 Special, the .44 magnum, the .44-40, the .38-40 and various other previously established calibers of comparable power.

However, the final approval or veto of any new caliber lies with the buying public and nine years and a bit later, it looks as though some have given the nod to the partisans of the .41 magnum, because it has been adopted by a number of police departments and — perhaps more important — has been bought with the hard-earned cash of numerous civilian customers.

When it became a pretty good bet that this was the way the tide was swinging, Sturm, Ruger & Company brought out their Blackhawk in the .41 magnum chambering. It had been available in .357 magnum and .44 magnum prior to that. A beefed up and flossified version of the .44 magnum had been available as the Super Blackhawk — regarded by a sizeable cadre of handgun enthusiasts as a modern classic. Many of these would have welcomed the .41 version in the super category — with its unfluted cylinder, larger grip, straightbacked trigger guard, and other desirable refinements. However, it was the standard Blackhawk in which the .41 was offered so that's the version we used in what was, essentially, a review of progress in the reloading of the .41 magnum caliber in the years since its introduction.

When the caliber first was introduced, we received the six-inch barreled Model 57 Smith & Wesson, together with a set of RCBS reloading dies and did not receive any empty brass or loaded cartridges for a matter of several weeks after that. We scanned through Lyman's Handbook of Cast Bullets in search of suitable slugs in the proper .410-inch diameter and found three that looked — and later proved — quite adaptable. These were the No. 410214 and No. 410426, as shown in the book, plus a shortened version of the No. 412263 with its lower driving band and grease groove eliminated. Though the fact is not widely known, Lyman can and will furnish any of their mould designs on special order with a specified part of its base missing. The cutting tool used in forming the mould cavity — called a "cherry," by the way — simply is not inserted as deeply and the resulting mould will produce a shorter, lighter bullet.

We became impatient to burn powder in the new .41 and, lacking only the brass, we painfully cobbled some together out of .30-30 brass, which has a similar head dimension. We don't recommend the technique but we produced eleven custom-made cases which lasted until the shipment of genuine .41 loads arrived from Remington like the U.S. Cavalry galloping over the crest in the last reel of an old movie.

The old .41 Long Colt cartridge, now nearly defunct, will drop out of sight in the chamber of the .41 magnum since its rim diameter is a trifle smaller than the boring of the .41 mag chamber. The .41LC had a barrel with a groove diameter of approximately .401-inch and took the same diameter of bullet as the .38-40 although the .41LC generally was loaded with a "step-heel" design of bullet which had a shank of .386-inch diameter that fitted inside the case mouth with the .401-inch portion being exposed. The .41 magnum, on the other hand, achieves that rare consistency between designation and diameter since its groove diameter is .410-inch. Bullets for the .41 magnum likewise are sized to .410-inch diameter by most of the reloaders who work with this caliber.

Smith & Wesson offers the .41 magnum in two versions: the Model 57, in either bright blue or nickel, with 4, 6 or 8-3/8-inch barrel and one-eighth-inch red ramp front sight with a micrometer click rear sight that is adjustable for windage and elevation. There's a white outline around the rear notch and it's a good rig for shooting under conditions of poor visibility. Later, S&W introduced their Model 58, in a Military & Police version in blue or nickel finish. The Model 58 has a one-eighth-inch ramp front sight, matted to prevent glare, and the rear sight in a milled slot in the top of the receiver, non-adjustable as is customary in their M&P design; it's available with a four-inch barrel only.

The Ruger Blackhawk currently is offered in a choice of .357 magnum or .41 magnum caliber, either size with barrel length of 4-5/8 or 6½ inches. There also are .30 carbine versions in 7½ only plus a .45 LC/ACP in 4-5/8 or 7½-inch barrels.

We chose to get the version of the .41 Blackhawk with the shorter barrel, feeling that the slight sacrifice in velocity was balanced by compactness and convenience. Besides, we had a six-inch Model 57 Smith & Wesson and it offered a good chance to compare velocities through both the short and long barrels.

Four cavity mould by Hensley & Gibbs with five of their .41 designs. From left are the No. 258 semi-wadcutter; No. 263 round nose; the No. 256 semi-wadcutter; the No. 253 flat nose; No. 255 wadcutter.

Smith & Wesson loaned us a Model 58 so that we could round out the comparison with its four-inch barrel. We welcomed the chance since this is the version of the 41 magnum that has been adopted for standard issue by an ever-growing number of police departments and it offered a chance to find out how assorted loads checked out as to point of impact with the fixed sights on the Model 58.

Somehow, a reloader never seems able to find as many empty cases as he thinks he should have so we added to a meager supply by buying a box of primed empty cases from a local emporium.

The dies used were our original set of RCBS, which includes a tungsten carbide sizing die. It leaves the case in perfect condition, without the unsightly ridge just above the head which is left by some of the earlier carbide sizing dies...especially when used on the .357 magnum. Second of the RCBS dies is a combination that decaps and flares the mouth to receive the base of the bullet without shaving lead. Third and final die is the one that seats and crimps. If you wish to seat the bullet to a desired depth without crimping, then crimp as a fourth operation, it's a simple matter to accomplish this with the third die by screwing the body up in the press so that the case mouth isn't crimped, running the seating stem downward to provide proper seating depth; after this you reverse the procedure, screwing the die body down until it puts the desired amount of crimp on the mouth, meanwhile having run the seating stem up so it doesn't contact the nose of the bullet.

It's quite important to perform a good strong crimp for the .41 magnum, particularly if the bullet tip projects up nearly flush with the front surface of the cylinder, as many of them do, and/or if the powder charge is one that will deliver considerable recoil. A light crimp will allow the bullets to work forward out of the case from the force of recoil as the first few rounds are fired and if the tip projects ahead of the cylinder, it will hang up the whole shebang when that chamber's turn comes up since the projecting tip won't clear the rear of the barrel.

Despite the need for heavy crimps, reloading life of the .41 brass has been better than might be expected. Some of the present cases have been reloaded upward of thirty times apiece and we've yet to lose a case to the split-neck virus, nor have we annealed them or taken any other steps beyond simply running them in and out of the dies.

Frankly, we like the .41 magnum as a caliber and can recommend it without reservation to any handgunner interested in a moderately beefy cartridge that offers broad flexibility through reloading. It's a good-natured, omnivorous sort of cartridge that will work surprisingly well when fed a bewildering variety of components. For example, there are upward of thirty different powders that can be used with some degree of success. Primers for this caliber are those designated as Large Pistol size by their manufacturers.

In the bullet department, the .41 buff now has a wide variety from which to choose. Lyman has added five new designs to the three previously mentioned. Hensley & Gibbs offer five new designs while SAECO has one. Accuracy Bullets, Markell and Green Bay Bullets have added the .410-inch diameter to their respective lines of cast and lubricated bullets while Speer offers two versions of half-jacketed, with solid or hollow points. Some of the items offered by the makers of cast bullets are similar or identical to those from Lyman, H&G or SAECO moulds. The choice of weights, readily available, ranges from the 166-grain Hensley & Gibbs No. 255 upward to the 242-grain Lyman No. 410426. Weights here are only approximate and will vary according to the composition of the bullet metal, these being taken with a hard mix consisting of wheel weights with added tin.

Considerable discussion has been published on reloading the .41 magnum. For example, the interested reader is referred to a six-page article in the 1966 edition of The Gun Digest. It lists, on page 262, a number of loads ranging upward in power to one with 22.0 grains of Hodgdon's H-110 powder behind the 242-grain No. 410426 Lyman round nose bullet; this load, chronographed from the six-inch Model 57 S&W, delivers 1445 fps and 1120 foot-pounds...which is only slightly less than the rated energy for the .44 magnum in standard factory loading. This particular load is somewhat more potent than most of those seen listed elsewhere and we doubt not that the pressure is substantial. However, Dean Grennell loaded and fired many rounds of this load and has experienced no signs of excessive pressure such as difficult extraction in his own Smith & Wesson Model 57. Reloaders who wish to try this particular load may elect to reduce the powder charge to 18.0 or 20.0 grains for a start and work up from that point. It also should be noted that this load works best when high-energy primers are used, such as the CCI No. 350 "magnum," and that H-110 ignites and burns best when the base of the bullet is seated right down to the surface of the powder charge to minimize the air space within the cartridge without, necessarily, compressing the powder itself.

It's an accurate load in the Model 57 and it displays astounding capabilities for penetration. Grennell once tried six rounds through a junked '56 Ford and five went completely through both front doors from side to side at fifty yards while the sixth hit an arm rest on the far door and didn't quite make it. Suffice to say, it would be adequate for any ordinary highway patrol uses. When checked through the Ruger, we got the same velocity – 1445 fps – with this load, and 1420 fps out of the four-inch S&W Model 58.

By way of comparison, the two factory loads both use 210-grain bullets. According to P. O. Ackley – in Volume II of his Handbook for Shooters & Reloaders, page 224 – the medium speed, lead bullet factory load carries 6.7 grains of Bullseye while the high speed, jacketed soft-point

Lyman moulds were used to make these .41 bullets. From left, they are: No. 410214 shortened, 410426, the 41028, 41032, 41026 and maker's No. 41027 hollow base.

Liz Stevens peers through gaping hole blasted in cake of soap by backward-loaded No. 41027 hollow-base wadcutter and 4.5 grains of AL-120.

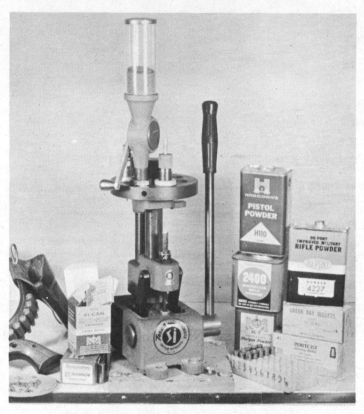

Texan's seven-station turret press was used to make up test loads, with dies and rotary powder measure by RCBS, including carbide sizing die.

load uses about 21.0 grains of 295 Ball powder. Presumably, the latter is similar to the No. 295HP Ball powder which Winchester-Western marketed briefly a few years ago. It's also similar, but not identical to Hodgdon's H-110 powder which Hodgdon designates as spherical type. This is nice powder to use, because it meters smoothly and uniformly through most measures.

We chronographed the two factory loads through a six-inch S&W Model 57 and got readings of 1007 fps for the lead bullet and 1382 fps for the soft-point. Mr. Ackley, in his book just mentioned, lists the following data for the two factory loads:

	LEAD BULLET	SOFT-POINT
10-inch test barrel	1135 fps	1600 fps
8¾-inch revolver barrel	1050	1500
6-inch revolver barrel	990	1350
4-inch revolver barrel	940	1250

The reload with 22.0 grains of H-110 behind the 242-grain Lyman No. 410426, at 1445 fps, gives an extra 32 grains of bullet weight and a sixty-three fps gain in velocity over the factory round for a muzzle energy of about 1120 foot-pounds...as compared to 888 foot-pounds which is the actual energy of the factory soft-point load as checked on our chronograph; this is a substantial gain of 232 foot-pounds and you might liken it to shooting something with the factory soft-point and hitting it simultaneously with a slug from a .38 Special since an average load in that caliber carries about 232 foot-pounds.

Considerable load data for the .41 magnum already has been published in various sources. The Ackley book alone lists over 115 different loads for it in bullet weights from 105 to 240 grains.

For the high-velocity load, we gravitated toward the Hensley & Gibbs No. 255 wadcutter, which weighs approximately 166 grains when cast hard. For propellant, we chose Alcan's AL-5 shotshell powder, which repeatedly has proven a good choice for peak velocity with light bullets from short barrels; primers were Alcan large pistol size. Results of numerous test rounds were:

Grains of AL-5	Ruger 4-5/8"	S&W M57 6"	S&W M58 4"
13.2	1400 fps		
13.7	1450		

14.7	1500	1540	1465
15.7	1578	1550	
16.2	1580	1590	
17.0	1628	1660	1615

The seventeen-grain charge should be regarded as maximum; it is definitely too much for the Model 58 Military & Police and, for other guns, it should be approached with caution at the risk and discretion of the reloader and/or shooter. Figures would be closely comparable for the same charges with Lyman's No. 410214 which is a blunt nose design similar to a wadcutter only minus the sharp shoulder. The No. 410214 weighs from 168 to 172 grains depending on the alloy.

The Lee Loader kit offered for the .41 magnum incorporates the No. 069 Lee dipper, with a capacity of .069 cubic inch, being identical to Lee's old No. 410M dipper. This measures out 12.4 grains of AL-5 and we used that charge behind the Lyman No. 41027; this is a 220-grain hollow base wadcutter design and we loaded it backwards into the case, with the cavity to the front and found that the 12.4 grains of AL-5 from the Lee dipper gave 1450 fps at the muzzle.

Other powders, with the same dipper and the same bullet gave performance as follows: 10.0 grains of Herco for 1320 fps, a potent load with moderate pressures; 12.7 grains of AL-7 for 1420 fps; 15.2 grains of No. 2400 for 1275 fps and 10.5 grains of Unique for 1440 fps. All of these appeared suitable as to pressure for use in the Model 58 and, of course, in the Ruger and Model 57 as well.

We wanted to donk a cake of Fels Naphtha with the cup point load to show its remarkable expansion but had to drop the charge clear down to 4.5 grains of AL-120 before it left enough of the soap to be recognizable. At around 1400-plus, it simply covered the surrounding terrain with a thin film of soap flakes!

Lyman's bid for a .41 mag target wadcutter is their No. 41026, a 200-grain, plain base design. Unfortunately, its designer incorporated a generous length of full diameter lead ahead of the crimping groove. His plausible theory was that this would guide it accurately through the throat of the chamber. While this sounds good on paper — they claimed one-hole groups at twenty-five yards with 4.0 grains of Red Dot — the average reloader usually is disillusioned to discover that he can't drive the loaded rounds into his chambers with a polo mallet unless he seats the bullet about a sixteenth of an inch deeper than the normal crimping groove. The hollow base wadcutter, Lyman No. 41027, has the same obstructing band at the front although this does not bother when you're loading it backwards as just described, since the base of the driving band is narrow enough so that you can crimp it into the bottom grease groove with no trouble.

Lyman lists several designs for the .41 magnum in their current catalogs, plus a semi-obsolete number which is available, though not presently shown. The number 410214 is a small wadcutter which comes out at around 170 grains, depending upon the alloy used for casting. The 410214 is unusual in that it has a flat tip with rounded edges, rather than the traditional sharp-cutting front edge. However, it's a good, accurate bullet for light loads in this caliber.

Other Lyman designs — from current catalogs — are the 41026, a 199-grain full wadcutter; the 41027, a similar wadcutter, but with a conical hollow-base; the 41028, a flat-tip which comes close to duplicating the shape of the factory loaded bullets for this caliber; the 41032, a 212-grain semi-wadcutter with a plain base and the 410610, a gas-checked semi-wadcutter of about 210 grains. Weights on the 41027 run 220 grains, 212 for the 41028 design.

Green Bay Bullets offers the No. 256 Hensley & Gibbs — a good little 197-grain semi-wadcutter — plus the Lyman No. 41026 wadcutter and proprietor Dick Bienzen recommends the H&G design over the long-shouldered Lyman.

Markell makes two of the H&G designs: the No. 256 in either plain lead or copper plated and the No. 255, their 166-grain wadcutter, unplated. The unplated versions are, of course, hardened to prevent bore leading.

Accuracy Bullets offers the 220-grain semi-wadcutter designed by Elmer Keith; this is practically identical to the H&G No. 258, with a single, square-cornered grease groove. The Lyman No. 41032 is also similar but it has a rounded grease groove; even so, it's hard to knock from the mould because of all the other squared corners.

Speer offers the two half-jacket designs: a 200-grain hollow-point for which they recommend either 18.5 grains of AL-8 (1377 fps) or 21.0 grains of H-110 (1381 fps) as the most accurate charges in their tests. The 220-grain Speer half-jacket is said to give best accuracy with 19.0 grains of No. 2400 at 1362 fps.

SAECO has a 230-grain semi-wadcutter which they designate as their No. 14: it has a single, square-bottom grease groove and a crimping groove.

In addition to the No. 255 and 256 designs discussed here, Hensley & Gibbs offers their semi-wadcutter No. 258 at 222 grains; No. 263, a 218-grain round nose and No. 253, a 210-grain flat tip similar to the factory soft-point. If these quoted weights seem confusingly contradictory, it's due to the variation caused by different amounts of hardening metal such as antimony or tin used in the casting alloy; such metals, being lighter than lead, make for lighter bullets if present in higher percentages.

Remington lists their 210-grain lead bullet as a separate component available for reloading.

If you took all of the bullets presently available for the .41 mag and multiplied that number times the thirty-odd types of powder that can be used, and that number times perhaps five different charge weights for each...and that number times five or six available large pistol primers...that number times the three guns on hand...you would arrive at a fairly frightsome figure. To load and shoot five rounds of each possible combination plus another through the chronograph would take a large chunk out of the average reloader's lifetime. The current test series included twenty-eight different loads through the chronograph and many of these onto target. Since the latest sets of load data from Hercules and Alcan do not list the .41 magnum, we concentrated somewhat on their powders so as to provide the missing dope. Hodgdon and DuPont both include listings on the .41 in their latest data books so their figures were not duplicated except for exploring bullet weights that they didn't list.

There was a problem whose solution eluded us: we wanted to isolate one load that would hit at the point of aim at seventy-five feet with the fixed-sight Model 58 Smith & Wesson. Light bullets, as usual, struck low — by as much as a foot at that range — and most of the other loads which were tried through it were off to one side or the other, with the 242-grain round nosed No. 410426 Lyman coming about the closest to the bullseye. Unless you enjoy using "Kentucky windage," there's really nothing to take the place of adjustable sights although the difference in the cost between the Models 57 and 58 is considerable enough to offset this in the minds of many purchasers. This sort of thinking, in our experience, is commonly found in the minds of the city fathers who approve or veto expenditures for the budgets of police departments.

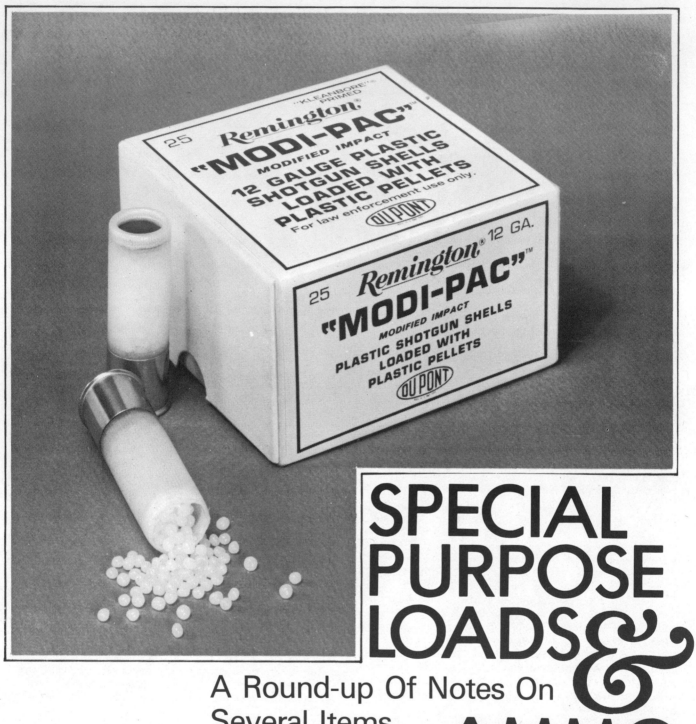

SPECIAL PURPOSE LOADS & AMMO

A Round-up Of Notes On Several Items That Defy Classification Elsewhere!

Chapter 16

THERE ARE SEVERAL types of ammunition for the police handgun and shotgun which can be purchased, ready for use or in the form of components for reloading, offering special performance for extraordinary police applications.

An example is the shot load for handguns, which can be handy to have for those peculiar, unpredictable situations which have a way of cropping up now and then in the day to day routine of police work. Sharply limited as to range and penetration, the shot loads spread quite rapidly from the short, rifled barrel of a handgun.

These factors combine to make it a strictly short-range

proposition, useful for flushing out an animal who has taken up an inaccessible position beneath a building, in a length of culvert or similar locations. Assume that you don't want to kill the animal on the spot — as would be done by a standard bullet — you just want to haze him out under his own power. The stinging effect of the fine-size bird shot in the handgun shot load can prove highly effective.

Remco Corporation, 1404 Whitesboro Street, Utica, New York 13502, makes the Remco shot cap: a suitable quantity of number 9 shot — size 6 or 7 available on special order — put up in a plastic capsule in four sizes, for handloading into brass for .38 Special, .357 magnum, .44 magnum, .45 Long Colt or .45 ACP. The same capsule doubles for both the .38 and .357 calibers.

Load data is furnished with the capsules, with Hercules Bullseye being specified for use in all calibers.

CALIBER	CHARGE WEIGHT	SHOT CAP WEIGHT
.38 Special	3.5 gr Bullseye	156 grains
.357 magnum	4.0	156
.44 magnum	7.0	250
.44 Long Colt	4.5	270
.45 ACP	5.0	150

The .45 ACP capsule is contoured so that it will chamber in the auto if fed by retracting and releasing the slide. However, usually the force of recoil is insufficient to work the action. As a result, we would suggest that it be single-loaded into the chamber and, if additional shots are anticipated, depend upon a magazine full of conventional ammunition. It may be necessary to work the slide to chamber the next round.

Shot loads are particularly useful in those localities where venomous snakes are common enough to account for an occasional call for the police to deal with the problem. The pattern spread is just right to do a good job on snakes from a comfortably safe distance; say six feet or so.

Speer/DWM, Box 896, Lewiston, Idaho 83501, offers a loaded shot round for use in the .38 Special — equally suited for firing in the .357 mag — which is put up in pocket packs of six rounds. This load is extremely effective, both as to velocity and spread. Our tests indicate dispersion of about one inch per foot of distance from the muzzle. For example, average diameter of the pattern is six inches at six feet, ten inches at ten feet and so on.

Muzzle velocity from a six-inch revolver barrel is right around 1100 fps, ample to bury the pellets out of sight in wood within twenty-five feet or so. The empty Speer capsules are available at considerably lower cost. These permit you to fill them with the shot size of your choice, or with any other appropriate compound such as oil pigments for marking purposes.

Once filled, they are easy to handload by means of conventional techniques. Speer suggests powder charges of 6.0 grains of Hercules Unique or 5.0 grains of DuPont SR-7625: either good for over 1100 fps in a six-inch barrel. Pressures developed by these loads are down around 13,000 psi, moderate in comparison to standard ball ammo in this caliber.

Speer does not recommend higher powder charges for use in the .357 magnum, noting that loading more powder merely lessens pattern performance with little gain in velocity. The same loads can be put up in .357 mag cases, if desired. Be sure to seat the capsules deeply enough not to project from the front of the chamber and give them a firm roll-crimp.

We should note that we've fired a great many of the

Although the armor-piercing bullet absolutely does not expand, this does not mean that it is any great pleasure to stop one! This is the half of a sectioned block of oil-base clay hit by one of the 9mm Luger KTW round – and hit hard.

Here's an engine block that was hit by an array of .357 magnum loads. The star-shaped smear was left by conventional metal-piercing load; gaping holes mark impact point of KTW loads.

Here's a closer look at the holes in the photo above. KTW loads tore through outer casting and put heavy dents in the cylinder walls.

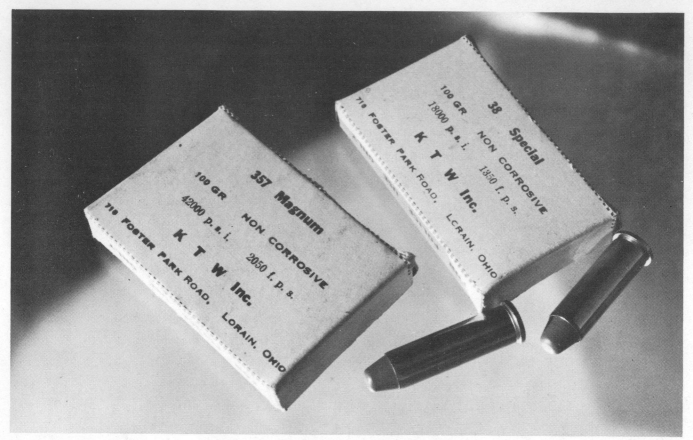

KTW loads for most calibers are put in in handy pocket packs of six rounds each. Bullets, as of 1972, have steel cores rather than original tungsten alloy. Bullets for .38 and .357 each are 100 grains: 1350 fps for the .38, 2050 fps for .357 magnum.

Speer capsule loads and have never had one fail to open upon leaving the muzzle. However, in occasional instances, the Remco capsules have reached the target intact. Needless to say, this could create a problem if non-lethal effect was intended since the intact capsule has at least as much punch as a solid bullet of the same weight; usually more. So it is suggested that — as with all unfamiliar loads — extensive testing be carried out to become acquainted with performance before adopting them for regular duty use.

In many cities, it is not uncommon for certain species of birds to pose a serious nuisance. Pigeons, crows and starlings are among those of which this may be true. Several control techniques have been tried but, as yet, few work as well as shooting a portion of the offensive horde. For obvious reasons, it is better that this be done as inconspicuously as possible, in the interests of friction-free public relations.

Since distances may extend to twenty-five yards or a bit farther, few guns work as well as the high-quality air rifles which combine accuracy, mild report and ample power to assure humane kills. Two dependable performers are the Sheridan and the recently introduced Smith & Wesson Model 77A. Both of these rifles are of the hand-pumped design, permitting excellent control over the amount of power delivered. Both are capable of accuracy adequate to assure hits on a pigeon at twenty-five yards, with enough remaining energy for dependable results at that distance.

There are pellet guns designed to operate on reservoirs of liquified carbon dioxide — CO2 — gas and, while these are more convenient, few if any have the power capabilities of the hand-pumped air rifles mentioned.

As was noted in the section under that heading, non-lethal weaponry often may or may not qualify for that term, depending upon the distance. No matter how light the projectile may be in weight, if it packs enough velocity, it can cause serious and/or fatal damage. At one time, wax bullets were much in vogue for practice and training purposes. As an experiment, one of these, in caliber .38 size — weighing about eleven grains — was loaded into a caliber .35 Remington cartridge and fired in a bolt action rifle of that chambering ahead of a charge of 14.0 grains of DuPont PB shotshell powder. At point blank range, the light wax slug proved amply capable of blowing a splintery hole completely through a piece of plywood, three-quarters-inch in thickness.

It is unlikely that there is a practical application for such a load, but it is noted to underscore the vital need for care and caution in the discharge of any projectile, no matter how light and innocuous it may seem. Even when the wax practice bullets have been loaded in the prescribed manner, with nothing but the primer for power, they have caused painful injury when striking the body through heavy clothing.

The foregoing is by way of introductory comments on Remington's Modi-Pac 12-gauge shotshell. The pellets in a shell number about 320 and are made of polyethylene plastic to approximately the diameter of a standard number 5 shot pellet. The total weight of the shot charge is only one-quarter ounce — about 95 grains — instead of the usual ounce and a quarter of standard shotshells.

For occasional specialized applications such as pest control in areas of high population density, the air rifle, such as this S&W Model 77A, offer a fine blend of low report, excellent accuracy and sufficient power to down crow-sized quarry.

Below: A graphic break-down on performance of the plastic pellet Remington Modi-Pac shotshell gives the rapid loss of velocity from point-blank range to distance of fifteen yards.

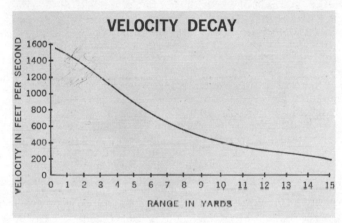

Performance of the Modi-Pac load is strongly dependent upon distance from the muzzle. Within the first nine feet, its effect is more than sufficiently lethal to provide adequate protection for the officer in the face of a determined and aggressive assailant. In fact, at three feet, its striking force and stopping power are equivalent to a point blank hit with a lead bullet from the .41 magnum. Thus, unlike some non-lethal weapons, the carrier is not vulnerable to close-range attack.

Variation of velocity with distance is shown graphically in the accompanying chart headed Velocity Decay. Leaving the muzzle at nearly 1600 fps, average velocity of the individual pellet has dropped to 1000 fps at a distance of four yards. By the time the pellets have traveled twenty-five yards, remaining energy is insufficient to penetrate a single thickness of common newspaper.

Suggested employment is by means of deflection firing — bouncing it from the ground into the aggressor's legs below the knee — at distances from three to fifteen yards. Typical pattern is ten feet in diameter at a distance of ten yards. In view of the hazard of eye injuries, discretion should be used in horizontal fire or shooting over the heads of an unruly crowd.

The Modi-Pac — short for modified impact — load has been engineered deliberately to produce an unusually large amount of muzzle flash, with a loud, sharp report. This is intended to enhance its psychological effect. Recoil is negligible but the Modi-Pac won't function in autoloading shotguns for that reason.

Available only as a loaded round and sold only to law enforcement agencies and military purchasers, the KTW metal-piercing ammunition is offered in six calibers: .380 auto, 9mm Luger, .38 Colt Super, .38 Special, .357 magnum and .30 M 1 carbine. In nearly every instance, the KTW load will penetrate twice as many thicknesses of metal as will the metal-piercing loads of other makes. Comparative charts are free upon request from the manufacturer: KTW, Incorporated, 710 Cooper-Foster Park Road, Lorain, Ohio 44053.

For convenience and economy, the KTW loads are packed in boxes of six rounds at a current price of $2 per box, except for the .30 carbine loads, which are packed seven per box at $3.50 per box.

Elsewhere in this book, under the discussion of bullet proof vests, there is a report on the rather singular effectiveness of the .38 Special KTW load which bored through steel plate that was merely dented by other factory loads, including several magnums. The remarkable penetration capability of the KTW load is secured without the development of abnormal breech pressures and at a rather moderate velocity.

The key factors seem to be the carefully developed shape of the bullet, the hard core and the teflon envelope which covers the foreportion to serve as a sort of lubricant during penetration. That part of the bullet which engages the rifling of the bore is enclosed in a copper-alloy jacket to prevent barrel wear.

Admittedly, the KTW load is expensive but its availability in specialized emergencies could make it a bargain at many times the price.

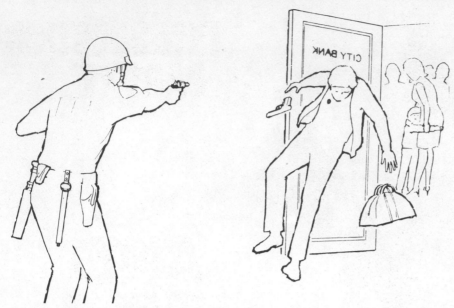

The epidemic of airliner hijacking, spawned in the Sixties and spreading into the Seventies, pointed out the need for a weapon system that would be highly effective at deactivating an armed and dangerous law-breaker as quickly as possible. The second specification for such a load made the solution more difficult: The walls of an airliner, pressurized at cruising altitude, are highly vulnerable if punctured. Should this occur, abrupt loss of cabin pressure can be an extremely serious matter.

Therefore, the need was apparent for a projectile which would terminate the threat of a dangerous felon without endangering other passengers and personnel or damaging the aircraft. Numerous other applications backed up the need for a closely comparable weapons system: hold-up

stake-out duty in stores and banks, court bailiffs, industrial security and so on.

The most promising answer that has turned up to date is an adaptation of the Stun Gun projectile — discussed elsewhere in this book under the heading of non-lethal weapons — with the implicit distinction that the Short Stop projectile is thoroughly lethal at short distances: within about fifty feet. By the time it has traveled over one hundred feet, the muzzle energy of 125 foot-pounds has dwindled to a mere 6 foot-pounds. That represents a velocity drop from over 1000 fps at the muzzle to about 190 fps at one hundred feet. Fired horizontally from shoulder height, the projectile drops to the ground in less than two hundred feet and is not apt to cause serious injury at half that distance.

A further good point is that the Short Stop load, manufactured by MB Associates, of San Ramon, California, does not require a special gun for firing. The Short Stop projectile is loaded into standard caliber .38 Special cartridge cases and can be fired in unmodified revolvers chambered for the .357 magnum as well as those for .38 Special.

The Short Stop projectile is, as noted, similar in principle to the one fired in the Stun Gun — which likewise is manufactured by MB Associates — except that the Short Stop projectile is lighter in weight and smaller in diameter, starting out at a much higher velocity. Opened out, the Short Stop is a pancake-shaped bag of tough cloth, weighing 70 grains and containing a small quantity of fine — size 12 — lead shot. Full diameter of the opened projectile is 1.2 inches.

When loaded into the cartridge and ready for firing, the cloth bag is folded to fit inside the case mouth and there is a thin plastic cap which protects the front of the load. Since this cap gives about the same contour as a conventional cartridge with a round-nosed bullet, it assists in rapid reloading of the cylinder by guiding the nose into the chamber.

Upon being fired, the bag travels up the barrel and a rapid spinning motion is imparted by the rifling in the bore. When the bag leaves the muzzle, the centrifugal force of this spinning motion causes it to open up and travel flat-side-foremost toward the traget. At the same time, the spinning stabilizes its flight path for better accuracy.

In addition to the applications mentioned before, the Short Stop load can be used to advantage in animal control work in densely populated areas.

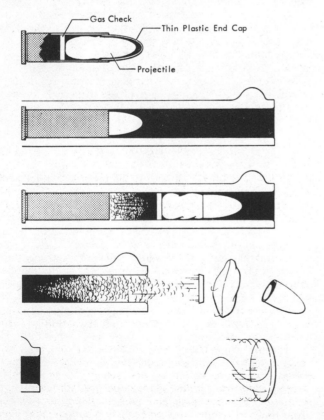

Gas Check
Thin Plastic End Cap
Projectile

Several firms have begun to offer Teflon coating for firearms on a commercial basis for protection. Some police departments have found this to be advantageous.

AND TO KEEP IT THAT WAY...

The Duty Weapon Can Be A Life Insurance Policy, If Premiums Are Kept Up!

*I*T IS POSSIBLE for a well made handgun to malfunction because of neglect and equally so due to improper maintenance. When a man finds the performance of his duties and his very life and well-being depending upon the reliable performance of a hunk of hardware, few would question that correct maintenance should receive its share of attention.

Rust and corrosion are the great enemies of firearm life and performance. The standard blued-steel finish is by no means proof against rust. In fact, some of the processes used in blueing steel are, themselves, a controlled form of rusting.

Some amount of water vapor always is present in the air and a sudden shift in temperature can and often does cause moisture to condense on metal surfaces — particularly when entering a warm, humid room after being outside at a cooler temperature. This, in itself, is enough to start the rusting process and, unless checked, it will continue getting worse progressively.

The real culprit, however, is salt — any of several salts, not necessarily common table salt or sodium chloride — which can be deposited on the steel surfaces in any of several manners. Normal human perspiration has a small content of various acids and salts, including sodium chloride. In some people, this percentage is considerably higher than normal. Let such a person touch an unprotected steel surface and the red-etched fingerprint can be seen plainly within a matter of hours or days.

It has only been within the last twenty years or so that the corrosive primer began being phased out of use and occasional lots of corrosive-primed ammunition still may be encountered in military calibers produced prior to about 1952. The .45 ACP and 9mm Luger military ammo are the two handgun calibers which, if produced before 1952, are most apt to have corrosive primers. The cut-off date of 1952 is by no means firm and uniform with all ammunition producers. There was a period of transition spanning from about 1950 to 1955 during which ordnance plants changed over to non-corrosive primers between lots of ammunition. The cautious procedure is, if in doubt, clean the gun thoroughly and apply rust preventive compounds.

Many a good barrel has been ruined, with possible damage to other parts of the gun, through neglect of this simple precaution. The old corrosive primers contained potassium chlorate and, when the primer detonated, this compound gave up its content of oxygen to support the reaction, leaving a residue of potassium chloride: a substance practically identical to common table salt.

Salt does not, in itself, cause steel or iron to rust. It is common to find that table salt becomes lumpy in the shaker from absorption of air-borne mositure and the same effect is what causes the trouble when minute deposits of salt are left on unprotected steel, whether as residue of firing by-products or from perspiration or similar contaminants. The salt attracts moisture and moisture rusts the steel.

In a similar manner, the black powder used in early firearms left a corrosive residue, requiring prompt cleaning and protection of iron and steel against the danger of rust. There is a popular belief that the introduction of non-corrosive priming and smokeless powder eliminated most if not all need for cleaning guns. This is by no means true.

The explosive compound used in modern, non-corrosive primers contains several materials including lead styphnate, any of several other explosive compounds and ground glass The last named substance is a major offender when deposited over friction-bearing parts as a firing residue. It's a necessary ingredient of the mixture since it provides heat through friction when the blow of the firing pin crushes the pellet of priming compound against the anvil of the primer. Without the content of ground glass in the priming compound, it would be difficult to duplicate the reliable ignition performance of the modern non-corrosive primer: difficult if not impossible.

The heat of the burning powder acts upon air-borne impurities to produce further deposits of harmful compounds after firing. Too, the by-products of smokeless powder are by no means as harmless to steel as often is supposed.

All of which points to the fairly obvious conclusion that you are not doing your duty weapon any favor by neglecting its routine maintenance and your inattention will hasten the day when it, in turn, may let you down. Too often, this can happen just when you need it most desperately.

In the opposite direction, you can speed the wearing process of a good handgun through improper, over-enthusiastic cleaning. In general cleaning materials and implements should not be harder than the steel surfaces being cleaned. This rules out, for example, steel wool as a bore cleaning swab, or emery cloth for use on the outer surfaces and similar dubious procedures.

Another unwise procedure to avoid is excessive use of the wrong oil in the wrong places. For example, thick, slippery coatings of oil inside the chamber, remaining at the time of the next firing, make it impossible for the sides of the case to adhere normally to the chamber walls at the peak of pressure. This allows the full rearward push of the explosion to be directed against the bolt face or frame and imposes much greater than average strain upon the frame and mechanism of the gun.

Again, contrary to popular beliefs, all oils do not necessarily protect against rust. Common engine lubricating oil, for example, is all but worthless as a rust preventive coating. So — unfortunately — are several other slippery compounds whose labels proclaim them to be lubricants and rust preventives. One such goop, found so widely that its name has become a household word or nearly so, will protect against rust only briefly, if at all; meanwhile, if it's coated on a steel surface, it becomes gummy and turns into a sort of horrible brown varnish, waxing progressively browner as the metal surface underneath rusts away.

Resist the temptation to experiment with automotive waxes as protection for external firearm surfaces. Often they make the polished blueing sparkle beautifully and they offer a modest amount of protection — right up to the moment you commence firing the gun to the point that it heats up the barrel and nearby areas. About this time, the auto wax is apt to take on general appearance of a pinto pony and, once baked on, it's not easy to remove.

We do not propose to list the unsatisfactory substances which should not be used in maintenance of firearms; it would be all but impossible to compile a complete listing of them and new ones appear constantly.

Rather, in the discussion that follows, we'll list several lubricants and preservatives that have proved themselves effective and satisfactory for this particular application. Again, the list is not complete and good new products will turn up on the market from time to time. Many of the better ones have gotten away from the inclusion of petroleum products. Unlike foodstuffs, it's not required that the ingredients be listed on the label but you'll find some with a long listing of materials that they do not contain: long enough to leave you wondering how they found something left to put in the bottle or can! Suffice to say, they did and it works.

So far as we know, no rust preventive compound provides eternal protection at the present state of the art. The best of them will protect for several weeks if the gun is not used, handled or fired — hardly applicable to the officer's duty weapon. After use and cleaning, a light coating of rust preventive and/or lubricant should be applied to the surfaces exposed to corrosion and/or wear.

The teflon coating, mentioned earlier in this book, offers one of the most permanent and satisfactory solutions to the corrosion problem; so does nickel plating or all-stainless construction. Cosmoline — widely used as a gun storage medium in the military services — affords virtually eternal protection but the gun so protected is out of service until someone devotes a vast amount of elbow grease to its cleaning.

So let's shift to discussing the specific steps, procedures and materials that will keep your hardware companion working better and longer. The odds are excellent that, if you take proper care of it, your duty weapon will stand ready to return the favor, should its authoritative services be required.

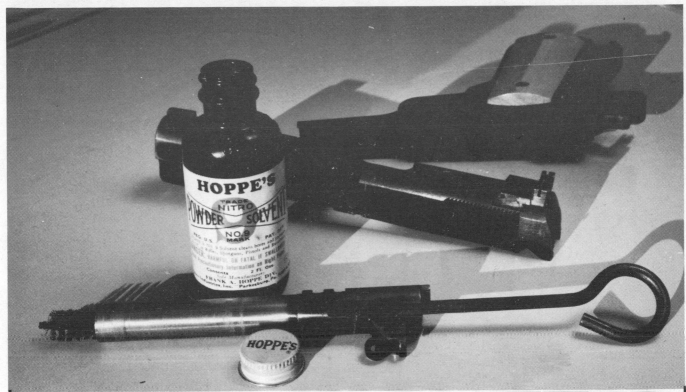

A MATTER OF MAINTENANCE

Keeping The Gun And Its Parts Moving Free And Easy Is More Than Half The Battle!

Chapter 17

A HANDGUN WITH a fouled bore usually will shoot at the expense of accuracy. Normal firing residue is not a severe problem in this respect, but lead fouling of the bore is highly detrimental to accuracy.

Cleaning a handgun after firing is a simple operation if metal fouling is not present. Attach a bristle brush to the end of the cleaning rod, moisten it well with a good bore-cleaning solution and scrub the length of the barrel with several strokes, applying more bore cleaner during the process, if necessary. As a rule, cleaning brushes with nylon bristles are preferable to those with bronze or brass bristles although non-marring metal bristles may be required if metal fouling has to be removed.

Each chamber of a revolver must be cleaned in much the same manner as the barrel itself. Take care, when running the brush through revolver chambers, that a loose bristle does not lodge between the front of the ejector star and the rear of the cylinder since this could prevent or interfere with lock-up of the cylinder in the same manner as discussed elsewhere regarding granules of unburned powder.

After the bore and chambers have been scrubbed thoroughly with brushes and bore cleaner, remove the brush from the end of the cleaning rod and install the patch holder. Push dry cleaning patches through the barrel and through each chamber of a revolver until the patches come out clean.

Inspect the bore and chambers under good light at this point. It may be helpful, in the case of revolvers, to hold a piece of paper or similar light-reflecting object behind the rear of the barrel to reflect illumination for inspection. All interior metal surfaces should appear bright and clean at this stage.

TSI-300 is a versatile synthetic that cleans, lubes and protects.

Though developed for black powder uses, this works with smokeless.

Companion TSI product cleans cartridge brass, retards future tarnish.

If metal fouling is present, or if powder deposits have built up in the chambers, it can be seen easily during inspection. Lead fouling usually will appear as darker streaks between the lands of the barrel rifling; more pronounced toward the rear of the barrel. While bullets having jackets of copper alloy can and do leave metal fouling in the bore, it is extremely rare for copper fouling to be as heavy as lead deposits.

Metal fouling may respond to further application of cleaning brushes and bore solvent and, usually, this is where the use of bronze bristle brushes will prove helpful. In extreme cases, more effective remedies must be applied.

One of the most useful and effective tools for removal of stubborn deposits is the Lewis lead remover from LEM Gun Specialties of College Park, Georgia. This consists of a rod with a T-handle and a rubber tip of correct diameter to which is affixed a circular patch of brass screen. The rod is inserted from the muzzle, the screen and plug assembly is screwed into the end of the rod and pulled toward the muzzle and out; repeating the process as required, with bore cleaner being applied to the brass screen each time.

The Lewis lead remover has a second attachment, a tapered plug which holds the brass screen in such a manner that it can be used to remove lead deposits from the forcing cone at the rear of a revolver barrel. Most revolvers will build up a quantity of bullet metal at this point and the improvement after treatment with the Lewis unit can be quite impressive.

In extremely stubborn cases of metal fouling, metallic mercury — quicksilver — is one of the most effective remedies. Mercury unites with many metals, including copper, lead and other metals used in cast bullets, to form a softer mixture called an amalgam. Metallic mercury is expensive and not too readily available, one source of salvage being the small, glass-enclosed switches used in some heating thermostats and similar controls.

If enough mercury is on hand, the barrel can be stopped tightly at one end by means of a cork or wooden plug. The barrel can be clamped in a vise with the open end uppermost and the bore can be poured full of mercury and allowed to remain until the fouling has been softened or dissolved. If only a small amount of mercury is available, the barrel can be stoppered tightly at both ends and the liquid metal can be worked about by tilting or careful shaking.

You may hear reports that the medicinal preparation known as blue ointment — used in the control of bodily parasites and containing some percentage of mercuric compounds — can be used to soften and remove bore fouling. We have tried it for this application and found it quite ineffective for the purpose.

Another problem fouling area is that point in revolver chambers just ahead of the case mouth. A build-up of powder residue may occur here and, if allowed to accumulate over a long interlude between thorough cleanings, it defies removal quite stubbornly. One of the more serious examples of this problem will occur in .357 magnum revolvers in which large amounts of .38 Special ammunition have been fired. The shorter case tends to build deposits in that gap between the mouth and the front of the chamber and, if left unchecked, it is apt to reach the point where .357 ammunition no longer can be chambered. The Lewis lead removing tool can be quite helpful and effective in dealing with this problem. Lacking such a device, various approaches can be tried. If a spare pistol cleaning rod is available, the handle or loop can be removed with a hacksaw, a brass cleaning brush installed in the forward end with the rear being chucked into an electric drill. Wet the bristles with bore cleaner and insert the brush into the chamber before turning on the drill, moving the brush back and forth as it

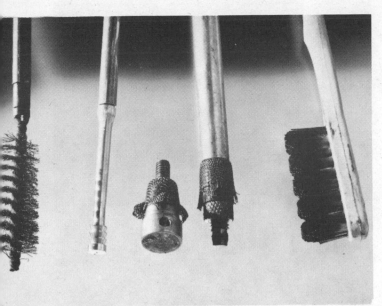

Cleaning aids, from left: bronze wire brush, patch holding tip, Lewis cone cleaner and bore swab, toothbrush that, wet with cleaner is handy for odd corners.

turns. Only if absolutely necessary, a small tuft of the finest grade of steel wool can be wound around the bristles to assist in removal of stubborn deposits in the front of revolver chambers.

Under no conditions should this technique be employed in the barrel. The steel used in most gun barrels is not particularly hard and damage to the rifling would result. It should be emphasized that the treatment just described is for use only when ordinary methods prove ineffective. A typical example might be the restoration of a recently acquired handgun which has suffered through a long period of abuse and neglect.

After the bore and chambers — or chamber, in the

Lewis lead remover here is being turned by T-handle to scrub away deposits of lead fouling in revolver forcing cone.

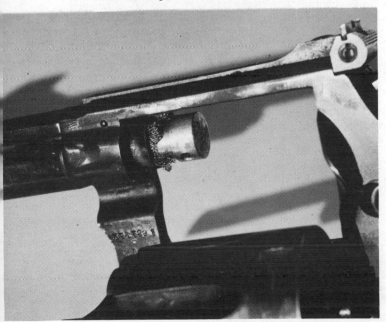

instance of autoloaders — have been thoroughly cleaned down to the bare steel, a light coating of a suitable rust preventive should be applied on a clean patch to protect the metal until the next time the gun is fired. Unless the gun is exposed to severe conditions such as rain, cleaning the bore is not necessary except after firing, although it is indicated in the course of routine periodic maintenance for guns which are stored for long intervals without being fired.

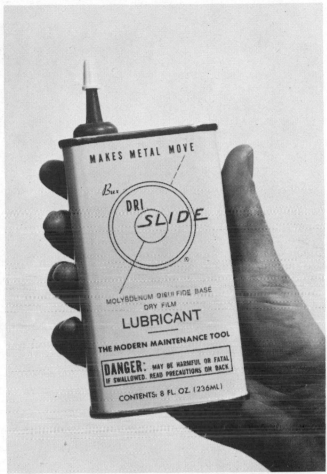

Temperature has little effect upon Dri Slide performance; it also fights rust.

Bore cleaner applied to a rag and/or an old toothbrush can be used to remove powder residue and similar foreign matter from the feed ramp of autoloaders and outer surfaces and this should be followed by a wipe-down with the selected rust preventive material. Again, reasonable discretion should be used, rather than slopping copious quantities of preservative all over the gun. Some of the preservative compounds, in excessive amounts, can prove harmful to the stock material or its finish, or can deteriorate the holster leather.

During routine maintenance, the cleaning and application of protective compounds should be followed by a check for loose screws, particularly in revolvers as these are prone to shake loose during firing or normal carrying. Screws, if present, in the sideplate, thumb latch or mounting of adjustable sights should be checked, as should the ejector rod. This is discussed and illustrated in an earlier chapter on the handgun mechanism. Screws securing the

WD-40 penetrates into metallic surfaces to displace moisture and leaves a coat of lubricant to minimize friction and wear.

G96 Gun Treatment as another multi-purpose preparation. It cleans, lubes and prevents rust.

stocks to the frame likewise should be checked for tightness as these can become loosened and, at such times, are distracting.

Hoppe's No. 9, long a popular and effective bore cleaner and solvent, works well for routine cleaning. The more drastic measures outlined previously should be reserved for those extreme cases that do not respond to regular bore cleaners. The Hoppe's cleaner has an ingredient which stains the swabbing patch greenish-blue if copper fouling is present in the bore. This affords a good test for the completeness of removing jacket fouling: Swab the bore with a patch generously wetted with Hoppe's, allow it to stand over night and run a clean, dry patch through. If it comes out with the distinctive color, this indicates that some trace of copper fouling remained.

It should be noted that Hoppe's No. 9 has no property of preventing rust. Therefore, after cleaning with this solvent, a light coating of protective material should be applied to the bore and exposed exterior surfaces.

There are materials which function quite well as combination cleaners and preservatives. A partial listing of these would include TSI-300, by Testing Systems, Incorporated, Brayco LSA Gunlube, by Bray Oil Company, Box 63908, Los Angeles, California 90063, and Micro-Mist, by Micro-Lube, Incorporated.

Colt makes a lubricant containing teflon, sold in pocket oiler tubes about the size of a fountain pen, with a carrying clip. This has a needle point dispenser for precise, waste-free delivery to the desired point. The Colt's Gun Lubricant will provide excellent protection against wear and friction over a broad temperature range.

Dri-Slide is a lubricant containing finely powdered

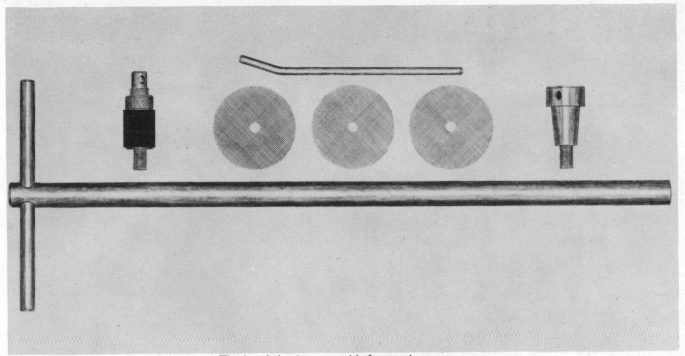

The Lewis lead remover kit for revolvers includes two heads: one for pulling through the bore, another to fit the forcing cone.

molybdenum disulfide in a liquid vehicle and is sold in pen-sized oilers or in flat cans with plastic spouts. The vehicle or medium evaporates, leaving a coating of micro-fine MDS particles clinging to surfaces in contact with each other. It is highly effective at reducing wear and friction and retains this property down through temperatures as low as any in which a firearm is apt to be used or carried. In addition to lubricating, it acts as a rust preventive also.

Bucheimer's cleaner and patch lubricant for black powder guns is sold in a pressurized can and functions well as a cleaner and rust preventive, even on firearms using smokeless powders. It is useful for removing the stubborn, caked powder residue from inside revolver chambers and, once applied, does not attract dust, dirt or sand. A single application is said to be good for about four months of protection. It also frees frozen parts, loosens rust, carbon residues, corrosion and metal fouling. Aerosol cans are in two and six-ounce sizes, with a screw-top pint can for volume users.

WD-40 is an excellent lubricant and rust-preventive, sold in aerosol dispensers and in several sizes of cans and drums, from three ounces to fifty-five gallons. In action, it displaces moisture to penetrate deeply into the pores of metal surfaces for long-term protection and lubrication.

Testing Systems, Incorporated, terms their TSI-300 a preparation for one-step gun care, noting that it performs the functions of eight separate compounds: rust remover, blueing preserver, stock conditioner, lube oil, solvent, cleaner/degreaser, corrosion preventive and wood preserver. Quite apart from that, it works quite well as a lubricant for resizing brass cartridge cases when reloading, being used in amounts so small as not to require removal after resizing. TSI-300 is sold in a 1¼-ounce, screw-top plastic bottle and in four and twenty-ounce aerosol dispenser cans. An additional product of the same firm is TSI-400 ammo brass cleaner; this removes dirt, corrosion and powder residue from fired cases and treats the surface so as to minimize future staining and corrosion.

Jet-Aer Corporation produces an extensive line of products for the shooter and sportsman under the brand name of G96, a complete catalog being available on request through the address given in the directory section. Their G96 gun treatment is a multi-purpose material in aerosol cans which cleans, lubricates and protects. It loosens and removes rust, lead and jacket fouling from bores and the lubricating ingredients do not leave gummy residues, meanwhile functioning from fifty degrees below zero to 350 above, F. The protective properties extend even to salt water spray.

Birchwood Casey likewise produces a broad assortment of gun care products, on which a complete catalog may be requested. Their Sheath is a polarized rust preventive, sold in aerosol cans and flat dispenser tins. A novel third application method is the disposable gun-wiping pads which are impregnated with Sheath: Wipe down the surfaces to be protected and discard the used cloth. The same firm's Dri-Touch is a non-tacky, instant-drying, water-displacing rust preventive which can be sprayed through the bore to provide effective protection until such time as it can be cleaned in the normal manner.

Other Birchwood Casey products include Gun Scrubber, a pressurized cleaning solvent for use on caked dirt, grease, oil and fouling; no rinsing is required. Their Heavy Duty Bore Solvent is a powerful cleaning agent with good rust preventive qualities and their Anderol synthetic gun oil provides non-gumming, high-viscosity lubrication from 60 degrees below to 300 above. It's sold in a four-ounce spout can or a three-ounce aerosol dispenser.

Several of these multi-purpose compounds were developed to meet the exacting requirements of the space program, but they can keep your duty weapon in tiptop condition on the earth's surface, just as well!

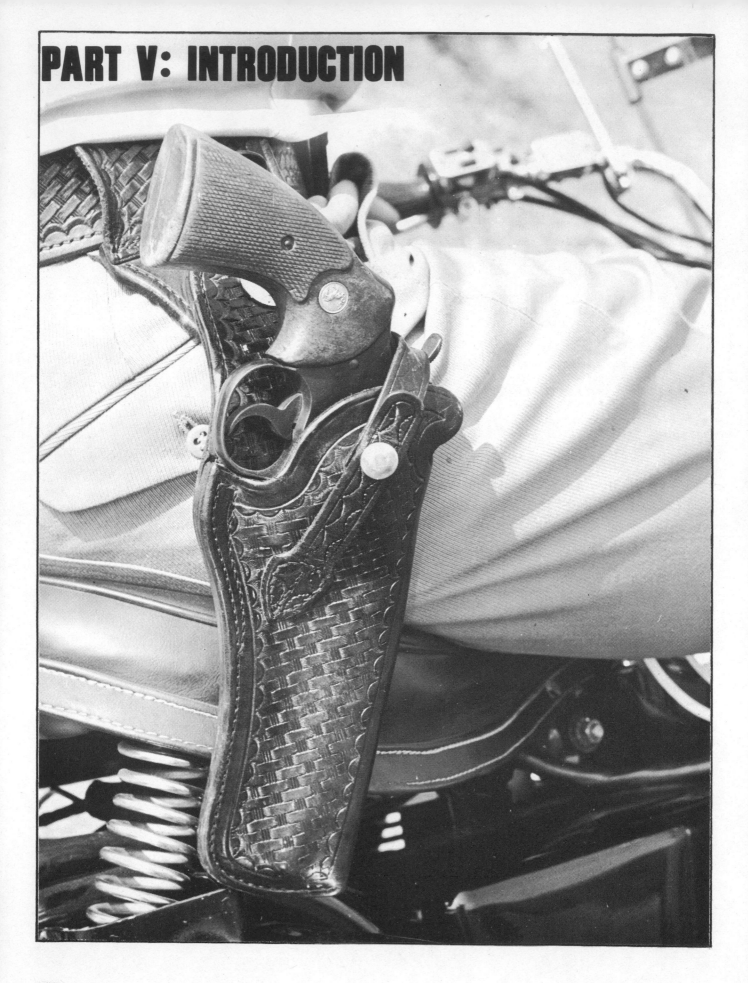

LEATHER FOR LAW GUNS

A Basic Item Of Gear For The Working Lawman, Holsters Can Be A Pleasure Or A Pain And Here Are Suggestions To Help In Making Sure It's The Former!

THE DICTIONARY DEFINES a holster as a mode of carrying a handgun or as a leather case for a pistol. Holsters are, however, like the handguns that they carry in the aspect that there is a great variety of styles and each style is best suited for a particular purpose. In the same respect the price range of holsters varies greatly also, from the cheap to modest to not-so-modest.

How effectively a holster carries a handgun and performs its intended purpose depends on a well thought out design, the best top quality materials available for its construction and the grade of workmanship used on it. No matter what a holster costs, $2.50 or $25, it is still "cheap" unless it is built well and effectively does the job it was intended to do. Although the price rarely affects how a holster is designed, it is in most cases a reflection of the quality of the materials used and the time spent in its making.

Many of today's manufacturers of leathergoods for law enforcement incorporate a wide variety of safety devices, straps, buckles and locks in the designing of their products. When selecting a holster the professional law officer knows, or at least should know, that some of the devices are potential trouble makers and steers clear of them. For instance, a steel spring utilized in the holster's construction that allows the officer to draw his pistol only when pushed in the right spot. This device could probably prevent the loss of the weapon during a scuffle, but what if the officer was faced with an emergency situation and had to quickly draw his handgun? Would the device work or would it let him down?

Professional law officers that have been at their work for a good number of years seem to prefer a holster of rather simple design, one that is styled to perform its intended purpose or duty without being gaudy. One feature that seems to be forever prevalent in holsters carried by lawmen is the quality. The extra wear of a top quality holster and belt combination through years of service will more than repay the officer that is willing to part with the extra cash that a good rig will cost.

When it comes to buying a piece of leather for carrying a handgun for duty purposes, there is no such thing as a bargain. Quality is synonymous with dependability and the lawman finds the latter feature one that cannot be done without. Cheap holsters, with their shoddy leather and ill thought out designs are booby traps and have no place in the law enforcement officer's life. Too many times an officer is let down by a three-dollar-terrific buy.

Selecting a suitable holster for any type of police work, plain clothes or uniformed, requires a considerable amount of looking and shopping around. Before looking, however, you should first predetermine what features the holster you are shopping for must incorporate. If the designs you examine lack a feature that you feel is a necessity or some-how doesn't quite measure up to your requirements, shop around some more. You should never sell yourself short and allow for the lack of a needed feature, the design must meet your needs or the holster isn't what you're looking for or want.

A good holster design is the end result of much study and testing by the manufacturers. Since safe holsters with their built in safety devices, straps, snaps and locks could prove to be more of a hazard to the officer faced with drawing his handgun during an emergency situation than they are beneficial to him, the manufacturers must practice a certain amount of give and take when designing a truly effective holster. There are, on the other hand, many desirable features that would surely enhance the design of any holster but would raise the price of producing such leathergoods to the point of being impractical for the average officer to purchase. Some especially designed rigs sell for as high as $100.

Many of the top designs are the creations of dissastisfied law officers, men who knew exactly what they wanted in a holster design but couldn't find it in any of the products on the market. Many of these custom designed holsters won such wide acceptance by lawmen that several of today's top leathergoods producers have stemmed from those individuals wanting to design and construct a better holster.

The belt, a much overlooked item, is nearly as important to the lawman as is the holster. Without the proper tight fit of holster to belt, the effectiveness of the entire rig is greatly hampered. The improper match becomes a trouble spot that should be avoided by matching the two from the start.

As with holsters, belts should be of good quality. A good belt will give an officer years of service with little, if any, sign of tearing, ripping, rotting or peeling. If the belt is constructed of top quality material it will readily take a high glossy shine and will keep it.

Unlike the gaudy and uncomfortable rigs of just a short decade ago, the police rigs of today are designed for both comfortable wear and eye appeal. The lawman working in plain clothes has available to him a wide variety of holsters that are simple to conceal and that avoid the slightest evidence of carrying a handgun. There are a number of reputable holster making firms that are now producing entire lines of leathergoods for the man behind the badge.

In the following chapters of this section we will discuss the suitability of police rigs from such firms as Bianchi, Smith & Wesson, Don Hume, Safariland, Lawrence and Colt. There are, of course, many other firms producing top-flight leather equipment for today's lawman.

Chapter 18

UNIFORMED DUTY HOLSTERS

Bill Jordan demonstrates the perils and pitfalls of a too-loose gun belt.

Here's The Run-Down On Working Law Leather!

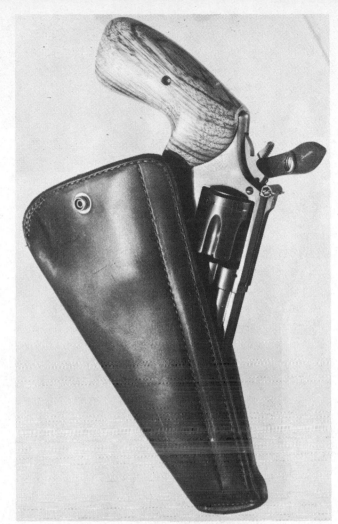

Bianchi's Break Front Model 27 (right) allows the revolver to be drawn by pulling the weapon forward, instead of the awkward conventional lifting motion. The Model 27 (below) is ideal for wear when riding in a patrol vehicle.

Tโ𝙾DAY'S LAW ENFORCEMENT equipment has come a long way. Today's lawman carries the finest double action revolvers or the most dependable automatic handguns that money can buy, drives extremely powerful high performance vehicles, and utilizes the technology of thousands of dollars worth of complicated electronic communications devices. Even with all this, the uniformed lawman of today is still faced with the daily burden of packing around several pounds of equipment on his waist.

For years, the peace officer packed around equipment that was outmoded at the turn of the century. In the last decade, however, the lawman has witnessed the introduction of many modern police rigs, designed expressly for his line of work.

When selecting a holster for duty, the uniformed officer must consider three basic features: does the holster's design include features for the safe carrying of a loaded handgun, does it afford efficiency and is it comfortable to wear for long periods of time? Perhaps security should be included as a separate feature, but a safe holster should also be a secure holster.

One of the top belt and holster manufacturers in the country, John Bianchi, has compiled a complete holster evaluation chart that makes determining the suitability of a holster's quality and design easier. With the possibility of having his life depending on the way he carries his handgun, the professional lawman should pay considerable attention to the questions on this chart.

The uniformed officer doesn't try to hide or conceal his duty revolver or automatic pistol and should be able to carry the weapon without fear of someone slipping up from behind and snatching it from his holster. Many designs are equipped with a variety of straps and snaps for the purpose of preventing just this.

The Bianchi Model 27 Break Front is a relatively new holster design that makes it virtually impossible for an officer to have his revolver snatched from his holster. An ex-cop himself, John Bianchi of Rancho, California, began his research for a holster designed to assure that an officer's duty revolver would be secure from grabbing hands more than a decade ago. The result was the Model 27.

As the name indicates, the Break Front does just that. Along the entire front edge of the holster is a slot through which the revolver is drawn. The holster is made of a double thickness of nine-ounce prime quality cowhide. The rigid construction of the Model 27 plus an ingenious built-in cylinder recess holds four-inch or six-inch barreled revolvers quite securely.

Instead of the usual awkward lifting motion necessary to draw revolvers from conventionally designed holsters, the handgun is drawn from the Break Front in one smooth continual forward movement. A three-quarter inch thick trigger housing makes it impossible for someone to snatch the gun out of the holster from the rear or from the side, with or without the carrying strap fastened.

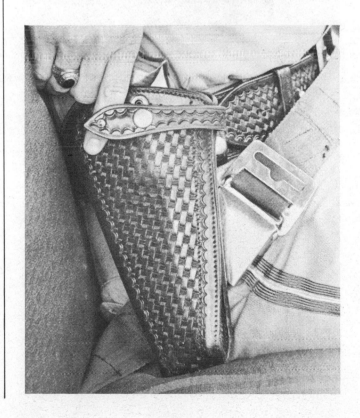

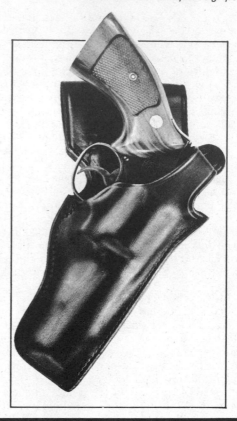

Safariland's Sight Track, a neoprene channel built into the forward edge of the holster, guides the handgun's front sight blade the entire length of the holster, eliminating hang ups.

Equipped with a thumb release snap, Safariland's Model 10-A affords added insurance from losing a duty handgun to grabbing hands. Snap is located forward of the weapon's grips.

Another Model 27, but manufactured by Smith & Wesson's leather company, incorporates a false snap on the front side of the holster that cannot be unfastened. The true snap is located on the belt side of the holster near the hammer and is released by applying thumb pressure. The false snap, however is what the would-be snatcher sees and it appears to be his only obstacle in taking the officer's revolver from him.

Holsters equipped with thumb released snaps, such as Safariland's Model 10-A Thumb Break, the S&W Model 28 Clam Shell and Bianchi's Speed Swivel auto pistol holster, all afford some protection from having a pistol taken away unexpectedly.

Safariland holsters have a built in sight track that make it difficult for anyone but the lawful carrier to remove the handgun from the holster. The front sight blade fits into and rides in a central neoprene channel located in the forward edge of the holster. A straight-forward draw by the officer will free the handgun and allow the weapon to be drawn smoothly and quickly, an unexpected tug from the side or rear will only bind it tightly enough to forstall the loss.

Prior to the Safariland sight track design, lining was not a practical option in handgun holsters of the conventional wrap-around design. Linings that offer soft and smooth protection for the officer's revolver become a hazard to him once they begin to wear through. Front sights tend to hang up on ragged linings and could put the officer on the spot should he ever have to draw his handgun in defense of his own life.

The sight track, however, allows the front sight to be guided clear of any lining surface and therefore eliminates the chances of having a hang up during drawing. As an extra precaution to preventing a ragged lining interfering with extracting the handgun from the holster, Safariland utilizes tough but soft and protecting sueded elk hide lining in their holsters. The lining is also sealed on its inner side to prevent bleeding through from the main holster leather, giving extra protection to the handgun during inclement weather.

Quality uniformed duty rigs, as are holsters of any other design, are custom molded for a certain handgun. This type of holster carries the handgun in the holster securely, allows the weapon to be drawn without any restricting pull, and permits the revolver or auto to be returned to the holster without having to force it back in.

The uniformed officer carries a holster that is one of two

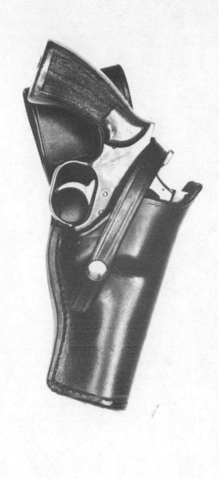
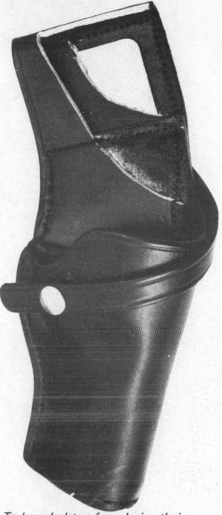

Uniformed duty holsters are of two principal designs, incorporating either a long or short shank. These two Don Hume holsters are good examples. The longer shank with swivel allows holster to be worn in the squad car.

To keep holsters from losing their rigidity, most top flight manufacturers usually include a reinforcing steel plate in their product's construction.

principal designs; one style fits directly onto the officer's belt and rides high upon his hip, while the other is suspended from his belt by a leather shank. The latter throws the butt of the handgun out and away from his body and hangs considerably lower than the holster of the first design.

Several of the shank design holsters presently being produced are built with a swivel located near the center of the shank. This swivel styling allows patrolmen to comfortably wear their rigs while cruising in a patrol vehicle.

There are many holsters that incorporate a steel reinforcing plate in the leather shank or in the belt loop. This steel plate adds to the rigid construction of the holster and prevents it from riding up as the revolver or automatic pistol is drawn.

The S&W Standard Border Model is one of the current designs that utilizes the reinforcing plate. Designed for minimum overall length, the Standard Border is constructed of heavy ten-ounce full grain cowhide and features full length metal plate reinforcement. This particular model is available in twenty different variations for S&W and Colt revolvers, plus the S&W Model 39 9mm Automatic. The Don Hume Jordan River holster is a similar design featuring

a reinforced shank. This holster also features a specially designed short drop shank that allows adequate car seat clearance.

Which style the officer wears is usually up to him to select. He should constantly know exactly where the butt of his handgun lies and should be able to grasp it, should he have to draw suddenly, without having to feel around for it or look down to see where it is. This a prime factor in selecting a holster, that is, finding a model that carries the handgun with the proper angle and pitch of the butt. The holster must be efficiently designed to warrant use while on duty.

The Lawrence Model 86, the Don Hume Uniform and Speed Swivel holsters and the Safariland Roberts Rangemaster Auto Swivel all feature shanks with swivels. The latter, a holster for carrying an automatic pistol, allows the hammer to remain cocked at all times. The safety strap on this particular model runs between the face of the hammer and the firing pin, making it impossible for the hammer to strike the firing pin while it is being carried. The Roberts Rangemaster is designed for packing the .45 Government Colt autoloader.

Safariland's Model 55 Thumb Break and Model 56

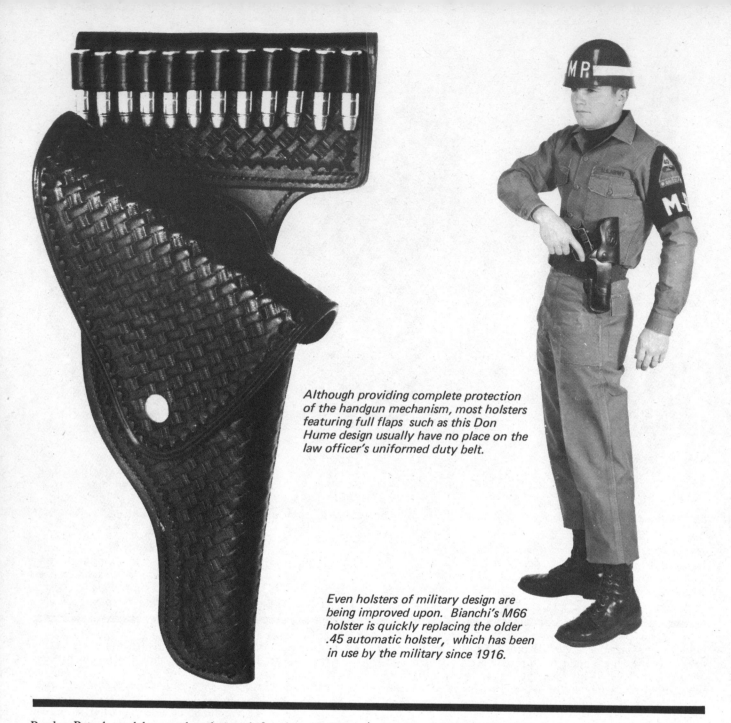

Although providing complete protection of the handgun mechanism, most holsters featuring full flaps such as this Don Hume design usually have no place on the law officer's uniformed duty belt.

Even holsters of military design are being improved upon. Bianchi's M66 holster is quickly replacing the older .45 automatic holster, which has been in use by the military since 1916.

Border Patrol models are also designed for the .45 Colt Auto, plus the S&W Model 39. The first is styled for fast drawing of the auto pistol. The design is styled so the handgun is angled with the barrel forward and the grips are to the rear, this styling plus the lower cut slot along the holster's front edge make this model very efficient. The Border Patrol, on the other hand, is styled so it rides rather high on the hip, as do most holsters of Border Patrol design. Instead of the rearward angle, this holster angles the pistol in just the opposite direction. The Model 56 is designed more for secure carrying rather than quick drawing, although the thumb release snap does make it possible to draw the pistol with little time lost.

Colt's Speed Holster is another design styled for fast drawing of their .45 Auto or the same handgun in Super .38 or 9mm. This holster will fit on belts up to two inches wide, it does lack one feature, however. There is no safety strap on this holster.

There is one feature that all law enforcement officers agree upon, and that is quality. The lawman wears his rig year after year, day after day and for hours upon hours. To remain serviceable and in good condition, a police rig must be constructed of premium quality materials and built with fine workmanship.

As previously mentioned, most of the top quality holsters are fitted for a certain model of handgun and will fit only that particular model. This is done by pressure moulding top quality leather to an actual frame and cylinder of that handgun model or to a cast mould of the weapon. To add years of life to the uniform police rig, most of the top leathergoods manufacturers today use only the best materials and put the rigs together with rugged double stitching.

In addition to the designs and features already discussed,

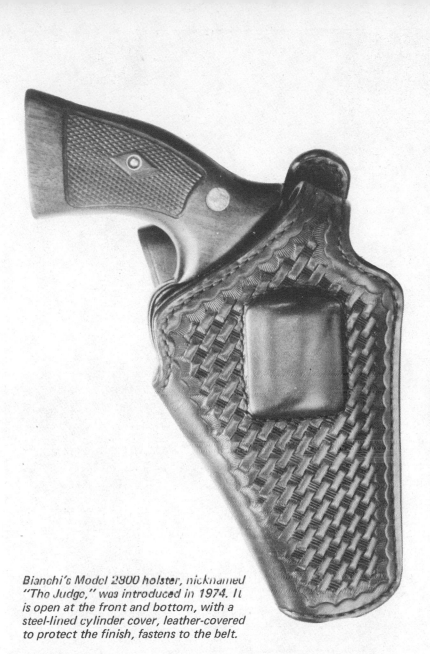

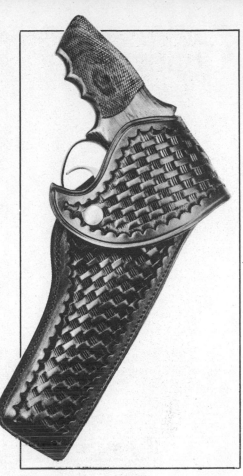

Flaps usually tend to hamper the speed with which a handgun is drawn; the Model 58 holster by Safariland is so styled that flap functions the same as a strap.

Bianchi's Model 2800 holster, nicknamed "The Judge," was introduced in 1974. It is open at the front and bottom, with a steel-lined cylinder cover, leather-covered to protect the finish, fastens to the belt.

there are holsters incorporating such features as flaps that cover the entire hammer and receiver or holsters that have built in cartridge loops right on their elongated belt loops.

The S&W Flap Swivel Model 18 and the Lawrence Model 85 Police Holster are two makes that feature full flap protection of a revolver's functioning parts. Many officers feel that the flap does not have any place on a police rig, claiming that it gets in the way when drawing the weapon. Safariland took this into consideration and now produces their quarter flap Model 58-B. This holster still features flap protection of the handgun's action, but instead of completely covering the grips it allows these to protrude from beneath the flap for easy grasping. The flap is then unsnapped much the same as a regular safety strap.

Holsters such as the Don Hume Swivel models with cartridge loops make use of otherwise unused space on the shank type holsters. Most of the holsters featuring cartridge loops have enough of the loops for carrying an extra six to twelve rounds in addition to those in the duty weapon. Holsters of this design also make it unnecessary for the officer to carry extra cartridge holders on his already weighted belt.

If the uniformed lawman's rig is properly matched and fits him correctly, he will wear it with a reasonable amount of comfort without being constantly reminded that he has the assembly on by a holster riding in the wrong place or being prodded by the butt of the handgun. The rig should fit so comfortably that the officer can go about his duties without constantly being conscious of the weapon on his hip.

Although the way a holster and belt match up and how a holster rides do affect the overall comfort of the rig, the belt plays the primary role in making the rig comfortable to wear for hours each day. We will discuss belts and other accessories in the last chapter of this section.

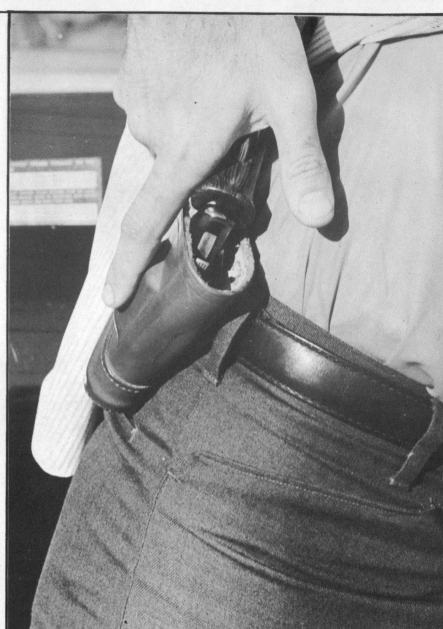

Chapter 19

Leather Designed To Keep Your Secret When You're Armed Wearing Plainclothes!

PLAINCLOTHES AND OFF-DUTY HOLSTERS

Bianchi's Model X15 shoulder holster is made for all popular handguns. The lower photo demonstrates how lower end is anchored by a loop to the belt.

Uɴʟɪᴋᴇ ᴛʜᴇ ᴜɴɪꜰᴏʀᴍᴇᴅ duty officer's forever visible police rig, holsters designed for plainclothes wearing are built for easy concealment. Special agents and off-duty officers sometimes are required to carry a handgun while on special assignments or for their own protection during their off-duty hours.

There are, of course, many factors that determine the suitability of the plainclothes rig, but concealment is perhaps the most important aspect to the man who will be carrying the gun. The detective or off-duty officer must be able to carry the handgun without an unsightly bulge betraying its presence. In addition to easy concealment, the holster must carry the handgun so as to allow quick and easy drawing of the weapon.

Most officers carry either a small automatic or a short barreled lightweight revolver for this type of work. Most of the holsters designed for plainclothes wearing are light in weight, partially skeletonized and form-fitted for a particular handgun from rugged materials. Some of these rigs are designed with a wide variety of straps and snaps for holding the handgun securely in place, others rely on nothing more than the snug fit of weapon to leather to hold it in place. Many officers feel the latter is asking for trouble since the friction-tight fit of the two eventually will begin to decrease with the wearing down of the leather surface. The result could be an embarrassing situation for an officer should his handgun slip from its precarious grip and fall to the floor.

Holsters such as Bianchi's Special Agent model shoulder holster are built with a heavy duty spring enclosed inside the leather flaps that securely grasp the revolver. Although this model carries the weapon in an inverted position, the tension of the spring will hold the handgun securely in place while the officer is engaged in even the most strenuous of activities. This particular holster carries the revolver so that it is angled to give the wearer easy and quick access without having to fumble and feel for the handgun's butt.

To combat loss of the handgun while involved in a scuffle when attempting to apprehend a suspect or while in a running pursuit of a suspect or any other related situation where the handgun is most apt to fall from the holster, Safariland and a few of the other leather companies use elastic in the construction of their shoulder holsters.

Safariland's Model 19 upside-down holster does this by housing the revolver's trigger guard in leather. To draw this holster, the officer must pull the gun forward and down. An elastic strap is located on the holster just above the revolver's receiver bridge and holds the weapon securely by pulling the leather tightly against the receiver and cylinder.

When evaluating the efficiency of any of the concealable plainclothes holsters, whether it be a shoulder holster, belt or waistband type, the officer must check the design to make certain that the holster carries the handgun close to his body, the butt in close and the hang such that both holster and weapon blend with the contours of the body. Again, the design should allow easy access to the revolver or auto without having to fumble around looking for the grips.

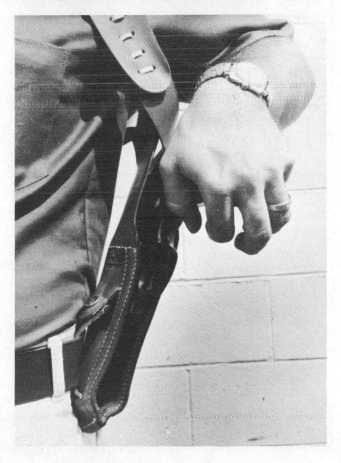

As previously pointed out, the snug fit between the handgun and the leather of the holster sometimes is not enough to warrant safe or practical carrying of a loaded weapon. Generally speaking, a holster that will securely carry a handgun, right side up or upside down, does not necessarily need a safety strap installed. The officer selecting this type of holster also should remember the fact that eventually this tight fit will begin to diminish through day after day wearing of the rig. Another foe of leather is age; the fibers of leather sometimes will soften and lose their rigidity through years of service, especially if the product has not been properly taken care of.

The way the rig fits is especially important. Belt holsters, both those of the typical straight draw or cross-draw design, of correct design and fitting hold the handgun fairly tightly and usually require a considerable amount of initial effort to break the holster's grip on the weapon during the draw. This sudden yank on the handgun's grips should be enough to release the weapon from the holster.

Any play — forward or backward movement as well as up and down motion — in the holster and belt during the draw will affect the speed and efficiency of the draw. Similarly, the cant of the holster is controlled to some degree by the fit of the holster to the belt. This cant produces the pitch of the handgun's butt, which must remain the same at all times, allowing the officer to know precisely where it is every time he reaches for it. The poor fit of a holster mounted on a belt that is too small or too thin allows the holster to be shifted easily to different positions and alters the cant of the gun each time it moves.

The same is true with shoulder holsters; the design must fit the officer properly or its efficiency is greatly impaired. In checking out a shoulder holster, the officer should be doubly careful, because a holster that hangs right and feels right while walking actually may allow the handgun to hang too far out from the body. In this situation, the officer has little, if any, control of the weapon when he bends over and the entire rig swings from its intended position.

Some shoulder holsters make it extremely difficult to draw the handgun when the man wearing it is sitting in a car or in a large cushioned chair. When selecting a holster of this styling, the officer should be sure to check out both the hang and the placement of the weapon. His selection should allow easy concealment while still making the handgun readily accessible.

In addition to removing the bulge of the holster from the average viewer's sight, officers wearing shoulder rigs have another problem to cope with: the problem of adjusting the buckles of the shoulder holster's straps so they don't show through today's light suit materials. Some officers adjust these straps until they fit just right, then cut out the buckles and snaps and sew the leather straps together. The result is a shoulder harness that lies flat under any material, eliminating any bulges or lumps.

The Lawrence Handy-Strap makes converting the regular belt-type holster into a shoulder rig not only easy but quite practical. As with many shoulder designs, the Handy-Strap is equipped with an elastic band that fits across the opposite shoulder. This draws the holster closer into the body and holds the entire rig securely in place.

On some shoulder rigs there are straps running from the harness or holster that can be securely anchored to the belt. This type of styling helps reduce the chances of having the rig shift its position or swing out unexpectedly when the officer turns swiftly or bends over to pick up something.

There is still a third type of plainclothes holster that we've not discussed to any extent: the inside the pants, waistband clip-on holsters. This type of holster offers the

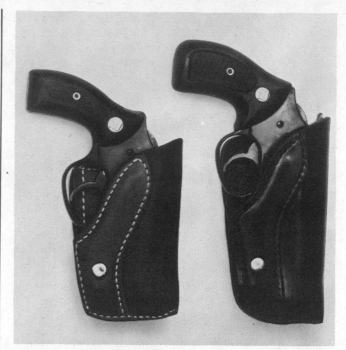

Holsters by Don Hume Leather Goods for the Charter Oak revolvers. Unit at right is for optional 3-inch barrel.

Here are details of harness straps as used on the Seventrees shoulder rig.

maximum in concealment of small automatics and short barreled revolvers.

These holsters, rarely designed to handle handguns with barrels longer than three inches, usually attach to the inside waistband of the officer's trousers by the means of a small clip or a steel spring reinforced leather clip. Several makes such as the Lawrence Model 22 have a detachable belt loop that crosses over the top of the waistband and is held securely in place by the belt. This particular model will also handle revolvers or autos with barrel lengths up to five inches.

This highly concealable rig allows the handgun to be drawn readily, without its pulling free of the waistband. Should this happen, with holsters featuring trigger housings especially, it would be extremely difficult for the officer to get off a shot that just may save his life. Another feature, although it may be found on a few of the waistband designs, is the lack of any sort of safety strap or locking device other than the tight fit of metal to leather in these holsters.

An overweight officer may find that the waistband

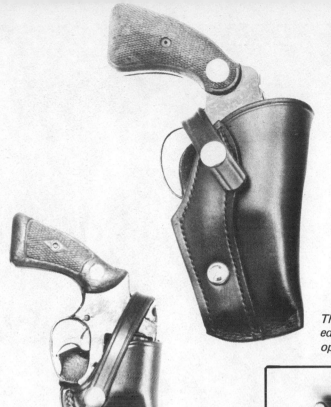

This design puts the gun inside pants waistline to blend better with body contours; strap holds leather to belt.

This Hume hoster is open up the left edge for cross-draw. Spring around opening plus strap secures revolver.

Hume holster above puts snap-strap over the hammer for straight-up draw.

This under-waistband model, for the M39 S&W, is by Seventrees, as is the revolver type appearing in photo above.

holsters are somewhat uncomfortable for him to carry. That accumulated fat on his midriff tends to envelope the holster and handgun, making it anything but efficient, let alone being an uncomfortable rig for him to carry. The joy of all the fine eating that put that extra weight there is soon forgotten when the officer is face to face with an armed suspect, especially if he grabs for his handgun and gets nothing more than a handful of fat.

The type of plainclothes rig that the officer selects should be the result of a considerable amount of time spent shopping and trying on. He should select the rig that combines comfort, efficiency and good concealment. These three features are actually synonymous. Without good concealment the rig would be far from being efficient. On the other hand, so would a rig that was anything but comfortable. The holster recommended by a friend on the force may fit him perfectly and, if the officer shopping for a plainclothes rig is of about the same body structure, the rig may be worth checking out. Just because it fits the friend, however, doesn't mean that his rig is perfect for everyone no matter how much he insists that it is "a

great rig."

As mentioned earlier in this chapter, modern holsters are formed to fit a certain handgun make. This is extremely important to remember when buying a concealable rig, many revolvers and automatic pistols have similar styling or receivers of relatively similar designing. The holsters that fit one, however, may or will not fit the other handgun. Also, some handguns may seem to fit a holster design, although that holster was not built for that particular gun. This should be avoided whenever possible since a slight deviation in the form of the holster well and the lines of the gun's receiver could possibly become a trouble spot in the future. The two may fit each other in the beginning, but an uneven match could wear the holster rather rapidly and soon render the entire rig useless.

Occasionally an officer will find it difficult and sometimes impossible to find a rig that will fill the bill of his needs. The only answer then is to turn to a specially made rig. These rigs invariably cost more than those of commercial make, since they are custom-made and fitted for the person ordering them.

Chapter 20

SPECIAL DESIGN HOLSTERS, BELTS & ACCESSORIES

When Nothing Commercially Made Fits, Try Something Different!

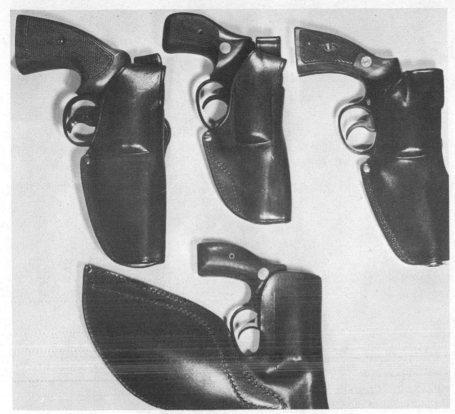

The three belt slots incorporated into the design of this special rig by Roy's Custom Leather Goods enables officer to wear handgun in FBI tilt or crossdraw position.

Featuring exposed trigger guards, these special design thumb release holsters, pinch-top (upper right), and pocket holster are made by Seventrees Holsters, Inc.

IT IS NOT UNUSUAL for a police officer to be required occasionally to attire in garb other than his uniform or the customarily worn suit during situations when he is expected to mingle undetected among crowds. For these special assignments, he sometimes finds it difficult to carry his handgun so that it is out of sight but still within easy grasping distance should he have need to draw it. For these infrequent cases, the man who is to perform the stake out or undercover work may find it necessary to carry a rig that has been especially made for that particular phase of work.

This is where the trouble actually starts; that is, finding a reputable holster maker that will give in to the officer's whims and design and make a holster individually fitted just for him. Out of the some forty to fifty commercial holster makers presently in this country, only a small handful take the time and trouble to produce these special rigs.

Even when you do find someone willing to custom fit you with a rig that varies greatly from any that are presently being commercially produced, you can well expect to pay dearly for the finished product. Specially-made rigs don't come cheap!

When designing a holster that is to have a special mission, the manufacturer must take several things into consideration. First, what kind of holster does the officer want or, better yet, need? Special rigs range from the various modified versions of the regular shoulder holster and other plainclothes rigs to such personally designed styles as a special overcoat pocket holster or one that straps to the officer's leg just above his ankle.

Occasionally an officer is dissatisfied with the way his shoulder holster carries his handgun or he may want the added attraction of magazine holders attached to the shoulder harness so that they ride under the opposite armpit. Perhaps this type of re-styling would be better classified as a modification instead of a specially made rig. Unless you are exceptionally talented at leather working, however, it still will require some doing to find a qualified cobbler or holster maker who will agree to do the modifying and it is nearly impossible to find a commercial holster-making firm that will do personal modification to any of their conventionally designed holsters.

Bianchi and Don Hume began as small home businesses, designing and building personally patterned rigs. Although many were simply of the uniform type, since commercially made quality was somewhat of a rarity just few short years ago, they were occasionally called on to make a holster that was completely different and far from being conventional.

Finding someone to produce a special rig for you will be hard, but not impossible. The undercover officer, taking the time to search for someone that will agree to blueprint him a specially designed outfit, eventually will find success. Sometimes the best place to start is by looking right in the phone book or in the yellow pages under leather or leather goods. There are almost always several firms that specialize in producing custom leather goods in any given area of the country.

Roy's Custom Leather Goods, Magnolia, Arkansas, pioneered the Pancake Holster, here for the Browning Hi-Power, with Pachmayr rubber grips, design offers excellent concealability.

Seventrees, Limited, is a New York leather goods firm that has on occasion given into the whims of officers needing a holster of special designing. This firm has occasionally produced personal modifications for certain members of the U.S. Secret Service.

As an example of this, Seventrees once produced for a member of the Secret Service a peculiar little revolver holster that was built for carrying inside his overcoat pocket. It was designed so that with one movement of his finger he positioned the trigger and, in seconds, could fire five rounds into the silhouette of a man at about twenty yards. What actually made the design so peculiar was the fact that he did the firing right through the overcoat!

Special rigs are built for a vast variety of reasons; concealability, comfort, efficiency and maybe for any deformities the individual officer may suffer. Whatever the reason, this type of police leather is difficult to find and always carries a premium price. If you are looking for a rig of this type here are a few pointers:

Make sure the design, which is sketched out usually before it is actually constructed, is exactly what you're looking for. Every modification done on the holster after it is once cut and assembled usually means a little more squeezing of the old wallet.

Decide beforehand which style of holster best fits your needs; belt holster, clip-on waist band or shoulder type rigs; cross draw, standard draw, inverted or conventional grips-up styling.

Security: will the handgun remain in the holster while involved in hand-to-hand combat, running or when jumping out of cars? Make sure that the builder has taken the effort to form the holster correctly to the handgun.

In the same aspect, will it be necessary to install a safety strap as additional insurance against losing the gun? Here again, it may actually defray the total cost of the rig by having straps, snaps or locks installed when the holster is first manufactured instead of having them installed at a later date.

Special rigs aren't always built for plainclothes work. Whenever a uniformed officer has a modification of any sort done to his uniformed duty rig, it thus becomes a specially built or modified version and qualifies it for classification as such. In short, a specialized rig is any holster or holster and belt combination that has for some personal reason been modified or built to personal specifications.

Today there is such a wide variety of commercially manufactured uniform type holsters and police rigs that specialized production of any sort is decreasing. There will always be the need for unusual holster designs since the use of some of the unorthodox styles is so limited that they

Safariland's new M254 Border Patrol holster is designed for carrying the .45 service auto cocked and locked; has jacket slot clearance and one-piece wrap around rear construction to insure maximum durability.

This Don Hume "Agent 9" is a prime example of how some special design holsters do nothing more than carry the handgun. Highly skeletonized, rig leaves the slightest trace of packing a handgun around, even under today's suits.

don't warrant mass production, or at least to be made in any great numbers. However, before questing for a holster maker who will build you a personal rig, check out the many holster-making firms located across the country. Just because your rig doesn't seem to fit right or provide the efficiency you desire from it, don't run out and throw away money on a high priced personal blueprint job. Thumb through a few catalogs and shop around to actually examine the many different styles now available. You may save a considerable amount of cash by doing so.

With This Waist Gear, Comfort And Quality Must Be Synonymous!

PROFESSIONAL MEN, as Ogden Nash once viewed, have no cares; whatever happens, they get theirs. It's quite obvious that Mr. Nash never experienced the pleasures of being a policeman, or at least never had entertained the idea of carting around several pounds of equipment snugly on his waist. This can become an unpleasant experience when riding in a patrol car or atop a powerful two-wheeler.

Equipment that doesn't fit properly or has a tendency to ride in the wrong position prodding the officer in the wrong places, or a rig that doesn't balance its weight evenly, can leave the officer with an attitude at the end of the day that can be classified as anything but pleasant.

For years officers were subjected to wearing equipment that was considered of standard styling and design, or so it was accepted as such. There wasn't much of a choice, since there were only a few companies involved in making police leather. After numerous surveys and much research, today's leather producers have examined the problems and dislikes of the modern lawman and have begun to do something about making a policeman's lot a little happier.

One of the biggest headaches, or so it seemed, was that of the massive metal buckle used on the standard Sam Browne belt. It was apparent that something should be done to change from tradition and eliminate this trouble spot. In addition to providing a natural aiming point, gleaming and glittering even in the poorest of light, the reinforced leather which held the buckle in place was uncomfortable. On some makes as much as six or more layers of leather were necessary in order to fasten the buckle in place, sometimes these belts are almost 1¾ inches thick at the buckle.

In searching for a suitable replacement for the accepted belt buckle, Safariland, Incorporated, makers of widely accepted police leathergoods, found Velcro — a material with which many of us became familiar on the sleeves of the old GI field jacket. This was just what they were looking for.

Rather than one material, properly this is a system composed of two different materials, called hook and pile. The hook is a swatch of fabric or material that has short curved projections made of tough elastic material protruding from it. The pile is a similar material, except that the fibers projecting from its base are looped and form sort of a coarse mat. When pressed together, even with a light pressure, the two surfaces adhere to each other readily. When engaged, the hook and pile hold with a more than adequate grip for securing the belt in place.

Safariland successfully incorporated Velcro into the production of their law enforcement leather. The application of the system is rather simple: A strip of the hook material is sewn to one area of the belt and a swatch of the pile is sewn on in the corresponding area, where the two are intended to make contact, where the old Sam Browne belt buckle was located.

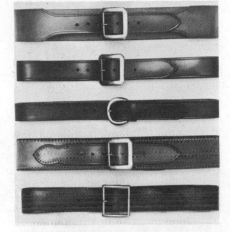

Bianchi makes a variety of belts, these are of either Border Patrol design or for dress wear.

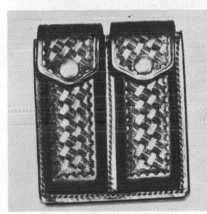

Ammo pouches come in many designs and styles. This pouch is for clip fed auto magazines.

Ready for duty, this Don Hume rig features key strap with flap, extra ammo pouches, handcuff case and short shank design holster. The belt is of the conventional Sam Browne design, entire rig features basketweave finish.

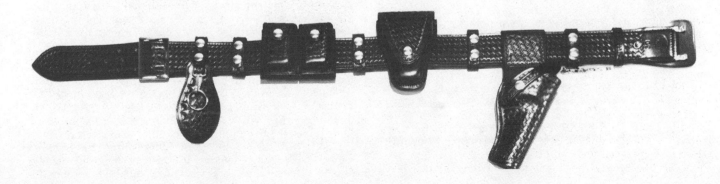

Many police departments have done away with the shoulder strap, but officers wearing this belt still are faced with the discomfort of its bulk. There are a few belts presently being offered that have reduced the bulk of the typical Sam Browne type belts. Many of these have gained acceptance into this elite field of men.

Bianchi's Border Patrol belt, although still a full 2½ inches wide, reduces some of the typical bulk common to almost all police belts by styling the belt and buckle with a sewn-on strap that travels through the reduced-in-size buckle. On the belts of Sam Browne designation, the entire belt travels through the buckle, making it exceptionally bulky and uncomfortable, especially if riding in a squad car: The buckle tends to prod the wearer in some mighty tender places at times.

Although the belt is the main piece of equipment when it comes to comfort, the designing of the accessories that go on the belt are of great importance. A pound here, an ounce there can add up to a lot of fatigue if the rig isn't properly matched and its weight evenly balanced.

Handcuff cases, cartridge holders, batons and baton carrying rings, flashlight holders, and strap-mounted key rings are just a few of the accessories you may encounter at one time or another, many of which are mandatory on some police forces.

To counterbalance the weight of the revolver on one hip, many officers place the added weight of extra cartridges or similar equipment on the opposite hip. Both the man on the beat and the lawman making his rounds in a patrol vehicle may also find that where this equipment is placed greatly affects how comfortably they can wear it, walking or sitting.

Perhaps the best means of wearing a uniformed holster and belt combination comfortably is to organize the added accessories so they are evenly balanced. Belt keepers that attach to both the uniformed duty belt and the trouser belt underneath help keep the weighted rig from riding down. Some of the belt straps double as key rings.

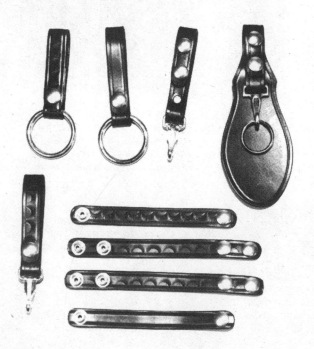

FOR MANY YEARS, the uniforms of most police organizations have been highly visible and purposely so. It was felt that high boots, multi-colored garb and bulky Sam Browne belts added to the authority of the officer's appearance. But there has begun a trend toward changing the visual aspect of the police officer, both for tactical and public relations reasons.

Lengthy research and development by the Los Angeles Police Department, among others, has resulted in extensive — if not always obvious — changes in its line-officers' uniform. Some of the most striking changes are evident in a holster and belt combination now in use. In keeping with its desire for a dark, slim-proportioned uniform appearance, LAPD has taken part in the design of a buckleless uniform equipment belt.

The Safariland Model 95 two-inch police equipment belt is described by the originator and maker, Safariland Leather Products, Incorporated, as the first real advance in duty belts since the turn of the century. The fact that the belt is buckleless (that is, its closure is not externally visible) is only an outgrowth of the search for an improved police belt design. It was believed a secure belt could be made that had a more logical fitting system than the arbitrarily inch-spaced buckle/tongue arrangement. In making a successful improvement over the old Sam Browne type, there is an inner closure, with an infinite number of possible sizes within the belt's overall size range (three ranges cover most sizes).

Some form of sliding buckle probably would lend itself to a similar design, but there are other reasons for leaving the hardware off. When a belt stretches, buckle readjustments make unsightly wear lines on the uniform belt. With no buckle, there are no such lines — and less polishing!

With pleasing lines and a neat surface comes a point more in keeping with police combat needs — lowered visibility. The brass buckle is a well placed target, even in reduced light. With the buckleless, the average officer may approve its extra edge of tactical efficiency.

Companions to this belt are Safariland's Sight Track holsters.

As the manufacturer puts it, the features of the Sight Track holster design stem partly from its two-sided construction, which is joined by a deeply channeled welting or "track." This neoprene or leather welt has a slot that encloses the front sight, without pressing or dragging on it. Toward the top of these holsters, this track is relieved to avoid interference with rear sights.

This construction is said to offer great frontal strength, because of its central reinforcement, as well as protection for the most radical sights, while offering a smooth, unimpeded draw. And this draw doesn't slice a strip of leather out of the front of the holster.

Not only the belt buckle is missing; all other items that used to be waist-high eye-catchers are removed or toned down as well. Velcro fabric fastener is extensively utilized in place of snaps, chains and studs.

Tests have shown that this closure material has a much longer useful life than any metallic snap and is, of course, soundless and non-reflective. The actual life expectancy of a closure made of Velcro is known to be on the order to 23,000 partings and resealings. Strength actually increases up to about the five thousandth closure, then levels off.

Along with silence, low visibility and durability must be mentioned Velcro's memory. If a Velcro flap is forgetfully left open, even a slight brush will re-seal it. This lends to

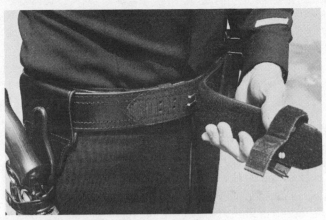

With Velcro replacing the older Sam Browne belt buckle, an officer no longer sports a natural aiming point. Sam Browne buckle would gleam even in poor lighting.

Safariland's Velcro system eliminates the problem of sagging duty belts. The hook and pile of the material form a strong bond that securely holds belt in place.

neatness and the security of belt equipment.

Research into police equipment matters considered the common snap. Experiments put the life expectancy of a snap at 3000 to 4000 closures, with a continuous decrease in strength from use to use. One day, whether it be on a cuff case, or more important a cartridge drop, the snap will fail.

The Model 95 belt meets tough purchasing specs, although developed in answer to requests for the most functional law enforcement belt for full-duty use. To get a slim silhouette and light weight without bulk — and without losing the feeling of substantial quality that lends to authority — Velcro, a sturdy brass hook-and-eye hidden closure and an extra, especially designed keeper at the other tip of the wrap-around belt are used.

Most of the units in use or under test also utilize an underbelt that presents a complete outer surface of Velcro pile that mates with other Velcro on the reverse side of the duty belt. This lighter inner belt also is reversible to straight leather-outside appearance and can be used as an outer dress belt for office or unarmed duties. In addition, being 1½ inches wide, it will carry an off-duty gun with ease. One unseen feature of the buckleless unit is the inner lining of heavy-gauge nylon webbing that runs throughout the duty belt, adding to its already considerable strength.

Although the belt first was put into the field by the Los Angeles Police Department, many thousands now are in use and on order from scores of localities. Users include: police departments in Covina, California; Los Alamitos, California; Kansas City, Missouri; Vienna, Virginia; Colorado Springs, Colorado; and even the Oakland, California, Parks and Recreation Department. Smaller units across the country have approved it for gradual phase-in as new recruits hit the streets. In addition, many single users are now in possesion of one.

As added insurance to keeping the belt riding in the proper place, belt keepers should be used. The low slung, fast draw look went out with such renowned lawmen as Wyatt Earp and, besides looking sloppy, the low riding of a handgun puts undue strain on the opposite hip. Belt keepers encompass the rig belt and the trouser belt or loops sewn on the trousers waist band at spots where the extra support is needed to compensate for the additional weight.

Of even greater importance is the placement of this equipment so as to give the wearer the maximum in efficiency. Handcuffs should be located in a position that allows the officers to remove them instantaneously and put them into operation when needed. Along the same line of thought, extra ammo also should be located in an easily accessible location.

If you suddenly found yourself in a situation where the speed at which you could utilize your cuffs or reload your weapon was of utmost importance, you undoubtedly wouldn't want to have to wrestle with a stubborn safety snap or fumble around feeling for the location of those objects. It is important that equipment of such importance be repeatedly located in exactly the same spot once it has been determined where it will be placed on the belt.

Stubborn safety snaps are hazardous and to prevent the chance of encountering one during a situation where it would be a problem and anything but desirable, these devices should be checked continuously and rechecked to assure that they are operating correctly. As on their belt, Safariland is utilizing Velcro in place of snaps and straps. The material fastens securely, holding the contents of equipment cases and pouches firmly in place, but readily available with a firm tug on a flap or tab.

Quality equipment invariably costs a little more, but the added dependability of top-flight rigs will more than repay you if you choose your equipment well. On the other hand, quality material is only as good as you maintain it.

COMING TO GRIPS WITH YOUR HANDGUN

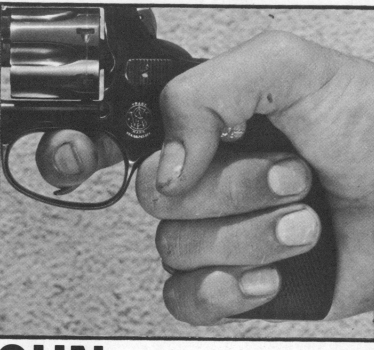

Those Small Pieces Of Wood Or Plastic Are Of Vital Importance Since, If They Are Just Right, They Tailor The Gun For Hand-Fitting Comfort And Accuracy!

THE ACCEPTANCE OF EXISTING standards is nothing new and, as with almost everything that is mass produced, factory-installed handgun grips are no exception. Manufacturers find that intricately made wooden grips do not lend themselves to modern, high speed mass production while trying to produce the best possible handgun at the most economical price.

Factory grips have shown little change in their styling over the past hundred years. As a rule, factory standards have left much to be desired when it comes to finding grips that come in a variety of sizes to fit hands of all sizes. You wouldn't want to purchase a handgun that featured grips that were so small that your pinky would be left without room to hang on, especially when firing revolvers or autos with exceptionally forceful recoil. Along the same line of thought, anyone with relatively small hands shouldn't entertain the idea of getting a handgun incorporating somewhat oversized stocks.

Most factory stocks, even those allowing room for the little finger to be included in the grip of the hand on the weapon, are so designed that the short little finger is not afforded any gripping action. The pinky must close around the front strap as far as possible without using a side hold; the gripping action of the finger is a major portion of the hand's strength on the weapon. Any design that forces this finger below the butt so that it is left out of play is illogical.

Recoil has a tendency to be of a rather sudden nature and thus hard to evaluate. If the hand is not placed properly so as to provide a tight and secure grip on the weapon, the result can be anything from cuts and bites, as the handgun walks smartly to the rear or jumps back and up due to the improper grip, to a simple smarting palm, the latter if you're lucky.

The palm swell is capable of absorbing a considerable amount of shock, providing it is distributed evenly. By correctly loading the palm of the hand with evenly distributed recoil, the damaging effects on the web of the hand are reduced greatly. In the event that a factory grip does not provide for well distributed recoil, it will most certainly affect the accuracy of succeeding shots once the first has been triggered.

The accuracy with which you shoot a revolver or auto should not be accredited solely to the length of the barrel, caliber of the handgun, or its make and model. The manner in which the flesh of the hand and contours of the stock match is of just as much importance as any of the qualities or features just mentioned. A good number of shooters who have been discouraged from shooting handguns, with the thought that they just weren't built for shooting these weapons, were probably the victims of stocks featuring poor design or a style that just didn't fit their hand. Perhaps as many as half the people who ever have fired a revolver have been prevented from becoming good, or even great, shots because of their inability to adapt to the standard factory installed handgun grips.

Many manufacturers claim to produce their handguns with stocks that are so designed that they fit shooters with "average" sized hands. How do you determine an average sized hand? Hands come in all sizes, small to extremely large, and therefore so should handgun grips.

When a stock is too large for the shooter's hand, such as are many of the factory installed target type stocks, for the average shooter the weapon feels bulky and awkward. Many shooters then blame the gun, when actually it is the grips that are causing all the problems. In the case of the big bore automatics and magnum revolvers, the shooter with hands that are not large enough to fit around the oversized grips for an effective hold will find the weapon extremely uncomfortable as well as inaccurate. An officer finding that standard factory grips are on the small side for him can sometimes find satisfaction, and in many cases accurate results, by switching to a regular pair of factory installed target-type grips.

For the most part, the hand must do the adjusting to achieve a suitable fit of the factory stock to the individual shooter. Although not a perfect fit, in some cases not even a suitable fit, through practice the average shooter can get used to the feel of the weapon and maintain some degree of accuracy with it. The standard factory grip usually is just two pieces of wood, walnut in handguns of better quality, that are fitted to the sides of the handgun frame. These wooden plates have little, if any, relation to the grip of the human hand, other than the fact that the fingers and palm of the hand envelope the grips in its grasp. Instead, the factory grips retain the contours of the steel frame and contribute little to the handling capabilities of the weapon.

Occasionally the stock will be of one-piece construction, sometimes of plastic or a synthetic material having similar density to that of wooden grips. Although grips made of top quality walnut are usually more desirable than plastic grips, the one-piece plastic stock sometimes actually offers better features than the wooden ones. Looks are nice, but efficiency is what counts when it comes to law enforcement work.

Reputable handgun manufacturers — Smith & Wesson, Colt, Browning, et al. — offer, to a small degree, a choice of grips featuring some variation in their design. This is usually just the choice of round or square butts on a particular model. Others, such as Dan Wesson Arms, give the purchaser a variety of grips featuring a choice of contours, and as with this particular manufacturer, they occasionally offer a grip blank that is factory inletted to fit the weapon's frame but leaves the contour shaping to the individual shooter. The Dan Wesson handguns also feature stocks that are interchangeable, as are the barrels.

Generally speaking, most of the pistol grips presently being installed on handguns in the factory are quite good. Most feature checkering of some sort or they are semi-contoured. On some handguns the grips may be adequate in length for the shooter, but lack the width needed to fill gap left when fired by men with large hands.

Several manufacturers turn out grip fillers that add to the feel of the stock and to the shooter's ability to handle the handgun. These are small adapters, usually made of a light alloy or rubber, which are held in place by a clip in the area between the rear of the trigger guard and the front of the grips. These are offered in various sizes and can offer an inexpensive but satisfactory solution to improving comfort and shooting control of the weapon.

When selecting a handgun for duty, check the feel of the weapon's grips. A duty weapon should incorporate stocks that will enable the officer to fire it from either hand should he be forced to do so. Grips that feature a contoured thumb rest that protrudes from the portion of the stock where it mates up with the handgun's receiver could make firing from the opposite hand difficult.

Suitable handgun stocks should feature a memory groove in the area where the trigger finger extends from the grip to the trigger. It is not true that a handgun's stock has to be oversized to be functionally acceptable, nor does it have to be undersized to make the handgun concealable. The important factor is that the stock must conform to the hand as well as to the frame of the gun. As a rule, stocks that feature excessive girth at the butt will most assuredly rob the shooter of good control, and as far as recoil is concerned, it is a meaningless addition to the weapon. Some stocks feature a memory groove on the thumb side of the stock which partially serves as a thumb-rest.

For one reason or another, a shooter may not be able to find a standard factory grip that will warrant use while on duty. To cope with these special demands and modifications there are several custom handgun stock manufacturers that will build personally fitted stocks for most any shooter and on occasion handgun manufacturers may deviate from their regular grip patterns and produce a custom handgun stock. These special designs will be discussed in greater detail in the following chapters in this section.

Mustang grips on an S&W Model 29.

Chapter 21

SPECIAL GRIPS FOR THE DUTY HANDGUN

When factory grips need replacing, these practical and often handsome handles are just the answer!

To COMPROMISE DOESN'T necessarily mean to give in to pressure and accept standards of less than desirable proportions. As the late Dwight D. Eisenhower once stated, "People talk about the middle of the road as though it were unacceptable. Actually, all human problems, excepting morals, come into the gray areas. Things are not all black and white. There have to be compromises. The middle of the road is all of the usable surface."

The late President in most probability wasn't thinking of handgun grips as he made this statement, but as with all other problems, the one of finding proper fitting grips can sometimes be solved by compromising and selecting a set of factory-installed target grips. Some handgun manufacturers even supply grip blanks that are already inletted and leave the contouring to the purchaser.

One such firm offering grips with excess wood that allows an officer to shape the stocks contours to fit him personally is Dan Wesson Arms of Monson, Massachusetts. Although these stocks are more than ample for use on the Dan Wesson revolvers just as they come from the factory, there is still enough wood for the shooter to make any slight modifications he may feel necessary to achieve a perfect fit of the weapon.

To meet the demands of the gun-buying public for handguns that have more than just one design of grips as standard equipment, all of the Wesson revolvers are available with a choice of five different stock designs.

Colt, Smith & Wesson, and a few of the other producers of fine law enforcement weapons offer as an option target grips for many of their handguns. On some of the models, they are available with or without checkering. Again, some of the oversized grips lacking checkering may have enough excess wood to warrant personal shaping of the grip.

As a standard factory alternate, Charter Arms offers an optional set of Bulldog grips for their small framed revolvers, the .38 caliber Undercover and the .32 caliber Undercoverette. The larger grips add greatly to the point control of the small handguns, making their use more practical as well as safer.

An important thing to remember when buying an oversized set of grips or when shaping a set yourself, is that you should insure that there isn't any excess wood which could interfere with the loading of the revolver or even the ejection of empty cases. The latter is an important step in speedy reloading of the cylinder, a feature that is important should an officer find himself engaged in a fire-fight.

If satisfaction can't be found with a set of commercially factory fitted stocks, about the only answer is to turn to one of the more reputable custom stock making firms. The

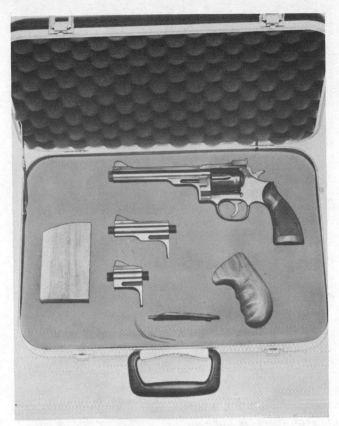

The Dan Wesson Arms firm offers their Model 12 in pack form, complete with an extra set of grips, three interchangeable barrels and a blank of quality grade walnut for making a set of custom home-made grips.

cost is usually somewhat higher than that of the factory replacement or target grips, but not so high as to make them not a reasonable choice. Then if you happen to be a craftsman, talented with the ability to manage home projects with some degree of quality, you can always make your own set of custom grips.

The grips on the left were identical to the factory grips on the right before being reshaped. A few of today's manufacturers leave enough wood for this purpose.

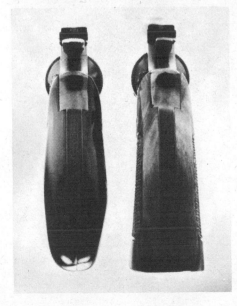

First, you'll need to select the proper wood to be used in the construction of the grips. Your selection is of vital importance, since the wood should be durable as well as finely figured so as to enhance the looks of the weapon on which the grips will be installed.

For a few dollars you should be able to pick up enough wood of suitable quality from a gunsmith or stock making firm. They usually have scrap pieces laying around that are left over from rifle or shotgun blanks. The best wood usually comes from the root and is more commonly referred to as burl. Quality wood should display fine figuration of the grain, which should be of rather dense nature but should not be so hard as to actually become brittle.

The piece of wood should be sawed oversize and somewhat thicker than is needed; for most pistols, the blank should be of double thickness. This allows the grain of each grip half to correspond with the opposite grip by sawing the double blank down the center.

To achieve the rough outline shape of the handgun's frame, remove the original stocks and trace an outline of the old grip onto the wood blank. When doing so, it should be kept in mind that the grain should run longitudinally, or from the uppermost part of the stock to the butt.

The tools necessary for making pistol grips are simple: A few files, consisting of a medium rasp and a couple of half-round files, a coping saw, an eleven-tooth carpenter's saw, a bench vise, several grades of garnet sandpaper for finishing and a minimum amount of good stock finish or varnish for the final coat.

With some practice and a little patience, custom home-made grips, like this set of laminated grips on a Colt Super .38 auto, can be made during leisure hours.

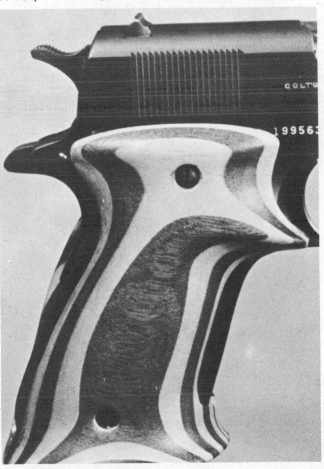

Once you have sawed the double thick blank down the center, you have two single grip blanks that are ready to be inletted for the handguns frame. Care should be taken to insure that the inletting is done precisely, since this is a deciding factor as to whether the finished grips will actually be satisfactory or just two more pieces of wood slapped onto the gun.

The rounded contours of the grip surface are obtained by using the wood rasp and files to remove excess wood in the area immediately to the rear of the trigger guard. As insurance against marring the blued finish of the back strap and trigger guard, this process should be done with the grips off the pistol, although it is possible to do this with them on the weapon. This is usually a tedious process that requires skillful use of both rasp and files.

After the grips begin to take shape, start using the sandpaper to remove the minute amounts of wood that are to be taken off, keeping in mind that once you shave off too much from a certain area you'll have to start all over to get the grips that you had originally planned to produce. During the final sanding with 400 to 600 grit garnet paper you will begin to notice the grain of wood becoming increasingly apparent. As a rule, the finer the final sanding, the more beautiful the grain of wood.

The next step is to apply the gunstock finish or varnish. This is a simple process when using one of the many finishing kits now available, but equally satisfying results can be had with the varnish if you take your time and do the job properly.

It is simple to obtain a beautiful high glossy finish, merely by following the instructions included in many of the stock finishing kits on the market today, such as Herter's Stock Finishing Kit and other kits available from Williams, Lyman, Birchwood-Casey and Brownell. An important facet towards obtaining a smooth finish, however, is to fill the pores of the wood, after a final sanding with 400 grit wet-or-dry abrasive paper. If these pores aren't filled properly, the finish most assuredly will have an overall pitted appearance.

In most of the stock finishing kits there is ample filler to accomplish this. When using linseed oil or when striking out on one's own, some type of wood filler is necessary. Usually this can be purchased separate from the kits at a reasonable price.

VARIETY MAY VERY well be the spice of life, but when it comes to finding a set of handgun grips that will give you a perfect fit, variety then in many cases becomes a necessity of life. Hands are different, grips are different; what perfectly fits one shooter doesn't necessarily mean that it will fit another even if the hands appear to be of about the same size.

There is a great number of quality handguns on the market that have proven themselves over and over under the most adverse of conditions. Many of these weapons are perfect choices for use while an officer is on duty or enjoying his off duty hours. Some lack one important feature, however, and that is they are not equipped with versatile quality grips.

Today there are a good number of custom handgun stock making firms located across the country. Many of which will replace, alter or improve most any design that is being presently produced or many of which that have been long discontinued from production.

In many cases the factory installed stocks on many of the small frame guns used for home defense or off-duty policemen don't provide for the consistent point-control

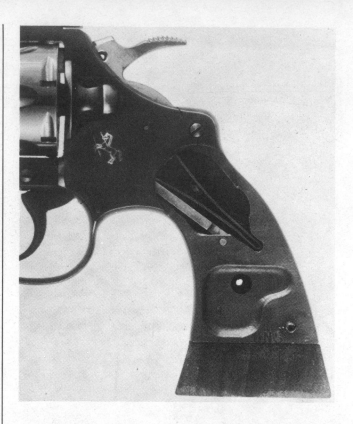

Here we see the difference between factory and custom grips, on the same short-barreled revolver, with the left stock removed to make the frame visible. Factory grip (top) follows contour of frame, extending downward for control by little finger, which is vital. Herrett's Shooting Ace stock, below, has wood added behind the frame in a carefully worked out proportion designed to prevent shooting too high during rapid, instinctive fire.

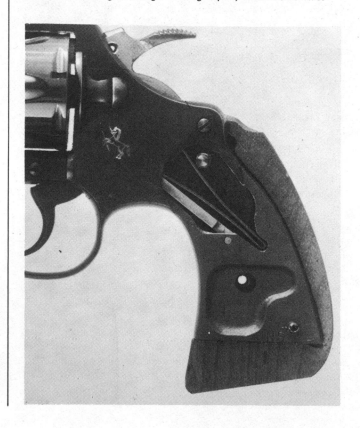

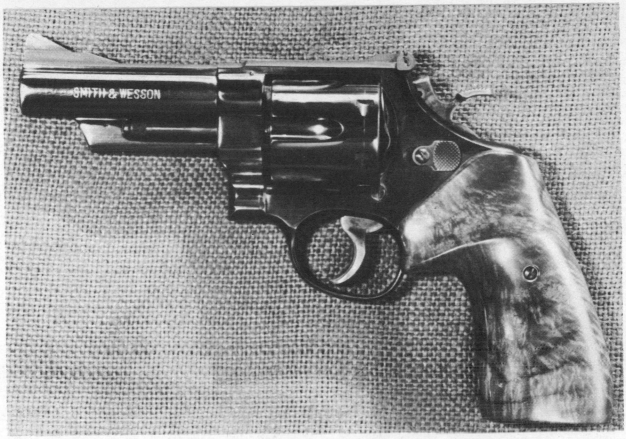

Even the flossiest, most expensive guns, such as this S&W Model 29, can be enhanced by well-made custom grips. This pair of Jordan Trooper stocks, by Herrett's, is a frozen explosion of glowing grain.

needed when firing the short barreled lightweight handguns. As a rule snub-nosed guns are not too accurate, especially when fired double action. Although they usually feature trigger pulls in excess of ten pounds, requiring some amount of effort to work the action and fire the revolver, their ineffectiveness is occasionally the fault of the inadequacy of the stocks that were installed during its production. In addition to the lack of control, the usually meager grips on these weapons don't provide for adequate distribution of the weapon's recoil, especially in the case of small revolvers of .38 caliber.

The statistics of the F.B.I. reveal that the typical average employment of the handgun is done at ranges of less than seven yards. When the stocks of these small framed revolvers and autos are substituted with a custom set that has been constructed so as to provide for better control of the weapon, it then becomes a logical choice for self-defense purposes. No one should assume the responsibility that goes with carrying any handgun unless they are reasonably proficient with its use.

Manufacturers of custom handgun stocks, such as Herrett's Stocks, Incorporated, of Twin Falls, Idaho, have spent months of research, firing thousands of rounds of ammunition, searching for grip designs that afford the shooter both comfort and efficiency at the same time. Many of the custom grips that have evolved from their studies offer the shooter the confidence he needs when packing his weapon while off duty, allowing him to properly control his weapon so he is no longer handicapped with an uncomfortable grip and thus usually poor accuracy.

Herrett's Shooting Ace stocks are so designed that they allow the shooter to deliver three or four well placed shots in less than two seconds. The secret is in the new back strap design, styled so that the gun points parallel with the arm when firing. There is no loss of time when seeking the target and increased speed is the result of the one hand point-control shooting.

For the larger framed duty revolvers, Herrett's Shooting Star stocks offer the officer the versatility of firing with either right or left hand, should the need arise. Although not a true target design, the memory grooves incorporated along both sides of the grips allow for positive placing of the trigger finger and a sort of thumb rest on the opposite side. These grooves are a prime necessity for better gun control.

There are more than a dozen custom stock making firms located across the country, and their prices vary greatly. You can expect to pay anywhere from a minimum of around eight dollars to a maximum of around thirty dollars for custom grips that are suitable enough to warrant installation on duty revolvers.

If, after examining some of the custom grips now on the market, you are still not satisfied and are not willing to part with the cash that a personally built set of grips will certainly cost you, why not design and build a set of your own? It's not as hard as it may seem and is an excellent project for your leisure off-duty hours at home, especially when bad weather limits your activities. Home built grips, to your own shaping and styling, are inexpensive to make and the end results are grips that are for you and you only.

PART VII: INTRODUCTION

Whether By Whim Or Necessity, Some Require A Gun That No Manufacturer Builds. Here Are Some Examples!

HANDGUN MODIFICATIONS

Swenson customizes heavy Colt autos to "Bobcat" version, complete with exclusive right/left-handed safety

NO MANUFACTURER makes a deliberate effort to turn out guns that are inadequate and unsatisfactory. You can feel certain that their standard models represent a careful refinement of designs intended to satisfy the greatest number of their customers to the fullest extent possible.

That's the key: Standard factory production is geared to fulfill the desires of the average gun buyer and you have to have a good prospect of selling a substantial number of units before the costs of designing and tooling can be amortized. This is no more than the finalization of cold commercial equations. Few enterprises the size of arms making factories are operated for any motive other than the earning of a profit for the workers, management and stockholders.

The flip-side of the coin is that customers are not turned out to blueprint specs on tool-maker's jigs in the same manner as the guns they buy. The guns may be closely similar to each other, but no two customers are alike to an appreciable degree.

Thus we find that, with fair frequency, a man becomes the owner of a gun and finds himself wishing that this, that or the other thing were different in some respect from the configuration it had been given upon leaving the factory.

The majority of such customizing operations do not have enough broad and general appeal to even remotely warrant offering as a factory-built option. In a few examples, pioneer remodeling has generated adequate market potential so that a factory version of the modification was offered.

One of the more outstanding examples of such a situation concerns the Government Model .45 auto pistol. It was designed for reliability rather than target accuracy and

mill-run samples of the big pistol deliver enough accuracy for ordinary purposes. Phrasing it another way, even the unmodified, as-issued .45 auto is capable of better groups than are most of the shooters who encounter it.

However, the .45 auto is fired competitively in target matches and the more dedicated shooters engage in sufficient practice so that they elevate their personal skill to a degree several levels above the in-built capability of the pistol. At first, there was a dedicated program of sifting and testing to pin down which one of several nominally identical pistols was capable of the best groups.

When the hand-culling process came to the end of its potential, mechanically gifted artisans began taking a long, thoughtful look at John M. Browning's basic design of the Government Model and the more bright-eyed researchers began to discover ways in which it could be made to group ever more tightly. About this time, the verb, "accurize," came into existence.

Meanwhile, back at Hartford, management at the Colt works was not unaware that it was possible to build a more accurate pistol on the basic design and the National Match grade .45s were being turned out prior to WWII. The accurizer's art reached new heights in the years immediately following the Hitler/Tojo fracas and the inevitable result was the Colt Gold Cup.

It was intended that this would fill the demand for a pistol that could be bought off the dealer's shelves and taken to the matches without further refinement. The puncturing of this bright dream should have been predictable: Customizers immediately began dreaming up ways to accurize the Gold Cup still further. And so it goes...and goes...

The Complete Customizing Chronicle Is Endless, But Here Are Some Of The More Popular Avenues That Have Been Explored!

Chapter 22

Snubbed M17 Colt revolver.

A TIME OF CHANGE

BACK AROUND 1960, Kleins Sporting Goods, in Chicago, acquired a batch of WWI relics in the form of Colt Model 1917 revolvers, chambered to accept the .45 ACP round — by means of the half-moon clips — or the .45 Auto Rim cartridge as produced under the Remington and Peters brand names.

A dozen-odd years to the rear, used handguns were by no means the briskly moving merchandise of today and surplus revolvers of the Kaiser War generated little beyond indifference in the average store browser. Half a decade later, thirty to thirty-five dollars still would get you clean title on a good, as-issued M17, be it Colt or S&W.

Something had to be done to that consignment of ancient Colts to enhance their market potential and someone must have suggested bobbing some pipe off the muzzle to convert them into one of the most awesome snub-nosed revolvers of all recorded history.

Hardly sooner suggested than executed. About three inches was cut from the front, leaving two and one-half inches of barrel, which extended slightly past the end of the ejector rod. A semi-circle of steel, with beveled edges, was affixed to the upper surface to replace the missing front sight and the new muzzle was crowned neatly.

We picked up one of these re-styled relics at — as nearly as memory recalls — something close around the twenty-five dollar mark. It retained the bulky lanyard swivel and it must be confessed that the relationship between the second-generation front sight and the point of bullet impact was — to put it as charitably as possible — rather casual.

However, the .45 Auto Rim cartridge has capability not to be dismissed lightly. When reloaded with the excellent Lyman cast bullet design number 452423 — a Keith-designed semi-wadcutter of around 250 grains in weight — even the shortened barrel could condense a lot of punch into a revolver of medium-compact dimensions.

We fiddled with the basic modification, as time permitted, over the course of the next few years. Removal of the useless lanyard swivel was a simple operation. Separating the rudimentary front sight required little beyond a few crafty dabs with a ball-peen hammer. Dressing down the top of the barrel with careful swipes of a fine-cut file, we silver-soldered a small, ramp-type sight in its place.

There followed a long and patient interlude of cut-and-try test firing, in the course of which the point of impact was worked ever into closer congruity with the line of sight. Meanwhile, every effort was made to retain eye-pleasing lines for the new front sight. Came the day that typical loads would cluster into a six-inch pattern around the point of aim at twenty-five yards and we proclaimed ourselves satisfied, crowning the operation with swabbed coats of cold blue to tone down the piebald appearance of the venerable ventilator. Though still far from a museum piece, its aesthetic charm had been improved, to say nothing of its functional efficiency.

In today's burgeoning handgun market, it would be no problem to show a profit on the original cash outlay but, if a modest value were to be set upon the man-hours expended, the 21st Century will arrive ahead of the break-even point.

If economic considerations are a factor in your thinking, remember that almost anything you do to modify original factory specs is quite apt to diminish the value of the gun for which you've parted with hard-earned and tax-paid dollar bills. As recently as 1970, we acquired clear title to a nice little Model 31 S&W in caliber .32 S&W Long for a prefunctory thirty-five dollars: well under the market value but made possible by the fact that a previous owner had trimmed the spur off the hammer.

In the process, something upward of twenty bucks has been trimmed off the gun's market value. The motive behind this particular alteration is fairly obvious: to eliminate the risk of having the spur catch on the edge of a pocket or other clothing during the draw.

The model 31 proved to be a rather charming and capable little item of ordnance. As with many S&W snub-noses, it could print some groups that many would find hard to believe — provided you cocked the hammer and fired single action. Sadly, this had been made into a somewhat chancy operation. You could start the hammer back by careful pressure on the trigger and catch the top with your thumb to continue cocking: most of the time. Every now and then, the trigger pressure wasn't quite careful enough and you got that sharp, yippy report when you weren't really prepared for it.

De-spurring the hammer of a revolver should be regarded as a one-way operation which rules out future use of single action firing. From then on, it's a gun for firing double action, pure and simple. If you change your mind, the gun can be sent back to the factory for replacement of the mutilated hammer and the cost will come extremely close to equaling the reduction in the gun's market value as of the moment you finished sawing off the first hammer spur.

We've discussed these two modifications in some detail to provide sharp delineation of a fairly significant point: Before you permit yourself to be carried away by your enthusiasm for a visualized modification of your handgun, give some sober reflection upon the strong likelihood that it will subtract from your net worth by reducing the intrinsic value of the gun. If you're lucky, the modification will prove pleasing and satisfactory to you. But don't be surprised and dismayed if other shooters don't see it from the same viewpoint.

It's your gun, so hacksaw and file away on it to your heart's delight, but plan on retaining ownership or losing money.

Along the way, try to keep a cool head and a touch of reasoned judgement. You'll see samples or photos of guns that have been modified in all imagineable manners. There once was a minor vogue for cutting away the front half of the trigger guard. The rationale for this was logical enough: It kept you from hanging up your trigger finger on the guard during an all-out emergency fast draw-and-shoot effort. Usually, this was accompanied by sawing off the hammer spur and sometimes the front sight, as well. The resulting end-product of all these well-intentioned ministrations was suited for little beyond what has been termed across-the-table shooting.

If you need an across-the-table gun and are prepared to accept the financial consequences, that's fine. Consider, though, that your hopeful modifications do little to retain the ability of the original design to weather hard useage.

Any minor blow to the remaining half of the cutaway trigger guard is apt to bend it upward enough so as to prevent the gun from being fired. The original, intact trigger guard is much sturdier, more resistant to the hard knocks it may encounter. Comes the real clutch and you discover that, instead of a functional firearm, you've wound up with a pretty ineffectual blunt instrument.

All of which is to say that almost any sensible handgun modification can be duplicated from factory stock. If it fills a justified need, the factories build it and are happy to sell you a copy. If you've reason to worry about snagging the hammer spur on the draw, S&W lists their hammerless, strictly double action Centennial or their shrouded-hammer Bodyguard. The hammer of the latter can be cocked manually, if desired, with rather less risk than would be assumed in trigger-cocking a de-spurred Model 31 or Model 36, for two examples. As noted in the catalog section of this book, Colt offers snag-free shrouded hammers on certain of their ultra-compact revolvers. All of these are standard factory production that do not carry the lost-value penalty of home-modified combat specials. You can buy them and re-sell them without undue loss of financial blood.

About one person out of every seven or eight — call it roughly fourteen percent — is more skilled when using his left hand instead of his right. Most auto pistols have been built for the benefit of the other six or seven north-paws in the general population. If you're a right-hander and question this observation, try manipulating a self-stuffer with your off-side hand and see how clumsy the operation becomes.

So far as we know, no one has converted a revolver to south-paw configuration but the basic revolver design is fairly ambidextrous in the first place. However, there are modifications for some of the more popular auto pistols and these can be thoroughly admirable and worthwhile if you favor the port-side paw.

Armand Swenson, of Gardena, California, installs a safety on the .45 Government Model Colt which can be manipulated with the right or left hand equally well. Unlike some of the farther-out modifications, this does not reduce the value of a .45 auto in the slightest and it makes that part of the operation equal in convenience for anyone who has at least one hand on either side.

The magazine catch of the .45 auto remains about as Browning first sketched it out in the early years of the present century and we know of no one offering a left-handed or ambidextrous catch. It does not present a really serious problem, as does the safety catch. It's not too inconvenient to shift the left index finger back and drop the magazine from a .45 auto but working the safety is quite another matter.

There is not too much that can be done to improve the performance of most revolvers, beyond installation of more comfortable and efficient grips and that is covered more completely in another section of this book. The .45 Colt auto and the Browning 9mm Hi-Power can benefit from skilled ministrations by becoming notably more accurate than the mill-run factory production but that falls more into the area of a target competitor's interests rather than in that of the working law enforcement officer. The accuracy standards of the unmodified production handgun are adequate for the usually hasty employment of typical duty shooting situations.

Replacement of the magazines in an auto pistol can be speeded and streamlined by inward beveling of the surfaces of the butt around the entrance to the magazine well and this is a useful and justified modification. A pad of leather can be cemented to the bottom of the magazine, serving the dual purpose of preventing damage to the empty magazine if dropped to the ground in simulated combat practice and making it easier, more positive to slam home a fresh magazine.

A self-cocking accessory for the .45 Colt auto is discussed in detail in an adjacent segment. As of press time, a New England inventor is developing a full-scale double action trigger modification of the same gun, equipping it with capabilities to equal those of such pistols as the Model 39 S&W but marketing plans and conversion details are not as yet resolved. Skilled welding can build up the engaging surface of the thumb safety on many auto pistol designs to make the disengagement of the safety easier, more positive and adjustable sights can be installed if the probable benefits seem to so warrant.

The key question to consider is whether or not a proposed modification will, in the long-term employment of your handgun, result in more gain in value and utility than loss through cost, effort and possibly hampering normal function. Be confident as to the answer before proceeding.

An Ingenious Accessory Adds New Versatility And Capability To This 61-Year-Old Veteran Handgun!

BELOVED, REVILED, admired, endured, adored and cussed-at, the old autoloading Colt Government Model, vintage of 1911, has used up its rightful quota of printer's ink — and then some — in the course of its long and turbulent career. Countless pages have been expended in singing its praises, with an equal if not greater number having been used up in cataloging its alleged array of vices, inadequacies, shortcomings and similar ornery traits.

With the appearance of auto pistols such as the Walther P-38 and the Smith & Wesson Model 39, critics of the old M1911 Colt added a fresh chapter to their vituperations: It took some little amount of time to get off the first shot. The so-called double action autos could be whipped from the holster and, with one stout yank of their trigger, could haul their hammer back to drop upon a chambered round, functioning in the usual self-cocking/loading configuration after that point.

The M1911 Colt offered a few choices in this matter; none of them entirely satisfactory. The optimum state of readiness involved carrying the gun with a live round in the chamber, hammer back and thumb safety lever up: the cocked-and-locked mode. Disadvantages included the possibility of getting the safety unlocked too soon and gouging a channel down your leg through over-hasty pressure on the trigger.

As an alternate, it could be carried with a live round in the chamber, hammer fully down: nominally a safe mode on the theory that the floating or inertial firing pin is slightly shorter than the distance between hammer face and cartridge primer. In actual fact, if the hammer is struck with sufficient force, the firing pin can be driven forward with enough energy to fire the round. Carrying the chamber loaded with the hammer on half cock is even worse because, if the half-cock notch is broken or defective, the hammer can drop with a fair chance of setting off the cartridge.

Which brings us to the mode of carry specified by most military agencies using the M1911: chamber empty, with seven rounds in the box magazine, hammer down. Putting it into action involves drawing from the holster, pulling the slide to the rear and releasing to cock the hammer simultaneously with chambering a round. The old GI holster, with its button-down flap, obviously never was designed for the primary purpose of getting the handgun into action with ultimate speed. The military philosophy seems to envision the likelihood that the carrier of the pistol will have some adequate amount of forewarning, so as to have the handgun out, loaded and ready before the situation calls for shooting. This hopeful assumption seems to include the condition that the carrier will have both hands free for drawing plus dragging back on the slide. True, there is a knack of pulling it partway from the holster, giving the butt a quarter-turn forward, pushing the muzzle down on a ledge in the GI holster to bring the slide back before completing the draw so that it can be done with one hand.

Turn the clock back to the early days of U.S. participation in WW II, down under — Sydney, Australia, year 1942 — a young sailor, Clarence A. Raville by name, is working the ordnance department of a newly organized USN supply depot. Aware that the existing design of the service auto is short of perfection, he launched forth on a long program aimed at development of an improved cocking system.

Many years and some eighteen different designs later, he marketed the device known as the Caraville Double Ace. It's priced at $39.95, which includes postage and insurance — add five percent sales tax for California residents — and it can be mailed to anyone; no federal firearms license being required since the basic device is not a firearm in itself.

Installation is fairly easy and simple. The unit can be put into any of the Colt autos built on the .45 service pistol frame — such as the .38 Super, the Commander models, Gold Cup and several foreign-made guns of the same pattern — with occasional minor modifications as described in the accompanying instruction sheet.

Contrary to typical expectations, the Double Ace, when installed, does not bring the hammer back from the full-down position. Raville explains the reason for this in literature supplied with the unit by noting that, with the hammer in full-down position, a sharp blow on the hammer spur can set off a chambered round. If you feel a need to verify this, he urges that an empty, primed case be used rather than a live round.

In order to function in the intended manner, with the Double Ace installed, the hammer must be drawn back to a point slightly behind the normal half-cock position of the unmodified pistol design. Raville designates this as the "standby mode." I prefer to say three-quarters-cock on grounds that the term is slightly more self-defining.

Call it by either name, when the hammer is on standby mode, it is not being supported by the original sear, although that component remains a part of the pistol mechanism. Support of the hammer in standby mode is taken over by a double ball-bearing sear located at the lower end of the drawrod of the Double Ace unit.

When in standby mode, it becomes virtually impossible for a round in the chamber to fire, except by deliberately mashing the Double Ace forward to the limit of its travel, holding it in that position and pulling the trigger. This can be verified by repeating the previous experiment: placing an empty, primed case — without powder or bullet — in the chamber, moving the hammer to standby mode and rapping smartly against the spur of the hammer with a mallet.

As the Double Ace is squeezed in against the frame of the gun, the hammer moves back to full-cock position and remains there. If the trigger is pulled with the Double Ace unit forward, a round in the chamber will fire. Assuming a loaded magazine is in place, it will reload automatically and, so long as the Double Ace unit is held forward, additional rounds can be discharged by releasing the trigger, then pulling it again in the usual manner until the magazine is empty.

If the hammer is cocked — either manually or via the Double Ace unit — and the hand pressure against the Double Ace is released, pulling the trigger causes the hammer to drop back down to standby mode. The half-cock notch of the original design remains in the system and will arrest the hammer — provided the trigger is not pulled — should any operating defect of the Double Ace unit release the hammer before it is cocked fully.

Should the shooter wish to lock the Double Ace unit out of operation for any reason, it can be squeezed forward, held there and a small locking pin can be moved to secure it in forward postion. This locking pin occupies the same position as the mainspring housing pin of the original design: one of the components replaced in installation of the Double Ace unit.

A further design feature permits the locking pin to render the pistol completely inoperable, if this should be desired for safety reasons. If the locking pin is moved over with the Double Ace unit in relaxed — that is, rearward — position, it becomes impossible to squeeze the DA unit forward and, as a result, impossible to fire the pistol until the inconspicuous locking pin is pushed a short distance back the other way to permit functioning of the Double Ace unit.

Thus the pistol can be put into non-firing configuration as a safety precaution, with a strong likelihood that it cannot be fired by anyone not familiar with the operation of the Double Ace unit. If further assurance is needed, a small padlock can be used, with its hasp inserted through a hole in the Double Ace unit and locked, thereby making the pistol totally unfireable until such time as the padlock has been removed.

With the Double Ace unit locked in forward position, the pistol returns to its accustomed operation, except that it does not have the grip safety feature. The thumb safety continues to function in the usual manner. An owner might prefer this configuration if, for example, firing the pistol at targets. Holding the unlocked Double Ace unit in forward position requires approximately three-quarters of a pound of effort and most shooters find that this is about the normal amount of squeeze applied to the handle when shooting the big auto. However, if a more relaxed grip is desired, the unit can be locked forward, as noted.

Four parts are removed from the original design during installation: the grip safety, hammer strut, mainspring housing assembly and mainspring housing retaining pin. If desired, the Double Ace unit can be removed, with the original parts reinstalled at any time, as often as the owner wishes. No change or modification is made in any standard parts of the pistol.

Occasionally, a non-standard part will be encountered, requiring minor modification or a replacement part. Nearly

Cutaway demonstrator (below) shows how Double Ace unit replaces standard grip safety, hammer strut, mainspring housing and retaining pin of original gun

Unit at left is in cocked mode; if released — as at right — it must be re-set by pushing against a solid surface.

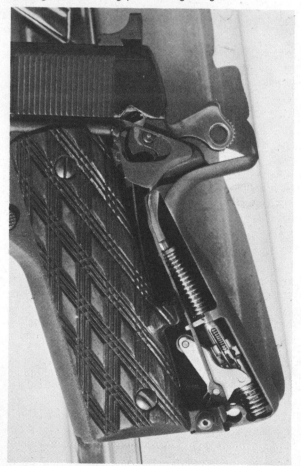

A dust cover encloses the gap, being held in place by the ingenious locking cross-pin for deactivating gun as discussed in text.

Hammer in the above photo is in carrying mode for use with the Double Ace. At this position, a round in the chamber cannot fire until DA unit is squeezed to cock the hammer and held in as trigger is pulled.

Clarence A. Raville began the long road to development of his Double Ace unit while serving with the Navy in Australia.

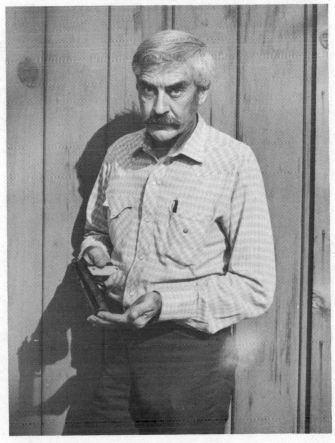

always, the part in question will be the hammer. The hammer supplied as standard equipment with Gold Cup models has a slightly different configuration which permits it to go "over the top" and back with the hammer cock notch out of engagement with the standard sear. Therefore, when installing the Double Ace on Gold Cups, it is recommended that a standard hammer be obtained and installed. A few of the hammers installed on the older M1911 Colts have a broad area at the rear of the hammer spur, extending far enough back to interfere with cocking via the Double Ace; such hammers must be modified by removal of a small amount of metal from the rear of the spur.

If the Double Ace unit is installed with one of the old, long-spur hammers and an attempt is made to operate it in the usual manner, the extremely strong leverage of the DA unit may warp the drawrod. If this happens, the hammer will drop back to half-cock, unless the trigger is pulled at the same time to the DA unit is depressed. If such a condition is noted, the unit should be returned to the manufacturer for adjustment — preferably accompanied by the hammer. The drawrod will be adjusted or replaced, followed by modification of the hammer to assure that it will function when reinstalled with the repaired unit.

A further minor modification of the basic Double Ace design is in the works, to be designated as the Mark II unit and, according to production plans, future delivery will be of the Mark II version exclusively. The most noteworthy change from the previous device is the addition of an externally adjustable trigger stop, by means of which a small hex-wrench — supplied with each unit — can be used to limit rearward trigger travel following release of the hammer. This feature should appeal to target shooting enthusiasts, having been a sales feature of the Colt Gold Cup models.

Once installed in the correct manner, the Double Ace has little effect upon normal operation of the auto pistol. Inherent accuracy remains the same, as does the trigger pull and similar characteristics carried over from the same gun, prior to its modification.

PART VIII: MISCELLANEOUS MATTERS

The Field Of Police Armament Is Anything But Static, As This Discussion Indicates!

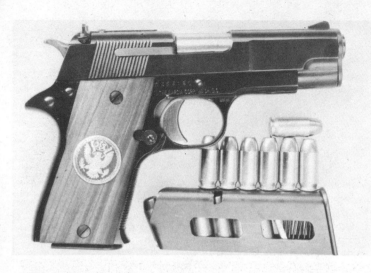

Imported from Spain by Garcia Sporting Arms, the Star Model PD holds seven rounds of .45 ACP in a compact, 23-oz. package, providing a lot of punch for the plainclothes officer or off-duty carrying. Checkered grips are standard, without the eagle seal on the custom set shown.

The Thomas .45 ACP auto, center, between a .25 ACP Raven and an M1911A1 Colt, is unusual in that each shot requires a full double-action pull of the trigger. It's made by H&N Mini-Craft, address on facing page. The black nylon grip adapter on the M1911A1 is made and sold by Auto Grip Enterprises, Box 7078, Burbank, California 91505 and is held on by the stocks.

Chapter 23
SINCE LAST EDITION

Sterling Arms introduced this prototype of a new double-action .45 ACP early in 1976. It has exposed hammer, target sights, staggered nine-round magazine capacity.

Heckler & Koch introduced a .45 ACP version of their Model P9S in early 1976. That's a cocking lever to the rear of the trigger guard and the trigger is double-action.

IN THE FOUR years since the publication of the first edition of Law Enforcement Handgun Digest, a number of the items discussed therein have ceased to be available. At the same time, at least as many more have been introduced. Indeed, several items have been introduced and dropped from production since last edition.

One of the earliest dropouts, discontinued shortly after publication of the first edition, was the Auto-Burglar; a 20-gauge, double-barreled shotgun/pistol. It would appear that this gun posed considerable interest for the typical reader, since a great many inquiries have been received as to the current address of the distributor. According to reports, the complexities of the paper work and attendant red tape involved in importing the Auto-Burglar — which was manufactured in Italy — became totally insurmountable, despite the distributor's firm policy of selling solely to law enforcement agencies.

Another gun in the first edition that generated a lot of inquiries was the GG-31 tear gas pistol. After some amount of patient sleuthing, we found that its manufacture and distribution has been taken over by Casady Engineering Associates, 560 Alaska Avenue, Torrance, California 90503.

The Pepper Fog tear gas generator discussed in the first edition is made and sold by Erie Chemicals, a division of Smith & Wesson, Box 520, Springfield, Massachusetts 01101. The same firm distributed the Mercox dart pistol, but it is our understanding that this gun has been discontinued.

Numerous references to Super Vel bullets and loaded ammunition remain from the first edition. The Super Vel Cartridge Corporation ceased operations late in 1974 and its president, Lee Jurras, moved to Roswell, New Mexico, to go into business as a custom pistolsmith, specializing in the Auto Mag. Several of the major ammunition makers have added loads to their lines, more or less comparable in power and performance to the original Super Vel loads. At the same time, such bulletmaking firms as Hornady, Sierra and Speer now offer bullets similar to those introduced and popularized by Super Vel.

The A&W diverter, a muzzle attachment for shotguns, designed to produce flattened rectangular pellet patterns on proportions of about four-to-one, as described in the first edition, remains in limited production. Information concerning it can be obtained from W. Gordon Wing at Box 22084, Houston, Texas 77027.

Since the first edition, there has been greatly increased interest in double-action autoloading pistols, particularly with staggered, large-capacity magazines in the heavier calibers, up to and including the .45 ACP. The Walther P-38 and the Model 39 Smith & Wesson were among the early examples of such guns, though both had straight, single-column magazines. S&W modified the M39 design by adding a staggered-column magazine to produce their Model 59.

Within quite recent times, both Heckler & Koch and Sterling Arms have produced new designs of .45 ACP double-action auto pistols. The German-made H&K guns are distributed in the United States by Security Arms Company, Limited, Suite 218, 933 North Kenmore Street, Arlington, Virginia 22201, while Sterling Arms can be reached at 4436 Prospect Street, Gasport, New York 14067.

Another double-action auto, designed by Frank S. Thomas, Jr., is being marketed by H&N Mini-Craft, Incorporated, 1066 East Edna Place, Covina, California 91724. Offered in 9mm Luger, .38 Colt Super and .45 ACP, it has a single-column magazine and can be used with magazines intended for the corresponding Colt Government or Commander models. The Thomas design is unusual in that every shot is fired by means of a double-action pull of the trigger;

that is, the action feeds a fresh cartridge into the chamber but the hammer or striker does not remain cocked in the usual manner. It is claimed this eliminates the change in trigger pull between the first and subsequent shots, and reduces the risk that a shot will be fired inadvertently when the gun is in cocked mode.

Many departments and arms-training supervisors have come to recognize the hazard that can stem from cocking the police revolver in typical duty situations. In fact, at least one large metropolitan police department has modified all of the double-action revolvers carried by its officers, so that the hammers cannot be cocked and the gun can be fired only by a deliberate double-action pull of the trigger. It is reported that this step virtually has eliminated the problems of unintentionally discharged revolvers.

An interesting new submachine gun has been introduced since last edition. It's called the American 180, which is mildly misleading, since it's manufactured in West Germany and its magazine capacity is 177 rounds of caliber .22 long rifle cartridges. At first thought, the .22 long rifle may seem an odd choice for a submachine-gun round, but the A-180 fires at a cyclic rate of around twenty to thirty shots per second. Taking the lower figure, based on a muzzle velocity of 1335 fps, that amounts to twenty bullets, weighing forty grains each, at 158 foot-pounds apiece for a total of eight hundred grains of lead at a muzzle energy of 3160 foot-

pounds. That's roughly equal, in weight and energy, to ten rounds of .38 Super Colt, or two rounds of .45-70.

The distributors of the A-180 offer it with a true laser sighting system that projects a thin beam of intense scarlet light. The spot is about one inch in diameter at one hundred yards. When properly sighted, the laser spot can be aligned with the intended target, requiring no more than a touch of the trigger to deliver hits to the spot. The U.S. distributor of the A-180 is American International Corporation, 103 Social Hall Avenue, Salt Lake City, Utah 84111.

A snub-nosed version of the A-180 has been developed and is being marketed by Ford Firearms Company, 3251 East Speedway, Tucson, Arizona 85716. With the stock detached, this offers a highly concealable weapon capable of delivering 7080 grains of lead — that's slightly over one pound — within an interval of from 5.9 to 8.85 seconds, at a total energy of 27,966 foot-pounds. The high cyclic rate of fire, combined with the ease of controlling the negligible recoil — literally, you can write your name on a board with it — and the Laser Lok sight add up to quite a combination of unusual capabilities. If the lawbreaker is aware of the laser's purpose, merely pinning the bright red spot on his person can have a highly demoralizing effect and usually offsets the need for actual firing.

At press time, High Standard Sporting Firearms of 1817 Dixwell Avenue, Hamden, Connecticut 06514, was developing a new line of double-action revolvers that they hope to have in production by mid-1977. Their large-frame model, called the Crusader, will be chambered in .44 magnum and .45 Long Colt, and possibly in .41 magnum, as well. A smaller-frame model will be made in .357 magnum.

The all-plastic Tayra holster, shown on page 268, no longer is manufactured. Many readers have written to inquire about the unusual checkered stocks shown on pages 265 and 268. To the present, we've not succeeded in identifying these grips. The Thompson spring-type holster, shown on page 261, no longer is made and the manufacturer is out of business. Somehow, the printer managed to get the photo of the under-belt holster on the upper right corner of page 265 inverted in the first edition, causing considerable comment and minor confusion.

Certainly, one of the factors provoking the greatest amount of comment has been the prices shown in the

Above, Mag-na-port Arms has cut the recoil-reducing slot seen on the top of the barrel near muzzle, with a matching cut on opposite side, as discussed in the text. Right, A-180 submachine gun is snub-nosed type chambered for the .22 long rifle, is shown with caliber .380 Ingram, one of the smallest SMGs now available.

catalog section of the first edition. The prices, as given, were correct in late 1971, but costs have escalated upward in varying degrees since then, often to surprising levels. The value of the dollar in international monetary exchange has been a contributing factor, as well as the overall upward trends in the cost of labor. An example is the ornately engraved Renaissance version of the Browning Hi-Power, priced at $284.50 in the first edition and currently quoted at $900, with fixed sights. The standard Browning, with target sights, now costs $288.95; more than the price of the Renaissance just four years ago!

Sturm, Ruger and Company brought out their double-action Security Six revolver late in 1970, followed by a compact, short-barreled version termed the Ruger Speed Six a few years later. Within the past couple of years, the same guns have been made available in stainless steel, as well. Priced well below comparable patterns by Colt or S&W, the Ruger double-action revolvers have won considerable acceptance among law enforcement personnel. The most recent modification has consisted of removing the hammer spur from the Speed Six, making it much less apt to hang up when drawn from a pocket. Both guns are chambered for the more powerful .357 magnum cartridge, being equally capable of handling the .38 Special, if desired.

Recoil control has come in for its share of attention. One of the most successful operators in this specialized field has been Larry Kelly, head of Mag-na-port Arms, 30016 South River Road, Mt. Clemens, Michigan 48043. The Mag-na-port modification consists of milling slots in the side of the barrel, near the muzzle, using an electrostatic discharge machine. The technique does not leave burrs inside the bore and does not change the ballistics. Early Mag-na-porting consisted of one slot on each side, at angles of about forty-five degrees upward. More recently, Kelly has been adding another pair of slots, angled straight to each side. The upper pair controls muzzle jump as well as recoil, while the lower pair operates solely to counteract recoil. Reduction of as much as thirty percent or more of net recoil has been determined by tests. The actual reduction depends on several factors, including barrel length, type of powder charge and so on.

It is indicative of our increasingly troubled times that the police officer's off-duty weapon has come to be employed ever more frequently and, as a direct result, there is much more interest in a really effective, readily concealable handgun. One wry observer has commented that the ideal off-duty gun would be the size of a lipstick, capable of firing twenty rounds of hot-loaded .45-70 cartridges. While far from realistic, it serves to point up the current trend of such guns.

An example of today's off-duty guns is the OMC .380 Back Up, from TDE Marketing Corporation of 11658 McBean Drive, El Monte, California 91732. With an empty weight of but eighteen ounces, this all-stainless auto holds five rounds in the magazine and a sixth in the chamber. Its barrel is rigidly attached to the frame, contributing to respectable accuracy at the typically short ranges associated with the use of such guns.

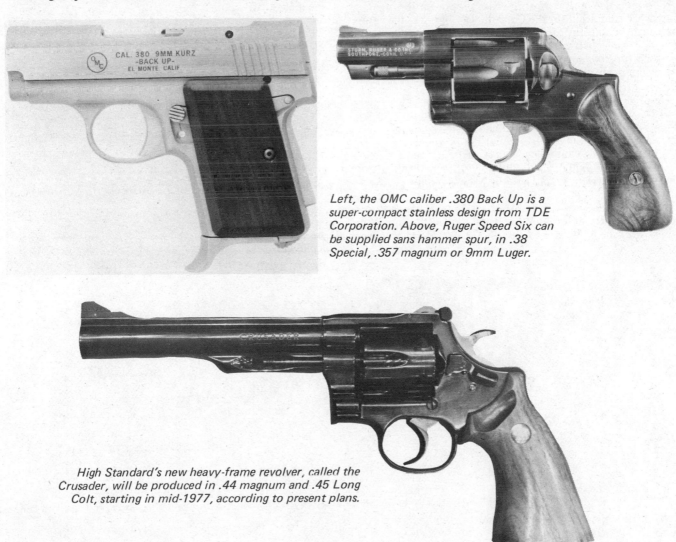

Left, the OMC caliber .380 Back Up is a super-compact stainless design from TDE Corporation. Above, Ruger Speed Six can be supplied sans hammer spur, in .38 Special, .357 magnum or 9mm Luger.

High Standard's new heavy-frame revolver, called the Crusader, will be produced in .44 magnum and .45 Long Colt, starting in mid-1977, according to present plans.

Still smaller is the .25 ACP Diane from Wilkinson Arms, 803 North Glendora Avenue, Covina, California 91724. The Diane weighs less than twelve ounces, measuring 4.2 inches in length by 2.95 inches in height and 0.875-inch in thickness. It holds six in the magazine and a seventh round in the chamber. At press time, designer Ray Wilkinson was developing a companion version to handle the .22 long rifle cartridge.

Colt's Detective Special, Agent and Cobra revolvers have been redesigned since the first edition, carrying a photo of the then-new Detective Special on the cover, went to press. The main changes have consisted of a heavier barrel, which incorporates a protective shroud for the ejector rod, as well as larger stocks in what has come to be termed the bulldog pattern. This new breed of snub-nosed Colts has won considerable popularity in the short time since its introduction.

Another growing trend has involved conversion of existing auto pistols to the double-action mode by modifying the mechanism. A discussion of Clarence A. Raville's Caraville Double Ace system for the .45 ACP Colt auto was included in the first edition and Raville continues to make and market this device, which the owner can install in accordance with the supplied instructions.

A different approach was worked out by L.W. Seecamp, Box 255, New Haven, Connecticut 06502, originally for the Colt Government and Commander models, more recently for the Browning Hi-Power 9mm. The Seecamp conversion results in a true double-action pistol, with the hammer being brought back and dropped by a long pull of the trigger, firing single action after the first shot or until the hammer is lowered again. In the Caraville Double Ace, the hammer must be kept in carrying mode — a notch farther back than the usual half-cock position — in order to be cocked before firing by squeezing forward on the lever that replaces the mainspring housing and grip safety of the original design.

Another pistolsmith firm specializing in double-action conversions, as well as shortening the barrel and/or magazine/grip dimensions for greater concealability, is Custom Gunshop operated by Austin and Frank Behlert at 550 Boulevard, Kenilworth, New Jersey 07033. That's a new address for the Behlerts and should it change in the next few years, try them at 33 Herning Avenue, Cranford, New Jersey 07016.

If the Behlerts offer bobbed-off and cut-down versions of the .45 auto, John A. "Bo" Clerke goes the opposite route. His firm, JAC Associates, Box 3355, Santa Monica, California 90403, offers barrels in stainless or chrome molybdenum alloys for the Government or Commander models in lengths of 5, 6 and 7½ inches, in calibers .45 ACP, 9mmP, .38 Super and .38/45 Clerke. The last is a necked-down wildcat cartridge on the .45 ACP case, operating with the standard .45 ACP magazine and requiring no further modification beyond changing the barrel. Clerke now is offering longer than standard slides to go with the longer barrels, either separately or in kit form.

Still another approach toward modifying performance of the venerable .45 auto has been taken by pistolsmith John Jeffredo, Jeffredo Gunsight Company, 1629 Via Monserate, Fallbrook, California 92028. He designed a wildcat cartridge he calls the .45 J-Mag, which is made from .30/06 or .308 brass to a case length of 1.025 inches. It positions the light, 185-grain JHP bullets, as made by Hornady and Sierra, farther forward for more reliable feeding. At the same time, Jeffredo supplies load data with his barrel conversion kits that will put the 185-grain bullets out of the muzzle at velocities slightly in excess of 1400 fps, with corresponding peak pressures listed in the data. Oddly enough, the longer chamber does not prevent use of standard .45 ACP ammunition in the modified barrel. The extractor supports the case sufficiently to assure reliable firing.

Another opposite extreme is the Kart .22 conversion unit for the .45 auto, marketed by United States Arms Corporation, Riverhead, New York 11901. The firm guarantees that the unit is capable of machinerest groups of one inch at fifty yards.

Above, right-hand side of Browning Hi-Power 9mm, as converted to double-action by L.W. Seecamp Company. Below, a Behlert-customized Smith & Wesson Model 39.

Wilkinson Arms' .25 ACP Diane features all-milled parts, concealed internal hammer, locking safety; weighs less than 12 ounces, 4.2″ long, holds six-plus-one rounds.

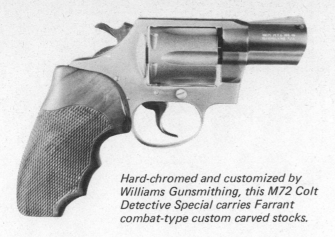

Hard-chromed and customized by Williams Gunsmithing, this M72 Colt Detective Special carries Farrant combat-type custom carved stocks.

Called "The Shadow," Bianchi's new holster can be furnished for up to 4" revolvers, autos up to Colt M1911A1.

Considerable efforts have been made toward improving performance of police handguns through modifying the ammunition. The usual desired objective in a pistol bullet is controlled expansion, coupled with effective penetration, with the bullet retaining as much of its original weight as possible.

Colonel Jack Y. Cannon took a sharply different approach in designing his new projectile, which is manufactured by Glaser Safety Slug, Incorporated (2903 Expressway/Box 1975, McAllen, Texas 78501) and distributed by Deadeye Associates (Box 1687, Opelousas, Louisiana 70570). The Glaser safety slug embodies a fairly conventional bullet jacket of gilding metal — an alloy of copper and zinc — but, rather than making the lead core of the bullet out of lead wire in the usual manner, Cannon coats No. 12 shot pellets with a silicone solution and compresses them into a solid mass in the swaging of the bullet to its final shape.

The purpose of the silicone coating over the shot pellets, which average about .050-inch in diameter and run about 2385 per ounce, is to prevent them from adhering to each other upon impact. The Glaser slug has a nose cap, made of teflon impregnated with twenty-five percent fiberglass, to seal the open area at the front of the jacket.

The Glaser safety slug is available for reloading into certain of the more popular rifle calibers. Likewise, it is made up as loaded ammunition or as a component for reloading in popular center-fire handgun cartridges. However, Col. Cannon restricts sales of the Glaser slug in handgun specifications to bona fide law-enforcement agencies only.

Multiple-bullet loads for handguns have been around for many years. Lyman makes a mould, No. 358101, for a stubby wadcutter bullet weighing about 75 grains, as cast. After sizing and lubricating, it is a simple matter to load two of these into a .38 Special case, or three into a .357 mag case. Any powder charge given in the manuals as suitable for the combined weight of the slugs in the particular cartridge can be used with good success. Care should be taken not to compress the powder charge heavily, since the front of the foremost bullet will be nearly even with the mouth of the cartridge case in most instances. The amount of dispersion of such loads will vary somewhat with individual guns and other related factors. At a distance of seven yards, it is common for all projectiles to print within a circle of hardly more than four or five inches, usually close to the aiming point.

Similar projectiles can be produced on the Swag-O-Matic bullet swaging press that was made by C-H Tool & Die Corporation (Box L, Owen, Wisconsin 54460) prior to the end of 1975. The .3565-inch diameter dies are used, with a full wadcutter nose punch, to produce a slug not much longer than the top of the half-jacket. Often it will be possible to find buckshot of a size that the pellet can be swaged into the half-jacket, resulting in a slug that fills the jacket, but does not have exposed lead in contact with the bore. Such slugs can be used for multiple loading in the same manner described for the Lyman No. 358101 cast bullet.

The slugs made up in the C-H Swag-O-Matic press tend to expand quite impressively at any reasonable velocity and have the effect of multiplying the cross-sectional area by a factor of from at least two to as much as eight times that of a conventional bullet. Naturally, there is some sacrifice as to depth of penetration.

For those lacking facilities or inclination to reload, a four-projectile cartridge is distributed by Michigan Fire Rescue Equipment Corporation (MFRE Corporation, 148 North Groesbeck Highway, Mt. Clemens, Michigan 48043) under the brand name of Quads. Introduced in a size that can be used in revolvers chambered for the .38 Special cartridge, the same load can be fired in the .357 magnum with equal effect. The .38 Quad loads are sold in fifty-round boxes or in six-round pocket packs. At present, MFRE is developing comparable Quad loads for other popular handgun calibers used in law-enforcement work.

Performance of the .38 Quad load, out of service-type revolvers, is outstanding. In most instances, the point of

Left-hand view of Seecamp's DA converted Browning HP, here fitted with Pachmayr Signature rubber grips. This gun has been accurized by pistolsmith Armand Swenson.

Favored in competitive combat matches, custom stocks by E.M. "Fuzzy" Farrant, 1235 West Vine Street, West Covina, California 91790, are available in rosewood, pau ferro, zebrawood or, as here, in Makassar ebony wood. See photo at right for frame modification needed on K-38.

Front corner of S&W K-frame butt must be cut to a bevel, as shown here, in order to accommodate the custom Farrant combat grips that improve pointing in double-action fire.

impact differs little if at all from that of conventional ammunition and the dispersion averages about three to four inches at twenty-five yards.

At the time the first edition of this book was published, early in 1972, Speer had brought out their shot capsules for use in the .38 Special and .357 magnum, with both loaded ammunition and empty capsules for reloading. Since that time, they have added shot capsules for the .44 Special and magnum, likewise available as loaded rounds or empty capsules. Given the facility for reloading, the empty capsules offer an attractive saving in cost. To the present, Speer loads the shot capsules only in .44 magnum cases, although it is a simple matter to fill the empty capsules with shot — No. 9 is the customary size — for reloading in .44 Special cases. The resulting load is a superb performer in the Charter Arms .44 Bulldog.

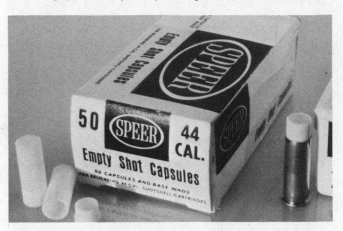

Introduced initially in a size for the .38 Special and .357 magnum, Speer has added a .44 shot capsule, available as loaded ammo or components for reloading purposes.

It has become ever more popular to carry a single shot load in one chamber of a revolver so that it will be first to fire, the theory being that the first shot can be gotten off in all possible haste, with a good chance of delivering a spray of pellets to the adversary so as to cause distraction, thus permitting more deliberate and accurate aim, should additional shots be required.

The March 1976 issue of AMERICAN RIFLEMAN, published by the National Rifle Association (1600 Rhode Island Avenue, N.W., Washington, D.C. 20036) carried responses gathered by the NRA to inquiries among the domestic makers of revolvers chambered for the .38 Special cartridge. The question centered upon the use of high-velocity .38 Special ammunition — usually termed +P — in the various makes and models of domestic revolvers.

Charter Arms responded that their six-shot Police Bulldog .38 Special will handle +P loads satisfactorily, but they do not recommend use of these loads in their smaller models, such as the Undercover.

Colt Industries does not recommend use of +P loads in their D-frame series, which comprises the Detective Special, Cobra and Agent. Presumably, use of +P loads in their larger models, such as the Diamondback, presents no problem.

Dan Wesson Arms approves the use of factory ammunition designated +P in any of their revolvers chambered for the .38 Special cartridge.

High Standard revolvers, Models Mark II and Mark III, are chambered for the .357 magnum cartridge and will handle +P .38 Special ammunition with no problem.

MFRE Corporation distributes these unusual but effective .38 Quad loads, firing four projectiles per pull of the trigger. Refer to the cutaway view appearing on page 291.

Smith & Wesson does not recommend firing +P .38 Special ammunition in any of their models having a frame made of aluminum alloy.

Sturm, Ruger & Company reports that the use of +P factory ammunition in .38 Special is completely acceptable in any of that firm's guns originally chambered for the .38 Special or .357 magnum cartridges.

Iver Johnson's Arms does not recommend the use of +P

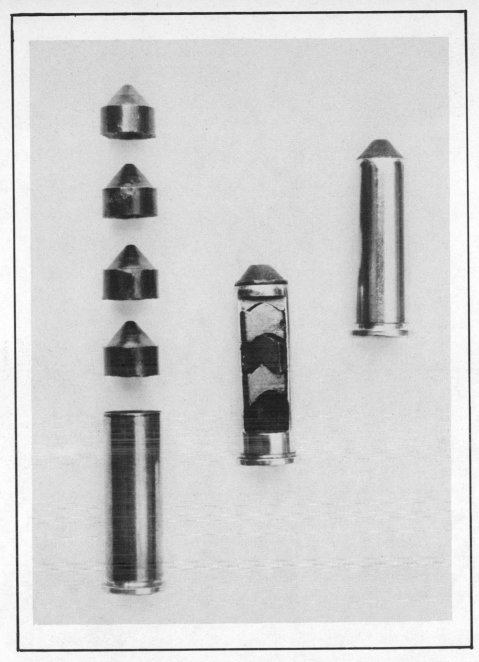

How to put twenty-four holes in the target without reloading your .38 or .357 six-shooter! The four .38 Quad projectiles have a combined weight of about 205 grains and are designed for firing in .38 Special or .357 magnum revolvers.

ammunition in any of their guns chambered for the .38 Special cartridge.

No information is available for the present as to acceptability of +P .38 Special ammunition in foreign-made revolvers of .38 Special caliber. It should be stressed that the foregoing discussion is concerned solely with factory-produced ammunition designated as +P levels of peak pressure. The +P loads are said to develop about 20,000 copper units of pressure (cup), as compared to the usual maximum pressures developed in standard .38 Special cartridges of about 16,000 cup.

In Chapter 14, several photographs show reloading equipment by Lachmiller. In 1974, RCBS, Incorporated (Box 1919, Oroville, California 95965) purchased Lachmiller Engineering, as well as the bullet mould making operations of Ohaus Scale Corporation. All of these items now are made by RCBS in their Oroville plant and distributed from there. The initials, if you'd wondered, stand for

Rock Chuck Bullet Swage, in honor of the swaging dies that were the firm's first product, discontinued from production many years ago.

Speer, Incorporated, was purchased in 1975 by Omark Industries, the same firm that had acquired Cascade Cartridge Industries (CCI) some years earlier. Speer no longer uses brass cases by DWM in their loaded ammunition, having substituted cases made in the United States. Both CCI and Speer continue operations in their original plants, and can be reached by addressing Omark-CCI/Speer, Box 856, Lewiston, Idaho 83501.

Both Browning and Amron have suspended production of loaded ammunition under their respective brand names since the first edition of this book appeared. The firm formerly known as Forster-Appelt, making equipment for reloaders and gunsmiths, has been reorganized as Forster Products, 82 East Lanark Avenue, Lanark, Illinois 61046; the same site occupied by the previous company.

Chapter 24

A GENTLE LOOK AT COMBAT

Spur-Of-The-Moment Shooting Is A Life And Death Thing In Reality; Now Emphasis Is Being Given In Practice

In the early days of the Indiana University police combat shoot, many methods of hip shooting were seen along the firing line.

AT FIRST GLANCE at the campus of the University of Indiana at Bloomington, this is the last place in the world where one would expect to find lessons being given in more efficient ways of shooting a felon.

Yet, amid the modern buildings and indoor tropical planters, police officers, FBI agents and coeds rub shoulders for several days each summer, during the International Combat Championships. These matches have been sponsored by the university and Colt's Fire Arms exclusively for law enforcement agencies.

Although the event is relatively young by comparison with the National Rifle Matches and other recognized national events, teams come from such widely distributed points as Hermosa Beach, California, Winnipeg, Canada, Florida and New York.

And unlike most sport shooting events, these matches are strictly for business; they are meant to help individual lawmen improve their shooting under combat conditions and to allow for an exchange of ideas which the lawmen carry back to their home precincts and put into operation.

Unlike bullseye shooting, where everything is fired from the off-hand position and with single action manipulation of the handgun, this course must be fired from the hip; the kneeling position, sitting, prone, from behind a barricade, both left and right-handed, and with double action as well as single.

In other words, any situation in which a police officer is likely to find himself in combat is covered in these matches. As this series takes place at ranges from seven to sixty yards, being fired under time conditions which include the interval taken to load and move from one position to another, there are obvious safety factors that must be given consideration. Most ranges space competitors approximately thirty feet apart as a safety measure, but this limits the number of shooters to about six in 150 feet. Since this is hardly practical for this match in which nearly four hundred competitors are entered, it is necessary to move the shooters as close to each other as practical, and have all firing from the same distance at one time.

Early in the series, officials broke down the overall time allotment into segments and allowed a specific time for each of the four yardages fired. Match officials under the

Uniformity of style by members of same law enforcement agencies is obvious in the four-man team competitions.

direction of Robert Borkenstein of the University of Indiana's Police Administration School did an outstanding job of preparatory work in planning for these matches, and it was generally agreed among competitors and observers that the facilities were as fine as could be wished for.

When targets and barricades are placed so close together for combat shooting, it is not always easy to distinguish your own target, but this problem was solved by using different colors for the barricades and appropriate target numbers. If you were firing from behind a red barricade, you

Above: Officers from several states take part in one segment of the contest, which is devoted to firing from behind barricade. They can shoot from either side.

would shoot at the target over the red numeral.

The combat course that was fired was devised after the Practical Pistol Course developed by the Federal Bureau of Investigation about 1949. This since has been adopted as the standard combat course for most police departments across the country.

At this match, it is called the Indiana University Practical Pistol Course and is fired in the following manner: Ten rounds double action hip shooting at seven yards in twenty-five seconds; fifteen rounds double action, kneeling using weak hand and strong hand at barricade at twenty-five yards in ninety seconds; twenty rounds single action sitting, prone, weak and strong hand from barricade at fifty yards in 2-¾ minutes. Finally, five rounds are fired single action prone position at fifty yards in thirty-five seconds.

All matches are fired on the Colt silhouette target, the X-ring being used in scoring by judges to break any ties.

Although this shooter may not be aware of it, were the silhouette target returning his fire, angled position creates a much wider target than were he faced head-on.

With the FBI course, the system is almost reversed. One fires the seven-yard phase, then moves to the sixty-yard marker instead of the fifty for the five shots. One continues the rest of the course from there, ending up at the twenty-five-yard line.

Overall time allowed for the FBI course is six minutes, ten seconds, which includes eight loadings and advancing from one position to another. The Indiana University course time allowance is only four minutes, thirty-five seconds, which includes six loadings and no position advancement.

Eligibility for the Bloomington matches is open only to full-time police officers falling in the category of federal, state, county, or municipal police departments; highway patrols; prison guards; deputy sheriffs or conservation officers; railroad or industrial police; bank or armored express guards. Members of the Armed Forces are not eligible, even though they may be assigned to military police duty.

Left: The value of the sitting position for combat shooting has been controversial and there seems to be no accepted position.

Captain Troy Woolf of Richmond, Ind., found sitting position uncomfortable, but he fired possible on the course.

Jeanne Bray, policewoman from Columbus, Ohio, added charm to one of contests at Bloomington, at the same time proving herself formidable competitor with 98.4.

Weapons fired in the matches must be .38 caliber revolvers with barrel lengths not exceeding six inches. No unusual alterations are allowed. The revolver must be holsterable and considered a duty weapon. Exceptions have been made in that .357 magnum weapons were allowed as long as .38 Special ammunition was fired in them.

Other rules for the matches were few and far between with the only written rule pertaining to seven-yard hip shooting. It stated: "At the seven-yard line (hip shooting position), point shoulder shooting will not be permitted. The shooting arm elbow must be perceptibly bent and the weapon below eye level." There is nothing in the rules against two-handed shooting.

From the twenty-five and fifty-yard distances, and par-

ticularly from the barricade, it is a shame to place the shoot in the category of a combat match. Barricade shooting was devised as a means of training officers to fire around the corner of a building, using the structure for maximum cover.

However, the match fired at the university allowed competitors to fire from a fully exposed position so long as·one hand was touching the barricade. We talked to a number of officers from all parts of the country, and learned that none of them train this way in their own departments, but that they fired with this technique in the match "because others were allowed to fire that way."

All of the competitors stated that they would like to see firm rules so that cover would have to be used when firing from the barricades.

Firing from the prone position is another segment in which rules would help. This position is intended to make the officer a smaller target, but a number of the participants didn't get the idea. To allow an officer to shoot from any position that does not afford maximum cover is a result of poor training and certainly should not be honored in a combat match.

Many of the shooters said that they had been taught this exposed brand of shooting while in the service this is true, but what they fail to remember is that in the service, they were taught with a rifle and at ranges up to five hundred yards.

Whenever a match of this scale — with so many contestants from so many sections of the country — can be conducted in a three-day span, it is obvious that someone has put in a lot of labor. The matches are approved by the National Rifle Association and a staff from NRA headquarters is on hand to observe. This group has come up with rules to apply to a NRA-approved police combat course.

In the initial outing, Bill Toney, former national handgun champion and chief range officer for this meet, conducted the match superbly, as did all of the other officials. The first match fired was the Individual Match, which was won by Constable Ron Allison of the Winnipeg, Canada, Police Department. He won with a 100-42X score. The second match was for four-man teams and was won by the Columbus, Ohio, police. This aggregation scored 397.6-162X out of a possible 400 points. Second place honors went to the White House team from Washington, D.C., which scored 397.6-145X. The third place team honors were won by another team from Columbus with 395.6-145X.

Match No. 3 was an experimental match fired on the Indiana University Experimental Target, which could be referred to as a bullseye match fired from combat positions and under combat time limitations. This match created a good deal of interest, if for no other reason than that it is different and challenging.

This was a twenty-four round match fired from the fifty-yard line with six shots being fired single action from the sitting, prone, weak and strong hand barricade in 2-¾ minutes. This match has one realistic point in its favor in that the shooter loads with six rounds and fires six from each position. Several shooters, it was noted, fired only five shots, then emptied their cylinders. This was through force of habit formed in shooting the regular Practical Pistol Course. Most instructors agree that five-shot courses are poor training and that an ideal course should be designed to load and fire six shots from each position.

The Number 4 Match was for the three highest teams from federal, state, county and municipal jurisdiction. High scores from the second match were used to select the three high teams from each enforcement plane. These teams again fired the Indiana University Combat Course, with the White House Police team coming up as winner.

This is a real team and shoots the entire course all double action. Most shooters feel they are handicapped by doing this, but the scores of the guardians of the President prove that with enough training, the combat course can be fired equally as well double action as single action. In fact, numerous instructors in law enforcement are advocating that the FBI course be changed to double action throughout, and we feel that this would be in the best interests of most officers.

Target shooters are trained to cock their handguns without thinking, but percentage-wise, there are not too many trained paper punchers in the police ranks. When under pressure, they are inclined to fire double action.

In conjunction with the matches, there are numerous meetings in which shooters have an opportunity to express thoughts and exchange ideas with other instructors.

Meetings of this type are helping standardize a nationwide combat course. That is the aim of the International Police Firearms Instructors' Association.

Combat matches may be new on the competitive level, but they are growing rapidly, and the coming year should see them spreading to new sections of the country — with standardized rules

On a more than slightly different plane, a group in the West have taken it upon themselves to introduce fun as well as precision into combat shooting.

Pitting Shooters Against Each Other May Seem Old West, But It Perfects Under-Pressure Techniques

Thell Reed, Jr., noted handgun handler, who taught fast draw techniques to Marines during Vietnamese war service, advances upon his target, hand low, ready for the draw.

This organization takes itself seriously and, under its founder, handgun expert Jeff Cooper, has done much to improve the concept of combat shooting. In the beginning, the organization was feeling its way and held its first competition nearly a decade ago. At first glance, it held some aspects of the fast draw sport, which was popular in that era. However, these were serious shooters, not primer poppers.

The Southwest Combat Pistol League held its first simulated dueling contest at the Wes Thompson Range in Southern California's Solidad Canyon, where forty-nine men — all claiming to be the fastest accurate shooters alive — showed up for a round robin double elimination shootout. In a shoot of this type, two men are matched against one another and are spaced about twenty feet apart and advance together toward two metal electronic targets that reg-

Harry Gregory, who was winner of this contest, used clamshell holster tilted at odd angle to handle S&W .38 Special.

A fast draw timer was used to determine which of the contestants got off first shot, but only hits counted.

ister which was hit first. Neither hand is allowed to touch the firearm during the walkdown and on a given command, such as the whistle used at this meet, each man must draw and fire until one scores a hit. The first shooting distance is approximately thirty yards. Each shooter is allowed to reload if he chooses, then the walkdown is resumed until the next command, which is given fifteen to twenty yards from target, whereupon they fire again.

If the same person wins from both positions, his opponent is considered shot down from that round. If the shooters are tied at this position, they continue the walkdown and fire again from about the seven-yard position. In this type of contest, speed and accuracy both are important. Most of the competitors prefer two-handed shooting, as they feel that they can obtain greater accuracy. As any gun of .38 caliber or greater bore may be used, there is quite a variety of handguns used.

The league has a point system devised that gives a greater

Onlookers throng the safety zone as shooters advance on their targets during early day combat shoot at Soledad Canyon in Southern California. This predated courses of serious nature.

number of points to wins obtained with the larger caliber guns, and although these specific points don't count for an individual contest, they add toward one's aggregate points for the year's events. The highest point winner is Top Gun after a year of contests. This honor was won for three years running by Eldon Carl of the El Cajon (Calif.) Police Department. Carl is considered by most men in this combat league to be the best pistol shot in America.

A large percent of the competitors were using single action .44 and .45 caliber guns with quick draw holsters, but another large group was using the .45 automatic.

The automatic has one definite advantage over the six-shooter in that its magazine will hold more rounds; this can be a deciding factor in a serious showdown, of course.

This contest is somewhat different from the type of combat shooting described at Indiana University and even more different from what one might see on the average police range. However, it can be — and in a few instances, has been — adapted to police training.

Most good police shooters should fare well in such competition, although we have talked to some who feel the police are not trained properly.

Other shooters, during that initial feeling-the-way-to-bigger-things contest expressed surprise that police officers would come to the shoot. However, there were numerous law enforcement types on hand, numbering some forty percent of the participants.

This event required about five and a half hours to come up with the winner and there was no wasted time between shootouts.

The event was well run and it constituted the best shooting program we ever have witnessed for keeping the spectators happy. By using a public address system and the visual electronic timer there never was any doubt as to precisely what was taking place. On a National Match Course or a Police Combat Course, not even the competitors know how they stand until hours after the match has finished. At some, you go home and wait for the mail before you find out the outcome. On several occasions, many of the spectators would disagree with the electronic timing device but in each instance wherein there was doubt, the contestants involved stated there could be no changing of the decision of the timer. What usually happened, according to Eldon Carl, was that a shot would hit the wire that was supporting the target. This would cause the spectators to believe there had been a hit. Other times, there would be a grazing shot that could be heard hitting the target but would not be a solid enough hit to register on the electronic device.

This dueling isn't a new idea, but has been used for several years by the FBI in its training program at Quantico, Virginia. At the FBI Academy they are training law enforcement officers and not holding a contest to see which man is best, so they do things a little different. They usually start at sixty yards or better, then advance all the way to the seven-yard line, being required to shoot from many different positions along the way. For all general purposes, the two systems are the same except that one is a training program, the other a competitive match.

Depending upon caliber, type of powder, barrel length, bullet weight and a few other factors, the muzzle flash from a handgun can be quite spectacular. Note the large amount of blazing gases escaping from the crevice between the front of the cylinder and rear of barrel, rendering silencers useless. Text discusses tactical employment of muzzle flash.

After Dark, It's A Whole New Ballgame!

NEW FOR NIGHT

THERE IS A classical reference to the effect that, in the hours of darkness, the powers of evil are exalted. The exact source eludes my memory, though it could have been Shakespeare; so many of such observations are credited to him. Certainly, it is an observation with which few policemen would be inclined to disagree. Night shifts and stretches of bad weather tend to be busy seasons for law enforcement personnel.

A major problem presents itself if it becomes necessary to employ firearms after dark in the line of duty, principally due to the difficulty of aiming with any pretense of accuracy. Back on page 97, there's a picture of one solution: Bushnell's Lite Site telescopic sight. It's quite effective, but its use is restricted to rifles or, at the outside, to shotguns. No comparable version is available for use on handguns.

Shortly after the first edition of this book was published, two police officers — Julio Santiago, a deputy sheriff for Dakota County, Minnesota, and Elliel Knutsen, a patrolman with the Apple Valley, Minnesota, police department — invented and developed a system they call the Bardot sight. That's pronounced bar-dot, not Bar-doh, as in Brigitte. The Bardot sight incorporates a radioactive isotope plus a lensing system, the exact nature of which remains a trade secret. It consists of a round dot on the front sight and a horizontal bar across the top of the rear sight. Both give off a subdued greenish glow. Unlike the conventional luminous material used for watch dials, the isotope used in the Bardot sight does not require previous exposure to bright light to energize it.

A minor complication connected with the Bardot sight is that possession and use requires certification from the Atomic Energy Commission or AEC. In many cases, the department has the required certificate for use with other radioactive materials utilized by the crime lab, so that having the Bardot sights covered is a simple matter.

Although the level of radiation of the Bardot sight is high enough to bring it under AEC jurisdiction, there is no hazard to health involved in carrying or using guns so equipped. The isotope has a half-life of thirty months. That is, after five years, visibility would be about one-quarter that of a new sighting unit. When installed, it is not conspicuous and the light emitted by the sight is not visible from the front.

Further details on the Bardot sight, which is sold only to accredited law enforcement agencies and their personnel,

The Bardot sighting system utilizes a radioactive material having a half-life of thirty months, plus a lensing arrangement to illuminate the sights, as simulated in the photo at right, above. In subdued light, a horizontal bar is seen across the top of the rear sight, with a glowing dot on the front sight, both are green in color. Photographs by M.J. Nelson.

can be obtained from the distributor, Caswell Equipment Company, Incorporated, 1215 Second Avenue North, Minneapolis, Minnesota 55405.

Working on a different approach, Cap Cresap, 21422 Rosedell Drive, Saugus, California 91350, developed the L-Tronic sight in 1973. The L-Tronic system employs no radioactive materials and thus is independent of AEC certification. Instead, it has small, solid-state light-emitting devices in the front and rear sights and these are powered by a small, rechargeable nickel cadmium battery located in the wood grip of the gun. A convenient pressure switch in the grip is depressed to switch the L-Tronic sights on.

Cresap uses units that emit a bright red light, since this color is highly visible and, at the same time, has minimum effect on night vision in the human eye. His initial designs were intended for use on revolvers but, as of early 1976, he has solved the technical problems connected with routing electricity from the battery in the grip up to sights on the slide of auto pistols. Likewise, installations can be made on AR-15 or M-16 rifles. The L-Tronic sights are guaranteed for a period of one year after installation and experience indicates that the trouble-free service life is much longer. One charging of the battery is good for about four months of normal use and the current design of recharging unit is different from that shown in the accompanying photo. The new charger plugs into a wall socket.

Details as to current costs and installation procedures can be requested from Cresap at the address given and should be accompanied by a stamped, self-addressed envelope.

The more lurid types of literature often show guns being fired on their cover illustrations and, almost always, a needle-thin pencil of flame is shown emerging from the muzzle. Photos made with the muzzle flash as the sole source of illumination display impressive blossoms of flame (pages 35 and 237). I had assumed that such displays of fireworks constituted a total liability for afterdark shooting

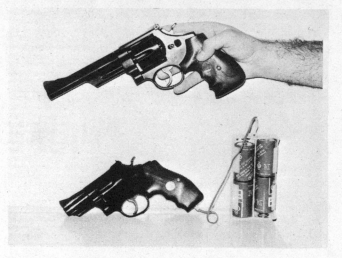

Two early examples of Cap Cresap's L-Tronic sighting system, which does not depend upon radioactive material. Battery recharger now uses 9-V battery or 110-V A.C.

because they betrayed one's location. Not necessarily so, according to Tom Ferguson, who has discussed the matter with fellow officers on the San Antonio PD who've been involved in lightless shootouts.

In a gunfight in a relatively small, dark room, say Ferguson's friends, the flash from your own gun can be used effectively as a means for seeing the location of your target and, as such, is much more distracting than a flashlight and considerably less apt to draw accurate return fire from the opponent.

It makes an interesting point for conjecture and poses the possibility that some manner of useful training simulation could be set up whereby firing is performed

An early model of the Laser-Lok, now redesigned to use an integral battery pack. It projects an intense beam of scarlet light which can be adjusted to coincide with point of impact.

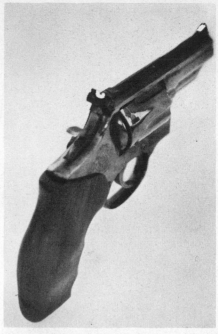

A closer look at the solid-state light emitting diodes of the L-Tronic sight. Red is standard color, yellow optional.

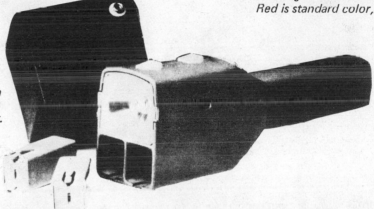

The Taser combined a flashlight with projectors of twin barb-tipped wires to deliver disabling shock out to 18 feet.

solely by the light of the muzzle flashes. The shooter should have his eyes focused toward the target's probable location, with the gun held so as to minimize the temporary blinding effect from the flash, thus increasing the chance of getting a good fix on the target.

Amount of muzzle flash varies considerably, according to the load and barrel length. Revolvers display substantial plumes of fire emerging from the gap between the cylinder face and the rear of the barrel — which points up the idiocy of putting silencers on revolvers! — and this may provide more light than the actual muzzle blast.

Recent technological progress has made some highly sophisticated equipment available for nighttime operations, including the sniperscope for use on rifles and the Starlight scope that amplifies even the faintest amounts of light electronically. Such gadgetry may be available to specialized SWAT teams of large departments, but systems such as the Bardot or L-Tronic sights are available at the level of the individual officer, whereas the more flossy hardware, with price tags well into the five-digit brackets, is a matter for departmental negotiations, not for private purchase.

The Laser-Lok sight was discussed in the previous chapter in connection with the A-180 submachine gun, that is handled by the same distributor. To the present, no comparable device exists for installation on handguns. I had an opportunity for first-hand testing of the A-180 fitted with the Laser-Lok sight and found it highly effective. However, it is necessary to have some threshold amount of illumination on the target in order to transfix it with the little red dot of projected light from the laser. In total darkness, you can see the dot but you can't tell what it's impinging upon.

The High Standard Model 10 police shotgun (page 112) customarily is fitted with a clamp device to which a police flashlight can be attached in such a manner that a slug or pellet pattern can be delivered to the area covered by the beam from the flashlight. This affords one more possibility for directing accurate fire under conditions of poor visibility although at the cost of considerable risk of drawing return fire.

With the characteristic onrush of technology, it seems likely that the future will produce remarkable new items with applications for aiding the policeman in protecting the public he has sworn to serve. The ideal device for a lot of emergency police situations would be one that produces an instantaneous but temporary and harmless paralysis. Thus far, the nearest approach has been the Taser; a device shaped somewhat like a flashlight but capable of projecting twin barbs for a distance of fifteen to eighteen feet. The barbs attach themselves to the target, after which a disabling current of electricity can be delivered.

Hailed at first as a great boon to mankind, the Taser has not worked out well and it has figured in committing crimes, rather than preventing them, all too often. As a result, many jurisdictions have outlawed the device for possession or use by civilians.

301

TODAY'S HANDGUNS

In putting together this section, guns have been included that were deemed suitable for personnel concerned with upholding and enforcing the law. Insofar as it was obtainable, relevant information is listed for each entry. The prices quoted were correct as of presstime — early 1976 — but past experience indicates that these will show varying increases with the passage of time.

With no more than rare exceptions, the manufacturers and/or distributors of these guns are happy to supply descriptive catalogs, price sheets and similar literature upon request. Usually, such information is offered without cost. Addresses of the manufacturers and/or distributors are given in the directory section of this book and inquiries should be directed to the individual firm concerned.

ASTRA CONSTABLE

BERETTA DOUBLE-ACTION

BAUER .25

BERETTA MODEL 951

ASTRA CONSTABLE: Calibers .22 LR, 10 rds.; .32 ACP, 8 rds.; .380 ACP, 7 rds. Barrel, 3½''. Weight, 26 oz. Stocks, moulded plastic. Sights, blade front, adjustable rear. Features double-action trigger; quick, no-tool takedown; nonglare rib on slide. .380 available in blue or chrome. Imported from Spain by Garcia. Blue, $150; chrome, $165.

BAUER .25: Caliber .25 ACP, 6 rds. Barrel, 2-1/8''; overall length, 4''. Weight, 10 oz. Stocks, plastic pearl or checkered walnut. Sights recessed, fixed. Features stainless steel construction, positive manual safety, magazine disconnect. With padded zipper case, $94.95.

Prices as of Spring, 1976; subject to change.

BERETTA DOUBLE-ACTION: Caliber .380 ACP, 13-rd. magazine. Barrel, 3¾''; overall length, 6½''. Weight, 23 oz. Stocks, smooth walnut. Sights, blade front, rear adjustable for windage only. Features right or left safety, reversible magazine release, free-falling magazine on release, non-snagging round hammer spur, inertia firing pin and no-tool takedown. Price not available at press time.

BERETTA MODEL 951: Caliber 9mmP, 8-rd. magazine. Barrel, 4½''; overall length, 8''. Weight, 31 oz. Stocks, moulded plastic. Sights fixed. Features crossbolt safety, external hammer; slide locks open after last shot. Prices from $260.

BERNARDELLI MODEL 60

BERNARDELLI MODEL 80

BROWNING MODEL 1935 HI-POWER

BUDISCHOWSKY TP-70

CHARTER ARMS BULLDOG

CHARTER ARMS POLICE BULLDOG

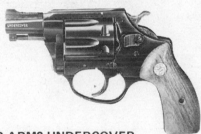

CHARTER ARMS UNDERCOVER

BERNARDELLI MODEL 60: Calibers .22 LR; 10 rds., .32 ACP, 8 rds.; .380 ACP, 7 rds. Barrel, 3½''; overall length, 6-1/3''. Weight, 26 oz. Stocks, checkered plastic. Sights, blade front, adjustable rear. Features manual safety and magazine disconnect, optional thumb rest grips ($10 extra). Imported from Italy by Kleinguenther's. Blue, $90.

BERNARDELLI MODEL 80: Calibers .22 LR, 10 rds.; .32 ACP, 8 rds.; .380, 7 rds. Barrel, 3½''. Weight, 26½ oz. Stocks, checkered plastic with thumb rest. Sights, ramp front, adjustable rear with white outline. Features hammer block slide safety, loaded chamber indicator, dual recoil springs, serrated trigger, inertia firing pin. Imported from Italy by Interarms. Blue, $149; Model 90 (same except for 6'' barrel), $169.

BROWNING MODEL 1935 HI-POWER: Caliber 9mm Parabellum (Luger), 13-rd. magazine. Barrel, 4.66''; overall length, 7¾''. Weight, 32 oz. Stocks, hand-checkered walnut. Sights, choice of fixed or fixed front and adjustable rear. Features external hammer with half-cock, inertia firing pin, manual safety and magazine disconnect. Blue, fixed sights, $272.95; blue, target rear sight, $288.95; fully engraved, chrome-plated Renaissance model with polyester pearl grips, fixed sights, $900; Renaissance with target sights, $920.

BUDISCHOWSKY TP-70: Calibers .22 LR, 6 rds.; .25 ACP, 6 rds. Barrel, 2.6''; overall length, 4-2/3''. Weight, 12-1/3 oz. Stocks, checkered plastic. Sights fixed, with full-length serrated rib. Features double-action, exposed hammer, manual safety and magazine disconnect. Has slide stop; action is held open after last shot. All stainless steel construction. Made by Norton Armament Corp., 41471 Irwin, Mt. Clemens, Michigan 48043. In .25 ACP, $125; in .22 LR, $135.

CHARTER ARMS BULLDOG: Caliber .44 Special, 5-rd. cylinder. Barrel, 3''. Weight, 19 oz. Stocks, checkered walnut. Sights, Patridge type front, fixed square-notch rear. Features wide trigger and hammer spur, chrome-moly steel frame, unbreakable firing pin and transfer bar ignition. Blue, $138.

CHARTER ARMS POLICE BULLDOG: Caliber .38 Special standard or +P, 6-rd. cylinder. Barrel, 4''; overall length, 7¼''. Weight, 20 oz. Stocks, hand-checkered American walnut. Sights, ramp front, fully adjustable rear. Features enclosed ejector rod, with full-length ejection of fired cases. Blue, about $135.

CHARTER ARMS UNDERCOVER: Caliber .38 Special (standard pressure), 5-rd. cylinder. Barrel, 2'' or 3''; overall length, 6¼''. Weight, 16 oz. Stocks, smooth walnut. Sights fixed with matted ramp front. Features wide trigger and hammer spur. Blue, round butt stocks, $104; with finger-rest Bulldog grips, $111; nickel, round butt, $115.

Prices as of Spring, 1976; subject to change.

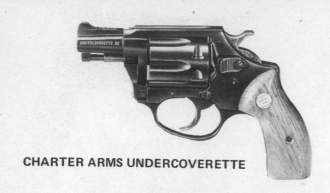

CHARTER ARMS UNDERCOVERETTE

COLT DETECTIVE SPECIAL

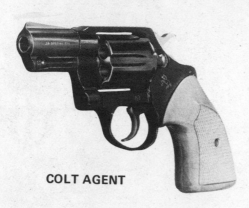

COLT AGENT

COLT COMMANDER

COLT COMBAT COMMANDER

COLT COBRA

COLT DIAMONDBACK

CHARTER ARMS UNDERCOVERETTE: Caliber .32 S&W Long, 6-rd. cylinder. Barrel, 2". Weight, 16½ oz. Blue only, $105; with Bulldog grips, $112.

COLT AGENT: Caliber .38 Special, 6-rd. cylinder. Barrel, 2"; overall length, 6-5/8". Weight, 16 oz. Stocks, checkered walnut. Sights fixed with matted ramp front and square-notch rear. Features grooved trigger. Blue, $141; with hammer shroud installed, $146.

COLT COBRA: Caliber .38 Special, 6-rd. cylinder. Barrel, 2"; overall length, 6-5/8". Weight, 16½ oz. Stocks, checkered walnut, round butt. Sights fixed with matted ramp front and square-notch rear. Features grooved trigger. Blue, $143; nickel, $162.

COLT DETECTIVE SPECIAL: Caliber .38 Special, 6-rd. cylinder. Barrel, 2"; overall length, 6-5/8". Weight, 22 oz. Stocks, checkered walnut, round butt. Sights fixed with matted ramp front and square-notch rear. Features smooth trigger, all-steel construction. Blue, $140; nickel, $149.50; optional hammer shroud, add $5.

Prices as of Spring, 1976; subject to change.

COLT COMMANDER: Calibers .45 ACP, 7-rd. magazine; .38 Super, 9-rd.; 9mm Luger, 9-rd. Barrel, 4¼"; overall length, 8". Weight, 27 oz. Stocks, sandblasted walnut. Features grooved trigger and hammer spur, arched mainspring housing, grip and thumb safeties. Sights fixed, glare-proof front blade, square-notch rear driftable for windage adjustment. Blue, $175.50.

COLT COMBAT COMMANDER: Same as Colt Commander, except steel frame instead of aluminum alloy. Weight, 36½ oz. Blue or satin nickel, $175.50.

COLT DIAMONDBACK: Calibers .38 Special and .22 LR, 6-rds. Barrel, with mentioned rib, 2½" or 4"; overall length with 4" barrel, 9". Weight, 24 oz. with 2½" barrel; 28½ oz. with 4" barrel. Checkered walnut stocks, target type, square butt, wide-spur hammer. Sights, ramp front, adjustable rear. Blue, $176; nickel (.38 only), $188.

COLT GOLD CUP NATIONAL MATCH, MK IV SERIES 70

COLT LAWMAN MK III

COLT GOVERNMENT MODEL MK IV/SERIES 70

COLT PYTHON

COLT OFFICIAL POLICE MK III

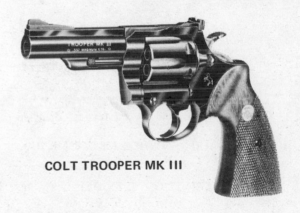

COLT TROOPER MK III

COLT GOLD CUP NATIONAL MATCH, MK IV Series 70: Caliber .45 ACP, 7-rd. magazine. Barrel with new design bushing, 5''; overall length, 8-3/8''. Weight, 38½ oz. Checkered walnut stocks, gold-plated medallion. Rear sight adjustable for windage and elevation; sight radius 6¾''. Finish, blue only. Choice of arched or flat mainspring housing. Wide, grooved trigger with adjustable stop, ribbed-top slide, hand fitted, with improved ejection port, $256.

COLT GOVERNMENT MODEL MK IV/Series 70: Calibers .45 ACP, 7-rd. magazine; .38 Super, 9-rd.; 9mm Luger, 9-rd. Barrel, 5''; overall length, 8-3/8''. Weight, 40 oz. Stocks, sandblasted walnut panels. Sights, fixed ramp front, square-notch rear driftable for windage adjustment. Features grip and thumb safeties, grooved trigger, collet-type barrel bushing for improved accuracy. Blue, $175.50; nickel (.45 ACP only), $192.

COLT OFFICIAL POLICE MK III: Caliber .38 Special standard or +P, 6-rd. cylinder. Barrel, 4''; overall length, 9-3/8''. Weight, 33 oz. Stocks, checkered walnut, service style. Sights fixed with matted ramp front and square-notch rear. Blue, $147.

COLT LAWMAN MK III: Caliber .357 magnum only, 6-rd. cylinder. Same as Official Police MK III, but with 2'' or 4'' heavy barrel. With 4'' barrel, weight, 35 oz. Blue, $149.50; nickel, $158.50.

COLT PYTHON: Caliber .357 magnum (handles .38 Spl.), 6 rds. Barrel, with ventilated rib, 2½'', 4'' or 6''. With 4'' barrel, 9¼'' overall length. Weight, 38 oz. Checkered walnut, target-type, square butt stocks, wide-spur hammer. Sights, ramp front, adjustable rear. Blue, $253; nickel, $282.

COLT TROOPER MK III: Caliber .357 magnum, 6-rd. cylinder. Barrel, 4'' or 6''. Overall length with 4'' barrel, 9½''. Weight, 39 oz. with 4'' barrel, 42 oz. with 6'' barrel. Stocks, checkered walnut, square butt. Sights, fixed ramp front, fully adjustable square-notch rear. Features grooved trigger. Blue, with target hammer and stocks, $188; same in nickel, $200.

Prices as of Spring, 1976; subject to change.

FIREARMS INTERNATIONAL MODEL D

INDIAN ARMS

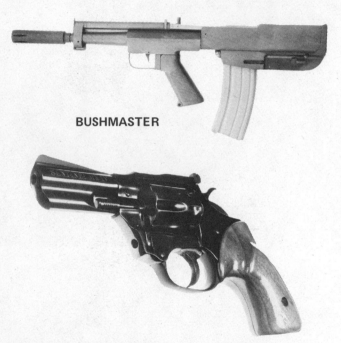

BUSHMASTER

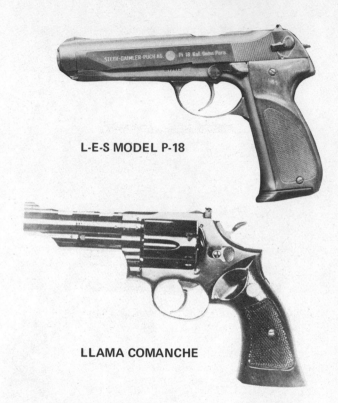

L-E-S MODEL P-18

HIGH STANDARD SENTINEL, MK II & MK III

LLAMA COMANCHE

FIREARMS INTERNATIONAL MODEL D: Caliber .380 ACP, 6-rd. magazine. Barrel, 3-1/8''; overall length, 6-1/8''. Weight, 20 oz. Stocks, checkered walnut. Sights, fixed blade front, square-notch rear, driftable for windage. Features loaded chamber indicator, all-steel construction, thumb safety which locks hammer, lanyard ring. Distributed by Garcia. Blue, $150.

GWINN FIREARMS BUSHMASTER: Caliber .223 Remington (5.56mm), 20 or 30-rd. magazine. Barrel, 11½''; overall length, 20''. Weight, 68 oz. Sights fixed. Stock, one-piece checkered plastic. Features grip swiveling 45 degrees to right or left, gas-operated, firing from closed bolt. Available as semiauto or selective fire to authorized users. Semi-auto, about $300.

HIGH STANDARD SENTINEL, MK II and MK III: Caliber .357 magnum, 6-rd. cylinder. Barrel, 2½'', 4'' and 6''. With 4'' barrel 9'' overall length. Weight, 38 oz. Stocks, checkered walnut, service or combat type. Sights fixed on MK II; fully adjustable rear on MK III. Features cylinder latch located in front of cylinder, with fast lock time. Blue finish only. MK II, $120; MK III, $154.95.

Prices as of Spring, 1976; subject to change.

INDIAN ARMS: Caliber .380 ACP, 6-rd. magazine. Barrel, 3¼''; overall length, 6-1/16''. Weight, 20 oz. Stocks, checkered walnut. Sights, fixed-blade front, square-notch rear driftable for windage adjustment. Features all-stainless steel, natural or blued finish. Double-action trigger; actions stay open after last shot. Optional lock with key to lock safety is integral with slide. Made by Indian Arms Corporation, 13503 Joseph Campar, Detroit, Michigan 48212. With or without safety lock, either finish, $185.

L-E-S MODEL P-18: Caliber 9mm Luger, 18-rd. magazine. Barrel, 5½''. Weight, 36 oz. Stocks, checkered plastic. Sights, fixed front, V-notch rear, driftable for windage adjustment. Features stationary barrel with polygonal rifling, gas-operated, double-action trigger, stainless steel construction with inertia firing pin and hammer-drop safety. Made in the U.S.A. by L-E-S, 3640 West Dempster Street, Skokie, Illinois 66676. Approximately $175.

LLAMA COMANCHE: Caliber .357 magnum, 6-rd. cylinder. Barrel, 4''; overall length, 9¼''. Weight, 36 oz. Stocks, checkered walnut with medallion, in grip-filling target pattern. Sights, ramp front on ventilated rib, click-adjustable, target-type rear. Features broad, serrated trigger and hammer spur; forged steel frame and floating firing pin. Distributed by Stoeger Industries. Blue, $169.95.

LLAMA LOCKED-BREECH AUTOS

MAUSER HSc

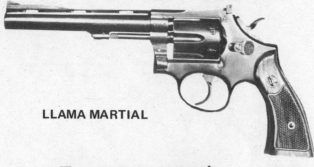

LLAMA MARTIAL

MKE MODEL TPK

LLAMA STRAIGHT BLOWBACK AUTOS

OMC 380 BACK UP

LLAMA LOCKED-BREECH AUTOS: Calibers .38 Super, 9-rd. magazine; 9mm Luger, 9-rd.; .45 ACP, 7-rd. Barrel, 5"; overall length, 8½". Weight, 40 oz. Stocks, hand-checkered walnut, with lanyard loop. Sights, Patridge front, square-notch rear, screw-adjustable for windage. Blue finish is standard, engraved, satin-blue, gold, damascened; simulated pearl grips available. Features ventilated rib, slide-top matted, serrated trigger, external hammer with wide spur, thumb safety, half-cock and grip safety. Distributed by Stoeger Industries. Prices, from $184.95.

LLAMA MARTIAL: Calibers .22 LR, .22 WMR, .38 Special (including +P loads), 6-rd. cylinder. Barrel, 4" and 6" in .38 and .22 WMR; 6" only in .22 LR; overall length, 9¼" or 11". Weight, 33 oz. with 4" barrel, 36 oz. with 6" barrel in .38; 40 oz. in .22 LR/WMR. Stocks, magna style, checkered walnut or simulated pearl. Sights, serrated quick-draw front on ramp, white-outlined square-notch rear, adjustable target type. Features forged steel frame with serrated front and back straps, wide target trigger and hammer spur, floating firing pin and ventilated rib, with matted top surfaces. Distributed by Stoeger Industries. Prices, from $139.95.

LLAMA STRAIGHT BLOWBACK AUTOS: Calibers .22 LR, 8-rd. magazine; .32 ACP, 8-rd.; .380 ACP, 7-rd. Barrel, 3.69"; overall length, 6½". Weight, 23 oz. Stocks, plastic with modified thumb rest; no lanyard loop. Sights, Patridge front; rear is screw-adjustable for windage. Finish, blue is standard, engraved, satin-blue and gold. Features ventilated rib with matted slide top, serrated trigger, external hammer with wide spur. Thumb safety, half-cock, grip safety and .22 LR (only) has magazine disconnect. Distributed by Stoeger Industries. Prices, from $129.95.

MAUSER HSc: Calibers .32 ACP and .380 ACP, both 7-rd. magazines. Barrel, 3-3/8"; overall length, 6.05". Weight, 23 oz. Stocks, checkered walnut. Sights fixed. Features double-action trigger, manual safety and magazine disconnect. Imported from Germany by Interarms. Blue, $199, nickel, $219.

MKE MODEL TPK: Calibers .32 ACP, 8-rd. magazine and .380 ACP, 7-rd. Barrel, 4"; overall length, 6½". Weight, 23 oz. Stocks, checkered black plastic. Sights fixed, low-profile blade front, square-notch rear, driftable for windage adjustment. Features double-action trigger with exposed hammer; safety blocks firing pin and drops hammer, if cocked. Extractor serves as loaded chamber indicator. Imported from Turkey by Firearms Center. Blue, $154; Armaloy, $184.

OMC 380 BACK UP: Caliber .380 ACP, 5-rd. magazine. Barrel, 2¾"; overall length, 5". Weight, 18 oz. Stocks, smooth zebrawood. Sights fixed, inset in channel of slide. Features thumb safety, grip safety; no magazine disconnect, all-stainless steel construction. About $200.

Prices as of Spring, 1976; subject to change.

PLAINFIELD MODEL 72

RAVEN ARMS MOD. P-25

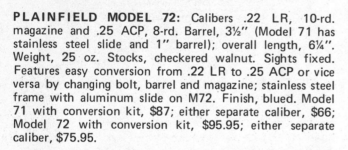

**RUGER POLICE SERVICE-SIX
MODELS 107, 108, 707 & 708**

RUGER SECURITY-SIX MODEL 117

RUGER STAINLESS SECURITY-SIX MODEL 717

RUGER SPEED-SIX MODELS 207, 208, 737 & 738

PLAINFIELD MODEL 72: Calibers .22 LR, 10-rd. magazine and .25 ACP, 8-rd. Barrel, 3½" (Model 71 has stainless steel slide and 1" barrel); overall length, 6¼". Weight, 25 oz. Stocks, checkered walnut. Sights fixed. Features easy conversion from .22 LR to .25 ACP or vice versa by changing bolt, barrel and magazine; stainless steel frame with aluminum slide on M72. Finish, blued. Model 71 with conversion kit, $87; either separate caliber, $66; Model 72 with conversion kit, $95.95; either separate caliber, $75.95.

RAVEN ARMS MODEL P-25: Caliber .25 ACP, 6-rd. magazine. Barrel, 2.44"; overall length, 4.85". Weight, 14 ½ oz. Satin nickel with simulated pearl stocks shown. Smooth walnut stocks now are standard. Sights fixed. Finish, blued, bright chrome or satin nickel, all at $55.

RUGER POLICE SERVICE-SIX MODELS 107, 108, 707 and 708: Calibers .38 Special (M108) and .357 magnum (M107), both 6-rd. cylinders. Barrel, 2¾" or 4". With 4" barrel, 9¼" overall length. Weight, 33½ oz. Stocks, checkered American walnut. Sights fixed, ramp front, square-notch rear. Features solid frame with integral barrel, rib and ejector housing. All-steel construction. Field strips without tools. Blue, M107 (.357), $130; M108 (.38), $112; M707 (.357, stainless steel, 4" only), $149; M708 (.38, stainless, 4" only), $135.

Prices as of Spring, 1976; subject to change.

RUGER SECURITY-SIX MODEL 117: Caliber .357 magnum, 6-rd. cylinder. Barrel, 2¾", 4" or 6". With 4" barrel, 9¼" overall length. Weight, 35 oz. Stocks, hand-checkered American walnut. Sights, ramp front, fully adjustable rear. Features music wire coil springs throughout; hardened steel construction; integral barrel, rib and ejector rod housing. Can be field stripped, using only a coin or the rim of a cartridge. Blue, $143.50.

RUGER STAINLESS SECURITY-SIX MODEL 717: Same as Security-Six Model 117, except stainless steel, with sights of black alloy for maximum visibility. Price, $167.50.

RUGER SPEED-SIX MODELS 207, 208, 737 and 738: Calibers .38 Special standard or +P (blue M208, stainless steel M738); .357 magnum (blue M207, stainless M737), all 6-rd. cylinders. Barrel, 2¾" or 4". With 2¾" barrel, 7½" overall length. Weight, 31½ oz. Stocks, checkered American walnut, round butt. Sights fixed, ramp front, square-notch rear. Features same basic mechanism as Ruger's Security Six. Hammer without spur available on special order. Model 207, $130; Model 208, $112; Model 737, $149; Model 738, $135.

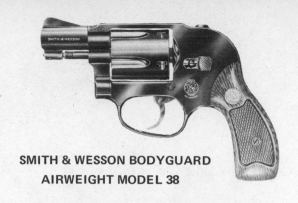

SMITH & WESSON BODYGUARD AIRWEIGHT MODEL 38

AIRWEIGHT (MODEL 37)

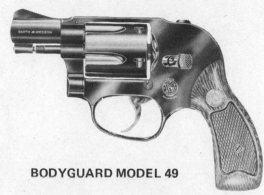

BODYGUARD MODEL 49

STAINLESS (MODEL 60)

SMITH & WESSON 38 CHIEFS SPECIAL (MODEL 36)

SMITH & WESSON 357 COMBAT MAGNUM MODEL 19

SMITH & WESSON MODEL 15 COMBAT MASTERPIECE

SMITH & WESSON BODYGUARD AIRWEIGHT MODEL 38 & BODYGUARD MODEL 49: Caliber .38 Special, 5-rd. cylinder. Barrel, 2''; overall length, 6-3/8''. Weights, Model 38, 14½ oz.; Model 49, 20½ oz. Sights fixed, with ramp front and square-notch rear. Stocks, checkered walnut, magna style. Model 38, blue, $115; nickel, $130; Model 49, blue, $113; nickel, $123.

SMITH & WESSON 38 CHIEFS SPECIAL (MODEL 36), AIRWEIGHT (MODEL 37), STAINLESS (MODEL 60): Caliber .38 Special, 5-rd. cylinder. Barrel, 2'' and 3'' (Models 36 and 37; 2'' only in Model 60). Stocks, checkered walnut, magna style, round or square butt. With 2'' round butt, 6½'' overall length; weight, 19 oz. (14 oz. for airweight). Sights fixed, with ramp front and square-notch rear. M36, blue, $111; nickel, $121; M37, blue, $115; nickel, $130; M60, $135.

SMITH & WESSON 357 COMBAT MAGNUM MODEL 19: Caliber .357 magnum, 6-rd. cylinder. Barrel, 2½'', 4'' or 6''. With 4'' barrel, 9½'' overall length. Weight, 35 oz. Stocks, checkered goncala alves, target type with square butt; round butt pattern available for 2½''. Sights, ramp front with 2½'' and 4'' barrels, fully adjustable rear with square notch, Patridge front sight with 6'' barrel. Blue or nickel, $167.50.

SMITH & WESSON COMBAT MASTERPIECE MODEL 15: Caliber .38 Special, 6-rds. Barrel, 2'' or 4''; overall length, 9-1/8'' with 4'' barrel. Weight, 34 oz. (loaded). Checkered, magna-type walnut stocks. Sights, ramp front, adjustable rear. Blue, $135; nickel, $145.

Prices as of Spring, 1976; subject to change.

SMITH & WESSON 32 HAND EJECTOR MODEL 30

SMITH & WESSON 32 REGULATION POLICE MODEL 31

SMITH & WESSON HIGHWAY PATROLMAN MODEL 28

SMITH & WESSON 41 MAGNUM MODEL 57

SMITH & WESSON 41 MILITARY & POLICE MODEL 58

SMITH & WESSON 44 MAGNUM MODEL 29

SMITH & WESSON 32 HAND EJECTOR MODEL 30:
Caliber .32 S&W Long, 6-rd. cylinder. Barrel, 2", 3" or 4".
With 4" barrel, 8" overall length. Weight, 18 oz. Stocks,
checkered walnut, magna style. Sights fixed, with ramp
front and square-notch rear. Blue, $107; nickel, $117.

**SMITH & WESSON 32 REGULATION POLICE MODEL
31:** Caliber .32 S&W Long, 6-rd. cylinder. Barrel, 2", 3" or
4". With 4" barrel, 8½" overall length. Weight, 18¾ oz.
Stocks, checkered walnut, magna style. Sights fixed, with
ramp front and square-notch rear. Blue, $107; nickel, $117.

**SMITH & WESSON HIGHWAY PATROLMAN MODEL
28:** Caliber .357 magnum, 6-rd. cylinder. Barrel, 4" or 6".
With 6" barrel, 11¼" overall length. Weight, 44 oz. Stocks,
checkered walnut, magna style. Sights, ramp front with
fully adjustable square-notch rear. Blue only, $140; with
target stocks, $147.50.

Prices as of Spring, 1976; subject to change.

SMITH & WESSON 41 MAGNUM MODEL 57: Caliber .41
magnum, 6-rd. cylinder. Barrel, 4", 6" or 8-3/8". With 6"
barrel, 11-3/8" overall length. Weight, 48 oz. Stocks,
checkered goncala alves, target type. Sights, red insert ramp
front, fully adjustable rear with square notch. Features
broad, grooved trigger and wide, checkered hammer spur.
Blue or nickel in 4" and 6", $235; same in 8-3/8", $241.50.

SMITH & WESSON 41 MILITARY & POLICE MODEL 58:
Caliber .41 magnum, 6-rd. cylinder. Barrel, 4"; overall
length, 9¼". Weight, 41 oz. Stocks, checkered walnut,
magna style. Sights fixed, ramp front and square-notch rear.
Blue, $130; nickel, $140.

SMITH & WESSON 44 MAGNUM MODEL 29: Caliber .44
magnum, 6-rd. cylinder. Barrel, 4", 6½" or 8-3/8". With
6½" barrel, 11-7/8" overall length. Weight, 47 oz. Stocks,
checkered goncala alves, target type, grooved target trigger;
broad, checkered hammer spur. Sights, red-insert ramp
front, fully adjustable rear with square notch. Features
presentation case included. Blue or nickel in 4" and 6½",
$235; 8-3/8", $241.50.

SMITH & WESSON 357 MAGNUM MODEL 27

SMITH & WESSON MILITARY & POLICE MODEL 10

SMITH & WESSON K-38 MASTERPIECE MODEL 14

SMITH & WESSON MILITARY & POLICE MODEL 10 HEAVY BARREL

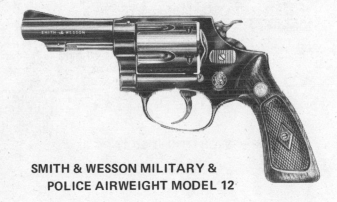

SMITH & WESSON MILITARY & POLICE AIRWEIGHT MODEL 12

SMITH & WESSON MILITARY & POLICE MODEL 13 HEAVY BARREL & MODEL 65

SMITH & WESSON 357 MAGNUM MODEL 27: Caliber .357 magnum, 6-rd. cylinder. Barrel, 3½", 5", 6" or 8-3/8". With 6" barrel, 11¼" overall length. Weight, 44 oz. Stocks, checkered walnut, magna style. Sights any S&W target front, fully adjustable square-notch rear. Blue or nickel in 3½", 5" or 6", $195; 8-3/8", $201.50.

SMITH & WESSON K-38 MASTERPIECE MODEL 14: Caliber .38 Special, 6-rd. cylinder. Barrel, 6" or 8-3/8". With 6" barrel, 11-1/8" overall length. Weight, 38½ oz. Stocks, checkered walnut, magna style. Sights, Patridge front, fully adjustable rear, square notch. Finish, blue only. With 6" barrel, $135; 8-3/8", $141.50.

SMITH & WESSON MILITARY & POLICE AIRWEIGHT MODEL 12: Caliber .38 Special, 6-rd. cylinder. Barrel, 2" or 4". With 2" barrel, 6-7/8" overall length. Weight, 18 oz. Otherwise same as regular Model 10. Blue, $114; nickel, $129.

SMITH & WESSON MILITARY & POLICE MODEL 10: Caliber .38 Special, 6-rd. cylinder. Barrel, 2", 4", 5" or 6". With 4" barrel, 9¼" overall length. Weight, 30½ oz. Stocks, checkered walnut, magna pattern, round or square butt. Sights fixed, with ramp front and square-notch rear. Blue, $109; nickel, $119.

SMITH & WESSON MILITARY & POLICE HEAVY BARREL MODEL 10: Same as regular Model 10, except for 4" ribbed barrel. Weight, 34 oz. Blue, $109; nickel, $119.

SMITH & WESSON MILITARY & POLICE HEAVY BARREL MODEL 13 & MODEL 65: Same as regular Model 10 and M10HB, except offered in 4" barrel only in choice of .357 magnum or .38 Special, both 6-rd. cylinders, square butt stocks only. Blue, $120; stainless steel Model 65, $145.

Prices as of Spring, 1976; subject to change.

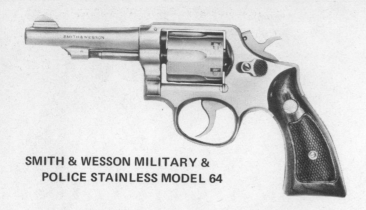

**SMITH & WESSON MILITARY &
POLICE STAINLESS MODEL 64**

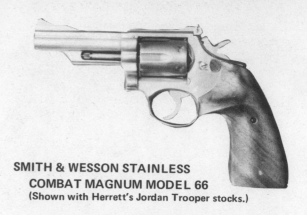

**SMITH & WESSON STAINLESS
COMBAT MAGNUM MODEL 66**
(Shown with Herrett's Jordan Trooper stocks.)

SMITH & WESSON MODEL 39

**SMITH & WESSON STAINLESS K-38
COMBAT MASTERPIECE MODEL 66**

SMITH & WESSON MODEL 59

SMITH & WESSON MODEL 25 TARGET

**SMITH & WESSON MILITARY & POLICE STAINLESS
MODEL 64:** Caliber .38 Special, 6-rd. cylinder. Barrel, 4";
overall length, 9½". Weight, 30½ oz. Stocks, checkered
walnut, magna style. Sights fixed, ramp front, square-notch
rear. Features satin finish stainless steel construction with
square butt. $135.

SMITH & WESSON MODEL 39: Caliber 9mm Luger, 8-rd.
magazine. Barrel, 4"; overall length, 7-7/16". Weight, 26½
oz. without magazine. Stocks, checkered walnut. Sights,
ramp front, rear adjustable for windage. Features double-
action trigger, magazine disconnect; if safety is put on when
cocked, hammer drops and is blocked. Frame is aluminum
alloy with lanyard loop. Slide locks open on last shot. Blue,
$148.50; nickel, $164.

SMITH & WESSON MODEL 59: Caliber 9mm Luger, 14-rd.
magazine. Barrel, 4"; overall length, 7-7/16". Weight, 27½
oz. without magazine. Stocks, checkered nylon. Sights,
ramp front, rear adjustable for windage. Features double-
action trigger, staggered-column magazine. Furnished with
two magazines. Blue, $178.50.

Prices as of Spring, 1976; subject to change.

**SMITH & WESSON STAINLESS COMBAT MAGNUM
MODEL 66:** Caliber .357 magnum, 6-rd. cylinder. Barrel,
4"; overall length, 9½". Weight, 35 oz. Stocks, checkered
goncala alves, magna style, target-type. Sights, ramp front,
fully adjustable, square-notch rear. Features satin stainless
steel construction, with grooved trigger having adjustable
stop. $185.

**SMITH & WESSON STAINLESS K-38 COMBAT MASTER-
PIECE MODEL 67:** Caliber .38 Special, 6-rd. cylinder.
Barrel, 4"; overall length, 9-1/8". Weight, 34 oz. (loaded).
Stocks, checkered walnut, magna style. Sights, ramp front,
fully adjustable square-notch rear. Features satin finish
stainless steel construction, grooved trigger with adjustable
stop. $152.

SMITH & WESSON TARGET MODEL 25: Caliber .45 ACP
or Auto Rim, 6 rds. Barrel, 6½" heavy target type; overall
length, 11-7/8". Weight, 45 oz. Stocks, checkered walnut,
target-type. Sights, Patridge front, adjustable rear. Broad
target trigger, wide-spur hammer. Blue, including case,
$215.

STAR MODEL BKS STARLIGHT

STERLING MODEL 300

STAR MODEL PD

STERLING MODEL 400

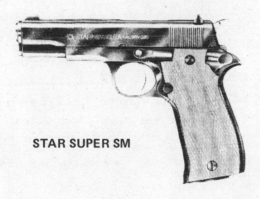

STAR SUPER SM

**THERMODYNAMIC SYSTEMS
TDA INTERNATIONAL POLICE**

STAR MODEL BKS STARLIGHT: Caliber 9mm Luger, 8-rd. magazine. Barrel, 4¼". Weight, 25 oz. Stocks, checkered plastic. Sights fixed. Features manual safety and magazine disconnect, with external hammer. Imported from Spain by Garcia. Blue, $160; chrome, $170.

STAR MODEL PD: Caliber .45 ACP, 7-rd. magazine. Barrel, 3.8"; overall length, 7". Weight, 25 oz. Stocks, checkered walnut. Sights, ramp front, square-notch rear, adjustable for windage and elevation. Features grooved, nonslip front strap, nylon recoil buffer, inertia firing pin and thumb safety. Slide locks open on last shot. Imported from Spain by Garcia. Blue, $210; chrome, $220.

STAR SUPER SM: Caliber .380 ACP, 10-rd. magazine. Barrel, 4"; overall length, 6-5/8". Weight, 22 oz. Stocks, checkered plastic. Sights, blade front, rear adjustable for elevation and windage. Features loaded chamber indicator and thumb safety. Imported from Spain by Garcia. Blue, $145; chrome, $155.

STERLING MODEL 300: Caliber .25 ACP, 6-rd. magazine. Barrel, 2½"; overall length, 4½". Weight, 13 oz. Stocks black or white plastic. Sights fixed. All-steel construction. Blue, $69.95; nickel, $74.95.

STERLING MODEL 400: Caliber .380 ACP, 7-rd. magazine. Barrel, 3¾"; 6½" overall length. Weight, 24 oz. Stocks, simulated walnut, checkered. Features double-action trigger and all-steel construction. Blue, $129.95; satin nickel, $134.95.

THERMODYNAMIC SYSTEMS TDA INTERNATIONAL POLICE: Caliber .357 magnum, 6-rd. cylinder. Barrel, 2½" or 4". With 4" barrel, 9½" overall length. Weight, 39 oz. Stocks, Pachmayr Signature black rubber, fully checkered. Sights fixed, ramp front and square-notch rear. Features broad, grooved trigger and wide, grooved hammer spur, with ventilated, matted barrel rib integral with frame, all-stainless steel construction, music wire coil springs and hex-socket screws. Made in U.S.A. and distributed by EMF Co., Inc., Box 1248, Studio City, CA 91604. Approximately $130.

Prices as of Spring, 1976; subject to change.

THOMAS DA

DAN WESSON MODEL 8-2 & MODEL 14-2

WALTHER MODEL PP

DAN WESSON MODEL 9-2 & MODEL 15-2

WALTHER MODEL PPK/S

WILKINSON ARMS DIANE

THOMAS DA: Calibers 9mm Luger and .38 Colt Super, 7-rd. magazine; .45 ACP, 6-rd. Barrel, 3½''; overall length, 6-3/8''. Weight, 33 oz. Stocks, smooth walnut (checkered plastic may be offered later). Sights, fixed ramp front, square-notch rear driftable for windage adjustment; target-type rear sight optional at unspecified added cost. Features double-action trigger pull on every shot, stainless steel construction. Made in U.S.A. by H&N Mini-Craft, 1066 E. Edna Pl., Covina, CA 91724. Estimated price, approximately $250.

WALTHER MODEL PP: Calibers .22 LR, 8-rd. magazine; .32 ACP, 8-rd.; .380 ACP, 7-rd. Barrel, 3.86''; overall length, 6.7''. Weight, 23½ oz. Stocks, checkered plastic. Sights fixed, with white markings. Features double-action trigger; manual safety blocks firing pin and drops hammer if cocked. Loaded chamber indicator for .32 and .380, finger rest and extra magazine. Imported from Germany by Interarms. Finish, blued. In .22 LR, $212; in .32 and .380, $199; engraved models from $600.

WALTHER MODEL PPK/S: Identical to Walther Model PP, except barrel is 3.27'' and overall length is 6.1''. Prices same as for Model PP.

Prices as of Spring, 1976; subject to change.

DAN WESSON MODEL 8-2 & MODEL 14-2: Calibers .38 Special standard or +P (Model 8-2), .357 magnum (Model 14-2), all 6-rd. cylinders. Barrel, 2½'', 4'', 6'' or 8''; Quickshift interchangeable as to length. With 4'' barrel, 9¼'' overall length. Weight, 34 oz. Stocks, checkered walnut grain Powerwood in four Quickshift designs. Sights fixed with ramp front and square-notch rear. Features interchangeable barrels, four interchangeable stocks, few moving parts and easy disassembly. Satin blue, with 2½'', 4'' or 6'' barrel, $130; same with 8'' barrel, $143.

DAN WESSON MODEL 9-2 & MODEL 15-2: Calibers .38 Special standard or +P (Model 9-2); .357 magnum (Model 15-2), all 6-rd. cylinders. Barrel, 2½'', 4'', 6'' or 8''; Quickshift interchangeable as to length. With 4'' barrel, 9¼'' overall length. Weight, 36 oz. Stocks, checkered walnut grain Powerwood in four Quickshift designs. Sights, serrated ramp front and fully adjustable square-notch rear. Features Quickshift interchangeable barrels and stocks, few moving parts, easy disassembly, bright blue finish only. Model priced with choice of 2½'', 4'' or 6'' barrels (add $37 for 8'' barrel); Models 9-2H & 15-2H (bull barrel), $168; Models 9-2V & 15-2V (ventilated rib), $188; Models 9-2VH and 15-2VH (ventilated rib, bull barrel), $188.

WILKINSON ARMS DIANE: Caliber .25 ACP, 6-rd. magazine. Barrel, 2-1/8''; overall length, 4.2''. Weight, 11¾ oz. Stocks, checkered plastic. Features all-milled steel construction, positive manual safety, concealed hammer, separate ejector, threaded barrel support bushing. Sights recessed, fixed. $115.

FIREARMS DIRECTORY

While many of the manufacturers included in the listings below are not engaged primarily in supplying equipment to law enforcement agencies, their addresses are included inasmuch as some of the products they produce or market may find use in police firearms training programs or by the individual officers in pursuit of their duties.

AMMUNITION (Commercial)
Alcan Shells (See Smith & Wesson Ammunition Co.)
Cascade Cartridge Inc., (See Omark)
Federal Cartridge Co., 2700 Foshay Tower,
  Minneapolis, Minn. 55401
Frontier Cartridge Co., Inc., Box 906, Grand Island, Neb. 68801
Omark-CCI/Speer, Inc., Box 856, Lewiston, ID 83501
Remington Arms Co., 939 Barnum Ave., Bridgeport, CT 06602
Service Armament, 689 Bergen Blvd., Ridgefield, N.J. 07657
Smith & Wesson Ammunition Co., 3640 Seminary Rd., Alton, IL
  62002
Speer, Inc. (See Omark)
Weatherby's, 2781 E. Firestone Blvd., South Gate, Calif. 90280
Winchester-Western, 275 Winchester Ave., New Haven, CT 06504

AMMUNITION (Custom)
Ammodyne, Box 1589, Los Angeles, Calif. 90053
B&K Custom Rel. Serv., Rte. 1, Lake 13, Farwell, Mich. 48622
BRI, 116 Main St., Sebastopol, CA 95472
Bill Ballard, P. O. Box 656, Billings, Mont. 59103
Jerry & Betty Bird, Box 10183, Corpus Christi, Tex. 78410
Caldwell's Loading Serv., 1314 Monroe Dr.,
  N.E., Atlanta, Ga. 30306
Russell Campbell, 219 Leisure Dr., San Antonio, Tex. 78201
Cumberland Arms, 1222 Oak Dr., Manchester, Tenn. 37355
Custom Ammo & Gunsmithing, 390 S. Main, Moab, Utah 84532
Custom Ammo Service, Box 15531, Santa Ana, CA 92705
F. W. Ellis Sport Shop, RFD 1, Box 139, Corinth, N.Y.
Ellwood Epps, 80 Kind St., Clinton, Ont., Canada
Steve Filipiak, 1270 So. Raleigh, Denver, Colo. 00219
H.P.K. Co., Inc., 3750 Ridge Rd., Highland, Ind.
R. H. Keeler, 1304 S. Oak, Port Angeles, Wash. 98362
L.E. Jurras & Associates, Box 846, Roswell, NM 88201
KTW, Inc., 710 Cooper-Foster Park Road West, Lorain, OH 44053
  (armor-piercing loads)
Dean Lincoln, 390 S. Main, Moab, Utah 84532
MB Associates, Bollinger Cnyn. Rd., San Ramon,
  CA 94583 (Short-Stop)
MFRE, Inc., 140 N. Groesbeck Hwy., Mt. Clemens, MI 48043
  (Quad Loads)
Pat B. McMillan, 4908 E. Indianola, Phoenix, Ariz. 85018
Mansfield Gunshop, Box 83, New Boston, N.H. 03070
Man-Tol Shells, Box 134, Bunnell, Fla. 32010
Moody's Reloading Serv., 2108 Broadway, Helena, Mont. 59601
Numrich Arms Corp., 203 Broadway, W. Hurley, N.Y. 12491
Robert Pomeroy, Morrison Ave., East Corinth,
  ME 04427 (custom shells)
Sanders Cust. Gun Serv., 2358 Tyler Lane, Louisville, Ky. 40205
Shot Shell Components, 365 So. Moore, Lakewood, Colo. 80226
3-D Co., Box 4411, Lincoln, Neb. 68504
James C. Tillinghast, Box 568, Marlow, N.H. 03456
True-Blue Co., 1400 E. Palmer Ave., Glendale, Calif. 91205 (blanks)
Walmax Inc. (See True-Blue)

AMMUNITION (Foreign)
Ammodyne, Box 1859, Los Angeles, Calif. 90053 (RWS)
Canadian Ind. Ltd. (C.I.L.), Box 10, Montreal, Que., Canada
C-I-L Ammunition Inc., P. O. Box 831, Plattsburgh, N.Y. 12901
Gevelot of Canada, Box 1593, Saskatoon, Sask., Canada
Hy-Score Arms Co., 200 Tillary, Brooklyn, N.Y. 11201
Paul Jaeger Inc., 211 Leedom St., Jenkintown, Pa. 19046
S. E. Lazlo, 200 Tillary, Brooklyn, N.Y. 11201
NORMA-Precision, 153 Van Ness Ave., Lansing, N.Y. 14882
Stoeger Arms Corp., 55 Ruta Ct., So. Hackensack, N.J. 07606

BODY ARMOR
American Body Armor and Equipment Co., 100 Ricefield Lane,
  Hauppauge, NY 11787
Armorshield (Federal Laboratories Inc., Saltsburg, PA 15681)
Armour of America, P.O. Box 1405, Beverly Hills, CA 90213
Blauer Mfg. Co., Inc., 160 N. Washington Street, Boston, MA 02114
Burlington Industrial Fabrics Co., 1345 Avenue of Americas, New
  York, NY 10019
Capps & Sons Ltd., 500 W. LaFayette Street, Jacksonville, IL 62650
Davis Aircraft Products Co., Inc., Scudder and Woodbine Avenues,
  Northport, NY 11768
HLB Security Electronics, Ltd., 211 E. 43rd Street, New York, NY
  10017
Paul Johnson Police Supply, 811 Hulman Street, Terre Haute, IN
  47802
Kansas City Custom Uniform Co., 301 W. Tenth Street, Kansas
  City, MO 64105
Law Enforcement Associates, Inc., 88 Holmes Street, Belleville, NJ
  07109
Levinson's, 2231 Front, Cuyahoga Falls, OH 44221
Life Shield Vest Co., 3425 Gratiot Avenue, Detroit, MI 48207
Mandall Shooting Supplies Inc., 7150 E. Fourth Street, Scottsdale,
  AZ 85252
Maryland Police Supply, Inc., 7112 Darlington Drive, Baltimore,
  MD 21234

Merson Uniform Co., Inc., 254-8 Canal Street, New York, NY
  10013
MFRE Corp., 148 N. Groesbeck Hwy., Mt. Clemens, MI 48043
Protective Apparel Corp. of America, 333 Sylvan Avenue, Engle-
  wood Cliffs, NJ 07632
Protective Materials Co., York and Haverhill Streets, Andover, MA
  01810
Quick Arms & Supply Co., 445 Atwood Avenue, Cranston, RI
  02920
Rachman Mfg. Co., 1135 Moss Street, Reading, PA 19604
Safariland Leather Products, 1941 S. Walker Avenue, Monrovia, CA
  91016
Second Chance, Box 578-A, Central Lake, MI 49522
Caleb V. Smith Uniform Co., 132-10 89th Avenue, Richmond Hill,
  NY 11418
Smith & Wesson, 2100 Roosevelt Avenue, Springfield, MA 01101
Sol's Stores of Aliquippa, 475 Franklin Avenue, Aliquippa, PA
  15001
Some's Uniforms, Inc., Paramus, NJ 07652
Strong Uniform Co., 14 W. 17th Street, New York, NY 10011

BULLET & CASE LUBRICANTS
Alpha-Molykote, Dow Corning Corp., 45 Commerce Dr.,
  Trumbull, Ct. 06601
Birchwood-Casey Co., Inc., 7900 Fuller Rd.,
  Eden Prairie, Minn. 55343 (Anderol)
Cooper-Woodward, Box 972, Riverside, Cal. 92502 (Perfect Lube)
DAI-Wing, Box 22084, Houston, TX 77027 (Spray lube)
D.R. Corbin Mfg. Co., Box 44, North Bend, OR 97459 (Swaging
  lube)
Green Bay Bullets, 233 N. Ashland, Green Bay,
  Wis. 54303 (EZE-Size case lube)
Herter's, Inc., Waseca, Minn. 56093 (Perfect Lubricant)
Javelina Products, Box 337, San Bernardino,
  Cal. 92402 (Alox beeswax)
Jet-Aer Corp., 100 Sixth Ave., Paterson, N.J. 07524
Lyman Gun Sight Products, Middlefield, Conn. 06455 (Size-Ezy)
Micro Shooter's Supply, Box 213, Las Cruces,
  N. Mex. 88001 (Micro-Lube)
Mirror-Lube, Box 693, San Juan Capistrano, CA 92675
Nutec, Box 1187, Wilmington, Del. 19899 (Dry-Lube)
Pacific Tool Co., Drawer 2048, Grand Island, NE 60801
Phelps Rel. Inc., Box 4004, E. Orange, N.J. 07019
RCBS, Inc., Box 1919, Oroville, Calif. 95965
SAECO Rel., Inc., Box 778, Carpinteria, CA 93013
Scientific Lubricants Co., 3753 Lawrence Ave.,
  Chicago, Ill. 60625
Shooters Accessory Supply (SAS), Box 250, N. Bend, Ore. 97459
Testing Systems, Inc., 2836 Mt. Carmel, Glenside, PA 19038

CHOKE DEVICES & RECOIL ABSORBERS
Contra-Jet, 7920 49th Ave., So., Seattle, Wash. 98118
DAI-Wing, Box 22084, Houston, TX 77027 (A&W shotgun diverter)
Herter's Inc., Waseca, Minn. 56093 (Vari-Choke)
Lyman Gun Sight Products, Middlefield, Conn. 60455 (Cutts Comp.)
Mag-na-port Arms, 30016 S. River Rd., Mt. Clemens, MI 48043
Pendleton Dekickers, 1210 S. W. Hailey Ave.,
  Pendleton, Ore. 97801
Poly-Choke Co., Inc., Box 296, Hartford, Conn. 06101
St. Louis Precision Products, 902 Michigan Ave.,
  St. Louis, Mich. 48880 (Gun-Tamer)

CHRONOGRAPHS AND PRESSURE TOOLS
Avtron, 10409 Meech Ave., Cleveland, Ohio 44105
B-Square Co., Box 11281, Ft. Worth, Tex. 76110
Chronograph Specialists, P.O. Box 5005, Santa Ana, Calif. 92704
Herter's, Waseca, Minn. 56093
Micro-Sight Co., 242 Harbor Blvd., Belmont,
  Calif. 94002 (Techsonic)
Oehler Research, P. O. Box 9135, Austin, Tex. 78756
Sundtek Co., P. O. Box 744, Springfield, Ore. 97477
Telepacific Electronics Co., Inc., 3335 W. Orange Ave.,
  Anaheim, CA 92804
York-Cantrell, 30241 Rosebriar, St. Clair Shores,
  Mich. 48082 (pressure tool)

CLEANING & REFINISHING SUPPLIES
Ammodyne, Box 1589, Los Angeles, Cal. 90053 (Gun Kote)
Birchwood-Casey Chem. Co., 7900 Fuller Rd.,
  Eden Prairie, Minn. 55343
Bisonite Co., Inc., Box 84, Buffalo, N.Y. 14217
Jim Brobst, 299 Poplar St., Hamburg, Pa. 19526 (J-B Compound)
Geo. Brothers, Great Barrington, Mass. 01230 (G-B Linspeed Oil)
Browning Arms. Rt. 4, Box 624-B, Arnold, Mo. 63010
Burnishine Prod. Co., 8140 N. Ridgeway,
  Skokie, Ill. 60076 (Stock Glaze)
C & R Distr. Corp., 449 E. 21st So., Salt Lake City, Utah 84115
Cherry Corners Gun Shop, 8010 Lafayette Rd., Rte. 1,
  Lodi, Ohio 44254 (buffing compound)

Clenzoil Co., Box 1226, Sta., C. Canton, O. 44708
Corrosion Reaction Consultants, Inc., Dresher, Pa. 19025 (Mask)
Craftsman Wood Serv. Co., 2727 S. Marry, Chicago, Ill. 60608
Custom Industries, 18900 Detroit Ave., Lakewood, O. 44107
Dex-Kleen, Box 509 Des Moines, Ia. 50302 (gun wipers)
Dri-Slide, Inc., Industrial Park, Fremont, Mich. 49412
Dry Film Gun Coatings, 1521 43rd St., W. Palm Beach, Fla. 33407
Electromation Comp. Corp., 11 Lincoln St., Copiague, N.Y. 11726 (ultra-sonic cleaning tank)
F & J Derusting Co., Inc., 247 Westcott Dr., Rahway, N.J. 07065
Forty-Five Ranch Enterpr., Box 1080, Miami, Okla. 74354
Frye Industs., 1318 N. Broadway, Santa Maria, Cal. 93454
Garcia Sptg. Arms Corp., 329 Alfred Ave., Teaneck, N.J. 07666
Gun-All Products, Box 244, Dowagiac, Mich. 49047
Frank C. Hoppe Div., P. O. Box 97, Parkesburg, Pa. 19365
Hunting World, 247 E. 50th St., New York, N.Y. 10022 (P-H Safari Kit)
J & G Rifle Ranch, Turner, MT 59542
Jet-Aer Corp., 100 Sixth Ave., Paterson, N.J. 07524 (blues & oils)
K. W. Kleinendorst, Taylortown Rd., Montville, N.J. 07045 (rifle clg. rods)
Knox Laboratories, 2335 S. Michigan Ave., Chicago, Ill. 60616
LPS Res. Labs. Inc., 2050 Cotner Ave., Los Angeles, Calif. 90025
Carl Lampert Co., 2639 So. 31st St., Milwaukee, Wis. 53215 (gun bags)
LEM Gun Spec., Box 31, College Park, Ga 30337 (Lewis Lead Remover)
Liquid Wrench, Box 10628, Charlotte, N.C. 28201 (pen. oil)
Lyman Gun Sight Products, Middlefield, Conn. 60455
Lynx-Line Gun Products, Box 3985, Detroit, Mich. 48227
Marble Arms Co., 1120 Superior, Gladstone, Mich. 49837
Micro-Lube, Inc., 8505 Directors Row, Dallas, Tx 75247 (Micro-Mist/Solv)
Micro Sight Co., 242 Harbor Blvd., Belmont, Ca. 94002 (bedding)
Mill Run Prod., 1360 W. 9th, Cleveland, O. 44113 (Brite-Bore Kits)
Mint Luster Cleaners, 1102 N. Division, Appleton, Wis. 54911
Mirror-Lube, Box 693, San Juan Capistrano, CA 92675
Mistic Metal Mover, Inc., R.R. 2, P. O. Box 336, Princeton, Ill. 61356
Mitchell Chemical Co., Wampus Lane, Milford, Conn. (Gun Guard)
New Method Mfg. Co., Box 175, Bradford, Pa. 16701 (gun blue)
Numrich Arms Co., West Hurley, N.Y. 12491 (44-40 gun blue)
Nutec, Box 1187, Wilmington, Del. 19899 (Dry-Lube)
Outers Laboratories, Box 37, Onalaska, Wis. 54650 (Gunslick kits)
Ponsness-Warren, Inc., Box 186, Rathdrum, ID 83858 (STOS grease)
R.E.I., 101 Wolpers, Park Forest, Ill. 60466 (whale oil lube)
Radiator Spec. Co., Charlotte, N.C. 28201 (liquid wrench)
Reardon Prod., 323 N. Main St., Roanoke, Ill. 61561 (Dry-Lube)
Reese Arms Co., R.R. 1, Colona, IL 61241 (Dry-film lube)
Riel & Fuller, 423 Woodrow Ave., Dunkirk, N.Y. 14048 (anti-rust oil)
Rig Products Co., Box 279, Oregon, Ill. 61061 (Rig Grease)
Rocket Chemical Co., Inc., 5390 Napa St., San Diego, Calif. (WD-40)
Rusterprufe Labs., 605 Wolcott St., Sparta, Wis. 54656
Service Armament, 689 Bergen Blvd., Ridgefield, N.J. 07657 (Parker-Hale)
Sheldon's Inc., Box 508, Antigo, Wis. 54409 (shotgun brushes)
Silicote Corp., Box 359, Oshkosh, Wis. 54901 (Silicone cloths)
Silver Dollar Guns, 7 Balsam St., Keene, N.H. 03431 (silicone oil)
A. D. Soucy, Box 191, Ft. Kent, Me. 04743 (stock finish)
Southeastern Coatings, Ind., (SECOA), Bldg. 132, P.B.I. Airport, W. Palm Beach, Fla. 33406 (Teflon Coatings)
Sportsmen's Labs., Inc., Box 732, Anoka, Minn. 55303 (Gun Life lube)
Sun Ray Chemicals, 371-39th Ave., San Francisco, Calif. 94121
Surcon, Inc., P. O. Box 277, Zieglerville, Pa. 19492
Taylor & Robbins, Box 164, Rixford, Pa. 16745 (Throat Saver)
Testing Systems, Inc., 2836 Mt. Carmel, Glenside, PA 19038 (TSI-300)
L. B. Thompson, 468 E. School Ave., Salem, O. 44460 (Rust bluing/browning)
C. S. Van Gorden, 120 Tenth Ave., Eau Claire, Wis. 54701 (Instant Blue)
WD-40 Co., 5390 Napa St., San Diego, Ca. 92110
W&W Mfg. Co., Box 365, Belton, Mo. 64012 (shotgun cleaner)
Webber Gage Division, 12900 Triskett Rd., Cleveland, O. 44111 (Luger oil)
West Coast Secoa, Inc., 3915 U.S. Hwy. 98 So., Lakeland, Fla. 33803
Williams Gun Sight, 7389 Lapeer Rd., Davison, Mich. 48412 (finish kit)
Winslow Arms Co., P. O. Box 578, Osprey, Fla. 33595 (refinishing kit)
Woodstream Corp., P. O. Box 327, Lititz, Pa. 17543 (Mask)

COMPONENTS — BULLETS, POWDER, PRIMERS
Accuracy Bullet Co., 2443 41st St., San Francisco, Calif. 94116 (Perfecast bullets)
Bitterroot Bullet Co., Box 412, Lewiston, Ida. 83501
Centrix, 2116 N. 10th Ave., Tucson, Ariz. 85705
Kenneth E. Clark, 18738 Highway 99, Madera, CA 93637 (Bullets)
Colorado Custom Bullets, Rt. 1, Box 507-B, Montrose, Colo. 81401
D.R. Corbin Mfg. Co., Box 44, North Bend, OR 97459 (Bullet jackets)
Division Lead, 7742 W. 61 Pl., Summit, Ill. 60502
DuPont, Explosives Dept., Wilmington, Del. 19898
Elk Mountain Shooters Supply, 1719 Marie, Pasco, WA 99301 (Alaskan bullets)
Forty Five Ranch Enterprises, Box 1080, Miami, Okla. 74354
Godfrey Reloading Supply, R.R. 1, Box 189, Brighton, Ill. 62012 (cast bullets)
Green Bay Bullets, 233 No. Ashland, Green Bay, Wis. 54303 (lead)
H.P.K. Co., Inc., 3750 Ridge Rd., Highland, Ind. 46322 (cast bullets)
Hercules Powder Co., 910 Market St., Wilmington, Del. 19899
Herter's Inc., Waseca, Minn. 56093
Hi-Precision Co., 109 Third Ave., N.E., Orange City, Ia. 51041
B. E. Hodgdon, Inc., 7710 W. 50 Hw., Shawnee Mission, Kans. 66202
Hornady Mfg. Co., Box 1848, Grand Island, Neb. 68801
N. E. House Co., Middletown Rd., E. Hampton, Conn. 06424
Lyman Gun Sight Products, Middlefield, Conn. 06455
Markell, Inc., 4115 Judah St., San Francisco, Calif. 94112
Meyer Bros. Wabasha, Minn. 55981 (shotgun slugs)

Michael's Antiques, Box 233, Copiague, L.I., N.Y. 11726 (Balle Blondeau)
Miller Trading Co., 20 S. Front St., Wilmington, N.C. 28401
Norma-Precision, 153 Van Ness Ave., Lansing, NY 14882
Nosler Bullets, P. O. Box 688, Beaverton, OR 97005
Omark-CCI/Speer, Inc., Box 856, Lewiston, ID 83501
Oregon Ammo Service, Box 19341, Portland, Ore. 97219
Robert Pomeroy, Morrison Ave., East Corinth, ME 04427
Precision Mfg. Co., 1440 S. State College Blvd., Bldg. 5, Suite M, Anaheim, CA 92806
Rainbow Prod., P. O. Box 75, Wishram, Wash. 98673 (bullets)
Remington-Peters, 939 Barnum Ave., Bridgeport, CT 06602
S. W. M. Bullet Co., 1122 S. Cherry St., Port Angeles, Wash. 98362 (17 cal.)
Sierra Bullets Inc., 10532 S. Painter Ave., Santa Fe Springs, CA 90670
Smith & Wesson Amm. Co., 3640 Seminary Rd., Alton, IL 62002
Speer, Inc., (See Omark)
George W. Spence, 202 Main St., Steele, MO 63877 (Custom formed cases)
Taylor Bullets, P. O. Box 21254, San Antonio, Tex. 78221
James C. Tillinghast, Box 568, Marlow, N.H. 03456
Winchester-Western, 275 Winchester Ave., New Have
Xelex Ltd., Hawksbury, Ont. Canada (powder)

GUN CASES, CABINETS AND RACKS
Alco Carrying Cases Inc., 601 W. 26th St., New York, N.Y. 10001
Amer. Safety Gun Case Co., Holland, Mich. 49424
Aremac Co., 101 N. Verity Parkway, Middletown, O. 45042
Artistic Wood Specialties, 923-29 W. Chicago Ave., Chicago, Ill. 60622
Morton Booth Co., Box 123, Joplin, Mo. 64801
Boyt Co., Box 1108, Iowa Falls, Ia. 50126
Brewster Corp., Old Lyme, Conn. 06371
Browning Arms Co., Rt. 4, Box 624-B, Arnold, Mo. 63010
Castle Sptg. Gods., Inc., 498 Nepperhan Ave., Yonkers, N.Y. 10701
Challanger Mfg. Co., 94-28 Merrick Blvd., Jamaica, N.Y. 11433
Cincinnati Ind. Inc., (Cindus), Cincinnati (Lockland), O. 45215
Coladonato Bros. Box 156, Hazleton, Pa. 18201
Dutton's 7840 Phillips Highway, Jacksonville, Fla. 32216 (single rack)
Ellwood Epps Sporting Goods, Clinton, Ont., Canada
Farber Bros., Inc., 821 Linden Ave., Memphis, Tenn. 38101 (truck pouch)
Ferrell Co., Rte. 3, Gallatin, Tenn. 37066 (Redi-Rack)
Flambeau Plastics Corp., 801 Lynn, Baraboo, Wis. 53913
Gun-Ho Case Mfg., Co., 110 East 10th St., St. Paul, Minn. 55101
Gun Racks, Inc., P. O. Box 22675, Houston, Tex. 77027
B. E. Hodgdon, Inc., 7710 W. 50 Hiway, Shawnee Mission, Kans. 66202
Ithaca Gun Co., Terrace Hill, Ithaca, N.Y. 14850
J-K Imports, Box 403, Novato, Cal. 94947 (leg 'o mutton case)
Jumbo Sports Prods., P. O. Box 280-Airport Rd., Frederick, MD 21701
Kolpin Bros. Co., Inc., Box 231, Berlin, Wis. 54923
Marble Arms Corp., 1120 Superior, Gladstone, Mich. 49837
National Sports Div., 19 E. McWilliams St., Fond du Lac, Wis. 54935
Nortex Co., 2821 Main St., Dallas, Tex. 75226 (automobile gun rack)
Paul-Reed, Inc., P. O. Box 227, Charlevoix, Mich. 49720
Penguin Assoc. Inc., Box 97, Parkersburg, Pa. 19365
Precise Imp. Corp., 3 Chestnut, Suffern, N.Y. 10901
Pretto Cabinet Co., 1201 E. Walnut, Oglesby, Ill. 61348
Protecto Plastics, Inc., Box 37, Wind Gap, Pa. 18091
Richland Arms Co., 321 W. Adrian, Blissfield, Mich. 49228
Saf-T-Case, Box 10592, Dallas, Tex. 75207
San Angelo Die Castings, Box 984, San Angelo, Tex. 76901
Buddy Schoelkopf, 4100 Platinum Way., Dallas, Tex. 75237
Sile Distr., 7 Centre Market Pl., New York, N.Y. 10013 (leg o'mutton case)
Stearn Mfg. Co., Div. & 30th St., St. Cloud, Minn. 56301
Sure Shoot'n, Box 195, Jacksonville, Ill. 62650
Western Holder Co., Box 33, Menomonee Falls, Wis. 53051
Woodstream Corp., Box 327, Lititz, Pa. 17543
Yield House, Inc., RFD, No. Conway, N.H. 03860

GUN PARTS, U.S. AND FOREIGN
American Firearms Mfg. Co., Inc., 5732 Kenwick Dr., San Antonio, Tex. 78238 (clips)
Badger Shooter's Supply, Owen, Wisc. 54460
Federal Ordnance Inc., P. O. Box 36032, Los Angeles, Calif. 90036
Gunner's Armory, 2 Sonoma, San Francisco, Calif. 94133
H&B Gun Corp., 1228 Fort St., Lincoln Park, Mich. 48166
Hunter's Haven, Zero Prince St., Alexandria, Va. 22314
Bob Lovell, Box 401, Elmhurst, Ill. 60126
Numrich Arms Co., West Hurley, N.Y. 12491
Reed & Co., Shokan, N.Y. 12481
Sporting Arms, Inc., 9643 Alpaca St., So. El Monte, CA 91733 (M-1 carb access)
N. F. Strebe, 4926 Marlboro Pike, S.E., Washington, D.C. 20027
Triple-K Mfg. Co., 568-6th Ave., San Diego, CA 92101

GUNS (Foreign)
Armoury Inc., Rte. 25, New Preston, Ct. 06777
Atlas Arms, Inc., 7952 Waukegan Rd., Niles, Ill. 60648
Browning Arms Co., Rt. 4, Box 624-B, Arnold, Mo. 63010
Centennial Arms Corp., 3318 W. Devon, Chicago, Ill. 60645
Century Arms Co., 3-5 Federal St., St. Albans, Vt. 05478
W.H. Craig, Box 927, Selma, Ala. 36701
Charles Daly, Inc., 90 Chambers St., New York, N.Y. 10007
Firearms Imp. & Exp. Co., P.O. Box 691 Biscayne Annex, Miami, Fla. 33152 (I.N.A. Arminius)
Flaig's Lodge, Millvale, Pa. 15209
J.L. Galef & Son, Inc., 85 Chambers, New York, N.Y. 10007
Garcia Sptg. Arms Corp., 17801 Indian Head Hwy., Accokeek, MD 20607
Gevelot of Can. Ltd., Box 1593, Saskatoon, Sask., Canada
Gold Rush Guns, 2211 Clement St., San Francisco, Ca. 94121
H.F. Grieder, Box 487, Knoxville, Ill. 61448 (Hammerli)

Interarms Ltd., 10 Prince St., Alexandria, Va.
22313 (Mauser)
Intercontinental Arms, 2222 Barry Ave., Los Angeles,
Calif. 90046
International Firearms Co., Ltd., Montreal 1, Que., Canada
International Distr., Box 7566, Miami, Fla. 33155
Ithaca Gun Co., Terrace Hill, Ithaca, N.Y. 14850 (Perazzi)
JBL Arms Co., Box 323, Dover, Pa. 17315
J-K Imports, Box 403, Novato, Cal. 94947 (Italian)
Paul Jaeger Inc., 211 Leedom St., Jenkintown, Pa. 19046
Kleinguenther's, P. O. Box 1261, Sequin, Tx. 78155
L.A. Distributors, 4 Centre Market Pl., New York, N.Y. 11201
Jos. G. Landmann, 2308 Preetz/Holstein, W. Germany (JGL)
S.E. Laszlo, 200 Tilary St., Brooklyn, N.Y. 11201
Liberty Arms Corp., Box 306, Montrose, Calif. 91020
Mars Equipment Corp., 3318 W. Devon, Chicago, Ill. 60645
Navy Arms Co., 689 Bergen Blvd., Ridgefield, N.J. 07657
Pachmayr Gun Works, 1220 S. Grand Ave., Los Angeles,
Calif. 90015
Parker-Hale, Whittall St., Birmingham 4, England
Precise Imp. Corp. (PIC), 3 Chestnut, Suffern, N.Y. 10901
Savage Arms Corp., Westfield, Mass. 01085 (Anschutz)
Security Arms Training Affiliates (H&K guns), Suite 1004,
1815 N. Fort Myer Dr., Arlington, Va. 22209
Simmons Spec., Inc., 700 Rogers Rd., Olathe, Kans. 66061
Stoeger Arms Co., 55 Ruta Ct., S. Hackensack, N.J. 07606
Tradewinds Inc., P.O. Box 1191, Tacoma, Wash. 98401
Weatherby's, 2781 Firestone Blvd., So. Gate, Calif.
90280

GUNS, U.S.-made
American Firearms Mfg. Co., Inc., 5732 Kenwich Dr.,
San Antonio, Tex. 78238
Armalite, 118 E. 16th St., Costa Mesa, Calif. 92627
Auto Mag (See TDE Corp.)
Caraville Arms, P.O. Box 377, Thousand Oaks, Calif. 91360
Charter Arms Corp., 430 Sniffens Lane, Stratford, CT 06497
Colt's, 150 Huyshope Ave., Hartford, Conn. 06102
Commando Arms, Inc., Box 10214, Knoxville, Tenn. 37919
Day Arms Corp., 7515 Stagecoach Ln., San Antonio,
Tex. 78227
Harrington & Richardson, Park Ave., Worcester,
Mass. 01610
High Standard Mfg. Co., 1817 Dixwell Ave., Hamden,
Conn. 06514
Ithaca Gun Co., Ithaca, N.Y. 14850
Iver Johnson Arms & Cycle Works, Fitchburg, Mass. 01420
Marlin Firearms Co., 100 Kenna Dr., New Haven,
Conn. 06473
O.F. Mossberg & Sons, Inc., 7 Grasso St., N. Haven,
Conn. 06473
Numrich Arms Co., W. Hurley, N.Y. 12491
Plainfield Machine Co., Inc. Box 447, Dunellen, N.J. 08812
Potomac Arms Corp., P.O. Box 35, Alexandria, Va.
22313 (ML replicas)
Raven Arms, 5060 N. Calmview Ave., Baldwin Park, CA 91706
Remington Arms Co., 939 Barnum Ave., Bridgeport, CT 06602
Savage Arms Corp., Westfield, Mass. 01085
Sears, Roebuck & Co., 825 S. St. Louis, Chicago, Ill. 60607
Seventrees Ltd., 315 W. 39th St., New York, N.Y. 10018
Smith & Wesson Inc., Springfield, Mass. 01101
Sterling Arms Corp., 2206 Elmwood Ave., Buffalo,
N.Y. 14216
Sturm, Ruger & Co., Southport, Conn. 06490
TDE Corp., 11658 McBean Drive, El Monte, CA 91732 (Auto Mag,
.380 Back Up)
Thompson-Center Arms, Box 2405, Rochester, N.H. 03867
(Contender pistol)
Universal Sporting Goods, Inc., 7920 N. W. 76th Ave., Medley,
FL 33166
Ward's, 619 W. Chicago, Ill. 60607 (Western Field brand)
Weatherby's, 2781 E. Firestone Blvd., South Gate,
Calif. 90280
Dan Wesson Arms, 293 S. Main St., Monson, Mass. 01057
Wilkinson Arms, 803 N. Glendora Ave., Covina, CA 91724 (Diane
pistols)
Winchester Repeating Arms Co., New Haven Conn. 06504

GUNSMITH SUPPLIES, TOOLS, SERVICES
Alley Supply Co., Carson Valley Industrial Park, Gardnerville, NV
89410
American Firearms Mfg. Co., Inc., 5732 Kenwich Dr.,
San Antonio, Tex. 78238 (45 Conversion Kit)
B-Square Engineering, Box 11281, Ft. Worth, TX 76110
Bonanza Sports Mfg. Co., 412 Western Ave., Faribault,
Minn. 55021
Bob Brownell's, Main & Third, Montezuma, Ia. 50171
Maynard P. Buehler, Inc., 17 Orinda Hwy, Orinda, Calif.
94563 (Rocol lube)
Clymer Mfg. Co., 14214 W. 11 Mile Rd., Oak Park, Mich.
48237 (reamers)
Dremel Mfg. Co., P.O. Box 518, Racine, Wis. 53401 (grinders)
DAI-Wing, Box 22084, Houston, TX 77027
Edmund Scientific Co., 101 E. Glouster Pike, Barrington, N.J. 08807
Forster Appelt Mfg. Co., Inc., 82 E. Lanark Ave., Lanark,
Ill. 61046
Keith Francis, Box 343, Talent, Ore. 97540 (reamers)
Gopher Shooter's Supply, Box 246, Faribault, Minn.
55021 (screwdrivers. etc)
Jeffredo Gunsight Co., 1629 Via Monserate, Fallbrook, CA 92028
(Ctge. trap butt pad)
Ruhr-American Corp., S. Hwy 55, Glenwood, Minn. 56334
A.G. Russell, P.O. Box 474, Fayetteville, Ark. 72701
(Arkansas stones)
Williams Gun Sight Co., 7389 Lapeer Rd., Davison,
Mich. 48423

HANDGUN ACCESSORIES
Bianchi Holster Co., 100 Calle Cortez, Temecula, CA 92390
(Revolver speedloader)

B.L. Broadway, 1503 Jasper, Chula Vista, Calif.
92011 (machine rest)
C'Arco, Box 2943, San Bernardino, CA 92406 (Ransom pistol
machine rest)
Case Master, 4675 E. 10 Ave., Miami, Fla. 33013
Central Specialties Co., 6030 Northwest Hwy., Chicago,
Ill. 60631
Dade Screw Machine Prod., 2319 S.W. 7th Ave., Miami, FL 33127
(Speedloaders)
R.S. Frielich, 396 Broome St., New York, N.Y. 10013 (cases)
Frontier Ballistics, Box 1412, Hutchinson, KS 67501 (Feather
Touch speedloaders)
HKS Tool Prod. Co., 132 Fifth Ave., Dayton, KY 41074 (Six
Second speedloaders)
Hunt Eng. 121-17th St., Yucaipa, Calif. 92399 (Multi-Loader)
R.G. Jensen, 16153 ½ Parthenia, Sepulveda, Calif.
91343 (auxiliary chambers)
Matich Loader, Box 958, S. Pasadena, Calif. 91030 (Quick Load)
Pachmayr, 1220 S. Grand, Los Angeles, Calif. 90015 (cases)
Platt Luggage, Inc., 2301 S. Prairie, Chicago, Ill.
60616 (cases)
Juels Reiver, 4104 Market St., Wilmington, Del. 19899 (cases)
Safariland, 1941 S. Walker Ave., Monrovia, CA 91016 (Revolver
speedloader)
Second Six, Box 215, South Laguna, CA 92677 (Revolver
speedloader)
M. Tyler, 1326 W. Britton, Oklahoma City, Okla.
73114 (grip adaptor)

HANDGUN GRIPS
Beckelhymer's, Hidalgo & San Bernardo, Laredo, Tex. 78040
Caray Sales Co., 2044 Hudson St., Ft. Lee, N.J. 07024
Custom Combat Grips, 148 Shepherd Ave., Brooklyn, N.Y. 11208
J.M. Evans, 5078 Harwood Rd., San Jose, Calif. 95124
E.M. "Fuzzy" Farrant, 1235 W. Vine Ave., West Covina, CA 91790
Fitz, Box 49797, Los Angeles, Calif. 90049
Herrett's Stocks, Box 741, Twin Falls, ID 83301
Hogue Custom Grips, Box 1001, Cambria, Calif. 93428
Mershon Co., Inc., 1230 S. Grand Ave., Los Angeles,
Calif. 90015
Mustang Grips, 28030 Del Rio Rd., Temecula, CA 92390
Sanderson Custom Pistol Stocks, 17965 Fenton, Detroit,
Mich. 48219
Jay Scott, 81 Sherman Place, Garfield, N.J. 07026
Sile Dist., 7 Centre Market Pl., New York, N.Y. 10013
Sports, Inc., 5501 Broadway, Chicago, Ill. 60640 (Franzite)
John W. Womack, 3006 Bibb St., Shreveport, La. 71108

HOLSTERS & LEATHER GOODS
American Sales & Mfg. Co., Box 677, Laredo, TX 78040 (holsters &
gun belts)
Bacon Holsters, Box 1466, Rosemead, CA 91770
Berns-Martin, Box 335, Elberton, Ga. 30635
Bianchi Holster Co., 100 Calle Cortez, Temecula,
Calif. 92390
Boyt Co., Box 1108, Iowa Falls, Iowa 51026
E.A. Brandin Saddle Co., Rte. 2, Box 243-A, Monroe,
La. 71201
Brauer Bros. Mfg. Co., 817 N. 17th, St. Louis, Mo. 63106
Browning Arms Co., Rt. 4, Box 624-B, Arnold, Mo. 63010
J.M. Bucheimer Co., Airport Rd., Frederick, Md. 21701
Cole's Acku-Rite, Box 25, Kennedy, N.Y. 14747
Colt's, 150 Huyshope Ave., Hartford, Conn. 06012
Hoyt Holster Co., P.O. Box 1783, Costa Mesa, Calif. 92626
Don Hume, Box 351, Miami, Okla. 74354
The Hunter Co., 1215 12th St., Denver, Colo. 80204
Jet Holster Corp., 4 Centre Market Pl., New York, N.Y. 10013
Jumbo Sport Prods., P.O. Box 280, Airport Rd., Frederick,
Md. 21701
George Lawrence Co., 306 S.W. First Ave., Portland, Ore. 97204
S.D. Myres Saddle Co., Box 9776, El Paso, Tex. 79988
Red Head Brand Co., 4100 Platinum Way, Dallas, Tex. 75237
Roy Baker's Pancake Holsters, Box G, Hwy. 132, Magnolia, AR
71753
Safariland Leather Products, 1941 S. Walker Ave., Box 60,
Monrovia, CA 91016
Safety Speed Holster, Inc., 910 S. Vail, Montebello,
Calif. 90640
Seventrees, Ltd., 315 W. 39 St., New York, N.Y. 10018
Sile Distr., 7 Centre Market Pl., New York, N.Y. 10013
Smith & Wesson Leather Co., 2100 Roosevelt, Springfield,
Mass. 01101
Whitco, Box 1712, Brownsville, Tex. 78520 (Hide-A-Way)

METALLIC SIGHTS
B-Square Eng. Co., Box 11281, Ft. Worth, Tex. 76110
Bo-Mar Tool & Mfg. Co., Box 168, Carthage, Tex. 75633
Maynard P. Buehler, Inc., 17 Orinda Highway, Orinda,
Calif. 94563
Chicago Gun Center, 3109 W. Armitage, Chicago, Ill. 60647
Christy Gun Works, 875 57th St., Sacramento, Calif. 95819
Art Cook Supply, Rte. 2, Box 123B, Laurel, Md.
20810 (Illum. gunsight)
Cap Cresap, 21442 Rosedell Dr., Saugus, CA 91350 (Illuminated
pistol sights)
Firearms Dev. Lab., Box 278, Scotts Valley, Calif. 95060
Jeffredo Gunsight Co., 1629 Via Monserate, Fallbrook, CA 92028
(Folding leaf sight)
Lyman Gun Sight Products, Middlefield, Conn. 06455
Marble Arms Corp., 1120 Superior, Gladstone, Mich. 49837
Merit Gunsight Co., P.O. Box 995, Sequim, Wash. 98382
Micro Sight Co., 242 Harbor Blvd., Belmont, Calif. 94002
Miniature Machine Co., 212 E. Spruce, Deming, N.M. 88030
Oxford Corp., 100 Benbro Dr., Buffalo, N.Y. 14225 (Illum Sight)
C.R. Pedersen & Son, Ludington, Mich. 49431
Redfield Gun Sight Co., 1315 S. Clarkson St., Denver,
Colo. 80210
Simmons Gun Specialties, Inc., 700 Rodgers Rd., Olathe,
Kans. 66061
Slug Site Co., 3835 University, Des Moines, Iowa 50311
Williams Gun Sight Co., 7389 Lapeer Rd., Davison, Mich. 48423
W.H. Womack, 2124 Meriwether Rd., Shreveport, La. 71108

MISCELLANEOUS

Ammo Pouch, Creed Ent., 13167 E. Garvey Ave., Baldwin Park, Calif. 91706
Bore Collimator, Alley Supply Co., Carson Valley Industrial Park, Gardnerville, NV 89410
Bore Collimator, Collins Co., Box 40, Shepherdsville, Ky. 40165
Cartridge Boxes, Llanerch Gun Shop, 2800 Township Line, Upper Darby, Pa. 19083
Cartridge Boxes, MTM Molded Prod. Co., Box 14092, Dayton, Ohio, 45414
Cartridge Boxes, Shooters Supplies, 1589 Payne Ave., St. Paul, Minn. 55101
Cartridge Box Labels, Milton Brynin, Box 162, Fleetwood Sta., Mt. Vernon, N.Y. 10552
Cartridge Box Labels, Jasco, Box 49751, Los Angeles, Calif. 90049
Cartridge Box Labels, Peterson Label Co., P.O. Box 186GW, Redding Ridge, Conn. 06876
Cartridge Carrier, N.H. Schiffman, P.O. Box 7373, Murray, Utah, 84107
Case Gauge, Plum City Ballistics Range, Box 128, Plum City, Wis. 54761
Chrome Brl. Lining, Marker Mach. Co., Box 426, Charleston, Ill. 61920
Distress Flares, March Coulter Co., Box 333, Tecumseh, Mich. 49286
Ear-Valv, Sigma Eng. Co., 11320 Burbank Blvd., N. Hollywood, Calif. 91601
Flares, Colt Industries, Huyshope Ave., Hartford, Conn. 06102
Flares, Goble Assoc., Box 1057, Escondido, Calif. 92025
Flares, Intercontinental Arms, 2222 Barry Ave., Los Angeles, Calif. 90064 (MBA)
Gun Lock, Bor-Lok Prods., 4200 California St., San Francisco, Calif. 94118
Gun Lock, E & C Enterprises, P.O. Box 823, So. Pasadena, Calif. 91030
Gun Lock Chain, Lundy Corp., 1123-24 Davenport Bk. Bldg., Davenport, Iowa 52801
Gun Lok, 4780 Old Orchard Trail, Orchard Lake, Mich. 48034
Gun Socks Covers, E & C Enterprises, P.O. Box 823, So. Pasadena, Calif. 91030
Gun Socks Covers, East-Tenn Mills, Inc., Box 1030, Johnson City, Tenn. 37601
Hearing Protector, American Optical Corp., Mechanic St., Southbridge, Mass. 01550 (ear valve)
Hearing Protector, Bausch & Lomb, 635 St. Paul St., Rochester, N.Y. 14602
Hearing Protector, David Clark Co., 360 Franklin St., Worcester, Mass. 01601
Hearing Protector, Curtis Safety Prod. Co., Box 61, Webster Sq. Sta., Worcester, Mass. 01603 (ear valve)
Hearing Protector, Hodgdon, 7710 W. 50 Hiway, Shawnee Mission, Kans. 66202
Hearing Protector, Sigma Eng. Co., 11320 Burbank Blvd., North Hollywood, Calif. 91601 (Lee-Sonic ear valve)
Hearing Protector, Wilson Prods., Div. P.O. Box 622, Reading, Pa. 19603
Hollow Pointer, Goerg Ent., 3009 S. Laurel St., Port Angeles, Wash. 98362
Magazine Clip (Colyer), Great Northern Trading Post, 13001 Hwy. 65 NE, Rte 4, Anoka, Minn. 55303
Magazine Clips, Amer. Firearms Mfg. Co., Inc., 5732 Kenwich Dr., San Antonio, Tex. 78238
MINI Lights, Avery Corp., Box 99, Electra, Tex. 76360
Personal Firearms Record Book, Box 201, Park Ridge, Ill. 60068
Portable Gun Rest, Central Specialties Co., 630 Northwest Hwy., Chicago, Ill. 60631 (Gun-Rak)
Recoil Pads, etc., Mershon Co., Inc., 1230 S. Grand, Los Angeles, Calif. 90015
Recoil Pads, Pachmayr Gun Works, 1220 S. Grand Ave., Los Angeles, Calif. 90015
Recoil Reducer, J.B. Edwards, 269 Herbert St., Alton, Ill. 62002
Rifle Rests, Edw. L. Bagrosky, 13451 Philmont Ave., Philadelphia, Pa. 19116
Rifle Rests, E.L. Beecher, 2155 Demington Dr., Cleveland Hgts., Ohio 44106
Rifle Rests, Cole's Acku-Rite Prod., Box 25, Kennedy, N.Y. 14747
Rifle Rests, E-N Gun Prod., 1015 Van Hoy Ave., Winston-Salem, N.C. 27104
Rifle Rests, Frontier Arms, Inc., Box 2593, Cheyenne, Wyo. 82001
Rifle Rests, The Gun Case, 11035 Maplefield, El Monte, Calif. 91733
Rifle Rests, Harris Engr., Inc., Box 305, Fraser, Mich. 48026 (bipods)
Rifle Rests, Rob. W. Hart & Son, 401 Montgomery St., Nescopeck, Pa. 18635
Rifle Rests, Rec. Prods., Res., Inc., 158 Franklin Ave., Ridgewood, N.J. 07450 (Buttspipod)
Rifle Rests, Ten Ring Mfg. Co., Box 157, New City, N.Y. 10956 (RifleMate)
Rifle Rests, Basil Tuller, 29 Germania, Galeton, Pa. 16922 (Protektor sandbags)
Rifle Rests, W. H. Womack, 2124 Meriwether Rd., Shreveport, La. 71108
Rubber Cheekpiece, W.H. Lodewich, 2816 N.E. Halsey, Portland, Ore. 97232
Sharpening Stones, Russell's Arkansas Oilstones, P.O. Box 474, Fayetteville, Ark. 72701
Shooting/Testing Glasses, Clear View Sports Shields, P. O. Box 255, Wethersfield, Conn. 06107
Shooting Glasses, Bushnell Optical Corp., 2828 E. Foothill Blvd., Pasadena, CA 91107
Shooting Glasses, M. B. Dinsmore, Box 21, Wyomissing, Pa. 19610
Shooting Glasses, Mitchell's, Box 539, Waynesville, Mo. 65583
Shooting Ranges, Shooting Equip. Inc., 2001 N. Parkside Ave., Chicago, Ill. 60639
Shotgun Recoil Kit, CHB, 3063 Hiram, Wichita, Kan. 67217
Shotgun Sight, bi-ocular, Trius Prod., Box 25, Cleves, O. 45002
Shotshell Catcher, Old Mill Trap & Skeet, 300 Mill Ridge Rd., Secaucus, N.J. 07094 (Seymour)
Targ-Dots, Peterson Label Co., P.O. Box 186GW, Redding Ridge, CT 06876
Trap, claybird, Deerback Prod., 8239 Hayle Ave., Dallas, Tex. 75227
Trap, claybird, Outers Lab. Inc., Box 37, Onalaska, Wis. 54650
Trap, claybird, Trius Prod., Box 25, Cleves, O. 45002

PISTOLSMITHS AND MODIFIED HANDGUN PARTS

Alamo Heat Treating, Box 55345, Houston, Tex. 77055
Allen Assoc., 7448 Limekiln Pike, Philadelphia, Pa. 19138 (speed-cock lever for .45 ACP)
Bain and Davis Sptg. Gds., 559 W. Las Tunas Dr., San Gabriel, Cal. 91776
Bar-Sto Precision, 633 S. Victory Blvd., Burbank, CA 91502 (Bar-Sto barrels, stainless springs)
Behlert & Freed, Inc., 33 Herning Ave., Cranford, N.J. 07016 (short actions)
R. M. Champlin, Stanyan Hill, Wentworth, N.H. 03282
F. Bob Chow, Gun Shop, 3185 Mission, San Francisco, Calif. 94110
J. E. Clark, 7424 Broadacres Rd., Shreveport, La. 71109
J.A. "Bo" Clerke, Box 3355, Santa Monica, CA 90403 (Stainless barrels, long slide kits)
Custom Gunshop, 33 Herning Ave., Cranford, N.J. 07016
Day Arms Corp., 7515 Stagecoach Lane, San Antonio, Tex. 78227
Alton S. Dinan, Jr., P. O. Box 6674, Canaan, Conn. 06018
Dan Dwyer, 915 W. Washington, San Diego, Calif. 92103
Giles' 45 Shop, Rt. 1, Box 47, Odessa, Fla. 33556
H. H. Harris, 1237 So. State, Chicago, Ill. 60605
Gil Hebard Guns, Box 1, Knoxville, Ill. 61448
Jeffredo Gunsight Co., 1629 Via Monserate, Fallbrook, CA 92028 (.45 J-Mag conv. kits)
L.E. Jurras & Associates, Box 846, Roswell, NM 88201
Macs Accuracy Serv., 3260 Lakewood So., Seattle, Wash. 98144 (.45 ACP)
Mag-na-port Arms, 30016 S. River Rd., Mt. Clemens, MI 48043 (Customizing Rugers)
Rudy Marent, 9711 Tiltree, Houston, Tex. 77034 (Hammerli)
Maryland Gun Exchange, Inc., Rte. 40 W., RD 5, Frederick, Md. 21701
Match Arms Co., 831 Mary St. Springdale, Pa. 15144
Pachmayr Gun Works. 1220 S. Grand Ave., Los Angeles, Calif. 90015
Clarence A. Raville, Box 377, Thousand Oaks, CA 91360 (.45 accessories)
L.W. Seecamp, Box 255, New Haven, CT 06502 (DA conversions of Colt, Browning)
Geo. E. Sheldon, 7 Balsam St., Keene, N.H. 03431
R. L. Shockey Guns, Inc., 1614 S. Choctaw, El Reno, Okla. 73036
Silver Dollar Guns, 7 Balsam St., Keene, N.H. 03431 (.45 auto only)
Sportsmens Equip., Co., 915 W. Washington, San Diego, Calif. 92103
Armand D. Swenson, Box 606, Fallbrook, CA 92028 (.45 accurizing, customizing)
Williams Gunsmithing, 704 E. Commonwealth, Fullerton. CA 92631 (Hard chroming, porting, customizing)

RELOADING TOOLS AND ACCESSORIES

Alpha-Molykote, Dow Corning Corp., 45 Commerce, Trumbull, Ct. 06601
Anchor Alloys, Inc., 966 Meeker Ave., Brooklyn, N.Y. 11222 (chilled shot)
Automatic Reloading Equipment (See Rosann Enterprises)
B-Square Eng. Co., Box 11281, Ft. Worth. Tex. 76110
Bair Reloaders, Inc., 57 Glendale Avenue, Akron, OH 44308
Bill Ballard, P. O. Box 656, Billings, Mont. 59103
Belding & Mull, P. O. Box 428, Philipsburg, Pa. 16866
Blackhawk East, C2274 POB, Loves Park, Ill. 61111
Bonanza Sports, Inc., 412 Western Ave., Faribault, Minn. 55021
Brown Precision Co., 5869 Indian Ave., San Jose, Calif. 95123
A. V. Bryant, East Hartford, Ct. 06424
C-H Tool & Die Corp., Box L, Owen, Wis. 54460
Camdex, Inc., 15339 W. Michaels, Detroit, Mich. 48235
Carbide Die & Mfg. Co., Box 226, Covina, Calif. 91723
C'Arco, P. O. Box 2943, San Bernardino, CA 92406 (Ranson rest)
Carter Gun Works, 2211 Jefferson Pk. Ave., Charlottesville, Va. 22903
Cooper-Woodward, Box 972, Riverside, Calif. 92502 (Perfect Lube)
D.R. Corbin Mfg. Co., Box 44, North Bend, OR 97459 (Bullet swaging eqpt.)
Division Lead Co., 7742 W. 61st Pl., Summit, Ill. 60502
W. H. English, 4411 S. W. 100th, Seattle, Wash. 98146 (Paktool)
Ellwood Epps Sptg. Goods, 80 King St., Clinton, Ont., Canada
Fitz. Box 49797, Los Angeles, Calif. 90049 (Fitz Flipper)
Flambeau Plastics, 801 Lynn, Baraboo, Wis. 53913
Fordwad Inc., 4322 W. 58th St., Cleveland, Ohio. 44109
Forster Products, 80 E. Lanark Ave., Lanark, IL 61046
Gopher Shooter's Supply, Box 246, Faribault, Minn. 55021
The Gun Clinic, 81 Kale St., Mahtomedi, Minn. 55115
H & H Sealants, Box 448, Saugerties, N.Y. 12477 (Loctite)
Hart Products, 401 Montgomery St., Nescopeck, Pa. 18635
Hensley & Gibbs, Box 10, Murphy, Ore. 97533
Herter's Inc., RR 1, Waseca, Minn. 56093
B. E. Hodgdon, Inc., 7710 W. 50 Hiway, Shawnee Mission, Kans. 66202
Hollywood Reloading, Inc., 19540 Victory, Reseda, CA 91335
Hulme Firearm Serv., Box 83, Millbrae, Calif. 94030 (Star case feeder)
Independent Mach. & Gun Shop, 1416 N. Hayes, Pocatello, Ida. 83201
JASCO, Box 49751, Los Angeles, Calif. 90049
J & G Rifle Ranch, Turner, Mont. 59542 (case tumblers)
Javelina Products, Box 337, San Bernardino, Cal. 92402 (Alox beeswax)
Jay's Sports Inc., Menomonee Falls, Wis. 53051 (powd. meas. stand)
Kexplore, Box 22084, Houston, Tex. 77027
Kuharsky Bros., 2425 W. 12th, Erie, Pa. 16500 (primer pocket cleaner)
Lachmiller Engineering (See RCBS)
Lee Engineering, 46 E. Jackson, Hartford, Wis. 53027 (Lee loaders)
Lee Precision, Rt. 3, Highway U, Hartford, WI 53027 (Bullet moulds)
L. L. F. Die Shop. 1281 Highway 99 N., Eugene, Ore. 97402
Ljutic Industries, 918 N. 5th Ave., Yakima, Wash. 98902
Lock's Phila. Gun Exch., 6700 Rowland, Philadelphia, Pa. 19149
J.T. Loos, Pomfret, Ct. 06258 (primer pocket cleaner)
Lyman Gun Sight Products, Middlefield, Conn. 06455
McKillen & Heyer, Box 627, Willoughby, O. 44094 (case gauge)
Paul McLean, 2670 Lakeshore Blvd., W., Toronto 14, Ont., Canada (Universal Cartridge Holder)
MTM Molded Prod. Co., P O. Box 14092, Dayton, OH 45414
Magma Eng. Co., P. O. Box 881, Chandler, AZ 85224
Marquart Precision Co., Box 1740, Prescott, AZ 86301 (Case neck turning tool)

Mayville Eng. Co., Box 267, Mayville, Wis. 53050 (shotshell loader)
Merit Gun Sight Co., P. O. Box 995, Sequim, Wash. 98382
Minnesota Shooters Supply, 1915 E. 22nd St., Minneapolis, Minn. 55404
Multi-Scale Charge Ltd., 3269 Niagara Falls Blvd., N. Tonawanda, NY 14120 (Univ. charge bar for MEC shotshell loader)
Murdock Lead Co., Box 5298, Dallas, Tex. 75222
National Lead Co., Box 831, Perth Amboy, N.J. 08861
Normington Co., Box 156, Rathdrum, Ida. 83858 (powder baffles)
John Nuler, 12869 Dixie, Detroit, Mich. 48239 (primer seating tool)
Ohaus Scale Corp., 29 Hanover Rd., Florham Park, N.J. 07932
Omark-CCI/Speer, Inc., Box 856, Lewiston, ID 83501 (Primers, bullets, cases)
Outdoor Research Co., Box 401, Abilene, KS 67410 (Case polishing compound)
Pacific Tool Co., Drawer 2048, Grand Island, NE 68801 (Loading presses, eqpt.)
C. W. Paddock, 1589 Payne Ave., St. Paul, Minn. 55101 (cartridge boxes)
Vernon Parks, 104 Heussy, Buffalo, N.Y. 14220 (loaders bench)
Perfection Die Co., 1614 S. Choctaw, El Reno, Okla. 73036
Personal Firearms Record Book, Box 201, Park Ridge, Ill. 60068
Phelps Reloader Inc., Box 4004, E. Orange, N.J. 07019
Ferris Pindell, Connersville, Ind. 47331
Plano Gun Shop, 1521B 14th St., Plano, Tex. 75074 (powder measure)
Plum City Ballistics Range, Box 128, Plum City, Wis. 54761
Ponsness-Warren, Box 1818, Eugene, OR 97401 (Shotshell reloaders)
Marian Powley, 19 Sugarplum Rd., Levittown, Pa. 10956
Quinetics Corp., Box 13237, San Antonio, TX 78213 (Inertia bullet puller, universal shell holder)
RCBS, Inc., Box 1919, Oroville, Calif. 95965
Raymor Industries, 5856 So. Logan Ct., Littleton, Colo. 80120 (primer mag.)
Redding-Hunter, Inc., 114 Starr Rd., Cortland, N.Y. 13045
Remco, 1404 Whitesboro St., Utica, N.Y. 13502 (shot caps)
Rifle Ranch, Rte. 1, Prescott, Ariz. 86301
Rosann Enterprises, 2901 W. Coast Hwy., Newport Beach, CA 92660 (Auto reloading eqpt.)
SAECO Rel. Inc., P. O. Box 778, Carpinteria, Calif. 93013
Shoffstalls Mfg. Co., 740 Ellis Place, E. Aurora, N.Y. 14052
Shooters Accessory Supply, Box 250, N. Bend, Ore. 97459 (SAS)
Sil's Gun Prod., 490 Sylvan Dr., Washington, Pa. 15301 (K-spinner)
Rob. B. Simonson, Rte. 7, 2129 Vanderbilt Rd., Kalamazoo, Mich. 49002
Star Machine Works, 418 10th Ave., San Diego, Calif. 92101
Strathmore Gun Spec., Box 308, Strathmore, Calif. 93267
Texan Reloaders, Inc., P. O. Box 5355, Dallas, Tex. 76222
Vibra-Tek Co., 2807 N. Prospect St., Colorado Springs, CO 80907 (Case polisher)
W. S. Vickerman, 505 W. 3rd Ave., Ellensburg, Wash. 98926
Weatherby, Inc., 2781 Firestone Blvd., South Gate, Calif. 90280
Webster Scale Mfg. Co., Box 188, Sebring, Fla. 33870
Whitney Sales, Inc., Box 875, Reseda, CA 91335 (Hollywood presses, eqpt.)
L. E. Wilson, Inc., Box 324, Cashmere, Wash. 98815
Zenith Ent., RFD, Nordlund, WA 98358 (Primer depth mike)
A. Zimmerman, 127 Highland Trail, Denville, N.J. 07834 (case trimmer)

SCOPES, MOUNTS, ACCESSORIES, OPTICAL EQUIPMENT

Alloy Supply Co., Carson Valley Industrial Park, Gardnerville, NV 89410
American Import Co., 1167 Mission, San Francisco, Calif. 94103
Anderson & Co., 1203 Broadway, Yakima, Wash. 98902 (lens cap)
Bausch & Lomb Sptg. Gds. Div., 174 N. Daisy, Pasadena, CA 91107 (Scopes)
Bridge Mount Co., Box 3344, Lubbock, Tex. 79410 (one-piece target mts.)
Brownell's, Inc., Rt. 2, Box 1, Montezuma, IA 50171
Len Brownell, Box 25, Wyarno, WY 82845
Browning, Rt. 1, Morgan, UT 84050 (Scopes)
Maynard P. Buehler, Inc., 17 Orinda Highway, Orinda, Calif. 94563
Bullitco, Box 40, Shepherdsville, Ky. 40165 (Scope collimator)
Burris Co., Box 747, Greeley, CO 80631 (Scopes, mounts, iron sights)
D. P. Bushnell & Co., Inc., 2828 E. Foothill Blvd., Pasadena, Calif. 91107
Butler Creek Corp., Box GG, Jackson Hole, WY 83001 (Supreme snap-open lens covers)
Chilford Arms Mfg. Co., 9 First St., San Francisco, Calif. 94105
Kenneth Clark, 18738 Highway 99, Madera, Calif. 93637
Collins Co., Box 40, Shepherdsville, Ky. 40165 (Scope collimator)
Colt's, Hartford, Conn. 06102
Compass Instr. & Optical Co., Inc., 104 E. 25th St., New York, N.Y. 10010
Conetrol, Hwy 123 South, Seguin, Tex. 78155
Continental Arms Corp., 697 5th Ave., New York, N.Y. 10022 (Nickel)
Davis Optical Co., P. O. Box 6, Winchester, Ind. 47934
Del-Sports, Main St., Margaretville, N.Y. 12455 (Kahles)
Diana Imports, Main St., Margaretville, N.Y. 12455 (Habicht)
Don's Gun Shop, 128 Ruxton, Manitou Springs, Colo. 80829 (claw mtg. rings)
Duo-Gun Prod., 3213 Partridge Ave., Oakland, Calif. 94605 (mount)
Flaig's, Babcock Blvd., Millvale, Pa. 15209
Freeland's Scope Stands, Inc., 3734 14th, Rock Island, Ill. 61201
Bert Friedberg & Co., 820 Mission St., San Francisco, Cal. 94103
Griffin & Howe, Inc., 589 8th Ave., New York, N.Y. 10017
Herter's Inc., Waseca, Minn. 56093
J. B. Holden Co., Box H-1495, Plymouth, Mich. 48170 (Ironsighter)
The Hutson Corp., P. O. 1127, Arlington, Tex. 76010
Hy-Score Arms Corp., 200 Tillary St., Brooklyn, N.Y. 11201
Paul Jaeger, 211 Leedom St., Jenkintown, Pa. 19046 (Nickel)
Jana Intl. Co., Box 1107, Denver, Colo. 80201
Jason Empire, 1211 Walnut, Kansas City, Mo. 64106

Jeffredo Gunsight Co., 1629 Via Monserate, Fallbrook, CA 92028 (Scope mounts, rings)
L.E. Jurras & Associates, Box 846, Roswell, NM 88201 (Handgun scope mounts)
Kesselring Gun Shop, Box 350, Rt. 1, Burlington, Wash. 98283
Kuharsky Bros., 2425 W. 12th St., Erie, Pa. 16500
Kwik-Site, 27367 Michigan, Inkster, Mich. 48141 (rings)
Forster Products, 80 E. Lanark Ave., Lanark, IL 61046
T. K. Lee, Box 2123, Birmingham, Ala. 35201 (reticles)
E. Leitz, Rockleigh, N.J. 07647
Leupold & Stevens, Inc., P. O. Box 688, Beaverton, Ore. 97005
Jake Levin and Son, Inc., 1211 Walnut, Kansas City, Mo. 64106
Lyman Gun Sight Products, Middlefield, Conn. 06455
Marble Arms Co., 1120 Superior St., Gladstone, Mich. 49837
Marlin Firearms Co., 100 Kenna Dr., New Haven, Conn. 06473
Mashburn Arms Co., 112 W. Sheridan, Oklahoma City, Okla. 73102
Maverick, 13901 W. 101st, Lenexa, KS 66215 (Scopes, mounts, binoculars)
O. F. Mossberg & Sons, Inc., 7 Grasso Ave., North Haven, Conn. 06473
Normark Corp., 1710 E. 78th St., Minneapolis, Minn. 55423 (Singlepoint)
Numrich Arms Corp., West Hurley, NY 12491 (Mounts, rings)
Nydar Div., Swain Nelson Co., Box 45, Glenview, Ill. 60025 (shotgun sight)
PGS, Peters' Inc., 622 Gratiot Ave., Saginaw, Mich. 48602 (scope shields)
R. J. Enorec Inc., 175 N. 5th St., Saddle Brook, N.J. 07662 (bullet mould)
Pachmayr Gun Works, 1220 S. Grand Ave., Los Angeles, Calif. 90015
Pacific Tool Co., Box 4495, Lincoln, Neb. 68504
Ed Paul's Sptg. Goods, Inc., 172 Flatbush Ave., Brooklyn, N.Y. 11217 (Tops)
Pickering Co., 2110 Walnut, Unionville, Mo. 63565
Precise Imports Corp., 3 Chestnut, Suffern, N.Y. 10901 (PIC)
Premier Reticles, Ocala, Fla. 32670
Ranging Inc., P. O. Box 9106, Rochester, N.Y. 14625

Redfield Gun Sight Co., 5800 E. Jewell Ave., Denver, Colo. 80222
Riedl Rifle Co., 15124 Weststate St., Westminster, CA 92683 (Scope bases)
S & K Mfg., Co., Box 247, Pittsburgh, Pa. 16340 (Insta-mount)
Sanders Cust. Gun Serv., 2358 Tyler Lane, Louisville, Ky. 40205 (MSW)
Savage Arms, Westfield, Mass. 01085
Scope Inst. Co., 25-20 Brooklyn-Queens Expressway West, Woodside, N.Y. 11377
Sears, Roebuck & Co., 825 S. St. Louis, Chicago, Ill. 60607
Selsi Co., 40 Veterans Blvd., Carlstadt, N.J. 07072
W. H. Siebert, 22443 S.E. 56th Pl., Issaquah, Wh. 98027
Southern Precision Inst. Co., 710 Augusta St., San Antonio, Tex. 78215
Stoeger Arms Co., 55 Ruta Ct., S. Hackensack, N.J. 07606
Swift Instruments, Inc., 952 Dorchester Ave., Boston, Mass. 02125
Tasco, 1075 N.W. 71st, Miami, Fla. 33138
Thompson-Center Arms, P. O. Box 2405, Rochester, N.H. 03867 (handgun scope)
Tradewinds, Inc., Box 1191, Tacoma, Wash. 98401
John Unertl Optical Co., 3551-5 East St., Pittsburgh, Pa. 15214
United Binocular Co., 9043 S. Western Ave., Chicago, Ill. 60620
Universal Sporting Goods, Inc., 7920 N. W. 76th Ave., Medley, FL 33166
Vissing Co., Box 437, Idaho Falls, Idaho 83401 (lens cap)
H. P. Wesson, Box 181, Netcong, N.J. 07857 (eyeglass apertures)
Weatherby's, 2781 Firestone, South Gate, Calif. 90280
W. R. Weaver Co., 7125 Industrial Ave., El Paso, Tex. 79915
Williams Gun Sight Co., 7389 Lapeer Rd., Davison, Mich. 48423
Carl Zeiss Inc., 444 Fifth Ave., New York, N.Y. 10018 (Hensoldt)

TARGETS, BULLET & CLAYBIRD TRAPS

Black Products Co., 13512 Calumet Ave., Chicago, Ill. 60627
Caswell Target Carriers, Box 344, Anoka, Minn. 55303
Cole's Acku-Rite Prod., Box 25, Kennedy, N.Y. 14747 (Site Rite targets)
Detroit Bullet Trap Co., 2233 N. Palmer Dr., Schaumburg, Ill. 60172
Dupont Target Co., Dupont, Ind. 47231 (motorized target carrier)
Gopher Shooter's Supply, Box 246, Faribault, Minn. 55021 (Lok-A-Leg target holders)
Millard F. Lerch, Box 163, 10842 Front St., Mokena, Ill. 60448 (bullet target)
National Target Co., 4960 Wyaconda Rd., Rockville, Md. 20853
Outers Laboratories, Inc., Onalaska, Wis. 54650 (claybird traps)
Peterson Label Co., P. O. Box 186GW, Redding Ridge, CT 06876 (paste-ons)
Police Ordnance, 3027 Enterprise St., Costa Mesa, Calif. 92626 (Multi-Rotating target system)
Professional Tape Co., 355 E. Burlington Rd., Riverside, Ill. 60546 (Time Labels)
Ranger Arms Co., Box 704, Gainesville, Tex. 76240 (paper targets)
Recreation Prods. Res., Inc., 158 Franklin Ave., Ridgwood, N.J. 07450 (Butts bullet trap)
Remington Arms Co., Bridgeport, Conn. 06602 (claybird traps)
Scientific Prod. Corp., 5417A Vine St., Alexandria, Va. 22310 (Targeteer)
Sheridan Products, Inc., 3205 Sheridan, Racine, Wis. 53403 (traps)
Shooting Equip. Inc., 2001 N. Parkside Ave., Chicago, Ill. 60639 (electric range)
Sterling-Fleischman Inc., 176 Penna Ave., Malvern, Pa. 19355
Time Products Co. (See Prof. Tape Co.)
Trius Prod., Box 25, Cleves, O. 45002 (claybird, can thrower)
Valentine Equip. Co., 2630 W. Arthington, Chicago, Ill 60612 ("Crazy Quail" clay target game)
Winchester-Western, New Haven, Conn. 06504 (claybird traps)
Wisler Western Target Co., 1685 Industrial Way, Sparks, Nev. 89431 (NRA targets)
X-Ring Prod. Co., Outers Lab., Onalaska, Wis. 54650 (traps)

FIREARMS   DIRECTORY